DRAGON
ON OUR
DOORSTEP

DRAGON ON OUR DOORSTEP

MANAGING

CHINA

THROUGH

MILITARY

POWER

PRAVIN SAWHNEY

& GHAZALA WAHAB

ALEPH

ALEPH

ALEPH BOOK COMPANY
An independent publishing firm
promoted by *Rupa Publications India*

Published in India in 2017
by Aleph Book Company
7/16 Ansari Road, Daryaganj
New Delhi 110 002

ISBN: 978-93-82277-26-2

1 3 5 7 9 10 8 6 4 2

Printed and bound in India by Replika Press Pvt. Ltd.

For India,
the land of our birth, our pride and hope

To Sophie,
with warm regards,
Sharala and
Pravin

CONTENTS

SECTION VI
Building Military Power

SECTION VII
Tibet

SECTION VIII
The Insurgencies Within

SECTION IX
The High Seas

PROLOGUE

Let alone China, India cannot even win a war against Pakistan. And this has nothing to do with the possession of nuclear weapons—the roles of nuclear and conventional weapons are separate in the war planning of India, China and Pakistan.

The reason India would be at a disadvantage in a war with Pakistan is because while Pakistan has built military power, India focused on building military force. In this difference lies the capability to win wars. Military force involves the mere collection of 'war-withal', that is building up of troops and war-waging materiel; military power is about optimal utilization of military force. It entails an understanding of the adversaries and the quantum of threat from each, the nature of warfare, domains of war, how it would be fought, and structural military reforms at various levels to meet these challenges. All this comes under the rubric of defence policy (also called political directive) and higher defence management, which in India's case is either absent or anachronistic and in urgent need of transformation.

A measure of this can be gauged from the then Defence Minister Arun Jaitley's comment on Pakistan in October 2014. He said, 'Our [India's] conventional strength is far more than theirs [Pakistan's]. If they persist with this [cross-border terrorism], they'll feel the pain of this adventurism.' Given that the Pakistan Army unabashedly continues its proxy war against India, Jaitley and his successors should wonder why the mere 6 lakh strong Pakistan Army is not deterred by the 13 lakh strong Indian Army. Even after twenty-six years of proxy war, the Indian leadership continues to confuse military force with military power and, consequently, dismisses Pakistan as an irritant, based on number-crunching. If India were to undertake military reforms, the army alone could reduce 300,000 troops over three to five years, and the defence services would be able to provide optimal value without an increase in annual defence allocations.

Military power has geopolitical implications. Pakistan today is sought after by the United States, China, Russia, Iran, Saudi Arabia, Afghanistan, the Central Asian Republics and the littoral countries of South Asia. It has emerged as a critical geopolitical pivot on the Eurasian chessboard. India, on the other hand, remains an important but certainly not geostrategic player. While geostrategic players have the capacity, capability and national will to exercise influence beyond their borders to impact geopolitical affairs, geopolitical pivots are nations whose importance is directly proportional to the number of geostrategic players that seek them out.

US strategist Zbigniew Brzezinski wrote in his book *The Grand Chessboard*, 'It should also be noted at the outset that although all geostrategic players tend to be important and powerful countries, not all important and powerful countries are automatically geostrategic players.'

India's northern frontiers, both on the east and the west, are not what Indian policymakers imagine them to be. Since 1963, China has supported Pakistan with war-withal—conventional and nuclear—to keep India boxed in on the subcontinent. This has ensured that India's foreign policy remains shackled by the two military lines with Pakistan and China. Understanding the dynamics of these military lines in peace and wartime is not a mere defence matter. It is critical to India's relations with major powers and will help India think strategically through a top-down approach—something it has never done because of lack of understanding.

Today the partnership between China and Pakistan—where both need the other equally—has two serious implications for India. First, since the military power of both has achieved interoperability, which far exceeds that of the US and the North Atlantic Treaty Organization (NATO) forces at the height of the Cold War, India's military strategy of a two-front war is no longer relevant. Interoperability is the ability of two armed forces to operate with ease as one whole in a combat environment. This helps strengthen deterrence, manage crises, shape battlefields and win wars. The invigorated Pakistan military—which would be supported by China's People's Liberation Army (PLA) in all conventional war domains (land, sea, air, space, electromagnetic and cyber) without showing its hand—is the new military threat facing India.

The other implication is geopolitical. From the time China supplied Pakistan with war-waging equipment (nuclear and conventional) to keep its strategic rival India imbalanced in South Asia, Beijing's strategy, since 2013, has evolved in keeping with its global ambitions. China, set on replacing the US as the foremost geostrategic player in this century, has forged a deep, all-encompassing relationship with Pakistan. As a result, from being a lackey, Pakistan has emerged as China's most trusted and crucial partner for its geostrategic designs, which are unfolding through the wide-sweeping

One Belt One Road (OBOR) project. The OBOR project seeks economic connectivity both on the Eurasian continent and in the Asia-Pacific and Indian Ocean regions. China has deduced that the viability and success of its OBOR project hinges on the flagship China-Pakistan Economic Corridor (CPEC), which will link Kashgar in China to the Gwadar Port in Pakistan. China believes, and with reason, that the triumph of the CPEC will convince the world that its OBOR is not an amorphous concept but a result-oriented venture which will change the balance of power in the world.

This is the reason China now desires that India and Pakistan have peace. After Pakistan, China wants India to become part of the OBOR project, which President Xi Jinping has been marketing as a win-win mechanism for China and the region. As more Asian countries, and Russia, jump on China's OBOR bandwagon, they recognize that the unsettled India-Pakistan relationship—with Kashmir as the millstone—is preventing the region from realizing its economic and political potential. Speaking at the first session of the Indian External Affairs Ministry-supported Raisina Dialogue in March 2016, former Sri Lankan President Chandrika Kumaratunga said as much: 'The conflict between India and Pakistan has prevented South Asian integration for a long time. There have been disastrous consequences because of Indo-Pak mistrust. The need is for cooperating more than making security concerns an excuse for not cooperating.'

Kumaratunga was clearly speaking for other Asian countries, too, which have no issues with Pakistan and hence cannot empathize with repeated Indian attempts to turn Pakistan into an international pariah. Even Afghanistan, which has suffered Pakistani machinations as much as India, if not more, understands the importance of Islamabad for regional stability and economic prosperity as China unleashes its ambitious connectivity plans with Pakistan's help.

India cannot look forward if its neck is arched backward. Instead of viewing China and Pakistan as two separate adversaries bound by an unholy nexus, India needs to understand that the road to managing an assertive China runs through Pakistan—both strategically and militarily. Only this will ensure space for India in Eurasia. For this reason, an Indian study about managing China should begin with an understanding of Pakistan's security policy and military power. Whether we like it or not, the path to India becoming a leading power is through Pakistan. Without optimal regional integration through the South Asian Association for Regional Cooperation (SAARC), which has not happened since its inception, India cannot claim its rightful place in Asia and the world—a void which China has been stepping into boldly for several years now.

If India can grasp this reality, it will be able to understand China's grand strategy for global domination. While it encapsulates a fierce contest for supremacy with the US, a war between the two is ruled out. Since the US and China are both nuclear weapon powers with capabilities to hit each other's homeland, there are few political objectives that would be achieved by war. Moreover, as former US Secretary of State Hillary Clinton famously said, 'you don't go to war with your bankers'; going to war with China will carry a huge domestic cost for the US. Besides, the US's closest allies in Europe and Asia, which have colossal trade and commerce with China, are unlikely to support the war option.

Furthermore, the US-led Asian security architecture which China hopes to replace with its own is predicated on different principles with little possibility of a clash of trajectories. The US-led system, set up after World War II, is based on military alliances, strategic partnerships and close defence ties with Asian nations to ensure that time-tested rules of law in all domains, especially on the sea and in the air, are followed by all. Pivoted upon military power, which is the US's strength, this architecture assesses victories and setbacks through direct confrontations.

China seeks a new regional security architecture based on its economic strength—the OBOR connectivity being its manifestation. It hopes to bring economic prosperity to nations who would join hands with it. In return, China seeks deference to its views from nations who benefit from the OBOR initiative. Avoiding direct confrontations, China places a premium on psychological victories. With this approach, Beijing has succeeded in drawing into its orbit nations that traditionally have strong military ties with the US.

The two approaches to global power are condensed in the US's Group of Two special relationship offer to China, and Beijing's call for a 'new model of major country relations' with the US. The US wants China to become a part of the existing security architecture as a leader in partnership with Washington. It is another matter that the US is not known to partner with other nations—it believes in its leadership role and would not forsake it willingly. China, on the other hand, wants the US to accept the new global leadership model where two divergent security architectures led by major geostrategic players could coexist. Consequently, tensions between the two will remain, heightening the suspense about which system will eventually prevail.

Make no mistake: China is both a revisionist and irredentist state, which for decades kept a low profile in order to build national power under the US's Asian security benediction. Making use of globalization and the interconnected world, China, in 2008, decided to become assertive since it was by then a recognized economic power.

Between 1978 (with Deng Xiaoping's accession) and 2008, when China sought peace and stability for building national power, it worked simultaneously through a multipronged strategy to trounce its rival, India, for leadership in Asia. Through a series of bilateral agreements crafted to place India at a disadvantage on the contentious border dispute between the two countries, China has made India extremely vulnerable in the north and east. Beijing was aided in this effort by India's appeasement policy, which began after the death of Prime Minister Indira Gandhi and continues to date. India's political and military leaders, in cahoots with its diplomats, have sold falsehoods to their own people on the border issue. The cases in point are the various border intrusions and transgressions by China, which are strictly one-sided, with the Indian Army being a mute spectator.

Today the disputed border holds back India's rise and impacts India's ties with Pakistan, and consequently the entire Asian neighbourhood, which views the border dispute as a consequence of Indian timidity. Understanding how India reached this stage where Chinese troops are able to saunter at will across the border with little protest from India is critical to managing China.

Similarly, there is a need to reassess Pakistan, where the army controls the foreign and security policies. Unlike the Indian military, which was sidelined by Prime Minister Jawaharlal Nehru, the Pakistan Army took centre stage after the 1947–48 war over Kashmir and hence it learnt early on to think strategically. Just as Pakistan President General Ayub Khan offered a joint defence pact to India in September 1959 against rising communism, which was rejected by Nehru, it is time now for India to take a bold step forward. For this, India must review Kashmir politically, militarily and strategically. The interests of India, Pakistan, China and the people of Kashmir converge here. Sure, no party will give up its stakes, though give and take are both possible and doable under the overall rubric of the Kashmir resolution. Removing this one bottleneck will open the floodgates of opportunities not only for India but the entire region.

Resolution of the Kashmir issue will bring India many benefits. One, it will render the military line irrelevant, thereby freeing up a large number of troops from their perennial tours of duty in the region. It will also give India the moral space to address the Tibetan issue with greater self-confidence.

Despite India being home to the Dalai Lama, the Tibetan government-in-exile and the largest Tibetan diaspora, the Government of India has had an unsure and inconsistent approach to the Tibetan issue. It has been unable to convert the humanitarian crisis into a strategic advantage vis-à-vis China, primarily because of its sensitivity on the Kashmir issue. India has believed that if it keeps off the Tibetan issue, China will reciprocate by not openly supporting Pakistan on Kashmir. However, this has not worked. The China-Pakistan combine has changed the narrative of Kashmir and it will continue to change to India's disadvantage as the CPEC progresses through the northern parts of Kashmir.

Once India addresses the aspirations of the Kashmiri people, it can then urge China to do the same with Tibet. After all, China's dream of connectivity and prosperity cannot be fulfilled if a large section of its population remains restive and disconnected. This display of decisiveness and confidence will enhance India's stature. It will also give India its rightful space in Asia, which it has craved historically.

At the moment, the suspicious bilateral relationships between India-Pakistan and India-China have not only stymied India's stature in the neighbourhood but have also reduced India's ties with other countries to a zero-sum equation, whereby smaller nations try to play India against China or Pakistan for their narrow and immediate gains. This is also the reason why the multiple insurgencies in the Indian Northeast continue to find safe havens abroad.

While China no longer directly abets dissent within India—it is too big to do that—its tacit support encourages countries like Myanmar to keep the insurgencies alive. What's more, a network of arms smugglers based in Yunnan province of China ensures that small arms are never in short supply amongst the insurgents. As a result, insurgency in the northeastern states of India has turned into an industry of sorts. Proliferation of arms from Yunnan to the Northeast via Myanmar has resulted in the proliferation of insurgent groups as well, with several of them not even making demands for resolution on the government, content as they are with extortion or siphoning off a portion of the Government of India's funds. Clearly, in this situation, peacemaking is akin to shadow-boxing. It doesn't require genius to see how these multiple insurgencies are sapping India's national resources, including manpower. Even more dangerous is the growing nexus of weapons and training between left-wing extremists (who have been extending their tentacles into the Northeast) and local insurgent groups.

Of course, these problems will not disappear with the resolution of the border issues on the east and the west. But it is possible that improved ties with China and Pakistan, and consequently, an Asian cooperative framework will eventually turn off the tap of supplies—financial and equipment—to the dissenters; once the virtues of the common good become evident, nations will not be tempted to resort to reductionist or Machiavellian foreign policies. It is a truism that a secure homeland is imperative for building and projecting national power.

Confounded by the Himalayan conflicts, many Indian analysts now talk of moving away from them without seeking a resolution. Taking recourse in ancient and medieval Indian maritime history, they argue that India has always been a seafaring nation. Indian mariners used the sea to expand the national footprint from the Horn of Africa in the west to Indonesia in the east. Hence, India needs to reclaim its maritime legacy and once again become the master of the oceans, not merely the Indian Ocean, but the Western Pacific as well. To fit this narrative, these analysts attribute mythical capabilities to the Indian Navy.

There are two major flaws in this scenario. First, it resorts to a selective reading of history. In the ancient and medieval period, no single country straddled the Himalayas in the north and the Indian Ocean in the south. There were several independent kingdoms, each following its own trajectory. So even as the Chola kings of present-day Tamil Nadu were making trading, cultural and religious forays into the Indian Ocean, the kingdoms in northern India were grappling, mostly unsuccessfully, with invaders from the west and north.

The second flaw is that it does not take the present reality into account. Just as India finds itself hamstrung in the Himalayas by the China-Pakistan partnership, the situation is no different in the Indian Ocean. China woke up to the importance of the Indian Ocean well before India did. In the last decade, since 2005 to be precise, when the term 'string of pearls' was coined, it has strung together a chain of friendly ports all along India and beyond: Myanmar in the east, Sri Lanka in the south, and the Maldives and Tanzania in the west. Of course, the lynchpin of all these is Gwadar in Pakistan, from which the CPEC will run onwards to Kashgar in China's Xinjiang region.

The options before India in the ocean are just as limited as they are on the land. And both require a cold assessment of present capabilities and an imaginative road map for the future. If India does that, it will realize that it needs to build military power instead of fooling itself through bean counting and bravado. It also needs to make the military a part of foreign policymaking. This will not be easy. Indian political leaders have traditionally been inept at handling military power, especially now that nuclear weapons are in the picture. Moreover, bureaucrats and diplomats, who constitutionally are in the policymaking loop, will be determined to keep the military leadership on the fringes.

A close alignment of India's national security and foreign policies is essential for India's rise. For one, as we know, India has disputed borders, and for another, the two main adversaries give prominence to military power. Thus, India needs to reassess its approach to foreign policy. Prime Minister Narendra Modi's foreign policy of ignoring Pakistan and positioning India as China's rival in Eurasia will yield little. India will not be able to translate its huge potential into real clout without building military power, a strong component of which is an indigenous defence industry to support strategic objectives. An absence of these implies that India's relations with major powers like the US and Russia will remain suboptimal at best and tentative at worst. This is not what important nations that aspire to become geostrategic players do. India cannot become a leading power in the world unless it becomes a power of consequence in Asia first.

This book argues that a strategy based on an understanding and building of military power provides the road map—never considered by India—for both peace and stability in the region as well as India's transformation from an important power to a geostrategic player. Both Pakistan and China are central to this strategic vision.

GAMES THE CHINESE PLAY

I[*] gained an important insight into China at a dinner in Beijing hosted by the Chinese Army for visiting Indian journalists in August 2012. At the Ministry of National Defence (MND), after an interesting though frustrating day—the Chinese talk in parables, leaving the listener wondering about the real message—I was seated next to a widely travelled senior colonel (brigadier rank officer) of the People's Liberation Army. I asked him about the popular Chinese game called wei qi (also known as Go) and how it differed from chess played in India and around the world.

Giving a strategic twist to it, he told me, 'In today's world, it is difficult to hide capabilities. What wei qi teaches is the art of hiding intentions, which should never be disclosed.' He smiled, and as an afterthought added that the Chinese were fond of both games. Next evening, spending some

---

[*]Pravin Sawhney.

time in a popular market, I discovered that no shops sold chessboards, but wei qi was readily available. A shopkeeper confirmed that chess was not popular with the Chinese public.

At the culmination of my visit to Shanghai, I was presented by the MND information office with two slim booklets titled *The Wisdom of Sun Tzu* and *The Great Wall*. Sun Tzu is a key architect of China's distinctive military theory which is in harmony with wei qi. The central message of Sun Tzu is to develop strategic thought that places a premium on victory through psychological advantage and preaches avoidance of direct conflict. The second booklet suggests that China has no expansionist designs. This was mentioned to me by a PLA officer who added that the Chinese fight only when their core interests are affected.

In consonance with wei qi, hiding intentions, or deception, is central to Chinese foreign and security policies. For example, during my week-long stay in China I travelled to Beijing and Shanghai; Chinese military officials took pains to convey the message that their enemy was the West, especially the United States. India was a close friend with whom China desired a strategic partnership. This was done without my asking and often out of context.

During the visit to 1 Armoured Regiment (brigade) outside Beijing, the commanding officer, Senior Colonel Su Rong, said that in simulation training the home forces were depicted in red, while the enemy was shown in blue. With a grin, he pointed to a soldier practising simulation shooting and said the tank he was seeking to destroy was the US's Abrams. The PLA soldier, he added, can fight better on a fourth of the food consumed by a US soldier. And unlike the US, which dropped nuclear bombs, Chinese soldiers would fight only in self-defence.

While listening to Su Rong I tried to figure out who my real hosts were: the Chinese foreign office, their journalists' association or the military? The invitation had come from the first secretary, press section, at the Chinese Embassy in New Delhi. Extending the invitation on behalf of the All China Journalists' Association (ACJA), the caller asked me to join a group of 'senior Indian journalists' to visit China. The proposed dates did not suit me, so in less than forty-eight hours the Chinese graciously shifted the dates by a fortnight.

Why did the journalists' association not invite me directly and why were the dates changed to accommodate me? When I asked the Chinese press officer about the programme, he said the detailed itinerary was being worked out and would be provided on arrival in Beijing, adding that this was an opportunity to meet with Chinese officials and visit some defence installations.

It turned out that I was among the first Indian journalists invited for interaction with the PLA. This was part of their overall transparency drive which started sometime in the 1990s. Until then, China, under Communist rule, was a closed society where the dictum was to lie low and work hard. Its definition of deterrence was different from what was understood in the West. For Western countries, deterrence meant showcasing military capabilities to warn off adversaries; for China, deterrence meant hiding capabilities to leave the adversary guessing.

Things started to change when China, conscious that it had become a risen power constantly on the global radar, decided it needed to open up and become transparent. This had been accentuated by an interdependent world shrunk further by the information revolution. The world's focus on China was clearly in two areas: defence and diplomacy. China opened its State Council (council of ministers) Information Office in 1990, established the Foreign Ministry's Press Information Office in 2001 and set up the Ministry of National Defence (MND) spokesperson system in 2008. Both the state council and foreign ministry information offices are grand buildings with posh facilities and extremely efficient staff. I was told that there are nearly 900 foreign journalists living in Beijing alone. The daily press briefing (packed with foreign journalists) that I attended could well have been at the US State Department; the only reminder that it was Beijing was the language being used. The spokesperson spoke in Chinese and translation headsets were provided on each desk.

Xi Yanchun, the chief information officer at the State Council Information Office, was a bright lady in her thirties who had worked in the US media for four years and had been in her current job since 2002. Xi was happy to talk about China's public relations system. 'Before 2002 there were no press conferences; and the news releases, if any, were ad hoc. There was no mechanism,' she recalled. 'Now this office does a variety of things, from issuing press releases to organizing press conferences and briefings, to interviews and replies to emails and of course publicity on the Internet,' she said. With a smile she added that it was still difficult to get officials to understand the importance of media interaction. The staff under her had increased and many people had been sent to the US and the UK for 'Internet training'. She admitted that after the Foreign Ministry and MND opened their own information offices, few journalists came to the State Council Information Office. 'Those two offices are considered important,' she added, rather ruefully.

While the Chinese government was opening up gradually, there was also an irrepressible urge to control the media. This message was given to us as well. 'Indian media should exercise overall restraint when talking about China so as not to impede improvements in bilateral relations,' senior editor Zhu Shouchen, executive secretary and member of the Board of Leadership, All China Journalists' Association, told us blandly. He spoke at length about the 'code of conduct' followed by the ACJA. Most of the Chinese media are members of the ACJA organized into 494 media committees under six major regional centres across China. Each regional centre contributes a vice chairman to the Board of Leadership of the ACJA. The ACJA has three tasks: to train journalists, teach them to abide by the code of conduct and facilitate foreign journalists in China.

Any lingering doubts on Chinese media and journalism were cleared by senior editor Wang Lan of the multi-billion dollar Wen Hui group in Shanghai. The code of conduct, she said, meant journalism with Chinese characteristics. 'My media group is open to healthy criticism of the government on health, education and science and technology matters,' she said. Earlier, a senior editor at the *China Daily* newspaper office in Beijing admitted that every evening a government-constituted board cleared what news would go into the paper.

The week-long China visit was devised to convey several messages to the visitors. The first day provided the opportunity to ask questions to senior PLA officers at the MND. How long is China's border with India? Colonel Guo Hongtao, staff officer of the Asian Affairs Bureau, Foreign Affairs Office, MND, who had participated in the Special Representatives (SRs) talks on border resolution, replied with an air of finality, 'China's border with India is 2,000 kilometres long.' The colonel confirmed what was known but not believed, at least in India.

Months before the visit of Prime Minister Wen Jiabao to India in December 2010, China had decided to unilaterally announce its perception of the border. That came as a bolt from the blue for India. With this border pronouncement China had virtually shut the door on border negotiations. Moreover, the Chinese stance compelled India to announce its own perception of the border, which it said was 3,488 kilometres long. The difference in the two border perceptions is a whopping 1,488 kilometres— so large that neither side will be able to trade so much land for peace. Perhaps this would not be required since to date India hasn't protested to China about its theoretical gobbling up of Indian land.

The PLA leaders indicated that China's claims on the disputed border were more complex than are understood in India. 'Indian security forces have made more intrusions into Chinese territories than we have made into India,' said Major General Yao Yunzhu, director of the Centre of China-America Defence Relations, PLA Academy of Military Sciences. She was referring to India's state of Arunachal Pradesh, which Beijing says is South Tibet, a part of China. By her logic, Indian troops posted in Arunachal Pradesh are in occupation of Chinese territory.

The next day, during the visit to the foreign office, Ma Jisheng, the deputy director general, Information Department, Ministry of Foreign Affairs, asserted, 'All reports [in Indian media] of Chinese ingressions are false. The border issue is difficult and will not be resolved soon. We should give more time to political and diplomatic aspects. It requires wisdom on both sides to make sure that border talks are not made difficult with media spotlight. With more mutual cooperation and mutual understanding we will have the magic to solve the border issue. For people who doubt one another, it is difficult to solve problems. But for people who like one another, it is easier to solve problems. Therefore, we should keep the border issue on one track and on another track we should continue working in other areas. For example, trade.'

There was an extraordinary consistency in what the PLA (Ministry of National Defence) officials and diplomats (Ministry of Foreign Affairs) said on the disputed border issue. Unlike in India, not only is the PLA authorized to speak on the politically sensitive border issue, it has an extremely important if not the leading role in policymaking.

Another important message was imparted during the visit to the National Museum in Shanghai. Drawing attention to paintings when China was subjected to colonial rule in the mid-nineteenth century by Britain, France, Russia and later Japan, our guide told us that it was a period of deep humiliation for the Chinese people. Starting with the Opium Wars it ended with Mao's China. But this was not the real point that was driven home. Speaking in English, the museum guide and our language interpreter compared China and India under colonial rule and questioned how Indians could view their colonial period as favourable. Unlike all Chinese, many Indians believe that colonialism had 'many positives' about it, they averred.

All the PLA officials I met were reluctant to talk about Pakistan, which they said was a bilateral relationship between China and Pakistan. The need, they said, was for India and China to have more bilateral cooperation and openness. An interesting bilateral issue that the PLA is keen to pursue is military-to-military relations. According to Colonel Hongtao, 'A breakthrough has been achieved in military relations between China and

India. Both navies have done rescue operations together, the armies have done joint anti-terrorism training, and defence institutes have invited experts to talk with one another. This is leading towards peaceful coexistence.'

The future, he added, is bright. 'We need to consolidate what has been achieved in the last ten years, we should maintain and broaden visits, we should continue with security and defence mechanism talks, and we should find ways to expand mutual cooperation.' It does not need a genius to figure out that the PLA, through greater military transparency, is keen on gaining information about the Indian military's capability, training and morale, and growing military ties between the Indian and US militaries.

Discussing military cooperation between India and China, the PLA officials said that bilateral interactions were much less than what China had with other countries, including with the US. Major General Yunzhu observed, 'The 1962 [war] memory should be forgotten in India.' The PLA is conscious that the trauma and humiliation of India's 1962 war with China has contributed immensely to a trust deficit between the two countries. India, on the other hand, has yet to fully grasp two truths about the 1962 war.

From China's perspective, the border war was not about territory. Had it been so, the PLA, after routing the Indian Army in the Eastern Sector (NEFA), would not have unilaterally gone back to positions held by them before the war. The border war was the consequence of Mao Zedong's frustration and anger at having handled the Tibet issue badly by allowing the Dalai Lama to flee to India. Nehru not only welcomed the Tibetan leader with open arms, he also gave him and hundreds of his followers asylum in India. Once Nehru, who had already incensed Mao, implemented the ill-conceived Forward Policy and made provocative remarks by ordering the Indian Army to throw out the PLA, the ground for war was laid.

The other issue connected with the 1962 war was that China, unlike India, views military power as a part of diplomacy and not separate from it. Taking their cue from Mao's famous dictum that 'power flows from the barrel of a gun', Chinese leaders see no dissonance between use of force alongside negotiations for good results. The PLA understands the importance of military power and places a high premium on it.

HOW WE GOT HERE

On the evening of 6 August 1947, with the partition of the subcontinent looming, a party to bid farewell to officers assigned to the Pakistan Army was in full swing in Delhi. On the menu, apart from food, were choked emotions, frequent hugs and promises to stay in touch forever. None of the officers present could imagine that anything in the world could break apart this camaraderie.

However, Lieutenant Colonel S. H. F. J. Manekshaw was in no hurry to join in the bonhomie. Posted in the sensitive Military Operations branch dealing with the distribution of army units between the newly formed Pakistan and India, he had the all-important job of sorting out the paperwork. All documents connected with the North-West Frontier Province (NWFP, present-day Khyber Pakhtunkhwa) were to go to the Pakistan Army. But before putting away the documents for the Pakistan Army, he made photocopies for safekeeping, which was standard military procedure. Only after he had done this did he leave for the party, unaware that in the weeks to come, his simple military drill would become part of history.

On 14 August 1947, the subcontinent was officially partitioned. The violence that ensued did not leave the two armies untouched. On 22 October 1947, supposed tribal fighters invaded Kashmir, ostensibly to liberate it from India. The invasion and the subsequent signing of the Instrument of Accession by Kashmir's Maharaja Hari Singh with the Union of India brought the Indian Army into the war. In less than two months, the once inseparable comrades became deadly enemies.

At the time, the Indian officers fighting the invaders didn't know that amongst the tribals were their former colleagues. It wasn't until Manekshaw made a chance discovery while poring over the documents he had photocopied that realization dawned: some of the personnel from the army units in the NWFP fought alongside the tribal fighters. It was highly likely that one such officer was the mysterious General Tariq, the mastermind of Operation Gulmarg—the planned invasion of Kashmir.

Pakistan's Quaid-e-Azam (Great Leader), Mohammad Ali Jinnah, wanted Muslim-majority Kashmir to be part of Pakistan, without which his idea of Pakistan as the homeland for Muslims was incomplete. Given the reluctance of Hari Singh, the Hindu ruler of Kashmir, to join either of the two dominions, India or Pakistan, Jinnah was desperately looking for a way to force Kashmir to join Pakistan without officially revealing his hand. His trusted lieutenant, Prime Minister Liaquat Ali Khan, came to his rescue when he engaged a middle-level army officer, Colonel Akbar Khan (then on leave from General Headquarters, Rawalpindi), to mastermind a clandestine plan to capture Kashmir. Given the secrecy, Akbar Khan assumed the name General Tariq after Tariq ibn Ziyad, the legendary Muslim warrior who captured Spain and after whom the Rock of Gibraltar is named. Akbar's plan was code-named Operation Gulmarg.

Akbar became the informal interface between Pakistan's civilian and military leaderships, both of which were aware of what was going on, though neither would admit so publicly. Akbar Khan co-opted fellow officer Colonel Sher Khan from the Military Intelligence Directorate who suggested that tribal fighters from the NWFP, who had strong ethnic, martial and religious ties with Muslims from Poonch, be employed in Operation Gulmarg. Within days of the declaration of independence, the Muslims from Poonch, or Poonchis as they were called, revolted against the ruler, Hari Singh, for his high-handed tax collection practice. To quell the revolt, Hari Singh sent his Jammu and Kashmir (J&K) state forces to silence the Poonchis. The tribals from the NWFP were to assist the Poonchis against the ruler. Given the meagre J&K forces, it was assumed that the tribals, supported by the regular Pakistan Army masquerading as volunteering ex-servicemen, would capture Srinagar, the capital of Jammu and Kashmir. Then the puppet government installed there would request Pakistan for military help, which would then assist in the creation of Azad (free) Kashmir.

Akbar Khan's plan suited General Headquarters, which had senior British officers as well. As there was a paucity of senior officers in both the Indian and Pakistani armies, British officers were pressed to stay on until December 1947—nearly 3,000 of them volunteered do so until December 1947. The two nations had picked their commanders-in-chief in early August 1947: General Sir Robert Lockhart for the Indian Army and General Sir Frank Messervy for the Pakistan Army. The British commander-in-chief of the Pakistan Army was not inclined to openly support a clandestine operation against Kashmir, although he was aware of it.

Thus, under Operation Gulmarg, 4,000-odd tribesmen from the NWFP invaded Kashmir, with Muzaffarabad as their first stop, on 22 October 1947. This was no ragtag assemblage of guerrilla fighters in trucks and tractors, but men who were well provided for: they carried rifles, mortars, machine guns, mines, ammunition, rations, petrol and even medical supplies, materiel that a regular army would carry. Moving purposefully, they reached Baramulla town on 26 October. Srinagar was just 56 kilometres away.

Once there, the marauders lost their heads. Instead of capturing Srinagar town and its airstrip, which was the shortest lifeline between Delhi and Srinagar post-haste, the 'liberators' succumbed to their base instincts. They plundered Baramulla town and raped the women, with many of them carrying the hapless women back as war spoils.

This unplanned diversion by the tribals in Baramulla gave the shocked Indian government time to retrieve the situation. Alarmed by the invasion, the dithering Maharaja Hari Singh gave up the idea of independence and hurriedly signed the Instrument of Accession with India on 26 October, thereby legally paving the way for Indian troops to land on the Srinagar airstrip on the morning of 27 October. Over the next fourteen months the war was fought in all three J&K provinces—Jammu, Kashmir and Ladakh—until the United Nations-sponsored ceasefire came into effect on 1 January 1949. Under international mediation, the two warring sides finally terminated operations with troops holding territories under their control. And the military-held ceasefire line, arbitrarily cutting across villages, fields and rivers, came into being.

What lessons were learnt on both sides?

Ironically, civil-military relations took different trajectories in the two nations. As a junior army officer, Akbar Khan was appointed military advisor to Liaquat Ali Khan. Observing the political leadership from close quarters, Akbar Khan was apparently not impressed during Operation Gulmarg. The political leadership also probably had greater faith in his acumen than in its own abilities, as he, along with other Pakistani officers, was allowed a free hand in running the campaign. Moreover, as General Headquarters in Rawalpindi was closer to the war theatre than the civilian government in Karachi, the Pakistan Army assumed ownership of the war and its consequences. Thus, the acceptance of the ceasefire by Karachi, which created the Ceasefire Line (CFL), disallowing the whole of Kashmir to become part of Pakistan, did not go down well with Akbar Khan and his ilk. They felt betrayed by Liaquat Ali Khan's government.

The government was not the only recipient of military scorn.

The debauchery of the tribals which prevented the seizure of the Srinagar airstrip convinced the Pakistan Army that if they had had army regulars close on the heels of the ragtag tribals (who certainly provided the initial surprise) Srinagar and eventually the Kashmir Valley would not have been lost. In the Pakistan Army's view, the government should not have used the tribals as a fig leaf to avoid being seen as aggressors.

The absence of multiple plans that covered all eventualities was further exposed when the Indian Army was airlifted from Delhi into Srinagar on 27 October 1947. Taken aback by this development, Jinnah changed his mind and urged the Pakistani commander-in-chief to immediately send regular soldiers to save the situation. But the officiating commander-in-chief, General Sir Douglas Gracey (Messervy was on leave), refused, making it clear that, if forced, all British officers would immediately leave the Pakistan Army. Jinnah gave in. Unlike the Indian Army, there were more British officers in senior positions in the Pakistan Army. Akbar Khan, however, felt that the British should not have been permitted to dictate terms. After all, it was the Pakistani officers who fought in Kashmir during the war.

Making matters worse, Jinnah passed away on 11 September 1948; however, so far as the Pakistan Army was concerned Jinnah's dream of making Kashmir a part of Pakistan did not die with him, as the 1965 war with India showed. It became imperative for General Headquarters, Rawalpindi, to complete the unfulfilled agenda of the Partition—the merger of Kashmir with Pakistan. Gradually, the civilian government's hold over Pakistan's national security policy was usurped by the army. This led to the famous Rawalpindi Conspiracy Case (an attempted Soviet-backed coup d'état against the government of Liaquat Ali Khan), followed by the assassination of Liaquat Ali Khan and finally the army coup in October 1958 which installed Field Marshal Ayub Khan as Pakistan's president and chief martial law administrator.

Despite its disdain for the tribals, the Pakistan Army realized the merit of using them and other irregular troops as the first line of offence to be backed up by regular troops. While this pattern of war helped it offset the Indian Army's numerical advantage, it also put the onus of aggression on India. After all, the Indian Army's retaliation against Pakistan-supported irregulars would force Pakistani regulars to reluctantly join the war to defend the nation's honour. This method was improved and perfected in subsequent wars on Kashmir, from 1965 to 1999.

Once the Pakistan Army decided to take charge of Jinnah's Kashmir agenda, it assessed that its intelligence gathering must improve. On two occasions, it had been caught off guard—Jinnah's terminal illness and the sudden airlift of the Indian Army into Srinagar. Both events changed not just the course of war, but the discourse on Kashmir.

Thus, Pakistan's Inter-Services Intelligence (ISI) agency, with representatives of all three defence services (army, air force and navy), was formed in 1948 by the amalgamation of the Intelligence Bureau (for internal intelligence) and Military Intelligence (for external espionage). Its roles and organization expanded over time under various army chiefs. Being an integral part of General Headquarters, it has always been headed by a three-star army officer, and while reporting to the prime minister as part of its set-up, it has unflinching loyalty to the army chief.

India learnt different lessons from the Kashmir war. Nehru wrote to Liaquat Ali Khan on 22 December 1947 giving details of the regular Pakistan Army's support to the NWFP tribals and sought a quick end to hostilities. Getting no reply even after repeated goading, India, on Nehru's instruction, took the matter to the United Nations on 1 January 1948, arguing that the world body should intervene at the earliest to end hostilities as it could lead to an international conflict.

In complete denial (which became its signature style), Pakistan insisted that the so-called invaders were Azad Kashmir forces who had nothing to do with the state. Throughout 1948, as the Indian Army grappled with the Kashmir war, Nehru remained occupied with scoring brownie points at the United Nations. This created a wide chasm between India's political and military leaders. A consequence of this was that while the battles were fought valiantly, the larger war, bereft of strategic or political guidance, was dictated by the Pakistan Army. Failing to get Nehru's attention, top military commanders were compelled to seek instructions from the civilian bureaucracy.

Nehru's desire to avoid war was disturbing, especially when it became clear that the Pakistan Army's involvement was all-pervasive right from the beginning. Two instances will illustrate this point.

One, the Indian Army's commander-in-chief, General Lockhart, who had been the NWFP governor before taking up this post, was informed in a telephone conversation by his colleague General Gracey about plans being finalized at General Headquarters for the impending tribal attack on Kashmir. Lockhart neither informed Nehru nor prepared the Indian Army for it. Once Nehru came to know about the matter, he replaced Lockhart with General Sir Roy Bucher on 1 January 1948, the day India took the conflict to the United Nations. Ideally, Nehru should have replaced Lockhart with the senior-most Indian officer, Major General K. M. Cariappa, desisted from going to the United Nations, and involved himself with the progress of the war.

Two, Major O. S. Kalkat, who had opted for the Indian Army, but was still posted at General Headquarters, accidentally chanced upon the plans of Operation Gulmarg in early October. Escaping to Delhi on 19 October 1947, he narrated the plans to his senior officers. No one believed him. The attack happened according to the plan.

Despite innumerable odds, both the Indian Army and the Indian Air Force gave a brilliant account of themselves. By October 1948, the tide of war had tilted in India's favour, and Cariappa, who had taken over as the overall commander for J&K operations from General Dudley Russell on 20 January 1948, had made plans to clear the Pakistan Army completely from Kashmir by the summer of 1949. Unfortunately, the ceasefire and the Ceasefire Line came into force on 1 January 1949, setting the stage for the next war over Kashmir in 1965.

Much changed on the security front for Pakistan and India in the interim. After the end of World War II in 1945, a series of military alliances were formed to counter the threat from the Communist countries. The threat from the Union of Soviet Socialist Republics (USSR) was followed by the Communists' takeover in China on 1 October 1949. The US soon extended its containment strategy to West and Southeast Asia in the 1950s in the form of two military alliances: the Southeast Asia Treaty Organization (SEATO) and the Central Treaty Organization (CENTO). Pakistan, sensing the opportunity to get close to the US, so it could obtain arms to fight India, joined both.

President (General) Ayub Khan, who took over power in October 1958, came to meet Nehru in Delhi on 1 September 1959 with a military proposal. If India accepted Pakistan's terms for settlement of the J&K dispute, he, on behalf of Pakistan, was ready to discuss joint defence with India. According to him, the Chinese occupation of Tibet, and the USSR's influence in Afghanistan had made the northern flanks of both Pakistan and India vulnerable to Communism, and hence the need for joint defence.

Nehru declined Ayub Khan's offer—given his non-militaristic thinking, he was opposed to military alliances. Instead, he championed the non-aligned movement meant to keep equidistance from the two power blocs, NATO and the Warsaw Pact.

Nehru's pacifist attitude, his aversion to military groupings and his proclivity for seeking non-violent solutions did not help the growth of the

Indian military, especially the army, whose responsibilities had increased with the creation of the Ceasefire Line (CFL) in Kashmir. The bureaucracy, led by the Indian Civil Services, endeared itself to the prime minister and sought to marginalize the chiefs of the defence services. This was done by abolishing the designation of the commander-in-chief in 1955. It was argued that the commander-in-chief, who was next to the viceroy in status and headed the British Indian Army, had become irrelevant after Independence. The three service chiefs of the army, air force and navy were instead renamed as chiefs of staff. What was lost in this transition was a unified authority that would advise the prime minister (as the head of the government) on military matters, a shortcoming that remains to this day and is purportedly responsible for the woeful higher defence organization which is unable to meet the needs of modern warfare.

Moreover, after the military takeover in Pakistan in 1958, the fear of a similar military coup in India caused the civilian bureaucracy to further marginalize the defence services by fuelling the paranoia of a coup in the political dispensation. Consequently, the three service headquarters of the army, air force and navy were relegated to being attached offices or departments of the Defence Ministry. Under the Government of India 1961 order, the Ministry of Defence (MoD) was to conduct its business as laid down in the Second Schedule of the Allocation of Business Rules and Transaction of Business Rules. According to these rules, 'the responsibility for the defence of India, including preparation for defence by the armed forces including army, navy and air force, has been vested in the defence secretary who heads the Department of Defence'. The heads of the three defence services were not recognized under these government rules. Except for the routine day-to-day running of the armed forces, which included discipline and limited financial powers, all other issues were to be sent to and decided by the civilian-staffed MoD, a situation that exists even today.

The Pakistan Army, in comparison, became powerful as it was seen as the ultimate guarantor of the sanctity of the CFL in Kashmir against India; this helped its perspective in strategic and geopolitical terms much beyond planning and fighting wars.

MASSACRE IN THE MOUNTAINS
The Chinese invasion of Tibet on 25 October 1950 was a cataclysmic event for India, just as the takeover of China by the Communist People's Liberation Army (PLA) under Mao Zedong on 1 October 1949 was for the world. With the buffer of Tibet gone, China, for the first time in history,

was knocking on the northeast frontier of India. What separated China from India in 1950 were the mountain ranges—the Karakoram in the west and the Himalayas in the east.

With the invasion, Mao had crushed the British doctrine of suzerainty. Under this, the powerful British India—which saw little need to define sovereignty or the border with Tibet as both China and Tibet were weak and fighting each other for supremacy—was content with the administrative concept of suzerainty which determined the limits of British India's political and military influence.

This allowed British India to enjoy privileges from a weak neighbouring state without discharging sovereign duties of defining and defending the border with China or Tibet, whichever was stronger. So while China and Tibet flexed their muscles against each other for control over Tibetan territory, all British India did, since the famous (Francis) Younghusband expedition to Lhasa in 1904, was maintain trade agencies in Yatung, Gyantse and Gartok in Tibet, rest houses, post and telegraph lines, and a small garrison of soldiers at Yatung and Gyantse. While British India passed these privileges on to India in 1947, Nehru, in a goodwill gesture in 1950, surrendered them to Communist China in return for nothing.

In 1950, India, as the successor of British India, was not strong, while Tibet was too weak to challenge Communist China. This shift in the balance of power should have concerned Nehru, but he was unperturbed. However, two other men were worried: the army chief, General K. M. Cariappa, and the home minister, Sardar Vallabhbhai Patel.

After the Chinese occupation of Tibet, Cariappa was keen to strengthen the country's defences—with airfields, roads and military camps—right up to the border with Tibet. With this in mind, he met Nehru and told him that India should prepare itself militarily against China's expansionist designs in the future. Nehru flared up. He told Cariappa that it was not the business of the commander-in-chief to tell the prime minister who was going to attack where. Cariappa was told to focus on Kashmir and Pakistan.

But Patel could not be brushed aside as easily. On 7 November 1950, a month before his death, Patel wrote a detailed letter to Nehru explaining that the Chinese occupation of Tibet had increased the threat to India as there was no agreed border between the two. Consequently, Nehru set up the Himmatsinghji Committee to recommend military and non-military measures to strengthen the border and integrate the people of the North-East Frontier Agency (NEFA), today's Arunachal Pradesh, with India.

In private, Nehru confessed that he was against a two-front military build-up, as it would dilute military attention away from Pakistan. For this reason, he maintained that Pakistan was the military threat, while China and India as the two great emerging nations in Asia could resolve their differences with goodwill and diplomatic means. So after Patel passed away, Nehru and his men pretended that there was no border problem with China (incidentally, India was the first country to recognize the People's Republic of China on 30 December 1949). This suited Peking (Beijing), which, preoccupied with internal problems and fighting the Korean War with the United States since 1950, was content playing Nehru's game of 'let's pretend' till the opportune time.

In a fraternal Hindi-Chini bhai-bhai (Indians and Chinese are brothers) spirit, Nehru made a goodwill visit to China in 1954 and both sides signed the Five Principles of Peaceful Co-existence or Panchsheel Agreement on Trade and Intercourse. According to Foreign Secretary T. N. Kaul, who was involved in the drafting of the 1954 agreement, India wanted it for twenty-five years, while China wanted it for a mere five years. Eventually, the two sides settled for eight years, the exact duration of the period of bonhomie between the two countries. The compromise period of eight years was the time China needed to strengthen its control over Tibet and build the infrastructure to fight a border war with India. To be fair to China, its focus was and still remains Tibet. While open to a border resolution with India, Peking did not want to be unprepared in case India flexed its muscles. Unfortunately, this is what Nehru did.

After numerous border skirmishes and unrest within Tibet, the year 1959 was a turning point in bilateral relations. After an armed revolt in Tibet was ruthlessly crushed by China's PLA, the Dalai Lama (along with his followers) escaped to India on 31 March 1959 and was granted political asylum at his request. This was the proverbial last straw for China. Consequently, it took two steps: first, stockpiling for a war with India began in earnest. This was done over three years, the minimum time then needed to prepare war logistics for a limited campaign in the Himalayas. Second, the PLA began nibbling at Indian territories. Between August and October 1959, there were three serious clashes at Khenzemane, Longju and Ladakh. When the government could no longer hide these critical events, Nehru told an incredulous nation that the army had been ordered to take corrective measures, when in reality the army was completely out of its depth.

The corrective measures were the ill-conceived Forward Policy, where the military was ordered to establish forward posts with disregard for tactics and sustenance. This was done at the behest of the intelligence agencies and

Nehru's own belief that China would not go to war; a physical occupation of land was considered enough to deter the PLA. Worse, on 12 October 1962, Nehru, on his way to Colombo, told the media at the airport that he had instructed the army to put an end to Chinese incursions. The headlines the following day shouted that the army had been ordered to throw out the Chinese.

An incensed China called India's bluff by launching simultaneous attacks in the Eastern Sector (NEFA) on what was called the McMahon Line (the boundary between British India and Tibet as agreed by the Simla Accord of 1914) and in the Western Sector (Ladakh in Kashmir) on the disputed border on 20 October 1962. For the Indian Army, it was catastrophe on the McMahon Line. As the Indian Air Force was instructed not to participate in the war for fear of further escalation, all army posts, which were forward (there were no roads or tracks there) and air supplied, were left without essential supplies. By the end of November, Brigadier J. P. Dalvi, commander of 7 Brigade that was in charge of NEFA, was taken prisoner and the entire army top brass was on the run. Indian defences crumbled, the higher defence organization headed by Nehru in Delhi ran for cover and the Chinese army appeared invincible. The rout was total.

The prestige of the Indian Army was partly salvaged in battles on the western front. In Ladakh, 114 Brigade was prepared—it fought well and remained undefeated till the end. The Chinese announced a unilateral ceasefire on 21 November 1962, withdrew to their pre-war positions on the McMahon Line, but moved forward towards their 1959 claim line in Ladakh, where a 320-kilometre military-held Line of Actual Control (LAC) from Daulat Beg Oldi to Demchok came into being. The humiliation of India by China was the beginning of the alliance between China and Pakistan.

And what were the lessons learnt by India? None.

Discarding realpolitik, India, in spite of the 1962 war and opposition from the United States, continued to support the Peking government (as opposed to the Taiwanese) to represent China in the United Nations until its admission on 25 October 1971. By so doing, India hoped to improve relations with China. Unmindful of India's magnanimity, China moved closer to Pakistan. The two signed a treaty on 2 March 1963 under which Pakistan illegally gifted to China 5,475 kilometres of territory in the Hunza region, namely the Shaksgam Valley of Pakistan-occupied Kashmir (POK), which was close to the Karakoram Pass. With this move, China acquired a position deep within Kashmir, from where it could exert military pressure over the rest of the state.

It was lost on Nehru that for meaningful interaction with non-status quo nations like Pakistan and China, credible military muscle should back diplomacy. Talks from a position of relative military weakness can only result in a series of tactical gains at best; at worst, they lead to a hardening of positions.

Given Nehru's attitude towards military power, civil-military relations hit an unprecedented low and never quite recovered thereafter. Frustrated with Defence Minister Krishna Menon's neglect of defences against China, army chief General K. S. Thimayya tendered his resignation to the prime minister on 31 August 1959. Promising to look into the matter, Nehru persuaded him to withdraw his resignation. In Parliament, however, he chastised his army chief and had little reproach for Menon.

More than anything else, India wrongly assessed the reason for the war. For China, the hostilities were not about the border dispute but Tibet. China was frustrated by the Dalai Lama's escape to India, and angry that India had given him asylum. In his memoirs, *My Land and My People*, the Dalai Lama has given three reasons why China coveted Tibet. They wanted Tibet's vast area to accommodate the fast-growing Chinese population; the large untapped mineral reserves in Tibet could be exploited for China's development; and, most importantly, China intended to dominate Asia. If this had been understood, Nehru would have followed Patel's and Cariappa's advice to both strengthen border management and resolve the border dispute, which was possible in his lifetime. The 1962 war and the clandestine nexus between China and Pakistan may not have developed.

KASHMIR ONCE MORE

The 1965 war between India and Pakistan resulted in a political and military stalemate. Political because the Tashkent Declaration after the war sought to settle the immediate war issues rather than the reason behind the war: Kashmir. Military because the Ceasefire Line formed after the 1947–48 war remained intact without change—proof that neither side had won the war.

In his book *War Despatches*, Lieutenant General Harbakhsh Singh, general officer commanding (GOC) of the Western Command responsible for the entire war front, wrote, 'With the exception of the Hajipir offensive, none of the remaining thrusts were pushed to a successful conclusion… Most of our offensive actions fizzled out into a series of stalemates without achieving decisive results.'

One such offensive that revealed the incompetence of India's senior leadership and the initiative of its junior leadership happened on 7 September

1965 when a leading infantry column (3 Jat) of the Indian Army reached the outskirts of Lahore and asked for reinforcements to press ahead. While tasked to occupy the east bank of Ichhogil Canal (the Pakistan Army's obstacle system for the defence of Lahore), they managed to cross the canal and reached the gates of Lahore.

Both the Pakistan Army and the Indian Army were shocked. The Pakistan Army could not conceive that the enemy had managed to breach its defences. Heavy strafing by the Pakistan Air Force was ordered to save face. The senior leadership of the Indian Army was equally dumbstruck by the initiative and success of the junior leadership. What followed was dithering, piecemeal reinforcements, tardy cooperation with the Indian Air Force and finally orders from the brigade commander for the Indian column to withdraw instead of pressing home its advantage.

Yet another example of India's weak leadership was in the Chhamb sector where the Pakistan Army made a major irregular forces' thrust supported by heavy artillery fire on 14 August. The bombardment cost the life of the 191 Infantry brigade commander, Brigadier B. F. Master. While the forces' ingress was contained, the Indian leadership failed to appreciate the terrain advantages the Indian forces had over Pakistan in this sector, as well as the fact that Pakistan's armoured formation was close at hand in Sialkot and Kharian. Indeed, the Indian leadership failed to see that Chhamb would be a major war arena and were taken by surprise by Pakistan's armoured thrust during Operation Grand Slam on 1 September 1965. India's newly raised and inducted 10 Division lost Chhamb and just about managed to save the Akhnoor Bridge, the sole communication link to Jammu.

Thus, India's overall war effort showed numerous shortcomings: poor strategic and operational intelligence, indecisive higher defence organization, reactive thinking, inability to exploit operational opportunities, lack of directive style of command (where junior leadership is allowed to take the initiative), and little agreement between the army and the air force. All these weaknesses exist even today with each defence service having its own doctrine and ideas about how to defend territory.

Pakistan's 1965 proactive war aim was to complete the unfinished agenda of the 1947–48 war: to annex Kashmir. This was to be done in three phases—one in Gujarat and two in Kashmir. The Gujarat phase was conceived by the Pakistan supremo, President General Ayub Khan, to bring territorial disputes between India and Pakistan into the international limelight and to test the new weapons systems acquired from the US after Pakistan joined the US-led SEATO and CENTO.

Taking advantage of its territorial claims in the Rann of Kutch in Gujarat, the Pakistan Army took advantage of India's laxity in guarding the disputed area (a similar mistake by India led to the 1999 Kargil conflict). While India's timely reaction minimized the damage, the Pakistan Army had the opportunity to test its new weapons. Under the aegis of Britain's Prime Minister Harold Wilson, the two sides, both members of the Commonwealth, signed the Kutch agreement in July 1965 amidst fanfare and bonhomie and agreed to restore the status quo ante as on 1 January 1965. This set the stage for the war in Kashmir.

Pakistan's 1965 Kashmir war plan followed the 1947–48 script: irregulars followed by regulars. Originally, the war was meant to be limited to Jammu and Kashmir. The Pakistan Army raised a guerrilla force which was led by regular officers under the overall command of Major General Akhtar Hussain Malik. Numbering about 30,000, and called the Gibraltar Force, it was divided into columns which were to infiltrate into Kashmir through various ingress routes. For example, the Salauddin column with Srinagar as its objective was meant to capture the Srinagar airfield and the radio station. They were then to publicly invite Pakistan to liberate Kashmir. Heeding the call, the Pakistan Army would attack with tanks and artillery across the southern end of the CFL (called the Working Boundary by Pakistan), which comprised hills and plains and cut off Jammu from the mainland. The plan was based on two simple principles of war: surprise and initiative.

The infiltrations started on 8 August, the day Kashmir was celebrating the festival of Sufi Pir Dastgir. The same week, people were to assemble in Srinagar to mark the anniversary of the arrest of Sheikh Abdullah in 1953. Pakistan's guerrilla force was to mingle with the crowds and incite them to raise anti-India slogans. Instead, finding foreigners amongst them, people handed them over to the police. Other infiltrating columns met with a similar fate. Undeterred by the failure of his initial plan, Ayub Khan went ahead with the second act and launched Operation Grand Slam on 1 September 1965 in the Chhamb-Akhnoor sector. India, its intelligence agencies and the military were caught by surprise.

What saved India from embarrassment was the support of the people of Kashmir and Prime Minister Lal Bahadur Shastri's go-ahead to the army to broaden the war beyond the J&K theatre to relieve pressure from Pakistan's point of choosing. Ayub Khan had not bargained for this. While losing Chhamb, the Indian Army opened the Punjab front, which broadened the war.

The twenty-two-day war between India and Pakistan in 1965 went wrong for President Ayub Khan because he was mistaken in his critical assumptions. In his attempt to grab those parts of Kashmir that Pakistan could not in 1947–48, Ayub Khan presumed that the people of Kashmir would welcome the Pakistani intruders. They did not. Instead, they helped Indian security forces nab the outsiders. Then, China did not open the second front against India; it simply made a few threatening noises. Moreover, in spite of the 1962 debacle, the Indian Army, at tactical levels, valiantly rose to meet the Pakistani challenge. And last but not least, Ayub Khan calculated that in the absence of the towering presence of Nehru, his little-known and mild-mannered successor, Lal Bahadur Shastri, would surrender on Kashmir.

The opposite happened. Shastri stood his ground on Kashmir and let the military run the operations. In an exceptional saga of grit and determination, Haji Pir was captured by 68 Infantry Brigade under Brigadier Zorawar Bakshi. Unfortunately, after the ceasefire, Shastri, in a goodwill gesture towards Pakistan, returned it at the post-war Tashkent Summit with Ayub Khan.

In the end, honours were shared equally by the two sides. Pakistan lost territory in Jammu and Kashmir, while India lost land in Khem-Karan and Chhamb. Shastri, by supporting the military effort, helped the army recover some of the honour it had lost in the 1962 war. However, his giving away of Haji Pir to the wily Ayub Khan showed that India continued to decide its border policy without any input from the military, which is meant to defend it.

A MOMENT FOR INDIA

The 1971 India-Pakistan war was not about Kashmir, yet it provided the mechanism for the Kashmir resolution. P. N. Dhar, Prime Minister Indira Gandhi's closest advisor in the 1970s, wrote, 'The transformation of the ceasefire line into the line of control was the core of India's solution to the Kashmir problem. The de facto line of control was meant to be graduated to the level of de jure border.'

The Kashmir solution was the outcome of the thirteen-day war, the first full-fledged war fought in the east and west with Pakistan amidst hectic geopolitical and geostrategic jostling. The war created the new nation of Bangladesh.

It started as Pakistan's domestic problem which sucked India into the conflict. In March 1971, the Pakistan Army started a military crackdown in East Pakistan (now Bangladesh). The reason was elections in Pakistan where the Awami League party of Sheikh Mujibur Rahman had swept the polls in

East Pakistan (which had more seats in Pakistan's National Assembly, given its population). The Pakistan People's Party, led by Zulfikar Ali Bhutto, had emerged as the single largest party in West Pakistan, but in sheer numbers trailed the Awami League. Bhutto refused to accept that the Awami League should rightfully form the next government in Pakistan. He instigated the president, General Yahya Khan, to crack down on Bengalis, many of whom had migrated from India. To escape brutal army repression, refugees from East Pakistan started pouring into India. The international community did little to help, as India struggled to provide food and shelter to 6 to 8 million refugees. Meanwhile, the Awami League (which was banned after the election result) set up an armed wing, the Mukti Bahini, which was helped by Indian security forces to tackle the atrocities unleashed by the Pakistan Army. But it was soon clear that just providing support to the guerrillas would not be enough to stop the genocide that was taking place in East Pakistan. The Indian Army would have to move in. The only way out for a harassed India was to send its army into East Pakistan to help the Mukti Bahini stop military high-handedness there.

Meanwhile, other developments were taking place at a fast pace. Unknown to the world, Yahya Khan arranged the secret visit of Henry Kissinger, US President Richard Nixon's national security advisor, to China in July 1971, which thawed the strained relations between the two countries. While the resultant rapprochement between the US and China was welcomed across the globe, their combined backing of Pakistan added to India's discomfiture. Determined to stop the massacres taking place in East Pakistan and the relentless influx of refugees into India, Indira Gandhi, on 9 August 1971, signed the Treaty of Peace and Friendship with the Soviet Union, thus bringing the global confrontation between the superpowers to the subcontinent. It was clear to the US and China that the Soviet Union would intervene in support of India if either joined the imminent war between India and Pakistan.

Underestimating Indira Gandhi's resolve, Yahya Khan mobilized his army against India. The Pakistan Air Force struck Indian airfields on 3 December 1971. War was joined. India's military aims were modest and, unlike in the previous wars, were clearly spelt out: to liberate East Pakistan and cause high attrition to Pakistan's war machinery in the west.

Given the logistical nightmare of bridging the distance between West and East Pakistan, across India, it was evident that Pakistani troops in the east would be hard-pressed for reinforcements. So the Pakistani military strategy was the opposite of India's: to fight holding battles in the east and embark on an offensive in the west. To its own surprise, the Indian military in the east moved faster than envisaged. Despite the waterlogged battlefields, as East Pakistan was riverine, the Indian Army moved in from three directions, demonstrating excellent paradrop and good cooperation between the army and the air force. Dacca fell sooner than planned. On 16 December 1971, just thirteen days into the war, Pakistan's Eastern Army Commander, Lieutenant General A. A. K. Niazi, signed the Instrument of Surrender in Dacca. An unprecedented 93,000 Pakistani forces (57,000 regular troops and 36,000 paramilitary personnel) were taken prisoner.

War in the west was a different story. While some spectacular battles were fought and won at the tactical level, the overall Indian campaign was marred by a number of glaring shortcomings. Lack of military intelligence, interference from headquarters, the inability to take quick decisions and react to last-minute changes in plans, piecemeal rather than bold reinforcements, being unable to switch forces speedily between formations, and lack of good coordination between the army and air force restricted Indian gains. Notwithstanding all this, India created history by liberating East Pakistan and midwifing a new nation called Bangladesh.

Probably the most significant territorial gains by India in the Western Theatre were made in north Kashmir, where Indian troops captured 586 square kilometres of territory in Shyok Valley and Kargil. These were incorporated into India when the Ceasefire Line was named the Line of Control (LC) after the Simla Agreement of July 1972. In hindsight, it is strange that India, which gave importance to north Kashmir, should have left the LC unmarked beyond map point NJ 9842. The Karachi Agreement of 1949, which had created the Ceasefire Line, mentioned that beyond map point NJ 9842, the line would run northwards. No one would have imagined that this mistake would, in the 1980s, become the basis of the Siachen conflict between India and Pakistan.

It would not be incorrect to say that India failed to convert its victory on the battlefield into gains at the negotiating table in Simla where an agreement was signed between Indira Gandhi and Pakistan's President Zulfikar Ali Bhutto on 3 July 1972. Pakistan had lost its eastern wing in the war, its army was demoralized, President Yahya Khan had resigned on 20 December 1971 and 93,000 of its troops were prisoners of war. It was under these circumstances that Bhutto had come to make peace with Gandhi in Simla. Instead of twisting his arm, Gandhi decided to be magnanimous in victory.

Bhutto accepted that a resolution on Kashmir was necessary. Going further, he suggested that the CFL be called the Line of Peace, which, over time, could be accepted as the international border. However, the time for all this was not opportune, he insisted. Considering that Pakistan was traumatized by the loss of its eastern wing, it would be better if issues such as prisoners of war and territories were decided first. In a step-by-step approach, the two nations could develop overall relations to then tackle the Kashmir resolution.

The wily Bhutto outsmarted Gandhi, who, without a written commitment, accepted his word. The only thing India got was the formal commitment that issues between India and Pakistan would be resolved bilaterally through talks. But even bilateralism was discarded in favour of opportunism by Bhutto's successors whenever it suited them. The only outcome completely accepted by the two sides was the status of the Line of Control, where in accordance with the Simla agreement, the United Nations' military observers became unnecessary.

GLACIAL CONFLICT

The ongoing Siachen Glacier conflict between India and Pakistan is extraordinary in numerous ways. It is being fought on the highest battlefield in the world at an average height of 20,000 feet. Started on 13 April 1984, it has been the longest running conflict in the world in recent memory. It is the only conflict where fighting inclement weather rather than the human enemy takes a greater toll on lives. It is also the only conflict started by the Indian Army which is completely dependent on the Indian Air Force for its sustenance. And contrary to the argument put forth by many analysts, it is not a low-hanging fruit that can be plucked to improve India-Pakistan relations.

The 76-kilometre-long Siachen Glacier in north Kashmir is on no-man's land. Both during the 1949 Karachi Agreement which created the Ceasefire Line and the 1972 Simla Agreement which converted the Ceasefire Line into the Line of Control, the military line running across Jammu and Kashmir was left undecided in north Kashmir beyond map coordinates NJ 9842. The reason: both sides felt that the glaciated areas, being uninhabitable, need not be bothered about. This was a mistake. Commanders on both sides tasked with agreeing to the military line on maps (delimitation) and identifying it on the ground through surveys (demarcation), should have realized that with improved technology, unoccupied territory would get occupied by the side which could take preemptive action. This is what happened with the Siachen Glacier, wedged in the shape of a triangle between Pakistan to the west and China to the east.

The race started in the late 1970s in a rather innocuous way. Finding Siachen to be an exciting mountaineering prospect, foreign mountaineers sought permission from both India and Pakistan, which held territories in the region, for permission to venture there. As the Indian authorities were reluctant to allow foreigners to go to Siachen, more mountain expedition organizations sought Pakistan's permission. Subsequently, presuming Siachen to be a part of Pakistan, United States Air Force maps and certain reputed world atlases started showing it as part of Pakistan. Once the Indian Army came across these maps, it sent out military reconnaissance patrols into the area. To its horror, it ran into Pakistani Army patrols there.

While the Indian Army was still mulling over how to respond, Pakistan's northern sector commander sent a signal to his Indian counterpart on 21 August 1983, which read, 'Request instruct your troops to withdraw beyond Line of Control south of line joining NJ 9842, Karakoram Pass NE 9410 immediately. I have instructed my troops to show maximum restraint. But any delay in vacating our territory will create a serious situation.' This signal, which became the tipping point, was shared by the then Indian Northern Army Commander, Lieutenant General M. L. Chibber, with the authors in a detailed interaction in November 2004.

According to Chibber, Army Headquarters approached Prime Minister Indira Gandhi for permission to deny the glacier (which they were claiming) to Pakistan. While giving the green signal, Gandhi made it clear that the army action should be carried out in a manner which would not escalate into an all-out war. With these political instructions, Chibber decided to occupy the only three passes (Sia La, Bilafond La and Gyong La), at heights between 18,000 to 23,000 feet, on the Saltoro Ridge, which is the western edge of the Siachen Glacier, facing Pakistan. This was in consonance with the 1949 Karachi Agreement, which delimited the CFL till map point NJ 9842, and thence running to the north (Saltoro Ridge was in the north). Preparation for a modest occupation of the passes, to be called Operation Meghdoot, began with Chibber's Chief of Staff, Lieutenant General P. N. Hoon, shopping for tents, ski boots, and other glacier-related equipment and clothing in Europe in December 1984. Hoon was taken aback to find a senior Pakistani delegation shopping for similar items there. This was enough reason for the Indians to act speedily to preempt the Pakistanis for the race to Siachen, which they did.

When the authors asked Chibber about the strategic significance and military plan of Operation Meghdoot, he scoffed, 'Siachen does not have any strategic significance. The strategic importance being talked about is all invention.' According to him, 'The military plan was to occupy the three passes with platoon group strength (fifty to sixty soldiers) each for summer months only. During this period the troops were to be maintained totally by air. We appreciated that given the adverse climatic conditions, during winter months, neither side would want to occupy these passes.'

Chibber was wrong in his geopolitical assessment. Siachen's strategic significance lies in the fact that after 1963, when China got a foothold in north Kashmir, both countries have sought to increase their common border in Kashmir. What Indira Gandhi had in mind was to deny a free run to Pakistan and China in north Kashmir.

Generals Chibber and Hoon got the military plan wrong too. Instead of occupying the glacier at high altitude above 10,000 feet, where survival itself is a feat, the Indian Army should have occupied flat areas in the west (Dansum) at a lower altitude of 10,000 feet, which was then lightly held by the Pakistan Army. This would have provided three military advantages: one, instead of a single logistics lifeline on the glacier itself for distant posts at upto 23,000 feet, the Indian Army would have had numerous logistics options to support the posts. Two, troops on the glacier would not have been tightly squeezed on both sides, by Pakistan on the west and China on the east. This has limited the Indian Army's space for manoeuvre in case of hostilities with both or either (see Chapter 9 Threat to Ladakh). And three, Indian casualties owing to extreme weather at high altitude would have been minimal. Moreover, it would have been far easier to evacuate troops by air for medical reasons.

Hoon responded to the above critique by saying that occupying territory west of the glacier would have meant aggression, since the 1949 Karachi agreement clearly mentioned that beyond map point NJ 9842 (the northern end of the CFL), the line should run northwards—which was along the Saltoro Ridge presently occupied by India. However, his contention is not correct. Since map point NJ 9842 was identified on the ground by the Indian survey team only in July-August 1985, how did Hoon know in April 1984 from where the line would go northwards on the ground? The truth is that the mistakes by Indian generals—of not delineating the military line north of NJ 9842 in 1972 when the Line of Control was agreed, and by Chibber and Hoon of having occupied the glacier—have cost India dear.

Why wouldn't Pakistan occupy passes vacated by India?

'In my experience as the deputy director general Military Operations during the delimitation of the Line of Control after the 1971 war, Pakistanis were prone to transgressing the LC. But once it was occupied by the Indian troops, they usually went back to the original line. The basic issue was who reaches the passes first,' Chibber said. Once Indians had occupied the passes, Chibber said, he got an intelligence briefing on Pakistan's extensive preparations for Siachen in May 1984. 'At that stage we concluded that occupation of passes would need to be permanent.'

Chibber's candid admission said a lot about the poor army leadership, and its understanding of war and geopolitics. Chibber and Hoon betrayed a lack of geopolitical understanding by basing their military planning on the wrong assumption that there was no requirement for a permanent occupation of the Siachen Glacier. Occupation of the passes was considered enough to deter Pakistani troops from reaching the Saltoro Range. The Indian military leadership failed to appreciate the nature and quantum of Pakistani reaction to an Indian occupation of Saltoro passes. On one hand, the nature and quantum of protracted conflict was assessed wrong. On the other, two basic military rules were simply overlooked: that logistics planning is always more important than strategy in war, especially in high-altitude mountainous terrain; and operations at high altitude are different from those in the mountains. A medically proven fact, which was vividly demonstrated in the 1962 war, was that no human acclimatization is possible at extreme high altitudes; survival depends wholly on individual disposition and good fortune.

The simple truth remains that Operation Meghdoot was not a well-thought-out military plan, but a panic reaction, reminiscent of the pre-1962 Forward Policy against China, when posts were occupied without ensuring their logistics lifeline. Panic was created by Pakistan's action, as its former army chief, General Mirza Aslam Beg, later conceded: in 1983, Pakistan's Special Services Group chased Indian scouts from the glacier. Thus, while the race for the militarization of Siachen was started by Pakistan, Indian Army leadership thoughtlessly occupied the Saltoro Range with the incorrect strategy of 'hold the passes'.

Notwithstanding this, India, over time, has managed to create the perception that occupation of the glacier itself was a sensible move. Few realize that this is not correct. Sandwiched between two adversaries, Siachen in north Kashmir is militarily vulnerable, with the prospect of a limited two-front war being high in this area.

A PYRRHIC VICTORY

The 1999 Kargil conflict—a bold gamble by General Pervez Musharraf—

was based on two assumptions: one, the LC marked on maps and signed by commanders of the two sides in 1972 after the Simla Agreement was on small-scale maps, which, by existing survey facilities could be off by between 2 to 10 kilometres on a large modern map. Pakistan played up this technical shortcoming of the original and existing maps when making its case that its troops, though inside territories traditionally held by India, were within the LC on Pakistan's side in the Kargil sector of Ladakh.

Two, Musharraf took advantage of large unoccupied gaps (nearly 120 kilometres in the Kargil sector) during winter months to move his paramilitary force, the Northern Light Infantry, to forward positions, far ahead of where they should have been. As most of the LC in the Kargil sector was in high-altitude (between 12,000 to 18,000 feet) terrain, as a normal practice, forward posts were held by Indian troops (that too lightly) in the summer months; in the winter months (about six to eight months), they were left unoccupied on the assumption that the LC was agreed on maps and on the ground. Moreover, as this mostly snowbound area was assessed (since 1972) by the Indian Army to have minimal conventional threat, during the summer months, when infiltration was more likely, posts were held mostly for ground observation purposes.

Pakistan's case has been explained by Musharraf in his memoir, *In the Line of Fire*. He wanted to avenge the Indian Army's 1984 occupation of Siachen by capturing unoccupied or thinly held areas in the Kargil sector. (He conveniently overlooked the fact that Siachen, unlike Kargil, was in no-man's land in the north beyond the mutually agreed LC.)

With this driving him, he ordered his local troops from the area (though listed as paramilitary, the Northern Light Infantry is indistinguishable from the regular Pakistan Army with similar weapons, training and leadership) to adopt what he called a 'forward defensive posture' under Operation Badr by moving ahead of the traditional LC and preparing and occupying military positions on heights (supported by massive firepower from the rear) during the 1998–99 winter months. The troops were to coordinate with mujahids who were further inside Indian territory to ensure that Indian troops were unable to get back to their original posts. 'We wanted to dominate the areas held by the freedom fighters', is how Musharraf puts it. In his judgement, this was to be a fait accompli. (Musharraf was aware that the Indian Army was woefully short of capabilities in terms of equipment, training and, importantly, mindset for conventional war.)

This tactical manoeuvre was to provide the Pakistan Army with major military (operational) gains. By occupying forward positions in the Kargil sector, the Pakistan Army would be able to observe and disrupt (through firepower) at numerous places India's only road lifeline—National Highway 1A—from Srinagar to Leh. This would isolate Ladakh from the Kashmir Valley. Moreover, with the occupation of forward locations (firm bases in army parlance) adjacent to the Siachen Glacier, the road link to India's Siachen Brigade Headquarters (responsible for the war effort of Indian troops on the Siachen Glacier) would get snapped, forcing India to vacate the glacier sooner rather than later.

While this was a brilliantly conceived tactical plan, Musharraf failed to appreciate that India would fight hard to ensure that Siachen was not severed nor Ladakh threatened. Given the necessity to maintain secrecy, Musharraf kept the Pakistan air force and the navy out of the loop. Even within the army, only selected people knew what was going on. The Pakistan military was unprepared for a total conventional war.

This was the case for the Indian military as well, with the army being the least prepared. India's Northern Command (responsible for Jammu and Kashmir state) leadership proved to be a complete let-down, with Army Headquarters being no better. Nine years of counterterrorism operations in J&K starting in 1990 had perhaps made the senior army leadership forget that their raison d'être was to prepare, train and fight a conventional war.

Considering that the first intrusions—occupation not infiltration—in the Kargil sector were detected on 6 May 1998, Lieutenant General Kishan Pal, the general officer commanding, 15 Corps (responsible for Kashmir Valley and Ladakh), told the Unified Headquarters meeting (of all security forces including the army, paramilitary, state police and intelligence agencies) on 14 May that 'the situation was local and would be dealt with locally'. Based on this input, Defence Minister George Fernandes told the media that the infiltrators would be thrown out in forty-eight hours. And the Vice Chief of Army Staff, Lieutenant General Chandra Shekhar, dissuaded his boss, the Chief of Army Staff, General V. P. Malik, who was on an official tour to Poland, from cutting short his visit. When more intelligence inputs poured in, Chandra Shekhar, in a desperate attempt to cover up the army's folly, tried hard to persuade the air force to provide attack helicopter support without the knowledge of the political leadership, to hit the intruders who had dug in inside Indian territories. The IAF chief, Air Chief Marshal A. Y. Tipnis, refused. He made it clear that the use of air power needed clearance from the government as it would enlarge the conflict from a local to an all-out war.

The seriousness of the situation was realized when the IAF finally joined the army's operation (Operation Vijay) on 26 May. Before the air force came in, army units ordered to evict the intruders suffered very heavy casualties; after the conflict ended, as many as forty-eight officers and all ranks from these units faced a court of inquiry on charges ranging from command failure to cowardice to desertion.

Commenting on the period from 16-26 May, Malik, in his book, *Kargil: From Surprise to Victory,* wrote, 'I felt that the movement of additional units and sub-units at the brigade and divisional level had been done in haste. The hastily moved units and sub-units had neither adequate combat strength nor logistics support. They were being tasked at brigade and divisional levels in an ad hoc manner without any detailed planning.' Of the official figure of 527 dead and 1,363 wounded, the maximum were during this period.

Once it was evident that a greater military effort would be required to dislodge the entrenched intruders, the government on 25 May allowed the use of air power with two caveats: ground and air forces were not to cross the LC, and the area of operations must remain restricted to the Kargil sector. Malik writes that while the nuclear weapons factor was not discussed by the political leadership during the conflict, it must have weighed on their minds for the Vajpayee government to issue such political instructions.

The Indian Army faced its moment of truth: it was not prepared for war. Malik writes, 'Besides weapons and equipment, the ammunition reserves for many important weapons were low.' There were shortages everywhere, from transport fleet to oils, lubricants and greases, winter clothing for troops, artillery guns, and so on. The situation was so alarming that Malik, in reply to a media question on 23 June, when operations were at a precarious juncture, conveyed his helplessness to a surprised nation saying, 'We will fight with whatever we have.' His comments got worldwide coverage, with Vajpayee admonishing Malik in private that he should have restrained himself. Meanwhile, bureaucrats from the defence ministry were either busy ringing up friendly nations (Russia and Israel in particular) to urgently despatch spares and ammunition, or were themselves on flights to buy the items.

While the IAF and the navy were placed on high alert, the army's dilemma was how to balance its resources: not only was a strong attacking force required, but concurrently a strong defensive posture had to be adopted on the entire western front to discourage the Pakistan Army from enlarging the conflict. Malik gambled. He moved a preponderance of artillery (firepower), which is the mainstay of any operation, from other formations including strike (offensive) corps to Kargil. Malik also moved additional troops to Kargil, thereby denuding the capabilities of other critical theatres which would have become vulnerable had Pakistan launched an all-out war. According to him, 'nearly fifty fire units (900 guns) comprising artillery guns, howitzers, mortars and one rocket battery were employed in the area of operations'. All 100 Bofors guns with the army were brought to Kargil.

In Musharraf's words, 'As few as five (Northern Light Infantry) battalions (6,000 men), in support of freedom fighter groups, were able to compel the Indians to employ more than four divisions (50,000 men), with the bulk of the Indian artillery coming from strike formations meant for operations in the southern plains. The Indians were also forced to mobilize their entire national resources, including their air force.' There was panic in the Indian establishment given that Musharraf seemed determined to fight it out.

Then the tide turned as a result of two events far away from the theatre of war. India's National Security Advisor Brajesh Mishra met with his US counterpart, Sandy Berger, in Europe on 16 June and told him that it would be difficult to leash the Indian military forces for long. Dreading the nuclear factor, the US took Mishra seriously and despatched a powerful team to meet Prime Minister Nawaz Sharif with advice to withdraw his troops to the Line of Control. Sharif panicked and sought a meeting with President Bill Clinton; the two met in Washington on 4 July 1999 with Sharif agreeing to withdraw his troops.

China played a powerful behind-the-scenes role in support of Pakistan. During the seventy-seven-day conflict, Chinese forces did offensive patrolling in Ladakh ensuring that India did not withdraw the acclimatized troops (a total of 3,500 on the Chinese front) of 114 Brigade at Dungti for Operation Vijay against Pakistan. Moreover, at the start of the conflict, Musharraf was in China and the Chinese military official in charge of operational support equipment including ammunition was in Rawalpindi. The inference was obvious: the Chinese were ready to support the Pakistan military with war-withal (operational sustenance) alongside exerting pressure on the disputed border with India. As a result of US and China actions, the war did not spiral out of control.

In the aftermath of the conflict, the Indian Army raised the new 14 Corps at Leh (Ladakh) on 1 September 1999 as, according to Malik, 'We need a credible dissuasive posture in Ladakh till the LC and the Siachen dispute with Pakistan, and the boundary question with China, are fully resolved.' This is not all. In order to occupy vacated posts in the sector, 8 Mountain Division (12,000 troops) was told to hold, at altitudes above 12,000 feet, the entire Kargil sector throughout the year. As 8 Division was earlier responsible for counter-insurgency operations (CI ops) in Kashmir before getting sucked into Kargil, thirty new Rashtriya Rifles (See Chapter Line of Constraint) units (each with 10,000 troops) were raised to fill the void in counter-insurgency grids. Thus, the Indian Army raised about 30,000 more troops from within its own resources, further depleting availability of officers in units and reserves of small arms, ammunition and equipment meant for war (war wastage reserves). While unable to make territorial gains in the Kargil sector, Musharraf managed to raise the burden of the Indian Army by forcing its troops to hold an additional 120 kilometres of the Line of Control throughout the year.

The two core lessons from the Kargil conflict for India and its armed forces (especially the army) remain unlearnt. One, as the Pakistan Army—which controls its nation's terms for peace and war—has enormous potential to spring (military) surprises, the Indian military should be prepared at all times to fight and win a conventional war. At the political level, this implies an understanding of military power, including nuclear power, and how wars will be fought between adversaries holding military lines. At the military level, the need is for adequate war wastage reserves, training, mindset and capability for joint operations in an intense all-out war.

Two, Ladakh, where the conflict was fought, is extremely vulnerable to a two-front offensive, whatever its shape or form. Moreover, Pakistan, given its strategic relationship and growing military interoperability with China, will, unlike in previous wars, have the advantage of fighting a prolonged campaign without much depletion of its operational sustenance.

The biggest takeaway for India should have been to acknowledge that Kargil was an aberration (not a war) and a pyrrhic victory. India paid a heavy price for evicting the mujahids and Pakistan's then paramilitary forces from its soil.

OPERATION PARAKRAM FAILS

Five terrorists belonging to the Pakistan-based Lashkar-e-Taiba (LeT) and Jaish-e-Mohammad (JeM) attacked the Indian Parliament, then in session, on 13 December 2001. Prime Minister Atal Bihari Vajpayee told a shocked nation that India, which had been fighting terrorism for a decade, would now enter the final stage of a do-or-die battle. Two days later, India gave Pakistan a list of three demands: stop all activities of the LeT and JeM, take their leadership into custody and freeze their financial assets.

Musharraf swiftly rejected India's demands. On 17 December, Vajpayee chaired a meeting of the Cabinet Committee on Security which was attended by the chiefs of the three defence services to review the situation. On

18 December, the three chiefs again met Vajpayee and Brajesh Mishra, his national security advisor, and were told to prepare for a war with Pakistan. On being asked by the army chief, General S. Padmanabhan, who was also chairman of the Chiefs of Staff Committee, what the government expected from the war, Vajpayee told him that the army would be fully briefed later. So the 1.3 million strong army started its mobilization under Operation Parakram (valour). The ten-month-long military stand-off finally ended on 16 October 2002 without a shot being fired.

Once mobilization orders were given, for the army, it meant a full-scale war was in the offing, something it had not experienced since 1971. Going by the union war book, soldiers' leaves were cancelled, troops were ordered to join units forthwith; civilian trains were cancelled and made available for troop movement; road transport was hired in large numbers for immediate military duties; reserve stocks of equipment and ammunition were taken out from depots and distributed to units, and so on. It took the army over two weeks to move from peace stations to the war locations.

By 6 January 2002, the army was ready to cross into Pakistan across the LC in J&K and the international border. The military plan was to cross the LC with multiple thrusts to occupy territories in Pakistan-occupied Kashmir (POK), thereby inhibiting infiltration. Advantage was taken of the fact that the Indian Army had a large number of troops (since 1990) in J&K, and the Pakistani reserve forces for this theatre were far away on the western front fighting the US-led Operation Enduring Freedom in Afghanistan. However, if Pakistan found the pressure unbearable in POK and decided to enlarge the war beyond J&K, its efforts would be checkmated by India's Operation Parakram. It was argued within the army that as the war aims were limited to J&K, Pakistan would not feel pushed to the wall to contemplate the use of nuclear weapons.

Meanwhile, Musharraf, who was completely surprised by India's actions, agreed to US President Bush's suggestion to publicly declare that he would rein in the terrorists and would not allow his territory to be used against India. This mollified India a bit. Then the unexpected happened. Elements of India's 2 Corps (offensive) were spotted by a US satellite around 8 January as being too close to the border for Pakistan's and the US's comfort. In a sudden development, Lieutenant General Kapil Vij, the corps commander, was immediately replaced for taking the initiative. This sent the entire army command into a tizzy wondering what the mobilization was all about. In a first of its kind, the perplexed army chief, General Padmanabhan, held a press meet on 11 January announcing that mobilization for war was complete and the armed forces were awaiting the political nod. The political leadership neither gave the go-ahead for war nor asked the army to demobilize.

Weeks turned into months and things changed on the ground. Musharraf ordered the counter-mobilization of his army and moved his reserves from the west to the east against India; China shipped two squadrons of forty new F-7MG aircraft to beef up the Pakistan Air Force in addition to supplies of operational logistics such as spares and ammunition; and Pakistan reportedly moved its ballistic missiles forward and two of them, capable of delivering nukes, were test-fired.

Having lost the element of surprise, as Pakistan took countermeasures in POK, the Indian Army, between January and June, modified its war plan. Nearly three divisions (30,000 troops) were moved from the east against China to the vulnerable Jammu corridor, where the army had traditionally used its 1 Strike Corps. Once Jammu was beefed up, all three strike corps were moved to Rajasthan, the idea being that in a battle of attrition where the Indian offensive forces were larger, the Pakistan Army's mainstay, its strike corps, would be destroyed and, maybe, territory captured in the desert could be used as a bargaining chip in the aftermath of war. Thus, according to the new plan, the main battle was to be fought in the Rajasthan desert and not in POK.

The LeT yet again provided the trigger for war. Its terrorists attacked an army camp in Jammu on 14 May, killing soldiers' families including more than thirty women and children. Without waiting for the government's reaction, an agitated Padmanabhan said that the time had come for India to act. Vajpayee joined in the domestic mood and thundered that Pakistan would be taught a lesson; Musharraf also dug in his heels and threatened India. The US and other Western countries issued advisories to their citizens in the subcontinent to leave as war appeared imminent. At this stage, Brajesh Mishra telephoned his US counterpart, Condoleezza Rice, and told her, 'I cannot contain the war lobby here [Delhi] without some help.' According to Rice, as mentioned in her memoir, *No Higher Honor*, she got President Bush to persuade Musharraf to make a public announcement that Pakistan would rein in the militants. After all the posturing by both sides, this was a bit of an anticlimax; nevertheless, it was time for India to demobilize its army.

It, however, took another four months as the government needed a face-saver to do so—this finally came in the shape of a National Security Advisory Board review held on 16 October which concluded that all objectives of Operation Parakram had been met. Given the official figures of 798 dead, ₹8,000 crore spent and massive wear and tear of equipment, what objectives were met?

Union External Affairs Minister Jaswant Singh declared that India's coercive diplomacy had been successful. Months later, Vajpayee admitted that India was close to war on two occasions: in January and June 2002. Importantly, he conceded that not going to war in January 2002 (when Musharraf was not ready and Indian war aims were limited to POK) was a mistake.

Unknown to the world, plenty was happening within the army. According to former army chief General V. K. Singh, 'The very first few days of Operation Parakram exposed the hollowness of our (army's) operational preparedness.' Once mobilization was ordered, Singh writes in his autobiography, *Courage and Conviction*, 'Northern Command further compounded the problem by declaring that it needed time for the troops—who were mostly deployed in counter-insurgency role—to reorient themselves.' How could the army have achieved its war aim of multiple thrusts in POK in January 2002 when its troops were 'untrained', were not mentally prepared for a conventional war, and lacked crucial equipment and weaponry? Fortunately, these questions were not put to the test.

The situation on the international border was equally grim. Singh, who was a brigadier in 11 Corps in Jalandhar, writes that after the war in January 2002 was postponed, troops were ordered to adopt a defensive posture and lay mines in front of them to discourage the enemy from attacking. 'Then the problem started, as it soon became apparent that there had been no check on quality control. A large number of mines had fuses that wouldn't fit and, in true army style, the men would try and force the fuse in. Mine after mine exploded, killing men in numbers that were shockingly high,' Singh writes, explaining why the Indian Army had high casualties without a war. He adds poignantly, 'Helplessly, the army kept sitting on the border, its men and equipment both victims of attrition. Training schedules had gone out of the window and after a while we seemed to be at war with ourselves.'

Operation Parakram was a total disappointment on three counts. One, India's 'coercive diplomacy' failed miserably as Pakistan still continues to support terrorism. As American thinker Joseph S. Nye explains in his book *The Future of Power*, 'If threat from coercive diplomacy is not credible, it may lead to costs to the reputation of the coercing state. Threats are costly when they fail, not only in encouraging resistance in the target, but also in negatively influencing third parties observing the outcome.' Two, the Indian Army's unpreparedness for war exposed its blunted conventional capabilities. And, three, the complete breakdown of communication between

India's political and military leadership, which had started with the 1947–48 war, stood exposed. The Vajpayee government did not tell the army why it was being mobilized; this was essential considering that for the army, mobilization unambiguously means war. Worse, the army chief started mobilization without knowing what political objectives were hoped to be achieved by war.

◆

What we intend to do in the book is provide an overview of key aspects of our struggle with China, followed by an in-depth study of the many smaller components of these issues that deserve to be appraised in detail. The book is therefore divided into sections, which look at the macro issues and chapters within these sections go deep into problems that make up the key issues that India has to contend with. As we have made clear, the problem with Pakistan is inextricably linked with the China problem and we have studied that as well.

DRAGON ON OUR DOORSTEP

Chapter 1

THE CHINESE THREAT

Two weeks after Prime Minister Narendra Modi's visit to China in May 2015, National Security Advisor (NSA) Ajit Doval said, 'For bilateral relations with China, border [resolution] is a critical and vital issue.' While emphasizing that 'deterrence is necessary to avoid conflict [with China]', he added, 'India has to work on a larger plan on how to tackle China'. The realization that the disputed border is India's Achilles heel and deserves substantial weightage had dawned on the NSA, who is considered close to Modi.

Fifteen years ago, India's President K. R. Narayanan—probably the most informed, sagacious and troubled man regarding the threat to India from China—had famously and publicly disagreed with the Chinese leader of the time about the ongoing problems between the two countries. During his March 2000 visit to Beijing, in response to Chinese President Jiang Zemin's remark that 'time and patience are needed to overcome problems left by history', Narayanan had said, 'it is true these are problems left over by history, but these problems need to be resolved and not left over to history'.

Narayanan—India's first ambassador to China after diplomatic relations were restored between the two countries in 1976; the first chairman of the China Study Group set up by Prime Minister Indira Gandhi a year earlier in 1975; and minister of state for external affairs in Prime Minister Rajiv Gandhi's Cabinet during the 1986–87 Sumdorong Chu crisis—was acutely conscious that India, since 1950, had a 'frontier' rather than a 'border' with China. The word 'frontier' is defined as the limit of a nation's political and military influence, while 'border' denotes the territorial limit of national sovereignty. The situation today remains the same; the disputed border is neither delimited (agreed on maps) nor demarcated (agreed on the ground).

Narayanan was aware of the role of military power in Communist China's thinking. The Communists came to power in China on 1 October 1949. They consolidated their hold over Xinjiang province the same year.

As we have seen, India, in a goodwill gesture, hastened to recognize the People's Republic of China on 30 December 1949. And weeks before China entered the Korean War, the PLA marched into Tibet in October 1950 to complete China's unification.

Three lessons emerged from these events. One, even as a weak, isolated nation, Communist China meant business and shunned dithering. Two, the PLA, which spearheaded the Communist takeover of China, would remain a key element in Beijing's (or Peking as it was then known) policymaking. And three, from the security perspective, with Tibet gone, China for the first time in history was knocking at the frontiers of India. As mentioned earlier, what separated China from India in 1950 were the mountain ranges—the Karakorams in the west and the Himalayas in the east.

Narayanan was mindful of how China with deft diplomacy at an opportune time had ensured peace with Russia by quick resolution of its border dispute after a thirty-year hiatus. This allowed China to withdraw its forces from the Russian border and enter into a defence and technology relationship with Moscow through a 'strategic partnership' to upgrade its archaic arsenal. At a frenetic pace, which started with Soviet President Mikhail Gorbachev's visit to China in May 1989, through the political upheavals of the break-up of the Union of Soviet Socialist Republics, the two sides settled their border dispute in the Eastern Sector in May 1991; it was ratified in February 1992. The Western Sector border talks were held between China, Russia and three Central Asian Republics (Kirgizstan, Kazakhstan and Tajikistan) and the border agreement was signed in September 1994.

Starting with the visit of US President Richard Nixon to Beijing on 21 February 1972, China, by 1994, had neutralized its two major adversaries— the US and the Soviet Union—and settled its border disputes with all countries except India and Bhutan. Narayanan, a seasoned diplomat, knew too well that Chinese procrastination with regard to India had less to do with history and the complexity of the border dispute than with eliminating a potential rival for supremacy in Asia.

Today, the disputed border is India's Achilles heel. Through a series of policy blunders by numerous prime ministers since Independence, India has made itself extremely vulnerable to China's risen status, deep pockets and formidable military power. On the one hand, India's military weakness in border management—where a catch-up is not possible—has ensured that it is unable to deter China from going ahead with its version of a 'forward policy'—through regular border transgressions which have increased with each year since the signing of the ill-considered 1993 Border Peace and Tranquillity Agreement. Two decades of Chinese-style forward policy concluded in successful military coercion in April–May 2013 when the Chinese intruded into Indian territory in the Depsang Valley of north Ladakh and left by choice after three weeks. In the process, without firing a shot, they altered the disputed border in that sector beyond their own 1959 claim line.

On the other hand, rhetoric apart, India, for fear of increased PLA aggression on the border, should hesitate to balance China strategically by joining multinational groupings that seek to moderate Chinese expansionist designs. For example, while India has sought close political and security ties with the United States and Japan, prudence demands it be careful that they remain suboptimal or tactical in nature. Getting too close to either or both could incite China to become more aggressive at the disputed border. India today is militarily and by extension strategically vulnerable because of the border dispute with China. This is what makes the border dispute India's core concern, something that cannot and should not be placed on the back-burner. Two prime ministers—Jawaharlal Nehru and Indira Gandhi—understood this. One was inflexible, the other, preoccupied with other issues.

Indira Gandhi understood that Chinese actions are never stand-alone but are linked to international and regional events. When Chairman Mao Zedong decided to start the 1962 war, he made sure through secret parleys that the US would not come to India's rescue by opening the Taiwanese front against China. Mao also got Soviet leader Nikita Khrushchev's nod under the proviso of the bilateral 1950 Treaty of Friendship and Alliance that the Soviet Union would not support India during the war. In any case, the looming Cuban missile crisis was a guarantee for Mao that Moscow would be too preoccupied with more pressing international matters to worry about a regional crisis.

Unfortunately, Indian prime ministers since Rajiv Gandhi have neither assessed the disputed border as India's core concern (which should be addressed with messianic zeal), nor understood the effect the border dispute has had on India's rising stature. There has instead been pressure within the establishment to make prime ministerial visits to China appear a grand success. Consequently, the appeasement policy followed by India has worked to China's advantage. The Chinese detest appeasement, which they view as a sign of weakness and exploit.

The genesis of the disputed border predates India's independence and the Communist government takeover in China. For convenience, the border is divided into three sectors: the Western Sector is India's Ladakh (Jammu and Kashmir) opposite Chinese Xinjiang (also called East Turkestan) and Western Tibet; the Middle Sector comprising the Indian states of Himachal Pradesh and Uttaranchal (now Uttarakhand) opposite Tibet; and the Eastern Sector is India's Arunachal Pradesh opposite Tibet. India's Sikkim state, located in the Eastern Sector, is not part of the border dispute as China considers it to be an independent nation which was forcibly integrated by India in 1975. In 2003, China modified this position by showing Sikkim as an Indian state on select maps; it has not, however, formally adopted this stance.

Desiring a linear border to supersede the existing frontier between British India and Tibet, a tripartite conference with representatives of China and Tibet was hosted by Sir Henry McMahon, the British foreign secretary for India, in Simla in 1914. It was a dubious meeting at which three lines denoting three boundaries were drawn on a map: the boundary between British India and Tibet; between Tibet and Bhutan; a boundary between the Outer and Inner regions of Tibet. Making matters even more problematic is the fact that lines drawn on a small-scale map can be up to 50 kilometres off on the ground when charted using modern survey technology. China never ratified the 1914 treaty which it claimed was initialled by its representative under duress, nor did it accept the division of Tibet. Moreover, China never promised autonomy to Tibet. This was an illusion maintained by British India and later by Nehru up to 1959.

In a well-documented book, A. G. Noorani makes two pertinent points regarding the Eastern Sector. One, in 1914, the Chinese did not object to the McMahon Line. Their sole objection was to the line dividing Inner and Outer Tibet. And two, while the Chinese atlas of 1936 claimed territory south of the McMahon Line, China officially first claimed territory south of the McMahon Line only in September 1959. That same year India officially spoke about the McMahon Line as the traditionally accepted border between China and India for the first time. Until then, Nehru's India, as the successor state of British India, had presumed China's acceptance of the McMahon Line.

The boundary issue in the Western Sector is more complex. In the war of letters exchanged between Nehru and Chinese Premier Zhou Enlai in 1959, Nehru wrote, 'The treaty of 1842 between Kashmir on the one hand and the Emperor of China and the Lama Guru of Lhasa on the other, mentions the India–China boundary in the Ladakh region. In 1847, the Chinese government admitted that this boundary was sufficiently and distinctly fixed.' Another version argues that the Ladakh–Tibetan border was defined in the Treaty of Tingmosgang in 1684. Officials from the Indian External Affairs Ministry appear to agree with both versions.

Three incidents, however, cast doubt on Nehru's claim of an agreed border in Ladakh. First, Noorani, based on archival studies, writes, 'Under Zakaraiah's [director of the historical division in the Defence Ministry] supervision, on 24 March 1953, a decision was taken [unilaterally] to formulate a new line for the boundary. Nehru's directive of 1 July 1954 was apparently in pursuance of that decision. It was a fateful decision. Old maps were burnt.'

Second, 'the British did not regard the Ladakh-Tibet treaty of 1842 as a boundary treaty which had defined the boundary of Ladakh. If they had, they would not have begun pleading with China to enter into negotiations to define the frontier, no sooner had they added the state of Jammu and Kashmir to their Empire in 1846, and pursued their efforts assiduously for well over half a century. They gave up, because China, for its own reasons, did not respond.'

And third, in April 1960, when Zhou Enlai came to India to seek a solution to the boundary dispute, Nehru sought his advisors' counsel. T. N. Kaul, a former foreign secretary who was close to Nehru, writes, 'Nehru actually came out of the negotiating room (with Zhou Enlai) and asked his senior officials why we are insisting on Kun-Lun range further East and not agree to the Karakoram range further West, as the Chinese claimed. His advisors said we have a cast-iron case and Kun-Lun range was better from the defence angle.' According to Kaul, Zhou got furious and threatened to reopen the whole border issue. Earlier China had indicated that it would agree to the McMahon Line 'as a de facto, though not a de jure border' if India agreed recognize the line that the Chinese claimed in Ladakh.

Noorani concludes, 'The northern and eastern boundary of Kashmir [were] not only un-demarcated on the ground but also undefined by a formal treaty or even an informal understanding. It was in dispute.' India (and before it British India) and China never had any boundary or understanding in the Western Sector.

In the Eastern Sector, India's traditional boundary, the McMahon Line, drawn up by the Simla Agreement of 1914, was unacceptable to China. The Middle Sector was least contentious and was settled de facto by the 1954 bilateral agreement between India and China on trade and intercourse (also called the Panchsheel Agreement) as both sides agreed to traders and pilgrims using the route passing through six mountain passes, namely, Shipki

La, Mana, Niti, Kungri Bingri, Darma and Lipu Lekh.

To be fair to China, twice—in 1959 and in 1960—Zhou offered a give and take compromise to settle the boundary question. The 'package' was that China was willing to accept India's claim in the Eastern Sector in exchange for China's claims in the Western Sector, essentially an acknowledgement of the status quo. However, Nehru's rigid stance of non-recognition of the Chinese viewpoint and non-negotiation made headway impossible. Nehru declared that India was open to minor sector-wise territorial adjustments, but no 'package deals', and until territorial adjustments were made, no normalization of relations was possible. India's unyielding position and muscle-flexing through the militarily illogical Forward Policy, in which, as we have seen, army posts were established in far-flung areas without logistics and communication backup, provided the trigger for the 1962 war and the end of diplomatic ties.

After India's defeat in the 1962 border war, Pakistan decided to cozy up to China by offering it traction in Gilgit-Baltistan (Northern Areas), which has a 480-kilometre common border with China's Xinjiang province. The boundary settlement was reached on 2 March 1963, following which China got a foothold on the Karakoram and a stake in the Kashmir dispute between India and Pakistan. However, to assuage India, which protested Pakistan's illegal gifting of Kashmiri territory to China—according to India, the area belonged to it following the Instrument of Accession signed by the J&K ruler on 26 October 1947—China reacted by saying that its border agreement with Pakistan was 'provisional'. Peking clarified that it would renegotiate its 1963 border agreement after the settlement of the Kashmir dispute with whichever country would possess it. China also said that it would remain neutral in the Kashmir dispute. However, in less than a year after the 1963 agreement, work started on the Karakoram Highway between China and Pakistan. The Nehru government was aware of this, but kept it under wraps till it became public knowledge with the announcement of the highway by China in 1978.

Between 1963 and 1965, the Chinese started building defence works on the Sikkim border with India following suit. Numerous warnings were given by China to India to stop trespassing into its territory in Sikkim, with India suggesting that a third-party observer be sought for verification. The PLA simultaneously started concentrating troops in the Chumbi Valley. It later transpired that the Chinese defence preparations in Sikkim and regular protestations were meant to ensure that Indian troops remained tied down on two fronts, with Pakistan and China. This helped Pakistan, even if psychologically, during the 1965 war. At the height of Indo-Pak hostilities, the Chinese issued a bizarre ultimatum to India on 16 September 1965. In addition to the pending complaint of India undertaking defence works in Chinese territory (which India claimed was in Sikkim), India was to return four Chinese border inhabitants, 800 sheep and 59 yaks seized by Indian troops on the China-Sikkim border.

Immediately after the 1965 war, China commenced activities on various fronts opposite Sikkim. Construction work started on the motorable Yatung-Chumbithang-Nathu La road, and shellproof living bunkers, communication trenches and gun positions were built at Nathu La, Jelap La and Cho La. The PLA installed loudspeakers at all these places, which blared round the clock and also started reminding Indian troops of their defeat in the 1962 war. The die was cast on 11 September 1967. The PLA opened fire on unarmed Indian soldiers who were laying barbed wire along the boundary at Nathu La, inflicting heavy casualties. The fire was returned, which resulted in artillery exchanges by both sides. India lost sixty-seven soldiers, while the exact PLA casualties are not known. After days of firing, with the barbed wire remaining intact at Nathu La, an uneasy peace returned. The Indian Army learnt the lesson that good border infrastructure was necessary to face the Chinese challenge.

Various generals approached the government for infrastructure building on the Chinese border, with Lieutenant General Sam Manekshaw being the first one to do so on becoming the 4 Corps commander after the 1962 war. Each time, Indian intelligence agencies thwarted their attempts saying that it would be seen as a provocation by China and lead to war. The then army chief, General T. N. Raina set up an expert committee in June 1975 comprising three officers—K. Sundarji (later army chief), K. V. Krishna Rao (later army chief) and M. L. Chibber—to take a view on the situation. Their task was to suggest a plan to build infrastructure, viable forward communications and defensive positions to ensure a robust defensive posture against China. The expert committee's report gathered dust till it was finally presented by army chief General K. V. Krishna Rao to Prime Minister Indira Gandhi in June 1981.

According to Krishna Rao, 'I must say that Prime Minister Gandhi had an excellent understanding of defence matters. She asked me how much time all this would take as we had no roads and we were required to build defences for big formations like brigades [3,500 troops in each brigade]. I said that the whole plan would take eight to ten years to implement. She asked what would be the implication of our action. I replied that, "this could lead to war." "So what?" she asked. I said we will fight it out. I told her that if the Chinese tell us to stop, we should not do so but continue building our defences.' The prime minister agreed but told the army chief that in the event of a war with China, Tawang in Kameng district of Arunachal Pradesh must not fall again as it did in the 1962 war. Before giving her assent, she asked the army chief if China would use nuclear weapons in a war with India. He answered that it was unlikely. Thus, Operation Falcon disguised as routine exercises in forward areas was launched to 'secure Indian Army's forward defences in Ladakh, in the Central sector, Sikkim, Bhutan, and the Northeast' in 1981.

Indira Gandhi is credited with another development regarding border management with China. An inter-ministerial group called the China Study Group was set up in November 1975 under K. R. Narayanan in order to keep the border situation under review and to assist in preparations for negotiations with China whenever they would commence. The group was also to define the Patrolling Limits Policy in the Eastern and Western sectors. In India's perception its security forces (Indian Army and Indo-Tibetan Border Police) were to conduct regular patrols on the border. Interestingly, Chinese troops, after the unilateral 1962 war ceasefire, 'withdrew from the territories [they] occupied as a result of the 1962 operations, with some exceptions particularly in the Western sector'.

Even before diplomatic relations were restored in 1976, both sides had, since 1970, expressed the willingness to thaw relations. The actual act was delayed because of the 1971 war which saw the birth of Bangladesh. Then, India under Indira Gandhi conducted the 1974 peaceful nuclear test, and despite China's strong protests, Sikkim, with the passage of the 38th Amendment Bill passed in Parliament on 23 April 1975, became the twenty-second state of the Union of India. Indira's firm handling of events both inside and outside India was not lost on the Chinese leadership.

With Indira firmly back in the saddle in January 1980, Chinese Vice Premier Deng Xiaoping during the course of an interview with Krishan Kumar, chief editor of *Defence News Service*, on 21 June 1980 offered a settlement of the border issue along the lines of the 1960 Zhou package. He also extended a warm invitation to Gandhi to visit China. Following this, both sides began the eight rounds of talks on the border issue starting December 1981.

In 1983, away from the media glare, a number of informal and confidential exchanges were made between the two governments to resolve the border dispute. According to former Foreign Secretary Shyam Saran, who was then posted in the Indian Embassy in China, Deng was keen that Indira Gandhi visit China. The Indian response was that it would only be possible if the border issue was resolved satisfactorily. China pointed to the Deng package proposal which was to formalize the status quo. Saran writes, 'Our counter was that something more than the status quo would be necessary given the previous blow to Indian psyche that the 1962 war had delivered.'

What was this 'something more' that Saran alluded to but did not elaborate upon? After the 1962 war, the PLA in the Western Sector (Ladakh) did not go back to its original pre-war positions like it did in the Eastern Sector (McMahon Line). Instead, it pushed forward and moved to its present positions running along the Karakoram Range. In the process, the PLA amalgamated Aksai Chin into its territory, and disregarded the Indian claim that the border should begin at the Karakoram Range and run along the Kunlun Range; the Aksai Chin region is between these two ranges. This is how, after the war, the 320-kilometre-long Line of Actual Control (LAC) came into being only in the Western Sector. The LAC, however, was still short of the Chinese 1959 claim line (varying between 2 to 20 kilometres); the gap between the present positions of the Chinese and their 1959 claim line became an unofficial demilitarized zone where both sides avoided sending patrols.

Against this backdrop, India's dilemma was that its Parliament had passed a resolution after the 1962 war to recover Aksai Chin from China. Indira's government thus found it difficult to accept China's post-1962 status quo offer which would imply accepting Aksai Chin as Chinese territory. In hindsight, the Indian response showed a lack of understanding of military power by Indian diplomats who doubled up as strategists. For a defeated nation to demand more than the status quo was unrealistic. Instead of an outright rejection, the need was to engage with China. Unfortunately, Indira, completely preoccupied by the Khalistan movement in the state of Punjab, which was supported by Pakistan, could not make it to China. With her assassination on 31 October 1984, India lost all hopes of a border resolution. Worse, the security component which was central to the border narrative was, to China's glee, replaced by diplomacy.

PRIME MINISTER RAJIV GANDHI VISITS CHINA
In December 1988, Rajiv Gandhi became the first prime minister to visit China after the 1962 war, thirty-four years after the visit of his grandfather, Jawaharlal Nehru, in 1954. The credit for the visit goes to Minister of

State for External Affairs Natwar Singh, who regarded it as the single most important achievement 'in [his] fifty years' involvement in foreign affairs and diplomacy'.

Two senior Cabinet ministers—External Affairs Minister P.V. Narasimha Rao and Defence Minister K. C. Pant—were amongst the numerous officials opposed to the visit. On Narasimha Rao's enquiry in a ministerial review of what was achieved by India, Natwar wrote, 'The Prime Minister had put an end to thirty-four years of diplomatic drought.' After the visit, Pant told Natwar, 'If the choice is between believing what the Chinese say and what my officers (senior defence brass) say I shall always believe my people.' Following the visit, the prime minister in a unilateral goodwill gesture (perhaps on Natwar Singh's advice) ordered a temporary cessation of Operation Falcon meant to strengthen border management along the disputed border, although the Chinese continued to strengthen their own positions with gusto. Indian generals were opposed to this and protested to Pant. Years later, India would pay the price for this dangerous unilateral goodwill concession to China.

Though path-breaking, the timing of Rajiv Gandhi's visit was not propitious. President Gorbachev's 1986 Vladivostok speech had thawed relations between the Soviet Union and China; Beijing was less wary of a Soviet-India alliance against it. Relations between the US and China were normalized. Therefore, settlement of the disputed border with India was no longer a priority for Deng Xiaoping's China.

On the domestic front, China was aware of Indian military activism under Rajiv Gandhi, most of which had gone awry. This included the 1987 Exercise Brasstacks against Pakistan, the Sumdorong Chu crisis which led to Exercise Chequerboard, and Operation Pawan in Sri Lanka in 1987. Moreover, in 1988 Rajiv Gandhi was on his way out, a battered man surrounded by failed domestic accords and the Bofors bribery scandal. It must be said though that Rajiv displayed a streak of his mother's firmness; despite everything he had to contend with, over the protests of China, he granted full statehood to Arunachal Pradesh in February 1987.

By 1986, China modified the Deng offer from the earlier status quo. Saran writes, 'The fresh Chinese position was that since the largest dispute was in the Eastern sector, India had to make meaningful concessions in the sector and the Chinese side would then make appropriate and corresponding concessions in the Western sector. Additionally, an explicit demand was now advanced for ceding Tawang. This remains the current Chinese position on the border dispute.'

The reason for China's changed position has been explained by IAS officer R. D. Pradhan, who writes, 'Before the seventh round that took place in Beijing in August 1986, the events of the summer of 1986 [the Sumdorong Chu crisis] struck at the root of the package that in a way served as a reference point for talks that began in 1981.' Both India and China drew different lessons from the Sumdorong Chu crisis which led to a troop build-up on both sides for a year, followed by de-escalation, with China blinking first. The Indian inference was that 'the Sumdorong Chu conflict showed the preparedness of the Indian Army to take on any eventuality to secure its border'. China, on the other hand, backed off to avoid direct conflict and to strengthen its border management and war-preparedness to defeat India psychologically through military coercion without fighting.

The shift in the Chinese position was indicative of the fact that they did not consider Rajiv Gandhi to be an imaginative, introspective and firm leader like his mother. The Chinese leadership was not impressed by the fact that Rajiv Gandhi had 413 Members of Parliament in the Lok Sabha; even though, as we have seen, Natwar Singh thought this was an ace up his sleeve.

Rajiv Gandhi's December 1988 China visit was high on histrionics and symbolism but low on substance. China's paramount leader Deng Xiaoping's forty-five-second-long handshake with Gandhi was read as an unusual achievement by India, while the fact that the two did not even mention the border issue was dismissed as trivial by Natwar Singh. Deng spent his meeting with Gandhi talking generalities: he underscored the need for the economic development of India and China, and to cultivate overall bilateral relations.

The border issue was instead discussed between Prime Ministers Gandhi and Li Peng. The latter stressed that China 'had decided to take concrete steps to resolve the boundary issue'. He added, 'Both sides should adopt positive attitude' and sought 'mutual understanding and mutual accommodation'. By 'mutual understanding', Li Peng meant 'understanding each other's viewpoint' and 'mutual accommodation' meant possibilities in give and take because 'the boundary had not been delimited or demarcated'.

China, however, ensured that its core concern on Tibet found fulsome mention during the Gandhi visit. In the joint communiqué, India repeated its 1959 position: India recognizes Tibet as an integral part of China, the Dalai Lama has only the status of a spiritual leader in India and no anti-China Tibetan activity would be permitted on Indian soil.

Rajiv thus reversed Nehru's and Indira's China policy by defusing India's core concern of seeking a resolution of border issues and substituted it with the Chinese desire to strengthen the overall relationship. The border management started by Indira was abandoned, and with it, the burgeoning role of the military leadership in border policymaking—a lacuna of the Nehru years, corrected by Indira—was curtailed. India's Ministry of External Affairs became the sole custodian of India's China policy, including the disputed border. Consequently, all border agreements thereafter demonstrated an ignorance of military understanding and its correlation with foreign policy.

The two achievements of the Rajiv visit flagged by the government were: one, Deng appeared to be extremely pleased with the first visit of an Indian prime minister to China after the 1962 debacle. And two, the two sides formed three joint working groups to deal with the boundary issue, economic relations, trade, science and technology. The perception of a successful Gandhi visit put successive prime ministers under pressure to show similar, if not better, results.

PRIME MINISTER P. V. NARASIMHA RAO'S VISIT

If Rajiv Gandhi's 1988 China visit downgraded the border dispute, Prime Minister Narasimha Rao's 1993 visit complicated the border resolution by adding an additional military line to the PLA's advantage.

Rao went back to the Nehru approach of minor territorial (sectoral) adjustments instead of a 'package deal' for border resolution. China responded by saying that the entire border should be called the Line of Actual Control, without prejudice to the border positions of the two sides. China told India that with the LAC in place, troops could be withdrawn sector-wise instead of waiting for the entire LAC and border agreements. The agreed sectors could then have 'mutual and equal security' as agreed by the two sides. The hand of the PLA was evident in the Chinese offer, while India—much like during the Nehru years—did not consult its army while making its border policy.

Rao and his civil advisors failed to understand that the LAC by definition would be easier to alter than a disputed border even if it was not agreed on maps or on the ground. The resolution of a disputed border is expected to follow tradition, history and the international principles of geographical determinants such as crest-lines and watersheds, which is not the case with the LAC. Being a military-held line, it can be changed by force.

The Rao government fell for the Chinese ploy and the two sides signed the Border Peace and Tranquillity Agreement during the prime minister's

China visit in September 1993. With a stroke of the pen, the entire disputed border was renamed the Line of Actual Control. Hitherto, the LAC had meant a mere 320 kilometres from Daulat Beg Oldi (DBO) to Demchok in Ladakh (Western Sector) which had come up after the 1962 war. In the Eastern Sector, India continued to refer to the border as the McMahon Line, a colonial term unacceptable to China. Thus, after the signing of the Border Peace and Tranquillity Agreement, the disputed border acquired three lines: the border as perceived by China; the border as understood by India; and the Line of Actual Control as agreed by both.

The Border Peace and Tranquillity Agreement added to the operational woes of the Indian Army in three areas: renaming of the border as the LAC, the sector-by-sector approach and the concept of 'mutual and equal security' (Article II of the agreement). For example, between 1962 and the 1993 agreement, there were two recorded border skirmishes or show of strength incidents: the 1967 series of firings at Nathu La and Cho La in Sikkim and the 1986–87 Sumdorong Chu crisis in Arunachal Pradesh. However, after the agreement was signed, and especially after India's nuclear tests in 1998 when relations between the two countries nosedived, the number of Chinese transgressions inside Indian territories increased manifold. India's figures show that Chinese transgressions (which they claim is patrolling within their own territories) have become brazen over the years. The PLA's version of 'forward policy' had begun and continues apace.

Starting in 1998, Chinese activities both in the Western and Eastern sectors continued to be aimed at asserting their claims up to their perception of the LAC irrespective of the mutually agreed 'disputed pockets' where both sides should be exercising equal levels of jurisdiction. For example, during the eighth meeting of the joint working group held in August 1995, the two sides had identified eight 'pockets of dispute' where both had differing perceptions on the alignment of the 1993 LAC and border. These were Trig Heights and Demchok in the Western Sector, Barahoti in the Middle Sector and Namka Chu, Sumdorong Chu, Chantze, Asaphila and Longju in the Eastern Sector. However, in 1998, the Chinese adopted an offensive posture in the Trig Heights area by constructing a road approximately 5 kilometres inside Indian territory. This was used by Chinese patrols to demonstrate their presence in the disputed area. This unprecedented movement was indicative of the Chinese intention of asserting their claim as part of a well-designed nibbling action. Violations inside Indian territories by the Chinese became routine, increasing with each passing year.

Similarly, though Pangong Tso in the Western Sector was not an 'agreed disputed area', since 1998 the Chinese started patrolling the lake in powerful boats. In 1999, they constructed a motorable gravel track from their post at Spanggur up to the southern bank of the lake. The Chinese indicated to local Indian commanders that their LAC ran about 6 kilometres inside Indian territory. The Chinese increased their activities in Rechin La, Siri Jap and Demchok in the Western Sector. Since 1998, they started slowly upgrading their infrastructure and moved up to their 1960 claim line at some places in the Western Sector. By early 2015, 'there were 12 areas of differences in LAC perception between the Indian and Chinese maps, which was far beyond the two mutually identified disputed areas—Trig Heights and Demchok—in the Western sector by the Joint Working Group on boundary in 1995'.

In the Eastern Sector, the Chinese repeatedly attempted to push their graziers intermixed with soldiers into Indian territory. Such incidents, that began in 1999, happened in Chantze and a number of times in the Asaphila and Dichu areas. Consequently, the PLA holds Indian ground in Asaphila and Maja in west Arunachal Pradesh. All these and numerous minor stand-offs have been reported by local commanders to the government through proper channels. China, in essence, has been trying to assert its claims or seek bargains on the basis of the de facto possession of pockets that are being grabbed through intrusions. It was no coincidence that China's heightened activities along the Sino-India border started in 1999 when India was at war with Pakistan in Kargil. Moreover, as we have seen, during Operation Parakram, the ten-month-long military stand-off between India and Pakistan, the PLA maintained pressure, especially in the Eastern Sector, to ensure that India found it difficult to divert maximum forces from the eastern front towards Pakistan.

China also beguiled India into accepting the sector-by-sector approach. A mutual troop withdrawal was delinked from the need to properly define the LAC. Instead, it was based upon a 'sector-wise approach'. Such an approach adopted by mandarins in the Indian foreign office makes little military sense. How can a military theatre commander pull out troops when he does not know what he is required to defend and what has been settled in his area of responsibility? A theatre commander should also know about his area of interest, meaning what his adjacent number is doing.

In the Indian context, it involves coordination amongst four army commanders: the Western Sector is the responsibility of the Northern and Western army commanders, the Middle Sector is the operational area of the Central army commander, and starting from the Nepal-Sikkim border the Eastern army commander takes on the disputed sector. The Chinese do not have this problem because the Tibet Autonomous Region (TAR) is a single theatre command. Simply put, until the entire LAC is mutually agreed upon, any troop withdrawal for India is unrealistic and is not likely to be accepted by the army; what's more, even the 1993 Border Peace and Tranquillity Agreement and its follow-on deal on 'Confidence Building Measures in the Military Field', signed on 29 November 1996 during the visit of Chinese President Hu Jintao, cannot be implemented. Doing so would jeopardize India's border management. Furthermore, even after the LAC is settled in its entirety, the Indian Army would find it difficult to reduce its presence in any significant way until the LAC is accepted as the border.

This is because the PLA's formidable airlift, road and rail capabilities have made the principle of 'mutual and equal security' for troop withdrawal as suggested in the Border Peace and Tranquillity Agreement meaningless. The Chinese have a dual operational advantage along the LAC: a growing capability to bring in troops quickly (thirty-four divisions, each with 12,000 troops within weeks); and, unlike India, they do not have to spend weeks acclimatizing their troops stationed in Tibet for operations on the high-altitude border.

Another issue that mocks 'mutual and equal security' is intelligence gathering. The PLA does not need to undertake reconnaissance missions by aircraft and unmanned aerial vehicles as it has high-resolution satellites with low visitation periods (the time a satellite takes to come back to the same point on completing its cycle) in both low Earth and polar synchronous orbits, as well as fixed reconnaissance satellites in sun synchronous orbits. India does not have comparable capabilities. Moreover, China has better human intelligence than India because the people near the border are of the same stock, and, unlike India, China is not an open society and can therefore bring more pressure to bear on its people as also camouflage its moves better. It is not surprising that China has been able to hide its surface-to-surface missiles in the Tibet Autonomous Region, something that India would find difficult to do close to the LAC.

PRIME MINISTER A. B. VAJPAYEE GOES CALLING

Continuing the trend of not displeasing China, Prime Minister Atal Bihari Vajpayee became the fourth Indian prime minister and the first non-Congress head of government to visit China in June 2003. In the first joint declaration signed between India and China after Independence, India formally accepted the Tibet Autonomous Region as a part of China. By doing so, it diluted the Dalai Lama's definition of autonomy within China.

In return, Vajpayee had sought a quid pro quo—formal Chinese recognition of Sikkim as a part of India. China refused to include Vajpayee's request in the joint declaration, but gave a verbal assurance that it would do so. Indian officials expressed satisfaction saying that China had de facto accepted India's request by agreeing to Changgu as a border trading point and Nathu La—both in Sikkim—as the passage for border trade between India and China. China also printed a few maps showing Sikkim in the same colour as the rest of India. Beijing, thus, hasn't given the formal recognition to Sikkim that India gave to the TAR.

A positive outcome to emerge from the Vajpayee visit—if indeed it could be called so—was China's acceptance of India's request to appoint politically empowered Special Representatives (SRs) to explore the framework of a boundary settlement. This replaced the official-level joint working group formed in 1988 which was devoted to the settlement of the border (as envisaged by Rajiv Gandhi) and later clarification of the LAC (after the 1993 Border Peace and Tranquillity Agreement) as it was felt that only a political approach could resolve the knotty border dispute. India's experience of Chinese deception had resulted in Vajpayee seeking the SRs route to resolve the border dispute. For example, when talks for the Middle Sector of the LAC began in 1998, China made boundary claims in four areas of Lapthal, Sangcha, Pulam Sumda and Kavriki in addition to the 1995-recorded difference in perception of the LAC in Barahoti. India and China had, in November 2000, exchanged maps of the Middle Sector—the least controversial of the three sectors—and they promised to exchange maps of the Western Sector in 2002. The Chinese did show their version of LAC maps of the Western Sector to the Indian interlocutors in 2002, but for unexplained reasons immediately withdrew the maps.

TEN YEARS OF PRIME MINISTER MANMOHAN SINGH

Compared with Indian prime ministerial visits, the visits of Chinese leaders to India have been preceded or accompanied by spectacular border announcements and unsavoury incidents. For example, when Chinese President Xi Jinping came to India in September 2014, while he was meeting with the Indian prime minister, PLA troops intruded into the Chumar area of north Kashmir. The exception was Prime Minister Wen Jiabao's India visit in April 2005, when the geopolitical context of the bilateral relationship had altered.

In 2005, the Indian economy was on the upswing and its naval power appeared robust. Delhi's relations with all major powers like Russia, Japan and the European Union were warm and its Look East policy was being welcomed by China's small neighbours. In addition, India's relations with the US were at their apogee: the US Secretary of State, Condoleezza Rice, on her maiden visit to India in March 2005, had announced that the US would help India become a major power (this eventually led to the signing of the July 2005 Indo-US joint statement whose high point was the civil nuclear deal).

Given this backdrop, and possibly fearing encirclement by an Indo-US strategic partnership, Wen, in order to wean India away from the US's orbit, signed two important agreements during his India visit: a strategic and cooperative partnership for peace and prosperity and the 'political parameters and guiding principles' for the settlement of the India-China boundary question as the first step towards border resolution. The other two steps had to do with the framework of the resolution and converting the agreed framework into a mutually acceptable border line. Delhi assessed the first agreement as the Chinese acceptance of India's risen status and the second was viewed as a positive first step achieved by the Special Representatives' talks towards border settlement. The guiding principles underscored the need to abide by the 'interests of population of border areas' and 'well-defined natural geographical features'. This was interpreted in India to mean that China would accept the McMahon Line as the border with minor adjustments, an assessment which was annulled by China within a year when its president came to India.

Wen's supposedly positive visit was followed by President Hu Jintao's visit to India in November 2006 which cast a long shadow over Chinese intentions on the border row. In April 2006, months before the president's arrival, Sun Yaxi, the Chinese ambassador in Delhi, created a stir by referring to India's Arunachal Pradesh as South Tibet and a part of China. This created an uproar in the Indian Parliament. Everyone forgot that China had first made territorial claims south of Tibet in 1959 when Nehru had asserted the McMahon Line as the border between India and Tibet. Earlier, China had objected to the 1914 Simla Agreement's division between Inner and Outer Tibet. Peking called the latter 'Zang Nan' or disputed area south of Tibet where it did not have control. Despite this knowledge, few had objected to Vajpayee's formal acceptance of Tibet as a part of China during his 2003 visit.

To diminish the impact of Sun Yaxi's statement, Indian experts argued that it was mere posturing; China was claiming Arunachal Pradesh whereas it would be satisfied with getting Tawang. The latter claim was first made by

China after Indira Gandhi's demise, saying that Tawang was the birthplace of the sixth Dalai Lama and hence a part of Tibet. What was not said was that Major R. Khathing of the Indian Army had evicted the Tibetan administration from Tawang and had established a subdivisional headquarters there on 12 February 1951. At the time, China had responded with a studied and significant silence.

The next bilateral visit which had an impact on the border question was the second visit of Premier Wen Jiabao in December 2010. On the eve of his visit, China announced that its border with India was 2,000 kilometres. Compelled to react to the unexpected Chinese move, S. Jaishankar, India's ambassador to China, told the media that India's disputed border with China was 3,488 kilometres.

What was the 2,000-kilometre-long disputed border that China was talking about? This is the total of the Middle Sector (554 kilometres), Sikkim (198 kilometres), and the Eastern Sector (1,226 kilometres), which adds up to 1,978 kilometres or 2,000 kilometres when rounded off. According to China's December 2010 announcement, it no longer has a border with India in the Western Sector or Ladakh (Jammu and Kashmir). Now if the Chinese do not have a border with India in Ladakh, then on whose territory do they have the LAC there? The Indian government and analysts ignored this moot question much in the same way that they misinterpreted the build-up leading to the major shift in China's Kashmir policy.

It was sometime in 2009 that the Chinese started issuing stapled visas to residents of Kashmir visiting China. Then, in July 2010, China refused a visa to Lieutenant General B. S. Jaswal, head of the Indian Army's Northern Command responsible for J&K, who was to lead a military delegation to China. Beijing told Delhi that as Jaswal was posted in Kashmir, which was a disputed territory, it would hurt Pakistani sensitivities if he visited China as head of the delegation. If, instead, he was sent as a member of the delegation, he would get the visa. Delhi did not agree to this.

Beijing finally acceded to India's request in January 2011 and started issuing regular visas to Kashmiris. India hailed this as a diplomatic victory, although we should have realized that after China had stated publicly that it did not have a border with India in J&K, it had no need to make a point through the use of stapled visas. Kashmir, China signalled, now belonged to Pakistan. Given this logic, Gilgit-Baltistan, by Chinese interpretation, was no longer disputed, but Pakistani territory. This explained the PLA's presence in Gilgit-Baltistan beginning 2011; when confronted, China claimed its civilian engineers were working on the upgrade of the Karakoram Highway joining

China's Xinjiang province with Pakistan's Gwadar Port. As the PLA numbers starting increasing, army chief General V. K. Singh finally went public and said there were 3,000 to 4,000 PLA soldiers in POK. Elaborating, the then Northern Army Commander, Lieutenant General K. T. Parnaik, confirmed that PLA footprints were increasing steadily, with their presence even sited along the Line of Control with Pakistan. Though not cartographically, the two military lines—the Line of Actual Control with China and the Line of Control with Pakistan—had, by 2011, become physically one for the Chinese troops who could straddle them with ease. For instance, the Border Security Force confirmed the presence of PLA snipers across the Jammu International Border or IB (called Working Boundary by Pakistan) in October 2014 when cross-border firing between India and Pakistan intensified within months of Narendra Modi becoming prime minister in May 2014.

As these twists and turns in the border saga continued, the fourth generation (since 1949 when the People's Republic of China came into being under Mao Zedong) of Chinese leadership gave way to the fifth in 2012. The fifth generation leadership had two peculiarities. First, the leadership—President Xi Jinping and Prime Minister Li Keqiang—which came to power at the 18th Communist Party Congress in November 2012 is the first to preside over a prosperous and risen China with more options than limitations and restraints which tied the hands of earlier leaderships. Such leaders were expected to follow proactive foreign and security policies, with the PLA in a decisive vanguard role. For this reason, President Xi, unlike his predecessors, assumed three powerful positions—the presidency, the post of general secretary of the Communist Party and chairmanship of the Central Military Commission (CMC)—at the same time. This should put to rest speculations that Jinping is not in firm control of the PLA, an explanation dished out by apologists for the Indian government.

Second, the PLA is likely to use all legal and psychological tricks to keep India chained to the border dispute given that it enjoys massive military advantages and close ties with the Pakistan military. To quote leading international scholar Roderick MacFarquhar, 'China would try and do business with India, through trade and investment, but they would view India as a country with a political system antithetical to their own, a natural ally of America or Japan or both, and, therefore, a country to be looked at with some wariness, a country for which the Chinese should crack the whip on the border when necessary.'

To take the disputed border story forward, days before Chinese Premier Li Keqiang was expected to arrive on his first visit to India, a platoon (about thirty soldiers) of the PLA, on 15 April 2013, intruded 19 kilometres inside Indian territory and pitched tents at Track Junction in the Depsang plains south of Daulat Beg Oldi in Ladakh (north Kashmir). The Chinese troops had found a gap in the surveillance grid of the Indian forces manning forward positions and slipped in. They stayed put for three weeks, finally leaving of their own accord on 5 May. During this period, in icy cold temperatures at heights of 16,500 feet, the PLA maintained its road and air (helicopter) logistics, including hot meals, with no interference from the Indian security forces. The latter, meanwhile, started the blame game with the Indo-Tibetan Border Police, which holds the first line of defence (observation), blaming the army (Ladakh Scouts) located behind it of little cooperation. The army, out of domestic (media) pressure to do something, pitched tents 300 metres from the PLA tents to monitor any Chinese activity.

India (unlike during the 1986–87 Sumdorong Chu crisis) did no troop build-up, nor warned the intruding PLA soldiers to vacate Indian land, nor blamed China for its blatant intrusion. India said that the intrusion was the result of a differing perception of the LAC. In an incredible statement flashed across televisions worldwide, Foreign Minister Salman Khurshid compared the intrusion with acne on the face. Delhi's diplomats worked overtime to resolve matters peacefully. From National Security Advisor Shivshankar Menon to mandarins of the External Affairs Ministry, all were busy working through a dozen existing bilateral communication channels. China smugly told India that for matters to be resolved, one more bilateral agreement was essential: the Border Defence Cooperation Agreement (BDCA), whose draft China had sent to India months ago. The PLA also asked that a few defence structures and Indian Army observation posts in the Chumar area in southern Ladakh (which overlooked China's Aksai Chin Highway) be dismantled, which was done.

Notwithstanding the ongoing crisis, Manmohan Singh and his Cabinet Committee on Security did not seek a briefing from the army chief, General Bikram Singh, for nineteen days. Without political direction, the general did nothing but repeat the tiresome cliché of different perceptions of the Line of Actual Control, which, of course, was not true on this occasion. The PLA had moved forward beyond its 1959 claim line. By doing so, China had substantiated its December 2010 declaration of not having a border with India in Ladakh. Throughout the three-week crisis, China maintained that its troops had not intruded but were on their own land.

A slew of high-level visits by high-ranking Indian politicians and bureaucrats to Beijing, including the National Security Advisor Shivshankar

Menon, Foreign Minister Salman Khurshid, Defence Minister A. K. Antony and Chief of Army Staff General Bikram Singh took place before October 2013 to show that relations between the two countries were normal; all this was in preparation for Manmohan Singh's October 2013 visit where the BDCA was signed. While repeating commitments made in previous bilateral agreements, the BDCA formalized that one side will not follow or tail patrols of the other side in border areas where there is no common understanding of the LAC. In reality this means that if a PLA patrol manages to find a gap anywhere in the 3,488-kilometre LAC (there is no understanding of the LAC alignment) and slips in—which is not difficult—the Indian Army would not follow or tail it by pitching tents close to them or obstructing its logistics line.

Given this restriction, the only option left for the Indian security forces (Indo-Tibetan Border Patrol and army) is to physically monitor the entire LAC without gaps so that Chinese intruders are stopped at the LAC itself and persuaded to go back through the 'banner drill'—blocking their way with banners marked 'you have crossed the LAC'—without provocation, use of arms or any means that can be construed as aggressive.

With this, the role of Indian forces on the LAC has been downgraded from guarding to policing, entailing huge manpower obligations. The term guarding suggests an inbuilt aggression resulting from heated exchanges and the possible use of arms. Policing, on the other hand, is a blocking activity requiring a disproportionately large force to control crowds or intruders.

Conscious of the huge manpower obligation that this would entail, India was dragging its feet on signing the Beijing-drafted BDCA until compelled to do so by the Ladakh intrusion. The BDCA has forced Indian security forces to police the 3,488-kilometre LAC round the clock with serious implications for India's border management, force allocations, annual defence allocations and war preparedness.

When asked whether the BDCA would place restrictions on India developing border infrastructure or enhancing military capabilities along the LAC, S. Jaishankar, India's ambassador to China, replied in the negative. Quoting from the BDCA preamble, which states the 'accepted principle of mutual and equal security', Jaishankar said that both countries were free to decide their respective security needs. This is not correct. The BDCA states that under Article I 'the two states shall carry out defence border cooperation on the basis of their respective laws and relevant bilateral agreements'. A relevant bilateral agreement like the 1993 Border Peace and Tranquillity Agreement states under Article II that the two sides 'will keep military forces by the principle of mutual and equal security to ceilings to be mutually agreed'.

The inference is clear: India cannot enhance military capability close to the LAC without China agreeing to it. Chinese deployment, with its excellent infrastructure and airlift capabilities, is not affected by this restriction. While there is no restriction on infrastructure building close to the LAC, the PLA, having moved the goalposts, has been objecting to Indian security forces' observation posts and towers close to the LAC. China has even expressed its displeasure at India's plan to construct a 1,800-kilometre industrial corridor in southern Arunachal Pradesh, which it considers a disputed area.

Following the Depsang incursion, the PLA did not allow Indian security forces to patrol up to its perception of the LAC in western Ladakh. As India did not want to escalate matters, its security forces have deliberately restricted the limit of their patrolling to a point well short of Track Junction where the PLA had pitched tents for three weeks. Thus the new 'limit of patrol' has become the new LAC in Ladakh, according to a report submitted by Shyam Saran, the chairman of the National Security Advisory Board, to the Prime Minister's Office.

Meanwhile, to formalize its Depsang gains, the PLA issued new 'battle maps' to its troops so as to facilitate their patrolling of new Chinese territorial claims. According to the *PLA Daily*, 'units were earlier using maps which were made between the Sixties and Seventies. To address this issue, the PLA's general headquarters started revision of maps in the second half of 2013.' Once the troops were familiar with the new battle maps and were in a state of military preparedness for border management and tackling conflicts on the new LAC, senior generals reportedly visited forward areas in north Ladakh close to the Karakoram Pass and areas ceded by Pakistan to China in 1963. In a rare gesture not seen in decades, a year after the Depsang incursion, General Xu Qiliang, vice chairman of the CMC, visited all PLA formations, from the highest military area commands to the smallest garrisons associated with the new LAC alignment in north Ladakh.

Watching the 2013 Depsang drama unfold, with India capitulating to China's terms of engagement, the BJP's prime ministerial candidate, Narendra Modi, in the run-up to India's general elections in early 2014, raked up the China issue in his public meetings, something that had never done before. By cautioning China to desist from its 'expansionist tendencies', he signalled that he would order a robust response to Chinese machinations if voted to power. The only way to halt these 'tendencies' was to get China to agree to the LAC ahead of the border resolution. Once the LAC was mutually agreed, PLA territorial aggressions would then constitute an act of war, something that China with its moralistic war philosophy of never being the aggressor but fighting only in self-defence, would be loath to do.

Once elected prime minister in May 2014, Modi welcomed high-level Chinese visits to India starting with State Councillor Yang Jiechi, who was appointed Special Representative for border talks with India. However, the most awaited Chinese leader's visit, watched and analysed across the world, was that of President Xi Jinping to India in September 2014. It turned out to be an unusual one with China professing friendship and flexing its muscles simultaneously. As mentioned earlier, while Xi was confabulating with Modi, about 1,000 PLA soldiers intruded inside Indian territory in Chumar in south Ladakh. Objecting to civilian infrastructure, they sought to build a road in the only area in Ladakh where the PLA is tactically not advantageously placed as compared with the Indian Army. The Indian reaction was swift and within days the two sides—with nearly 1,500 troops each and more arriving—faced off against each another. A visibly disturbed Modi confronted his Chinese counterpart, who promised to resolve the issue; however, nothing happened and the face-off continued.

During the joint press conference on the conclusion of the summit meeting, Modi publicly sought clarification of the LAC at the earliest. This was a clear departure—since the thawing of bilateral relations—from India's stance up to now, when it would routinely call for an early resolution of the border dispute. It was also an acknowledgement at the highest level that the signing of the 1993 agreement was a blunder which had complicated issues by aiding Chinese border transgressions; and a tacit acceptance by India that its border management will not be able to match China's anytime soon and that the Special Representatives' talks on border resolution had hit a dead end. Ignoring Modi's query, Xi replied that 'both sides were fully capable of ensuring that such incidents do not have a large impact on bilateral relations'.

The face-off in Ladakh continued even after Xi's three-day maiden visit to India and lasted a total of thirteen days. The terms of disengagement were not known immediately as the Indian government's public relations machinery obfuscated reality by comparing the two Chinese incursions in Ladakh—the three-week-long 19-kilometre incursion by the Chinese into the Depsang plains in April–May 2013 under Manmohan Singh's government and the two-week-long, 2-kilometre incursion by the Chinese into Chumar in September 2014 under the Modi government. It was overlooked that in the Depsang area, the Chinese have far better access than India, whereas in Chumar the Indians are better placed.

The cat was finally out of the bag when National Security Advisor Ajit Doval, who was appointed Special Representative for the eighteenth round of border talks in Beijing (on 23 March 2015), was to be briefed on his mandate for talks. In a high-level meeting chaired by Home Minister Rajnath Singh, it was decided that 'India will maintain [the] status quo at disputed pockets along the China border'. Modi, like Manmohan Singh, had reportedly accepted the new LAC in Ladakh, where the PLA had shifted the military line at both ends—Depsang Valley in the Northern Sector and Chumar in the Southern Sector. In essence, 'the PLA had incrementally occupied near 640 sq km [about 30 km by 21 km] in DBO, Chumar, and Pangong Tso'.

Since the stand-off in Depsang in April–May 2013, and the beginning of the eighteenth round of border resolution talks, the following developments have taken place: the two nations signed the Border Defence Cooperation Agreement (a Chinese requirement); India voluntarily reduced its patrolling limits in the Depsang Valley resulting in the new LAC; the PLA issued fresh tactical maps to its forces showing the new LAC; China, in recognition of their good work, promoted nine officers of the Lanzhou military area, responsible for the border in Ladakh, from senior colonel to the rank of major general on 12 January 2015; and India's Modi government quietly accepted the altered LAC.

Xi's September 2014 visit had dented Modi's image as a strong leader. Consequently, Modi adopted the dual approach of firmness and appeasement while dealing with the border issue. For his audience at home, Modi showed firmness by becoming the first prime minister in twenty-eight years to visit Arunachal Pradesh on its twenty-ninth statehood day in February 2015, and promised substantive economic assistance to the state which China maintains as disputed. Modi's presence in Arunachal Pradesh was vehemently protested by Beijing.

However, before leaving for his China visit in May 2015, Modi, in order to create the right atmospherics and bonhomie, gave an interview saying what the Chinese wanted to hear: 'The present priority of both nations is the economic welfare of their people. We have taken a conscious decision not to allow confrontation to escalate into conflict…in so far as the border is concerned, the most important point right now is that peace and tranquillity must not be disturbed.'

Past masters at the game Modi was playing, China gave it back in the same coin. While Xi broke protocol to welcome Modi in his hometown Xian rather than the capital Beijing, the *Global Times* newspaper, a Communist party mouthpiece, curtly advised the Indian prime minister to avoid 'playing dirty tricks', referring to his visit to Arunachal Pradesh a few months ago. Meanwhile, China's state television showed news of Modi's China visit with an Indian map minus Kashmir and Arunachal Pradesh as the backdrop. China, which relies heavily on symbolism, made it clear that bilateral relations would progress only on its terms; there was no need for Modi to bring up the need to define the LAC.

A digression to understand Chinese diplomacy would be instructive. According to Henry Kissinger, a long-term watcher of China, 'Chinese negotiations use diplomacy to weave together political, military and psychological elements into an overall strategic design. Diplomacy to them is the elaboration of a strategic principle. They ascribe no particular significance to the process of negotiations as such; nor do they consider the opening of a particular negotiation a transformational event. They have no emotional difficulty with deadlocks; they consider them the inevitable mechanism of diplomacy. And they patiently take a long view against impatient interlocutors, making time their ally.'

The impatient Modi, however, publicly brought up the issue of LAC clarification once again in China. Addressing students at the Tsinghua University in Beijing on 15 May 2015 in the presence of the Chinese foreign minister, he said, 'A shadow of uncertainty always hangs over the sensitive border region. It is because neither side knows where the LAC is in these areas. This is why I have proposed resuming the process of clarifying it. We can do this without prejudice to our position on the boundary question.' Modi did not stop at this. Three days later, while addressing the Mongolian Parliament, Modi, alluding to China, said that Asia 'is also a region that lives on the uneasy edge of uncertainty, of unsettled questions, of unresolved disputes and unforgotten memories'.

China responded by getting a middle-ranking official to reject Modi's public pitch for LAC agreement and instead called for a 'code of conduct' between the two nations. Meeting with Indian media, Huang Xilian, China's deputy director general of Asian Affairs, said, 'If we find that clarification of the LAC is a building block then we should go ahead. But if we find that it is a stumbling block it could complicate the situation further.' As far as China was concerned, the agreement on the LAC was a closed matter. The border resolution was a bridge too far.

The Chinese leadership had dismissed India's desire for mutual agreement on the LAC for two reasons. One, which has already been discussed, had to do with the Chinese announcement of December 2010 that it did not have a border with India in Ladakh (J&K); consequently, the LAC there with India had become meaningless. To ask China to agree to the LAC in Ladakh on what China now considers disputed territory between India and Pakistan is unrealistic.

And two, the LAC, by definition a military line, can be moved by force by either side. This helps Chinese troops undertake brazen LAC transgressions and intrusions. Such transgressions on an agreed LAC—a de facto border—would be an act of aggression tantamount to a declaration of war. Why would China lose the advantage of exercising military coercion by sauntering across the LAC at will?

In three-and-a-half decades, the chasm between India and China on the border dispute is glaringly visible. In 1980, China offered India the status quo formula for border resolution, which India refused. China was to accept the McMahon Line as the de facto border, while India was to forsake her claim to Aksai Chin and agree to the LAC in the Western Sector as the border with China. Today, China wants both Ladakh and Arunachal Pradesh!

The history of the border dispute shows that two prime ministers—Jawaharlal Nehru and Indira Gandhi—had the opportunity to resolve the issue. However, Rajiv Gandhi and Narasimha Rao made the border dispute a millstone around India's neck through their appeasement of China and abandonment of border management. Consequently, since 1993, China has pursued its brand of 'forward policy' through increased territorial transgressions resulting in the nibbling away of Indian land—by moving towards its 1960 claim line in the Western Sector, and by treating the LAC with derision by increasing areas of dispute in the Eastern and even the Middle sectors. Two decades of incremental transgressions, with India taking no steps to stop them, is helping China defeat India politically, psychologically and militarily. So, when India, at the height of the PLA intrusions in April–May 2013 said that 'India-China border areas continue to remain peaceful', it emboldened China to make more mischief, which it did in September 2014.

The bureaucrats who guide Indian policy from the External Affairs Ministry believe that China is merely posturing. According to Saran, 'One cannot see a solution that diverges significantly from the existing alignment of the LAC, and the longer the status quo continues the more likely is the LAC to eventually morph into a settled boundary.' Such assessments betray a lack of understanding of military power—the prime mover of foreign policy of non-status quo nations like China and Pakistan—and the role of strategic thinking in relations between nations.

For example, after the unfavourable international tribunal verdict on the South China Sea dispute in July 2016, China's top diplomat Yang Jiechi said, 'China cannot lose one centimetre of the area it claims. The sovereignty issue is China's bottom line.' Since Yang is both China's foreign minister and the designated Special Representative for border talks with India, New Delhi should mull over the inescapable conclusion: if China has refused to compromise over the South China Sea dispute which indirectly involves the United States's prestige, why would it compromise on the border dispute with India, especially when India stands alone and with questionable military power?

CHAPTER 2

LINE OF CONSTRAINT

The evening of 2 July 2003 in the Uri bowl on the LC with Pakistan in Kashmir began with routine shelling. The firing, which included illumination shells used to assist infiltrations across the LC, continued for two hours, after which the Indian side responded with interest. Next morning, a beaming brigade commander, Brigadier Ramesh Halgali, told the authors that accurate artillery fire had set a Pakistani ammunition point and petrol, oil and lubricant dump in Chakoti, across from the Uri bowl, on fire.

Before the ceasefire and LC fence, such tactical victories were a source of both joy and motivation. Tales of heroism travelled all along the LC to fire up other units to do one better. There was never a dull moment. It was unthinkable that Pakistani commandos could cross the LC and behead sleeping Indian soldiers, that too without fear of retaliation.

Given the unbridled nature of long-range artillery fire, those who were bound by duty to keep vigil at the treacherous forward posts preferred to keep their heads down. Warning boards such as 'The enemy observation post can see you', 'Drive carefully', 'You are in a shelling prone area', were taken seriously by both visitors and the officers escorting them. Since fair-weather friends could not be trusted, both sides traversed long back-breaking tracks from one post to another even if they were only a few metres away because any movement had to take place as far away from the enemy observation posts as possible. All this was routine. Shelling was so commonplace that it ruffled no feathers amongst the army brass or in New Delhi. On the contrary, the absence of shelling was a matter of concern and enquiry. Anxious commanding officers would intensify patrolling to get more information about the enemy. Has it pulled out its troops? Was the rotation of troops going on? Were they short of ammunition?

Life on the LC was as normal as it could be. The months between March and October witnessed maximum activity, and they were not of the shelling kind alone. The summer months were used for annual winter stocking to cater for the snowbound months when snow and avalanches block a large number of forward posts, tracks and roads. There are posts on the LC in the mountains that get buried under 25 feet of snow in winter. In some areas, the battalion headquarters remain cut off from their posts for about four to five months. It is an exacting task to keep lines of communication open when snow plays havoc not only with the telephone lines but also road transport.

While the upkeep of defences by both sides (India and Pakistan) was a continuous process, the making of new defences or the strengthening of existing ones invited instant fire. The Indian Army has three kinds of defences on the LC: steel permanent defences or fighting bunkers; ammunition permanent defences; and self-help bunkers made of stones. As a rule, most bunkers which are on the main enemy approaches are steel permanent defences; on an average, about 50 per cent of bunkers are steel permanent defences.

In the aftermath of the ten-month-long Operation Parakram, senior officers in Srinagar (15 Corps Headquarters) and Udhampur (Northern Command Headquarters responsible for the J&K theatre), were debating two issues. Inspired by the Border Security Force on the International Border (IB) in Jammu, the army vice chief, Lieutenant General N. C. Vij, had asked the Northern Command to fence likely ingress routes on the LC to check infiltrations. This was not an easy task as the enemy did everything possible (with heavy small arms and artillery fire) to thwart Indian troops from erecting the fence. Moreover, the officers themselves were divided on the issue; it was felt that the fence, however limited, would restrict the clandestine activities of our own troops across the LC whenever necessary.

The Northern Army commander, Lieutenant General Hari Prasad, told the authors, 'Our methods of interception have improved and we have started select fencing. This has put a lot of pressure on infiltrators.' He was encouraged by the fact that plenty of surveillance equipment meant to check infiltration had been procured on a 'fast-track' basis from Israel and France. These included handheld thermal imagers, handheld battlefield surveillance radars, thermal imaging integrated observation equipment, and so on. The mood in Delhi was clearly in favour of a fence on the LC.

The other issue being discussed was operations. Given the mountainous terrain in Kashmir, the war aim for 15 Corps would be to capture ground (heights) to improve the defensive posture. Two difficult military objectives in Kashmir could be the Lipa Valley (a prominent infiltration route in winters) and the Haji Pir Pass (the shortest route from Poonch in Jammu to Uri in Kashmir). The general officer commanding of 15 Corps, Lieutenant General V. G. Patankar, had little hesitation in saying, 'The strategic importance of Lipa Valley cannot be denied. We do have the Lipa Valley in mind.' The overall mood in the summer of 2003 in the J&K war theatre was to maintain an aggressive posture and work towards it. However, this was not what Army Headquarters, influenced by the political leadership, had in mind.

Even as the (internal) debate within Army Headquarters and field formations on whether to have an offensive or defensive posture was going on, the sudden announcement of a ceasefire on the LC by Pakistan on 24 November 2003, and its ready acceptance by India two days later, took the Indian Army and the country at large by surprise. Unknown to most Indians was the fact that the ceasefire was meant to prepare favourable ground for the ongoing backchannel talks for the Kashmir resolution by both sides. Equally unknown to the Pakistan Army at that time was the operational advantage the ceasefire would give them. The fencing, coupled with the counter-infiltration posture adopted by the Indian Army on the LC, reassured the Pakistan Army over time that its eastern front against India would remain trouble-free.

The 26 November 2003 ceasefire on the LC transformed the military line formed in 1972 after the 1971 war between India and Pakistan. Before the ceasefire, silence was the cause for concern; after the ceasefire, firing became the cause for concern.

LINE OF CONTROL

As we have seen, the 772-kilometre-long Line of Control runs from a place called Sangam close to Chhamb in the south up to map grid reference NJ 9842 in Ladakh in the north. It is peculiar in many ways. It is agreed on maps (delineated) but not on the ground (not demarcated). Since this left room for mischief by both sides to tactically adjust the line to its advantage, the LC has been prone to surprises (until the 2003 ceasefire). The 1999 Kargil conflict is the extreme example of the Pakistan Army pushing its luck too far.

Both ends of the LC are unstable. The northern end, which terminates at map point NJ 9842, resulted in the 1984 Siachen conflict. The southern end of the LC at Sangam does not join with the IB. Instead, there is the 189-kilometre-long quasi-LC between Sangam and Boundary Pillar 19 further south where the IB recognized by both countries begins. The quasi-LC in the Jammu division—called the Working Boundary (WB) by Pakistan and the International Border by India—was traditionally the revenue boundary between the erstwhile state of Jammu and Kashmir and undivided Punjab. Pakistan does not accept this portion as the IB as it faces Pakistan's Punjab. Recognizing it as the IB would imply that Pakistan accepts Jammu as the border; while accepting it as the LC would mean that the northernmost portion of Pakistan's Punjab is a military-held line, which can be altered.

Unlike the Line of Control, the International Border/Working Boundary is guarded by paramilitary forces: the Border Security Force for India and the Chhamb Rangers for Pakistan. The two armies hold defences just behind the paramilitary forces. According to rules of engagement mutually agreed to in 1960 and not broken by either side even with the creation of the LC after the 1971 war, artillery is not used at the WB/IB during peacetime. Even at the height of hostilities short of war, both sides have restricted the exchange of fire to small arms (rifles, machine guns, small-calibre mortars and other light weapons held by paramilitary forces). Once a war begins, paramilitary forces on both sides immediately come under the command of their respective armies.

The peacetime arrangement on the WB/IB has created a dilemma for India. Unlike the Chhamb Rangers, which are officered completely by the regular Pakistan Army, and which as a result share the army's military ethos, tactics, weapon systems and training, the Border Security Force, under the union Home Ministry, has its own cadre, with Indian Police Service officers holding the top slots. This implies that during peacetime, the Border Security Force and the army (under the union Defence Ministry) follow different channels of communication with minimal operational interaction between the two.

Unfortunately for India, the area between Chhamb and Sialkot, which is the traditional battlefield between India and Pakistan, is part of the WB/IB. In both the 1965 and 1971 wars, India lost Chhamb to Pakistan, which at present occupies it up to the west bank of the Munnawar Tawi River. Given the military importance of the area, the army effectively occupies 10 kilometres of the IB here, while the Border Security Force is left with a 179-kilometre-long stretch to guard. The Indian Army, thus, is directly responsible for guarding a total of 782 kilometres of the border with Pakistan—772 kilometres of the LC and 10 kilometres of the IB in Jammu.

Nearly 271 kilometres of the LC meanders through thickly vegetated plains and semi-mountainous terrain in Jammu division up to the Pir Panjal Range and falls in the area of responsibility of the army's 16 Corps at

Nagrota. North of Pir Panjal and up to the Zoji La pass, 450 kilometres of the LC is mountainous, with heights of up to 11,000 feet. It is the responsibility of the Srinagar-based 15 Corps Headquarters. Most of the high-altitude area starts beyond the Zoji La pass and runs into Ladakh. The 238-kilometre stretch of the LC here is the responsibility of 14 Corps, formed after the 1999 Kargil conflict.

INDIAN ARMY: 1990 TO 2016

The 13-lakh strong Indian Army faces two difficult challenges. One is the no-war-no-peace (NWNP) environment in Jammu and Kashmir, and the other is a probability of 'hot war' with Pakistan and China, both requiring different mindsets, equipment and training. Unfortunately, the NWNP combat, which is inward-looking, takes priority because it is the present reality and the army has honed its skills at it for twenty-six years since 1990.

Today, nearly 30 per cent of the army is in the J&K theatre under the Northern Command Headquarters in Udhampur, while an equal number prepares itself to replace those in the NWNP zone after four-week reorientation training in defensive counter-insurgency operations (CI ops) at two corps battle schools in the troubled state. Considering that NWNP is the only familiar battle zone, it is here that generations of officers have come of age and won awards, promotions, prestige and status. A retired general summed up the preference for NWNP: 'Today, general-ship is about fighting small wars,' he told the authors. This explains the long list of decorations that follow most senior army officers' names, something which their predecessors who participated in actual wars did not have. Field Marshal Sam Manekshaw, who won the 1971 war for India, was awarded a mere Military Cross.

Moreover, with all our present generals only having donned the uniform after the last war in 1971, preparedness for 'hot war' is an elusive concept which is more notional than real. Unless the army's prioritization gets reversed, India's territorial integrity will be severely affected. India, after all, has three military-held lines—the 772-kilometre Line of Control (LC) with Pakistan, the 126-kilometre Actual Ground Position Line (on Siachen Glacier), which Pakistan calls the Line of Contact, and the 3,488-kilometre LAC with China—which require boots on the ground to provide good border management, credible deterrence and an offensive posture for war. The present army is overworked and overstretched and poses little threat to either adversary. This is borne out by the uninterrupted infiltration by terrorists from Pakistan across the LC since 1990, and China's successful military coercion in April–May 2013. Strong political leadership is needed to get the army back to its basics: training for its primary task of preparing for 'hot war'.

The twenty-six years of the army's involvement in counter-insurgency operations in J&K has witnessed six distinct phases. The first phase from 1990–96 was the most difficult with numerous twists and turns. During army chief General S. F. Rodrigues' tenure from 1990–93, large numbers of the regular army were inducted for the first time in Kashmir for internal security operations. General Rodrigues maintained that the increased deployment of the army was an 'aid to civil authority' and not for counter-insurgency operations. The implication was that the army would leave the Kashmir Valley as soon as the situation was brought under control to allow the civil administration to function.

Pakistan, meanwhile, was in no mood to let go of the opportunity to foster insurgency in the Valley. So Prime Minister Benazir Bhutto declared from Muzaffarabad in April 1990 that the accession to Pakistan was the only option open to Kashmiris. Pakistan also told the United States that it feared that the massive induction of the Indian Army into J&K would be used to spring a surprise attack on Pakistan across the Line of Control. This led to the US's 1990 Robert Gates (deputy national security advisor under President George H. W. Bush) mission to the subcontinent when numerous confidence building measures between India and Pakistan, including the once-a-week telephone conversation between the two director generals of military operations, were agreed.

The Gates Mission put India on the back foot with little hope of the Indian Army crossing the LC. Moreover, Kashmiri youth had started to cross over into POK for training to liberate the Valley. From 1990–93, the militants had the upper hand, with the Indian media reporting 'liberated zones' in the Valley. Credit, however, must go to General Rodrigues, as despite the odds, by early 1993 the army had managed to bring insurgency in the Valley under control. The army came down with a heavy hand. Human rights were given short shrift. (The army, however, maintains that its human rights record, with a few exceptions, was exemplary.)

The Indian Army's tactical successes forced Pakistan's ISI to change its strategy of support to the insurgency through five well-thought-out steps. One, by 1993, radical Hizbul Mujahideen replaced the Jammu and Kashmir Liberation Front; and well-equipped mercenaries from Afghanistan, Syria, Libya and Algeria found their way into the Kashmir Valley by negotiating high mountain passes in the north. The foreign mercenaries were a determined lot who took on both the paramilitary forces and the Indian Army in pitched battles to support the indigenous Hizbul. Alongside, the Laskhar-e-Taiba, created in 1990 in Afghanistan with headquarters in Muridke (near Lahore), was encouraged to commence operations in Kashmir.

Two, Pakistan shifted terrorist training camps from POK to Afghanistan in 1993 as the US, under India's insistence, came close to declaring Pakistan a state sponsoring terrorism.

Three, to relieve pressure on insurgents in the Valley, the ISI took advantage of the communal divide in Jammu. With the Muslims of Doda having an affinity with those in the Valley, it proved an excellent place to provide succour and sustenance to insurgents on the run in the Valley across the Pir Panjal range. The towns of Doda, Kishtwar and Bhadarwah are contiguous to the thinly populated mountainous areas of Himachal Pradesh, which also became a good hiding place. By the beginning of 1994, the situation in Doda had deteriorated considerably. To operate in Doda, the army wanted the Disturbed Areas Act followed by the Armed Forces (Special Powers) Act (AFSPA), which since 1990 had been applied in the Valley and a 20-kilometre belt along the LC in Poonch and Rajouri districts, to be extended to Doda at the earliest. This was done.

Four, international concern over human rights violations in Kashmir reached a high point in February 1994 when Prime Minister Benazir Bhutto raised the issue at the United Nations Commission for Human Rights in Geneva. Meanwhile, India set up a National Human Rights Commission in October 1993, followed by the army establishing a human rights cell to look into human rights violations by the army. And, five, Pakistan helped create the Hurriyat Conference, an umbrella organization of twenty-seven militant groups, mostly pro-Pakistan, with dubious and untested political clout, in May 1993.

The year 1993 could have been a turning point for the Kashmir insurgency. The new Chief of Army Staff, General B. C. Joshi, who took office on 1 July 1993, was determined to meet the problem head-on. Unlike his predecessor, he refused to call the Kashmir problem a 'law and order' issue, implying that the governor, retired General K. V. Krishna Rao (the state was under governor's rule), be disallowed to dictate to the army in the troubled state. General Joshi asked Prime Minister P. V. Narasimha Rao in August 1993 for permission to hit insurgent bases in POK and conduct raids on Pakistani posts close to the LC, especially south of Pir Panjal. He reasoned that no additional troops were needed for these tasks. And such proactive action would help raise the morale of the troops, put

Pakistan on the defensive and help sever growing ties between the people and the radical mujahids operating in Kashmir. The timing was opportune as insurgency had not yet spread to Jammu division, the Hurriyat was not formed and the army had the militants under manageable control.

General Joshi was of the firm conviction that the army should not continue in counter-terrorism operations for long, but go back to its primary task of external defence. He said as much to the prime minister. Rao, however, made three strategic mistakes. The first, and perhaps the most fatal, was to accord primacy to military action over political initiatives to address the Kashmir issue; he ignored the fact that military action alone cannot defeat an insurgency.

The second mistake was ordering the army to maintain a strictly defensive posture along the LC. While this was lauded as a war avoidance measure, the result at the operational level was that the initiative passed completely into the hands of the insurgents and their Pakistani handlers. The latter dictated the rates of engagement, infiltration, areas to be activated and to what purpose, including methods of initiation. The 1999 Kargil conflict was a result of it.

The third mistake was that the army and paramilitary forces were never told what was expected of them. In military terms, this is called end state, specifying what results are expected or desired by an active deployment of military force. In later years, when counter-insurgency ops became a comfort zone for senior officers, they would concoct unrealistic reasons for continuing with the ops.

Prime Minister Rao backed Governor Rao to the hilt, making it clear to the defunct state administration and the army that he wanted to hold parliamentary and state assembly elections in J&K at the earliest. He was not interested in a political resolution of the Kashmir problem which had led to the insurgency. The state elections were eventually held in 1996 amidst widespread reports that the security forces had helped rig the Kashmir elections through bogus voting.

Meanwhile, taking stock of the situation, General Joshi revived the idea of the Rashtriya (National) Rifles, mooted in 1987 by Minister of State for Defence Arun Singh and Chief of Army Staff General K. Sundarji: a regular army with another name to beef up numbers, but with a temporary paramilitary status which remains to this day.

As it became clear that the army would have to be in J&K for longer than he had wished, General Joshi decided to raise large numbers of RR units from within the army, with the intention of saving time (by dispensing with getting the government's approval for new raisings). Even as a portion of the army was to become the RR, he was keen to not use the Northern Command and even Strike Corps reserves for counterterrorism operations in J&K. A total of 40,000 troops under thirty battalions and ten sector headquarters (brigade headquarters) were ordered to be raised in nine months starting January 1994 by milking existing army units and using war wastage reserves.

The raising of 40,000 RR troops in record time was a nightmare for the army. At a time when the army was struggling to maintain equipment levels because of the sudden collapse of the Soviet Union, war wastage reserves with the army for vehicles, tentage and small arms were depleted to precarious levels. To cater to the force's lack of cohesiveness (as they were gathered from disparate units) General Joshi became the honorary 'colonel of the RR regiment' to ensure the best troops and officers came to it. As the RR units took three to five years to stabilize, regular troops including reserve forces and Special Forces continued to be employed in counterterrorism roles.

Being aware that RR would have to operate amongst the people under the media glare, General Joshi issued strict dos and don'ts to troops to check human rights violations. He also decided to raise a psychological operations division under a major general rank officer drawing from officers of the Military Intelligence and Operations Directorate, that would report to the Vice Chief of Army Staff, to counter the insurgents' propaganda. This was the beginning of the Army Liaison Cell which, over time, transformed into the present Directorate General of Public Information. The way it operates now is not what it was intended to be. The Army Liaison Cell was meant to assist the media with timely and accurate information to counter militants' propaganda, and not to project senior army officers as the Additional Directorate General of Public Information and its affiliate organizations at lower command levels do now.

◆

The sudden death of General Joshi was a setback to the army's determination to go back to its primary task on the LC. It also marked the second phase from 1994–98 under the Chief of Army Staff, General Shankar Roychowdhury, when the army consolidated its hold on CI ops under difficult conditions: the Rashtriya Rifles after its rapid expansion was showing unmistakable signs of distress; the flow of hardened foreign militants into Kashmir increased progressively; the army's strategy of 'winning hearts and minds' under Operation Sadbhavana was viewed with suspicion by the people; and the United Headquarters—formed in May 1993 by union Minister of State for Home Rajesh Pilot with retired Lieutenant General M. A. Zaki as its chairman—was not working, as various security forces failed to cooperate with one another.

An elaboration on the RR during this period is necessary. Compared to the motivated militants, the RR lacked cohesion, motivation, good communications and weaponry. There were several instances of soldiers running amok. Cases of soldiers inflicting self-injuries as a way of being eased out of the Valley were not uncommon. The commanding officers of most RR units were simply not communicating with their troops. There was a discernible decrease in discipline and patience. Round-the-clock vigilance, lack of sleep and an all-pervading fear was taking its toll on the troops. Added to this was a shortage of young officers. Over a series of meetings with senior officers of the Northern Command, the following reasons were found to be responsible for the existing state of affairs: command breakdown, battle fatigue, overall shortage of young officers, peacetime administration found to be overloaded, environmental stress, a debilitating work culture, general disturbance, troops succumbing to enemy propaganda, officers using any method to get postings cancelled, and inadequate allowances for troops combating insurgency in the state.

Between 1995 and 1998, as many as six regular brigades were sucked into counter-insurgency operations. Little thought was given to the fact that these were reserves of the Northern Command, a fact which must have comforted Pakistan when planning the 1999 Kargil conflict. The Indian Army was to pay dearly by losing many more lives during the Kargil conflict, because these soldiers had to reorient themselves from conducting CI ops to fighting a conventional war.

The army, however, patted itself on the back for having done yeoman service in the conduct of the 1996 assembly elections and the installation of the Farooq Abdullah government in October 1996. This landmark event convinced the army leadership of its role in the running of the state administration. Kamal Mustafa, Farooq Abdullah's younger brother, told the authors that the army had then approached Chief Minister Farooq Abdullah with a strange proposal. It wanted senior army officers to fill the posts of deputy commissioners and commissioners in the state. The suggestion was immediately shot down by the union home minister, L. K. Advani.

◆

The 1999 Kargil conflict was the third and crucial phase in the army's involvement in CI ops. A number of lessons should have been learnt by then, yet few were sought let alone learnt by the army leadership. The army was caught off guard by the conflict and had difficulty in reorienting itself to conventional operations. With the sudden shifting of attention of 15 and 16 Corps commanders towards conventional war, the RR was rendered headless. By extension, the United Headquarters, which was formed to institutionalize cooperation and coordination between all security forces, especially the RR and paramilitary forces (Border Security Force and Central Reserve Police Force), and had been less than optimally functional since its inception in May 1993, was rendered defunct. This meant a grave threat to the internal lines of the army's communications for soldiers fighting on the LC. Therefore, to provide command and control to the RR troops and support to United Headquarters, Army Headquarters ordered the shifting of RR Overall Force Headquarters (OFH) from Delhi to Srinagar in June 1999 under its director general, Lieutenant General Avtar Singh, as overall force commander (OFC). The OFH was an administrative headquarters looking after the welfare of troops and not their operations.

This triggered a host of problems. Chief Minister Farooq Abdullah refused to accept Lieutenant General Avtar Singh as his security advisor, as Singh was unfamiliar with the situation on the ground. Moreover, the paramilitary forces in the state argued that the director general RR, in his avatar as OFC, could not dictate terms. In less than ninety days, the post of OFC, RR, was dissolved and Avtar Singh moved back to Delhi as director general RR, with most of the Overall Force Command's staff getting posted to the newly raised 14 Corps Headquarters near Leh (Ladakh).

This episode presented two challenges: first, the director general RR knew little about the operational aspects of RR. And second, the paramilitary forces that accepted the corps commanders who are security advisors to the state chief minister refused to accept the director general RR as operationally any better than themselves. Consequent to this, the army after the Kargil conflict decided that the general officers commanding of 15 and 16 Corps would be responsible for the dual tasks of traditional defence and counter-terrorism ops both in war and peace.

What lessons did the army learn from the Kargil conflict? It raised two additional counter-insurgency force headquarters to combat militants. The Kilo force headquarters was raised in September 1999, and the Romeo force headquarters came into being in January 2000. These moves demonstrated the army's resolve to continue with CI ops all by itself if necessary.

The idea of a greater involvement of paramilitary forces in both CI ops and in the security of internal communication lines during war was glossed over.

◆

Even as the infiltration of hard-core militants increased after Pakistan's defeat in the Kargil conflict, the army was also recovering from the jolt of the unexpected limited war. This impacted most on the field commanders, who became restive, setting the stage for the fourth phase. In 2000, in a replay of the early 1990s, the army at the lower levels was raring to go, having been encouraged by Chief of Army Staff General V. P. Malik's enunciation of the doctrine of a 'limited war', which was publicly endorsed by Defence Minister George Fernandes.

Thus, in a tacit understanding, while the senior brass in Kashmir turned a Nelson's eye, the units adopted a calibrated offensive action across the LC to engage the Pakistan Army and to sanitize areas of infiltration. For example, on 22 January 2000, fighting in the Chhamb sector left sixteen Pakistani soldiers dead. While both sides blamed the other, the truth was that Indian troops, in strength, attacked a Pakistani post and overran it. Similar instances occurred in Akhnoor, Mendhar, Kotli, Naushera and Pallanwala between January and August 2000. It was payback time on the Line of Control.

Indian commanders on the LC started justifying the need for such action on the grounds that Pakistan must face local military defeats. It was argued in private that body bags going home under the glare of cameras would compel the Pakistan Army to rethink its proxy war in Kashmir. Local artillery commanders said that in addition to punitive raids by infantry and Special Forces on Pakistani posts, more Bofors regiments should be inducted into J&K. Heavy artillery pounding of Pakistani positions in areas where infiltration occurred would be a morale booster for Indian troops.

Given this situation, General Malik, in August 2000, said that chances of a war with Pakistan were high. His assessment was based on the thinking that Pakistan might, in anger, retaliate in strength which could result in a full-scale limited war. The army chief's public statement was enough for the Indian political leadership to get alarmed. Thus, barring a few incidents in 2013 and 2014 when the Indian Army conducted raids across the LC, the unstated calibrated offensive action policy came to an end by April 2001.

To appease the army, the government cleared the raising of more RR battalions in January 2001. For the first time, a separate financial allocation was made for the RR in the annual defence budget. The proposal to raise thirty more RR battalions, six each year, was accepted. Two additional force headquarters and eight sector headquarters to control the additional forces were to be raised accordingly. This marked the end of the army's proactive strategy.

The following years saw the army justify the merits of a defensive mindset, and the benefits of counter-insurgency and anti-infiltration ops done by sixty-four RR battalions controlled by five force headquarters. Like the earlier period of 1994–98, the chasm between officers and men grew once again, but for entirely different reasons. The erstwhile dissonance within the RR is no longer there; they are functioning well. Instead, mutual respect between officers and men, which is the raison d'être of an army unit the world over, had diminished. This had to do with living in constant fear, day in and out, in a war-like environment, where the troops got little rest and relief from the punishing routine of patrols and ambushes. This is the main reason for growing instances of soldiers committing suicide.

◆

The fifth phase of the army's internal involvement in J&K began with the end of Operation Parakram in October 2002 and lasted until the arrival of Prime Minister Narendra Modi's government in May 2014. During this period, four events motivated the army to continue in the counter-insurgency role. These were the 26 November 2003 ceasefire on the Line of Control and Actual Ground Position Line (Siachen); Operation Fence (Deewar) or Anti-Infiltration Obstacle System since 1 July 2004; the release of the army's 'sub-conventional warfare doctrine' during General J. J. Singh's tenure in January 2007 by Defence Minister A. K. Antony; and the two successful state assembly elections of 2002 and 2008.

The LC ceasefire offer was a masterstroke by Pakistan's General Pervez Musharraf. By the silencing of firepower, especially artillery guns, all artillery units in the J&K theatre were suddenly short of hands-on training. Until the ceasefire, all artillery units had a battery (six guns) ready to fire salvos at short notice; the artillery fire was a morale booster for troops on the LC. The artillery guns were now lying in sheds with gunners doing counter-insurgency duties.

A sense of frustration born out of the unending and punishing CI role was gripping the soldiers. All the soldiers that the authors spoke with immediately after Operation Parakram said they were happier training for conventional war. With the LC ceasefire, General Musharraf had achieved his strategic purpose of tiring out the Indian Army by luring it to fight an elusive enemy rather than train for combat with the real one. This was not all. General Musharraf had directed his Director General, ISI, Lieutenant General Ashfaq Kayani, to take terrorism from the J&K theatre to mainland India. India was to witness many deplorable terrorism attacks supported by the ISI to a greater or lesser degree with the 26 November 2008 Mumbai attacks being the boldest of them all.

The announcement of the 26 November 2003 ceasefire on the LC also ended the debate on what military posture the army should adopt. Should it be offensive with tactical level defence or total defence? The army chief, General N. C. Vij, ordered the Northern Command to fence the LC. The fence was erected at a breakneck pace in the 16 and 15 Corps sectors. Given the meandering nature of the LC, the run of the fence varied from place to place from being right on the LC to up to 5 kilometres inside it.

Comprising four layers of iron pillars of decreasing heights of 12, 9, 7 and 5 feet, the fence has a total of seven concertina wires thrown between them. A direct current provided by 2.5-kilovolt generator sets placed every 500 metres along the entire fence partially electrifies it on the enemy side. An added sensor, a wire, on the fence connects it to the nearest headquarters and is meant to indicate trespassing. According to an engineer officer, the electrification system and the touch-sensor are primitive, being high on maintenance and low on detection. The fence is nowhere near the best in the world, like the fence on the United States-Mexico border which has computer consoles all along it to provide physical details of trespassers. While the cost of the entire fence was conservatively estimated to be ₹800 crore in 2005 at Army Headquarters, its recurring annual maintenance cost has been expensive both in terms of manpower as well as financial outlay.

Maintaining the fence has not been easy on the troops. It has not been cost-effective in the higher reaches in the winter months where the snow is 20 to 40 feet deep and the fence gets washed away. Only a small window is available in the summer for repairing the fence; two battalions of army pioneers (about 2,000 men) with ponies and mules are employed every year in addition to other support services to ensure that work is finished in time. This task obviously is at the cost of the annual winter stocking effort of the forward posts in high altitudes which, too, have the same window for work. For these reasons, in 2011–12, 15 Corps did a successful pilot project of replacing the fence with permanently buried wooden shrapnel (called punjis in jungle warfare) as the obstacle to deter infiltration. The project did not go far since the top army brass at Army Headquarters have found it difficult to disband the fence which had been controversial from the beginning.

The idea of a fence had been in circulation for many years before the LC ceasefire came into being. The Border Security Force erected one on the India-Pakistan border from Gujarat to Rajasthan and another on the India–Bangladesh border. But the army was never receptive to the idea of erecting a fence as it was found effective only against illegal immigrants and is a police tactic. According to army chief General S. Padmanabhan (General Vij's predecessor), 'When Vij asked my opinion on the fence, I told him that this idea had been there since 1993. The reason why it had not been implemented so far was that it was unsuited for the terrain along the LC. Moreover, a fence would instil a defensive mind-set in our troops.'

Considering the repeated efforts to restore the fence, how effective has it been? A senior field commander candidly admitted, 'If somebody is determined to get across, you cannot stop him. He will always find a way to overcome hurdles like fence.' Major General V. K. Singh (later army chief) conceded this when he said, 'The army is not the only one to learn. The infiltrators too have been quick to learn. The infiltrators come with insulated rubber gloves, ladders, insulated pliers and even poles to jump over the fence. There are instances where infiltrators have successfully burrowed under the fence to get through.'

Once Operation Deewar was completed, but before the army could settle down into the new arrangement of having fenced itself in and improved its defences by building more impregnable steel permanent defences than were available earlier, tragedy struck on 8 October 2005. A massive earthquake with its epicentre in POK wrought unimaginable destruction. The scale of havoc was much more on the Pakistani side than the Indian side. When the authors visited 15 Corps in Srinagar and nearby areas a fortnight after the earthquake, people were full of praise for the Indian Army, which had accorded priority to them over itself by putting their homes and hearths together. While anxious about the state of their own defences, army officers took solace in the fact that as 'constructions on the other side had been completely flattened, there was little possibility of aggression from their side'.

The restoration by both sides provides a picture in contrast. On the Indian side of the LC, priority was given to erection of the fence and to Operation Sadbhavana—the army's strategy of helping the local population. While defences were restored, they were barely improved. In POK, the division of labour was discernible. While the Jamaat-ud-Dawa (the umbrella organization of Lashkar-e-Taiba) volunteers devoted themselves to assisting the civilians, the Pakistan Army gave special attention to building good forward defences (more steel permanent defences), all of which were connected by communication trenches. Given the accurate and long-range surveillance equipment and lethal weapons available on both sides, the communication trenches would enable uninhibited troop movements between defences. The Indian side lacked good communication trenches, and had a mix of steel permanent defences and concrete trenches which would get blasted by direct fire from Pakistan.

◆

The argument that the fence is cost-effective, because it prevents infiltration, continues to be made by senior officers. While attributing benefits to the anti-infiltration obstacle system, the Indian Army is unwilling to concede its biggest drawback: it has instilled the Maginot mentality. Any worthwhile military commander the world over will attest that a fortification induces a false sense of security and stifles the attacking spirit of an army. With the silence of artillery guns and fencing on the LC, the Indian Army's mindset has decisively transformed from an offensive to a defensive one, focused on fighting terrorism in Jammu and Kashmir. This has given respite to the Pakistan Army to continue with its missions without worrying about Indian retaliation.

The release of the army's 'sub-conventional warfare doctrine' in January 2007 was the official indication that CI ops would have priority over 'hot war'. By 2009, the basic training at army schools of instruction (Indian Military Academy and Officers Training Academies) was changed from teaching tactics for conventional war to CI ops. The message for young men aspiring to become army officers was that CI ops would be their basic task.

To underline this point, the doctrine was updated by army chief General Bikram Singh in 2013. During a visit to Srinagar in March 2014, the 15 Corps commander, Lieutenant Gurmit Singh, took pride in telling the authors that he was responsible for updating the CI ops doctrine. The priority of commanders responsible for the Valley was evident when General Singh listed his five operational tasks, four of which were directly linked to CI ops. These were: 'prepare for conventional conflict; maintain moral domination on LC and anti-filtration; maintain effective counter-insurgency grids; have proper perception management; and provide maximum assistance to the people (awam)'. On conventional war preparedness, he admitted to numerous weapons shortages, especially dug-in ammunition sites.

Meanwhile, the successful 2002 and 2008 assembly elections convinced the army brass of their indispensability to the political process in the state.

Just when the army was conjuring up reasons to continue with CI ops, 2013 witnessed the maximum ceasefire violations on the LC. Five soldiers were shot dead in Poonch in August 2013 close to where a soldier was beheaded by Pakistan's forces in January. For the first time since the ceasefire of 26 November 2003, the tranquil International Border in Jammu saw an unprecedented exchange of fire between August and October. This placed the government on the back foot with the opposition parties accusing it of being soft against Pakistan's increased belligerence. The situation led to the government announcement that the army had been given a free hand to deal with Pakistan's violence on the LC.

Consequently the army changed its tactics at the LC in two ways. A portion of the Rashtriya Rifles was moved from the hinterland to the LC to strengthen the anti-infiltration grid, and forward troops were ordered to return Pakistani fire with interest. According to the army leadership, the focus of operations had shifted from the hinterland to the LC. As there were fewer terrorists in the hinterland, the need was to decimate them at the LC itself by strengthening the anti-infiltration grid.

The authors, with the army's permission, visited two infiltration-prone areas: 25 Division (in 16 Corps) which is hilly, and has thick foliage, in the Jammu sector, and 28 Division (in 15 Corps) in mostly high-altitude areas in the snowbound region of north Kashmir.

With a frontage of 243 kilometres, 25 Division extends from Surankot to Pir Panjal. The division was in a counter-insurgency role on the LC where soldiers undertook two tasks: area domination and ambushes. With the abatement of insurgency in the Jammu division (hinterland), nearly 12,000 troops from the RR had been moved forward to the LC. With this, the division had woven a formidable, if not impregnable, two-tier counter-insurgency grid, the first tier provided by the forward deployed troops on the LC itself, facing Pakistani posts within 300 metres to 1.5 kilometres along the entire frontage. The RR troops brought from the hinterland formed the second tier behind the fence. Five BSF battalions (each with 1,200 troops) of 16 Corps were deployed in an anti-infiltration role.

All army troops were visually networked at various levels—company, battalion, brigade, and so on—to ensure all had a real-time picture of their areas. Equipment available for surveillance included handheld thermal imagers, handheld battlefield surveillance radars, thermal imaging integrated observation equipment, long-range reconnaissance and observation systems and DIGI-scope, which allowed reasonably good visibility at night and during rough weather to detect infiltrations in real time. Once detections were made, a plethora of weapons (excluding artillery guns) were available for instant use in both area domination and punitive roles. These included 81-millimetre mortars, 84-millimetre rocket launchers, 51-millimetre mortars, 106-millimetre recoilless guns, heavy, medium and light machine guns, anti-material rifles, KPWT tank guns in ground roles, and even anti-aircraft and air defence guns in ground roles. In short, there was a seamless anti-infiltration network which included real-time surveillance, detection and punitive means.

The general officer commanding, 25 Division, Major General V. P. Singh, told the authors, 'We lay seventy to seventy-five ambushes each night, in addition to area domination patrols. About 60 per cent of soldiers remain awake and there is a stand-to at 2 a.m. every night where everyone is required to be on his post.' The story in 28 Division was similar, with variations for the peculiarity of the terrain.

The following observations were made by the authors after the two visits. The first issue concerned the soldiers' habitat. For forward deployed troops, no more than 50 per cent defences of all types and communication trenches are shellproof, lacking in desired security and cover for troops. Next, large numbers of RR troops moved forward to anti-infiltration obstacle systems were living in tents in freezing temperatures without proper toilets and water supply. Most of the surveillance devices being used by the troops were over a decade old (they were purchased from Israel after the 1999 Kargil conflict) and needed replacement or upgrades. Moreover, given that 25 Division had nearly seventy-five patrols and ambushes each night, troops were not getting adequate rest nor minimum comfort to perform their tasks well. The story in 28 Division was the same.

This was not all. All troops—in front of the fence, at the fence and behind the fence—were focused on counter-insurgency operations rather than conventional operations. According to Lieutenant General Mohinder Puri, who had to orient his troops within days to switch from CI ops to conventional war during the 1999 Kargil conflict, 'While CI ops require immediate and expeditious response with rapid planning lest militants create havoc, conventional ops require deliberate and unwavering coordination not only amongst those assaulting, but also with the array of supporting arms and services, including the air force.' The contention of the army leadership that troops in CI ops get hands-on training for 'hot war' is misleading.

Serious training for 'hot war' requires a nod from the political leadership. There are major conventional war objectives earmarked by the Indian Army—like Haji Pir, Kotli, Mirpur, Bimber, Mangla, and so on—to be captured across the LC. These will either help improve the Indian army's tactical posture or deny good infiltration areas to the Pakistan army. India has numbers in its favour and minimal risk of Pakistan's nuclear redlines here. What it lacks is a serious review of the defensive counter-infiltration mindset, for which it needs not only support but also direction from the political leadership. This has not happened.

Perhaps the single most important reason why Pakistanis are not deterred despite large numbers of Indian troops on the LC is the inward oriented mindset of the army. All forces are focused on an anti-infiltration role. And given the punishing routine of ambushes, patrols and constant observation round the clock for infiltrators, the Indian troops pose no threat to the enemy, which is apparent in their deployment and routine. The Pakistani forces facing India are in two tiers of Mujahid with regular POK battalions behind them. The Mujahid or the 'son of soil' forces have six companies (each with about 120 men) which carry out patrols, though less strenuous than the Indians, to ensure the sanctity of the LC. The POK battalions are free and train for 'hot war'.

◆

All that changed with the coming of the Modi government in May 2014 was perception. For example, the so-called surgical strikes on 29 September 2016 were low-calibre counter-terror operations which had been done before. As foreign secretary S. Jaishankar clarified in his briefing to the Parliamentary Standing Committee on External Affairs, this time the government decided to make it public, accompanied by tough statements from its senior ministers warning Pakistan of dire consequences. In fact, unlike its predecessor, the Modi government confirmed that the army's major task would be CI ops. Speaking in the Rajya Sabha on 22 July 2014, Defence Minister Arun Jaitley praised the army for its CI ops, concluding that 'innovative troops deployment, efficient use of surveillance and monitoring devices and fencing along the LC have enhanced [the army's] ability to detect and intercept infiltration'.

Encouraged by the government's praise, the army decided to upgrade the fence. The Northern Army Commander, Lieutenant General D. S. Hooda, told the media in August 2015, 'The new fence will be twice as effective as the existing one. It will be hard to breach.' The construction of the new fence began in April 2016 in the 28 Division sector (Tangdhar, Keran and Gurez) in high-altitude areas which sit astride the major infiltration route. Better material and structural changes will ensure minimum snow damage. The fence will have integrated sensors to detect intrusions; standard military coils layered between rows of stronger pickets will be thicker so that they won't bend under the weight of the snow. By 2019, the army plans to extend the new fence to 350 kilometres in the Valley at a cost of nearly ₹500 crore.

Encouraged by the Modi government's enthusiastic backing of the army's counter-insurgency role, the army chief, General Dalbir Singh, when asked by the authors in January 2015 how long the army would continue CI ops in J&K said that internal security was the domain of the union Ministry of Home Affairs, implying that this question should be asked of them. In his view, the political and military objectives were the same.

British General Rupert Smith, in his exceptional book *The Utility of Force* based on his extensive CI ops experience, wrote, 'It must always be remembered that the political objective and the military strategic objectives are not the same, and are never the same; the military strategic objective is achieved by military force whilst the political objective is achieved as a result of military success.'

Given General Smith's wisdom, it becomes clear that the Indian Army is fighting a war of diminishing returns in the Kashmir Valley. In the absence of political initiatives to address the Kashmir issue, the army leadership should be worried because unending CI ops will take their toll on the troops' morale, mindset and preparation for war. Surprisingly, it is not so. This is because the senior-most army leadership appears to have convinced itself that its bread and butter is CI ops. Preparedness for conventional war in J&K, which according to the Indian Army doctrine is the responsibility of the Northern Army commander and the Chief of Army Staff, has long been given short shrift.

This has worked to the Pakistan Army's advantage. For this reason, it has judiciously ensured that despite violations, the 26 November 2003 ceasefire stands. And it has allowed the rebuilding of the battered LC fence by not firing on Indian troops who are carrying out the repairs.

The use of small arms fire is a violation of the ceasefire whereas the use of artillery would lead to the ceasefire being called off. By keeping the violations below the ceasefire agreement threshold, the Pakistan Army has ensured that the Indian Army remains committed to fighting terrorism within its borders.

CHAPTER 3

NIGHTMARE ON THE LINE OF ACTUAL CONTROL

The Tawang monastery (also referred to as Galden Namgye Lhatsem, which means celestial paradise) in Tawang district is Asia's second oldest and largest monastery after the Potala Palace in Lhasa. Belonging to the Gelugpa sect of Tibetan Buddhism, the Tawang monastery was founded by Merag Lama Lodre Gyatso in 1680.

The story goes that the local Buddhist monks, including Merag Gyatso, went to meet the fifth Dalai Lama in Lhasa and requested him to visit them. He told them that while it might not be possible for him to visit them in this lifetime he would certainly visit them in his next birth. When the delegation returned, Merag Gyatso, along with his white horse, started wandering through the mountains to meditate and find a place fit to receive the Dalai Lama. During one of his meditative sessions, his horse wandered away. When Merag Gyatso awoke from his meditative spell he went to look for the horse and found him standing on the mountaintop that is now the seat of the monastery. He called the monastery Tawang—or found by the horse. Subsequently, a small township developed around the monastery and adopted the same name.

The monastery was completed in a year and the Dalai Lama kept his word. The sixth Dalai Lama, Tsangyang Gyatso, was born in the Urgelling monastery very close to Tawang. Though he moved to Lhasa once he was recognized as the Dalai Lama, the Tawang monastery's credibility and hence sacredness was established, given that it was sanctified by the Dalai Lama himself.

Today, for the Buddhists of the Gelugpa sect to which the present Dalai Lama belongs, Tawang is a place for pilgrimage, second only to Potala Palace. And since Lhasa is no longer easily accessible to a large number of Buddhists, especially those with allegiance to the present Dalai Lama, Tawang acquires additional significance.

In addition to its political and spiritual importance, Tawang is militarily sensitive too. In 1985, a year after the assassination of Prime Minister Indira Gandhi, China withdrew the Deng Xiaoping proposal to formalize the status quo, and made a fresh claim on the entire Tawang Tract, which comprises the monastery and the whole of West Kameng district from the McMahon Line up to Dirang, including the highest mountain pass in this region, Se La at 13,700 feet. The Tawang Tract would provide China's PLA easy access to the Assam plains, rendering India's defences in East Kameng untenable and jeopardizing the security of India's northeastern region.

For this reason, border management and the defence of Tawang has been critical for India. Tawang constitutes the Indian Army's centre of gravity in the Eastern Sector. With this weighing on his mind, Indian Army chief General K. Sundarji deployed an infantry division (12,000 soldiers) comprising three brigades (about 3,500 soldiers each) ahead of Tawang to protect it during the 1986–87 crisis with China. Even though after the 1988 visit of Prime Minister Rajiv Gandhi to Beijing, India unilaterally downgraded the Chinese threat and redeployed the troops for internal stability operations in the1990s, theoretically, the division remained earmarked for the defence of Tawang.

Once the PLA improved its infrastructure in the Tibet Autonomous Region (TAR), its territorial transgressions rose sharply, especially after India's 1998 nuclear tests when India cited China as the reason for conducting the tests. In the face of China's improved border management, India was suddenly faced with the need to prioritize infrastructure development and building up of troops in this sector, especially given the fact that the disputed border was neither agreed on maps nor on the ground.

The problems for the Indian Army were manifold as the Line of Actual Control with China was not a consequence of war, but, ironically, of peace. It is the only example in military history where a military line had been created not because of fighting but because of a desperate need to maintain peace and stability. The September 1993 agreement placed the enormous responsibility of guarding the 3,488-kilometre LAC on the army and the Indo-Tibetan Border Police (ITBP) force in a complex two-tier arrangement.

While earmarked troops for China were brought back from J&K in 2007, the army, as a result of the LAC, also assessed the need for more troops in this sector. The army made a case for the urgent raising of two new divisions, one for Tawang and the other for the rest of Arunachal Pradesh. In the first force accretion sanctioned by the government since 1983, two divisions—71 and 56—were raised in the record time of two years by using stores, equipment and weapons from the war wastage reserves.

The new Tawang division had just about settled into its role when the authors visited Tawang in August 2010 to assess border management at the place where it matters the most. The authors spent a few days (actually a couple of days were required to reach Tawang from Tezpur, a distance of a mere 350 kilometres, because of the slush-filled, landslide-afflicted virtually non-existent road) with the officers of 190 Mountain Brigade (from 5 Mountain Division, permanently based at Tenga Valley short of Se La which was forward deployed during the 1986–87 crisis).

The 190 Mountain, or the 'Korea Brigade' as it is popularly called, is permanently posted at a high altitude, with posts ahead of Tawang located at 10,000 feet to over 18,000 feet. The other two brigades of the division have permanent defences on these heights which are regularly maintained during the 'operational alert' period: the time when formations cross the Se La ridge line and occupy their operational defences for maintenance and familiarization. Considering that the army has adopted an extreme forward posture, road communications are unsatisfactory. The Korea Brigade occupies over 200 posts ahead of Tawang, many of which are devoid of tracks on which vehicles can run. Troops march for anywhere from a few hours to two days from the roadhead, a mere dirt track, to reach their posts. They often carry their own essential supplies. The employment of locals as porters or the heli-drop of loads are a temporary reprieve and would be unsustainable during war.

Logistics also have an impact on the living conditions of the troops. The shelters used by troops during acclimatization are inadequate for extreme winter conditions. Moreover, as permanent accommodation at each acclimatization area is limited, troops when inducted in large numbers are forced to stay in tents before occupying forward defences. Such a situation adversely impacts the soldier's fighting capability.

Troops here are conscious of the three tactical advantages of the opposing Chinese border guards. As we have seen, one, the Chinese side has proper gravel roads right up to the LAC. The difference in road communications on the two sides can be seen at the army post at Bum La where the Chinese and Indian troops meet for border personnel meetings. It is stark and disturbing. The Chinese have deliberately avoided making a 'black top' or cemented road as the gravel allows better water drainage during monsoons, and it puts pressure on the Indian side to not make 'black top' roads on its side. Indians cannot build gravel roads because the terrain, which is extremely sloping, does not allow it; and also because lack of resources holds them back. In any case, according to officers posted at Tawang, the Chinese have the capability to easily construct up to 45 kilometres of 'black top' road in ninety days.

The other advantage enjoyed by the Chinese troops is psychological. They seem to be under no pressure to maintain round-the-clock forward vigil. Chinese border guards' (paramilitary forces) force levels in forward positions are inversely proportionate to Indian troop deployments. The Chinese are content with using a plethora of tactically networked surveillance means which are monitored regularly. They rely on technology much more than the Indian side. The closest PLA garrison is about 50 kilometres in depth at a place called Le. Besides, Lhasa being an important communication hub is very well provided for and connected by oil pipelines and road network.

Weather and terrain also favour the Chinese. As we have pointed out earlier, unlike Indian troops who have to go through the rigours of three-stage acclimatization each time they come to occupy forward defences, the Chinese on the Tibetan plateau at heights of 16,000 feet and above are always acclimatized. The terrain on the Chinese side has a gradual gradient as compared to the Indian side which suffers from what the army calls 'friction of terrain'. This leads to frequent landslides, which cause havoc when it rains. A monsoon campaign in this area would hugely benefit the Chinese troops. According to senior tactical commanders, including general officer commanding, 5 Mountain Division, Major General Anil Ahuja, whom the authors met in August 2010, the Border Roads Organisation had set 2012 as the deadline for the construction of a two-lane road to Tawang and beyond. That has not come about.

The single-lane road to Tawang at most places is nothing more than a dirt track where vehicles routinely get stuck for hours. Troops travelling on this road are required to carry dry rations for a minimum two days as a precautionary measure for unforeseen delays. Given the state of the road, weather uncertainties at Se La, which has to be crossed by the troops living to the south of it, and anxiety in case of hostilities, the troops would be exhausted well before facing the enemy.

If this was not enough, the October 2013 agreement has aggravated India's border management problems by downgrading border guarding tasks to border policing duties. While 'border guarding' allows the use of firearms to stop intrusions, 'border policing' is about setting up check posts to curb intrusion by presence and persuasion at likely ingress points, which could be anywhere on the LAC. The policing job requires more troops on the ground to be able to monitor every conceivable infiltration point.

As the Border Defence Cooperation Agreement was signed under the shadow of the PLA's successful military coercion in April–May 2013 in north Ladakh, the government, in sheer fright, expeditiously cleared the long pending request of the Indian Army for more troops for the LAC. Thus, the raising of the Indian Army's 17 Mountain Corps, which commenced on 1 January 2014—a total of 90,000 soldiers to be inducted afresh—and was scheduled to be done over eight years (by 2022) was not a well-considered decision but a mindless political act in the hope that it would ward off the PLA threat.

Playing to the gallery, the army leadership has called it the 'mountain strike (offensive) corps' with no one questioning how troops would strike in high-altitude areas (at heights of 10,000 to 18,000 feet where all the troops are deployed) where survival itself is a feat. Moreover, if the 17 Corps was indeed an offensive corps, shouldn't the army have coordinated with the Indian Air Force for air cover for its moving land columns? In a first, after the Defence Ministry had cleared the army's proposal for the raising of 17 Corps, the objections came from the defence finance official (the representative of the Finance Ministry in the Defence Ministry), which asked for the IAF's opinion to be sought. The IAF then added its own airlift requirement to support the new corps.

In reality, 17 Mountain Corps has two parts to it: accretion forces and Army Headquarters Reserves. The accretion forces totalling 30,000 troops are meant to fill in operational gaps (policing duties) both in the Western and Eastern sectors. The remaining 60,000 troops would constitute 17 Mountain Corps; to be called Army Headquarters Reserves, these troops, to be posted in faraway locations (Panagarh, West Bengal) would be used in peacetime for rotation purposes to provide rest and relief to troops on policing duties on the LAC.

Consider a scenario where Indian and Chinese forces play a game of crossing the Line of Actual Control. As we have seen, the two sides have agreed (as per the 1993, 1996 and 2013 agreements) to a few rules: neither side will add numbers (military personnel) without the consent of the other side; both sides are free to cross the 3,488-kilometre-long line from anywhere without violence or use of force (implying unnoticed); and once players of one side cross the line, the other side will not follow or tail or chase them. The game, though seemingly fair, is enormously one-sided because of the multiple advantages that the Chinese forces enjoy. Although they have already been mentioned, it is worth going over them once again to stress the point we're making.

The Chinese forces do not stay close to the LAC but in proper accommodation in the rear where they are rested with ample time to plan their crossings and reprisals should they become necessary. Being mobile and with good access roads right up to the LAC, they move swiftly and with ease. A plethora of sensors and tactical level technology along the line helps Chinese forces keep an eye on their opponent's movements. While they do not expect the opponent to cross the line, Chinese forces have positioned their sentries (border guards or militia) at a few select places both to monitor the sensors and hold down the opponent—should they have the gumption to cross the line—until reinforcements arrive in quick time.

Indian forces on the other hand live in the vicinity of the line at freezing heights round the year because they do not have roads and tracks close to it. In some places, it takes a march of four to six days for troops carrying their belongings to reach the line. As infrastructure is non-existent, a maximum number of troops are required on the LAC with minimal gaps to ensure the Chinese are stopped at the line itself.

The outcome of this diabolical game being played regularly by the Chinese forces on the LAC is demoralizing for Indian troops on the ground and humiliating for the nation, which does not even accept the ground realities, seeking escape in euphemisms and semantics. According to Kiren Rijiju, the union minister of state for Home Affairs, there have been '1,612 transgressions between 1 January 2010 to 4 August 2014, but no intrusions'. The minister does not mention a single transgression by Indian forces and none have been reported in the Chinese media either.

Going by the official record, there were thirty-four transgressions each month in the last four years, which translates into almost one a day. On the one hand, the Chinese forces, having made a joke of the LAC, harass Indian forces with their sheer audacity. On the other hand, Indian forces, who are unable to cope with their policing duties against an opponent, are perplexed as to why India does not defend the line with full might. In an undeclared war, where shots are not fired, Indian forces are being psychologically defeated by the Chinese forces almost on a daily basis.

As we have seen, the blame for this rests with India's political leadership which since 1998 has adopted an appeasement policy towards China. According to George Fernandes, India's defence minister in May 1998 when the Vajpayee government conducted the nuclear tests and cited China as the prime reason for doing so, 'I do not think India has ever, including now, taken what China is doing or can do to our national security very seriously.'

In April 2008, when the Manmohan Singh-led United Progressive Alliance government was in power in New Delhi, the authors spoke with Kiren Rijiju, the Bharatiya Janata Party's Member of Parliament from Arunachal Pradesh (West) who in May 2014 became the minister of state in the union Home Ministry of the Modi government. 'In 2005, when I first raised the issue of Chinese incursions in Arunachal Pradesh, the government simply dismissed my assertions,' Rijiju told the authors. 'I raised the issue again in 2006 and the government flatly denied that any incursion has taken place. But within months, the director general of the Indo-Tibetan Border Police (ITBP) said there have been frequent Chinese incursions into our territory, with 146 in 2007 alone. Now even the army chief concedes that incursions have taken place. Why did the government then deny it when I first raised the issue?

'Now the government is citing unsettled border and Line of Actual Control not being demarcated as the reason for these transgressions. But I disagree with this stance. The land belongs to the people or the village community. If I am an Indian and the land belongs to me, won't that land belong to India? I agree that the McMahon Line has not been clearly demarcated or agreed on the ground. Yet an understanding exists that people living on this side of the line are Indians and our traditional grazing lands, ponds, mountains and our sacred places are in Indian territory. Since 1962, the Chinese have been gradually occupying our patches of land. This is what I call creeping incursion,' Rijiju complained.

He added, 'There is a pattern in which they are doing this. During regular flag meetings at the border, India and China mutually agree on certain areas as being no-man's land where no activity should take place. While India faithfully adheres to this agreement, Chinese sometimes send their soldiers on regular patrol or disguised as shepherds to put a mark or a cement post there to mark their territory. This is what I call incursion. My constituency is Arunachal West, where we have the maximum dispute with China. All the areas like Tawang, Bomdila, Kameng, Subansiri, etc. fall in my constituency, which is why I come to know of these incursions on my visits to my constituency.

'The problem is that whenever an incident takes place in the remote areas, the Indian Army covers up the issue. Take the example of the incident that happened [in 2007] in the Tawang district. Traditionally, there used to be a Buddha statue somewhere close to the McMahon Line which the local people used to revere. The Chinese always objected to this. Last year, the Indian Army placed the statue at the spot where the people believed it ought to be. The Chinese blasted it. Nobody reported this matter. The government kept quiet. This convinces me that the Government of India is not serious about its national security. Perhaps they are overcautious because the fear psychosis of 1962 still persists in their minds, which is why when it comes to China, the government hushes up anything that is remotely unpleasant.

'We have the courage to summon the ambassador of the US only because he wrote a letter to West Bengal government commenting on the state economic policy. But the Chinese ambassador to India, sitting on Indian soil, twice made a statement that the whole of Arunachal Pradesh was Chinese territory. Forget about condemning him, the government didn't react at all.

'Our major problem is lack of infrastructure. Our forces go out to patrol in a group of 15 or say 20. On the other hand, the Chinese come in the strength of 300 to 400. They have the roads and airfields to facilitate their movement. You can imagine the morale of our men when they come face to face with this huge number of enemy troops in a remote border area where there is no civilian population for miles. We cannot match their number because we do not have the basic infrastructure to support it, like the Chinese. We do not have roads, airports or telecommunications connectivity. Reaching the forward areas is itself a back-breaking and time-consuming activity for our troops. There are remote areas on the border which are not accessible to us due to lack of infrastructure. Meanwhile, the Chinese have a free run there as their roads stretch right up till the McMahon Line. To make matters worse, our government is oblivious to this problem. I intend to raise it as a privilege issue in Parliament.'

The authors met George Fernandes in April 2008 with Rijiju's viewpoint. At this time they reminded him that in 2000, when Mukut Mithi, the Congress chief minister of Arunachal Pradesh, had spoken about continued PLA intrusions, he had rebutted him by saying it was not true. Fernandes conceded that 'politics and constraints as the defence minister' had made him say so.

Asked why the government in his time did not review the 1975 Patrolling Limits Policy decided by the China Study Group (set up by Prime Minister Indira Gandhi), Fernandes said, 'Defence is not decided by the defence minister alone. Everything has to go through the prime minister [at the time A. B. Vajpayee].' After the 1962 war and the unilateral Chinese withdrawal till the McMahon Line (which, as we know, China does not recognize as the acceptable border), China had said that both sides would observe an informal 20-kilometre demilitarized zone on either side.

After the renaming of the border as the Line of Actual Control under the 1993 agreement, Chinese troops, since 1999, had been regularly violating the commitment.

Even more demoralizing than the Chinese bullying on the LAC is the Government of India issued Patrolling Limits Policy, which has not been reviewed since its inception by the China Study Group in 1975. The Patrolling Limits Policy laid down the limits beyond which Indian troops were not allowed to patrol. A self-imposed restriction, the policy stipulates that Indian troops stay well short of the Indian perception of the LAC. In some areas, like Asaphila and Wangdong (venue of the 1986–87 crisis), the troops stay almost 20 kilometres inside the LAC, giving ample opportunities to the PLA to intrude unchallenged.

On condition of anonymity, field commanders of 5 Mountain Division confirmed this, adding that troops were demoralized by such orders. The ITBP troops, which provide the first line of observation ahead of the army in Arunachal Pradesh, confirmed similar instructions for them. George Fernandes confirmed to the authors that 'the Vajpayee government did not want to review the patrolling limits as it may have displeased the Chinese'. Successive governments of Manmohan Singh and Narendra Modi too found the issue too hot to be tinkered with.

While this is a big impediment to the security forces discharging their duties in peacetime, it will prove to be a blunder in case of a crisis, for the simple reason that the other mechanisms for surveillance during peacetime also have severe limitations. Given the inclement weather and poor visibility for nearly 200 days of the year, aerial surveillance by satellites and unmanned aerial vehicles is unsatisfactory.

The standard Indian response, by politicians, military and paramilitary officials and diplomats since 1999 when China intensified transgressions, incursions and intrusions culminating in the 2013 April–May three-week sit-in on Indian territory, has been identical. Either transgressions are denied or if that is not possible, an alibi is found in the fact that the LAC is not agreed, hence 'both sides transgress into each other's territory'. This is not true. All transgressions have been one-sided. Indian troops do not go anywhere close to their own perception of the LAC. If they were doing so, wouldn't the Chinese have similar forward deployments like India on the LAC?

China's audacity on the border management issue has grown in direct proportion to India's eagerness to keep things under wraps. For example, during a visit by the authors to China in August 2012, Ma Jisheng, the deputy director general, Information Department, Ministry of Foreign Affairs, said, 'All reports in the Indian media on Chinese transgressions are false.' During the April–May 2013 stand-off in north Ladakh, the Chinese official spokesperson maintained that Chinese troops had not transgressed but were on their own territory.

If the main issue of India's weak-kneed responses to China's bullying is set aside, successive governments since 1988 have made attempts to tackle other aspects of border management with China. For example, the Vajpayee government set up a task force on border management, whose recommendations were incorporated in the Group of Ministers report released in February 2001. Three useful recommendations were: 'one border one force', 'single point control' and 'speedy development of infrastructure', especially roads in the border regions.

It was argued that one border guarding force should be responsible for the entire LAC with China. Until then, the ITBP looked after the LAC in Jammu and Kashmir, Himachal Pradesh and Uttaranchal. The border in Sikkim and the LAC in Arunachal Pradesh were the responsibility of the army and Assam Rifles combined, with the latter being under the operational control of the former. While the army and the Assam Rifles functioned well, there were problems of coordination between the ITBP and the army which was deployed in the rear. The ITBP reported to the army through the circuitous route of the Home and Defence ministries. In peacetime, the ITBP is required to have mere coordination with the army; it is only in war that the ITBP comes under direct control of the army. Considering that the PLA, since 1998, has resorted to offensive patrolling on the LAC, there were instances in the Western Sector when the ITPB was inadequately equipped to challenge the PLA, and by the time the army's Rapid Response Force (formed in 1999) could respond, the damage had been done. The Group of Ministers report, therefore, had said that the entire LAC should be the responsibility of the ITBP alone. After much dithering, the ITBP was finally given the responsibility of the entire LAC in 2005.

The second recommendation of a 'single point control' was not accepted. It had been argued by the task force on border management that in view of aggressive patrolling by the PLA, the need was for border guarding rather than border policing. As border guarding is possible only by a 'single point control', it was suggested that the ITBP come under the operational control of the army until the final resolution of the border dispute. Thereafter, the ITBP could go back to reporting to the Ministry of Home Affairs. Another reason why this is required is that, unlike the army, the ITBP constable retires at the advanced age of sixty years, which is a severe handicap for troops in far-flung high-altitude posts, which are physically challenging.

The army pointed to the four advantages of implementing 'single point control':

- It would ensure optimal utilization of resources;
- Patrolling activities would be coordinated better;
- An immediate response to an untoward incident could be optimally ensured with the help of the army's Rapid Reaction Force; and
- It was observed that flag and scheduled border meetings with Chinese sector commanders were attended by representatives of both the army and the ITBP, with no clear-cut areas of responsibilities. Once this problem was removed, a more focused approach could be adopted by sector commanders.

Surprisingly, the resistance to this advice came from the External Affairs Ministry which said that such a move might annoy China which could interpret it as leading to an accretion of forces by India. The army argued in vain that as all paramilitary and border guarding forces in China were directly under the PLA, China could not misinterpret a similar Indian arrangement.

After the signing of the Border Defence Cooperation Agreement in 2013, whereby border policing replaced border guarding, the ITBP sought an accretion of forces. They made the case that since the army was raising a new mountain corps the ITBP too should have more numbers for rest and relief. In January 2015, the union home minister announced an additional forty-nine battalions (each battalion with 1,200 troops) taking the total to sixty-nine. The central issue of 'single point control' remained unresolved.

For effective border management, the Cabinet Committee on Security in May 1999 sanctioned the construction of twenty-seven General Staff (GS) or operationally urgent roads (to be paid for from the defence budget) which were recommended by the China Study Group based upon two considerations. First, there were posts in the Western Sector that were air-maintained. For example, the entire sub-sector north is not connected by road. Secondly, most roads in other sectors, especially the Eastern Sector, remain about 80 to 150 kilometres short of the LAC, and it takes between four to six days for troops to reach the posts there. In order to address these infrastructural shortcomings, which directly impinge on good border management, the China Study Group had said that work on these operationally necessary roads should be finished by 2007. This was not done during the ten years of the Manmohan Singh government from 2004–14. The Director General, Border Roads Organisation, Lieutenant General A. T. Parnaik, explained why the roads had not been built, 'The delay is on account of forest and wildlife clearances, difficult terrain, limited working period because of weather, paucity of material, and natural disasters like flash floods.' According to Border Road Organisation sources, by August 2016, work on most of the important roads had still not begun.

The task force on border management had suggested assistance from other available construction agencies in the country for expediting road construction in border areas. At the very least, airlift by suitable helicopters of the Indian Air Force, or those procured on lease, should have been pressed into service to lift engineering and earthmoving equipment along the alignment of roads to be able to tackle construction at a number of points simultaneously. It is, after all, critical that India regularly patrol up to its perception of the border all along the LAC, especially in the more disputed Western and Eastern sectors. In addition to the General Staff roads, which are an operational priority, there is a need to address other roads and highways to ensure that troop movement, when required, is not stalled by the vagaries of the weather. At present, the situation on the ground is abysmal.

The Modi government also showed concern for road-building on the China border. In a statement in Parliament, Defence Minister Manohar Parrikar gave the following commitment to the nation regarding critical (General Staff) roads: sixteen roads in 2015; seventeen roads in 2016; nine roads in 2017; and four in 2018. Most of these roads, however, have not been made because in Delhi, 'the director general of military operations was reportedly against building roads close to the border for security reasons (the Chinese could use it to move fast inside Indian territory once war was joined)'.

India's existing border management has too many shortcomings which emboldens the PLA which in turn leads to more disputes. The latter compel India to further reduce its patrolling limits, and China feels confident of shifting the LAC without firing a shot. With such ground realities, why would China go to war with India over the border dispute?

China has taken the high moral ground by seeking peace and stability on the disputed border through numerous confidence building measures at various levels. At the top is the annual Special Representatives (SR) meeting. Next, there is the Working Mechanism for Consultation and Coordination formed in 2012 to discuss border patrolling and management. In addition, there are military-to-military confidence building measures at the level of the border forces. There are hotlines and established procedures for formal flag meetings between the sector and brigade commanders at five meeting points on the border.

The next structure for confidence building measures is the Annual Defence Dialogue (ADD) headed by India's defence secretary and a PLA representative from the Chinese Ministry of National Defence.

The ADD is a platform for extensive talks between the two militaries on defence cooperation, LAC management, military engagement and sharing of perspectives about the evolving regional and security situation. The annual army exercise, called Hand-in-Hand, between the two sides since 2009 is decided by this forum. In addition, there are annual visits by defence officials.

Given its excellent border management, and all bilateral agreements tilted in its favour, coupled with India's timidity, China has the upper hand without question. India is also extremely vulnerable, militarily speaking. To say, as columnist C. Raja Mohan does, that 'despite anxieties on frequent incursions across the disputed portions of the Sino-Indian border, there is no violence on the un-demarcated Line of Actual Control that separates forces in the Himalayas', is to live in a state of denial. Only those who do not understand military power can draw comfort from this. For others, it's a nightmare.

CHINA'S GRAND STRATEGY

CHAPTER 4

COLD START TO A HOT WAR

In December 2009, shortly before he retired in March 2010, army chief General Deepak Kapoor said that the army would prepare capabilities to fight a two-front war—against Pakistan and China. His statement drew sharp criticism from the then Pakistan Army chief, General Ashfaq Kayani, but China remained silent.

Soon after, the authors met with senior army officers to better understand General Kapoor's statement. What our investigations have shown is as follows. After the Pakistan Army-supported Lashkar terrorists struck Mumbai on 26 November 2008, the Indian military concluded that a swift war with Pakistan was feasible. It would be a blitzkrieg. Or what, in the words of former COAS General N. C. Vij, is known as the 'Cold Start' doctrine, a swift, surprise strike across the border as soon as a decision was taken to wage war. With the Indian Air Force in the lead, the Indian Army was ready to cross the International Border. In an operational surprise, a nondescript Pakistani hamlet, Fort Abbas in southern Punjab, facing India's Rajasthan very close to the border, could fall before the Pakistan Army chief, General Kayani, a Punjabi, realized that Punjabi land, howsoever small in area, had been occupied by the Indian Army. Considering that most of the Pakistan Army comes from the Punjab province this would be a huge psychological blow to Kayani and the Pakistan Army. Even if the Indian Army lost its edge in conventional capabilities, when compared with the Pakistan Army, the combined combat power of the Indian Army and the IAF was superior for a quick, hard-hitting, shallow penetration and occupation of Fort Abbas. According to the scenario that was discussed, the Indian Army's strike corps could reach the border within six to eight days, the time it would take Kayani to move 30 per cent of his army reserves from the Afghanistan front towards India. It was estimated that about 180,000 Pakistan army troops, reserves for the India front, were committed on the Afghanistan front and on counter-insurgency duties in

Federally Administered Tribal Areas.

While it is debatable whether the war scenario discussed at the Army Headquarters in the aftermath of 26/11 was realistic or naive, in our opinion, a couple of aspects of it deserve attention. When Prime Minister Manmohan Singh met the three service chiefs (General Deepak Kapoor, Air Chief Marshal F. H. Major and Admiral Sureesh Mehta) on 29 November 2008, three days after the terrorist onslaught began, he told the military leadership to prepare for war and await further orders. Not once were nuclear weapons mentioned by the prime minister or the service chiefs. The prime minister, however, was concerned about China's reaction.

Perhaps Prime Minister Manmohan Singh's concern about China compelled Defence Minister A. K. Antony to amend the February 2009 operational directive—a confidential document issued to the three services— to mention capability building for a two-front war. Having headed the Northern Command before he shifted to Army Headquarters as the vice chief prior to his appointment as the chief, General Deepak Kapoor was acutely aware of Chinese transgressions across the LAC in Ladakh. Unlike his predecessor, General J. J. Singh, who was fixated on CI ops, Kapoor, since becoming army chief in September 2007, had been pressing the Defence Ministry for acquisitions for the China front.

With pride, Kapoor mentioned in an interview to the authors that he obtained government sanction to raise two new divisions in record time (the last raising of 29 Infantry Division was in 1983). These mountain divisions (56 and 71 Mountain Divisions) were raised and placed under the Eastern Army Command facing China by March 2010, the month Kapoor retired. As we have seen, the army plans cleared by the Manmohan Singh government, approved the raising of a corps headquarters (17 Mountain Corps), two more mountain divisions and armoured brigades in the thirteenth defence plan (2017-2022). Huge amounts were to be spent on building infrastructure, accommodation, equipment and ammunition storage facilities against China. By the fourteenth defence plan (2022–27), the army hoped to have its first air assault division: 54 Mountain Division has been earmarked for this role.

The Indian Air Force, according to its accretion plans to cater for China, got its authorized combat squadron strength increased from 39.5 to forty-two squadrons (each with twenty aircraft) by 2025. The IAF hoped to raise it to forty-five combat squadrons; the wish list being fifty-five combat squadrons. In addition, the government sanctioned massive infrastructure to include airfields, advanced landing grounds and ammunition storage sites in the Eastern Sector.

Asked whether the Tibet issue was a likely reason for war with China, one of the senior officers said only the boundary dispute could result in a crisis or war with China. The Dalai Lama and the Tibet issue will not lead to conflict as India will not up the ante on these matters. India has a non-confrontational attitude towards China as China is more powerful.

Asked why, according to media reports, the army had submitted its accretion plan for China to the government without taking the IAF on board, the senior officer disclosed that there was no combined services' thinking (by the chiefs of staff committee) on the threat from China. No paper had been prepared. The threat matters more to the army because of the Line of Actual Control and the lack of infrastructure. After all, the gains and losses showed most on the ground. Like the army, the other two services had their own concerns. The navy was concerned about the PLA Navy's growing capabilities. The air force was focused on strategic reach. Regarding the army's war preparedness, the senior officer said that the army was about ten years behind China in preparedness on the disputed border. It had started work in a focused way but the gap was not likely to be overcome. The officer concluded that 1962 would not be repeated, an assertion which has been made by all army chiefs.

There was more than one view within the Air Force on the threat China posed. Air Headquarters in New Delhi had one perspective and the Eastern Air Command in Shillong, responsible for Tibet, had another. Even within the senior echelons in New Delhi, there was dissonance about the nature and magnitude of the threat. As Air Chief Marshal P. V. Naik told the authors, 'There is no Chinese threat in the near term [however], they [Chinese] will continue to keep us under pressure'. When asked to explain what was meant by 'near term', the quantification of time was given in an indirect fashion. 'The Chinese will be reluctant to get into a hot war with us as the global sympathy will be with the underdog [India] and this will not help them... We are ten years behind [the Chinese] in capability and infrastructure building and now we are making up the deficiencies,' he added.

Another senior officer at Air Headquarters in New Delhi had a different view. He said, 'It is inconceivable for two major nuclear powers to go to war... As territorial gains will not happen, why would China enter into a war with India?'

However, according to a senior officer at Eastern Air Command, 'The military preparedness of any nation is directly proportionate to its enemy. Had India seen China as its primary threat all these years, its military muscle would have been robust enough to cater for not only Pakistan but a two-front challenge. Considering that India is seen as a major emerging power in Asia, a push of ten days to India by China would settle matters and announce China as the sole power in Asia. The Chinese have already created good infrastructure to support military operations (in the Tibet Autonomous Region). What stops them from showcasing their technology at a time of their choosing?'

Another senior commander at the Eastern Air Command said, 'The Chinese will demonstrate their soft capabilities (electronic warfare, cyber and space), gain the initiative by striking first, and make the swift limited war appear like a political event where they were compelled to defend their motherland against India's aggression.'

Since both the army and air force agreed that they had to build infrastructure against China, the army's perception of the China threat is instructive. According to the army, it had assessed three levels of military threat from China: low, medium and high. In the low-level threat, the PLA has been assessed to field five to six divisions (each with 10,000 to 12,000 soldiers) on the LAC against the Indian Army. The medium-level threat envisages eight to twelve divisions. The high-level threat could be eighteen to twenty divisions staring us in the face. While the PLA is capable of mobilizing up to thirty-four divisions on the LAC against India, the saving grace is that given the terrain limitations, it would be difficult for them to bring more than eighteen to twenty divisions against India at the same time.

The army's war plans against China appear to be based on the high-level threat where the PLA could mobilize up to twenty divisions against the Indian Army. The army today, including the new raisings in March 2011, has a total of nine mountain divisions and one infantry division (each Indian Army division is 12,000 troops, more than the PLA as they have to cater for logistics; the PLA's mobile forces only have the fighting component) and three independent brigades (about 4,000 troops each). Add to this the new raising of 17 Mountain Strike Corps. The 17 Mountain Strike Corps will have two infantry divisions and various support elements. The army also hopes to shift a few formations from the west against Pakistan to the east against China, if needed.

The IAF would have two important functions in the war with China: fight the air war, and support logistics and troop movement of the army in the build-up to war and during war both into and within war theatres. In the absence of reasonable infrastructure in terms of railheads and roads (both national and military roads, called General Staff roads, leading to the border) supporting the army will probably be the major task of the air force. For this purpose, the IAF has since 2008 built or activated numerous advanced landing grounds for fixed-wing aircraft and helicopters in the Western and Eastern sectors.

On the two-front war, the army had assessed that in the event of a war with Pakistan, China was not likely to open its front with India. It would back Pakistan much more than it had done on earlier occasions with political and diplomatic support, and with war-withal including the uninterrupted supply of stores, spares and ammunition. However, if there is war between India and China, Pakistan would certainly take advantage of the opportunity by opening a war front with India.

COLD START DOCTRINE

The Indian Army's Cold Start Doctrine remains at the heart of hot war with Pakistan. Army chief General N. C. Vij, however, failed to realize that the Cold Start Doctrine—a phrase he coined for a war with Pakistan, perhaps on the spur of the moment while responding to the media—would generate international concern and help Pakistan project itself as hapless and in need of tactical nuclear weapons to stop the Indian juggernaut. As director general of Military Operations during the Kargil conflict and vice chief of army staff during Operation Parakram, Vij understood India's politico-military functioning in crisis and war.

The lesson of the Kargil conflict, according to the then army chief General V. P. Malik, was that a limited war in time, space, objectives and force levels was possible under a nuclear overhang. The challenge was to dovetail this lesson with that of Operation Parakram: how to mobilize offensive or strike formations quickly to deliver a hard-hitting punch all along the border without crossing Pakistan's nuclear redlines. This was done by Cold Start.

As we have explained, Cold Start meant instant crossing over into enemy territory once the decision to wage war was taken. Cold Start implied surprise, provided war preparedness existed to maintain the swift tempo of operations. Given Pakistan's elongated geography and high-profile assets close to the border, Cold Start envisaged that Pakistan would panic when faced with this sudden onslaught. However, India was forced to revisit Cold Start when Pakistan said such a strategy would force it to use tactical nuclear weapons. Vij got rapped on his knuckles by the political leadership for not consulting them on Cold Start. Within months, Cold Start was renamed 'proactive strategy', which is what it was. But Pakistan has stuck to the Cold Start coinage as it projected India as the aggressor.

The proactive strategy is meant to reduce the Indian Army's war mobilization time, and retain the element of surprise with phases of offensive actions crafted to unhinge the enemy so that it makes wrong operational assessments and commits its reserve forces (strike formations) early in war which could then be decimated by air and land firepower.

A bit of background is essential to grasp the strategy. Since no loss of territory is acceptable to both sides in politically vital Punjab, the Indian and Pakistani armies have an identical operational stance—in the form of holding or pivot corps and offensive or strike corps—which is unique to them.

India's standard holding corps—with three divisions or 38,000 to 40,000 troops—are deployed in linear fashion on the border (as the Line of Control with Pakistan is a military line, it can be shifted by force even during peacetime, unlike a border which is inviolable during peacetime as per international law). These are meant to ensure that the enemy is stopped or delayed at the border and does not get an easy breakthrough and gain the initiative before our own strike corps join the war. In the 1990s, it was realized that once our own strike corps entered enemy territory through the bridgehead (military terminology for access point) made by the holding corps, the latter had little employment in war. To utilize the holding corps better, they were given more combat power and renamed pivot corps—their task now was to stop or delay enemy ingress, build a bridgehead for our own strike corps and help in its breakout into enemy territory to reach its objective(s).

The problem arose because of geography. Pakistan operates on interior lines and could mobilize its holding corps to move into battle locations in seventy-two to ninety-six hours. Its strike corps could be mobilized for crossing the border simultaneously. Since the Indian Army operates on exterior lines of communication, its strike corps are spread across the hinterland. While it can mobilize its pivot corps in seventy-two to ninety-six hours, the strike corps would take between ten to fifteen days. Historically, this provided a tremendous advantage to Pakistan in the initial stages of war. However, the problems will be accentuated as any war is expected to be short and swift (lasting no more than two weeks) since international pressure for a ceasefire on account of nuclear weapons would be enormous.

The war, it was reasoned, could not wait for India's lumbering strike corps to move into battle positions for their offensives or counter-offensive strategies to show results. Therefore, instead of the counter-offensive strategy (followed in the 1965 and 1971 wars) for deep thrusts inside Pakistan that the Indian Army had traditionally planned, the new strategy would be proactive or offensive and envisaged shallow penetrations across the entire international border.

The proposed action would have three elements. The holding corps, which as we have seen, has been renamed pivot corps and provided with enough combat punch, will have the ability to be launched within forty-eight to seventy-two hours, establish a bridgehead and break out to shallow depths (10 to 15 kilometres) along the entire International Border. Meanwhile, eight to ten integrated battle groups—each a division-size self-contained force around an armoured brigade—drawn from the three strike corps will be launched within ninety-six hours in an escalatory mode. The integrated battle groups will build on the successes of the pivot corps and go deeper into enemy territory depending on the theatre of operations. The idea was that forces on the LC would remain self-sufficient. Different contingencies were to be catered for all along the border, and whoever achieved results would be backed. This would allow the Indian Army to exercise a range of options rather than an all or nothing approach. In turn, this would allow time and flexibility for shaping the response at the political level as also the desired end state. After all, multiple divisional-sized integrated battle group thrusts stand a better chance of quick penetration and of upsetting the enemy's organic cohesion through surprise, speed and decision dilemma, quite like the effectiveness of the 1940 German blitzkrieg.

Finally, the strike corps, while retaining enough combat capabilities despite shedding the integrated battle groups, and with its command and control and ethos intact, would get up to seven days to decide (depending on how the war progressed and how soon and where the Pakistan Army decided to launch its offensive corps) from where to be launched. Once launched, the strike corps would take under its command all elements of the integrated battle groups and pivot corps available along the axis.

Another important element of the proactive strategy would be to shape the non-linear battlefield in depth by firepower (artillery and air force) and Special Forces. The name of the game would be fire-strikes instead of troop strikes in depth. Once the battlefield was pulverized by fire-strikes, the strike forces could then be used to punch hard.

India has three strike corps, namely, 1, 2 and 21, against Pakistan's two—1 and 2 Corps. During peacetime, the Indian Army's strike corps 1, 2 and 21 train with the Southwestern, Western and Southern commands respectively. The Indian Army was also considering having an army strategic command to centrally hold long-range potent firepower assets like the BRAHMOS (the name is a combination of Brahmaputra and Moskva rivers) cruise missile, and conventional ballistic missiles like Prahaar required for targets deep inside enemy territory.

In short, the mobilization time for offensive formations was reduced by two methods: the appropriate forward location of certain portions of reserves called integrated battle groups, and a review of the Operational Rail Move Plan to move the remaining elements of the strike corps faster. Incidentally, the Operational Rail Move Plan was tested for the first time after the 1971 war during Operation Parakram. The integrated battle group is a good concept as it will add depth to the battlefield. But to have a successful integrated battle group, problems of command and control, operational logistics and air defence will need to be overcome. If the group is to move rapidly it must not carry a great deal of baggage and structures that might otherwise be desirable for the management of an organization of its size. For this reason, and to exploit the military options on the LC, the redrawing of command boundaries for better command and control was done.

The raising of the Southwestern Command (on 15 August 2005) and 9 Corps (on 1 September 2005) resulted in the redrawing of command boundaries against Pakistan. With the creation of 9 Corps, the Northern Command (responsible for J&K) was relieved of its responsibilities in the plains sector in Jammu division. The job of 16 Corps (of Northern Command) became more focused, so much so that its 10 Division at Akhnoor, a mostly defensive formation, now has the capability to seriously threaten the southern flank of Pakistan's 10 Corps (responsible for Kashmir).

Similarly, the operationally important Shakargarh Bulge that earlier was the responsibility of two army commands (Northern and Western) is now with the Western Command. Up to three acclimatized mountain divisions with an ad hoc corps headquarters (that was moved during Operation Parakram from the Chinese front to Jammu and Kashmir against Pakistan) would now be available at short notice for tasking in the Jammu region.

With the Indian Army's proactive strategy and restructuring of command boundaries, operational options have increased, especially in the area between Chhamb and Sialkot that is the traditional battlefield between India and Pakistan. In both the 1965 and 1971 wars, India lost Chhamb to Pakistan. Now, there is the possibility of seriously threatening Pakistan's Marala Headworks, where the waters of the Munnawar Tawi, Chenab and Tawi rivers join in Pakistan, as well as the very heartland of Pakistan—Punjab.

India's strategic advantage in this critical zone of operations is that

Pakistan calls it a Working Boundary (opposite the Jammu International Border) and not the International Border. This area then would be treated as part of the Jammu and Kashmir theatre which has the Line of Control. This implies that if Pakistan took the war from J&K outside to the International Border to release pressure, it would get labelled as the aggressor in the war. Similarly, the Indian Army's options have increased in the Thar Desert in Rajasthan in the south for shallow ingress.

The strategies of the army's Cold Start Doctrine are theoretical. The reality is different. The Indian Army's corps showed much less flexibility than the Pakistan Army's in the 1971 war in shedding or adding (called detachments and attachments) smaller units quickly during operations, which is what Cold Start is about. Moreover, all exercises done from 2005 onwards to practise Cold Start are about testing commanders rather than ensuring that the troops understand operational flexibility—changed war aims and operational options and what needs to be done. Most exercises are skeleton order (reduced strength) and stage-managed. War-gaming is mostly notional as things like network centricity, heavy volumes of firepower, operations in a nuclear, biological and chemical environment, joint-ness between army and air force for successful air-land battles, and so on, are hypothetical rather than real.

The Pakistan Army, meanwhile, has moved 25 per cent of its forces close to the border in permanent locations to meet operational surprises. It has reconfigured operational organizations (called order of battle) and practised war scenarios to thwart the Indian challenge. It has also reinforced its canal obstacles; strengthened the air force and its air defence network involving ground-based weapons; moved its cantonments forward, thereby further shortening its internal lines of communications; strengthened 100 per cent forward defences with permanent steel bunkers; and improved its land mines capacity, capability and training. More than anything else, as has been mentioned, it brought tactical nuclear weapons into the war discourse. After 26/11, sometime in 2009, retired Pakistani army officers turned analysts started talking about tactical nuclear weapons as the answer to India's Cold Start. This set alarm bells ringing in the West, which, steeped in Cold War theology, concluded that there was the possibility of the early use of nuclear weapons in a war between India and Pakistan. Not lacking bravado, senior Indian analysts started presenting war scenarios of the Indian Army fighting through battlefields burnt and charred by tactical nuclear weapons.

Ammunition was added by Pakistan's former head of the Strategic Plans Division—responsible for nukes under the Pakistan Army—over fifteen years, since its inception in December 1998. Lieutenant General Khalid Kidwai spoke about radical change in Pakistan's nuclear policy: from credible minimal deterrence to full-spectrum deterrence. Pakistan's 60-kilometre range Nasr ballistic missile, he said 'was meant to close the gap at the tactical level (of conventional war) which India's Cold Start hoped to exploit'. Nasr was supposed to carry battlefield tactical nuclear weapons with less than a 5-kiloton yield to halt Cold Start at the border itself.

The moot issue that the Indian military was not capable of victory (whereby reasonable political and military gains could be made by war) in a conventional war with the Pakistan military was omitted by both sides. The Indian side created the perception of a militarily strong nation, while the Pakistanis used India's fallacious argument to further buttress their ballistic, cruise and armed unmanned vehicles inventory and fissile material. Why would Pakistan use tactical nuclear weapons in war when it could beat India's Cold Start with its conventional capabilities? Given its elongated geography and high density of population close to the border, it would be suicidal for the Pakistan Army to use nuclear weapons on its own soil.

An evaluation of conventional war preparedness of both sides should not be based on bean counting of manpower, weapons and equipment as is commonly done by scholars. It must take into account what comprises military power: political directions; command and control; sustenance (entailing stores, spares, ammunition and other war-withal); organization for war; operational doctrines; state of readiness; professional training; mindset and morale of troops; weapons and equipment. Bean counting of assets and focusing on acquisitions alone is a misleading and meaningless exercise which contributes little towards overall war preparedness.

Since a war is fought at three levels, each must be clearly understood to deduce the likely outcome. The strategic level of war is defined and executed by the political leadership and the services' headquarters working together under the rubric of higher defence management, responsible for identifying the overall political objectives to be gained by war. Once these are given out to the armed forces, they will enable the military leadership to make the required allocation of land, sea and air forces along with their strategic sustenance and logistics backup systems to achieve the required objectives. An efficient, inclusive and responsive higher defence management will strengthen the operational level of war which determines the outcome of war.

The operational level of war is where tactical battles fought in a particular area or theatre are given a coherent design and tackled as a whole. This intermediate level of war translates strategic aims into a workable military method of fighting in a theatre of war. In the Indian context, the army command is the operational level of war. In the Pakistan Army, which does not have army commands, two corps are grouped together as Army Command North and Army Command South for operational purposes.

The actual combat occurs at the tactical levels. A corps with three to four divisions, each with nearly 12,000 troops, is called a major tactical level. Minor tactical battles are fought by divisions, brigades, battalions and lower sub-units. Combat is entered into by combining the assets of infantry, armour, artillery, engineers, signals, aviation and so on in a joint arms effort. A corps is the minimum level where the IAF is operationally involved with the army.

The success in a war between India and Pakistan depends on the operational level of war. In the 1965 and 1971 wars, both militaries were nearly matched at this level of warfare. A country can be successful at the operational level of war because of good higher defence management, firepower, coordination for strategic sustenance, training, mindset, morale and surprise despite fewer numbers in terms of manpower and equipment.

To understand why India cannot defeat Pakistan in conventional war, it is necessary to compare all levels of war.

STRATEGIC LEVEL OF WAR

At the strategic level, Pakistan's General Headquarters at Rawalpindi brooks no interference from the civilian government in Islamabad on national security issues. Much of the substance for diplomacy with India, China, Afghanistan, the US, Russia, the Central Asian Republics and the Middle East is dictated by Rawalpindi. Matters of war and peace, especially with India, are decided by the Pakistan Army alone. Pakistan's higher defence management is controlled by Rawalpindi.

Pakistan's nuclear policy, weaponization options, delivery vehicle choices and control of fissile material are completely and unambiguously with the Pakistan Army. Strategic sustenance for conventional war—which includes defence allocations, arms purchases, indigenous war materials production, war planning and strategic intelligence—are well coordinated, quick and under Rawalpindi. The Pakistan Army is the only army in the world which has perfected the capability to fight simultaneously on two dissimilar battlefields: conventional and sub-conventional (terrorism).

The director general Military Operations, director general ISI and director general Strategic Plans Division report to the army chief. Given the unprecedented command and control at the strategic level, General Headquarters enjoys wider choices in planning and execution at the operational level of war amounting to strategic- and operational-level war surprises and rules of engagement. With the ISI directorate under it, General Headquarters has complete knowledge of terrorism in India in J&K and the mainland. Without the Pakistan Army's permission, nothing moves across the Line of Control.

The Pakistan Army's biggest advantage is in the nuclear weapons domain under its control. On the one hand, there is seamless integration of conventional and nuclear forces' plans into operationally deterrent forces by the organization called the Strategic Plans Division. On the other hand, 'conventional war plans would be independent of nuclear forces'. Since the Pakistan Army continues to build its conventional war capabilities even after the 1998 nuclear tests, it has little reason to use nukes early in war. The focus of the Pakistan military will be in strengthening the operational level of war where it has advantages over India.

An opposite system exists in India where the higher defence management is at odds with the tasks it is required to perform. Since the defence forces are outside the government, they have little interaction with the political leadership in peacetime and little say in the acquisition of conventional weapons. The defence services have little knowledge and understanding of their own nuclear weapons and Pakistan's nuclear redlines (which should be decided jointly by the political and military leaders). As India does not have an efficient indigenous defence industry, war supplies are not assured. Moreover, there is uncertainty about how conventional war and internal stability operations would be fought since the two are under different union ministries—defence and home.

The political leadership which would decide the terms of war engagement understands neither nuclear weapons nor military power. Its responses would be slow, tardy, ad hoc and piecemeal rather than bold and substantive if the countries were to go to war. Pakistan scores heavily over India at this level of war.

OPERATIONAL LEVEL OF WAR

Five issues have altered the operational level of war in Pakistan's favour.

Line of Control Fence: As we have seen, there are layers of fence in Jammu and Kashmir, which have instilled a defensive mindset in Indian troops. The first layer is on the LC around which the Indian Army has built its operational deployments in three tiers—one ahead, one along and the third tier behind the fence. The second layer of fence is around all army units in J&K. Since there have been instances of terrorists attacking army units, the perimeter defences built around fences have been strengthened depending upon their proximity to the LC. The army plans to have more fences inside the Valley by 2019. These fences in J&K force the Indian Army to combat within its own territory with the fence becoming its physical, mental and psychological limit of war-fighting. This leaves the Pakistan Army with time, energy and resources to devote itself to training for war.

The Indian Army leadership claims it will be able to switch from counter-insurgency operations to conventional war with ease. Three reasons repudiate such assertions. One, in all crises since 1990 (the Kargil conflict and Operation Parakram), the Indian defence services, especially the army (the other two have not been tested) have been found unprepared. Two, since the army leadership is not focused on conventional war, the building of war wastage reserves has not been a priority. If anything, the army scraped the bottom of the barrel by using depleted war wastage reserves to raise the 17 Mountain Corps against China. And three, unlike the Pakistan military, there is little intra (within the army and the air force) and inter-services (between the army and the air force for joint operations especially in mountainous and high-altitude regions where major results are expected in the next war) training.

Army's Internal Logistics Lines: In the event of a war with Pakistan, the Indian Army's internal communication lines for the movement of troops and war logistics would be dangerously vulnerable. This is because Kashmiris have been further alienated by the Modi government. This was borne out by the defiance of thousands of Kashmiri people who participated in local militant Burhan Wani's funeral in July 2016. Since most of the Indian Army engaged in counter-insurgency ops will be compelled to withdraw and move forward to defend the Line of Control, and as no other security forces have enough training to replace the army, the Indian Army will be fighting two different wars on two different fronts—within Kashmir and against the Pakistan Army.

Cruise Missiles: Given the enormous benefits that cruise missiles have over ballistic missiles and aircraft, Pakistan's Ra'ad and Babur are game changers in war. Cruise missiles are cheap, unstoppable, accurate, difficult to detect and have few technology transfer restrictions associated with them. China, since the 1990s, has paid special attention to the acquisition of land, air and sea cruise missiles. China has turbofan technology for cruise missile propulsion which allows maintenance of subsonic speeds (less than the speed of sound) at distances of 2,000 kilometres. The Ra'ad and Babur cruise missiles are of Chinese origin.

Test-fired in August 2007 from Mirage III EA fighter aircraft, the Ra'ad is a 350-kilometre range air-launched cruise missile that has been inducted into the Pakistan Air Force. Ra'ad's stand-off capability will help it reach Delhi without hindrance from the Indian Air Force defences.

The test-firing of the Babur Land Attack Cruise Missile on 10 August 2005 and its induction into the Pakistan Army in 2008 was another game changer. India does not have a comparable capability. Babur's production line was acquired by Pakistan's National Development Complex from China's state-owned China National Precision Machinery Import and Export Corporation, implying its availability in large numbers in the Pakistan Army's inventory. The stated range of Babur is 500 kilometres, which could be extended to 2,000 kilometres because of turbofan propulsion. Babur's twin advantages are its turbofan propulsion and navigation and guidance system. It is accurate to within 10 metres at 500 kilometres. Moreover, the missile can fly at low altitude, posing a severe detection challenge even for airborne radars due to ground clutter. Regarding war-fighting, the Pakistan Army is expected to fight both the contact battle and the deep battle with Babur being the main source of disruptive firepower. Babur with conventional warheads would be the weapon of choice to counter India's Cold Start Doctrine.

Interoperability: This is the ability of two armed forces to operate together in a combat environment with ease as one whole. With China's support, interoperability will help Pakistan strengthen its deterrence, manage crises, shape battlefields and win wars against India. The Pakistani and Chinese armies and air forces have achieved interoperability, unmatched even by the US-NATO alliance at the height of détente in the 1970s when the Soviet Union's threat to Western Europe was at its peak. Even the two navies have taken steps in this direction with the proposed acquisition of eight Chinese submarines by Pakistan by 2018.

Interoperability starts with commonality of equipment. At present, most of Pakistan's strategic and the bulk of its conventional war capabilities are of Chinese origin. Strategic nuclear weapons, tactical nuclear weapons, ballistic and cruise missiles, unmanned aerial vehicles, fighter aircraft and tanks, to intelligence, surveillance and reconnaissance capabilities, and so on, have been given either clandestinely or at rock-bottom prices by China to Pakistan. It is no secret that the majority of Chinese defence hardware and software exports are to Pakistan.

The second step involves regular upgrades and an uninterrupted supply of spares without which a war cannot be sustained. In military terms, this is referred to as strategic and operational sustenance. During the 1999 Kargil conflict, the Pakistan army chief, General Pervez Musharraf, was in China seeking both political and diplomatic support and operational sustenance for his military gamble. That uncertain situation has disappeared with the opening of an all-weather land route. The Karakoram Highway is being upgraded into a four- and six-lane highway with China's assistance since December 2010, ever since China announced that it did not have a border with India in Jammu and Kashmir.

China has constructed sixteen airstrips on the Karakoram Highway, primarily for enhancing airlift capability for military support. China is also laying optical fibre cable for secure communications along the Karakoram from Rawalpindi to the Khunjerab Pass. Moreover, China has given the Pakistan military access to the high-resolution capability of its phase one BeiDou navigation system (equivalent of the US's Global Positioning System). Phase two of BeiDou, with a total of thirty-five satellites, has been launched, again with Pakistan as the partner country.

The third step for interoperability involves mission compatibility and is intrusive and intensive. In this, the two militaries understand each other's doctrines, force structuring, operational planning and art of war through regular visits and high-end exercises. The last step is familiarity with terrain where combat is expected. Once achieved, interoperability will bring standardization, integration, cooperation and synergy.

The Chinese and Pakistani air forces, with equipment compatibility, have since March 2010 undertaken the Shaheen series of air exercises over POK. According to reports, the two air forces shared digital data links during these air manoeuvres, implying the ability of the pilots of the two sides to communicate while in the air. Besides joint exercises, the two armies regularly visit each other's operational areas.

The two Special Forces have also been conducting the Warrior series of joint exercises in high-altitude areas since 2012. In military terms, while both sides have developed air capabilities to pound targets in high-altitude areas using Chinese satellites and special aperture radars, the two Special Forces could, through vertical envelopment (capability to drop and operate behind enemy lines), capture areas in depth, upsetting the linear battlefield. India has not dovetailed interoperability between the two adversaries into its thinking and operational planning.

Chinese Workers in Pakistan: Having announced in 2013 that the 2,395-kilometre China–Pakistan Economic Corridor will be the flagship of Chinese President Xi Jinping's spectacular One Belt One Road economic plan, thousands of Chinese are working on connectivity, power and industrial projects in Pakistan. They are in Gilgit–Baltistan, POK and along the entire border with India. This development has serious war implications, as Chinese workers could be collateral damage if India attacks Pakistan from the air and on land. Consider the following scenario:

Presuming that after another terrorist attack similar to 26/11 by the Pakistan military, the Indian Army unleashes its Cold Start Doctrine into Pakistan supported by air power and long-range land firepower—290-kilometre BRAHMOS and 150-kilometre Prithvi missiles, 70-kilometre Smerch and 40-kilometre Pinaka multi-barrel rocket launchers. Chinese civilian casualties in Pakistan will be unavoidable.

What will China do? It is unlikely to open a second front against India. However, the PLA could order its potent mobile rapid reaction forces to be readied, and place its war assets on high alert. This will place India under intense psychological pressure with the spectre of a two-front war staring it in the face. The PLA, meanwhile, will increase aggressive patrolling—a euphemism for border transgressions and intrusions—on the Line of Actual Control.

This will lead to a catch-22 situation for the Indian Army. It will not be able to move any troops from east to west (against Pakistan). On the contrary, war assets and troops belonging to the China front which have been moved to face Pakistan will need to be sent back post-haste. China will react harshly to any increase in Indian troops' strength or war assets close to the LAC as under the 1993, 1996 and 2013 bilateral treaties this is permissible only 'with mutual consent'. Violation of the treaty by India will be an act of war, and China's stated policy is to fight in self-defence.

If India does not increase troops on the LAC, Chinese troops, taking advantage of the 2013 Border Defence Cooperation Agreement, which does not allow 'tailing or following' of patrols once inside the adversary's territory, will induct hordes of forces through innumerable gaps in the 2,000-kilometre border in Arunachal Pradesh, or 'South Tibet' in Chinese parlance.

Like the April–May 2013 three-week intrusion in the Depsang plains (north Ladakh), numerous Chinese columns will cross into Arunachal Pradesh, without fear of being 'tailed or followed', pitch tents and occupy Indian land without firing a shot. Interestingly, the PLA had practised the occupation of the Indian Air Force's advanced landing ground during its

Strike series of exercises in 2010. If India attempts to force Chinese troops to go back, it will be war. If it does not, it will be national humiliation and India's international standing will nosedive.

The situation will be equally dim in the Kashmir Valley. As with the 1999 Kargil War, the Indian Army will be compelled to bring troops to the Line of Control by giving up on counter-insurgency operations in most of Jammu and Kashmir. The void left behind will not be filled by paramilitary forces because the army, with disdain for the latter's professionalism, has refused to hand over internal security duties to them during peacetime. Hence, the army's internal lines of communication will be extremely vulnerable to terrorist attacks.

Let's assess the Line of Control with Pakistan and the border where the Pakistani military will have three major advantages over the Indian military. One, given the interoperability of the Pakistan Air Force and the Pakistan Army with the PLA, where the two sides have reached the end game of fighting combat missions together, the Pakistani military will have the capability to fight a long duration war. Moreover, there will be an uninterrupted supply of spares, ammunition and air and land strike platforms from China for the Pakistani military.

The second operational advantage of the Pakistani military will be in electronic warfare, which the PLA considers the fourth dimension of combat after land, air and sea. According to the US Defense Department's 2015 report to Congress, 'PLA electronic warfare strategy focuses on radio, radar, optical, infrared and microwave frequencies in addition to adversarial computer and information systems.' Given the interoperability between the two militaries, the implications for the Indian military are obvious. The PLA will be able to jam communication, radar and satellite equipment, rendering the Indian military's command and control ineffective.

The third advantage will be in the plethora of long-range conventionally armed cruise and ballistic missiles (provided by China) available with Pakistan to halt India's Cold Start at the Thar border itself. Although Pakistan's Lieutenant General Khalid Kidwai had spoken about full-spectrum deterrence, hinting at the use of tactical nuclear weapons as the response to Cold Start, it is a ruse. When the Pakistani military has the twin advantage of PLA support and an edge at the operational level of war, why would it use nukes and that too on its own territory knowing full well that it has high-profile targets close to the Indian border? (Lahore is 40 kilometres from Amritsar.) As has been pointed out, Pakistan's Babur, Ra'ad and Nasr/Hatf-IX cruise and ballistic missiles will be game changers. Not by their use, but because of the absence of any bilateral understanding on ballistic and cruise missiles, India will worry about them being nuclear.

The wily Pakistanis have spoken about full-spectrum deterrence and tactical nuclear weapons merely to draw the world's attention to Kashmir, where the world fears a conventional war could end up in a nuclear weapons exchange.

TACTICAL LEVEL OF WAR

The 2015 Comptroller and Auditor General (CAG) report tabled in Parliament said that the Indian Army's ammunition stocks were below acceptable risk levels; 125 of 170 types of ammunition were not available. Responding to the news, the Northern Army Commander, Lieutenant General D. S. Hooda, said 'there is some shortage of ammunition', adding that 'day-to-day operations would not be affected. But if you are looking at war time, then you need to build up huge amounts of stocks'. He, however, did not admit that the army lacked the training and mindset for war, which was a major observation flagged by the 1999 Kargil War Committee Report after the localized conflict the same year.

It is well-known that the Indian Army was unprepared for war during the 1999 localized Kargil conflict. Remember the famous statement made by the then Chief of Army Staff, General V. P. Malik? During Operation Parakram, it was the army's good fortune that the Vajpayee government succumbed to US pressure and did not go to war with Pakistan in January 2002. Little known to him and the nation was the fact that the Northern Army Commander, Lieutenant General R. K. Nanavaty, had told the then army chief, General S. Padmanabhan, that he lacked adequate equipment and ammunition for war. In the aftermath of the 26/11 attacks when New Delhi was mulling over strong retaliatory action, there were reports that the army chief, General Deepak Kapoor, had expressed concerns to both Prime Minister Manmohan Singh and Defence Minister A. K. Antony about equipment and ammunition deficiencies.

The army has been unprepared for war since at least 1993 when army chief General B. C. Joshi ordered massive Rashtriya Rifles raisings. According to *FORCE* magazine, which did a comprehensive article after speaking with those who have knowledge of the matter, there is a very real concern that the Indian Army may not have ammunition to fight the next war (with Pakistan, not to mention China) beyond three to five days. Holdings for all types of missiles and anti-tank ammunition are critically low. Stocks for artillery (70 per cent of fuses needed for firing are unavailable) and ammunition for armoured fighting vehicles are unlikely to last beyond four to five days of intense war. War wastage reserves for most ammunition categories do not exist.

This is not all. Mission reliability of mechanized vehicles is poor. The artillery is obsolete and inadequate; air defence is antiquated; armour is unreliable due to regular barrel accidents caused by a mismatch between indigenous barrels and ammunition; army aviation helicopters need urgent replacement; and night fighting devices are insufficient.

These concerns have been voiced several times by high-ranking officers. The leaking to the media of General V. K. Singh's letter of 12 March 2012 to Prime Minister Manmohan Singh is one such instance.

The IAF fares no better than the army. It has critical deficiencies in combat aircraft, training aircraft, simulators, air defence and network-centricity. Most of all, the joint-ness in operations between the army and the air force, which is a critical requirement at the operational level for a short and swift war, is absent. This was obvious from the last localized Kargil conflict that the two services fought together. Instead of a single operation, the army's operation was named Vijay (victory), while the IAF campaign was called Safed Sagar (white sea, alluding to the snow-covered mountains). Moreover, the army and air force have different war doctrines on how a war would be fought.

In war, apart from the defence of national airspace, concepts of joint air, land and sea warfare are expected to remain largely theoretical. In practical terms, there would be separate campaigns developing on land, air and sea, which would not be in close concert with one another. Joint planning and the conduct of operations without unity of command is not a feasible proposition. This would lead to much waste and duplication within the three services. The biggest casualty would be the outcomes and end results, which are at a premium in a short war.

To conclude, the Pakistan military scores heavily over the Indian military at the strategic level of war. It has, for the first time, acquired a decisive edge at the crucial operational level of war and remains ahead at the tactical level of war. Given this situation, what would India do in case of a 26/11 type of terrorist attack or even the September 2016 terrorists' attack on the Indian Army's brigade at Uri near the LC? The war option would certainly not achieve the desired result of ending Pakistan's proxy war in J&K. If anything, it could escalate matters by bringing China, by default, into the war matrix. The reality is that India and its military are not prepared for such nightmarish scenarios.

CHAPTER 5

WAR IS NOT AN OPTION

China has ruled out war over the disputed border with India. The dispute has not been listed by China as a core or major concern over which it could go to war. According to Major General Yao Yunzhu, the director of the Centre of China-America Defence Relations, PLA Academy of Military Sciences, 'As both sides have agreed to have peaceful borders, the [Indian] focus should not be on the border issue.'

There are however two scenarios where China might be forced to go to war: in self-defence, or to protect its assets and interests abroad (given the expansive One Belt One Road project across continents, this probability is high).

As has been pointed out earlier, if India were to renege on any bilateral agreements, China would have reason to fight in 'self-defence'. With China, it's always heads I win, tails you lose. This is not bullying, something India tried with Pakistan during Operation Parakram and failed. This is military coercion, the capability to make an adversary comply without resistance. Successful military coercion is always backed by tangible military power, the essentials of which show in higher defence management.

The latter is country-specific and its nuances determine how envisaged wars will be fought and won. This is because higher defence management impacts at the strategic and operational levels of war. Most nations would hesitate to dwell too much on their higher defence management, especially when making a presentation to a potential rival audience. Not China. Instead, senior PLA officials took pains to explain China's higher defence management to the Indian journalists it invited in July 2012.

◆

With the arrival of the fifth generation Chinese leadership under President Xi Jinping, the country's higher defence management has undergone major military reforms starting 3 September 2015, in line with China's military strategy unveiled in May 2015. Meant to assist the expansion of China's global footprint as encapsulated in the China Dream and to meet the new threat (from the US), the 2015 military strategy made three revelations. It placed the focus on stand-off weapons, outer space and cyberspace. The implication was that the Chinese would place greater emphasis on non-contact war rather than a contact war which provides a warning period to an adversary to monitor the PLA's war preparation and accordingly adjust its own war waging capabilities to meet the threat. This PLA stance of non-contact war would also help in military coercion by placing the emphasis on psychological rather than physical victory.

The other first was the decision to move beyond coastal defence to the open seas. This announcement formalized what was already visible since 2008 with increasing frequency—the PLA Navy's aggressiveness in the South and East China seas and, importantly, its forays into the Indian Ocean with ships and submarines in the garb of anti-terrorism and anti-piracy operations to protect its commercial interests across the sea lanes.

The third revelation was in the nuclear domain. While removing any ambiguity on its nuclear weapons doctrine of no-first-use, no nuclear weapons against non-nuclear states and nuclear free zones, no participation in a nuclear arms race and commitment to maintain minimum nuclear deterrence, the PLA stated its decision to modernize its nuclear weapons capability. According to the May 2015 military strategy, 'China will optimise its nuclear force structure, improve strategic early warning, command and control, missile penetration, rapid reaction, and survivability and protection, and deter other countries from using or threatening to use nuclear weapons against China.' China watchers saw in this a move towards the militarization of outer space—anti-satellite capabilities, ballistic missile defence and use of space for faster detection and neutralization of hostile missiles and better navigation of its own long-range missiles—and the use of multiple nuclear warheads (by miniaturizing warheads), a capability that China has possessed since the 1990s.

In addition, China, like the United States and Russia, is working on a new type of weapon called a hypersonic glide vehicle. The latter will be able to travel up to 17,000 miles per hour, and manoeuvre erratically to avoid anti-missile defences, and given its speed will have high energy on impact which itself would act like a bomb even without an explosive warhead. Unlike a ballistic missile which travels in a parabolic arc, the hypersonic vehicle will glide once separated from its booster rocket. The hypersonic vehicle will make the requirement of nukes and contact war with India unnecessary.

While insisting that its new military ideas had a defensive profile, the PLA justified them as being in support of China's grown geo-economic status. According to the strategy paper, the PLA will maintain credible strategic deterrence, safeguard overseas interests and those in the domains of outer and cyberspace, in addition to participating in regional and global stability operations to maintain world order.

Against this backdrop, the essence of China's higher defence management is as follows.

The Central Military Commission (CMC) is China's highest military command and control organization, standing at the apex of the military (nuclear and conventional) chain of command and military-industrial complex. It commands the PLA, a 2.3 million strong regular force; the 660,000-strong People's Armed Police Force; and 8 million militia. Before Xi's reforms, the CMC had twelve members, eight of whom were from the PLA. These were the chief of General Staff Headquarters, chief of PLA Air Force (PLAAF), chief of PLA Navy (PLAN), chief of PLA Second Artillery (PLASA), head of General Political Department (GPD), head of General Logistics Department (GLD), head of General Armament Department (GAD) and the defence minister heading the Ministry of National Defence. There were three vice chairmen and the chairman of the CMC.

Given the new defensive posture, Xi's military reforms have given importance to joint-ness (ability of stakeholders to work in synergy for optimal results) both at the highest CMC level (for policymaking and administration) and at the operational level of war (for combat). Joint-ness at the CMC level is meant to strengthen Xi's hold over the PLA. This would ensure that the PLA, which would play an important role in the One Belt One Road project, remains corruption free, professional and obedient to the Communist party. Joint-ness at the highest combat level would ensure that the PLA wins wars by optimizing capabilities. With an emphasis upon unity in command, the PLA is expected to give equal weightage to all services on land, sea and in the air.

With this in mind, at the CMC level, the four former headquarters, namely, General Staff Headquarters, General Political Department, General Logistics Department and General Armament Department have been replaced by fifteen departments of the Commission. These are: Joint Staff Department (JSD), Political Work Department (PWD), Logistics Support Department, Equipment Development Department, Training and Administration Department, National Defence Mobilization Department, General Office,

Agency for Offices' Administration, Office for Reforms and Organizational Structure, Office for International Military Cooperation, Office for Strategic Planning, Audit Office, Discipline Inspection Commission, Politics and Law Commission, and Science and Technology Commission.

The breakdown of four headquarters into fifteen departments of the Commission implies two things: one, previous departments which were perhaps unwieldy have been streamlined for more focused results and monitoring. And two, new subjects have been added which were earlier not needed since the PLA's roles and missions were limited to continental defence. For example, the Office for International Military Cooperation has been necessitated by the PLA's new role in support of the One Belt One Road project. The task of this agency is increased military cooperation, counter-terrorism, and so on, between the PLA and security forces of countries on China's One Belt One Road map. Similarly, the Discipline Inspection Commission would ensure zero corruption within the PLA. Officers of this agency would regularly visit command headquarters and field formations to audit disciplinary cases, and submit a report card regularly to the CMC. This would ensure a corruption-free PLA and even more importantly a corruption-free image of the PLA abroad.

In addition to the fifteen departments of the Commission, PLA headquarters involved in combat support would continue to report to the CMC. Three of these have been renamed and two new ones added. These are the General Staff Headquarters (renamed the Joint Staff Department), the PLASA (renamed PLA Rocket Force) and GPD (renamed Political Work Department). The two new combat support headquarters are the PLA Army Headquarters (PLAA HQs) and PLA Strategic Support Force. While the post of defence minister with some change in responsibility has been retained, the number of vice chairmen of the CMC has been reduced from three to two (Generals Fan Changlong and Xu Qiliang).

The Political Work Department is unique to the PLA. No other military in the world has a similar representation. The PWD is a clear indication that the PLA is not apolitical: it is answerable to the Communist Party and not the state. Considering that the political officers are PLA officers doing party work and not party functionaries in army uniform inside the PLA, it suggests that the PLA has more weightage in civil-military relations, which has been the traditional stance of Communist China. When the authors asked Senior Colonel (brigadier) Su Rong, commander 1 Armoured Regiment (brigade), if having political officers in the PLA Army—an organization that aims to become a professional, high-tech force—was an aberration, his reply was, 'Political officers are needed for unity [between PLA and civilians]. It is important to be professional and have an ideology too. We believe that human beings are as important as equipment. It is because of this unity that PLA soldiers deliver more with less food. A PLA soldier needs just one-fourth of the food that a US soldier needs, to do his task well.' According to him, this arrangement helped enhance the PLA's interest in local affairs. Civilians in turn learn about military affairs—this helps them when they need to mobilize local populations in the event of hostilities and also helps them understand how civilian infrastructure can be used for war. As the PLA's political wing has clout outside the military, it helps Chinese Communist Party members understand the PLA better. There are six political commissars in each regular army division (8,000 soldiers) and one each in a regiment (equivalent of an Indian brigade). At the battalion level, the political officers are called directors and each PLA Army company has a political instructor.

The renaming of the General Staff Headquarters as the Joint Staff Department is meant to bring genuine joint-ness within the PLA with equal representation of high-ranking officers from all three services, that is, PLA Army, PLA Air Force and PLA Navy. The head of the Joint Staff Department is expected to have three functions: he will provide single point advice to the chairman, CMC. He will provide the secretariat to the Joint Command of the Commission in the form of Joint Operations Command Centre during crisis or war. When functioning from the Joint Operations Command Centre, the chairman, CMC, will be designated as the commander-in-chief, CMC joint command. The third role of the Joint Staff Department head will be to seamlessly integrate conventional and nuclear war plans. Since China has adopted a nuclear no-first-use policy, operational planning will be separate for nuclear and conventional warfare.

Given its high-profile task, the Joint Staff Department head is expected to have a higher status than other heads of services and will be hand-picked by the CMC chairman. A senior PLA officer explained to the authors that Joint Staff Department and theatre commands alone will not bring joint-ness for war. Since 2010, PLA officers at various levels have been attending interservice courses to understand each other's core competencies. Select officers are being posted on the staff of other services.

Next, the PLASA has been renamed as the PLA Rocket Force. This could have been done for two reasons. China's nuclear weapons assets, which were earlier seen as an extension of the artillery, now have been delinked from that, suggesting a more professional title for strategic assets which are under modernization in order to provide credible deterrence. The new name also suggests that Rocket Force would only have nuclear assets under it, including strategic nuclear submarines and strategic bombers. PLA's medium (under-300 kilometres range) and short-range missiles which use conventional warheads would be under the exclusive command of theatre commands. The PLASA was responsible for dual-use missiles with both nuclear and conventional warheads.

In its 1996 military demonstration against Taiwan and all subsequent training exercises, the PLA has left little doubt about how it intends to use conventional ballistic missiles. The latter will be used in conjunction with the PLAAF to allow the air force to retain sorties for strike and air superiority missions. The conventional missiles' targets would be heavily protected communication centres, weapons delivery sites and aircraft carrier battle groups. It is axiomatic that conventional ballistic missiles would be employed in the initial stages of a conflict from widely dispersed sites.

An important and long awaited reform has been the creation of PLA Army Headquarters similar to PLA Air Force Headquarters and PLA Navy Headquarters. Hitherto, the General Staff Headquarters, headed by a PLAA officer, was seen as both PLA Army Headquarters and joint command headquarters. The raising of new PLAA Headquarters indicates two things: one, the traditionally superior status of the PLAA within the PLA has been downgraded with the PLAA becoming like the other two combat services, PLAAF and PLAN. This is in sync with the PLA's thinking of fighting combined armed operations involving all three defence services. And two, there is the possibility in the future that some theatre commands could have overall PLAAF and PLAN commanders instead of the present system where all come from the PLAA.

As part of the reforms, the PLAA (ground forces) will shed 300,000 troops over five years (2015–20) to become a lean and professional force for modern warfare. According to the state-run *Global Times*, the ratio of ground, air and naval forces will finally be 2:1:1, a major shift from the present 4:2:1.

A new PLA Strategic Support Force has been created. This will bring all space, cyber, electromagnetic and technical assets, which are critical for information warfare, under one roof. These will be in support of combat operations both for continental defence and for expeditionary forces. The PLA Strategic Support Force will integrate support forces of different services to improve efficiency and save costs.

Regarding the operational level which directly impacts the outcome of war, new theatre (zone) commands have been formed. The seven MRs or Military Area Commands in Shenyang, Beijing, Lanzhou, Jinan, Nanjing, Guangzhou and Chengdu have been reduced to five theatre commands responsible for north, south, west, east and central theatres. The new theatre commanders—responsible for joint command, joint operations and joint logistics in war—will report to the CMC. Each theatre command will have subordinate PLAA, PLAAF and PLAN commands which will command their respective services' troops during peacetime and be responsible for dual training—intra-service to hone core competency and interservice for joint operations. The administrative and war-withal needs of subordinate PLAA, PLAAF and PLAN commanders will be met by their respective headquarters. Thus, theatre commanders will be the highest operational commanders responsible for war, while the three services' headquarters as the highest staff headquarters will ensure their subordinate commands are provided for war.

Specific to India, the Lanzhou and Chengdu Military Area Commands have been merged into the Western Theatre Command to improve joint planning, logistics and operations across the Tibet Autonomous Region. The importance of unity of command and joint operations for a short and swift war are major war-winning factors. In addition, China has created a new and unique Tibet Military Command specifically for a land war with India. The commander-in-chief, Tibet Military Command, has been placed under the PLAA Headquarters based in Beijing for administrative, including outside resources, and logistics, needs. Since China has resolved twelve of its fourteen land disputes, the PLAA Headquarters will ensure that all the PLA resources are made available against India and Bhutan (which has a special military relationship with India). For operations planning and actual combat, the Tibet Military Command will be under the Western Theatre Command based in Chengdu.

The commander, Tibet Military Command, has dedicated capabilities from the army, air force, missiles, air defence and Special Forces, as well as more plentiful support in terms of war logistics, specialized equipment for high-altitude warfare, and so on, within his area of responsibility. The commander, Tibet Military Command, trains all forces together for decided war missions. He also has under him all border guards (the equivalent of India's paramilitary forces) and militia (equating roughly with India's Territorial Army) to ensure internal stability within the Tibet Autonomous Region.

The Tibet Military Command's area of responsibility includes India's Arunachal Pradesh and a part of Ladakh. Most of Ladakh, including

Aksai Chin, is the responsibility of Lanzhou Provincial Command based in Xinjiang. Unlike the Tibet Military Command, the commander of Lanzhou Provincial Command has only border guards and militia under him. The regular troops and war resources are directly under the Western Theatre Command. According to Chinese experts, the Lanzhou Provincial Command commander may also get upgraded in rank and stature to the Tibet Military Command. However, this is unlikely. Since China says it does not have a border with India in Ladakh, it may allow Pakistani forces to take the lead against India in the Kashmir war theatre by providing military support without showing its hand. This is why the two allies have developed interoperability.

Regarding Special Forces, when asked why like the PLAA and PLAN, the PLAAF did not have special purpose (Special Forces) units, Colonel Yujun said, 'PLAAF does not need special purpose units as they are inbuilt into its organization.' Based in Henan province in central China, the 15th Airborne Corps is meant for independent strategic missions: limited power projection and deep strike manoeuvrability. The 15th Corps' missions include occupying strategic points behind the enemy, destroying the enemy's key communication hubs and preventing his supporting forces from reaching the front. The 15th Corps troops are supplemented by PLAA and PLAN special purpose (Special Forces) units, which are under theatre commands and are trained to fight behind enemy lines, engaging in sabotage, reconnaissance and other unconventional operations. They receive extensive parachute training. In addition to the special purpose (Special Forces) clandestine missions, the theatre commands have integral army aviation units to supplement the 15th Corps' strategic effort, demonstrating a major shift from horizontal thrust to vertical envelopment.

While China's defence minister (a retired PLAA officer) is a member of the CMC, the Ministry of National Defence (MND) has nothing to do with hard-core military work. In Colonel Yujun's words, 'The MND, under the state council (council of ministers or government) is the leading administrative organ of national defence undertakings. It is responsible for public relations; military cooperation with friendly foreign militaries; and in consultation with the CMC, it is authorized to mobilize PLA reserve force (militia) which is the backbone of the regular army.' He added, 'The militia is an organic part of the armed forces and performs combat readiness support and defensive operations and assists in social order.' During peacetime, training and administration of the border forces and militia which was the responsibility of the National Defence Mobilization Department, which reports directly to the CMC is now under theatre commands.

According to Colonel Yujun, the PLA is building capability to win local wars in conditions of informationization (a term used by the PLA to mean that all three defence services, the navy, air force and the army are networking) by strengthening the composite development of mechanization and informationization with the latter as the leading factor. This explains the two-step approach of the PLA: mechanization which has been achieved and informationization that it hopes to complete by 2020. Considering that all PLA forces are meant for mobile operations, the objective is to have lean, deadly forces—or what is known as the teeth component. The operational logistics or the tail factor is an entity by itself and is fully geared to support combat at various levels.

To address logistics, which are critical to an intense battle, the theatre PLAA, PLAAF and PLAN subordinate commands have taken important steps: the creation of a single supply system for the theatre and incorporation of nearby civilian supply depots to assist logistics in times of emergency. All PLAAF, PLAN and PLAA forces in the theatre can draw rations and fuel supplies from a single point. Moreover, massive storage sites have been created for holding ammunition reserves in the various operational theatres where forces would fight their wars.

For conventional war, the PLA chain of command runs from commander-in-chief, Theatre Command to the commander-in-chief, Joint Command of the Commission, President Xi Jinping, through the head of the Joint Staff Department. For nuclear war, the chain of command is the head of the PLA Rocket Force to the commander-in-chief, Joint Command of the Commission, President Xi Jinping, also through the head of the Joint Staff Department. The Joint Staff Department is expected to advise the commander-in-chief, Joint Command of the Commission, of transition from conventional to nuclear war.

COMPARISON WITH INDIAN MILITARY

Worryingly the PLA scores over the Indian military at all levels of war. At the strategic level, China has at least six advantages over Indian defence services. The first is good and quick decision-making, with enormous flexibility before and during a war. This has been made possible by close politico-military interaction and the PLA's deliberate and proactive thinking as a non-status quo power.

In India, there is no institutionalized system for the prime minister to get military advice on security and defence matters, with his Cabinet

Committee on Security colleagues understanding little of military power. It is an open secret that while ordering mobilization of the Indian Army against Pakistan (Operation Parakram), Prime Minister Vajpayee did not tell the army chief, General S. Padmanabhan, what was expected from the armed forces—war or just a show of strength. After the 26 November 2008 attacks in Mumbai, Prime Minister Manmohan Singh did not seek military advice for three days while the country was under siege and virtually paralysed. National security advisors in the Prime Minister's Office have either been former diplomats or police officers, with none—with the exception of Brajesh Mishra during Vajpayee's tenure—having shown brilliance in strategizing.

The PLA's second advantage over India is the possession of tactical nuclear weapons. While China has a no-first-use nuclear policy and considers strategic nukes as political weapons, non-possession of tactical nuclear weapons will continue to deprive India of an appropriate level of deterrence against China. This remains a serious operational shortcoming.

The PLA's third advantage over Indian forces is in strategic sustenance or the ability to fight a high tempo (speed of operations) war with optimal wherewithal for a long duration. It is one thing to have a much higher annual defence allocation—the PLA's defence budget for 2015 was reportedly US$ 139.5 billion against India's US$ 39.2 billion, excluding PLA acquisitions from outside. It is quite another thing to have a robust indigenous defence industrial base, something that China has and India does not. The Central Military Commission ensures a high level of war preparedness during peacetime.

Outer space is another area where the PLA is strides ahead of India. China demonstrated its anti-satellite capability first in 2007 by destroying its own legacy satellite with a land-based interceptor. This alarmed the US. Considering that the US has hundreds of military and commercial satellites in space, it desires good space situational awareness. China's anti-satellite capability could smash satellites into smithereens, leaving clouds of debris, which would adversely affect much-needed situational awareness. Such an act cannot be construed as an act of war. But it would play havoc with space supported Command, Control, Computer and Intelligence (C3I) systems.

In 2013, China 'launched three small satellites into orbit as part of Beijing's covert anti-satellite warfare programme'. These satellites have the capability to co-orbit, or enter into the orbit of other satellites, and 'with a retractable arm, they can be used for a number of things—to gouge, knock off, or grab passing satellites. This is part of a Chinese "Star Wars" programme'. India does not have anti-satellite capability, making its space programme—for commercial and military purposes—extremely vulnerable. For example, India's strategic missiles, the Agni series, with ranges from 700 to 5,000 kilometres would be largely dependent on space-based detection and tracking capabilities, which if destroyed by anti-satellites will render the ballistic missiles blind to incoming hostile nuclear missiles.

The PLA's fifth advantage is potent cyber warfare capabilities, something that India, still grappling with cyber-defence know-how, lacks. Ironically, the US, which launched the information revolution with the Internet in the 1990s, is now at its wits' end to meet the Chinese cyber challenge. According to Chinese Senior Colonel Xu Weidi of the PLA University of National Defence, who has engaged with the US at different cyber forums, 'No one will win the battle in the cyberspace and hence no one should engage in cyberwar. We should focus on security in cyberspace.'

The Chinese have been mulling over cyberwar since 1988, around the time that the Internet was invented. According to the US expert Joel Brenner, Shen Weiguang, now regarded as the founding sage of Chinese information warfare, told his perplexed PLA audience at the National Defence University, 'If we could destroy the enemy's political, economic and military infrastructure by putting virus-infected microchips into their systems, we could achieve the greatest of all strategic objectives. This could destroy the enemy's will to launch a war or wage a war.'

Brenner puts matters into perspective. He writes, 'Since 2002, the PLA has been actively creating Information Warfare militias, recruiting from universities, research institutes, and commercial IT companies, especially telecom firms. We [the US] know that China's Academy of Military Science has endorsed the formation of cyber-militia and directed the PLA to make the creation of such units a priority. In some cases they undergo light military indoctrination.' He adds, 'The Chinese see conflict on all fronts—but they do not see conflict as inconsistent with cooperation where interests intersect. For the US military, Command, Control, Communications and Intelligence (C3I), might be its greatest strength. But the Chinese saw that C3I was fragile, so it was also the American military's point of greatest vulnerability. Just as control of information had been the key to the American victory, paralysing or corrupting information systems would be the key to preventing American victory.'

Against this backdrop, Indians need to cast their minds to 2009 when reports of various Indian government military and civilian websites being hacked started emerging. The finger of suspicion in all cases pointed to China.

Considering that all three defence services, the navy, air force and the army are networking (informationization) themselves, they are proportionately making themselves vulnerable to cyberwarfare.

The PLA's sixth strategic advantage lies in the blurring of India's two military lines—the Line of Actual Control with China and the Line of Control with POK, which followed China's annulment of its border with India in Ladakh. Since then, PLA soldiers have reportedly been seen in Pakistan-occupied Kashmir, and by October 2014 close to the Jammu International Border. The open movement of PLA soldiers across the Karakoram road and POK will not allow the Indian Army to shift its war assets from one front to another in case of a crisis with either adversary, give a deeper foothold to China in the Kashmir dispute, and help the PLA provide sustained operational logistics support to Pakistan in case of a war with India. Moreover, Chinese economic and military activities in north Kashmir including Gilgit-Baltistan have gathered pace. Pakistan has raised a special security division (about 15,000 troops) for security of the China-Pakistan Economic Corridor—thus the Special Forces of China and Pakistan have been operating together presenting an unprecedented strategic challenge to India.

OPERATIONAL LEVEL OF WAR

The PLA has overwhelming superiority over the Indian military at the operational level of war. There is little likelihood of the gap narrowing even after the Indian Army and the IAF are provided with their planned acquisitions till the thirteenth defence plan (2022). The gap will only widen. Here are seven reasons why the PLA will remain unmatched and far superior at this level of war.

The most important reason is the PLA's excellent border management. It has good rail lines and roads (and overall infrastructure) right up to the LAC. The rail line from Lhasa has been extended to Shigatse and further to the Nepal border. China also plans to construct rail lines up to the Indian border; these are expected to be completed by 2020. By 2020, China will have both rail and road links available right up to the LAC.

There is unity of command between the PLAA and the border guards (Militia)—the latter is commanded by regular PLAA officers. Unlike the Indian Army which holds the LAC in strength, as we have seen, the PLAA is usually nowhere to be seen. The Chinese border guards hold positions sparingly in small groups along the LAC. According to the PLA's official spokesman Colonel Yang Yujun, 'The militia performs combat readiness

CHINA'S CENTRAL MILITARY COMMISSION COMMAND STRUCTURE

Central Military Commission (CMC) →

Total Members: 23

CHAIRMAN, CMC: XI JINPING

Vice Chairman	2
Members (PLA) (Total 22)	Heads of 15 departments →
	Commander, PLAA
	Commander, PLAAF
	Commander, PLAN
	Commander, Rocket Forces (Nuclear Forces)
	Commander, Strategic Support Force (Cyber, Electromagnetic and Space Assets)
Defence Minister	1

→ Northern Theatre Command
Eastern Theatre Command
Central Theatre Command
Southern Theatre Command
Western Theatre Command
★ *Tibet Military Command (Lhasa)*
★ *Lanzhou Provincial Command*

Joint Staff Department (JSD)

- Tri-service Secretariat for Joint Operations in Crisis and War
- Custodian of Conventional and Nuclear War Plans
- Provides Seamless Integration of Conventional and Nuclear War Plans

Political Work Department

Logistics Support Department

Equipment Development Department

Training and Administration Department

National Defence Mobilisation Department

General Office

Agency for Offices Administration

Office for Reforms and Organisational Structure

Office for International Military Cooperation

Office for Strategic Planning

Audit Office

Discipline Inspection Commission

Political and Law Commission

Science and Technology Commission

- Nuclear war chain command runs from CMC to JSD and Rocket Forces HQs
- Conventional war chain command runs from CMC to JSD to Theatre Command

support and defensive operations.' What that means can be seen at Tawang, one of the two critical places in the Eastern Sector which cannot be lost in a war, the other being the Siliguri corridor below Sikkim (still formally disputed).

The second PLA advantage is the war theatre itself. The Tibet Autonomous Region, a single PLA theatre with complete unity of command, faces four Indian Army commands and two Indian Air Force commands on the disputed border. The Chinese Western Theatre Command at Chengdu is pitted against the Indian Army's Northern, Western, Central and Eastern army commands, plus the IAF's Western and Eastern air commands. Given the comparable command profiles, the PLA will elicit much better responses and flexibility. China's overall forces commander (commander-in-chief, Western Theatre Command) will retain control at every step of the conflict escalation ladder. No amount of operational coordination between the six senior Indian commanders can equal a single theatre commander's firm grip over war with direct access to the nation's political-military leadership—the Central Military Commission.

As we have seen, even the terrain favours the PLA. The Indian troops have to undergo an excruciatingly long three-stage acclimatization process over fourteen days (six days for stage one at 10,000 feet, and four days each for the remaining two stages at 12,000 feet and 15,000 feet); the PLA, being already on the plateau (10,000 feet and above), has no such requirement. Probably the only advantage talked about for India has been the high altitude of PLA Air Force airfields in the Tibet Autonomous Region. Taking off from such heights, PLAAF fighter aircraft will not be able to carry a full weapons load. This is no longer true. According to interviews the authors have carried out with senior Indian Air Force officers, the PLAAF has reportedly developed special tyres for their aircraft that will help them carry more weaponry.

Moreover, the PLA's twin operational advantages are its Special Forces (each service has its own units skilled to do what they should: operate behind enemy lines) and impressive airlift capabilities. The PLA's vertical envelopment prowess, which involves capture of the enemy's advanced landing grounds in high altitude, was demonstrated during Exercise Stride-2009, which had the IAF brass worried. What if the PLA was to capture an Indian advanced landing ground close to the LAC? What if the PLA's Special Forces dropped directly in the Brahmaputra and the Indus valleys?

India's Special Forces and airlift capabilities are extremely modest as compared with those of the PLA. To prevent such a situation, the Indian Army and the IAF need to allot high priority to an integrated air defence, as has been the case in the west against Pakistan. This is the defensive part. Regarding offensive capability, the Indian military is undecided. The IAF has procured C-130J aircraft for special operations. But how skilled and trained the air force and army's Special Forces are remains a question. It is a pity that the Indian Army's Special Forces are being regularly used as commandos for counter-terrorism tasks in Jammu and Kashmir.

The PLA's fifth advantage is its conventionally armed ballistic and cruise missiles. In comparison, India's conventional missile programme is rudimentary. India deployed a few indigenous liquid-propellant 150-kilometre Prithvi ballistic missiles in the east. However, given the operational drawbacks of liquid propellants, Prithvis have been proposed to be replaced by indigenous 150-kilometre solid-propellant Prahaar missiles, which have yet to be accepted by the Indian Army. The PLA's large number of ballistic and cruise missiles with good accuracy and varying ranges cannot be matched by India, and are the biggest worry for the IAF.

Even the supersonic BRAHMOS land attack cruise missile (with the capability to cross mountains because of its steep-dive trajectory) against China will have two limitations: one, their fewer numbers will not match China's large quantity of cruise missiles. And two, they are a joint venture between India and Russia and given the close ties between Russia and China, Moscow, in case of India-China hostilities, might be reluctant to support BRAHMOS with spare parts and other required accessories.

The sixth advantage of the PLA is its mobile forces. Unlike Indian formations, the PLA forces are lightly armed for rapid deployments with enough logistics, ammunition and missile storage arrangements in the Tibet Autonomous Region to support a fast battle. Moreover, the PLAAF regularly trains in two modes: one, the PLAA and PLAAF exercise in their theatre both separately to sharpen their core competencies and together to sharpen joint-ness skills. The PLAA and PLAAF have been exercising with the Pakistan Army Special Forces and the Pakistan Air Force in POK since 2009 in the series of exercises called Warriors, Stride and Shaheen.

The seventh advantage is unmanned aerial vehicles (UAVs). China, today, has an impressive array and probably the largest number of UAVs (i.e. more than the US) in the world. It is also developing hypersonic UAVs and unmanned combat aerial vehicles (UCAVs) for near-space, Earth orbit missions. All this is meant to give real-time battlefield transparency to the PLAAF with serious implications for Indian military planners.

Consider a scenario where China decides to go to war with India. It will first unleash its offensive space and cyber capabilities which will destroy or blind the Indian military's intelligence, surveillance and reconnaissance assets. The PLAAF will simultaneously use its plethora of UAVs and UCAVs to identify and destroy communication nodes and command and control hubs. Next, the PLAAF will use its mobile ballistic and cruise missiles (with conventional warheads) according to its 'forward defence' stance, where the rear and front of the battlefield will be attacked together. The battle space, thus, could be hundreds or thousands of kilometres. The whole idea of the three-pronged assault will be to nearly paralyse the IAF. If not complete air dominance, the PLAAF has the capability to achieve large swathes of air superiority quickly enabling it to then turn its gaze towards the land battles.

At the tactical level, the PLA has overwhelming numbers (the PLAA is 2.3 million strong as compared to the 1.3 million strength of the Indian Army, committed to both the Pakistan and China borders). The PLAAF has 1,500 fighter aircraft against the IAF's 500 fighters. The PLA has far too many force multipliers: electronic support measures, defensive and offensive electronic warfare equipment, battlefield command and control systems, increased surveillance capability on the battlefield and precision-guided munitions. It also has innovative fire application means with electronic control and observation systems. India lags behind in all these aspects because equipment for the Western Sector against Pakistan has been given greater priority over mountain formations facing China.

If the Indian Navy decides to support the land battles against China, India, given the numbers of various types of submarines alone—strategic and conventional—with the PLAN, would open up an extremely dangerous front. In case of hostilities, the Indian Navy could expect to see Chinese submarines, guided missile frigates and maritime aviation moving around in the Bay of Bengal. When asked how the Indian Navy would match up to the PLAN in a war, nearly all admirals, in private conversations, candidly admit that it would be extremely difficult.

CHAPTER 6

CHINA'S GRAND STRATEGY

To a world steeped in the discourse of the Cold War where words like 'combative' and 'cooperation' appear incompatible, the Chinese strategy is baffling. Can a major power employ an oxymoronic strategy of 'combative cooperation' and proclaim its rise as a powerful nation as peaceful?

While most policymakers and analysts would disagree with such contradictory postulation, long-time China watcher Henry Kissinger believes China to be in a different league from the Western style of strategizing. Chinese strategy, according to Kissinger, exhibits three characteristics: 'meticulous analysis of long-term trends, careful study of tactical options, and detached exploration of operational decisions'. This approach to statecraft, he believes, is in sync with China's distinctive military theory where 'Chinese thinkers develop strategic thought that places a victory through psychological advantage and preaches the avoidance of direct conflict'. As China puts a high premium on political and psychological victories rather than pure military triumph, its diplomacy has little difficulty in pursuing peace and hostility at the same time.

Even if such theorizing is difficult to accept, it does help explain Xi Jinping's China Dream, unveiled in 2013, anchored on a new approach to international relations, based not upon a zero-sum game but a win–win formula of mutual cooperation, mutual trust and mutual understanding. Following a different format of power politics based on economic rather than military power, China is determined to portray its growing national power (that includes economic, technological, national resources, military power and diplomacy) as benign and meant for the security of the general good. By means of this strategy, unprecedented in history, China is resolved to become the world's pre-eminent power.

The China Dream implies the rejuvenation (or rise) of the Chinese nation through a better life (material and cultural) for the Chinese people. This requires bilateral, regional and global cooperation in economy, trade, investments, connectivity, energy and strategic security.

The China Dream is premised on fundamental issues. China has sought greatness through 'rejuvenation', which harks back to history and tradition. Since the formation of Mao's Communist China in October 1949, this has been the basic impulse that has motivated successive generations of leaders (since Mao, the country's leadership had changed every ten years). Each generation of leaders has faithfully followed the line that no single leader is responsible for the transformational changes in China. Rather, each new leadership is responsible for rejuvenating Chinese society.

In Mandarin, the word for China is 'Zhong-guo' which literally means the middle state, a state which straddles both north-south and east-west of the universe. According to Chinese scholars, China once dominated East Asia through its Confucian philosophy (based on the sayings of Chinese philosopher Confucius who lived in 6 BCE). The Confucian system meant that China did not dominate the region through acts of plunder and conquer. Rather, its neighbours paid tribute to China because they 'recognized' its greatness. In its present-day avatar, Confucian thought would mean that China as a risen major power would expect its neighbours, both near and far, to defer to the Chinese viewpoint. The return of Confucianism is exemplified by China having set up over 108 Confucius Institutes in Asian countries by May 2016.

The fact that China's leaders for decades have eschewed the personality cult and promoted continuity was borne out by the 3 September 2015 grand military parade held in Tiananmen Square to mark China's victory over colonialist Japan in World War II. In a meaningful gesture, Xi Jinping took the PLA's salute with two predecessors—Jiang Zemin and Hu Jintao—standing next to him. This was the Chinese leadership's method of conveying that Xi's strategic plans—which threaten to upstage the United States-led Western system of governance set up after World War II—had its origin in the earlier leaderships.

Looking back, the year 2008 appeared to be the turning point when China decided to abandon Deng Xiaoping's approach of maintaining a low profile and began silently building national power by integrating itself globally through trade and commerce. The great economic crisis of 2008 with its origin in the West, led China to believe that its own systems, which showed continued robust economic growth, were better. The 2008 Beijing Olympic Games at which China won the maximum gold medals demonstrated its soft power through the will and discipline of the Chinese people. Moreover, the protracted wars in Afghanistan and Iraq showed the muddled Western—especially US—thinking on war and peace. China concluded that it was time for it to conduct its foreign policy based on actual rather than perceived or potential national power.

A manifestation of this important conclusion was the expanded roles and missions of the PLA under the new defence policy released in 2010. China set up its official spokesperson system in the MND in 2008 for increased transparency. Anti-piracy voyages by the PLAN to the faraway Gulf of Aden traversing the entire Indian Ocean region started the same year. It was also in 2008 that China took the decision to take on combat roles for its peacekeeping forces under the UN. Until then, for two decades, China's contribution was limited to providing hospital and support staff.

In 2012 China clarified two further threats facing the PLA in addition to the existing two—the imbalance in strategic military power had increased China's land and maritime threats. While US President George Bush had in 2005 ordered an additional aircraft carrier and 60 per cent of US submarines to be moved to the US Pacific Command responsible for the Asia-Pacific region, it was under President Barack Obama that the US in 2010 spoke of the 'pivot' to the Asia policy, which was soon replaced by the benign word 'rebalancing' to checkmate the growing Chinese maritime challenge in the Western Pacific. The other existing threat was from social transformation where China had to guard against the three evils of terrorism, extremism and secessionism.

The new threats were to 'China's interests and facilities abroad, and China's investments abroad'. China's May 2015 military strategy paper made it clear that 'the security of overseas interests concerning energy and resources, strategic sea lines of communication, as well as institutions, personnel and assets abroad, has become an imminent issue'.

In hindsight, the PLA's preparations had started in 2008 for the new fifth generation Chinese leadership (under Xi and Li) to unfold the China Dream and its visible manifestation: One Belt One Road (OBOR). This also explains why Xi, unlike his predecessors, on assuming power in November 2012 took over simultaneously as the chairman of the Central Military Commission so that the PLA reforms kept pace with progress on the OBOR. As an aside, numerous (US) analysts who declared that Xi was the first leader since Mao to have assumed personalized dictatorship and moved away from the path of an institutionalized system of governance as advocated by Deng, might not be entirely correct.

The other issue underpinning the China Dream is the OBOR. Even as it leveraged its stupendous economic might and downplayed its military strength (which was no match for the US or Russia), China's aggressive push for dominance hinged on Xi's strategically important OBOR economic plan, which had strategic, political and security implications for the world.

The OBOR was unveiled by Xi on 7 September 2013 in Astana (Kazakhstan) as the Silk Road Economic Belt (the land component), and on 3 October 2013 in Indonesia as the 21st Century Maritime Silk Road (the maritime component). Officially called the Silk Road Economic Belt and the 21st Century Maritime Silk Road, the shorter title of the project is One Belt One Road.

Earlier, Chinese Prime Minister Li Keqiang had offered the Bangladesh-China-India-Myanmar (BCIM) economic corridor to India in May 2013, and proposed the setting up of the China-Pakistan Economic Corridor (CPEC) on his visit to Pakistan the same month. The BCIM and CPEC were suggested by the Chinese leadership before the OBOR grand plan into which they were meant to be integrated. China has proposed four other corridors to nations along the OBOR path. These are China-Mongolia-Russia; China-Central-and-Western Asia; China-Indochina; and the new Eurasian land bridge.

The uniqueness of OBOR is that it combines the visions of British geopolitical theorist Halford Mackinder who in 1904 put forward the theory of the Eurasia land mass being the pivot of the world, and the American thinker Alfred Mahan who talked about the strategic importance of the seas. The OBOR vision is about connecting land (Belt) and sea (Road) across Asia, Africa and Europe through a network of roads, rails, coastal and port infrastructure and oil and gas pipelines, through policy coordination, and unimpeded trade and monetary circulation supported by the China-backed Brazil, Russia, India, China and South Africa (BRICS) New Development Bank, Asian Infrastructure and Investment Bank (AIIB), Silk Route Fund, and so on.

According to China's National Resource and Development Commission—responsible for the OBOR—report released in March 2015, 'the initiative to jointly build the Belt and Road enhancing the trend towards a multipolar world, economic globalization, cultural diversity and greater IT application, is designed to uphold the global free-trade regime and the open world economy in the spirit of open regionalism'. Seventy nations having expressed a willingness to be part of the OBOR, China intends to strengthen its political and military relationship with each of these nations. China hopes that bilateral economic, political and security relationships with the OBOR nations would transform into a seamless regional and perhaps transcontinental security architecture which would challenge the US's strategic and military power by providing an alluring alternative.

Meanwhile, despite opposition from the US and Japan, by April 2015 fifty-seven nations had opted to join the China-led AIIB as founding members. These included the Association of Southeast Asian Nations (ASEAN) the UK, France, Germany and Italy. According to former US Treasury Secretary Larry Summers, the AIIB's establishment 'may be remembered as the moment the US lost its role as the underwriter of the global economic system'. The AIIB's governing principle that holds that the largest contributor to the multilateral organization gets the largest say in running it would ensure that China, which has initially committed US$ 50 billion of the total US$ 100 billion, would rule the roost.

COMBATIVE COOPERATION

The South China Sea (SCS) crisis in 2014–16 exemplified China's 'combative cooperation' doctrine of expansionism with Chinese characteristics. In tune with Deng Xiaoping's twelve-character policy which he had circulated amongst the country's leaders, China weighed its options (against the US) and decided to use its economic prowess and favourable geography to challenge the US's global clout. Challenging the US's military power would need a different approach over the long haul.

China's claimed nine-dash (nine points joined on water) line in the SCS is the first of its kind. Throughout history nations have claimed territory and then the sea surrounding them; China did the opposite. After Japan's defeat in World War II, China (during the Kuomintang regime) drew an eleven-dash line in the SCS in 1946, which after modification under the Communist regime was formally presented as the nine-dash line in May 2009 to the United Nations as historically its maritime territory.

China's claim of most of the SCS, through which more than US$ 5 trillion of global trade passes each year, was challenged by Vietnam, Malaysia, the Philippines, Indonesia, Brunei and Taiwan with claims of their own. These nations, interlocked with intense trade and commerce with China (the combined trade between China and ASEAN in 2014 stood at US$ 480 billion with a target of US$ 1 trillion by 2020), were not willing to succumb to China's military coercion which began in 2008 with land reclamation in the SCS. Concluding that the existing order was threatened by China, the US announced its pivot to Asia policy, which meant, among other things, the moving of military assets to further strengthen its US Pacific Command, responsible for the Asia-Pacific and Indian Ocean regions.

As we have seen, the pivot to Asia policy was subsequently more benignly renamed as the 'rebalancing strategy'. Undeterred, China continued with its assertiveness in the East China Sea over the Diaoyu Islands dispute with Japan; and to the ASEAN nations' consternation started building artificial islands on rocks and reefs in the SCS. To its already stated core concerns— Taiwan and Tibet—over which China had indicated it would go to war, China added four major concerns, namely, Xinjiang, Hong Kong, Diaoyu Islands and the South China Sea. It was not made clear if China would go to war over major concerns as well. Clarity on this crucial issue came after 12 July 2016 when the United Nations-backed Permanent Court of Arbitration in The Hague announced its decision wholeheartedly in favour of the Philippines and against China.

Meanwhile, the PLA's muscle-flexing in the East China Sea led Japan to strengthen its alliance with the US and re-examine its pacifist constitution which prohibited Japanese self-defence forces from operating outside its territory. With the SCS issue getting complicated by the US's rebalancing strategy, China was suddenly pitted against the world's most powerful nation. The ASEAN nations caught between the US and China were compelled to exercise patience since too much was at stake if they antagonized China.

As perceptions matter, numerous prestigious US think tanks stuck to the US strategy being a 'pivot', which has a military connotation, ignoring its new name, 'rebalancing strategy', and started analysing the US military power pitted against PLA capabilities in the SCS as a zero-sum game. China took full advantage of the war-like scenarios painted by the US thinkers to project itself as an altruistic nation seeking peace and development through the China Dream. Speaking in the context of the South China Sea, Xi Jinping, declared in 2013, 'All other countries [alluding to the US], please do not expect that China will trade off its core interests, nor expect that China will swallow the bitter pill of being injured in terms of sovereignty, security and prosperity.'

Placed on the back foot by its own analysts, US officials, both civilian and military, had been at pains to explain that rebalancing was not a pivot. According to J. Stapleton Roy, former US ambassador to China, 'The purpose of rebalance was to reassure friends and allies that the US had the hard will and resources to stay engaged in the region. The rebalance was meant to be compatible with China's rise in the region. Unfortunately, because of budgetary cuts, the non-military aspects (to be run by the US State Department) did not get funding while military activities got the funding.' He added, 'The Trans-Pacific Partnership will now provide the economic aspect to rebalancing and China is open to join it.' (In his election speeches US President Donald Trump had promised to bury the TPP, which is seen as an Obama initiative.) Questioning the Chinese interpretation of US rebalancing, Roy asked, 'How can the US contain China when it has a US$ 500 billion annual trade with it?'

While explaining rebalancing, Admiral Harry Harris, the US commander-in-chief, Pacific Command (PACOM), who would in May 2015 scoff at China's land reclamation as 'the great wall of sand' said, 'Rebalancing is real. By the end of 2020, the US will have 300 ships, 60 per cent of which will be in the Pacific (55 per cent are presently in the region), while 60 per cent of the submarines are already here. We will invest in new capabilities and strengthen our alliances and partnerships.' He added, 'Rebalancing serves diplomatic, economic, strategic and military interests. However, the most important component is economic not military. We will have a forward presence when it comes to humanitarian needs and for this we will have bilateral readiness programmes with various countries.'

Admiral Harris had made two points. The US PACOM would be the centre of US military power in this century, and hence provide the rebalancing to Asia. It took the US a while to understand that Chinese strategy for global ambition was the antithesis of the Soviet Union's approach. Beijing could retain unending initiative with its blow hot and blow cold moves, baffling the opponent about what lay ahead.

China's narrative of why the SCS was important for it was explained by two senior officials, a diplomat and a senior PLA officer. According to Ambassador Wu Jianmin, the Chinese member of the Foreign Policy Advisory Board, 'China has historical rights to these islands. China is on the rise. Its claims are indisputable as China was the first to come to these islands. Unlike the earlier rising powers, the US, UK and France which expanded their territories, China has never done it. It has not objected to other claimant nations (ASEAN) strengthening their areas. Since China is the largest trading nation (in the region), is it possible for China to not have a presence in South China Sea?'

A more nuanced answer was provided by Major General Yao Yunzhu, the director, Centre for the China-American Defence Relations. 'China is the largest stakeholder for the safety and security of SLOCs [sea lanes of communication]. Since 2013, China's trade [mostly maritime] exceeded US$ 4 trillion which is 12 per cent of the world trade. China has largest trading partnerships with 120 countries and it has largest shipping fleet. Moreover, China has learned lessons from the 1980s Iraq-Iran war and the earlier Suez crisis on the importance of having secure SLOCs especially at choke points like the Straits of Malacca and Hormuz. Then there is piracy, natural disasters and environment challenges to contend with. China opposes militarization of SLOCs and would like to play a larger role for making rules for maritime security.'

By May 2015, things were heating up in the SCS. While conceding that ASEAN claimants had strengthened their claimed territories, US Defense Secretary Ashton Carter accused China of reclaiming 3,000 acres of land (five islands in less than eighteen months) and of building military runways and port facilities there. The immediate trigger for provocation was the building of two multifunctional lighthouses in the disputed Spratly Islands by China in October despite US warnings. Following this, the US announced that it was considering regular 'freedom of navigation' operations by sending its surface ships within 12 nautical miles (the territorial limits under international law) of Chinese reclaimed land unless China agreed to dismantle the lighthouses and halt further reclamation. While cautioning the US against provocation, China refused to dismantle the lighthouses and infrastructure that had already been built as it would have dented the credibility of its growing military power.

Instead, China did two things. It pre-empted US military manoeuvres by taking a high moral stand, of peace and development, and it sought to develop fissures within ASEAN, which works by consensus, by offering political and economic goodies and security guarantees. If China could successfully woo nations in the West Pacific, which oppose its assertiveness, through One Belt One Road, it would make the US case for greater engagement—rebalancing—unnecessary.

Speaking at the Xiangshan Forum on 17 October 2015, General Fan Changlong, China's top general and vice chairman of the Central Military Commission, said, 'China will never adopt war-like policy. We will not recklessly use force even when the issues affect our sovereignty. Some countries [the US] worry that the construction [in the South China Sea] is not for peaceful purposes. The projects were mainly intended for civilian use and the projects will not affect freedom of navigation in SCS. Instead, they will enable us to provide better public services to aid navigation and production in the SCS. We believe that justice and peace should prevail and the principles of United Nations charter must be maintained. Yet, the shadow of war is hovering [because of US actions]. China is at a crucial stage of its peaceful development. China wants peace and will never seek expansionism.'

A day before General Fan responded to the US's imminent freedom of navigation challenge at the closeted meeting with ASEAN defence ministers in Beijing, China proposed a confidence building measure in the form of a joint drill with ASEAN nations for a Code of Unplanned Encounters at Sea (CUES) to ward off maritime miscalculations (the Chinese and the US navy follow the CUES protocol). China also proposed building a community of common destiny for ASEAN nations by the end of the year; this was done in December 2015. In addition, China offered to hasten joint efforts to advance the 2002 agreed DOC (Declaration on the Conduct of parties in the South China Sea) understanding to the legally binding and definitive COC (Code of Conduct for parties in the South China Sea).

Within ten days of the Xiangshan Forum, the US, on 27 October, carried out its freedom of navigation operation within 12 nautical miles of China's reclaimed land in the South China Sea. While the event passed off peacefully with two Chinese vessels tailing the guided missile frigate USS *Lassen* at a safe distance, the Chinese Admiral Wu Shengli cautioned the US chief of naval operations, Admiral John Richardson, against similar provocations which could 'spark war'. With both sides having done their bit—China not dismantling military facilities and declaring that it would hasten the building of more infrastructure and the US showing military resolve to support allies and freedom of navigation in the region—it was back to business. Both sides confirmed that as a part of the planned military-to-military cooperation, the US's top official in Asia-Pacific, PACOM Commander Admiral Harry Harris, would visit China in November 2015.

A few weeks after the US's show of strength in the SCS in November 2015, Xi visited Vietnam and Singapore to harmonize their own connectivity plans with the OBOR. The message he delivered was 'Asia should be for Asians' and that China and its neighbours were mature enough to resolve differences without outside [US] help. Moreover, in a historic first (since Taiwan and China split in 1949) Xi met the Taiwanese President Ma Ying-jeou on 7 November 2015 in Singapore. While most analysts concentrated on the symbolism of the meeting, no diplomatic encounter, especially one between the Chinese and Taiwanese leadership, could be bereft of substance. Beijing could well be hoping to dilute and eventually make the US's Taiwan Relations Act 1979—under which the US is legally bound to protect Taiwan's security—superfluous. This could take decades to materialize but a beginning had been made.

Against the backdrop of Xi's desire for building an Asian community of shared destiny, ASEAN and Taiwan by becoming part of it, could over time find more virtue in economic progress through the OBOR. Perhaps a decade or two hence, China's 'combative cooperation' doctrine might worry Western Pacific nations less. According to US strategist Zbigniew Brzezinski, China's rise will affect the Taiwan issue, which in turn will unsettle the US's position in the Far East. The impact will also be felt in Japan.

The gains of China's 'combative cooperation' in the SCS crisis were all too evident. By April 2016, China had positioned its anti-aircraft missiles, landed a military aircraft on reclaimed land, built a runway and shelters for military fighters and transport aircraft and, above all, had announced plans to provide a floating nuclear power station to support the massive infrastructure in the SCS. The US, meanwhile, announced regular freedom of navigation manoeuvres and overflights to comfort its regional allies. China called the US's actions provocative.

On 12 July 2016, the much awaited verdict of the international tribunal—to which the Philippines had taken the case of China riding roughshod over its claims in the SCS with Beijing, calling the proceedings illegal, refused to participate—was announced. The verdict declared that China's claims were not backed by evidence. China immediately rubbished the tribunal's verdict. Within a few days of the verdict, at the ASEAN foreign ministers meet held in Vientiane (Laos), Cambodia, on China's urging, warned ASEAN nations that the joint communiqué after the event would not be issued if it carried any reference to the UN-backed tribunal which had unequivocally declared Chinese occupation in the SCS illegal. Worried about their bilateral trade with China, the 2016 ASEAN foreign ministers' joint communiqué did not mention the damning ruling against China. Instead, a separate statement between China and ASEAN spoke about freedom of navigation and overflights, and the need to resolve disputes bilaterally through mutual discussions.

Once this was done, China announced that it would carry out naval drills and air patrols close to the South China Sea for which the area would be closed to outside traffic for a week. General Fan Changlong visited the Southern Theatre Command responsible for the South China Sea and exhorted troops to exercise well and be prepared for war. Meanwhile, Chinese state television showed new long-range naval missiles for the first time. This was during the visit to China of the US's Chief of Naval Operations in the Pacific Command, Admiral John Richardson.

Two inescapable conclusions from the events in the South China Sea were: one, China did not dismantle its infrastructure in the SCS nor did the US compel it to do so. Because of different ideological approaches to military victory, it was a win–win for both—the US was focused on the impact of military power, China on decisive psychological gains. China has built strong points in the form of (military and civilian) infrastructure in the SCS, which over time will help it reinforce ownership of the strategic islands—expansionism with Chinese characteristics.

The SCS dispute is not about massive untapped resources in the SCS that China would be unwilling to share with the ten smaller ASEAN countries. It is also not about freedom of navigation through the world's busiest sea lanes of communications that the US, with its military pivot (or re-balancing) to Asia, proposes to safeguard against a belligerent China. For China, it is about breaking free from its strategic confinement to gain unfettered access to the Western Pacific. To be the foremost power in Asia, China must become a maritime power in the Asia-Pacific and Indian Ocean region, in addition to being a land power.

And two, China's four major concerns had been elevated to the level of core concerns which, whatever be the implications, it would not relent on.

IS A CHINA-US CONFLICT INEVITABLE?

Colonel Liu Mingfu's answer to whether there will be outright conflict between the US and the China is a resounding yes. Liu, a military hardliner at China's National Defence University, wrote in his 2010 book, *China Dream*, that 'no matter how much China commits itself to a peaceful rise conflict is inherent in US-China relations'. According to him 'the biggest threat that China faces today is the military crisis. There is a huge gap in the military between China and the US. China needs a military rise in addition to its economic rise. China must be prepared, both militarily and psychologically, to struggle and prevail in a contest for strategic pre-eminence.'

The book was criticized for being too hawkish by Chinese analysts and critics and did not sell well. However, when President Xi in 2013 wrote his book, also called *China Dream*, and emphasized the need for major reforms in the military, attention went back to Liu's book which had stressed China's military rise. The Mandarin version of Liu's book flew off the shelves and the first English edition was printed in the US in 2014 as there was worldwide interest in understanding the path China might choose to build its military power.

By extrapolating from current and past trends, we can surmise that China's military rise will be in two simultaneous phases: one visible—building a new Asian security architecture around the OBOR, the other less visible—building military power to challenge the US's hard power directly, perhaps after 2050. Phase one in support of the OBOR has necessitated military reforms within the PLA for a transformational shift from continental defence to expeditionary or out-of-area operations. China's 'combative coexistence' for expansionism with Chinese characteristics would be the preferred doctrine.

Moreover, the PLA's UN peacekeeping in combat roles since 2008 (to help train for securing One Belt corridors) will complement the PLAN's role of securing the One Road sea route with experience gained since 2008 in anti-piracy operations in the Gulf of Aden. Interestingly, China's One Road route follows the one taken by commercial vessels sailing across the Indian Ocean and Western Pacific. The PLA has stepped up work in humanitarian assistance and disaster response as well.

Phase two, where China is expected to exhibit military power (Liu's *China Dream*) upfront will depend on the progress of phase one. According to the 2015 US annual report to Congress issued by the office of the US secretary of defense, 'China is investing in capabilities designed to defeat adversary power projection and counter third-party—including US—intervention during a crisis or conflict.'

For phase one reforms, Xi's announcement at the 3 September 2015 military parade and China's May 2015 military strategy provide valuable clues. Citing support to global peace and development, Xi, at the September 2015 military parade announced a reduction in PLA strength by 300,000 and contribution of 8,000 PLA troops for UN peacekeeping missions. China's Ministry of National Defence clarified that troop reduction would be of support staff and not fighting forces. In addition to contributing troops for peacekeeping, the PLA would train 2,000 foreign troops for UN peacekeeping missions.

China's May 2015 military strategy paper updated the 2004 military strategic guidelines from fighting 'local wars under conditions of informationization' to fighting 'informationized local wars'. As we have seen, informationization means network centricity where all weapon platforms on land, sea and in the air are connected in real time for obtaining a complete picture and command and control of assets. This involves a secure information transmission network with optical fibre communications as the mainstay and satellite and short-wave communications as assured backup.

The differences in the 2004 and May 2015 strategy papers denote a shift in the PLA's roles and missions from continental defence to expeditionary tasks (out-of-area operations). In continental defence, though not a critical requirement, local wars should ideally have complete informationization.

For expeditionary forces to fight successful local wars, they should have assured informationization.

Since the emphasis is on 'winning informationized local wars, highlighting maritime military struggle and maritime preparation for military struggle', it points towards securing the Maritime Silk Road across the Indian and Western Pacific oceans. Building expeditionary forces for fighting 'informationized local wars', through military reforms which are under way would yield the following:

- Smaller integrated forces with mobility and lethality. Mobility is being achieved by converting bigger divisions to smaller brigades with boosted overall combat capabilities. Lethality needs interoperability amongst command and control systems, combat forces, support systems, and making intelligence, transmission and guidance effective and rapid.
- Focus on army aviation, strategic and operational lift, and Special Operations forces for building expeditionary forces.
- To reorient PLAA 'from theatre defence to trans-theatre mobility' for multifunctional combat operations.

In addition to building expeditionary forces, the PLA is expected to dwell on two critical issues. The first is greater military diplomacy, which involves regional dialogues and cooperation on maritime security, humanitarian aid and disaster relief, and combating non-state actors (terrorists and pirates) on land and sea. The PLA plans to do this with increased training for and participation in UN peacekeeping missions as well as participation in bilateral and multilateral military engagements and exercises. The Xiangshan Forum since 2006 by the PLA, which in 2014 was upgraded to 1.5 track (which accords it semi-official status), is also a part of it.

Since China's military modernization has the potential to reduce US military technology advantages, there is global interest in China's military budget and approach to modernization. According to the US's 2015 annual report to Congress, 'China's officially disclosed military budget grew at an average of 9.5 per cent per year in inflation-adjusted terms from 2005 through 2014, and China will probably sustain defence spending growth at comparable rates for the foreseeable future. For an arms importing nation, China exported arms from 2009 to 2013 totalling approximately US$ 14 billion. In 2014, with exports of US$ 5.16 billion, China was the fifth largest exporting nation after the US, Russia, Sweden and France.

The second issue concerns the need for a positive image of the PLA with increased visibility in support of the OBOR. This explains the massive anti-corruption drive launched by Xi after taking over as chairman of the Central Military Commission. As many as thirty general rank officers have reportedly been sacked or are under investigation on corruption charges. During the 3 September 2015 military parade, in an unusual sight, the PLA columns were led by general rank officers. This indicated that senior military officers will be held accountable for training and discipline, two basic requirements for soldiers.

BUILDING MILITARY POWER

China's approach to building military power has been unique. Unlike Western nations where there is perpetual debate on whether capability leads ideas (strategy) or the other way round, in Chinese thinking, the quest for technology advancement and search for theory have gone hand in hand.

In the post-Mao era, while appreciating the importance of weaponry, Deng Xiaoping—credited with Chinese modernization starting in 1979—modified Mao's theory of 'People's (guerrilla) War' to 'People's War Under Modern Conditions' through an Active Defence stance in 1985. Active Defence indicated that after blunting the enemy's first attack, the PLA would launch large-scale counter-offensives. Deng also developed his thinking on warfare based on four possible scenarios: small wars (at the border), medium-sized conventional wars, full-scale conventional wars under conditions of nuclear deterrence, and nuclear wars. Deng ruled out the possibility of the last two types of wars considering that China's relations with both the United States and Soviet Union were stable. This implied that the PLA could be reduced substantially and preparedness for war—unlike the decades under Mao Zedong—could become peacetime work. The PLA launched a number of reforms such as massive force reduction and restructuring of its fighting forces for better command and control for fighting essentially on its own soil. The Great Wall of China syndrome had inculcated a defensive mindset.

Since China's theme was the high probability of local or regional wars, the PLA, according to government-supported Chinese literature, in 1985 identified seven hotspots on China's periphery: Taiwan, the South China Sea, the Koreas, the Indian border, Tibet, Xinjiang and Inner Mongolia. The PLA in the early 1990s considered its strengths vis-à-vis India as possession of nuclear weapons, especially tactical nuclear weapons, an effective missile strike capability, good interior lines of communication (infrastructure development), huge superiority in conventional weapons, and quality of officers and men.

In Deng's thinking, strategic nuclear weapons were considered political rather than military weapons. As China had the least number of nukes amongst declared nuclear weapon states, it adopted the nuclear policy of minimum nuclear deterrence: China would not be the first to use nukes, and would not use nukes against non-nuclear weapon states.

With time and in keeping with world trends, successive Chinese leaders revised and improved upon Deng's theory of warfare. Impressed with the US's spectacular show of technology ('revolution in military warfare') during the 1991 Gulf War against Saddam Hussein's Iraq, China, in 1992, under President Jiang Zemin as the chairman of the Central Military Commission, modified its military theory to 'Future War under High-Tech Conditions' through the forward defence stance. The replacement of the words 'People's War' with 'Future War' suggested a shift from quantity to quality of equipment and a better understanding of a high-tech battlefield.

Forward defence, a variation of the active defence stance, was a major shift from seeking positional defence on their own territory to forward deployment in areas of dispute. Because a high-tech war by definition is an offensive war, the thinking aimed to take on the enemy from a great distance. This broadened the concept of defence to mean some sort of limited power projection. The operational stance to be followed by military commanders thus changed from 'defence as overall posture, offence as the supplement' to a mix of 'both offensive and defensive capabilities'.

On nuclear weapons, in 1995, Chinese literature indicated that the doctrine of minimum nuclear deterrence was changed to one of limited nuclear deterrence, suggesting a war-fighting capability. The limited deterrence would involve capabilities to deter conventional, theatre and strategic conflicts as well as conflict control. China also amended its no-first-use policy of nuclear weapons to make it applicable only to member states which had signed the Nuclear Non-Proliferation Treaty and nuclear weapons-free zones. With a limited nuclear deterrence doctrine in place, China became at par, without saying so, with the United States and Russia which remain committed to the use of tactical nuclear weapons.

Of the estimated Chinese nuclear arsenal in the 1990s (about 500 warheads), about 200 were strategic warheads with the rest being tactical. Tactical nukes were reportedly deployed at about twenty places in China, including Tibet. These types of nuclear weapons include low-yield medium artillery fission rounds, enhanced radiation weapons of low yield, and low-yield fission tactical warheads.

The next wave of Chinese reforms in military theory was influenced by developments in the US, the only world power expected to thwart China's global ambitions. These were the arrival of the Internet at the turn of the twentieth century; the 2001 declaration by US President George Bush to lead the US towards space militarization; and building of the ballistic missile defence. It was clear to China that warfare would now be in six domains—land, air, sea, outer space, electromagnetic spectrum and cyber. It was also clear to China that with its relatively inferior military-technological base (the 1989 Tiananmen crisis had resulted in a worldwide arms embargo), it would have to resort to asymmetrical warfare. Instead of seeking an edge over the US's state-of-the-art ships, aircraft carriers and aviation assets, which was not possible, China decided to invest in missiles to attack the US's vulnerability. US strategists called these Chinese missiles Anti-Access Area-Denial weapons. Moreover, in line with the forward defence stance, China decided to build robust airlift capabilities.

Building on the gains made in science and technology (indigenous, acquired or stolen), China's military theory, made public at the beginning of the century, spoke of 'mechanization and informationization' with mobile-operations as the preferred stance. According to a PLA document, the shift was 'from quantity and scale to quality and efficiency, from a manpower-intensive model to a technology-intensive model with the overall approach being mechanization as the foundation and informationization as the focus'. The PLA's mobile forces or Rapid Reaction Forces would be technology intensive, with real-time ability to communicate and fight in all war domains.

CHINA DREAM

Since a nation's grand strategy is the means to obtain long-term objectives, what could be China's objectives by 2050 and the means to attain them? While undertaking such an assessment is dicey, it may not be so in the case of China which has perhaps revealed its hand. Not many would disagree that China's objective by 2050 would be to become the major power in Eurasia through the China Dream using the OBOR. This would assure its 'peaceful rise' through the use of its economic might and geography. China would employ a 'combative cooperation' doctrine for expansion (in support of OBOR) to derive psychological and political rather than military gains.

We have been talking of China's grand strategy called China Dream throughout this chapter and it will be useful to know when and how it began. China Dream's real start was in the 1980s when China decided to build its national power. While the blueprint for China's four modernizations (in the fields of agriculture, industry, national defence, and science and technology) was crafted by Premier Zhou Enlai in 1963 (after the 1962 border dispute with India), it was adopted in 1978 by Deng Xiaoping.

By the turn of the century, China, by taking advantage of the peace and stability in Asia, had made breathtaking progress on its four modernizations under US patronage. So much so that the dragon was showing signs of coming into its own by challenging the very system which had assisted its rise. Asserting that China's rise is 'irresistible', Qian Qichen, China's long-serving vice minister of foreign affairs in the 1980s and 1990s, wrote in his book *Ten Episodes in China's Diplomacy*, 'As long as China continues to grow, Sino-American relations will change in our favour.' The big question before the international community, especially the US which was most threatened, was: will China's rise be peaceful?

With uncertainty looming large, in May 2009, Admiral Timothy J. Keating, the US Pacific Command chief, reportedly met up with India's Chief of Naval Staff, Admiral Sureesh Mehta, in New Delhi to discuss the import and consequences of an off-the-cuff remark made by a Chinese admiral. The Chinese admiral had recently told Keating, 'You [the US] take Hawaii East and we [China] will take Hawaii West and the Indian Ocean. Then you will not need to come to the Western Pacific and the Indian Ocean and we will not need to go to the Eastern Pacific. If anything happens there, you can let us know and if something happens here, we will let you know.' The proposed deal envisaged that after China had its own aircraft carriers, the Pacific region could be divided into two areas of responsibility. Robert Kaplan, in his seminal book, *Monsoon,* noted, 'A one-ocean navy in the Western Pacific makes China a regional power; a two-nation navy in both the Western Pacific and the Indian Ocean makes China a great power, able to project force around the whole navigable Eurasian rim-land.'

Since nothing that the Chinese say is in jest, the US was rightly anxious. As we have seen, in order to avoid another Cold War, the US proposed the Group of Two (G2) system (an informal special relationship between the US and China) to China where both nations could work together, taking collective decisions. The G2 system was informally proposed in January 2009 by former US National Security Advisor Zbigniew Brzezinski during a lecture in China to mark the thirtieth anniversary of the establishment of formal Sino-American diplomatic ties. It was soon endorsed by the Obama administration with Hillary Clinton, the US Secretary of State, putting her weight behind the G2 system proposal.

However, China was not impressed by the G2 offer as it had different plans. During US President Barack Obama's China visit in November 2009, Chinese Premier Wen Jiabao told him that China preferred a multipolar world. What he did not say was that China aimed to displace the US as the global power in the twenty-first century. With the unusual combination of being a developing nation, which also had the second largest economy in the world, China resolved to position itself as the leader of the developing world which was committed to peace and progress with all who shared its vision, with an emphasis on cooperation with the nations of Asia, Africa and Latin America.

Specific to India, China's unstated rival in Asia, as has been pointed out, the core of the China Dream runs through the China-Pakistan Economic Corridor, the flagship of the OBOR. Addressing the Pakistan Parliament on 20 April 2015, President Xi focused on the importance of a China-Pakistan economic corridor, which would allow China access to the Indian Ocean and make Pakistan the geopolitical pivot for Afghanistan, Iran, the Central Asian Republics, Gulf countries and the Caspian Sea onward to Europe.

After the 1999 Kargil War with India, Pakistan's General Pervez Musharraf had approached China in 2000 to fund the development of a deep-water port at Gwadar. He had two objectives in mind. He could finally realize the dream of his predecessor and military ruler, Ayub Khan, who in the 1960s 'saw Gwadar as an air and naval hub that would be an alternate to Karachi and that, when set alongside Pasni and Ormara, would constitute a string of Arabian Sea bases making Pakistan a great Indian Ocean power athwart both the subcontinent and the whole Near East'.

China accepted Pakistan's offer and completed the first phase on the Gwadar Port project in 2006. In 2007, Pakistan (on China's advice) gave the contract to run the port for forty years to Singapore's Port of Singapore Authority. Once Xi announced his One Belt One Road vision with the China-Pakistan Economic Corridor as its centrepiece, Pakistan abruptly cancelled the contract with the Port of Singapore Authority and in April 2015 gave a forty-three-year contract to the Chinese Overseas Port to run all commercial affairs of the Gwadar Port free-trade zone.

Gwadar is a deep-sea port next to the Strait of Hormuz, the critical oil route in and out of the Persian Gulf, and it lies 120 kilometres from the Iran border. Since taking over the port, China has announced the building of a 3,000-kilometre railway line linking Xinjiang with Gwadar. On the one hand, China will be able to send up to 85 per cent of its shipments via Gwadar instead of the Malacca Strait; on the other hand, the China-Pakistan Economic Corridor will provide China with a huge market for exports to Pakistan.

Musharraf's other objective was to add the PLA's capabilities to Pakistan's conventional military strength against India. This has been realized through the China–Pakistan Economic Corridor which has military implications—the land war threat to India has increased and a maritime threat is staring it in the face. Far from supporting the land war, the Indian Navy will find it difficult to even protect India's commercial vessels in its area of responsibility. As a result of China's moves, both overt and covert, there will soon come a time when the Indian Ocean will no longer be India's ocean.

THE CHOICES BEFORE INDIA

CHAPTER 7

THE CHOICES BEFORE INDIA

Jaswant Singh, former union minister of External Affairs, Defence and Finance, belongs to that rare breed of senior politicians who are also prolific writers. In one of his many books, *India at Risk*, he described India's continental dilemma in these words, 'There is a direct interrelationship, a consequence, on account of which the principal purpose and objectives of our foreign policy have been trapped between four lines: the Durand Line; the McMahon Line; the Line of Control (LC) and the Line of Actual Control (LAC). To achieve autonomy, an absolute necessity in the conduct of our policy, we have to first find an answer to this strategic confinement.'

Technically, the McMahon Line does not exist any longer. After the signing of the Border Peace and Tranquillity Agreement with China in September 1993, India agreed to convert the entire border into the Line of Actual Control, overriding the McMahon Line. The Durand Line, historically British India's frontier with Afghanistan, is now the contentious border between Pakistan and Afghanistan. It does not affect India nor does India have any role to play here. The lines that should perturb Indian policymakers on account of their intractable nature are the Line of Control with Pakistan and the Line of Actual Control with China. But because policymakers cannot find a solution to these lines, they tend to combine them with other issues, thereby diluting the focus on them.

The key to India's rise as a leading power or geostrategic player is buried underneath these two military lines, the LC and the LAC, especially now, when they are converging in north Kashmir. As we have shown, the Chinese and Pakistani militaries have achieved interoperability and hence one will support the other in any conflict. This issue assumes urgency since, like Pakistan, where the army runs the country's policy towards India, the PLA, since the coming of President Xi Jinping in November 2012, is set to assume global visibility. The PLA will protect the Chinese people and the assets and interests associated with the One Belt One Road worldwide.

This makes it critical for India to (a) understand military power and its role in defining a nation's standing in the world, and (b) to craft a winning strategy in order to become a geostrategic player of consequence.

Defined in strategic terminology, India is an important and powerful nation. But, as we have seen, it is not yet a geostrategic or leading power with the capability, capacity and national will to influence geopolitical events in its neighbourhood, Asia and the world. China is a geostrategic player determined to displace the US as the foremost geostrategic power in Asia and the world. While the clash of interests between the US and China is inevitable, the challenge for both will be to manage their strategic relationship especially in the Asia-Pacific and Indian Ocean region which would be the pivot for global power in this century. As part of their strategic calculation, both will woo India: the US to balance China; China to wean India away from the US's orbit in the region.

To derive maximum benefit from the US-China power tussle, India should be aware of three truths: it cannot have a cooperative-competitive bilateral relationship with China (as Indian leaders routinely claim) until China realizes that its military coercion on the LAC is not cost-effective. Two, close ties between China and Russia with the common strategic objective of checkmating the US's influence in Asia will strengthen with time. The combined weight of the two geostrategic players—one a military superpower and the other an economic superpower—will impose enormous pressure on the US to woo India to consolidate its rebalancing in the Asia-Pacific and Indian Ocean region. And three, to become a geostrategic player, India needs to invest time and money in indigenous high-end technology research in strategic systems, defence and aerospace which no country, however close, will part with.

Caught between the US and China, India will have three strategic options. The first would be to align with the US—de jure or de facto—to limit China's strategic options and military forays into the Indian Ocean region. De jure would amount to sacrificing India's strategic autonomy. De facto would displease China with implications on the LAC. However, this option, being an attractive one, could be adapted and folded into the second option as necessary.

The second option for India requires devising a formulation which, given its potential, transforms it into a leading power. However, since India has shown little interest in strategizing and in understanding military power, this option will require a statesman for a prime minister, a leader with a breadth of vision and the ability to execute it. Sadly, we have never had such a person at the helm after the titans who led the Independence movement.

The third option will be to have a foreign policy with more optics than substance. This option, however, will eventually prove to be counterproductive and dangerous. Not only will India's rise be inhibited, war with Pakistan could become a possibility since Pakistan, a non-status quo nation, is unlikely to accept drift on the resolution of the Kashmir issue. And China, through strategic encirclement, will bust India's overestimation of being a great nation.

Prime Minister Narendra Modi, who assumed office in May 2014 with unprecedented political capital, seemed to have chosen the third option. On completion of one year in office, Modi, who had been active and assertive in his relationship with major powers, said, 'Thus far we have been a balancing power, always seeking others' favours. How long can we continue to do that? Why don't we grow into a global player? It is clear in my mind we are no more just a balancing power, but a global player. We speak on equal terms with all, whether it is the US or China. Today we approach the world with greater self-assurance. We have shown the confidence to engage all major powers simultaneously and effectively.'

According to Modi's foreign secretary, S. Jaishankar, the 'personal chemistry [of the prime minister] has emerged as an important tool in our diplomatic kit. It is therefore time to ask ourselves whether India should raise the level of its ambitions, are we content to react to events, or should we be initiating them or even driving them. Should we remain a balancing power or aspire to be a leading one? Diplomacy involves management of contradictions in international politics, and the pursuit of contradictory goals. In India's current position, it is possible to make a case for simultaneous pursuit of multiple relations which create a virtuous cycle where each one drives the other higher. So, it is time for greater activism…confidence leads to initiatives and drives strategy.'

Speaking at the Raisina Dialogue, supported by the Indian External Affairs Ministry in Delhi in March 2016, Jaishankar summed up the government's foreign policy as 'Act East, Think West'. Act East would place emphasis on connectivity (with geopolitical implications), trade and manufacturing, and would take place in two phases. Since the South Asian Association for Regional Cooperation (SAARC) had not been successful mainly because of Pakistan's hostility towards India, Delhi would consider subregional solutions under bilateral and trilateral arrangements. A case in point being the Bangladesh-Bhutan-India-Nepal (BBIN) matrix. Nations like Myanmar and ASEAN members would be included in this phase for a strategy-driven (i.e. to checkmate China) outcome.

BIMSTEC is an example of the Modi government's approach towards extra-regional cooperation. The Bay of Bengal Initiative for Multi-Sectoral Technical and Economic Cooperation is an international organization involving south and southeast nations, namely Bangladesh, India, Myanmar, Sri Lanka, Thailand, Bhutan and Nepal.

Regarding the Indian Ocean region, Delhi intends to improve connectivity and security ties through shared coastal surveillance and military exercises with the Indian Ocean Rim Association, set up in March 1997, comprising coastal states bordering the Indian Ocean. In phase two of Act East, which India hopes to launch in a decade, the focus will be on increased trade and manufacturing with Japan and South Korea.

On Think West, India will build economic and security relations with the Middle East region (Saudi Arabia, Iran, United Arab Emirates, Kuwait, and so on) that has around 8 million Indian expatriates, and is a big trading partner and major source of energy. For this, India will concentrate on the International North-South Transport Corridor project. The Iranian port of Chabahar, which India has been developing, will bypass Pakistan and provide connectivity (through road and rail) to Afghanistan, the Central Asian Republics and Russia. In India's estimation, this move will counter Pakistan's Gwadar Port being developed with China's assistance.

The military will be used to provide heft to India's Act East and Think West policy. The Indian Navy, whose area of interest traditionally stretched from the Persian Gulf to the Malacca Strait, will extend its diplomatic role to include the Arab states, Iran and the ASEAN nations. Moreover, all three services will provide humanitarian assistance and disaster relief and carry out military exercises with friendly nations to support India's diplomatic reach. Never mind whether India has the military capacity and capability to become the net security provider in the Indian Ocean region and also be in support of the Act East and Think West foreign policy. Delhi, in principle, has committed itself to do so. In pursuance of this objective, India, to China's annoyance, signed the 'Joint Strategic Vision for the Asia-Pacific and the Indian Ocean Region' with the US in January 2015.

Jaishankar made it known that India under Modi was undertaking connectivity as the hard-wire policy through mutual consultations with all countries. This was necessary since there was no agreed Asian security architecture. China, on the contrary, was pushing its connectivity agenda unilaterally through the One Belt One Road project. For instance, China had disregarded India's objection to the China-Pakistan Economic Corridor which passes through Pakistan-occupied Kashmir.

All of the foregoing is well and good, but oddly, there was no mention of military power by India's prime minister and his top diplomat for the conduct of foreign policy which aspires to be proactive rather than remain reactive. Would the world have worried about China's rise if its defence budget was not soaring decade after decade? Would the US have cared so much about China if it was not building asymmetrical warfare capabilities to blunt its powerful military? Would the US Navy have developed the idea of a 1,000-ship navy by partnering with other states to maintain freedom of the seas and building collective arrangements that promote mutual trust? Closer home, would the PLA have done what they do on the Line of Actual Control and would Pakistan pursue its relentless terrorism if India had credible military power? This is why despite all the activity and noise surrounding the Modi government's policies we consider it the flamboyantly dangerous strategic option we have referred to earlier in the chapter and not the second option which would have had real teeth and would have propelled the country into the ranks of geostrategic players.

India's attitude towards military power is puzzling seeing it has military lines to guard against two nuclear armed neighbours with strong conventional war capabilities. It is lost on India that China and Pakistan have devised smart military power, which calls for an understanding of warfare and how to achieve desirable objectives with minimal loss.

As we have seen earlier in the book, to a world familiar with the fourth generation of warfare, China has gone beyond and added the fifth generation and baffled its biggest adversary, the United States. It is worth exploring this concept in some detail. The first generation of warfare reflected the basic tactics of line and column as followed by the Mughal armies. The second generation relied on massed firepower and ended with World War I. The third generation gave importance to manoeuvre over attrition. This was reflected in the German blitzkrieg during World War II. Fourth generation warfare has narrowed the gaps between the front and rear of the battlefield. This has been done by the simultaneous unleashing of conventional war on the front and sub-conventional war (terrorism) in the rear. India's Army follows a mix of second and third generation warfare. Pakistan's Army has successfully demonstrated employment of fourth generation warfare which demoralizes the opponent's society.

China has moved to fifth generation warfare. According to the US thinker-author Joseph Nye, 'Chinese strategists, realizing that a conventional confrontation with the United States would be a folly, developed a strategy of "unrestricted warfare" that combines electronic, diplomatic, cyber, terrorist proxy, economic, and propaganda tools to deceive and exhaust American systems. As one Chinese military official puts it, the first rule of unrestricted warfare is that there are no rules.'

The generational changes in warfare have progressed in tandem with the domains in which they are to be fought. The expansion of domains is the consequence of advancements in technology. From three domains of warfare in the twentieth century—land, air and sea—three more have been added in the twenty-first century. These are outer space, electronic-magnetic space and cyberspace. Moreover, terrorism, which is the high point of fourth generation warfare, has blurred the distinction between external and internal threats. And fifth generation or unrestricted warfare has made an understanding of Chinese thinking essential to devise strategies to beat it.

Unfortunately, thinking strategically and developing an appreciation of military power are two major shortcomings of India's foreign policy. The evidence of this is strewn all across the Indian neighbourhood, where India, unconscious of the actual clout it brings to a relationship, overplays its hand and ends up a two-bit player. It tried to do so with dismal consequences in Myanmar, Sri Lanka, Nepal and the Maldives. A diplomat trying to justify this tendency of India throwing its weight around told the authors, 'Why shouldn't India expect its neighbours to take Indian sensitivities into account? We are a big country. And from time to time, we help them. The least they can do in return is factor in our concerns.' If our neighbours are neither deferential nor deterred, then clearly something is missing in our foreign policy. Also, this mindset betrays a very important aspect of foreign aid or support. Aid is seldom given to fulfil the needs of the recipient. It is given to meet the requirements—strategic in the case of nations—of the giver. Hence the underlying message is never articulated. And if the requirements are not met, you increase the aid or diversify it. This is not only the cardinal principle for the conduct of foreign policy, but of life as well. Even the scriptures say so. Our policymakers seem to have read none.

India is perhaps the only country in the world where foreign policy with nations having disputed borders—China and Pakistan—is made with disregard to military advice, especially when foreign service officers have little knowledge about military issues. This has been the root cause of failure of India's disputed border policy with China.

And India's defence policy?

India does not have a defence policy, however strange it might sound. A defence minister's most important task is to issue defence policy based on policy directives obtained from the Cabinet Committee on Security (CCS), and with advice from the services chiefs, to the Chiefs of Staff Committee (COSC). The CCS, headed by the prime minister, comprises the ministers of Defence, External Affairs, Home and Finance.

For professional outside advice, the CCS could order a Strategic Defence Review involving government and opposition party leaders, outside experts and independent think tanks. However, as nothing comes from the CCS, nothing gets forwarded. Deposing before the nineteenth Estimates Committee of the tenth Lok Sabha, the defence secretary in 1993 admitted that no policy directives had been issued to the defence services since Independence. This position remained unaltered under the Modi government which took office in May 2014.

The defence policy's cardinal responsibility should be to review military threats and assess what political objectives could be achieved by war. For instance, which is the bigger military threat—Pakistan, China or terrorism— and what prioritization ought to be accorded to them? What is the nature of the threat? Is it a short, swift and intense war or a prolonged war with Pakistan? Is it military coercion, or border war or an all-out nuclear war with China? Can all threats be handled together? Or should one threat be neutralized by other means? Which one should that be? What political objectives are being sought by war? What is the worst that could be expected from non-status quo adversaries like Pakistan and China who are in cahoots with one another?

Jawaharlal Nehru, India's first prime minister, had, after the 1947–48 war, concluded that Pakistan was the military threat. While conscious that China could not be trusted, he was unwilling to dilute the military attention on Pakistan. Hence it was decided that China should be engaged through political and diplomatic methods. The 1962 border war with China proved that his defence policy was wrong.

Ironically, despite the criticism of Nehru's China policy, no prime minister since has reviewed his assessment, especially when the world, China and Pakistan have transformed themselves in unimaginable ways. According to the perception of prime minister after prime minister, Pakistan continues to be India's primary military threat, while China has been assessed as a rival and a long-term challenge. With faulty threat assessments, military capabilities acquired to combat them cannot produce the desired political results. For this reason, raising the annual defence allocation—which analysts clamour for to build capabilities for misplaced threats—will not help. China reviews its threats regularly. Pakistan does not have the need to do so since

India has been recognized as the existential threat by General Headquarters, Rawalpindi.

With no defence policy, the authority for military capability building is vested in the defence minister's operational directive (ops directive). Until 2009, based on the assessed threat against Pakistan, in a bottom-up approach, the military leadership prepared the ops directive every five years, which the defence minister signed off on. Depending on the annual allocations, the defence services would fund their long-term acquisition plans and modernization.

This changed in 2009, when on the Indian Army's insistence, the ops directive, for the first time, instructed the defence forces to prepare capabilities for a two-front war. Not willing to give up its counter-insurgency role in Jammu and Kashmir, the army internally modified the ops directive to read 'two and a half front war'. Once the army declared its intentions to fight simultaneous conventional wars with Pakistan and China, as well as ensure internal stability within J&K by counter-insurgency operations, the IAF and the Indian Navy too sought additional capabilities. As we have seen, the IAF got its authorized strength of 39.5 combat squadrons (each with twenty aircraft) increased to forty-two combat squadrons, with a wish list of forty-five combat squadrons in the future. The Indian Navy's authorization of 170 ships in 2006 has been increased to 198 ships by 2027.

On the one hand, the clamour for more capability acquisition by the three services grew with time. For example, on military threats, Lieutenant General S. K. Gadeock, the commandant of India's prestigious Defence Services Staff College, wrote in 2014, 'In the short term, develop capability to thwart two and a half front threat by 2020. In the medium term, build credible force projection capability in the Indian Ocean Region by 2030. In the long term, attain military parity with China by 2050.' On the other hand, military capability failed to produce the desired political results. Neither did Pakistan feel compelled to stop cross-border terrorism across the Line of Control, nor did China halt its transgressions and intrusions.

Clearly India has assessed its military threats wrong, and instead of building military power, it is focused on building military force. As mentioned in the Prologue, the difference between the two runs deep. While military force involves the mere collection of war paraphernalia, military power is about optimal utilization of military force. It entails understanding the future of warfare, domains of war, how wars will be fought, and structural military reforms at various levels to meet the challenges. All this comes under the rubric of higher defence management, which in India's case needs transformation.

Instead of doing that, the defence ministry decided to reform the ops directive to include all stakeholders. Since 2011, the ops directive has been issued every two rather than five years. Instead of the services' headquarters, ops directive is now the charter of the Integrated Defence Headquarters (IDH) headed by a three-star officer. The IDH now gets inputs from three different streams which then produces a comprehensive security scan. In one stream, India's senior-most bureaucrat, the cabinet secretary summons the secretaries of all civil ministries to identify their vulnerable areas and vulnerable points. For example, the petroleum secretary gives lists of offshore assets which would be vulnerable in war. The IDH then does its research based on inputs from the Intelligence Bureau and other civilian agencies. Finally, the IDH convenes the three defence services' vice chiefs to prepare military vulnerable areas and vulnerable points. Once done, under the IDH, the national vulnerable areas and vulnerable points are compiled and the capabilities needed to protect them are added to the ops directive. The latter runs into hundreds of pages. Earlier it used to be just a few pages.

MILITARY THREATS TO INDIA

In the absence of a defence policy, the three services pick up leads from statements emanating from the Prime Minister's Office and the defence minister to guesstimate what the political leadership expects from the defence services. This is in addition to the defence minister's ops directive. This exercise is never easy as the signals could be conflicting and at times make little sense. Consider the following:

Addressing his maiden combined military commanders' conference in New Delhi in July 2014, Prime Minister Narendra Modi said, 'The threats are known but the enemy is invisible.' He called for 'effective deterrence to deal with terror' and the need for a 'United Nations comprehensive convention on international terrorism'. What were the senior officers of the three defence services to make of Modi's address to them which made no mention of the LC and LAC with Pakistan and China? That terrorism by itself was the military threat (to India), and India would spearhead an international drive to combat the menace?

Meanwhile, addressing the *Hindustan Times* Summit in New Delhi on 22 November 2014, National Security Advisor Ajit Doval remarked, 'India has to be ready for two-front war and build deterrence that ensures conflict is not an option for its adversaries.' Any discerning observer knows that a two-front war with nuclear weapons-armed China and Pakistan will be suicidal. It is a slogan rather than a government directive worthy of achieving results. Yet, no analysts, let alone policymakers, have questioned the unachievable task.

Equally ludicrous is the fight against terrorism. It is well-documented that terrorism in India has two fountainheads: the Pakistan Army and internal religious and economic fault lines. The Pakistan Army needs to be defeated in war or issues need to be settled through negotiations to end terrorism into India. Between 2004 and 2007, when backchannel talks between India and Pakistan were progressing well, terrorism across the Line of Control was nearly zero. Demands that Pakistan bring the 26/11 culprits to book or wanted terrorists like Dawood Ibrahim ensconced in Karachi be handed over to India are unrealizable.

STRATEGY FOR INDIA

If a two-front war is a fantasy, what are India's options for peace on the Line of Control and the Line of Actual Control? This requires a strategy which takes into account strategic goals, military threats and an understanding of adversaries, to arrive at the best available solution—shorn of individual or party ideology and leanings. According to Colin Gray, director of the Centre for Strategic Studies at the University of Reading in the UK, 'Making strategy is by far the most difficult and risky than making policy and war plans. By its very nature strategy is more demanding of the intellect and perhaps the imagination. Excellence in strategy requires the strategist to transcend simple categories of thought. Success in strategy calls for a quality of judgment that cannot be taught.'

India's strategy extrapolated from the top-down foreign policy with Modi's unmistakable signature on it has been: isolate Pakistan and position India as China's rival in Asia. To know whether this will deliver desired results of peace and stability on the LC and LAC so that India can concentrate on becoming a geostrategic player, Pakistan and China ought to be assessed.

Given its risen geopolitical profile, Pakistan qualifies as a major geopolitical pivot or balancing power. Geopolitical pivots, according to Zbigniew Brzezinski, 'are determined by their geography, which in some cases gives them a special role either in defining access to important areas or in denying resources to a significant player. Sometimes, the very existence of a geopolitical pivot can be said to have significant political and cultural consequences for a more active neighbourhood player.' For different reasons, three major powers who are also geostrategic players, namely, the US, Russia and China, have sought close relations with Pakistan.

The reality is that the Pakistan Army in Rawalpindi and not the civilian government in Islamabad matters to the world. Rawalpindi controls nuclear weapons, runs a professional military capable of strategizing, has been able to optimally exploit Pakistan's geography and has the potential to emerge as the leader of the Islamic world.

As we have seen, the reason the 6 lakh strong Pakistan Army has been able to take on and will in all probability be able to prevail over the 13 lakh Indian Army is because it strategizes. Rawalpindi has fulfilled the Indian Army's numerical advantage by developing expertise to fight on two battlefields—conventional and non-conventional. The answer to the Indian Army's Cold Start Doctrine was found in the acquisition of tactical nuclear weapons. Once India signed the 2005 civil nuclear agreement with the US, Pakistan enhanced the production of its fissile material. To beat India's purported indigenous ballistic missile defence capability, it increased the variety and range of its ballistic missiles, and acquired the long-range Babur cruise missile from China. After India declared the need to build capabilities to fight a two-front war (where India assessed the real enemy would be Pakistan) in 2009, the Pakistan Army sought and developed interoperability with the PLA. And to neutralize a possible quasi-alliance between India and the US in the Indian Ocean region as well as India's imminent sea-based deterrence, the Pakistan Army offered Gwadar Port to the Chinese Navy to have a free run in India's backyard.

Despite its defiance of the US on terrorism and refusal to compromise on the development of nukes, Pakistan received massive military largesse from Washington in 2016. Making the case for the US$ 860 million aid to Pakistan, the Obama administration wrote to the US Congress in February 2016, 'Pakistan lies at the heart of the US counter-terrorism strategy, the peace process in Afghanistan, nuclear non-proliferation efforts, and economic integration in South and Central Asia.'

Similarly, after the Yeltsin years, when it felt humiliated by the US and sought to champion Asia's cause, Russia's gaze fell on Pakistan. In 2004, Russia under Putin took the unusual step of supporting Pakistan. According to V. I. Trubnikov, the Russian ambassador to India, 'Our relations with Islamabad have their own agenda chiefly aimed at developing trade and economic ties and cooperation at the anti-terrorist front. They [Pakistan] have always been and will remain subject to our greater and traditional interest in stability in South Asia.'

By 2015, Russia-Pakistan relations had moved notches up with Russia selling four Mi-35 helicopters to the Pakistan Army. General Raheel Sharif, the Pakistan Army chief, visited Moscow in June 2015 where the two sides signed a general framework for interaction between the armed forces and security forces for capability building. Explaining why Russia had moved close to Pakistan, Denis Alipov, the Russian deputy chief of mission in India, said, 'Islamabad is a very important player in joint efforts to maintain regional stability, especially in view of the deteriorating situation in Afghanistan and growing threats of international terrorism fuelled by ISIS and rampant drug production. These efforts require collective counteraction and target-oriented capability building. These are exactly our reasons for recent supply of four Mi-35 helicopters.'

While both the US and Russia would like to see relations between India and Pakistan improve, they do not care much about Delhi's protestations of Pakistan's proxy war in India. It is one thing for the international community to support Modi's call for the adoption of the Comprehensive Convention on International Terrorism. It is quite another to accept Pakistan's case that it is a victim rather than a perpetrator of terror, thereby also accepting the spurious distinction that Pakistan makes between terrorists and freedom fighters.

Take the case of Afghanistan and Tajikistan (an important geopolitical pivot in the Central Asian Republics). On China's initiative, four nations, namely, China, Pakistan, Afghanistan and Tajikistan, signed the 'quadrilateral military cooperation and coordination mechanism' for counter-terrorism on 3 August 2016 in Urumqi, the capital of China's Xinjiang region. For all the noise that India makes about Afghanistan too being a victim of Pakistan's terrorism, the four nations agreed 'to cooperate in counter-terrorism situation evaluation, clue verification, intelligence sharing, counterterrorism capacity building, counter-terrorism joint training and personnel training'. Being part of this grouping on counter-terrorism, Pakistan, unlike India, would benefit more as the new member state of the Shanghai Cooperation Organization.

What does the Pakistan Army want from India? The Pakistan Army, with ownership of the Kashmir dispute since the 1947 war, wants to settle it on equal terms. Two wars, in 1947 and 1965, and two conflicts, Siachen and Kargil, have been fought over Kashmir. The proxy war or attack-by-infiltration by Pakistan Army-backed terrorists into Jammu and Kashmir has been in progress since 1990. The Indian Army cannot win this proxy war because the people of Kashmir are alienated. Why else have Indian security forces numbering over 300,000 been unable to eliminate 200 to 300 terrorists in the state? The Indian military cannot hit terrorist bases deep inside Pakistan-occupied Kashmir as it would lead to a war that it would have difficulty winning.

Former army chief General Shankar Roychowdhury made the point forcefully in his book, *Officially at Peace*, 'Our apparent tolerance towards these blatant terrorist attacks [from Pakistan in J&K] was actually due to the run-down in our military capabilities for decisive punitive action. Effective counter-offensive capabilities were the precise area where the Indian Army's potential had been greatly eroded.' This was written in 1994; things are worse now. For India, war with Pakistan is not an option.

Neither is it with China. As we have seen, Beijing views India not as an equal, but as a geopolitical pivot or balancing power in Asia. It has formulated a seven-pronged approach towards New Delhi: obfuscate the border dispute; do not define the LAC; disallow major political or diplomatic concessions; ensure through Pakistan that India remains a sub-regional player boxed in in South Asia; make India's neighbours deferential towards China by showering economic and military goodies on them; build its own military power by appropriate warfare strategy and higher defence management; and bind India with bilateral trade tilted in China's favour.

China's approach towards India has resulted in certain strategic military advantages for it. The first is successful military coercion which China first demonstrated in April–May 2013 when a few of its border guards walked into Indian territory in north Ladakh with India unable to do much. Since then China has exercised military coercion a number of times. For example, in April 2016, Beijing compelled New Delhi to withdraw the visa granted to Dolkun Isa, the Uyghur activist labelled a terrorist by China, who was to come to India to participate in a conference organized by the Dalai Lama.

Decades of India's appeasement policy towards China have been put paid to by Beijing's military coercion based on its military power. This cannot be offset by outside assistance to India—by New Delhi entering into close ties with the US. The argument made by analysts that India could balance China's military pressure on the land border with joint capabilities with friendly nations in the Indian Ocean is incorrect. Equally unsound is the argument that India could minimize the territorial threat from China by developing deep trade ties with it. China will not agree to such a trade-off. A case in point is the tug of war between China and the US in the South China Sea despite their trade ties. Yet another ludicrous argument is that India should intervene with its strategic partners (US) if its area of strategic interest—which now extends from the South China Sea to the Horn of Africa—is threatened (by China).

India's continental defence cannot be equated with maritime security because no nation will fight India's land war. India needs to develop a strategy that makes the cost of military coercion expensive for China.

China's military coercion is the direct consequence of the border dispute where China holds all the legal, psychological and military cards. This explains why China, which has resolved twelve land border disputes with fourteen nations, refuses to do so with India and Bhutan. Beijing, since 2014, has been in talks with Bhutan to resolve the issue relating to their common border by swapping territory to build additional military pressure on India and also to weaken the special relationship between India and Bhutan.

Another strategic-military advantage for China is in the Indian Ocean region. While demolishing the myth of it being India's own waters, China has expanded its footprints there. It started with the so-called 'string of pearls' strategy in 2005 where China assisted small littoral states in the Indian Ocean region with infrastructure development and financial and military assistance. The unveiling of the 21st century Maritime Silk Road project, in 2013 included Myanmar, Sri Lanka, the Maldives, Seychelles, Djibouti and of course, Pakistan's Gwadar, which would be the hub of China's commercial-cum-military activities. While these small nations are playing India against China to draw maximum benefits from both, in time, they will be compelled to show their preference. Given the extent of assistance provided to them by India and China, it is obvious which way the pendulum would swing.

To put this into perspective, China's deep pockets are helping it formulate an economy-driven Eurasian architecture where between the two heavyweights (Russia and China) Moscow has grudgingly accepted Beijing's lead. At the Shanghai Cooperation Organization meeting held in July 2015 in Ufa (Russia), on China's initiative, member states took an important decision—Russia's dream project, the Eurasia Economic Council, was integrated with China's ambitious Silk Road Economic Belt through large-scale infrastructure and technological projects. Given the economic sanctions on Russia (whose economy is, in any case, weak) since the Ukraine crisis, China stands to steer the integration to its advantage. China has already announced the opening of forty-six new direct air services in 2016 to countries along the Belt.

China's military anchor in the Indian Ocean will not happen anytime soon. Since China, focused on East Asia, will not divert its military capabilities to the Indian Ocean, it will be content with limited and selective port access, and better understanding of the littoral nations in the region. The need for navy bases will come once China has achieved its objectives in

East Asia and has built naval capabilities to match the US in the Indian Ocean region. Then it could either be a clash or an entente between China and the US where India could play an important role provided it is able to manage China now.

To do that, it would need to do much more than enlarging overall bilateral trade. For example, India's External Affairs Ministry signed the Enterprising Policy 2015 with the international department of the Communist Party of China. Under this, a mechanism was set up for Indian chief ministers to directly establish trade with China bypassing the central government in New Delhi. According to officials, this would help in the symbiotic economic relationship and marry China's excess manufacturing capacity with India's 'Make in India' campaign. By end 2015, Andhra Pradesh and Haryana had invested large sums in deals with China. Indian policymakers naively believe that massive bilateral trade and commerce with China will offset the negativity of the border dispute. This is unlikely.

Unless there is a cataclysmic event like the demise of the Soviet Union, a catch-up with China politically, economically and militarily is not possible for India. China is a permanent member of the UN Security Council and a nuclear weapon state under the Non-Proliferation Treaty. China's economy is five times that of India. Unlike India, whose economy is propelled by the service sector, China is a globally recognized manufacturing hub. China's indigenous shipbuilding is rated as the best in Asia, having surpassed South Korea's. India's capabilities in comparison are extremely modest.

According to Le Yucheng, the Chinese ambassador to India, 'China is the biggest trading country in the world. In 2015, the trade volume between Germany and China was over US$ 200 billion and that between China and the US amounted to US$ 550 billion. From 2011 to 2014, China attracted paid-in FDI of about US$ 500 billion. And its overseas investments reached US$ 116 billion in 2014, almost doubling the 2011 figures.' The International Monetary Fund agreed to include China's currency, the yuan, in the Special Drawing Rights by October 2016 (India does not have Special Drawing Rights). According to estimates, China could see the inflow of as much as over US$ 3 trillion into yuan assets over the medium to long term as successful inclusion of the yuan in the IMF reserve currency basket sets the stage for further opening of the country's financial markets.

◆

At this point, it would be useful to thread together everything we have touched upon in the previous chapters to show what India must do in the coming decades to successfully deal with the Chinese threat. As we have seen, without exception, all border transgressions on the LAC are from China to India. Indian soldiers hold heights from 10,000 to 18,000 feet along the LAC round the year. They undertake long duration patrols through icy tracks and slush for area domination in sub-zero temperatures trying to determine the Chinese presence close to the LAC. Indian commanders dread LAC transgressions in their area of responsibility as it reflects poorly on their record. China's border management advantages can be summed up as three Rs: roads or infrastructure; radar or technology rather than human patrolling; and reserves or the PLA's potent mobile forces.

China is not some distant challenge as it is made out to be. China is enervating India in consonance with Sun Tzu's maxim: 'Defeat the enemy without a battle'. In the long term, China, with increased international clout and military power could insist on settling the border dispute on its terms. Since it has already gobbled up 1,488 kilometres of disputed border (in Ladakh) without even a protest from India, what stops it from assuming a maximalist position on Arunachal Pradesh? Moreover, unless China is compelled to reassess its hardened position on the border dispute, India's foreign policy choices will remain constrained.

Good strategy dictates that between the two military lines, the LC with Pakistan is resolvable, the LAC with China is not. What should India do? Remove the LC in its present manifestation by making peace with Pakistan? This would not be easy because it involves the elimination of misplaced ideologies, prejudices and historical baggage. It bears repeating that this requires a statesman for a prime minister rather than a mere head of government with his or her own retrograde agenda.

The starting point of cooperation between India and Pakistan would have to be the resolution of the Kashmir issue. This makes strategic, military and economic sense. Khurshid Kasuri, Pakistan's foreign minister from 2004–07, was perhaps correct in writing, 'It is my belief that the raison d'être of the Pakistan Army is not permanent enmity with India; it is Pakistan's permanent security. And this implies secure borders, strong economy, and an inclusive and proactive foreign policy.'

Productive bilateral talks on Kashmir could, through nuclear confidence building measures, reduce chances of a nuclear war and an arms race. Moreover, the spectre of water wars, which owes more to mutual distrust than India's intentions to disregard the 1960 Indus Water Treaty, would dissipate. Pakistan, as the lower riparian state, has legitimate concerns regarding the intentions of a hostile India just as India has about China. Even if the two sides could resolve the Baglihar and Kishanganga projects on the Chenab River, there are many more hydroelectric dams planned by India in Kashmir.

Peace with Pakistan by resolving all the crises that have to do with Kashmir would be a first positive step for India to make China reassess its strategy of military pressure on the LAC or in the Indian Ocean. What makes this rather more than a pipe dream is that fact that, interestingly, China today wants India and Pakistan to resolve their problems and support the OBOR. While India should be open to cooperation with China, it should be on dignified terms where China has no choice but to recognize India, however grudgingly, as a leading power in Asia.

For this, as we have shown repeatedly, India will need to build its own military power, review its Tibet policy, honourably resolve internal insurgencies, build close ties with the US bilaterally and trilaterally by including Japan to combat common threats in the Asia-Pacific and Indian Ocean regions, and strengthen the Act East policy by deepening relations with ASEAN and other littoral nations. As these options comprising India's grand strategy unfold, India would have more space to make the SAARC productive. It should then seriously consider how its Act East policy and China's OBOR plan could be harmonized for mutual benefit. In a globalized world, this would be a win-win for India.

Proper handling of the LAC by India would certainly make peace and stability on the LAC less nerve-racking by reducing psychological pressure on the political leadership and soldiers policing the disputed border at high altitudes. And this will not come from the innumerable border confidence building measures, most of which have been instituted at China's behest. The confidence building measures do not prevent border transgressions by China; they only help in preventing a border crisis from escalation, something that China in any case would not do. When China can achieve its objective with military coercion, why would it go to war?

Moreover, an agreement or meaningful interactions on the LC with Pakistan (involving the whole of Kashmir across the divide) would help India discuss the strategic Northern Areas (Gilgit-Baltistan) with Pakistan. Since the settlement of the LC and genuine stability on the LAC would reduce the trust deficit that India has with Pakistan and China, numerous benefits could accrue. The negativity of the Pakistan-China nexus for India that began with Pakistan ceding a portion of the Northern Areas to China in 1963 would abate. India might assess the China-Pakistan Economic Corridor and the Chinese OBOR less as a threat and more as something that would benefit the larger neighbourhood and the world: a road to regional prosperity and gateway to Afghanistan, the Middle East, the Central Asian Republics, Central Europe and Iran. Chinese President Xi Jinping has listed the China- Pakistan Economic Corridor as the flagship of his OBOR plan.

Make no mistake: China and Pakistan are embarked on rewriting the rules of geopolitics in Afghanistan, the Middle East and India's neighbourhood. The situation in Afghanistan is unsettled. The Afghan Taliban, whose return to power is a possibility, appear willing to listen to the Pakistan-China duo provided the foreigners (the US and its western allies) leave their country. Similarly, with China and Pakistan by their side, the possibility of securing peace between arch-rivals Iran and Saudi Arabia with the alluring prospect of the revival of the Old Silk Route through the OBOR looks tantalizing. This is not all. Reports indicate that Pakistan's Gwadar Port will get linked through a railway line with the Iranian port city of Chabahar. Where does this leave India's investments and dreams of linking up with Central Asian Republics bypassing Pakistan through Chabahar?

At the very least, three bilateral issues where India and China could have done better if India had handled the border dispute properly are worth considering. While India's Act East policy and China's OBOR and BCIM economic corridors are about trade, financial integration, better connectivity and policy coordination amongst Asian nations, there is deep suspicion and reluctance on India's part to jump on the Chinese bandwagon. This is because of certain problems with the OBOR in its present avatar. The most obvious is one we have touched on the fact that its key artery, the China-Pakistan Economic Corridor, runs through POK which India considers its territory. Two, India worries that joining the BCIM (India insists that the BCIM and OBOR are separate issues) which might connect with China's One Belt (land route) would encourage Beijing to push Delhi to join the One Road (maritime route). India considers the One Road which passes through its backyard and connects with the Gwadar maritime hub in Pakistan as detrimental to its security. Three, the BCIM is seen as China's method of influencing India's Northeast—which has tenuous physical links with the mainland—through its economic might with obvious political implications. And four, India believes that joining the China-supported connectivity projects, when it has a few of its own, would undermine its own Act East policy. While India has joined the China-sponsored AIIB and BRICS New Development Bank (the official argument is that India with its large economy will benefit these institutions), it is hesitant to be a part of the Chinese agenda.

This explains India's dilly-dallying on the BCIM, which was offered by China before its expansive OBOR plan unfolded. India, since 2013, has still not completed its half-track study (by a joint secretary) to conclude whether it should join the BCIM. New Delhi's grouse at a deeper level is that China has not endorsed its Act East policy.

The other bilateral issue where suspicions linger is China's Zangmu hydropower dam over the Brahmaputra River (called Yarlung Zangbo River in Tibet) which was completed in October 2015. This is the largest dam built at a high altitude and is reported to provide 2.5 billion kilowatts of electricity per year. China says it is a run-of-the-river project and has agreed to share hydrological data and assistance in emergency management (flood data) with India, as it is the lower riparian state. It has, however, turned a deaf ear to India's demand of providing it with lean period data and that a cooperative framework be worked out between the two sides to assuage India's apprehensions. For instance, India fears that China may divert the river water or build large water storage facilities, both of which will affect India's entire northeastern region which is fed by the Brahmaputra.

Another issue where the unresolved border looms large was the first bilateral meeting on disarmament, non-proliferation and arms control held in April 2015 in Beijing, ahead of Modi's China visit in May. China is the only permanent member of the UN Security Council which does not accept India as a state with nuclear weapons and continues to demand that India sign the nuclear Non-Proliferation Treaty as a non-nuclear weapon state as per UN Security Council Resolution 1172 of 6 June 1998. It was after years of prodding by India that China agreed to take the first baby step where the two sides exchanged views on global technology regimes and conference on disarmament held under the aegis of the UN.

As China does not recognize India as a nuclear weapon state, it has refused to discuss bilateral issues such as respective nuclear doctrines, proliferation of Chinese nuclear and restrictive technologies to Pakistan, and China's May 2015 white paper on the Indian Ocean region. Even as India legally remains outside the Non-Proliferation Treaty, New Delhi hopes to eventually have a full-fledged dialogue on nuclear and conventional doctrines with China, which at present does not appear to be possible.

With genuine stability with China and Pakistan, India will be able to devote itself wholeheartedly to the development of national power—especially hard power, comprising economic and military power. The latter is critical for India to conduct foreign policy as a leading rather than a balancing power. India as a leading power will have more foreign policy options and opportunities; with time it could become an indispensable state for stability in the Asia–Pacific and Indian Ocean regions, something it aspires towards. Moreover, it will achieve strategic autonomy to conduct foreign policy in a multipolar world.

SECTION IV

KASHMIR

CHAPTER 8

POLITICAL GAMES AT WORK

The long queues outside the polling booths during Kashmir assembly elections have long been touted as proof of normalcy in the state. For nearly two decades, the faces of cheerful women lining up in orderly queues have been hailed by the Government of India as a sign of Jammu and Kashmir limping back to normalcy. Lulled by these images, the country's leadership periodically convinces itself that there is no problem in the state. Given that the state has been 'limping back to normalcy' since 1996, when the first elections were held after the armed insurgency began in 1989, it runs the risk of either getting a permanent limp or developing gangrene.

'Elections are not about the Kashmir issue. They are about day-to-day problem redressal,' Professor Abdul Ghani Bhat, leader of the Muslim Conference political party and a senior ideologue of the All Party Hurriyat Conference (Mirwaiz), told the authors in April 2014. Nestling a kangri close to his body to ward off the unexpected chill, he added, 'People criticize Omar Abdullah for having wasted six years [as chief minister]. I say he is a very good man. But even if an angel comes down from the heavens to govern Kashmir, he will fail. This is a problem that needs resolution by coming together of India, Pakistan and the people of Kashmir.'

As is the wont of politicians, Professor Bhat always has an audience of a few people at home, even if he meets you by appointment. And he pauses to deliver his punchline to ensure that he has the maximum attention of his listeners. 'Even today, India can resolve this issue by talking to Pakistan and the people of Kashmir. In a few years, it will have to talk with China too,' he said with a conspiratorial wink.

Why China?

'Why not,' he retorted. 'China is also a stakeholder. It is in possession of a part of Kashmir. And it is making huge investments in other parts,' he said, alluding to Pakistan-occupied Kashmir and the Northern Areas, also known as Gilgit-Baltistan, which is under Pakistani control. After a long pause, during which he appeared to be weighing his words carefully, he gave his concluding remarks on the subject with a flourish. 'China says that it does not have a border with India in Kashmir. Those who can think will understand what this means,' he said.

Professor Bhat is one of the few Kashmiri politicians, mainstream or otherwise, who talks of China staking a claim to Kashmir. And his is not a hollow claim. Apart from the fact that China is in physical possession of four valleys in the undivided state of J&K—Shaksgam, Raskam, Shimshal and Aksai Chin—its all-weather relationship with Pakistan has ensured that over a period of time both the Chinese technical workforce as well as the military have easy access to those parts of Kashmir which are under its control. According to Senge Sering, a human rights lawyer from Baltistan and currently president of the Institute for Gilgit-Baltistan Studies based in the United States, 'China is involved in mining of heavy metals and uranium, [building of] rail, roads, strategic build-up, airstrips on highways, tunnels with dual purpose missile storage capacity, fibre optics... and other similar projects [in Gilgit-Baltistan].'

While the people of POK are ethnically similar to those of the Kashmir Valley, about 40 per cent of the inhabitants of Gilgit-Baltistan are Tibetan in origin. In Ladakh (excluding the Kargil division), 90 per cent of the population has Tibetan antecedents. Once upon a time, both Baltistan and Ladakh were a part of the Dogra kingdom. Moreover, the Muslims (mainly Shia) of Gilgit-Baltistan share their culture and history with the people of Kargil, as all these were valleys on the ancient Silk Route. Over the years, many Uyghurs have also settled in these areas, in addition to Tajiks. Seen without the national boundaries, right from northern Afghanistan to Xinjiang, across Gilgit-Baltistan and Kargil-Ladakh, people have more or less similar ethnic roots.

As of now China is investing heavily in all the regions contiguous to Ladakh, where it has been indulging in creeping encroachment, both from the north as well as the south. While northern Ladakh is a vast high-altitude desert where not even a 'blade of grass grows', southeastern Ladakh has settled villages on both sides of the LAC. Given the sheer remoteness of the region and topographical distance from mainland India, there is no way of determining the extent of trans-LAC communication between the border villages. On the surface, while fascinated by the promise of development and prosperity, local people are wary of China at the moment.

Interestingly, Ladakh has long clamoured for the status of a union territory. Except for political history, it shares nothing with either Jammu or Kashmir. Even in the elections, whether parliamentary or state assembly, Ladakh usually votes for the national mainstream parties, usually the Congress, though in the parliamentary elections of 2014, it voted for the BJP. The insurgency in Kashmir, which gradually made its way into the Jammu region, has passed Ladakh by. But now with China knocking on its door, and building military infrastructure, Ladakh faces a very real threat.

While discounting China's claim to Kashmir, Mirwaiz Umar Farooq, chairman of the All Party Hurriyat Conference (M), said in reference to the short-lived Chinese policy of issuing stapled visas to the residents of Kashmir, 'The people of Kashmir have no animosity towards China, which has become increasingly supportive of our cause.'

Professor Bhat is poet-philosopher-politician all rolled in one. He talks in pithy proverbs, folklore and innuendos. But he doesn't talk without purpose. Unlike most of his ilk in the Hurriyat Conference he maintains that issues like elections, Article 370, Armed Forces (Special Powers) Act (AFSPA), release of political prisoners, etc. are confidence building measures. They will create harmonious atmospherics, but will not go very far. 'Addressing these issues is like taking the water out from a well in which a dog has died. We need to take the dog out,' he said.

The first genuine effort towards starting a political process—or devising a rope to take the dog out—was made by Prime Minister Atal Bihari Vajpayee, when he extended a hand of friendship to Pakistan on 18 April 2003 in a public address during his visit to Srinagar. Vajpayee didn't stop at friendship. Just before boarding his flight to Delhi, when a journalist at the Srinagar airport asked him whether the talks would be within the ambit of the Indian Constitution, Vajpayee made a sweeping gesture with his hand and said that he was willing to talk to anyone within the framework of humanity. Pakistan, under President Pervez Musharraf, responded in kind by announcing a ceasefire on the LC on 26 November 2003.

The overtures to Pakistan were followed by the first ever meeting between the Deputy Prime Minister and Home Minister L. K. Advani with the All Party Hurriyat Conference (M) in January 2004. It was an icebreaker, with the APHC leaders going back with a lot of optimism. They met again in March with the promise that serious talks would start with the third meeting. That never happened as the BJP-led National Democratic Alliance lost the elections and the Congress-led United Progressive Alliance came to power.

Meanwhile, the government in Kashmir had changed too. Mufti Mohammad Sayeed, whose daughter Rubaiya Sayeed was abducted in

December 1989 (when he was the union home minister) by the first insurgent group, the Jammu and Kashmir Liberation Front (JKLF), had led his party, the People's Democratic Party (PDP) to victory in the election held in 2002. His slogan was 'healing touch', which immediately connected with the people. As a counter to the National Conference's autonomy proposal, the PDP presented a 'self-rule' document in 2007. That didn't go far either.

Though there was much breast-beating in Kashmir when Vajpayee lost the elections, as people had come to believe that with him at the helm in Delhi and President Musharraf in Rawalpindi resolution was imminent, Manmohan Singh's government did not belie those hopes. At least not then.

Within months of assuming office, Singh visited Kashmir and announced the withdrawal of troops in November 2004. Some troops did withdraw; though in reality, only the troops which were inducted in haste during the Kargil conflict of 1999 were sent back to their original locations. But as a feel-good factor it worked. This was quickly followed up with the commencement of the Srinagar-Muzaffarabad bus service (April 2005), opening of a few meeting points along the LC to enable divided families on either side to meet and the beginning of Round Table Conferences (RTCs) between Delhi and the Kashmiri people. The first RTC, chaired by Manmohan Singh, was held on 25 February 2006. As the government had invited a cross section of Kashmiris, including traders and trade union leaders, the separatist politicians stayed away. However, they attended the second RTC on 25 May 2006, again chaired by the prime minister.

As a consequence of the second RTC, five working groups were announced. The first working group was to focus on confidence building measures within the state and issues like the rehabilitation of those affected by militant violence in the state. The second group was to work out mechanisms for strengthening trans-Line of Control relations by introducing trade as well as free movement of people. The third group's focus was on economic development, creation of jobs for the youth (thereby trying to draw them into the mainstream) and also restoring inter-regional economic balance within the state. The fourth group's responsibility was to draw up the principles of good governance by making the state administration more responsive, accountable and transparent. It was also to work on local self-governance (Panchayati Raj) and implementation of the Right to Information Act. The fifth, and the most important working group, was to find ways to strengthen centre-state relations. It was to look into the gradual dilution of the special status that J&K enjoyed within the Indian Constitution and to see how best the aspirations of the people from the three regions of the state could be met.

The prime minister invited Kashmiris to give their suggestions to the fifth working group on how lasting peace in the state might be achieved. Member of the All Parties Hurriyat Conference (M) and leader of the People's Conference, Sajjad Lone, who subsequently joined mainstream politics and won the state assembly elections in 2014 from Handwara and became a minister in the PDP-BJP alliance government, put together a comprehensive document titled 'Achievable Nationhood' and sent it to the Prime Minister's Office. Nothing more was heard of it. 'I did not even get an acknowledgement of receipt,' Lone complained bitterly.

All the working groups submitted their reports to the government, but barring the cosmetic implementation of a few proposals, nothing much came of them. While the centre-state report was shoved out of sight, the proposals on confidence building measures (CBMs) became part of the public discourse in Kashmir. The centrepiece of the CBMs was the withdrawal of troops and the revocation of AFSPA.

Even as the government was keeping the people in good humour, Manmohan Singh and Musharraf were engaged in a dialogue on Kashmir, as part of the overall Composite Dialogue between the two countries. The basis of the dialogue was Musharraf's publicly espoused four-point formula, outlined below, which aimed at a Kashmir resolution taking Indian, Pakistani and Kashmiri sensitivities into account. While Pakistan did not want the status quo to continue, India did not want the lines (LC) to be redrawn. The middle path that the two pursued aimed, in Singh's words, to make borders irrelevant.

A quasi non-official, referred to as backchannel, discussion commenced between former diplomats Satinder Lambah and Tariq Aziz to work out a proposal based on that formula which envisaged creating regional councils in all five regions of Kashmir—Jammu, the Valley and Ladakh in India; POK and Gilgit-Baltistan in Pakistan. The councils were to govern themselves and coordinate with each other as well as with India and Pakistan on larger issues. This way the borders would become irrelevant over a period of time. Going step by step, it implied porous borders in Kashmir with freedom of movement for the Kashmiris; 'self-governance' within each region of Kashmir; phased demilitarization of all regions; and finally, a 'joint supervisory mechanism', with representatives from India, Pakistan and all parts of Kashmir, to oversee the plan's implementation.

Apparently, by early 2007, the two sides were very close to drafting a proposal which could be sold to both countries. By late spring 2007, the air in the Kashmir Valley was pregnant with anticipation. Talking to local journalists in Srinagar in April 2007, Mirwaiz Umar Farooq said that the governments of India and Pakistan would announce the resolution by September 2007. The diplomats were also working on finalizing a visit by Manmohan Singh to Pakistan in late 2007, where the broad contours of the resolution would have been announced.

However, even as the proposal was being readied, Musharraf's political hold started to unravel. Manmohan Singh's visit was put off till such time as Musharraf regained his stability. Musharraf's position continued to deteriorate and he eventually resigned in early 2008. Manmohan Singh never went to Pakistan, and the draft proposal remained just that—a draft, with enormous possibilities.

Kashmir–watchers believe that this was the closest the Government of India came to resolving the Kashmir issue. A WikiLeaks exposé of a US embassy cable (dated 21 April 2009), in which Manmohan Singh is reported to have told the visiting US delegation led by then House Foreign Affairs Committee Chairman Howard Berman that 'we had reached an understanding in backchannels', confirmed as much. After holding his counsel for a few years, Satinder Lambah, one of the authors of the draft proposal, made a reference to the process in a talk he delivered at the Institute of Kashmir Studies, University of Kashmir, Srinagar, on 13 May 2014.

Emphasizing that this talk was his personal opinion, Lambah told his audience, 'A solution to the Kashmir issue will substantially enhance India's security, strengthen the prospects for durable peace and stability in the region and enable India to focus more on the rapidly emerging long-term geopolitical challenges. It will relieve the burden that our security forces have to shoulder in terms of lives and resources. It could provide a boost to the Indian economy in a variety of ways, open a market with one of the world's largest populations, restore our historical links to Central Asia and Eurasia and contribute to enhancing our energy security through improved connectivity with West Asia and Central Asia.'

Subsequently, in an interview to the *Hindustan Times* on 16 October 2015, Lambah finally spoke about the backchannel process. He said, 'What we were working on agreed there would be no reference to the United Nations resolution or a plebiscite in Kashmir. Both sides had agreed that borders cannot be redrawn.' In the same interview he also said, 'Mumbai was a very unfortunate incident and that did stop the dialogue. There was a break but we had already finished most of the work by then. After the Mumbai attacks, there were limited [backchannel] contacts but what was agreed on by the Musharraf government was not disowned by the successive governments [headed first by the PPP under Yousaf Raza Gillani and currently by Nawaz Sharif].'

Yet, curiously enough, during his talk at the University of Kashmir he also said that, 'After three wars and long periods of disagreements, it is essential that any agreement must ensure that the Line of Control is like a border between any two normal states. There can be no redrawal of borders.' If the LC is to become like a border between 'two normal states', how could it then be irrelevant as Prime Minister Manmohan Singh said?

Did it then mean that having walked Musharraf's talk, India started to develop cold feet about the pace and scope of the talks? That the government became unsure whether the deal could be sold to the country as a win-win and not a sellout to Pakistan? Finally, was India really serious about the resolution or was it simply playing along with Pakistan to see how far the talks would go? According to a former home secretary Madhukar Gupta, who was in office when the 'backchannel' talks were under way, 'Who knows what sorting out Kashmir means, what resolution means? A resolution will evolve with time; it cannot be forced.'

His successor, G. K. Pillai, was a bit more forthcoming. He said, 'As far as I understand, the Government of India thinks that as long as violence in Kashmir is kept under manageable limits, the matter will resolve on its own over a period of time. In the waiting game over Kashmir, India has the capacity to out-wait Pakistan.'

In hindsight, this statement appears closer to the truth, primarily because Manmohan Singh was heading a coalition government, with disparate partners. It is difficult to imagine that he could have presented to Parliament a draft proposal for the resolution of Kashmir when his own government was not on board with it. Being a parliamentary democracy, shouldn't the Indian government have prepared both Parliament and the people of the country for what could have been a change in the status of Kashmir? Moreover, unlike Pakistan, where Musharraf sounded out his senior military commanders, including ISI chief Kayani who succeeded him as army chief, and foreign ministry bureaucrats in early 2007, who subsequently gave extensive interviews to the international media, in India the mention of the backchannel talks remained in the realm of gossip. Even after Musharraf's 'ignominious' exit, when his successors were in the loop on the Kashmir backchannel, what stopped the Government of India (it was the same government that conducted the talks) from picking up the threads? After all, despite the breakdown of the Composite Dialogue after the 26/11 Mumbai attacks, talks did resume on trade after 2010. Clearly Musharraf's exit provided the Government of India with an escape route too.

Once this opportunity was lost, the situation in Kashmir started deteriorating again, with one difference. Starting with the summer of 2008, the militant violence was replaced by street violence, in which angry Kashmiri boys, as young as eleven, engaged the state police and the Central Reserve Police Force (CRPF) in pitched battles, with the former throwing stones and the latter resisting through tear gas shells and sporadic firing. The trigger changed every summer, but the end result was always the same: a heap of dead civilians. This phase of vicious street fighting culminated in the violent summer of 2010, which left 120 boys dead, all victims of the so-called riot control equipment of the CRPF and the state police.

Since talks of a resolution were dead, the union government once again resorted to buying time, during which it hoped that wounds would heal. After the violent summer of 2010, it appointed three interlocutors, Dileep Padgaonkar, Radha Kumar and M. M. Ansari, to talk to a cross section of people in the state and come up with recommendations to meet the genuine aspirations of the people. The interlocutors submitted their report to Home Minister P. Chidambaram in October 2011. After sitting on the report for a few months, the Ministry of Home Affairs uploaded it on its website. That was the end of the report, which recommended among other things, release of youth (charged with pelting stones at security forces) arrested under the draconian Kashmir Public Safety Act (PSA), revocation of the AFSPA, reduction in the presence of the armed forces and winding down of the Indian Army's Sadbhavana programme, which the report said was undermining the civilian government.

Meanwhile, in November 2011, the government announced the formation of two more committees, one at the centre and another in the state to look afresh at the controversial AFSPA and how it could be revoked. Nothing more was heard of those committees either. The fate of the working groups created in 2007 was somewhat similar.

All this lends credence to the assumption that the Government of India, irrespective of the party, believes that there is no Kashmir issue that needs to be resolved. While the previous government preferred ambiguity in this respect, the Modi government, has made it clear that as far as Kashmir is concerned, Pakistan is off the table; and as far as Pakistan is concerned, Kashmir is off the table.

This doesn't mean that the government does not want good relations with Pakistan; in fact, it wants very good trade relations with Pakistan. Even as the government called off the foreign secretary-level talks in August 2014, it was facilitating visas for Pakistani traders to attend a trade meet in India.

Ironically, the Indian foreign office referred to the bilateralism instituted by the Simla Agreement of 1972 while cancelling the foreign secretary-level talks as the Pakistan high commissioner had entertained Kashmiri separatists before the talks. Even if one discounts the fact that Kashmiri separatists are personae non gratae for the new government despite the fact that in its earlier term the NDA government started the process of talking to the separatists, the spirit of the Simla Agreement itself underlines the process of Kashmir resolution by taking the people of the state into confidence.

Soon after the agreement was signed, Prime Minister Indira Gandhi had 'opened a dialogue with Sheikh Abdullah... India was in effect meeting the demand of separatist Kashmiris for representation at Indo-Pak negotiations on Kashmir via simultaneous but separate talks with Sheikh Abdullah'.

While the Simla Agreement envisaged the way forward for a resolution, it still needed to be done formally. And the political aspirations of the people had to be addressed. The Indira Gandhi-Sheikh Abdullah Accord of 1974 sought to satisfy the aspirations of the Kashmiri people as a step towards the final resolution, but over time it was whittled away as petty politicking got in the way.

Today, instead of building on the legacies of its predecessors, the BJP government is trying to chart a new path by introducing communal consciousness in an already unstable situation by raising issues like enforcing the archaic law banning beef, the status of Article 370, the creation of special colonies for Kashmiri Pandits and retired Indian Army soldiers, besides reclaiming the ancient Hindu legacy of the state. It is true that Kashmir has an extremely rich history of Hinduism to which, over time, Islamic traditions were added to such an extent that they overwhelmed the ancient legacy in sheer numerical terms.

Yet, the two coexisted. And despite efforts by radicals on both sides to sully this confluence, even today many Muslim Kashmiri writers and poets of a certain age use Hindu metaphors and imagery in their work as evidence of the religious syncretism of the region. It is understandable that people with a sense of legacy, as well as Kashmiri Pandits, would want to reclaim and revive this tradition; just as people who feel that they are under siege would try to resist this reclamation for fear of being overwhelmed. Conversation and understanding can overcome these hurdles.

However, when politicians want to be part of the revival exercise, it is bound to lead to conflagration as has been happening in the state since the BJP–PDP government came to power after the 2014 assembly elections. Adding volatility to this already dangerous situation, is the union government's refusal to talk about the resolution. A party's professed position is one thing, a government's commitment is quite another. The BJP may be committed to the complete integration of Kashmir with India, but the Government of India has committed itself to the final resolution of Kashmir with Pakistan. It has also repeatedly stressed that all stakeholders will be taken on board and these include the people of Kashmir. While once upon a time it meant the elected representatives of the people (as in the state government), by repeatedly engaging with the Hurriyat Conference after it came into being in 1993, the Government of India conveyed the message that even non-elected politicians were stakeholders.

Hence, Kashmiri politics will always revolve around resolution. Especially when the Kashmiris were led to believe that a resolution, acceptable to them, was around the corner. To use the level of violence as a parameter to determine normalcy is to fool oneself. The Kashmir issue predates the violent insurgency that started in 1989. The present reality is that Kashmir is too dangerous a place to play religious games. In this tinderbox of frayed emotions, divisive politics will create havoc. Moreover, as experience shows, when moderate people are deliberately discredited or marginalized, extremists step in to fill the void. The polarized vote bank in Kashmir, which delivered the Jammu region to the Bharatiya Janata Party and the Valley to the People's Democratic Party, has further deepened the internal rift between the three regions of the state.

While the Jammu division may have a substantial Hindu and Sikh population, nurtured carefully into a constituency by the BJP's sister organizations such as the Vishwa Hindu Parishad and the Bajrang Dal, the majority, howsoever slender, is still Muslim. If religion becomes the defining factor in the politics of the state, civil society will further lose its civility, and the consequences may be too horrible to even contemplate.

Already, Kashmiri society has started to change. Kashmiri youth today are extremely vulnerable and susceptible to radicalization. The armed insurgency is in its twenty-eighth year. Everyone in the Valley below the age of twenty-six has seen nothing but violence, curfews, cordon and search operations, humiliation and uncertainty. Their entertainment avenues are limited to spending time at mosques or playing cricket or football in one of several graveyards dotting the state, provided there is no curfew or crackdown that day.

They are not radical people right now, only hugely insecure youngsters, who, for want of anything else, have entrusted their judgement to the so-called religious wise men. And here lies the danger. The process of radicalization does not happen in isolation. It needs a mind made receptive by religious indoctrination to take root. The first step is always an obsessive commitment to the fundamentals of religion and blind faith in the local preacher. The second step is the cause that cultivates and fans the sense of injustice.

Innumerable examples of this exist in the case studies of young men in different European states who wake up one day to enrol themselves for jihad, earlier in Afghanistan and now in Iraq and Syria. The biggest mistake that the West has made in addressing the issue of radicalization is to dismiss the cause. It is almost impossible for a person, with the promise of a fulfilling life ahead, to choose death without a cause. Since we usually emulate the West, we are making the same mistake in Kashmir—dismissing insurgents as either misguided youth or denouncing them as terrorists, as if they are operating completely without a context.

For the burgeoning youth of Kashmir, the cause was always there. Now it is being nurtured through careful religious indoctrination. 'In the last twenty years, madrassas have mushroomed all over the state. Most of them are one-room tenements,' a middle-level police officer posted in south Kashmir told the authors. According to him, there is no accounting of their funding or syllabi, despite the fact that everyone knows that money comes from West Asia, especially Saudi Arabia. 'The successive state governments have had a hands-off approach, saying that since they do not take any money from the state, the government has no control over them. But in the interest of the future of the state, some sort of auditing must be carried out of these madrassas,' he said.

Posted in the part of the Valley that in recent times has had the highest number of youth picking up guns, the police officer had done his homework. In 2015 alone, sixty-five boys from south Kashmir joined militant groups, essentially the Hizbul Mujahideen. And with the exception of one who was a police constable, the rest were young, semi-educated, unemployed boys with an obsessive commitment towards ritualistic religion. Needless to say their favourite haunts were the mosques.

◆

Islam arrived in India in all its various permutations and combinations over a period of time. However, in Kashmir, it was the Sufi strand of Islam which caught on, primarily because the Sufis rejected little and embraced everything. The so-called syncretism of Kashmir or Kashmiriyat emanated primarily from Sufi thought, which combined metaphysics with the religious. There was no conflict in coexistence with other faiths and practices despite the fact that Kashmir, as a society, was deeply religious, whichever be the religion. Even when revisionist, or what is referred to as reformist, Islam swept through the world, including parts of India, in Kashmir it could not make much of a mark.

However, years of exposure to violence has changed all that. While in absolute terms, Sufism may still be the dominant strain of Islam in Kashmir, newer and more exclusivist sects have emerged as the favourite of the young. There are many reasons for that.

One, the puritan sects demand little intellectual investment from their followers. All they ask is absolute and complete adherence to their interpretation of the Quran and the Hadith. Today, there are so many Hadiths, quite a few compiled by people two generations removed from Prophet Muhammad, that even contradictory injunctions can be justified by quoting some obscure text. Even the ones that can be rightfully attributed to the Prophet were relevant in the context in which they were said or occurred. They cannot hold up under all circumstances.

Two, given the long list of proscriptions, following the religious path becomes very arduous for devotees, leading to the feeling that they are on the right path. After all, isn't the righteous path more difficult? This is something akin to performing a pilgrimage on a daily basis. Moreover, this makes one aspire for paradise even more fervently.

Three, an increasing number of young people are technology-savvy. A technical mind prefers a simplistic religion with clear-cut tasks and goals. The amorphous, informal and all-encompassing Sufi thinking simply urges each individual to walk his or her own path. It is not formulaic but enables voyages of discovery, not the sort of thing a certain kind of young person is looking for. This is also the reason why the easiest people to get radicalized have studied technology. Their minds are already trained to learn and execute formulas and equations.

The biggest concern here is that the youth which is relentlessly exposed to such a puritanical form of religion ceases the habit of independent thinking and becomes susceptible to indoctrination. Puritanism, by definition, implies intolerance for dissent and different viewpoints. Since the puritan is convinced that only he is on the right path, he has only two choices. Either get others onto your path through proselytizing (Dawah) or simply shun them. It is also not difficult to justify to oneself that since the others are already doomed in the hereafter, their fate in this world is of little consequence. Religious violence is just the next step.

While this is universally applicable, for India this is the most worrying reality of Kashmir today, because the failure to resolve the issue has now ladled religious extremism into the already churning cauldron of political discontent. The insurgency exposed the Kashmiri to foreign forms of puritan Islam which disparaged the indigenous and inclusive religion followed by the locals.

As the offshoots of the so-called Wahhabi/Salafi line of Islam started to take root in Kashmir, several Kashmiris the authors have spoken to over the years have alleged that the formation of some moderate Islamic sects in the state owe their existence to the government. This was because the state believed this would be one way of countering the Saudi brand of Islam. According to the locals, the Ahle-Sunnat Dawat-e-Islami sect (a derivative of the Barelvi sect) has been New Delhi's gift to Kashmir.

What the state failed to foresee was that even a moderate sect is a sect nevertheless. To increase its base and to keep its flock from wandering over to a different sect, it has to perforce preach intolerance of other sects. Imagine a society divided into religious communities of a few hundred thousand, each convinced that only it is right. That would be a radical society the likes of which has hitherto not existed in the subcontinent. Weekly waving of the ISIS (Islamic State in Iraq and Syria) flag is not a measure of radicalism; it is just disillusionment and helpless anger.

This probably weighed on Prime Minister Modi's mind. In the second week of July 2015, the government sent Asif Ibrahim, former director, Intelligence Bureau, and special envoy for counter-insurgency (CI) and extremism, to the Valley to assess the extent of radicalization. He was accompanied by Dineshwar Sharma, director of the Intelligence Bureau. A few days later, National Security Advisor Ajit Doval also visited Srinagar and met the same set of people: governor, chief minister, 15 Corps commander, director general police, J&K, inspector general police, Kashmir zone, and inspector general police, CID. It is not known what they discovered, but whatever it was it has been guiding the government's uneven steps on talks with Pakistan. Despite its unwillingness to include the Kashmir issue in the talks, it has been unable to keep it out.

That said, it continues to ignore the fact that Pakistan will not allow the issue to be put on the back-burner.

For instance, the protests that followed the killing of Burhan Wani, the twenty-one-year-old Hizbul Mujahideen commander, by Indian security forces on 8 July 2016 were yet another example of Pakistan exploiting Indian fault lines in Kashmir. The moment the news of Wani's death spread, the entire Valley erupted in an outpouring of grief and protests. By the government's own assessment, over 200,000 people joined in Wani's funeral prayers, though local journalists claim a figure of half a million. Such numbers are unheard of, even in a place where people are known to honour militants killed by Indian security forces as martyrs. Yet, the government, both the union, and at its behest the state, continued to treat sustained street protests as a law and order problem created by Pakistan. As opposition parties rallied around the government to present a united front against Pakistan, all failed to notice how the present crisis was unprecedented, at least for three reasons.

One, for the first time, protests and violence has spread to all districts of the Valley, including the border areas. In the past, whether it was the violent nineties or the ugly events of 2010 (when nearly 120 youth were killed in police and CRPF firings over three months), Kashmir has always had islands of calm unaffected by the chaos elsewhere. Not this time.

Secondly, unlike the past, this time, people were not merely picketing bunkers or public property, they were marching towards the camps of the security forces and attacking them. The rage is directed towards not just the security personnel but all those civilians who are seen to be on the side of the Indian state, including elected legislators. According to some reports, the Kashmiri Members of the Legislative Assembly (MLAs) went into hiding to escape the brunt of public anger. So much so that when the Peoples' Democratic Party MLA, Khalil Bandh, was injured in one of the protests, he could not be admitted to any civilian hospital but had to be treated at the army base hospital. Is this not the erosion of credibility of the people's representatives?

And thirdly, it has brought together the disparate factions of the separatists who are now speaking in one voice; they recently issued an appeal to all the hiding MLAs to switch sides. Now, whether this voice is at the behest of Pakistan is immaterial, because unity is strength. Moreover, as long as the separatists were disunited, the Government of India at least had a channel of communication with several of them, whom it called moderate. Not any longer.

Unfortunately, overwhelmed by the sense of the street, with relentless protests against 'terrorist' Burhan Wani's killing, all that the politicians in Delhi have been able to do is once again resort to nationalistic rhetoric and sloganeering. If only the government had imagination, it would have understood what Wani represented for the people of Kashmir. Of course, he was a radicalized youth who took up arms against the Indian state because of the atrocities he saw and suffered in his teens at the hands of the Indian security forces. But he was no renegade; by throwing away his mask and revealing his face, he raised the level of his so-called movement. He conveyed to his people that he had both courage and conviction to stand up for his cause; that he was neither a terrorist nor a mercenary. Those who mourn him do so out of genuine feeling. Of course, Pakistan has a role in the street protests and violence, but not in the outpouring of grief for Wani, whose face lent a new credibility to the insurgency. The Government of India killed a local hero, and resurrected a legend. And it doesn't even realize how this is changing the situation on the ground. The people are becoming increasingly restive because they had come so close to a semblance of permanent peace in the halcyon years of 2005–08. The Government of India can of course commit more troops to quell the turmoil, but it will be at a military cost.

Military considerations aside, an unresolved Kashmir shackles India, holds it back through two military-determined lines, undermines its moral stature globally and increases its vulnerability to China. 'Just imagine,' said Professor Bhat, 'if the Kashmir issue is resolved, the biggest thorn in India-Pakistan relations will be removed forever. Kashmir, and along with it, India and Pakistan, will prosper because of open trade through a network of roads and mountain passes linking it with Central Asia, Afghanistan, Tibet and even China. Economic prosperity will curb the tendency towards religious extremism too.' And perhaps, with this cross-linking of economic activities, China will become less of a threat to India.

It may be a flight of fancy, but it's a dream worth nurturing. The state of Jammu and Kashmir is the only place that gives Pakistan and China a physical link-up. While any Kashmir resolution with Pakistan will not remove the connection, it is likely to reduce its volatility. Most importantly, it will relieve the Indian Army from its counter-insurgency role. Perhaps then it will be able to look at the big picture emerging on India's north and east.

As we have seen, in 1965 when Pakistan tried to raise the Kashmir banner, the locals stood with India. Yet instead of cashing in on its biggest advantage in the Valley—the people's support—India squandered it away by opportunist politics, thereby giving Pakistan a foothold inside Kashmir. Thereafter small pockets of resentment have grown into full-fledged insurgency. Today, even if the Government of India takes all kinds of ameliorative measures to meet the aspirations of the people, a resolution without Pakistan is no longer possible; and with the China-Pakistan Economic Corridor, China's stakes will also grow in the Valley. As will the desire of the average Kashmiri to jump on the CPEC's economic bandwagon, which promises growth and prosperity.

The Government of India's policy of status quo has been yielding diminishing returns, because both Pakistan and China have been working extremely hard to change the ground situation. While an honourable and cooperative resolution is still in the realms of possibility today, Chinese activities in Ladakh are changing the situation so rapidly that in a few years this option may no longer be there.

CHAPTER 9

THREAT TO LADAKH

If there is one place where foresight has converged with geography, it is Ladakh, the only area where China and Pakistan have forged a physical link. It is also the only place where the threat of a two-front war against India is in the realm of possibility and not mere conjecture. And this is one confrontation that has been in the making for close to half a century.

Within months of assuming power, the Communist government of China occupied Aksai Chin, securing its land corridor to Xinjiang. During the 1962 war with India, it further pushed its claims to secure areas west of Karakoram (northeastern Ladakh). This was meant to provide depth for the land route to Xinjiang from mainland China. A year later, it persuaded Pakistan to cede the Shaksgam Valley in north Kashmir so that feeder roads to the Karakoram Highway (connecting China and Pakistan) could be constructed, linking Kashgar in Xinjiang with Gilgit. China assuaged Indian protests by saying that it considers Gilgit-Baltistan disputed territory and will renegotiate the land agreement with the country that gets control of the region after the resolution of the Kashmir issue. Incidentally, for all these years that China has been in border talks with India it has deliberately not discussed the western portion of the Karakoram with India.

But in December 2010, China changed its mind. It announced that it did not have a border with India in Ladakh. Thereafter, Pakistan signed an agreement with China for the development of the Gwadar Port which would be connected to Xinjiang through the famous China-Pakistan Economic Corridor (CPEC) running through north Kashmir.

Like the stones on the wei qi board, where each player tries to surround the opponent in such a manner that he is left with no option but to surrender, China and Pakistan have been encircling Ladakh, limiting India's options with each patient move. It is only a matter of time before the two strategic partners decide to inflict the final blow. From their perspective, they have reasons to do so.

The reason for Pakistan is India's new stance on Jammu and Kashmir. Instead of the Kashmir resolution (an international dispute listed at the United Nations), India, under Modi in August 2016, declared its intention to get back the Kashmir territory under Pakistan (and China) occupation. Interestingly, India has merely 42,000 square miles under its control while China and Pakistan have a total of 47,645 square miles under their control. China, which regards the CPEC (that runs along the disputed Kashmir territory under Pakistan control) as important for its global rise is not pleased with India's altered position on Kashmir.

Therefore, the Pakistan Army's strategic objective for a localized war in north Ladakh could be to provide depth to the CPEC; the political objective could be to make India's hold over the Kashmir Valley tenuous; the military objective could be to force the Indian Army out of the Siachen Glacier; and the diplomatic objective could be to draw the international community's attention to the possibility of a full-scale war between adversaries with nuclear weapons. China would surely welcome depth for the CPEC.

Given China's capabilities and Pakistan's acquired expertise, the localized conflict in north Kashmir could be a non-contact war. However, before we see how the conflict might play out, it is important to see how even geography is against India in this area.

Of the six major mountain ranges in the region—Kunlun, Pamir, Hindu Kush, Karakoram, the Great Himalayas and the Pir Panjal—India has traditionally given importance to the Great Himalayan Range, which until the 1962 war was considered impregnable. Pakistan and China, with a keener sense of geography, have understood geopolitics better and hence the importance of the Karakoram. Pakistan's understanding was the takeaway from the British who grasped the geopolitics around the old Silk Route which passed along the base of the Siachen Glacier towards the Karakoram Pass and onto East Turkestan (now Xinjiang in China).

The Karakoram Range, more formidable than the Great Himalayas, can be crossed only through two prominent passes. The KK Pass (18,176 feet) in the east is more difficult, but is the shortest route from Leh (capital of Ladakh) to Xinjiang. Interestingly, the Pakistani version of NJ 9842 (the northernmost point of the LC) running eastward (trigger for the 1984 Siachen war) terminates at KK Pass. The KK Pass, which has witnessed exchange of trade and religion between Ladakh and East Turkestan through the centuries, was accepted (though not formally) as the border between British India and China. The canny British kept pressing China to agree to the boundary further east along the Kunlun Range, which Peking never agreed to. Then, as now, the Leh-Sasoma-Sasser Ridge crossing at Sasser La-Daulat Beg Oldi-KK Pass is the main route that connects Leh with Chinese territory. The Sasser Ridge roughly separates the Siachen Glacier from east Ladakh.

In the absence of a road it takes Indian troops anything from eighteen to twenty-five days to trudge the treacherous track along Sasoma, Sasser La to Chungtash, Margo and Burtse near Daulat Beg Oldi (DBO) where, until April 2013, the Indian Army only had a company (about 100 soldiers) in place. The Indian Army has a vehicle relay service on this route—once troops cross the Sasser La and come to Chungtash they are ferried onwards towards DBO in vehicles. DBO is 16 kilometres south of the Karakoram Pass.

The Indian Army has opened up another route to reach DBO. It runs from Tangtse northwards to Darbuk and then goes along the Shyok River, crossing it at two points—one downstream and the other upstream—to finally reach DBO. In the summer months, between May and October, this route is unavailable as the Shyok River gets flooded because of the melting glaciers, making crossing it downstream impossible. During this period, only the Sasoma route is available to reach DBO. Efforts are on to make this easier road route (where troops do not have to walk with loads) available throughout the year.

According to a July 2016 media report quoting Colonel B. S. Uppal who is posted there, 'while work on the 255 kilometres Darbuk-Shyok-DBO is progressing with a 150 kilometres bridge from Darbuk over Shyok river under construction, the complete road would be made only by 2022'.

Given such topography, extreme weather conditions at altitudes of 18,000 feet and above, and lack of infrastructure on the Indian side, it is a mammoth task for the Indian Army to guard DBO and surrounding areas including the Depsang Plain. Called the sub-sector north (SSN), this area is extremely vulnerable to ingress by the PLA as they have roads on their side right up to the LAC.

The other pass on Karakoram is Khunjerab (15,397 feet) in the north, across which the famed Karakoram Highway runs. The distance between the Khunjerab and Karakoram passes is a mere 18 kilometres. The southern end of Shaksgam Valley is close to the northern tip of the KK Pass. The Karakoram Range provides depth to China's western region and the restive Xinjiang province; provides good observation into most of Ladakh (especially the Siachen Glacier) held by Indian troops; and gives China a firm foothold into the bilateral Kashmir dispute between India and Pakistan. For Pakistan, the Karakoram Range provides the land route to China, which opens up military options against arch-enemy India.

The Karakoram Range has two mountain spurs running southwards. The Sasser and Saltoro ridgelines are on the eastward spur. While the Siachen Glacier lies between the Sasser and Saltoro ridgelines, the Saltoro Ridge—a distinct watershed feature in the area—separates Indian and Pakistani forces which have been fighting for the Siachen Glacier since April 1984. The other offshoot spur has glaciers which run westwards into the Pakistan-occupied area converging into the flat space at Dansum at 10,000 feet.

Coming back to the war, the PLA has constructed a road from its garrison having battalion strength (1,000 troops) near the KK Pass to its post on the pass. From atop Teram Sher Glacier, west of the KK Pass, the north and central portions of the Siachen Glacier are in full view. What stops the PLA from helping the Pakistan Army with good observation from Teram Sher Glacier? Aided by the observation provided by the PLA, the Pakistan Army, could fire its Babur cruise missiles (with conventional warheads in large numbers) to both interdict the Indian Army's logistics lifeline from the base camp to the glacier and on troops' positions itself. The contention of the Indian Army that they would retaliate with BRAHMOS missiles is unrealistic. Given the defunct infrastructure and limited deployment spaces which would be under Pakistani counter-fire, where would the BRAHMOS be positioned? Who would give them accurate coordinates to direct fire? What if the BRAHMOS kills Chinese citizens who are in POK?

This could anger China which might decide to throw its weight behind the Pakistan Army to enforce the NJ 9842-Karakoram line with national security implications for India. The PLA could share its asymmetrical military assets including anti-satellite capabilities, armed unmanned aerial vehicles and cruise missiles with the Pakistan Army through the Karakoram Highway. They could exercise all options short of air. The PLA Special Forces could occupy Fukche and even DBO advanced landing grounds. After the IAF activated these advanced landing grounds, China had protested to India. It will not be possible for the Indian Army to dislodge PLA forces from the advanced landing grounds without serious escalation. The PLA could move its forces to where they had come in April–May 2013 facing the Indian Army battalion in Burtse. With the Pakistan Army pounding Babur missiles, it will be difficult for the Indian Army to send logistics and troop reinforcements to the Burtse battalion. Any use of the IAF during this period will escalate matters forcing the PLA to fight in self-defence.

In a military pincer, Indian positions on the Saltoro Ridge and the Siachen Glacier could be outflanked. The Pakistan Army could attempt to capture NJ 9842 in sub-sector west presently held by India, and the PLA could sever India's operational logistics by land and air maintenance to sub-sector north facing the Chinese in Ladakh. In an area of little collateral damage, the two allies have the capability and reasons to send a powerful message to India.

The Pakistan Army meanwhile could attempt to send hundreds of terrorists across the Line of Control. The Indian Army, which would be reorienting itself from anti-infiltration to conventional war, would find it extremely difficult to deal with the terrorist influx. In a replay of the Kargil conflict, bureaucrats of the defence ministry would be flying across the globe to get ammunition, spares and other war-withal since the Indian Army would not have war wastage reserves to fight for long.

The above scenario could lead to two consequences: one, Indian troops after weeks of accurate pounding by Babur missiles, which would affect their lifeline especially if kerosene pipelines burst, could be forced to vacate the north and central glacier, partially or fully. Two, as the consequence of India's BRAHMOS firing which might kill Chinese workers, the PLA could take a tough position by quick mobilization, thereby further limiting India's options. Use of the IAF would be dangerous. Keeping the troops on the glacier without much overhead cover and logistics would be suicidal. Withdrawing them, which would be celebrated on Pakistani television, would be India's defeat.

This localized war could have three distinctive features: it would be slow and long-drawn-out rather than short, swift and intense; Pakistan would keep the war localized knowing that India lacks the capability to enlarge it; and it would be non-contact, implying no troops assaulting each other at high altitudes.

Yet the Indian Army, which raced to occupy the Siachen Glacier in haste lest the Pakistan Army reach there first, now believes that the situation is not so grim in north Ladakh. After conversations with senior officers of the armed forces, it is the authors' understanding that the army is somewhat less concerned about the situation in the area for the following reasons: One, as China has no political and military objectives in this area it has little reason to build up its troops there. Two, if the PLA indeed crosses the LAC, they will have problems on the Indian side: lack of infrastructure and lay-of-the-land where there are defiles and bottlenecks which will constrain them from moving linearly; they will then become easy targets of Indian Army fire. And, three, like the PLA in eastern Ladakh, the Pakistan Army on the other side will have similar problems.

The bottlenecks referred to above are Khapalu and Yargo-ferry (bridge), which provides operational logistics to Pakistani forces fighting for the Siachen Glacier. The Indian Army can hit these with accurate BRAHMOS steep-dive capability cruise missiles. Moreover, as the Indian Army stocks up to 270 days rations on the glacier itself, it will be an extremely long siege for the PLA and Pakistan Army combine to compel Indian forces to vacate Siachen. Reportedly, the Indian Army has war-gamed these scenarios.

When all is well, all war-gaming is done according to realistic and logical scenarios. But war games aside, could the Indian Army have even dreamt of the Pakistan Army carrying out the 1999 Kargil aggression? So long as vulnerability exists, a non-status quo power will always attempt to exploit it. In the 1999 Kargil conflict, large swathes of territories in high-altitude areas were left unguarded. At present, north Ladakh, especially sub-sector north, is extremely vulnerable to the PLA and the Pakistan Army.

Ladakh has featured prominently in all wars fought by India with Pakistan. After the 1947–48 war, the ceasefire line ended at map point NJ 9842 in Ladakh. During the 1965 war, territories gained in war were returned after the ceasefire. In the 1971 war, the Indian Army captured 22 kilometres in the Turtok sector (Ladakh) which it traded for Pakistan's gains made in the Chhamb sector. These two tactical changes resulted in the Ceasefire Line becoming the Line of Control after the 1971 war.

All these years, as India was fighting the Pakistan Army in the west on the Siachen Glacier, the eastern front facing China was quiet. This changed with the 2013 Depsang intrusion—India's eastern front became more dangerous than the western one. The PLA, without any fight, managed to compel India to alter the LAC in the area; it may only be a matter of time before the PLA shifts the LAC still closer to Sasser Ridge beyond China's 1960 claim line. The Indian Army on the Siachen Glacier (from 15,000 to 23,000 feet) wedged between the two—the Pakistan Army west of Saltoro Ridge and the PLA east of Sasser Ridge—would be hemmed in from both sides.

The folly of the Indian Army in having occupied the Siachen Glacier is obvious. As said earlier, had they instead occupied the lower flat area, Dansum, west of the Saltoro Ridge, they would have been better positioned—the troops would have been at lower heights and more than one logistics lifeline would have been available—to militarily take on the localized two-front threat.

Given the faulty occupation of the Siachen Glacier, the Indian Army is now constrained in the west against Pakistan on two counts: it has little room for manoeuvre, and it has a single logistics lifeline from the base camp of the glacier going northwards to supply troops perched on heights. This is an arduous climb for troops as they negotiate unpredictable terrain riddled with crevasses. Food supplies are airdropped both at the base camp and onto the glacier itself. The kerosene oil pipelines, which are critical to keep troops warm in inclement weather, are out in the open. In short, logistics without which troops cannot sustain themselves are easy targets provided good observation and accurate long-range fire is available to Pakistan.

Following the April 2013 Depsang incursion, the Indian Army took a few precautionary measures to meet the PLA challenge in eastern Ladakh. It increased the strength of troops to a battalion (1,000 soldiers) in Burtse near Daulat Beg Oldi to thwart a PLA thrust from sub-sector north of eastern Ladakh. Moreover, there are now three brigades (3,500 soldiers each) for eastern Ladakh, and a mechanized battalion of BMP-II near Leh. There are plans for one more infantry brigade and an armoured brigade (with over 100 tanks) in the theatre by the end of the twelfth defence plan (2012–17).

In July 2016, according to media reports, Indian Army officers said that they could not conduct the entire range of exercises since they didn't have the requisite firing ranges. This is a serious issue. Since tanks are nothing more than moving guns, the latter, if not calibrated by test-firings, will not fire accurately in rarefied high-altitude weather conditions.

The rarefied atmosphere will affect the functioning of missiles too. For example, the accuracy of Russian Kornet-E anti-tank guided missiles procured during the 1999 Kargil conflict with Pakistan suffered due to high altitude. They needed modification and recalibration for firing at that altitude. Since this was not done, 90 per cent of the missiles fired missed their targets. With the induction of anti-tank guided missiles and tanks, recalibration of weapons is a critical requirement. Another question which few have thought about is how the PLA would react to the provocation of the Indian Army test-firing weapons in east Ladakh. Indian Army officers concede that it will be difficult to stop a PLA thrust of six to eight divisions—each with about 10,000 mechanized soldiers from Lanzhou Military Region—across three axes along sub-sector north, sub-sector middle and sub-sector south. The PLA has formidable capabilities to mobilize its rapid reaction forces.

On the Indian side there is not much deployment space in the theatre; even the three brigades presently there are finding it difficult to be effective in the area. Then there is the problem of connectivity by land and air. Of the two road links to mainland India, the road through Himachal Pradesh (Manali-Leh road) is shorter and bypasses both the Jammu and Kashmir regions. But it is more treacherous, reaching altitudes as high as 17,400 feet (Tanglang La), is prone to landslides and is closed for a good part of the year. The other road meanders across the Pir Panjal Range, is longer and has lower altitude throughout with the highest pass at about 13,478 feet (Fotu La). On good days—the Manali route is open seventy to eighty days and the other route about one hundred days in a year—both demand a minimum of three days on the road. And if the weather packs up or there is a landslide, the journey could take much longer.

As far as air connectivity goes, the story is similar. The IAF plans to have Nyoma developed with a full-fledged runway and airport. Two more advanced landing grounds at Daulat Beg Oldi and Fukche have been developed. The question that few are willing to reckon with is whether the three advanced landing grounds will be available during a war. Build-up of troops is one thing, but to maintain air connectivity against a hostile PLA will be an entirely different matter.

The connectivity constraints will translate into operational limitations. The worst affected will be north Ladakh. Providing logistics and reinforcement to troops at Burtse would be extremely difficult. In addition, there are a total of 4.5 battalions (each with 1,200 men) of the Indo-Tibetan Border Police (ITBP) in eastern Ladakh which are the first line of defence (observation) ahead of the army. The ITBP is dependent on the army for its logistics supplies.

Then there is the issue of weather, which for most part of the day and year is not conducive to flying. This will affect intelligence, surveillance and reconnaissance by air, especially unmanned aerial vehicles. Moreover, as has been noted, the rarefied atmosphere will affect the functioning of missiles. And the troops themselves would require acclimatization, a three-stage, time-consuming procedure.

The Indian Air Force has two air bases—Leh at 10,680 feet and Thoise at 10,066 feet—straddling the Khardung La on the Ladakh Range (south of Karakoram) with overall control vested in the air officer commanding, J&K Headquarters, based in Udhampur. While both are full-fledged forward air bases, they have been involved round the clock since 1984 when the Siachen conflict began, in air maintenance of troops on the glacier and posts in sub-sector north facing China. The absence of roads in these areas has created an unusual dilemma for the IAF: how to continue with air maintenance, which is the lifeline for troops, to these areas even during hostilities, as well as actively participate in the air war.

While night flying is possible from both air bases, it has been limited to fixed-wing aircraft for air maintenance. Combat aircraft like the Su-30MKI have made daytime landings in Leh and Thoise, weather conditions permitting. There are three operational shortcomings which are underplayed here: altitude, air defence and training for war by itself, as well as with the army and with air-to-air refuellers. The weapon load carrying capacity of combat aircraft has been severely constrained especially when taking off from Thoise. Leh is more difficult than Thoise for combat operations. Leh, surrounded by mountains, provides a difficult funnel approach to aircraft. It would take hours of sustained and regular flying here to understand the problems of flying with and without weapon loads in high-altitude areas, the targeting profiles which are different from those in the plains, and to understand the operational logistics needed at these air bases.

The location of the two air bases poses serious difficulties for air defence. The answer lies in using these air bases as staging airfields with help from air-to-air refuellers. Regarding training for war, no air exercises by the IAF and those in support of the army have reportedly been held (unlike the Pakistan Air Force and the PLAAF). While officers say that war plans through joint staff work for cooperation between the air force and army exist, what good are they if they have not been validated by practical training? In reality, the situation since the Kargil conflict has not changed much.

If India wants to prevent a nightmarish scenario from developing in north Ladakh, it should: prepare for a major crisis leading to the escalation of hostilities in north Kashmir. Or it should pre-empt this with a good peacemaking strategy. Doing neither is suicidal.

CHAPTER 10

AFSPA AND OTHER DISCONTENTS

In the summer of 2007, with the state assembly elections due in a year and a half, Major General Ramesh Halgali, general officer commanding, 19 Division, based in Baramullah, looked fondly at the fruit-laden apple trees lining the highway and said, 'We have been here for far too long. The situation in the Valley is about as normal as it is likely to get given that the insurgents have safe havens across the border. We should now be going back to our primary task. I think the good time to do that would be after the assembly elections in 2008. By 2009, we must start pulling out progressively.'

Does the higher hierarchy in the army think that they should get out of counter-insurgency operations (CI ops) in Kashmir?

'Of course. The army doesn't want to do this forever. Our job is on the Line of Control,' he said. 'We must use the time between now and the elections to consolidate our gains and gradually hand over CI ops [being carried out by the army's CI force Rashtriya Rifles] to the CRPF [Central Reserve Police Force],' he said, still looking at the pre-harvest bounty of apples like an indulgent gardener through the window of his jeep. The cool breeze was redolent with the fragrance of ripe apples. Halgali (along with the authors) was driving back to his headquarters from a ceremony at which a dozen reluctant militants, who had crossed the LC into POK for training, had surrendered and now wanted to reclaim their old lives.

Kashmiri children returning from school, walking along the highway waved at the moving car. Halgali waved back, smiling wistfully. 'My mother loves spending the summer here. This place is beautiful and the weather so pleasant. She enjoys looking at the local girls,' he said, with an embarrassed grin. '"Look at their cheeks," she says, "they are like Kashmiri apples." She is going to miss all this once I am posted out.'

The general was indeed posted out within a few months but the army has continued with CI ops in Kashmir, a role it had accepted with reluctance when the rising tide of insurgency in 1989 had left the Government of

India both clueless and helpless. As usually happens in such circumstances, all that the government could think of at that time was 'call the army'. The government enacted the Armed Forces (Jammu & Kashmir) Special Powers Act (AFSPA), 1990 'to enable certain special powers to be conferred upon members of the armed forces in the disturbed areas in the State of Jammu and Kashmir'.

The army was chary of getting into another internal security situation. Army chief General S. F. Rodrigues, during whose tenure (June 1990–June 1993), a large number of regular army troops were brought into Kashmir insisted on calling it aid to civil power, and hence temporary in nature. He didn't think that the army would be in the Valley for a long time.

His successor General B. C. Joshi also felt the same way, though he understood that the army was conducting CI ops. As we have seen, to make the distinction between the regular army and a CI force (a token distinction, essentially to send out a message that the regular army was not involved in CI ops), he expedited the raising of Rashtriya Rifles (RR) for the J&K theatre in 1994. The idea of RR was first mooted in 1987 by the Minister of State for Defence, Arun Singh, and the Chief of Army Staff, General K. Sundarji, for the Northeast. Nomenclature apart, the RR was and remains regular army, but with a temporary paramilitary status.

These raisings over the next decade saw RR numbers rise with five Force Headquarters: Victor and Kilo in the Valley; and Romeo, Delta and Uniform in the Jammu division. Since it was expected to be a temporary job, the mandate for the RR remains ad hoc. The reluctant force gradually became comfortable in the new job and started convincing itself that this was indeed its main task, progressively coining new terminology, from 'attack by infiltration', 'low-intensity conflict', 'proxy war', 'irregular warfare' to 'hybrid warfare'.

The run-up to the assembly elections of 2008 perhaps saw the last of those reluctant officers. A number of them, both in New Delhi and Kashmir, spoke about the peaceful conduct of the elections as the benchmark to determine whether the army should recommend to the government that its secondary job (stabilizing the internal situation in Kashmir) was done and that it needed to get back to its primary job (conventional war-preparedness). With this, the government could progressively revoke AFSPA in the state.

The 2008 elections passed off peacefully, despite fears to the contrary. The voter turnout broke the previous record, just as the following elections in 2014 surpassed the 2008 turnout percentage. Within days of the culmination of polling, even before the results were announced, the National Conference's

Omar Abdullah, who was confident of forming the government, said, 'In view of peaceful elections, there is a case to be made for force (army) reduction in the state and a gradual increase in the role of the J&K police... There are areas now where this gradual withdrawal can take place... You don't need Pakistan to reduce the level of Rashtriya Rifles...'

Despite several political crises during the year, Chief Minister Omar Abdullah continued to urge revocation of the act, which is considered draconian, whether in Kashmir or the Northeast. In an interview to *FORCE* magazine in December 2009, he said, 'I believe that the revocation of AFSPA will happen in this government's term...the discussions to modify AFSPA are at a very advanced stage.'

However, what he had not bargained for was that the discussions had run into formidable resistance from the Indian Army, which refused to even consider modifications to the act. Lieutenant General V. R. Raghavan, who was one of the members of the Justice Jeevan Reddy Committee for the review of AFSPA, said, 'Blaming the Act is wrong. There is nothing in the Act that can be changed, but it should not be applied indefinitely.'

Even as the debate on AFSPA raged, serving army officers, including the chief of army staff, made their position known through periodic press statements throughout 2010. Meanwhile, the union government struggled over the Act, as a series of recommendations came out against AFSPA.

The three interlocutors appointed by the union government after the bloody summer of 2010 in the Valley recommended revocation of AFSPA in their report. Earlier, the prime minister-appointed Working Group on Confidence Building Measures in J&K had also recommended revocation of AFSPA. In fact, all committees ever appointed in any part of the country where AFSPA is operational have recommended its revocation. In 2013, the government appointed the Justice Santosh Hegde Committee to investigate extrajudicial killings in Manipur. In its report, the committee urged the revocation of AFSPA, as it noted that, 'Though the Act gives sweeping powers to security forces even to extent of killing a suspect with protection against prosecution, it does not provide any protection to the citizens against its possible misuse... Normally, the greater the power, the greater the restraint and stricter the mechanism to prevent its misuse or abuse. But in case of the AFSPA in Manipur this principle appears to have been reversed.' Such has been the groundswell against AFSPA, that the Justice J. S. Verma Committee appointed after the brutal gang rape of a young woman on 16 December 2012 in New Delhi to recommend more stringent laws against sexual crimes and violence, met women from J&K and observed that AFSPA legitimized 'impunity of systematic sexual violence' in places where it was in force. The committee recommended that the act be reviewed and revoked where possible. Moreover, in cases of sexual crimes, it recommended that offenders from the armed forces be tried under the civil law without the protection of AFSPA.

A former home secretary told the authors that in one of the Cabinet Committee on Security meetings Prime Minister Manmohan Singh had to play peacemaker between Home Minister P. Chidambaram, who favoured selective revocation of the act from Kashmir, and the Defence Minister A. K. Antony, who was vehemently opposed to it on the advice of the army. In several heated exchanges, the defence ministry's view prevailed repeatedly, because the government with no political resolution at hand didn't want to be on the wrong side of military advice, especially when that advice was followed by the frightening spectre of spiralling violence.

Building a doomsday scenario in the Unified Headquarters meeting held in Kashmir in November 2011 and chaired by Chief Minister Omar Abdullah, the Srinagar-based 15 Corps Commander, Lieutenant General Syed Ata Hasnain, gave a PowerPoint presentation to the assembled officials from the state police, CRPF and the Intelligence Bureau. One of his slides read, 'While the State people were seeking bijli, sadak, paani (electricity, roads, water), calls for lifting the AFSPA were coming from four categories: Pakistan, the Inter-Services Intelligence Directorate, terrorists and secessionists'. The miffed chief minister told the corps commander to leave the slide behind so that he could see 'where I fit in'.

As the chief minister upped the ante on AFSPA, the union government took refuge in obfuscation. First it said that AFSPA could only be revoked if the state government withdrew the Disturbed Areas Act. Given this liberty, Abdullah announced his intention of lifting the Disturbed Areas Act and AFSPA from four towns, two each in Jammu and Kashmir, namely, Jammu, Udhampur, Srinagar and Budgam. Faced with this ultimatum, the union government sought legal opinion and discovered that the power to revoke AFPSA rested with the state governor. The state government can only recommend to the governor, but the decision will be his based on the counsel of the union government.

To assuage the growing public outcry and to defuse the crisis, the government announced the creation of two more committees—a state and a central government committee—by the winter of 2011 to explore the manner in which the AFSPA issue ought to be dealt with while taking into account the sensitivities of the Indian Army. The two committees barely met.

In the midst of this, the Indian Army relied on a set of retired general-cadre officers to write articles in the media, setting new benchmarks. The first one was the US drawdown from Afghanistan by the end of 2015. The army argued that once the US forces left Afghanistan, the Taliban would have a free run and Pakistan would transfer the hardened fighters to Kashmir. The logic that the Taliban's first priority after the US exit would more likely be to consolidate its gains in Afghanistan and wrest power from the elected government in Kabul was lost on the army, which appeared to be determined to make the case for continuing with CI ops in Kashmir.

A year later the bar was set even higher, by a person no less than a former army chief. Writing in a national newspaper, he said that AFSPA could only be revoked once normalcy returned to Kashmir. And the sign of normalcy? When 'Kashmiri Pandits will feel confident enough to return… To my mind, the return of Kashmiri Pandits should be our real objective,' wrote the general. Of course, it escaped his attention that normalcy could not be enforced by the military, though a sense of security can be. Normalcy will only return with the resolution of the Kashmir issue with Pakistan.

In early 2015, with the Narendra Modi–led National Democratic Alliance government at the centre, the army raised the bar further. The condition for normalcy now has been set as the integration of Kashmiri people into the national mainstream. 'With very few terrorists left to eliminate, the path to conflict termination and ultimate victory over the adversary lies in smart operations where the contributory effort towards integration of the population is most focused. The task of the RR (Rashtriya Rifles) is to mainstream the entire J&K with rest of the nation. Until that happens the RR is there to stay in the state of J&K.'

The army's resistance to the lifting (even partially) of AFSPA in J&K rests on four arguments. One, it operates in a hostile environment. If it does not have the cover of AFSPA, which grants it immediate immunity against prosecution, then every day a few complaints or cases (true or fabricated) will be brought against it by the local population or vested interests among them. Then instead of doing its job, the army will spend all its time fighting court cases. Two, the army insists that though there may have been a few stray cases, the Indian Army does not commit human rights violations, so the fear of army personnel misusing the act to their personal advantage is exaggerated. Three, over the years, the Rashtriya Rifles have painstakingly built intelligence grids in the state, which have been instrumental in bringing violence under control. Lifting of AFSPA will render these grids untenable. If the situation deteriorates after the army's exit and it is called back again then creating new grids will take a long time and effort. And four, since the army physically holds the Line of Control and its convoys carrying personnel and logistics traverse the state, it needs AFSPA to ensure their safety.

There is a fifth factor, too, which is not voiced openly. The army has been in the counter-insurgency role in J&K for such a long time that it has developed a stake or, crudely put, a vested interest in it. As has been noted, an entire generation of army officers, now in the ranks of generals, has known nothing but CI operations in Kashmir. Their gallantry awards, perks, promotions and personal tales of heroism all come from Kashmir. In fact, a large number of recently retired officers have built new careers as security experts based on their experiences in Kashmir and frequently travel within India and abroad to give talks on the subject. Moreover, the US-led global war on terror and popular movies on counter-terrorist operations like hostage-rescue or raiding of terrorist hideouts, have glamorized CI ops in Kashmir to such an extent that in the last few years the army only talks of this in public forums. With these attendant benefits, the reluctance to leave is understandable.

However, of the four reasons offered by the army, only the first has some merit. On human rights, going by the army's figures, its record in J&K does not appear too bad, but that could be because no credible records have been maintained. Random figures of complaints and mitigation have been offered depending on the recipient of that information. In an interview with the authors in 2006 for an article on human rights, Major General Bobby Syed, the army's deputy director general for public information, said, 'Since 1994, there have been 1,200 charges of human rights violations against the army, of which 1,146 have been investigated and 56 are currently under investigation. 1,094 cases were found to be baseless and in the remaining 54, which were found to be true, punitive action has been taken.'

Yet in May 2008, in response to a right to information petition, the Ministry of Home Affairs said that no records of human rights offences were kept between 1989 and 1994 in Kashmir. Since then there have been 1,122 allegations of human rights violations against the security forces (including the army, paramilitary and the police) of which only 32 were found to be genuine.

Yet another figure was offered in 2004 by the then army chief, General N. C. Vij. He told the National Human Rights Commission that since 1990, 131 army personnel, including officers, have been punished for human rights violations in Kashmir.

In 2015, the International People's Tribunal on Human Rights and Justice in Kashmir and the Association of Parents of Disappeared Persons (APDP) brought out a report in which they accused more than 900 security personnel by name and unit for human rights abuses carried out between 1990 and 2014. The list included 150 officers of the Indian Army in the rank of major or above. The report also documented the extrajudicial killings of 1,080 people, in addition to cases of sexual violence.

Another set of statistics comes from the government of J&K, released in June 2011. According to this report between 1990 and 2011, over 43,000 people were killed in the state. Of these, while 13,226 were civilians killed by armed groups or in crossfire, 3,642 were killed by security forces.

Given the sensitivity of the issue, it is up to the army to answer its critics clearly. Discrepancies need to be eliminated and there needs to be complete transparency.

The third reason is flimsy. Most of the intelligence that the army generates comes from the border areas through the nomadic Gujjar (non-Kashmiri) tribes and these pertain to infiltration. In the hinterland, where the RR operates under the blanket of AFSPA, the primary source of intelligence is the state police and intelligence agencies. Intelligence gathering by its very nature demands secrecy and requires the operatives to remain incognito. No intelligence officer working amongst the people needs AFSPA, which will simply expose him.

The army has been conscious of its limitations, both in terms of intelligence gathering and image-building. In the late 1990s, it started with rudimentary welfare schemes to win the hearts and minds of the people, who after years of battering were both scared and hostile towards the army. The early efforts were determined by the local army leadership, which tried to reach out to the border and rural population by way of organizing periodic health camps, supplying water or building a bus stop. In return, the army expected people to come forward and give information on militants or 'over ground workers'. Letter box-like contraptions were placed in villages for people to quietly slip in papers with the requisite information.

By 2000, the programme coalesced into the organized and centralized Operation Sadbhavana with separate funding from the central government. The manifesto of Operation Sadbhavana tried to be all-encompassing and therefore was less than effective than if it had been specific. Vague objectives like 'Quality Education, Women Empowerment, Community and Infrastructural Development, Health and Veterinary Care, Development of

Gujjars/Bakarwals and Nation Building' didn't help the army to work on a sustained and focused plan.

The fifteen years of Operation Sadbhavana have resulted in thirty Army Goodwill Schools across the state where a total of 9,357 (about 10 per cent of the state's children) study. The devil, though, is in the details. Of the fifteen schools, only three qualify as intermediate schools, the rest being primary or secondary schools.

Despite substantial money and effort being spent on the programme—each RR battalion is given an annual allocation and targets—it has not been able to meet its primary requirements of image management and intelligence gathering. Perhaps, in addition to the vagueness of its objectives, the problem lies in the prefix 'operation' which brings to mind a military action, with not necessarily pleasant connotations. And also in the fact that underlying the supposed good deed is the motive of obtaining intelligence by getting people to tattle about their own to the Indian Army.

Unfortunately, intelligence sought through money is always dubious in nature, as the source usually resells the same information for a higher price. In Kashmir, locals who are seen currying favour with the army make many enemies from among their own people and hence have many scores to settle. In many incidents of human rights violations, the erring soldiers have often been led to the victims by the locals themselves, the supposed beneficiaries of Operation Sadbhavana. This was one of the factors weighing on the minds of the three interlocutors appointed by the Government of India after the tumultuous summer of 2010. Among their recommendations was the revocation of AFSPA and winding up of Operation Sadbhavana.

In an interview in November 2011, M. M. Ansari, one of the interlocutors, said, 'Operation Sadbhavana is further undermining the civil administration in the state...the army has become such an over-arching presence in the state that not many have noticed that it has encroached substantially into areas of administration and governance, which in the long run will be counterproductive. The delivery of basic public services cannot be the army's responsibility unless in the case of a natural disaster or other extreme circumstances.'

In sum, Operation Sadbhavana has not been able to achieve its primary purpose, that is, of winning over the hearts and minds of the people.

Conscious of the failure of Operation Sadbhavana, the government has progressively been curtailing its budgetary allocations; hence its scope is becoming more modest. 'We are not getting into infrastructure building anymore. All we do now is build culverts or roads in the border areas, as they are our requirements too. We are not even building new schools,' a senior officer posted in Srinagar said.

The strongest argument for the revocation of AFSPA, not only from J&K but from all the states where it is in force, is that it is gradually ruining the institution which has been held as the most honourable one in India. Even though the army fails to see it, the biggest victims of AFSPA are army personnel themselves. The overarching umbrella of immunity that the Act provides to uniformed personnel is progressively eroding their ethos and cutting edge. The absence of accountability has led to indiscipline in all ranks, from the lowest to the highest. Successive chiefs of army staff have voiced their concerns about growing indiscipline, insubordination and the loss of values, with at least two of them saying publicly that the army needs to go back to its basic code of ethics.

Such is the state of the Indian Army today that its officers take pride in comparing themselves with the paramilitary forces, of course, holding themselves as better than them. Lieutenant General Raghavan in an interview with the authors said, 'What was supposed to be a temporary arrangement has now become permanent, and the army is being converted into a constabulary.' The Justice Jeevan Reddy Committee sensed this when it wrote in its report that '…the armed forces of the union should not be so deployed, since too frequent a deployment, and that too for long periods of time, carries with it the danger of such forces losing their moorings and becoming, in effect, another police force, prey to all the temptations and weaknesses such exposures involve. Such exposure for long periods of time may well lead to the brutalization of such forces—which is a danger to be particularly guarded against.'

If indeed the army is serious about restoring its cutting edge and not ending up as a 'better' police force, it needs to recommend to the government that it must go back to its primary task. As far as CI ops in the hinterland are concerned, the CRPF can be progressively prepared to take on this task independently or in collaboration with the J&K police. The provisions of the Ranbir Penal Code, which provides legal cover to the J&K police, can be extended to the CRPF.

And the best way to reinforce the CRPF would be to bifurcate it, creating two forces: a counter-insurgency force for theatres like J&K, the Northeast and regions affected by left-wing extremism; and a central police force to support state police forces in law and order situations. As a CI force, the CRPF ought to be trained in the theatre training schools of the Indian Army, both in Jammu and Kashmir and the Northeast, probably by army personnel.

Reorganization of this force will call for some really tough decisions, cutting across vested interests, both of the services and the ministries (there is likely to be a tug of war between the ministries of defence and home affairs), because a CI force, trained, equipped and oriented on the lines of a 'para' military cannot reasonably be led by police officers. Since bringing in Indian Army officers will only lead to the creation of another Assam Rifles, the best solution would be to train cadre officers for command roles. A small percentage of vacancies can be created for army officers for lateral induction, but this number must remain small to ensure both upward mobility and motivation.

Even as this will free up a large number of troops for a conventional role on the LC, the withdrawal of the army from CI ops will also work as a huge confidence building measure within the state. Perhaps some kind of political process can then be initiated to seriously win over the hearts and minds of the people.

SECTION V

PAKISTAN

CHAPTER 11

THE DEMOLITION OF THE BABRI MASJID AND ITS AFTERMATH

The decade of the 1990s was the most defining one in the long history of the India–Pakistan hate fest. In the closing years of the previous decade Pakistan had finally succeeded in breaching the Indian grip on the Kashmiri psyche by demonstrating to the people of Kashmir that the bond between them and Pakistan has more dimensions than merely one of religion. Even as Pakistan expressed explicit psychological and moral support for the raging insurgency in the state (while clandestinely bankrolling it by diverting to it US funds meant for Afghanistan), in the early 1990s, it also managed to get a toehold in mainland India.

Once again, the links that were being forged between Pakistan and Muslims in mainland India had to do with a series of shortsighted moves by India that were taken advantage of by the enemy across the border. The campaign to assert Hindu nationalism, which peaked in 1992 with the demolition of the Babri Masjid on 6 December, had resulted in communal violence in most parts of northern and western India. Amongst the worst-affected places was Bombay, where over 900 people (nearly 575 of them Muslims) were killed in an explosion of communal hatred over a month and a half.

Despite the fact that these developments were greeted with shock and reactionary violence in the neighbouring countries of Pakistan and Bangladesh, the Indian government didn't think that the events were serious enough to merit executive action at the highest level. The Justice B. N. Sri Krishna Committee was set up to enquire into the violence. The task of rehabilitation of the victims was left largely to civil society, which could not go beyond providing material succour to the people left homeless and scarred; or holding intercommunity meetings to sort out what was believed to be a passing phenomenon. There was no serious attempt to understand the anger and alienation of the Muslim community.

Since communal, even caste, violence was not new to India, the prolonged Bombay riots were taken as par for the course. The Government of India did not realize (or preferred not to realize) that the post-Babri violence was unprecedented in many ways. One, the campaign for the demolition of the Mughal-era mosque had ratcheted up communal frenzy over a period of a few years, causing a deep cleavage in society. For the first time, wearing a religious identity like a badge of honour in public places had become rampant.

Two, sporadic riots had broken out in different parts of the country between 1990 till the actual demolition in December 1992. And even when there was no physical violence, the general atmosphere in northern and western India was steeped in fear and anticipation of terrible violence. In a horrifying 1992 documentary, *Ram Ke Naam,* filmmaker Anand Patwardhan captured the deliberate whipping up of religious passion, the latent violence and deep communal polarization that led to the eventual demolition of the mosque.

Three, while the Babri Masjid issue was centuries old (it was first raked up sometime in the 1850s, but became a dispute meriting official attention in 1946), it was only in 1986 when a district court ordered that its gates—shut since 1949 on Prime Minister Jawaharlal Nehru's orders—be opened and Hindus be allowed to pray inside that it turned volatile. Moreover, the newly formed Bharatiya Janata Party (the offspring of the defunct Hindu right-wing party, Jana Sangh) found in this a cause that would lead the party to power. The then president of the party, Lal Krishna Advani, made the Babri Masjid an issue of national importance, mobilizing people across the country. In 1990, he set off on a journey through India, starting from Somnath, to whip up the campaign for the demolition of what he called a disputed structure and the construction of a grand Ram temple in its place. The journey was called the Rath Yatra—an allusion to Lord Ram's victorious march to Ayodhya. Communal violence frequently tailed Advani's rath (a Toyota truck improvised to resemble a chariot).

Four, despite the fear of mass-scale violence, nobody really believed that a mob could actually pull down the sixteenth-century mosque in full glare of the state administration and international media. People, even those who wanted a grand temple built on the site, thought that the BJP campaign was mere political posturing. Perhaps the BJP did indulge in posturing. But the people it had mobilized throughout the country, who converged on Ayodhya on 6 December 1992 in response to the call given by the BJP and its sister parties like the Vishwa Hindu Parishad to perform kar seva (voluntary religious work), had no time for posturing. Slogans like 'ek dhakka aur do/ Babri Masjid tod do (give one more push and destroy the mosque)' had convinced the mob that that was the reason for the congregation.

Moreover, as a subsequently released video shot by the state intelligence agencies showed, the BJP's top leader, Atal Bihari Vajpayee, who later became prime minister, addressed the kar sevaks in Lucknow, about 135 kilometres from Ayodhya, and urged them to level the ground at the site by removing pointed stones. Vajpayee subsequently insisted that his speech was rhetorical in nature and not meant to instigate the mob, but at that time it was widely believed that by talking about the pointed stones he was referring to the domes of the mosque. The M. S. Liberhan Commission, which was constituted by the union government to enquire into the events leading to the demolition, did indict the senior BJP leadership in its report, submitted to the Government of India in 2009 seventeen years after the commission began its deliberation.

The communal violence that followed the demolition of the Babri Masjid wasn't of the kind seen in the country since Independence. It wasn't so much the violence that was different (people in this country have been killed for the faith they profess for decades now) as the sentiment that drove the violence. It was as if a historical wrong was being righted. The accompanying rhetoric was about the resurgent Hindu staking his rightful claim to the land that historically and religiously belonged to him. In Bombay, the feeling of dread and panic amongst the Muslims was amplified by the underworld community (disproportionately Muslim), which led the first phase of rioting after the demolition before the Shiv Sena took over.

Once the communal fires had been subdued, the state government went back to its somnolent state, completely oblivious to the simmering rage and fear amongst the Muslims. Urdu poet Khumar Barabankvi summed up the mood of the nation in these lines:

Ab na jale koi makaan, ab na uthe kahin dhuan
Aag lagi bujh gayi, aag dabi bujhaeye

(The homes are no longer on fire, there is no smoke
The flames of the fire have been doused, let us now douse the
simmering embers)

It wasn't just the loss of lives and property that was being mourned or the loss of a medieval structure. It was the fear of this setting the trend for the future of the intercommunity relationship between Hindus and Muslims, a relationship made even more complicated by economic interdependence.

In the spring of 1993, a consignment of contraband was smuggled into Bombay, facilitated by the well-oiled network of compromised state government officials from the port authority to customs and the police. The consignment was not gold or drugs. On 12 March 1993, thirteen bombs went off in different locations throughout the city, ranging from the stock exchange to five-star hotels, commercial hubs and the outskirts of the then international airport, killing 357 and injuring 717 people.

Terrorism had arrived on mainland India. The first terrorists were former criminals. Contacts in the Gulf emirate of Dubai had delivered the explosives that were set off. It is unlikely that Pakistan provided money for the operation and limited its involvement (before the bombs were set off) to the procurement of RDx and other weapons. But, after the attack, it gave asylum to Dawood Ibrahim (who India insists was the mastermind) and the rest of the perpetrators. Finally, Pakistan had found the chink in India's social and security structure, a gap it converted into an asset over the next few years.

With Indian fugitives as state guests, Pakistan had a gold mine of information about the chinks in Indian internal security, government/police officials who could be compromised, vulnerable places that could be developed as safe spots, etc. In addition to this, it also had access to a network of young men who inhabited the grey zones of society committing occasional crimes. These occasional foot soldiers did the groundwork, paving the way for Pakistani operatives to physically come to Bombay in an effort to influence the educated yet alienated Muslim youth.

'After the demolition of the Babri Masjid, things went completely out of control. The mafia and the foreign militants started approaching SIMI members and were even invited to their annual convention in Bombay. Despite resistance, there were voices within the organisation to declare a jihad. Gradually, by mid-90s, the moderates started leaving the organisation,' Saeed Khan, former president of the Bombay chapter of SIMI, told *FORCE* newsmagazine in an interview.

It took Pakistan over seven years to fully convert the breach of 1993 into a reliable asset. The first evidence of this was the attack on the Red Fort in Delhi in 2000 which was attributed to the Lashkar-e-Taiba (LeT), hitherto active only in J&K. Over the next few years, as terrorist attacks on various Indian cities became commonplace (a large number of them took place in Mumbai)—the most brazen of them was on the Indian Parliament in December 2001 which brought India and Pakistan to the brink of war—Indian intelligence agencies started to unearth sleeper cells established by Pakistan's ISI in several Indian cities. It also came across instances of mainstream Indian youth visiting Pakistan for rudimentary training either via Saudi Arabia or Dubai. This, obviously, was a first.

In the early years of terrorism on the mainland, Indian officials were prone to blame radicalization on the lack of education or employment amongst Muslim youth from a certain social strata, implying that the terrorists were mere mercenaries thereby delinking their acts from grievances and ideology. This misjudgement not only prevented the state from taking the right steps to address the issue, it actually helped in pushing the fence-sitters over the brink. After each attack, the police would routinely round up a few Muslim boys of a certain social profile (determined by the lawmakers' prejudice) and extract confessions from them, which were admissible as evidence in the courts under the anti-terrorism acts, whether the Terrorist and Disruptive Activities (Prevention) Act (TADA) or Prevention of Terrorism Act (POTA). This led to further alienation.

'If we look at triggers for radicalisation, I would say that two events— Babri Masjid and the communal carnage (again with maximum Muslim casualties) in Gujarat nearly a decade later—contributed 60 per cent,' former Home Secretary G. K. Pillai said. As an aside, a serious fallout of Muslim extremism was the conversion of Hindu radicalism into terrorism. So oblivious were the Indian investigating agencies of the growth of small, radical start-up Hindu outfits that when a series of attacks was mounted by them in different cities, the police as a matter of routine arrested Muslims as suspects; nine of them were released on bail in 2011 after spending five years in incarceration on charges of triggering bomb blasts in a Muslim cemetery in Malegaon (close to Mumbai) which killed thirty-seven Muslims on the day of the Muslim festival of Shab-e-Baraat. The special court granted them bail after the National Investigation Agency (NIA) decided not to oppose the bail plea, ostensibly because the only evidence against the accused was their confession given to the police.

Coming back to Pakistan's deep assets in India, the reason why the Indian establishment has not been able to effectively neutralize them is because of complete misdiagnosis of the malaise—either deliberately or out of sheer incompetence. Instead of understanding that Pakistan is taking advantage of the fault lines in India to weaken its social structures and widen the intercommunity differences to force it to the negotiating table on Kashmir, successive Indian governments have tended to conflate Indian conditions with international terrorism in an attempt to be one with the world.

This tendency started after 9/11 when India, even without being invited, allied itself with George W. Bush's war on terror. Since then, successive Indian politicians, from prime minister downwards, talk of global terrorism. The most recent example of this was Prime Minister Narendra Modi's executive intervention at the G20 Summit in Antalya, Turkey, in November 2015 where he once again urged the United Nations to define global terrorism in the wake of the attacks in Paris.

Perhaps this urge stems from the aspiration to be part of the big boys' club. Hence, after 9/11, Indian security experts started to raise the bogey of Al-Qaeda carrying out attacks in India. And Prime Minister Manmohan Singh took pride in saying that no Indian has ever joined Al-Qaeda. Today the same narrative is being repeated. Only Al-Qaeda has been replaced by the Islamic State (IS). Indian experts, military as well as civilians, have been parroting in chorus that India is vulnerable to IS attacks. So much so, a week after the IS attacks in Paris on 13 November 2015, the Indian Army's 16 Corps Commander, Lieutenant General R. R. Nimbhorkar, said in a media interaction, 'Yes, that [IS joining hands with LeT to launch attacks in India] can be a possibility as the motive of the terrorists is to spread their propaganda. They want their name and for that, they can do anything…'

Three days later, Lashkar-e-Taiba's spokesperson Abdullah Ghaznavi brushed off that possibility as propaganda by India. 'There is no scope for Al-Qaeda and IS in Jammu and Kashmir. Ours is a local indigenous struggle. The government of India…wants to defame our sacred struggle in the name of Al-Qaeda and ISIS. We have no world ambitions. Our sole objective is to force India to resolve the Kashmir issue in accordance with the United Nations resolutions,' added United Jihad Council's Jamil-ur-Rehman.

This Indian penchant for equating global terror with local terror was on view in July 2009 on the sidelines of the Non-Aligned Movement's summit at the Egyptian resort town of Sharm-el-Sheikh. Prime Minister Manmohan Singh and Pakistan Prime Minister Yousaf Raza Gillani issued a joint statement acknowledging that 'Both leaders agreed that terrorism is the main threat to both countries. Both leaders affirmed their resolve to fight terrorism and to cooperate with each other to this end. Both leaders agreed that the two countries will share real-time credible and actionable information on any future terrorist threats.'

The agreement was criticized in India because Pakistan had managed to sneak in a sentence about trouble in Balochistan (insinuating that India was fomenting it) immediately after the paragraph on the 26/11 attacks in Mumbai, where India had urged Pakistan to bring Pakistan-based perpetrators of the terrorist attack to justice. Ironically, the criticism was of the mention of Balochistan. They missed the nuance that while most of the terror attacks in India are orchestrated by Pakistan-based groups like LeT and Jaish-e-Mohammad, which are run by the ISI, all attacks inside Pakistan are carried out by Pakistan-based groups like Tehreek-e-Taliban Pakistan (TTP), Lashkar-e-Jhangvi, etc. which are inimical to the ISI. India has no role in them. So there is no way we can jointly fight terror beyond rhetoric.

We have to recognize the fact that the terrorism inside India is unique to our country and is more often than not perpetuated by Pakistan-created and nurtured organizations. It has little to do with the Taliban, Al-Qaeda or IS.

Contrary to what some experts say, perpetuating acts of terrorism is neither cheap nor easy. It requires money, human resources and intense planning. No organization can afford to waste that on areas which are of no interest to them. The Taliban's interest is Afghanistan. Al-Qaeda's was essentially the United States and its coalition partners. Islamic State wants control of the Levant (parts of Syria and Iraq) that used to be ruled by the Baathists. For them, India can be part of their overall bombast, but it cannot be part of their operations. The banner of jihad and khilafat are ruses to recruit foot soldiers. Of course, it wants to recruit young people from all over the world. Not for carrying out attacks in their home countries but to beef up their own numbers. The Indians who join IS do not come back to India after training to carry out attacks here like the Indian Mujahideen or LeT. They are operating (in whatever lowly capacity) in Syria or Iraq. Hoisting of IS flags by Kashmiri youth means little. It is part of the Friday protest ritual in downtown Srinagar to irk the Indian establishment. Once upon a time, Kashmiris waved Al-Qaeda banners too and even today they wave Pakistani flags. To take that as evidence of IS making inroads into India or Kashmir is a waste of intellectual time and resources.

Perhaps in this Indians need to take their cue from Pakistan which never loses focus of the key objective. At one of the Track II conclaves in Bahrain in the summer of 2015, where Indians and Pakistanis were hosted by one of the UK think tanks, Pakistani delegates brushed aside the fear voiced by Indians that IS may get a foothold in Pakistan. According to one Indian participant, the head of the Pakistan delegation said that there was no room for IS in Pakistan. While some Pakistani youth may get attracted to IS, it has no reasons to attack Pakistan.

The reasons our experts on terrorism try to link home-grown with global terrorism is largely because it is easier to do this than try to resolve the Kashmir issue or fix the alienation that is widespread in the Muslim community.

Addressing the freshly graduated Indian Police Service officers at the Sardar Vallabhbhai Patel National Police Academy in Hyderabad in 2006, Prime Minister Manmohan Singh said, 'The most dangerous threat today is terrorism. From an occasional footnote, it has become a hydra-headed monster. There are several strains of terrorism present, and you will need to keep abreast of developments in tackling this great danger.'

Yet there is very little of any consequence that the government has done as far as combating terrorism is concerned. In an interview to *FORCE* magazine, a former home secretary said that the weak links in India's battle against terrorism are ill-trained police and inept intelligence agencies, which simply do not get adequate, unbiased and prejudice-free information. Since Partition, partly out of communal prejudice and partly out of genuine fear of national security, Muslims were filtered out of intelligence agencies. Over a period of time, to overcome this shortfall, intelligence agencies infiltrated non-Muslim agents (pretending to be Muslims) into conservative mosques to keep tabs on what was happening. This has been a hit or miss approach, which worked sometimes, but mostly did not.

The main weapon the government uses in its fight against terrorism are harsh laws, although there is no empirical evidence to suggest that either of these laws—TADA or POTA—has been successful in combating terrorism. The reason for this is that any anti-terror law does not stop terrorists from carrying out attacks. It helps in convicting those who have carried out the attacks, provided they are caught. In theory this works as deterrence. But in practice the anti-terror laws in India have been misused to such an extent that the incarceration of innocents on trumped up charges is no longer an exception but the norm. And every time an innocent bears the brunt of the administration's prejudice, his community gets alienated even further.

The last National Democratic Alliance government's Prevention of Terrorism Act 2002, which was repealed by the United Progressive Alliance government in 2004, had left in its wake a long list of fake cases and encounters, essentially of the Muslim youth. A phrase made famous then by some members of the ruling party, 'while not all Muslims are terrorists, all terrorists are Muslims' gave a blanket permit to the police to harass Muslim youth whenever a terrorist incident took place. It is no state secret that thousands of Muslim youth even today are languishing in various prisons all over the country merely on suspicion.

A law like POTA actually compromised the professionalism of the police force by making it easy for them to eliminate so-called terrorist threats whether these were real or cooked up. All they had to do to get a conviction or put somebody away for years as an undertrial was to extract a confession. This eliminated the need for professional investigation into any incident. That this method of functioning had become deeply entrenched became evident when a number of terror cases unravelled after the National Investigation Agency started probing them.

After a bomb blast outside the Delhi High Court in 2011, then Home Minister P. Chidambaram had said that the media only picks on the cases where intelligence had purportedly failed. What about the cases where the intelligence works and the incident is prevented? Basically, what he was saying is that it is humanly impossible to track every lead because a majority of them are deliberately planted to send the agencies on a wild goose chase. Since the initiative is always with the terrorists, there are bound to be some misses.

There is truth in what Chidambaram had said then, but a greater truth is that prevention is still the best way of combating terrorism. A senior home ministry official told the authors that in the last few years intelligence gathering in India has become too dependent on technology. This dependence has undermined the importance of human intelligence. 'Technology or techint can be easily subverted,' he said. 'It cannot be a substitute for human intelligence. Unfortunately, our intelligence-gatherers have become lazy and too reliant on money. They don't realize that a person selling information to you can sell it to another for more money. Hence, we have a situation where different agencies source conflicting information from the same leads.'

Even the process of infiltrating mosques and vulnerable communities has limited utility. A better way would be to win the confidence and trust of the Muslim communities in such a manner that the influencers within the community start to believe that cooperating with the police will be in their larger interest. This clearly cannot be done if the police set up checkpoints in Muslim ghettos, harass the local people and treat all of them as potential terrorists.

Instead of a new terror law, national or international, we need better assimilation of Muslims into the mainstream. This will not only generate better preventive intelligence but will involve community leaders in leading and also policing the youth who have the potential of going astray.

Finally, despite all claims of professionalism, the police in India still look at the mood of the powers that be to assess which way the wind is blowing. If the government appears to favour community profiling for political ends, the police will be only too happy to comply.

Alienation never happens without provocation, as our history of the last three decades shows. What has changed today is that alienation of local Muslims is being exploited by Pakistan with great efficiency. The Indian government would do well to build the bridges first before it puts up the fence.

OLD ISSUES, NEW TRICKS

In the absence of serious, sustained and result-oriented talks with Pakistan, the two countries have been trudging the dreary path of confidence building, both in military and non-military areas. While military confidence building measures (CBMs) are necessary (and in government control), in the non-military sphere, the two governments usually play spoilsport, getting in the way of what would be natural CBMs.

Despite the vexed history between the two countries since Independence, the yearning for greater contact with each other amongst people on both sides of the border has remained strong. In the 1990s, even as Pakistan found two knives (Kashmir and terrorism) to inflict a 'thousand cuts on India' and the coldness between the neighbours increased the jingoistic voices among politicians on both sides, especially after India conducted its nuclear tests in May 1998 followed immediately by Pakistan, the people continued to meet one another.

Arriving in Delhi for a mushaira, while the political class on both sides was threatening annihilation, Pakistani poet Ahmad Faraz recited his newly composed poem *Dosti Ka Haath* (hand of friendship) to a spellbound Indian audience. He concluded his poem with these lines:

> Tumhare des mein aaya hoon doston ab ke
> Na saaz-o-nagme ki mehfil, na shaaiyri ke liye
> Agar tumhari ana hi ka hai sawal to phir
> Chalo main haath badhata hoon dosti ke liye

> (I have come to your country this time friends,
> not to enjoy soirees or recite poems
> If your ego is coming in the way, then, here,
> I extend my hand in friendship)

Indian poet Ali Sardar Jafri responded a few days later:

> Tumhara haath badha hai jo dosti ke liye
> Mere liye hai vo ik yaar-e-gham-gusar ka haath

(Your hand that has been extended in friendship,
is like the hand of a dear friend, who alleviates my pain)

He concluded the poem by extending this invitation:

Tum aao gulshan-e-Lahore se chaman-bardosh
Hum aayen subh-e-Banaras ki raushni le kar
Himalaya ki havaon ki taazgi le kar
Phir is ke baad ye puchhen ki kaun dushman hai

(You come redolent with the fragrances of Lahore's gardens;
we will bring the light from Banaras's dawn
Let us bring the freshness of Himalayan air and then ask,
who is the enemy?)

There is only so much that poets can do. Of course, the political atmosphere did not change, but the two poems became a talking point amongst artists, musicians, performers and human rights activists on both sides. The annual candlelight vigil at the Attari-Wagah border attracted even greater numbers on the Indian side, despite no reciprocation from Pakistan. Eventually these exchanges and interactions helped dissipate the dark clouds formed by the nuclear tests.

A few months later, in February 1999, Prime Minister Vajpayee embarked on an unprecedented journey. Accompanied by poets, actors, artists, activists, sportspersons and family members, Vajpayee boarded the inaugural bus to Lahore from Amritsar. People thronged the iron gates on both sides of the border, hopeful that something really historic was about to unfold. It did. On reaching Lahore, Vajpayee announced, 'India welcomes sustained discussions on all outstanding issues, including on Jammu and Kashmir... The solution of complex, outstanding issues can only be sought in an atmosphere free from prejudice and by adopting the path of balance, moderation and realism.'

In the official meeting subsequently, the two sides signed a number of agreements under the Lahore Declaration underlying peaceful coexistence. A memorandum of understanding aimed at preventing conflict was also signed. The MoU read, 'The two sides shall engage in bilateral consultations on security concepts, and nuclear doctrines, with a view to developing confidence building measures (CBMs) in the nuclear and conventional fields, aimed at avoidance of conflict.'

However, if civil society thought that it could guide the government on India-Pakistan relations, it was in for disappointment. For yet another mushaira, organized in April 1999 to celebrate the new-found love between the two countries, the organizers invited both Ahmad Faraz and Ali Sardar Jafri. The idea was that they would recite their poems in the presence of Delhi's elite. On the eve of Ahmad Faraz's departure from Pakistan, his government refused to issue him the no objection certificate, apparently required by all artists travelling to India. The following month, an Indian Army patrol out to verify information provided by nomads about Pakistanis occupying Indian territory in the Kargil sector of J&K ran into the Pakistan Army's troopers and Mujahids. The patrol never came back. Subsequently, the mutilated bodies of Captain Saurabh Kalia and five soldiers were handed over to the Indian Army by the Pakistan Army. The Kargil War had begun.

Despite this setback, the constituency for peace did not waver in its ardour. This is something extremely peculiar to India and Pakistan. The people to people contact, including trade and commerce, has always had a momentum of its own. If at all, the governments, especially the Pakistan government (even the democratically elected government has to take its cues from the army), usually play the negative role by thwarting them, with the idea of aligning these issues to the political mood of the country.

When Pervez Musharraf took over as Pakistan's chief executive and later president, sending Nawaz Sharif packing to Saudi Arabia after the debacle of the Kargil War, he initiated the peace process with India with much nudging from outsiders, including the United Nations Secretary General Kofi Annan, who urged the two sides to pick up the threads from the Lahore Declaration.

Musharraf came to Agra for a summit meeting with Vajpayee in July 2001 amidst great fanfare and gushing articles in the media about Musharraf's ancestral ties to India, including the house in old Delhi. However, the summit failed. Conspiracy theories about an external hand sabotaging it abounded. Subsequently various articles and books hinted that the Hindu right-wing organization, the Rashtriya Swayamsevak Sangh (RSS), was not happy with the way Vajpayee was running away with the peace process. Hence it used Deputy Prime Minister and Home Minister L. K. Advani to sabotage it. Others have suggested that Advani never wanted the summit to succeed, lest it enhance Vajpayee's status in India and abroad. After all, an overarching agreement with Musharraf that included the Kashmir issue would have been epochal. Musharraf left Agra disappointed.

When terrorists attacked the Indian Parliament on 13 December 2001, relations between India and Pakistan, which had barely recovered, nosedived. The Indian government mobilized the military (Operation Parakram), ostensibly for war. The Delhi-Lahore bus service was halted, and war rhetoric from both sides reached its peak. Relations settled down to a routine once Operation Parakram was called off after ten months. The bus service was resumed and Musharraf announced a ceasefire on the Line of Control on 26 November 2003. Though Vajpayee went to Pakistan for the second time in January 2004 to attend the SAARC summit, his meeting with Musharraf did not kick-start the stalled relationship.

A semblance of warmth returned when Manmohan Singh met Musharraf for the first time in New York on the sidelines of the UN General Assembly on 24 September 2004. The two sides even issued a joint statement, '[Manmohan Singh and Musharraf]…agreed that confidence building measures (CBMs) of all categories under discussion between the two governments should be implemented keeping in mind practical possibilities. They also addressed the issue of Jammu and Kashmir and agreed that possible options for a peaceful, negotiated settlement of the issue should be explored in a sincere spirit and purposeful manner…'

Even as backchannel talks on Kashmir started, several new initiatives to enhance the overall relationship were taken. These included cross-border bus services through Uri-Muzaffarabad (2005), Amritsar-Nankana Sahib and Poonch-Rawalkote (2006); and train services through Munabao-Khokhrapar (2005). The New Delhi-Lahore Samjhauta Express resumed service after forty years in 2006. Trade through these land borders also started during this period. And the biggest of all, the touchstone of India-Pakistan relations— cricketing ties—were resumed in 2006 after nearly seven years.

Since India was talking with Pakistan on Kashmir, as well as with the Kashmiris within, Pakistan had no problem in pursuing these CBMs between the two countries. In fact, the overall goodwill was helping Musharraf's image as being serious about resolving all outstanding issues with India. Prisoners and straying fishermen were frequently released by both sides. And a series of political CBMs, such as discussing the possibility of building gas pipelines—Iran-Pakistan-India (IPI) and Turkmenistan-Afghanistan-Pakistan-India (TAPI)—led to the overall sense that finally the two countries can coexist in peace and pursue an interdependent economic relationship.

One niggling issue however troubled the business community: restrictions imposed on tradable goods by Pakistan. Fearing that Indian goods would overwhelm Pakistan markets, the government in Islamabad had always maintained a positive list of items that could be imported from India. This list served another purpose. It allowed the government of the day to calibrate the relationship. Clearly, the Pakistan Army could not allow free trade to grow without the Kashmir resolution. That would have simply created a new vested group for better relations within Pakistani society.

Moreover, there was little progress on the so-called military CBMs like Siachen and Sir Creek. It seemed that everything hinged on the backchannel talks on Kashmir. However, the relationship unravelled just as quickly as it had grown. Musharraf got into trouble at home and his ability to deliver on the commitments became suspect. India started to drag its feet and the resolution of Kashmir never happened.

In August 2008, Musharraf quit office. The elections brought the Pakistan People's Party to power with the late Benazir Bhutto's husband Asif Ali Zardari as president. Musharraf had demitted office as chief of army staff a year earlier, appointing General Ashfaq Parvez Kayani in his place.

Preoccupied with the raging insurgencies in the North-West Frontier Province and Balochistan and the global war on terror in Afghanistan, Kayani adopted a hands-off approach as far as politics was concerned. And Zardari started to assert himself—the last flicker of the candle before it was extinguished.

At the UN General Assembly in September 2008, Zardari trashed the Pakistan Army's irregular troopers like LeT, JeM, etc. as terrorists who hunt in packs like wolves. He ridiculed the backchannel talks on Kashmir and offered to put the issue on the back-burner, focusing instead on trade and people to people contact between the two countries. This was music to Indian ears which had grown weary of too much focus on Kashmir. It also offered a respite from Musharraf directing the course of talks on the Kashmir resolution. India and the US both jumped on Zardari's dream machine, offering humanitarian aid and nudging him for early resolution of prickly issues like water sharing, Siachen and Sir Creek.

Then the Pakistan Army struck back, putting Zardari in his place, telling both India and the world that only it can run the country's India policy. On 26 November 2008, ten men, (apparently from the LeT and trained by ISI) armed with automatic weapons, explosives and dry rations sailed into Mumbai and held not just the city but the entire country to ransom for three days. When the carnage finally ended on 29 November, 164 people were dead.

Once again the relationship tanked and war rhetoric resumed. The threads of the talks during 2004–08 were never picked up. Since then India has insisted on Pakistan punishing the people behind the 26 November attack and Rawalpindi has been stonewalling the requests. The Kashmir issue has indeed been put on the back-burner. Interestingly, despite the freeze, both sides continued to honour the earlier agreements on nuclear and military CBMs.

A semblance of normalcy was restored by 2010, but the earlier warmth was no longer there. The only area where progress was made was in trade. In November 2011, Pakistan agreed to accord the Most Favoured Nation status to India. Prime Minister Manmohan Singh reciprocated by announcing his decision to initiate a Preferential Trade Agreement with Pakistan, which would progressively abolish customs duties on all traded goods from Pakistan. The following year, the Indian government issued a notification allowing Pakistan's industry to invest in all sectors in India barring defence, space and atomic energy. A month later the two sides agreed to ease the visa regime by creating new categories of visas like diplomatic, non-diplomatic, thirty-six hours transit visit, tourist visas, civil society, media, and business visas. Pakistan also converted the positive list of tradable goods to a negative list, allowing import of everything barring 1,200 items on that list. In January 2014, the commerce ministers of the two countries consented to sign yet another agreement: reciprocal Non-Discriminatory Market Access (NDMA), as the Most Favoured Nation status had not found favour with the Pakistani dispensation. However, both the relaxed visa regime and the NDMA did not materialize.

While all this created an illusion of conversation between the two countries, in reality the relationship died in November 2008. Since then the two sides have gone through the motions of talking, signing agreements and inviting each other, but always in the shadow of the Mumbai attacks. In all conversations or negotiations, irrespective of the context, the Indian side has always raised the issue of booking the perpetrators of 26/11, and the Pakistan side has made the usual sympathetic noises about the law taking its own course. Meanwhile, the Line of Control and International Border have become more volatile with frequent small-arms firing and ceasefire violations. In the heady years between 2004–08, because of peace on the LC and IB, villagers on both sides were allowed to cultivate their land right up to the border, well ahead of the fence. The army used to issue gate passes to the villagers to go through the fence in the morning and return in the evening. But since 2013, many villages, especially in the Jammu sector have either been evacuated or farmers instructed to stay well behind the fence.

Though the Pakistan Army suggested to the Indian government in 2009–11 that it must talk with them, probably to pick up the threads of the Musharraf-Manmohan Singh Kashmir interlocution, the Indians, not wanting to undermine the democratically elected government, refused to accept the invitation. Gradually the invitations stopped. Pakistan under Nawaz Sharif has gone back to its earlier position of a plebiscite and abiding by the UN resolutions. Having come so close to restoring normalcy in India-Pakistan relations, today, confidence building measures have been overtaken by new realities with the Pakistan-China clinch being the game changer. While military CBMs may still have some uses in preventing untoward incidents, the non-military CBMs have been reduced to tokenism.

This drift is likely to continue, and perhaps get worse as the attack on Indian Army's Uri brigade which killed eighteen soldiers on 18 September 2016 indicated. With Modi government making it clear that for it, the core issue worth discussing with Pakistan is terrorism; everything else (barring Kashmir) will follow, Pakistan's impatience will start to show more often. Yet the Indian government thinks that terrorism exists in a vacuum and can be dealt with in a vacuum. In fact, so enthused is the government about taking on terrorism, that on all his visits abroad Prime Minister Modi makes a case for fighting global terrorism together with the host country once he is through with urging people to invest in India. For Pakistan, the core issue remains Kashmir and everything else will flow from there. Under these circumstances, it is not difficult to imagine that challenges to internal security are only going to increase, whether lone wolf attacks or something else. A day after the seventh anniversary of the 26/11 attacks, Indian intelligence agencies claimed that they had received specific inputs about a meeting called by Pakistan's ISI in which thirty people from such terrorist outfits as LeT and JeM were instructed to carry out a spectacular attack in India sometime in December 2015.

Yet the world has not given up hope. At any given point there are at least twenty-five or more non-official dialogues (Track II) going on between India and Pakistan funded by the Western world. At one point in the 1990s, there were at least forty Track II dialogues underway in various parts of the world. Most of these started when the insurgency in Kashmir was in its most violent phase and the world feared that it could lead to a war between India and Pakistan. The fear only increased after the nuclear tests by the two countries and earned Kashmir the moniker of a 'nuclear flashpoint'.

With the experience of the Cold War, the West felt that it had a thing or two to teach Indians and Pakistanis about risk reduction and confidence building measures. Hence, one of the earliest Track II dialogues, the Neemrana Process, which started in 1991 and was funded by the US government and the Ford Foundation, adopted the approach of the Dartmouth Process between the US and Soviet Union. Participating Indian and Pakistani retired bureaucrats and other government officials were encouraged to think beyond the stated government positions on issues like Kashmir. But within a few years the sponsors lost their enthusiasm. They realized that while the participants hardly had original ideas, they also wielded very little influence with their respective governments.

This did not deter others from sponsoring similar jamborees. Through the 1990s several Track II dialogues, some focused purely on India and Pakistan and some with a broader focus of the South Asian Association for Regional Cooperation or India-Pakistan-China, started and wound up. Amongst the prominent Track II dialogues today are the Balusa Group, Chaophraya Dialogues, Pugwash Conferences, Friedrich-Ebert-Stiftung's India-Pakistan Dialogue and the International Institute for Strategic Studies' India-Pakistan-Afghanistan dialogue. All of them suffer from the same malady: they are a jamboree of retired personnel. Since most of their meetings are held in third countries, sometimes in exotic resorts, the participants treat it as a fully paid holiday over a couple of days. Even when the participants change, the issues under discussion remain the same. The biggest shortcoming of these meetings is that none of these dialogues have any traction with the concerned governments. At best, they make friends out of enemies, as in the case of retired military officers, but cause no change in the broader perspective.

In terms of influencing policy, the most successful one has been the Kashmir Study Group (KSG), founded in 1996 and funded by the US-based Kashmiri businessman M. Farooq Kathwari. In addition to Kashmiri experts from both sides of the divide, the group used to invite scholars and retired government officials from India and Pakistan. The US, Canada and Europe often sponsored their meetings and also sent observers. The KSG issued several papers on Kashmir resolution, one of which subsequently became the basis of Musharraf's four-point formula on which Ambassador Satinder Lambah and Tariq Aziz held backchannel talks on behalf of their respective governments and came within touching distance of a resolution.

Even today the KSG remains the best formula for Kashmir resolution, which was acceptable to both governments as well as the Kashmiri people. Since its collapse, nothing of any consequence has emerged. Given the nature of politics in the subcontinent, the India-Pakistan relationship really has no room for non-officials, leave alone third parties. In any case, it has been driven largely by initiatives from Pakistan, whether positive or negative. Most of the time, India has only responded to them. With a record like this, it is very unlikely that any confidence building measures can work in the absence of serious, result-oriented talks. Good days will not come anytime soon. But as Ali Sardar Jafri wrote after the 1965 India-Pakistan war:

Guftagu bandh na ho
Baat se baat chale

(Let the conversation not stop
Let one thing lead to another)

CHAPTER 12

THE PAKISTAN ARMY

There is an interesting anecdote that former US Deputy Secretary of State Strobe Talbott narrates in his book, *Engaging India*. Two days after the Indian nuclear tests in May 1998, Talbott and his team reached the US Central Command Headquarters located in Tampa, Florida, hoping to make a quick transfer to another plane for the long flight to Islamabad. (The US was keen to stop Pakistan from carrying out its own nuclear tests.) The team's departure was delayed inordinately because the US Ambassador to Pakistan, Thomas Simons, was unable to get through to his contacts in the foreign ministry and Prime Minister's Office.

Talbott writes, 'When his [Simons'] efforts proved unavailing, General Tony Zinni (US Central Command chief) put in a call to General Karamat (Pakistan Army chief), reaching him right away. Karamat professed astonishment that there was any obstacle to our departure and cleared the matter up in a matter of minutes. It was further evidence that the civilian leaders [Prime Minister Nawaz Sharif] were in a state of confusion, perhaps discord, and that the military called the shots in Pakistan.'

It was Pakistan Army chief General Jehangir Karamat who took the decision for Pakistan to conduct its nuclear tests to 'maintain strategic parity', as he put it, with India. Having demonstrated nuclear weapons capability, converting it into nuclear weapons under Rawalpindi's watch, was the natural next step. Strategic matters like Pakistan's nuclear policy, role of nuclear weapons, fissile stocks and policy, structures for strategic command and control, delivery systems, safety of nukes, future nuclear trajectories and associated geopolitics, and global non-proliferation regimes became the sole responsibility of the Pakistan Army.

Within weeks of the nuclear tests, the Pakistan Army was briefing the Pakistan foreign ministry on various aspects of its nuclear policy. To avoid the circuitous route of civilian leadership which in any case knew little, the US decided to talk directly with Rawalpindi on nuclear issues.

With the ownership of nukes, the stature of the Pakistan Army chief, both within and outside the country, was taller than that of the prime minister.

With nuclear weapons out in the open, the Pakistan military sought a more direct role in the country's governance It sought to use its nuclear weaponization to give it a larger role on the world stage. With this in mind, General Karamat, on 5 October 1998, publicly floated the idea of a national security council where, in an institutionalized fashion, the army would have a role in the political leadership in the government. Prime Minister Sharif saw this as an affront to the people's mandate, and asked General Karamat to resign, which he did on 7 October 1998. It opened the floodgates. General Pervez Musharraf toppled Sharif and took the country along a new path.

Once settled in the political seat after deposing Sharif, Musharraf's attention shifted to Kashmir. Having masterminded Kargil and failed to achieve much by force and guile, Musharraf, in his autobiography, *In the Line of Fire*, states, 'As early as 2001, I believed the time had come to turn over a new leaf.' His peace initiatives were as dramatic and out-of-the-box as his commando antics. On 24 November 2003, Musharraf announced proposals to improve relations with India, which India accepted. Starting 26 November 2003, which was Eid-ul-Fitr, both sides agreed to a ceasefire on the Line of Control, the Jammu International Border/Working Boundary and the Actual Ground Position Line/Line of Contact in Siachen.

After the Vajpayee government lost at the hustings, the Manmohan Singh-Musharraf duo took the peace process forward and instituted backchannel talks on Kashmir. Between 2004 and 2007, India, Pakistan and other stakeholders held intense discussions to fine-tune what Musharraf claimed was his four-element formula on Kashmir resolution. This comprised identification of regions of J&K that needed resolution; demilitarization; self-governance or self-rule; and a joint management mechanism with membership consisting of Pakistanis, Indians and Kashmiris.

Providing details of the backchannel talks, Khurshid Kasuri, Musharraf's foreign minister from 2002–07, who was privy to what transpired behind the scenes, confirmed in his 2015 book, *Neither a Hawk Nor a Dove*, what was known and not known. It was known that the four elements formula on Kashmir was acceptable to all stakeholders; this was the closest the two sides had ever come to an understanding on Kashmir. What was not known publicly was that the Pakistan Army was completely on board with the Musharraf peace plan. The senior army brass who met regularly to discuss progress on backchannel talks included 'the then DG-ISI, General Ashfaq

Pervez Kayani, later chief of army staff, the then vice chief of army staff, General Ahsan Saleem Hayat, and the chief of staff to the President, Lt Gen. Hamid Javed'.

Once Musharraf declared a ceasefire on the LC in Jammu & Kashmir in November 2003, which was necessary to take the Kashmir peace talks forward, he moderated the infiltration levels—they would increase or decrease depending upon progress on the talks. This was confirmed by Kasuri, who writes, 'We realized fairly early that the peace process with India could not survive, let alone thrive, unless cross LC movement was controlled. It was in this background that in 2005 and 2006, I started hearing in hushed tones at the Presidency and in some high-level meetings that centres had been set up to wean away militants from their past and impart skills to them which would help them integrate better in society.'

Kayani was instructed by Musharraf to stop cross-border terrorism into J&K. Indian Army officers confirmed that infiltration from POK was minimal if not zero during this period; it's another matter that they took credit for this. With guns silent on the LC and zero infiltration, the Pakistan Army felt the need to develop a few pressure points outside Kashmir to ensure Indian commitment on the Kashmir peace talks. The answer lay in exporting terrorism to mainland India. The requirement was to activate sleeper cells in Indian cities which would support LeT-induced mayhem whenever the ISI deemed it necessary. The years 2004–07 witnessed bomb blasts and other acts of terrorism across Indian cities.

After Musharraf had to ingloriously demit office, the next army chief, General Ashfaq Kayani, had the onerous task of restoring the credibility of the army within Pakistan. Kayani also had the responsibility for Pakistan's nuclear policy, and to carry forward Musharraf's Kashmir policy. The latter was not easy since neither Musharraf's successor, Asif Ali Zardari, nor India grasped the role of Rawalpindi on the Kashmir issue in a nuclearized Pakistan. Kayani was determined not to fritter away the spectacular progress made on the Kashmir resolution, but it was equally vital that the Pakistan Army was given credit for the Kashmir breakthrough.

President Asif Ali Zardari, however, did a turnaround on India policy. He spoke about improving overall relations with the focus on trade with India by putting the Kashmir issue on the back-burner. And then the 26/11 attack on Mumbai happened. There were many theories about why the Pakistan Army carried out 26/11: to put an end to Zardari's new-found love for India, to reassert Kashmir as the core concern or to inform India who they needed to talk with in Pakistan. The last theory comes closest to the mark.

In 2009, quite unexpectedly, the ISI chief, Lieutenant General Shuja Pasha, attended the Iftar party given by the Indian High Commission in Islamabad. There he met up with India's defence advisor and floated the idea of having parallel talks with the Pakistan Army alongside the civil dispensation. The idea got a lukewarm response from Delhi and did not go far.

This was expected as with a civilian government in Islamabad, India had difficulty in talking with the Pakistan Army for a number of reasons. The Pakistan Army, more than the political leadership, is seen as the enemy directly responsible for the proxy war in Kashmir. Moreover, the 26/11 terrorist attack in Mumbai was traced back to ISI handlers. Interacting with the Pakistan Army would imply that India had succumbed to their machinations. India prides itself as a democracy; hence, with an elected government in Islamabad direct talks with the army would not be in order. Also, India would not like to set a precedent by holding high-level government talks with the Pakistan Army fearing that with time, the Indian military—which is outside the security policymaking loop—would want to be inside it.

Finally, Indian diplomats detest the idea of sharing their exclusive space with military officers; notwithstanding the fact that the present warfare has complex nuances which the diplomats are ignorant about. For example, during the first round of talks held on 16 October 1998 in Islamabad on Strategic Restraint Regime, 'the Indian delegation had no military officer at the meeting. And the diplomats barely anticipated such an elaborate proposal… It became clear that India was prepared only to have generalised discussions on these issues'.

Despite India's politically correct arguments for talking with Islamabad and not Army Headquarters in Rawalpindi at the same time, the truth is that results will only accrue when the real power centre in Pakistan is addressed directly. This is how Pakistan works and India can do little about it. For example, years of structured bilateral talks under the rubric of Composite Dialogue with Islamabad have never moved beyond confidence building measures. The CBMs, by definition, are as good as the political will available on the two sides. When a civilian government in Pakistan talks peace with India, it has to look over its shoulders for its army's nod.

The US was conscious that not much would happen until a direct channel between New Delhi and the Pakistan Army was established. In his book, *The Dispensable Nation*, Vali Nasr, who was senior advisor to Ambassador Richard Holbrooke, the US special representative for Afghanistan and Pakistan, wrote, 'Holbrooke had persuaded General Kayani to agree in principle to talk with India over Afghanistan and Afghanistan only.' With this assurance, Holbrooke met the (unnamed) Indian diplomat over dinner in the US on 6 December 2010. According to Nasr, the Indian diplomat took this message to Delhi, and 'shortly thereafter, a message came from Delhi that [Prime Minister Manmohan Singh] had given the green light'. The meeting never took place as Holbrooke died within a week.

This is not all. According to Nasr, the idea of according the Most Favoured Nation (MFN) status between Pakistan and India had its origin in the Transit Trade Agreement (TTA) signed between Pakistan and Afghanistan in 2010. However, despite India according MFN status to Pakistan, the latter, while renaming it as Non-Discriminatory Market Access has still not reciprocated. Once Holbrooke realized that Afghani goods were popular in India, he, with difficulty, persuaded the civilian governments of Afghanistan and Pakistan to sign the TTA; he convinced Pakistanis that transit of trade between Afghanistan and India through their territory would benefit them as well.

Nasr writes, 'That he (Holbrooke) got the Pakistan military to give its okay was a mighty achievement... The TTA had given both India and Pakistan reason to expand beyond the Afghan trade connecting the two countries. Pakistan now saw it was possible to trade with an antagonist neighbour. Pakistan would grant India MFN trade status; Pakistan and India literally lifted entire clauses and passages out of the TTA to craft their own trade agreement.'

With Prime Minister Nawaz Sharif back in the saddle in June 2013, India's hopes to improve relations with Pakistan were rekindled—especially as this was something that Sharif had also desired during his election campaign. From India's perspective, what came in the way was closure to the 26/11 attacks; the perpetrators of the dastardly act that had taken 164 lives had to be punished. While promising justice, Sharif spoke about better ties with India and revived the talks about Most Favoured Nation (MFN) status to India for improved bilateral trade which had been hanging fire since 2011.

However, Pakistan's new army chief, General Raheel Sharif, who took office on 29 November 2013 adopted a hard stance on the Kashmir dispute. Small-arms firings from across the Line of Control, which had been a regular feature since the gruesome beheading of an Indian soldier, Lance Naik Hemraj, by Pakistani commandos in January 2013, intensified. The firings quickly spread to the International Border in Jammu, where in the first five months of 2014, there were 800 serious violations. Raising the pitch, Raheel Sharif went back to the traditional narrative of Kashmir being Pakistan's 'jugular vein' and sought its resolution under the UN Security Council resolutions. This was a walking back from the Musharraf position, who on 17 December 2003 had declared that 'in quest for a negotiated settlement of the Kashmir issue we have left the UN resolutions on plebiscite aside'. Despite the hardened stance, Raheel Sharif was careful not to use long-range artillery guns on the LC, which would have ended the November 2003 ceasefire and taken the two sides to the brink of war.

With bilateral relations at rock bottom, the Modi government assumed charge in May 2014. In a startling development, Modi invited Nawaz Sharif along with other SAARC leaders to his inauguration. Pushed to the wall by his strident army chief, Sharif, desperate to find space in Pakistan's India policy, readily accepted the Indian invitation. What followed were policy flip-flops by both sides; India, under Modi, not willing to talk Kashmir, and Islamabad being snubbed by Rawalpindi for not talking Kashmir.

The two sides agreed on the foreign secretaries meeting, which was cancelled by India at the last minute because the Pakistan high commissioner in India invited the Hurriyat leadership before the talks, the supposed third party in a bilateral process. India said that talks on terrorism had to be addressed before anything else. Displaying arrogance, senior Indian officials started talking about trade and connectivity with neighbours and SAARC minus Pakistan. Modi's Act East policy, repackaged from the Look East policy of the 1990s, was sought to be sold as a panacea for India's ills.

With relations strained for too long, the two prime ministers met on the sidelines of the Shanghai Cooperation Organization in Ufa (Russia) in August 2015. In a joint statement, the two sides agreed on three sets of talks: between the national security advisors, director general Border Security Force and Pakistan Rangers responsible for the Jammu International Border/ Working Boundary, and the two director generals of military operations to discuss peace on the LC. These did not materialize as India insisted on talking only terror, while Pakistan said that the Ufa statement had mentioned talks on 'other outstanding issues' as well, which implied Kashmir—the Pakistan Army's core concern.

Because the Kashmir issue was not mentioned clearly in the Ufa statement, Sharif got flak in Pakistan, especially from General Raheel Sharif, for the key omission. Although Prime Minister Sharif had appointed General Raheel Sharif, he forgot that the army chief was not dependent on him. In Pakistan, the army chief draws his strength not from the political dispensation that appoints him, but from three different sources: his relations with his nine corps commanders, his firm hold over nuclear weapons including delivery

Siachen Battle School for induction training of troops deployed on the glacier.

Road and rail bridges over the Brahmaputra, linking Lhasa with Shigatse.

China has built gravel roads right up to the LAC (at Bum La) instead of tar roads. This has two benefits. One, these roads are better able to withstand rain and snow at this altitude, hence are cost-effective. Two, this gives the Chinese the leverage to pressure India not to build pucca or black tar roads, as under various treaties both sides have agreed not to build permanent structures close to the LAC. India cannot built gravel roads because the terrain on the Indian side consists of sharp slopes and loose soil prone to slides, unlike on the Chinese side, which is flat plateau.

The Indian road leading up to Bum La near the LAC.

Tithwal is one of the few places in the Kashmir Valley where just a small sliver of a river, Kishenganga for Indians, Neelam for Pakistanis, divides Indian and Pakistani army posts. In fact, it is quite common for a binocular-wielding Indian soldier to look directly at a binocular-wielding Pakistani soldier across the river.

In several parts of the Kashmir Valley, the LC cuts through villages, leading to families being divided. In some areas the Indian Army posts overlook villages and defence installations in Pakistan-occupied Kashmir, in other parts, Pakistan overlooks Indian infrastructure.

Only one road connects Tezpur in the plains to Tawang, though the Border Roads Organisation has been trying to build another road for over a decade. This road is perpetually under construction. According to the Indian Army, this side of the Himalayan range consists of young mountains, which are prone to landslides and mudslides. There is also a limit to how much construction these mountains can take. Of course, another reason for the terrible state of the roads is poor technology and 'Indian rate of development'.

While the Chinese have fast attack craft to patrol their portion of the Pangong Tso in southeastern Ladakh, the Indian Army largely relies on ancient boats to guard one-third of the divided lake; some fast, imported boats have recently been inducted.

The authors were among the few journalists to visit INS *Hansa* in Goa in November 2010, the base for naval aviation when the first of the MiG-29K naval fighters, which now operate from aircraft carrier INS *Vikramaditya,* arrived. The naval pilots were only too happy to pose for the authors.

A C-17 Globemaster and two Su-30MKI fighters during the IAF Day parade in Hindan in 2014. The Indian Air Force, the second largest operator of this aircraft after the United States Air Force, operates ten Boeing-made C-17 strategic lift aircraft. The C-17 can carry over a hundred fully-equipped paratroopers for special operations. It can also carry heavy equipment including military vehicles. Most importantly, it can even land on unpaved runways. In November 2016, the IAF landed a C-17 aircraft at Mechuka in Arunachal Pradesh, about 29 km short of the LAC.

Chinese DF-15A Intermediate Range Ballistic Missile and CJ-10 Land Attack Cruise Missile. China will use both with conventional warheads to support the PLAAF.

Chinese-built HQ-9 Long Range Surface to Air Missiles. These have also been transferred to Pakistan.

Chinese JY-11B and YLC-2A radars.

T-90 tanks during the Indian Army's Exercise Sanghe Shakti in May 2006 in Punjab.

PHL-03 300mm Multi-Barrel Rocket Launcher. The Chinese-built MBRL are part of its long range artillery. The Chinese displayed all the five systems (IRBM, LACM, AIFV, LR-SAM radars and the MBRL) during their National Day Parade in October 2009.

PLAAF's ZBD-3 Armoured Infantry Fighting Vehicle of the 15 Airborne Corps. This corps, based in Henan province, has the capability to paradrop 25,000 fully-armed Special Forces with light armour, artillery and fighting vehicles behind enemy lines.

INS *Vikramaditya* during sea trials. After several delays, INS *Vikramaditya*, formerly *Admiral Gorshkov* of the Russian Navy, finally joined the Indian Navy in November 2013, after having signed the contract for its recovery and refurbishment in 2004. The Russian Navy had decommissioned *Admiral Gorshkov* after a fire on board and subsequently offered it to the Indian Navy in 1994.

INS *Talwar* was among the first made-to-order, state of the art frigates (3,500 tons) of the Indian Navy. The order was placed with the Russians in 1997 and the first ship was delivered in 2003. Two more followed. The authors visited INS *Talwar* in Mumbai in October 2004.

systems, and how well he manages to retain friendly terrorist groups, such as Laskhar, Jaish, Hizbul, and so on, in his war plans against India.

Meanwhile, the ice was once again broken at the Paris Climate Change Conference in December 2015 where the two prime ministers were seen talking with one another. Their brief interaction was quickly followed by a secret meeting between the two national security advisors accompanied by their foreign secretaries on 6 December 2015 in Bangkok. It was later disclosed that all subjects related to terror and Kashmir—being the area most affected by it—were discussed. Within days, the Indian Foreign Minister Sushma Swaraj flew to Islamabad to attend the Heart of Asia Conference on Afghanistan to which India had been invited. On her return, she informed Parliament that a 'comprehensive bilateral dialogue' covering more subjects than the earlier 'Composite Dialogue' suspended in the wake of the 26/11 attacks with Pakistan was necessary for regional peace. The two foreign secretaries would meet in early 2016 to discuss modalities for bilateral talks. However, terrorism in all its forms, with the focus on J&K state, would be discussed by the NSAs.

The 'comprehensive bilateral dialogue' format agreed to by the Modi government in December 2015 was unprecedented. The Pakistan Army had won while allowing India to save face. After the fiasco over the Ufa statement where India had insisted that only terrorism would be discussed by the two NSAs, on 22 October 2015 Rawalpindi replaced Pakistan's civilian NSA, Nawaz Sharif's appointee Sartaj Aziz, with the recently retired Lieutenant General Nasser Khan Janjua, considered close to Raheel Sharif. Therefore, while India had its way of holding talks between the NSAs in Bangkok, for the first time it was talking with the Pakistan Army.

India's NSA Ajit Doval, a police officer who had worked in the intelligence world, met Pakistan's Lieutenant General Janjua—a hard-core military officer who headed the ad hoc Southern Command and the 12 Corps which was responsible for counter-terrorism in Afghanistan and Balochistan—to determine the fate of the 'comprehensive bilateral dialogue'.

Given Pakistan's reality, it was important that the talks between the NSAs succeed. For if the Pakistan Army did not put its imprimatur on any decisions, it was unlikely to be implemented. But to talk directly with the Pakistan Army would be a challenge for the Indian interlocutor, since the aims of the two NSAs are incompatible. Doval would focus on confidence building because India under Modi (with his right-wing ideology), is not inclined to discuss the Kashmir resolution. Janjua, on the other hand, would concentrate primarily on conflict resolution.

While participating in the UN General Assembly on 1 October 2015, Sushma Swaraj said that the global community should focus on the political status of POK and the Gilgit-Baltistan region of the erstwhile princely state of J&K which had merged with India in 1947. Her statement was in keeping with the BJP's ideology of Greater India (Akhand Bharat).

Earlier in September 1998, L. K. Advani, the BJP senior leader who was India's deputy prime minister, elaborated on Greater India to Strobe Talbott. Talbott writes, 'The session with Advani was unnerving. He mused aloud about the happy day when India, Pakistan, Sri Lanka, Bangladesh and Myanmar would be reunited in a single South Asian confederation. Given India's advantages in size and strength, this construct, especially coming from India's highest-ranking hard-line Hindu nationalist, would have been truly frightening to all its neighbours, most of all Pakistan.'

The BJP's ideological mentor, the RSS maintains that unification of India, Pakistan, Bangladesh and Afghanistan, without the use of force, is possible. Unlike Vajpayee, who was a poet evasive on facts, Modi is a hard-core rightist, so there is little possibility of his government talking on Kashmir resolution which would usher in permanent peace and stability. True to his ideology, Modi, while reviewing the unrest in Kashmir following the killing of Hizbul commander Burhan Wani in July 2016, made it clear that India would only talk about the return of POK and Gilgit-Baltistan with Pakistan.

In December 2015, when Modi made a surprise stopover in Lahore while returning to Delhi from Kabul, L. K. Advani, while reiterating the need for peace, exhorted him to take the Vajpayee vision enshrined in the Lahore Declaration forward. The latter, signed in 1999, is generic on the need for bilateral talks on outstanding issues, including terrorism and Kashmir without resorting to war. This will not be acceptable to Rawalpindi, which under the Musharraf-Manmohan Singh formula, had moved substantively on Kashmir resolution.

Meanwhile, just when the stage was set for the January 2016 bilateral talks at two levels (NSA and foreign secretary), Pathankot happened. On 2 January 2016, terrorists belonging to Lashkar-e-Taiba attacked the Indian Air Force forward base in Pathankot. While three Indian soldiers were killed with no damage to fighter aircraft, the Modi government, equating the attack with the 26/11 Mumbai attacks, cancelled talks, pushing bilateral relations to a new low. It was made clear that terror and talks could not be held together; terrorists who attacked the air base had to be brought to justice for talks to commence.

Why did Lashkar attack the Indian air force base on the eve of the talks? Because the Pakistan Army, which had managed to grab centre stage through NSA talks, was not happy that its NSA was not informed by the Sharif government about Modi's unscheduled 2015 Christmas day visit to Nawaz Sharif's house in Lahore. For one, Rawalpindi would not allow Islamabad to hijack the core issue of Kashmir. For another, even when it had shown the way for meaningful bilateral talks (through NSA channel) to New Delhi, the latter gave primacy to talks with Pakistan's civilian government.

What is the way forward? While Indian analysts were divided on whether to talk or not with Pakistan, a few suggested that low-hanging fruits—like Siachen and Sir Creek—should be taken up once 'comprehensive bilateral talks' began. This approach would not bear results. Having been overtaken by events, Siachen is no longer 'low-hanging fruit'. It has become a complex issue, whose solution has become linked with the Kashmir resolution. The only confidence building measure acceptable to the Pakistan Army would be consistent bilateral interaction on Kashmir resolution.

In the absence of Kashmir resolution talks, the way forward to continue engagement with the Pakistan national security advisor would be to talk military confidence building measures enshrined in the Lahore Declaration's memorandum of understanding. These could even lead to Kashmir resolution in the future.

MILITARY CONFIDENCE BUILDING MEASURES

Military confidence building measures between India and Pakistan have three characteristics. One, whenever a destabilizing factor got introduced in the crisis-prone relationship, military CBMs were sought by both sides to stabilize the situation. In the 1980s, the destabilizing factor was Pakistan's nuclearization under General Zia-ul-Haq; in 1990, it was the beginning of the insurgency in Kashmir; in the mid-1990s, it was proliferation of ballistic missiles; and in 1998, it was the nuclear tests conducted by India and Pakistan.

Two, given the trust deficit, outside help, usually from the US, was welcomed by both sides to stabilize the situation. And three, unlike civilian CBMs, military CBMs, when agreed, have not been breached by either side.

India's large-scale 1986–87 military exercise Brasstacks, believed to be a cover-up for a sudden attack on Pakistan, and sharp Pakistani riposte, were held under the knowledge that both sides had acquired nuclear weapons capabilities. Pakistan's top scientist, A. Q. Khan, in January 1987 told prominent Indian journalist Kuldip Nayyar that they had the bomb. In

March the same year, General Haq confirmed to *Time* magazine that Pakistan had the technology to make the nuclear bomb whenever it wanted.India had conducted a peaceful nuclear explosion in 1974, and, since 1983 its nuclear programme had been weapon-oriented. Taking their cue from the availability of nuclear capability with both sides, leading defence analysts since the 1990 crisis have peddled the thesis that nuclear deterrence prevented conventional war between India and Pakistan. Pakistan's President Ghulam Ishaq Khan and General Mirza Aslam Beg publicly supported this thesis after their retirement in 1993. 'Far from talk of nuclear war, there is no danger of even a conventional war between India and Pakistan... As compared to previous years, there is no possibility of an India-Pakistan war now.' Three other prominent Pakistanis, diplomats Abdul Sattar, Agha Shahi and Air Chief Marshal Zulfikar Ali Khan made a similar claim, '1990 was one instance when Pakistan's nuclear capability deterred an Indian attack.' On the Indian side, General K. Sundarji was responsible for lending credence to this kind of thinking. He suggested that the three rounds of the India–Pakistan conflict (1947–48, 1965 and 1971) would not have occurred if minimum nuclear deterrence had been available at the time.

The nuclear assertions made by both sides were debatable. The reason for avoiding war had been that both militaries were nearly matched at the operational level of war. In a short conventional war, which had been envisaged against a nuclear backdrop, there were few worthwhile political objectives and military aims to be achieved by either side. If India had little to show in a short war, the loss of lives and huge finances did not make sense.

However, the period from 1987–90 saw the biggest exchange of delegations between India and Pakistan. Both countries signed the agreement on the prohibition of attack against nuclear installations and facilities in Islamabad on 31 December 1988, which was ratified on 27 January 1991. Since 1 January 1992, both sides have exchanged lists of their facilities covered under the agreement every year.

Following the 1990 crisis, and the arrival of the US mission to India led by Robert Gates, deputy national security advisor under President George H. W. Bush, three military CBMs were signed. One, a hotline between the two director generals of Military Operations was established with the understanding that each side would activate it once a week. While this CBM has not been followed with regularity, it has come in handy in times of crisis. Two, an agreement on advance notification of military exercises, movements and manoeuvres was signed. The agreement prohibits holding of exercises near the border and LC, and requires details of location, duration, size and type of exercise to be given. It also established procedures for addressing situations caused by changes in exercise parameters.

And three, measures were taken to prevent airspace violations and permitting overflights/landings by military aircraft. The latter agreement envisaged prior notice of supply dropping, mercy and rescue missions, and measures to ensure safety of air operations.

In the 1990s, when both India and Pakistan acquired ballistic missiles, India surprised Pakistan with the announcement of the indigenous Integrated Guided Missiles Development Programme (IGMDP) in 1983. It was no secret that the IGMDP was inspired and supported by India's indigenous space programme which was fairly advanced. The founder of the IGMDP, A. P. J. Abdul Kalam (later president of India), had worked for years on the Space Launch Vehicle programme.

With little technology base and expertise, Pakistan in 1987 decided to catch up. It adopted a three-pronged approach to resolve the ballistic missile dilemma after Zia-ul-Haq's death in an air crash in August 1988. Pakistan Prime Minister Benazir Bhutto offered a zero-missile status CBM to India repeatedly from 1988–96, which India did not accept. She urged the US to put pressure on India to stop or go slow on its indigenous missile development, which had a destabilizing effect in the subcontinent. This was successful as India's Prime Minister P. V. Narasimha Rao succumbed to US pressure. It was lost on the Indian leadership that with large numbers of ballistic missiles armed with conventional warheads, the balance for conventional war (at the operational level) would tilt decisively in India's favour, forcing Pakistan to reconsider its options on Kashmir.

Pakistan's third prong was the acquisition of missile production capability. In February 1989, Pakistan Army chief General Beg announced the test-firing of two indigenous missiles, Hatf-IA with a range of 80 kilometres, and Hatf-I with a 100-kilometre range. He added that Pakistan was developing the Hatf-II missile with help from a friendly country without naming China. Meanwhile, Pakistan's interim prime minister, Moeenuddin Qureshi, admitted in 1992 that Pakistan had got some missiles from China. These were Chinese M-11 missiles with a range of 300 kilometres capable of carrying 500-kilometre warheads, which were later renamed Hatf-III by Pakistan. By 1996, Pakistan had, with Chinese help, set up a production facility for Hatf-III missiles; with this, Islamabad stopped offering zero-missile status to India. Henceforth, for every missile test done by India, Pakistan would reply with a missile test of its own.

Pakistan also opened a second line of ballistic missiles with help from North Korea in 1998. The Chinese line had missiles with solid propellants, which were mobile but had range restriction. The North Korean line was with liquid propellant, which though less mobile could take the warhead to a greater distance.

With military instability owing to ballistic missiles still unresolved, both nations conducted nuclear tests in May 1998. By bringing nuclear weapons capability out in the open, the tests spurred an arms race. The move from nuclear capability to nuclear weaponization necessitated certain basic steps to be taken; delay in nuclear confidence building measures added to the trust deficit.

Weaponization implied putting into place a credible and flexible strategic command and control system. It also meant furtive building and stockpiling of fissile material ahead of the Fissile Material Cut-off Treaty. Ambiguity in Pakistan's nuclear-use policy required capability for different varieties of warheads and ranges of delivery systems to stay ahead of the adversary. It also demanded matching up with advances in India's technologies feeding its future nuclear trajectories.

Having unsuccessfully tried to stop Pakistan from conducting its tests to match India's nuclear blasts, the US, within eight weeks, was working with the Pakistan Army on an arms control regime. This was not difficult, as Pakistani nuclear interlocutors were well versed with the operational and technical aspects of nuclear arms control. This was not the case with India, where military officers were not part of the nuclear diplomacy and deterrence posture.

The Pakistani military officers in discussions with the US devised the Strategic Restraint Regime for South Asia. It consisted of 'three interlocking elements: (1) agreed reciprocal measures for nuclear and missile restraint to prevent deliberate or accidental use of nuclear weapons; (2) establishment of a conventional restraint measure; and (3) establishment of a political mechanism for resolving bilateral conflicts, especially the core issue of Jammu and Kashmir'.

Having worked out the contours of the regional stabilization regime, Pakistan soon got the opportunity to discuss it with India. In September 1998, Prime Ministers Vajpayee and Sharif met during the UN General Assembly in New York and decided to resume the Composite Dialogue stalled since the nuclear tests. Interlocutors on both sides agreed that under the segment of peace and security and confidence building measures, Pakistan would offer the Strategic Restraint Regime to India.

When the Indian delegation under Foreign Secretary K. Raghunath arrived for talks in Islamabad on 15–16 October 1998, both sides were in for a surprise when the dialogue, which was the first major discussion on security issues that included nuclear and conventional force arms control, started. According to Pakistani interlocutor, Brigadier Feroz Hassan Khan, 'The Indian delegation had no military officer at the meeting, and the diplomats barely anticipated such an elaborate proposal...it became clear that India was prepared only to have generalized discussions on these issues'. The Indian side refused to discuss conventional force doctrine and restraint as the delegation headed by Raghunath said India faced threats besides Pakistan.

India was unwilling to discuss conventional war capabilities with Pakistan. It only wanted to discuss nuclear and missile restraints and offered a 'no-first-use' doctrine agreement. This was unacceptable to Pakistan since, in its thinking, conventional war capabilities are linked to nuclear capabilities, and so they both need to be discussed together.

The situation altered in 2016 in two fundamental ways. With the Pakistan Army having plugged existing conventional gaps, a war between India and Pakistan is not possible. In order to meet the Indian Army's Cold Start Doctrine challenge, the Pakistan Army has taken two steps, one declaratory and the other meant to strengthen its conventional war capability. As we have seen, Pakistan has altered its nuclear doctrine from minimum deterrence to full-spectrum deterrence with the announcement of tactical nuclear weapons to stop India's purported mechanized offensive at the border itself. More relevant is its new concept of utilization of Pakistan Army reserves. The Pakistan Army has moved 25 per cent of its reserves in permanent forward defence positions. Moreover, it has trained to move one-third of its army from the Afghanistan border within seventy-two hours. Most importantly, it has acquired long-range turbofan propelled Babur cruise missiles to stop advancing Indian columns. India does not have a matching capability.

With the Cold Start Doctrine (for the plains) virtually neutralized by Pakistan, the pivot for the Indian Army's conventional war has shifted to the mountains. Indian troops are perched on mountains and high-altitude areas along the disputed borders with Pakistan and China. India has both military options and military threats here. For instance, threats to India from Gilgit-Baltistan (earlier Northern Areas) have increased as Pakistani and Chinese forces have fused at the Khunjerab Pass and the Wakhan Corridor further north, which provides China with the only land route to Afghanistan.

Given the geopolitical realities and threats to J&K, India, with a limited annual defence allocation of US$ 39 billion, should consider mutual arms reduction in the plains with Pakistan. Since the Indian Army has established a good defensive posture with reorganized forces called pivot corps and integrated battle groups in the plains, mutual and equal reduction of offensive forces would be a good idea that would interest the Pakistan Army. This will assist in arresting the burgeoning arms race and help with the resolution of the Kashmir issue too.

Unfortunately, it is probable that this idea will appeal neither to the Indian Army, which would resist its empire shrinking, nor to the diplomats, who would have to share space with military officers. However, whatever the Indian government does, it ought to be prepared to discuss military confidence building measures with Pakistan. Writing in *FORCE*, former Pakistan Army chief General Karamat suggested the following:

> The contours of a regional regime that includes reciprocal restraints on nuclear, missile and conventional force capabilities including a Joint Verification Committee or Commission (JVC) could be considered. This would mean a whole raft of confidence building measures meant to encourage conflict resolution and reduction of tension, nuclear deterrence related to conventional force imbalance and geographic constraints, arms control measures and an institutionalised crisis management arrangement... While asymmetrical proportionate force reduction may be a future option there could be consideration for designating of low-force-zones at some stage, strike force numbers and locations and a system of notifying and monitoring movements from peace locations to combat assemblies.

The mechanism for such talks is available under the Lahore Declaration signed between the two countries on 21 February 1999. The operative part of the Lahore Declaration is the memorandum of understanding which broadly tackles four security related issues:

(1) Give prior notification with respect to ballistic missiles flights;
(2) Discuss respective nuclear doctrines and security concepts for confidence building in nuclear and conventional fields aimed at conflict avoidance;
(3) Set up a nuclear risk reduction centre to minimize risks of accidental or unauthorized use of nuclear weapons; and
(4) Improve existing channels of communications.

However, to participate meaningfully in such discussions, Indian interlocutors need an understanding of nuclear and conventional wars. Diplomats cannot do this without the participation of military officers. In India, since the political leadership holds the responsibility for using nuclear weaponry, it should know the complexities of future nuclear and conventional war domains. With this as the essential beginning, India could hope to build credible military power.

Building Military Power

Chapter 13

A NEW DECISION-MAKING STRUCTURE

In the previous chapters, we have seen how Pakistan has built military power both deliberately and sometimes inadvertently. Wars, coups and terrorism have been used to hone its military power. Today, despite its limited success against its adversary in the past, India is unlikely to be the victor in any conflict. In order to win, India has to build its military power and we will look at this in detail over the next few chapters. It must be stressed, though, that it is not in the interest of India to focus solely on building military power. As has been pointed out repeatedly, it is in our best interest to resolve the Kashmir issue by working out a permanent solution with Pakistan, stop alienating the Muslim community in the country so they are not drawn into terrorism and repeal draconian laws like AFSPA. But let us turn now to the most important ways in which military power is built.

The late defence analyst K. Subrahmanyam wrote, 'Politicians enjoy power without any responsibility, bureaucrats wield power without any accountability, and the military assumes responsibility without any direction.' Nations with military power should have politicians as the strongest component of the trio—politician, bureaucrat, and military officer—in their higher defence management. In India, they are the weakest. Consequently, bureaucrats wield power and the military is spectator to decision-making. This is at the heart of what ails India's defence and prevents it, despite its impressive military force, from becoming a military power. This state exists because India, since Independence, has never had a defence policy or political directive that informs its defence. Yet this singularly important issue has never found mention in any defence task force's recommendations.

Having spent years heading a think tank, Subrahmanyam, a bureaucrat, had developed an objective world-view which conceptualized a leading role for India in the nuclearized world. Given his grasp of political-bureaucratic-military issues, Subrahmanyam was the Vajpayee government's right choice to head a committee to review the 1999 Kargil conflict with Pakistan.

Despite having achieved the limited objective of evicting terrorists from Indian soil, the conflict had gone terribly wrong on numerous counts. Based on the recommendations of the Kargil Review Committee report, the government ordered four task forces; one of them was on management of defence, headed by Arun Singh, the union minister of state for defence in Rajiv Gandhi's government.

The report on management of defence was scrutinized by a panel of three senior politicians headed by the union minister for home, L. K. Advani, and their final recommendation for reforming the national security system was released as the Group of Ministers (GoM) report in February 2001. The implementation of the GoM report was half-hearted at best, as political and bureaucratic interests, and interservices rivalry came into play.

A decade later, in June 2011, the Manmohan Singh government set up the Naresh Chandra task force to review the GoM report on management of defence. Naresh Chandra was a former cabinet and defence secretary. While the recommendations of his task force were never made public, they found their way into the public discourse through members of the task force. Recommendations of both the Arun Singh and Naresh Chandra task forces had a serious limitation: while keeping the political leadership outside its brief, it suggested reforms for better interaction between civilian bureaucrats and military leaders. The need for a defence policy was omitted.

As head of the Ministry of Defence, the framing of the defence policy or political directive should be the defence minister's responsibility. The operational directive, the long-term perspective plans and annual defence acquisition plans of the three defence services and commonality of equipment monitored by the Integrated Defence Headquarters should flow from the defence policy.

The defence policy should be a two-way peacetime process with the defence minister as the central pivot. The Chiefs of Staff Committee (COSC) comprising the three service chiefs should provide the combined military assessment for prevalent military threats. The defence minister after interactions with the COSC takes the combined military assessment to the prime minister and the Cabinet Committee on Security (comprising the ministers of external affairs, home, defence and finance with the national security advisor as member-secretary) where the political and international aspects would be deliberated upon. For example, this group would consider the political objectives to be gained by war, and, if these were not worth the loss of lives and cost to the economy and international standing, what the other options would be.

It could be argued that the defence services already have the unsaid political directive: to defend India's sovereignty and territorial integrity. This formulation is too vague and does not answer numerous pertinent questions. For example, is it possible to fight a two-front war? If not, which war could be fought and which should be handled by other means? Will the war be fought on the enemy's territory and for what political objectives? How would the world react to the war? What about nuclear weapons? Shouldn't there be a seamless integration of the country's nuclear and conventional war plans, as in China and Pakistan? Who will assess Pakistan's nuclear redlines and should they be known beforehand to the political leadership, senior field commanders and the commander-in-chief of the Strategic Forces Command? Are the army's continuous counter-insurgency operations in Jammu and Kashmir distracting it from its primary task on the border? These and many more questions require the Chiefs of Staff Committee to interact with the defence minister, and the defence minister and the prime minister to consult with each other. Such interactions will demolish silos between the COSC, defence minister, scientists, the Cabinet Committee on Security members and the prime minister.

These discussions would also encourage the prime minister to meet the COSC on a regular basis to understand war preparedness. Prime Minister Indira Gandhi used to do this—both Field Marshal Sam Manekshaw and General K.V. Krishna Rao confirmed this in media interviews. According to General V. P. Malik, he as the chairman, COSC, had started informal interactions with Prime Minister Vajpayee during peacetime.

He writes, 'During these meetings of about thirty minutes duration, we (the three chiefs) shared views on important strategic and security-related matters over a cup of tea. The interaction helped in establishing rapport and developed a better understanding of the on-going strategic issues at the politico-military level. All of us realised the immense utility of such interactions.' The general added, 'The secretaries in the ministry of defence and the cabinet secretariat had expressed strong resentment (on these interactions), hence the meetings were discontinued.'

Worried about losing their clout with the political leadership, the bureaucrats prevailed upon an indecisive Vajpayee. Rather unusually, they managed to do so with Prime Minister Narendra Modi as well, despite his being projected as a strong and decisive leader. For instance, on coming to power in May 2014, Modi met with the three services chiefs, and it was reported that these interactions would be held once a month. These happened for two months and then were quietly dropped; the bureaucrats had won yet again.

Since the defence policy or political directive of the government to the armed forces would be issued by the defence minister, the 1961 Government of India allocation of Business Rules and Transaction of Business Rules would need to be amended by Parliament. Instead of the defence secretary (a bureaucrat) who heads the Department of Defence, the defence minister who heads the Ministry of Defence would be responsible for the defence of India.

Given that the defence minister would meet the Chiefs of Staff Committee regularly on defence policy and operational matters, the service headquarters, participating in policy formulation, would no longer remain outside the apex governmental structure. Reforms would become imperative to bring them too into the ambit of the Government of India allocation of Business Rules and Transaction of Business Rules. This would solve one of the key findings of the 2001 Group of Ministers report that 'the COSC has not been effective in fulfilling its mandate'.

Hence, the foremost fault of the Vajpayee government's action would get corrected. In May 2001, the Vajpayee government had announced that the services' headquarters, which were not part of the government, would become the 'integrated headquarters' of the defence ministry rather than remain its 'attached offices'. The change, at the behest of the bureaucracy, was cosmetic, since the service headquarters were given limited financial and administrative powers. They were not made part of the government's management loop, which would no longer be the case as the services headquarters would become a part of the government.

The defence policy made by the prime minister-headed Cabinet Committee on Security will provide the 'why' of war. Based upon the 'why' of war, the Chiefs of Staff Committee will prepare the operational directive dealing with the 'how' of war which will be issued under the defence minister's signature to the services' headquarters.

Making the prime minister and defence minister aware of military matters by bringing the COSC and its services' headquarters into the government loop will not be enough. Politicians in general and members of Parliament's standing committee on defence in particular too need to understand military matters. This would encourage sensible comments and parliamentary debates on defence to ensure India becomes a lean, efficient and technology-savvy military power. The next military reform, therefore, should be of the national security advisor—the bridge between the Prime Minister's Office and union ministers concerned with defence and internal security. The NSA is also the member-secretary of the National (Nuclear) Command Authority (comprising the same political members as the Cabinet Committee on Security), and is responsible for executing instructions regarding nuclear weapons given by the National Command Authority.

NATIONAL SECURITY ADVISOR

India's first national security advisor, Brajesh Mishra, being Prime Minister Vajpayee's alter ego, in 1998 (after the nuclear tests) had the liberty to decide his own brief. He chose to retain two divergent and important portfolios— the NSA and principal secretary in the Prime Minister's Office. As the NSA, his brief included nuclear weapons—nuclear policy, strategy and preparedness, defence (the three services' chiefs reported to him), foreign affairs and internal security. As the principal secretary all files marked for the prime minister went through him.

In June 2004, when Manmohan Singh's government assumed charge, 'the NSA's beat, with foreign affairs, defence and nuclear strategy was allotted to Mani [J.N.] Dixit, and internal security to [M.K.] Narayanan'. After Dixit's death, Narayanan, a former police officer, became the NSA, followed by Shivshankar Menon, a former foreign secretary. When the Modi government came to power, Ajit Kumar Doval, also a police officer with Narayanan's background, was appointed NSA. With the exception of Brajesh Mishra, who was a strategist capable of out-of-the-box thinking, other NSAs have stuck to their comfort zones—Narayanan and Doval focused on intelligence services and internal security while Dixit and Menon were fixated on foreign policy. The NSA's primary job of maintaining minimum nuclear deterrence—it was why the office was created in the first place—does not seem to have been given due importance.

When asked for advice following Dixit's sudden death, defence analyst Subrahmanyam suggested that the office of the NSA should be outside the PMO and that the NSA should not necessarily be a former government officer. He could be a scientist or an international relations expert. Taking their cue from this, the authors asked BJP Member of Parliament, retired Major General B. C. Khanduri, whether it would not be better if a bright young politician was appointed as the NSA. His response was lukewarm. According to him, 'A politician would prefer nurturing his constituency rather than being the NSA.' Perhaps. But the prime minister could resolve this dilemma by appointing a senior politician (with a proven track record) who is not keen on contesting elections. Between being a Member of

NATIONAL SECURITY ADVISOR'S PROPOSED TASKS AND ORGANIZATION

Tasks

1. Nuclear Weapons
2. Defence
3. Foreign Affairs
4. Internal Security Affairs
5. Head of National Security Council
6. Head of Executive Council of National Command Authority (NCA)
7. Member Secretary of Political Council of National Command Authority (NCA)
8. Operational Control of Special Forces Command
9. Custodian of Conventional War Plans
10. Custodian of Nuclear War Plans
11. To Advise the CCS on Seamless Transition from Conventional to Nuclear War
12. To Regularly Brief Members of Parliament of Defence Parliamentary Committee, etc.

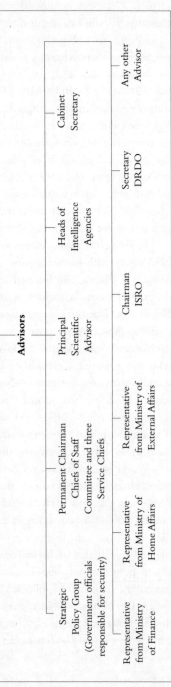

NSA (Politician)

De facto Chief of Defence Staff and Head of National Security Council

Advisors

Principal Scientific Advisor — Chairman ISRO — Heads of Intelligence Agencies — Secretary DRDO — Cabinet Secretary — Any other Advisor

Strategic Policy Group (Government officials responsible for security)

Representative from Ministry of Finance — Representative from Ministry of Home Affairs — Permanent Chairman Chiefs of Staff Committee and three Service Chiefs — Representative from Ministry of External Affairs

Parliament of the Upper House (Rajya Sabha) and the NSA, he might prefer the latter for two reasons: proximity to the prime minister, and union Cabinet status (which should be given).

A senior politician as the NSA would come to office with an open mind and huge political heft. His brief should include nuclear weapons, defence, internal security, foreign affairs and regular interaction with politicians associated with India's national security. His role would be both advisory and executive.

The NSA's office should be outside the PMO, and as head of the National Security Council, he could have members with knowledge on various subjects. The present National Security Council which advises the political members of the Cabinet Committee on Security is a three-tier structure. The first tier, called the Strategic Policy Group has serving officials associated with the execution of security policy. The second tier called the National Security Advisory Board (NSAB) consists of outside experts. The third tier is the National Security Council Secretariat. Since the government does not share classified information with outsiders, the Modi government has reconstituted the NSAB. With Ambassador P. S. Raghavan as chairman, the new NSAB is smaller in size and has been tasked with specific time-bound projects.

The NSA would provide the third advisory option to the prime minister on military matters, the other two being through the defence minister and direct interaction with the services' chiefs. Being a key player in the National Command Authority responsible for nuclear weapons, the NSA would understand the linkage between conventional war and the nuclear weapons option. As he would be responsible for conventional war plans (held by him and the permanent chairman, Chiefs of Staff Committee, to be appointed), nuclear war plans (held in his office), and internal security plans during crisis and war contingencies (prepared by the home ministry), the NSA with help from his secretariat would be the de facto chief of defence staff too.

CHIEF OF DEFENCE STAFF/PERMANENT CHAIRMAN, CHIEFS OF STAFF COMMITTEE

The creation of the Chief of Defence Staff (CDS) post was recommended by the 2001 Group of Ministers report. As the Chiefs of Staff Committee (COSC) had been ineffective, it was felt that the senior-most service chief, with elevated rank and stature, be made the CDS. Unlike the chairman, COSC, which was a rotational post with the senior-most service chief being a double-hatter (heading his own service and being chairman, COSC), the CDS—a five-star rank officer—would be a permanent post. While presiding over the deliberations of the COSC, the CDS would have his own tri-service secretariat run by his deputy, the vice CDS as the member-secretary, and discharge the following functions:

One, he would provide single-point military advice to the defence minister. Individual service chiefs would however continue to advise the defence minister on their service-related issues and could be invited to attend the Cabinet Committee on Security, if required. For example, if the CDS was a former air force chief, asking the army chief's advice on cross-border terrorism would be more effective.

The second function of the CDS would be to head the tri-service Strategic Forces Command (SFC) which was created on 4 January 2003. As head of the SFC, which would be run by a three-star rank commander-in-chief, the CDS would have overall administrative control—responsibility for managing the nuclear delivery systems—as distinct from operational control vested in the political leadership through the NSA.

The third function would be to improve the procurement procedure for intra-services and interservices for efficient utilization of defence allocations. And, finally, the CDS was expected to foster joint-ness amongst services. Since wars were expected to be short and swift, it was argued that the three services should fight the war together for optimal results. This required joint planning and joint training leading to fighting wars under a single commander.

The Group of Ministers directed the cabinet secretary to make recommendations regarding the relationship of the Chief of Defence Staff with the civilian officers in the Defence Ministry. The CDS, it was agreed, would be the 'principal military advisor' as distinct from the defence secretary designated as the 'principal defence advisor'. The latter, relegated to administrative tasks, would have the following functions—supervision of the department of defence; coordination between various departments of defence; coordinating finalization of the Long Term Defence Perspective Plan (of ten and fifteen years), five-year plan, and the annual budget for approval of the defence minister; and advising the defence minister on matters pertaining to Parliament, central and state governments, other ministries, and so on.

The above separation of powers amongst the civil bureaucrats and military officials though highly desirable was not acceptable to the bureaucracy. Building upon politicians' fears, born of ignorance, the bureaucracy scuttled the plan by arguing that too many powers in the hands of the CDS could result in the takeover of the government by the military, as was the case in Pakistan. Just as the idea of a military coup frightened the politicians, within the services, the air force resisted the creation of the CDS. It said that a CDS from the army who knew little about the air force's core competencies would be unhelpful to the growth and utilization of air power, which given technological advances had emerged as a strategic force capable of decisive results in war.

The result was a halfway house. Instead of the CDS, the government created the vice CDS post with a tri-service secretariat. A three-star officer, the vice CDS was made a non-voting member of the Chiefs of Staff Committee. Since there was no CDS, the question arose: vice chief to whom? To correct this anomaly, the vice CDS was redesignated as the Chief of Integrated Defence Staff, and was eventually changed to Chief of Integrated Staff to Chairman (CISC) of the Chiefs of Staff Committee. In day-to-day functioning, he is referred to as Chief of Integrated Defence Headquarters (IDH).

Just like his nomenclature, the role of the CISC has plenty of grey zones. He is answerable directly to the defence minister like the defence secretary, yet the IDH is not considered on par with the other four departments—the Department of Defence, the Department of Research and Development, the Department of Production and Supplies, and the Department of Finance—of the defence ministry headed by the defence secretary. Unlike the four departments of the defence ministry, the Integrated Defence Headquarters remains an attached office of the defence ministry, something like the secretariat, outside the government policymaking loop.

Given the locus standi of the IDH, the Defence Intelligence Agency under it too has an uncertain position in the defence ministry. The Defence Intelligence Agency, as distinct from the intelligence services of the three services headquarters responsible for tactical and operational intelligence, is charged with gathering strategic intelligence. Moreover, as the representative of the COSC, the Defence Intelligence Agency is supposed to advise the defence minister, the COSC, and provide services' overall intelligence inputs to the National Security Council as its member. The Defence Intelligence Agency is also to help the defence and foreign affairs ministries in the field of international cooperation. With so much on its plate, it is able to deliver only minimally because services' headquarters are reluctant to share intelligence with it, and defence attachés, who are supposed to be under it, continue to pay obeisance to their parent service. It is unclear if the Ministry of External Affairs even bothers to interact with it.

Next, take the case of the Andaman and Nicobar Command. Since it is directly under the COSC, for all administrative tasks, the Andaman and Nicobar Command approaches the IDH. On operational matters, nothing much happens as the service chiefs in the COSC accord preference to their own service over the Andaman and Nicobar Command. Created in 2001, the Andaman and Nicobar Command is the first tri-service command of the defence services meant to safeguard India's strategic interests across the Strait of Malacca into Southeast Asia. The commander-in-chief, Andaman and Nicobar Command, appointed by rotation from the three services, remains its biggest shortcoming. To expect a three-star commander-in-chief from the army and the air force to appreciate maritime issues, when the three services work in compartments, is unrealistic. To strengthen the Andaman and Nicobar Command operationally, which is essential since the People's Liberation Army Navy has made the Indian Ocean its playground, is an urgent need. The Andaman and Nicobar Command, while remaining tri-service, should be permanently under an overall naval commander.

The relationship of the IDH and Defence Research and Development Organisation (DRDO) is similarly muddled. The IDH formed the Horizon Core Technology Group with the DRDO with two aims. First, to know what technologies the DRDO thought would be relevant fifteen years ahead and how they would benefit the defence services. And second, for the DRDO to find out from the defence services what technologies they desired in their fifteen-year perspective plans. The arrangement has produced suboptimal results because the DRDO is part of the government loop with its secretary being advisor to the defence minister. And the office of the chief of the IDH is attached to the Defence Ministry.

However, there are three areas where the IDH, with the chiefs of integrated staff to chairman (CISC) as its head, has shown encouraging results. The first concerns management of nuclear weapons. The CISC prepares the nuclear targets list which is updated annually. The CISC gets the strategic target lists of the three defence services through the COSC, gets the opinion of the commander-in-chief, Strategic Forces Command, on the consolidated list, and once finalized hands it to the NSA for safe custody. The big lacuna in the system is that the CISC who prepares and finalizes the nuclear targets list works in isolation. He is unaware of the nuclear yields to weight ratios and accuracies which are known only to the scientists (DAE and DRDO) and the NSA.

The second issue concerns creation of more tri-service organizations in addition to the Andaman and Nicobar Command and the Strategic Forces Command. The CISC has under him the Defence Space Agency,

Defence Cyber Agency and the Defence Special Forces Agency, which was under way in August 2016. Headed by two-star rank officers, the Defence Space Agency interacts with the Indian Space Research Organisation; and the Defence Cyber Agency works closely with the National Technology Research Organisation under the union Home Ministry. Both the agencies are expected to be upgraded to commands awaiting the government nod. Once formed, the Space Command is expected to be headed by a three-star air force officer, and the Cyber Command to become the responsibility of a three-star army officer. What sort of relationship the two new commands would have with the CISC, who is also a three-star officer, remains to be seen. Ideally, both administratively and operationally these commands should be under the permanent chairman, Chiefs of Staff Committee (PCCOSC), when formed.

The Defence Special Forces Agency, which is sought to be raised, would be both different from and in addition to the Special Forces of the three services. It is expected to have direct recruitments and not lateral inductions from the services. While its administrative management could be with the CISC or PCCOSC, its operational control for strategic employment is expected to be with the NSA.

The third area where the IDH has made good progress concerns joint operations. Two doctrines—one for amphibious operations and another for joint operations for expeditionary missions—have been written and handed over to the COSC. While officers of the three services have worked out joint doctrines and operating manuals, much would depend upon interservices training.

Against this backdrop, the Naresh Chandra task force, which submitted its report in August 2012, made three suggestions pertaining to higher defence management. These were (a) creation of the post of permanent chairman, COSC; (b) establishment of a bureau of politico-military affairs; and (c) cross-posting of civil and military officers in the ministries of defence and external affairs.

The creation of the post of permanent chairman, Chiefs of Staff Committee—a four-star rank officer—for a fixed two-year term rather than a CDS found acceptance with the politicians and the air force brass. As he would not be the single point military advisor to the government, he would not have a higher status than the other three service chiefs.

The PCCOSC is a good idea and would further help what has been accomplished by various CISCs. Like the three service chiefs comprising the COSC, the PCCOSC too would be recognized by the Allocation of

Business Rules and Transaction of Business Rules. And the IDH, which he would head, would become on par with the other four departments of the defence ministry. This would have five major benefits.

One, as another department of the defence ministry, the IDH would no longer be the military secretariat of the department of defence. Its recommendations regarding defence planning, for instance, would go directly to the defence minister with minimal interference from the civil bureaucrats. This would obviate the need for cross-posting civil and military officers in the defence ministry as recommended by the Naresh Chandra task force and forcefully sought by numerous senior military officers. Interestingly, the Arun Singh task force on management of defence had rejected this suggestion as impractical.

Two, the PCCOSC would be better placed to work with the DRDO regarding the needs of the defence services and the utilization of technologies sought by the DRDO. Moreover, by becoming a voting member of the COSC, the interaction between the PCCOSC heading the IDH, an administrative headquarters, and the service chiefs heading operational headquarters, would improve substantially. Also, while the IDH would not decide what weapon systems each service should have, they would be able to clarify matters in the case of commonality of equipment like unmanned aerial vehicles, cruise missiles, air defence, and so on. Building a joint capability would give them better value for money and an edge over adversaries.

Three, the PCCOSC would administratively head tri-service commands like the Andaman and Nicobar Command, Strategic Forces Command and the expected Space, Cyber and Special Forces commands. The tri-service commands would provide a boost to joint-ness as officers and men who spend time here would better understand the core competencies of other services. Over time, interservice postings at various levels of field command should become a norm, perhaps, a necessary qualification for higher command positions. The defence services could then hope to develop genuine operational joint-ness necessary for swift and short wars. This, however, would take years to happen.

Four, the PCCOSC with a fixed two-year tenure and elevated rank and stature would be able to work better with the three services' chiefs. Working with the commander-in-chief, Strategic Forces Command, the PCCOSC and the services chiefs would contribute better towards a nuclear weapons targeting list than the present CISC.

Five, after superannuating from his post like the other services' chiefs at age sixty-two, the PCCOSC, given his experience with the COSC and as head of the tri-service IDH, could be appointed as tri-service advisor to the NSA.

The top-down conventional war chain of command will run from the prime minister-headed Cabinet Committee on Security to the defence minister to the PCCOSC and the service chiefs. The nuclear war chain of command will run from the prime minister-headed National Command Authority to the NSA to the commander-in-chief, Strategic Forces Command, with the PCCOSC and the three chiefs being in the loop. The NSA will provide the seamless integration of conventional war and nuclear war plans.

In summation, if the government were to frame a defence policy or political directive under the defence minister, have a politician as the NSA, and create the post of PCCOSC, India would improve its higher defence management substantially. All joint commands, namely, Andaman and Nicobar Command, Strategic Forces Command, Cyber, Space and Special Forces commands should administratively be brought under the PCCOSC. In operational terms, the command of Special Forces should be with the NSA, of the Andaman and Nicobar Command with the naval headquarters, while the rest (Cyber and Space Commands) could remain with the PCCOSC.

This would spur structural reforms within the three defence services. Instead of spending finances on capability building, the three defence services would be compelled to focus on threat-based acquisitions to accomplish defence policy goals. Capability building is done by nations like the US, who have secure borders, a vibrant indigenous defence industry and roles outside their national borders (expeditionary or out-of-area roles). India has none of these.

A word on three issues which are routinely debated is in order. With the PCCOSC in place, the chief of defence staff will not serve much purpose. The CDS debate should wait until the three defence services after structural reforms develop true joint-ness with an understanding of each other's core competencies at all levels of war. The other issue concerns the theatre commands. Since India has defined military threats and limited war assets, theatre commands are unnecessary. With a PCCOSC in place, the three services' chiefs can easily adopt multiple roles: they can be the top operational commanders and staff officers for their respective services and advisors to the prime minister, defence minister and the national security advisor.

The third issue concerns sea-based deterrence. In India, the scientists are the ones who can operate nuclear weapons, not the military. This raises pertinent questions about the functioning of nuclear armed submarines (called Ship Submersible Ballistic Nuclear, or SSBN) on deterrent patrol. Will the scientists be on board the SSBN (for which they will need military training) or will the SSBN go on patrol without nuclear weapons? This issue does not appear to have been resolved. For example, according to media reports, India's indigenous SSBN INS Arihant was commissioned into service in August 2016, but naval officers say it is not yet ready for deterrent patrols.

CHAPTER 14

THE INDIAN ARMED FORCES

The top-heavy Indian Army—the third largest in the world (after the US and China)—needs massive financial allocations for its modernization. As such financial resources will not be available now or at any time in the future, the key to making the army an effective and powerful fighting force is in the reduction of its numbers. This might seem counter-intuitive but it is a truism. Prime Minister Narendra Modi said as much while addressing the combined commanders' conference in December 2015. Six months later, Defence Minister Manohar Parrikar set up a committee headed by retired Lieutenant General D. B Shekatkar to suggest trimming the non-operational flab or the support elements of the army to restore the 60:40 balance between capital (for acquisitions) and revenue (pay and allowances) of annual defence allocations.

Since the army could not be singled out, Parrikar reportedly broadened the scope of the committee to include the air force and the navy. While the army's force level (combat strength) is based on manpower, and the force levels of the air force and the navy are based on equipment, the need is to trim the army's manpower and equipment of the air force and the navy.

To restore the desired balance between capital and revenue allocation was an impossible objective and Shekatkar knew it since he had conducted a similar exercise within the army decades ago. In the late 1990s, as head of the army's perspective planning directorate (which deals with futuristic operational posture and acquisitions based upon assessed threats) under the army chief, General V. P. Malik, he had recommended the reduction of 50,000 non-operational personnel over three years. The government welcomed the trimming. However, two years into this exercise the Kargil conflict broke out and all reductions were shelved; instead, the army's strength was increased for enhanced guarding duties on the military line.

A similar exercise has been ordered in 2016; the expected recommendations cannot be different from what was done by General

Malik. The committee will most likely suggest downsizing certain support, training and perhaps area and sub-area headquarters, clubbing of non-essential units such as military farms and the army postal service, merger of logistics units including outsourcing of vehicle repairs to the private sector, and so on. The reduction of upto 50,000 to 80,000 personnel would be possible; however, this cosmetic exercise (called a non-field force review) would not help the cause of bringing a balance between finances required for the upkeep of troops and building capabilities for them.

What is needed is a field force review for the trimming of operational flab based on specified political directives. This is unlikely to happen because the political leadership has not framed India's defence policy, and in its absence, the country's military leaders will fight fiercely to thwart the downsizing of their empires.

However, if the army were to carry out manpower rationalization through a field force review based on an honest assessment of the ground situation and the nature of war, it could move towards professionalism. As a consequence, suicide levels (due to combat in no-war-no-peace environment in J&K) within the army would come down, more qualified young men would join the army, and the possibility of war with Pakistan would diminish as there would be good reasons to initiate mutual arms reductions and for India and Pakistan to discuss a less hostile future. A discerning review of the ground situation would throw up the following conclusions.

As we have seen throughout the book, the ground situation since the last full-scale war that India and Pakistan fought in 1971 has altered in many ways. China is powerful and open about its strategic, military and diplomatic closeness with Pakistan. In military terms, Pakistan's strategic and operational sustenance for war is robust, implying the capability to fight a war of long duration. Moreover, the militaries of China and Pakistan have reached a high degree of interoperability—the ability to fight together for a common mission.

Both the Line of Control with Pakistan and the Line of Actual Control with China are live borders. In peacetime, the LC needs border guarding while the LAC needs border policing. In war, while the Indian military has numerous options on the LC, it has few on the International Border where Pakistan's full-spectrum nuclear deterrence has closed them. However, on the LAC, India does not have a war option; and China is unlikely to go to war with India over the border dispute.

The irrefutable conclusion for the Indian Army and the Indian Air

Force, which would fight the land war together, is that the pivot of war has decisively shifted from the plains to mountainous and high-altitude areas. Since high altitude refers to mountainous terrains from 10,000 feet upwards, where the survival of humans is itself a feat, contact war, where opposing forces clash with one another, is more or less passé.

The conflict is likely to be non-contact war where firepower from land and air assumes importance. Long-range artillery, ballistic and cruise missiles with conventional warheads would be used in abundance provided accuracies are good—India and Pakistan have traditionally avoided civilian casualties. Regarding air power, both manned and unmanned assets, preferably the latter, when available, would be used. More stand-off, smart and precision ammunition rather than dumb bombs would be used on well-fortified targets.

The non-contact war would have two major consequences. The contact and depth battles will be fought simultaneously with long-range firepower. This will make logistics trains carrying provisions for front-line troops, and command and control nodes, early and easy targets. Instead of linear battles, the side with better Special Forces which can be inserted vertically in depth (by air drops behind enemy lines) would show decisive results. Moreover, the side with superior intelligence surveillance and reconnaissance, outer space, cyber and electromagnetic warfare capabilities would influence the war outcome by faster target detection and destruction while denying the same to the enemy.

The Indian Army would do well to adopt a defensive posture on the Pakistan border, with firepower rather than manoeuvres taking precedence. The success of the Cold Start Doctrine is neither assured nor would show tangible results in terms of territory and attrition. Given the present state of preparedness, the hopes of the army taking the war (series of battles) into Pakistan is hogwash. There are serious operational shortcomings in terms of training, both within the army and jointly with the air force, as well as of equipment and ammunition. Moreover, Pakistan's countermeasures to thwart Cold Start and its tactical nuclear weapons threat cannot be ignored.

The LC provides opportunities for tactical adjustments and major gains provided the army and air force are trained and equipped to fight together under a common doctrine. Overall, it would be strategic defence on the border and limited counter-attacks on the LC. War objectives will be met both by long range fire-power and Special Forces used in battles deep inside enemy territory. Since such targets in depth on the mountainous terrain could be anything from 2 to 10 kilometres, they would need to be softened up with land-based and air firepower before Special Forces are injected behind the enemy's forward defences.

On the LAC with China, the Indian Army and Air Force can at best fight defensive battles. Unlike the 1962 war, India could end a war with honour intact provided it is prepared for it. At present, this is not the case.

More than anything else, the political resolve to fight with Pakistan or China, whatever the provocations, is not there. There are two reasons for this: India, unlike Pakistan, did not take necessary follow-on actions after the 1998 nuclear tests to become a nuclear weapons state seriously. While Pakistan did not yield to outside (read US) pressure to go slow with its nuclear weaponization, this cannot be said about India. Moreover, India's political leaders (who do not understand military matters) have difficulty in starting a war whose escalation dynamics they do not understand.

If war with Pakistan and China cannot deliver tangible results, why build military power? Because military power is not about war alone; it is about preventing war, deterring adversaries, exercising diplomatic and military coercion, and strengthening one's own political resolve to use military power as an essential component of foreign policy.

INDIAN ARMY
The long list of tasks that the Indian Army has taken upon itself—fighting sub-conventional, conventional and nuclear wars, participating in United Nations peacekeeping and military exercises with friendly nations, being the first responders in natural calamities, seeking a formalized role in disaster management, cleaning the Ganga, advising the government on combating left-wing extremism, regulating traffic in cantonments and everything imaginable where disciplined manpower could be used—would exhaust even a superhero. Clamouring for formal responsibility for Humanitarian Assistance and Disaster Relief (HADR) tasks from the designated National Disaster Management Authority set up in 2005, the army unabashedly solicits media favours to highlight its contributions. Given its manpower and pan-India reach, the Military Operations directorate at Army Headquarters has dedicated cells for HADR operations.

On the one hand, the overstretched army wants accretion of forces to do jobs which are someone else's responsibility. Its strength of one million in 1990, was 1.23 million and growing in 2015. Since 2012, the army has been eating into its annual capital outlay (meant for modernization and acquisitions) to provide for essential revenue needs (pay and allowances of soldiers). The ideal 60:40 ratio between capital and revenue expenditures has been reversed to 40:60. Unless stopped, the army, which complains about shortage of manpower including officers, will continue to burgeon. According to army chief General Dalbir Singh, 'The strength of the standing army is around 1.23 million… While this has skewed the ratio of funds heavily in favour of "revenue", it is unavoidable since the nature of security challenges faced by us necessitates boots on the ground.'

More worryingly, as is public knowledge because of various pronouncements by senior officers over the years, at the moment the army is unfit to fight and win a war. General Shankar Roychowdhury (1994–97) stated this in his book, *Officially at Peace*; General V. P. Malik's famous quote during the 1999 Kargil conflict that 'we will fight with whatever we have' is testament to this; and there is General V. K. Singh's letter to the prime minister in March 2012, to name just a few of the considered opinions in the matter that have been made public.

In office, all army chiefs have publicly maintained that the army is ready to give a befitting response to Pakistan. The claim is not borne out by facts and the pronouncements from top military commanders once they have demitted office. Media reports routinely decry the unpreparedness of the army to win wars. What little the army has as war reserves, for example, equipment, vehicles, spares and ammunition, it is using to raise more units—two divisions between 2009 and 2011, and a mountain corps. This means more manpower costs and less war preparedness. In a session with the parliamentary standing committee on defence in September 2014, army vice chief Lieutenant General Philip Campose was forthcoming on the need for augmenting force levels: 'Our analysis of the threat perception after fifteen years predicted that the way [China] has been getting more aggressive in resolving its disputes with neighbours, especially in view of what we have seen with its maritime disputes in the South China Sea, it was our attempt to make sure that we are fully prepared to deal with this threat if at any time [China] decides to raise the ante and get more aggressive.' In the same session, he admitted that to meet the 'fast time frame' the army used up some of its reserves.

The Parliament report tabled in the Lok Sabha in February 2015 chided the defence ministry for allowing the army to dig into existing war reserves without a separate allocation in the defence budget. In May 2015, the CAG's report pointed out the massive ammunition shortage in the army.

Worried about shortage of finances, Defence Minister Manohar Parrikar told the media in April 2015 that 'the government had frozen the cost of the new 17 Corps at ₹38,000 crore over next eight years and it would consist of 35,000 men'. He said that the previous government had estimated that it would cost ₹88,000 crore and have 70,000 men without making any budgetary allocation. However, in less than a year, the defence minister had reversed his stance. Speaking with the media on 13 January 2016, army chief General Dalbir Singh confirmed that 'a target was kept of nine years and we are on target to raise [17 Mountain Corps] by 2022'. The decision reversal by the government was reflective of the political leadership's unwillingness to know military matters.

The reality is that the army believes there will be no war. On 8 January 2015, on a visit to Kolkata, the general officer commanding, 15 Corps, responsible for the Kashmir theatre, Lieutenant General Subrata Saha, when asked why the army was not returning Pakistani fire with gusto said, 'After all, we have no plans to fight a war. So it's no use aimlessly firing across the LC.' His boss, the Northern Army Commander, Lieutenant General D. S. Hooda, admitted there was enough ammunition for day-to-day firing, but ammunition for war was a different matter.

The irony is that the people of India do not know what the army is supposed to do. The nation regularly pays homage to soldiers who die fighting terrorists or proxies inside Indian territory rather than fighting Pakistani soldiers or the real enemy on the border. The issue worth cogitating upon is that if the army takes on counter-terrorism operations, which should be the responsibility of state police assisted by paramilitary forces, who is to protect the borders? Should the nation be spending huge amounts of finances building a military force when what the army wishes to be is a glorified paramilitary force?

Had the defence minister ordered a field force review—instead of non-operational flab-cutting—these are the things that should have been looked at carefully:

On the LAC: Since the role of the security forces after the 2013 agreement has been reduced to policing on the LAC, the Indo-Tibetan Border Police (ITBP) as the first line of defence should assume greater responsibility. Except for Ladakh, where China says it does not have a border with India, and four agreed flashpoints elsewhere, namely, north Sikkim, Diphu, Bum La (Tawang), and Fishtail in the Eastern Sector, the remaining LAC should be policed by the ITBP. In February 2015, the Home Ministry announced that the ITBP strength was to be raised by forty-nine battalions; more should be done if needed. Except for a few pockets in depth, the army should be withdrawn from most of the LAC to return to its war role. The ITBP's policing task would be assisted by border confidence building measures already in place. The Chinese proposal of June 2015 for a 'code of conduct' in response to India's suggestion of defining the LAC for added peace and tranquillity on the disputed border should be considered.

In addition, troops of two army corps, namely, 3 and 4 Corps involved in counter-insurgency in the northeast region plus the Assam Rifles (army units funded by the union home ministry) should also revert to a war role. Once this is done, the army would have two tasks to perform: maintain and upgrade its defences, and conduct tactical level exercises. Under Article IV of the 1996 bilateral agreement between India and China, division level troops (12,000) are allowed near the LAC and up to brigade-group (5,000) can perform military exercises without notification to the other side. This would help in identifying gaps in war stores, equipment, ammunition, missiles, storage sites, and assist in coordination with the IAF. Once troops rehearse war tasks, their morale would be up. Moreover, higher headquarters of both the army and the IAF would be able to resolve their operational differences and have better coordination in a crisis. The overall results on the LAC would be astonishing. The army would become professional and confident.

On the Line of Control (LC): The army should adopt an offensive-defence posture on the LC. According to the National Security Advisor, Ajit Doval, the forces have three options: defensive option, which the army adopted in 2004 by fencing itself off; offensive option, which would be war; and the intermediate option of offensive-defence, which involves activities like aggressive patrolling, raids, use of Special Forces, increased firepower, and so on. The army had adopted this stance between 1990 and 2004 when the enemy was always on tenterhooks and on the lookout for surprises. The offensive-defence posture will have numerous advantages. It will raise the morale of one's own troops and keep the enemy nervous; since the focus will be on providing war-withal to field units, higher headquarters would seek fast-tracked and timely acquisitions from the government; and it would deter the Pakistan Army from raising the ante.

For an offensive-defence posture on the LC, three steps are required: the fence on the military line should be dismantled; troops should be reoriented to a war role from the present anti-infiltration role; and, in a phased manner, the internal stability or counter-insurgency operations should be handed over by the army to the paramilitary forces, for instance, the Central Reserve Police Force in J&K. These are actions that the army would take during war; taking them in peacetime would help deter Pakistan from continuous mischief across the LC.

The biggest advantages of an offensive-defence posture would be professionalism and the slashing of manpower. Once the army gives up its counter-insurgency role, the bulk of the 80,000 strong Rashtriya Rifles will become unnecessary. These troops could be moved to the proposed 17 Mountain Corps. And the finances allocated to 17 Mountain Corps could then be used for purchase of weapons and equipment for this corps.

Additionally, the army should revise its war wastage reserves—stocks of stores, ammunitions, fuel, and so on—which were meant for the 1980s' long-duration war with Pakistan. For example, according to the war wastage reserves, the army should have a forty-day supply of long-life category ammunition and twenty-one days' supply of short-life category ammunition such as anti-tank, rocket artillery and missiles to fight an intense war. Since war with Pakistan has been assessed to be short and intense, a drastic reduction of war wastage reserves is necessary.

The preparedness on the LAC with China also requires infrastructure in terms of roads and rail, which at present, are in a shambles. Since the Border Road Organisation has been unable to fulfil its commitments, the government should seriously consider other means, including assistance from foreign vendors.

On the border with Pakistan: Except for the Jammu International Border, there is little that the Indian Army—given Pakistan's full-spectrum nuclear deterrence—can do if there is war on the border. If pivot corps and the integrated battle groups have adequate punch for shallow penetration of 5 to 10 kilometres, this would amount to an offensive-defence posture. Given this, are three strike corps necessary? Yes, according to army chief General Bikram Singh. These provide deterrence, he said. The question he did not answer was deterrence against what? Shouldn't conventional war capabilities (offensive strike corps) deter sub-conventional war (terrorism)? The problem is that on the one hand, the Indian Army's offensive capabilities lack credibility on account of war-withal and lack of realistic training; on the other hand, Pakistan is confident about its conventional war capabilities, with fallback available through nuclear deterrence.

The answer for India lies in going back to professionalism. Once done, India could offer mutual reduction of offensive forces as military confidence-building measures to Pakistan. The Indian Army, to begin with, could reduce its strike corps from three to two potent corps by cannibalizing resources. It is known that at any given time one strike corps worth of equipment remains unfit for war on account of maintenance and upgrades.

Moreover, the Lieutenant General Shekatkar committee could suggest the reduction of about 50,000 to 80,000 troops by non-field force review.

Thus, by manpower and task rationalization, the army, through field force and non-field force review, could cut its existing strength by 300,000 troops in a phased manner over three to five years. This would get the army close to the ideal 40:60 ratio of revenue versus annual capital allocations making it easier to undertake modernization and acquire equipment.

A reduction in conventional war strength would spur India and Pakistan to consider the mutual reduction of nuclear capabilities. Unfortunately, India's insistence that its nuclear capabilities are independent of its conventional war capability against Pakistan since it has to cater for China as well is self-defeating. Catering for the worst case scenario of a border war where China has overwhelming conventional war superiority, it is debatable if India requires nukes for military use against China.

Once the reduction of army troops is decided, the army should move towards professionalism: its core competency. For armies worldwide it is combined arms operations, the ability to optimally bring together all its arms including infantry, artillery, engineers, Special Forces, army aviation, and so on, in a deliberate plan to achieve military objectives. The plans, depending on objectives and forces tasked, are rehearsed both without troops (to exercise commanders) and with troops; at corps and army level, the plans become interservice with the IAF being a part of the exercise. Combined arms operations with variations are relevant in all terrains. When these plans are made and rehearsed, capability requirements including ammunition and equipment are sought and it becomes the responsibility of various headquarters to ensure their availability. Genuine training for war is intrinsically linked with equipment and ammunition.

Since the army and the air force complement one another in a land war, it is necessary to assess the IAF doctrine, acquisitions and its implications.

INDIAN AIR FORCE

The transformational shift in the IAF came with the arrival of Russian heavy, twin-engine, multirole Su-30 aircraft in the 1990s, and the first air doctrine released in October 1995. From a tactical air force in support of the army in war, the IAF, having witnessed the spectacular role of US air power in the 1990 Gulf War, envisaged itself as a strategic force. Between 2000 and 2008, the IAF improved its doctrine by focusing on two war roles: strategic reach and parallel war.

The first role visualized that the IAF would become a global player to eventually emerge as an expeditionary force capable of deploying and operating in far-flung areas. The IAF considers the span from the Persian

Gulf to the Malacca Straits as its area of interest. The second role, specific to Pakistan, was meant to achieve decisive objectives in a conventional war limited in time and space against a nuclear backdrop.

Strategic reach implied acquiring a number of assets: superior platforms with air-to-air refuelling capability; network centricity to interlock long ranges, secure and real-time communications, command and control (command of war and control of firepower), beyond-visual-range weaponry and airborne warning and control systems for better early warning and assured air defence; aerospace command for exploitation of space; and strategic airlift capability. Alongside the assets, strategic reach requires working on three vital issues: regular and advanced bilateral and multilateral exercises with friendly major power air forces, firm support from the government, and a change of mindset within the IAF.

In reality, the IAF's exercises with friendly air forces remained limited to tactical settings for close combat manoeuvres to ensure that their own radars and avionics did not get compromised. Moreover, with little in writing from the government, the IAF leadership was never sure of how far it could go with friendly air forces.

The IAF owed its role of parallel war to lessons learnt from Operation Safed Sagar (1999 Kargil War) and Operation Parakram. The concept is to exploit the primacy of air power to shape the battlefield which would then enable the army to progress with its tasks without fear of enemy air attack. According to the IAF, the contribution of land forces would be able to improve only if they are consciously integrated into the counter air campaign, and train accordingly in peace. It does not mean that no other air campaign can be undertaken until air superiority is won. Instead it means that no other operation should be commenced if it is going to jeopardize the attainment of air superiority (achieved by a counter air campaign to be launched within forty-eight hours of a decision by government to go to war), or is going to use resources that should be used to attain air superiority. For this reason, even as the IAF undertakes counter air and air defence operations (these complement one another), its counter surface forces operations (in direct support of land forces) with the army could progress simultaneously.

While the concept is flawless and has worked worldwide, there are problems with it being implemented here since the Pakistan Air Force is steadily strengthening itself vis-à-vis the Indian Air Force. Let alone air supremacy or air superiority, the IAF will need to work hard for even localized air superiority. This is where the number of aircraft will always be an issue with the IAF even when it has superior multirole platforms. Better coordination with the army would also be needed.

Will the IAF be available for close air support operations in support of ground forces? According to senior officers at Air Headquarters, the air force would undertake 'effect-based operations to shape the battlefield and ensure limited air superiority'. This is suggestive of the reality that given scarce and multirole combat aircraft, and force multipliers in adequate numbers, the IAF will expend maximum effort on counter air operations with Battlefield Air Interdiction (BAI) operations getting the second priority. As the IAF is no longer a tactical air force, close air support operations will be the army's responsibility (the IAF will assist with attack helicopters). The basic difference between BAI and close air support lies in the proximity of targets to friendly forces and the control arrangements that are therefore needed. Unlike close air support operations, BAI missions require coordination in joint planning, they may not require continuous coordination during the execution phase. Moreover, close air support has its own problems, the major one being target acquisition, especially in high-altitude mountainous terrain. Similarly, the fog of war could lead to misidentification and fratricide (a lesson learnt during the 1999 Kargil War).

While the army and the IAF were grappling with operational problems of how to reconcile BAI, which the air force would carry out, and close air support operations, which the army wanted, the year 2009 saw both services turning their gaze to the China front. The IAF was suddenly faced with two operational dilemmas. With abysmal connectivity and the growing numbers of ground troops on the Chinese front, the IAF's massive involvement in peace and wartime operational logistics became inescapable. Moreover, it was evident that in high altitudes, where the army could not do much, the IAF would have the responsibility for dissuasive deterrence against China. In case it failed, the IAF would have to take the initiative to strike (counter air operations) to achieve 'limited air superiority'. The IAF sought a total of forty-two combat squadrons instead of the existing 39.5 squadrons, and the government accepted the requirement.

After successful IAF landings at three advanced landing grounds at Daulat Beg Oldi, Fukche and Nyoma right under the nose of the People's Liberation Army on the LAC from May to December 2008, New Delhi cleared the formation of the Apex Committee for the northeastern region in July 2009 with an initial funding of ₹2,000 crore. Headed by the Vice Chief of Air Staff, the committee—comprising members from the Defence Ministry, defence finance, defence estates, army and military engineering services, as well as a representative from Arunachal Pradesh—was responsible for improving the plethora of used and unused airfields and advanced landing grounds in the region. The entire region is strewn with airstrips made and used by US forces during World War II. A total of ten airfields and eight advanced landing grounds were identified. While the airfields are at Chhabua, Bagdogra, Kalaikunda, Hasimara, Jorhat, Tezpur, Panagarh, Purnia, Mohanbari and Kumbhirgram, the advanced landing grounds are at Vijaynagar, Mechuka, Tuting, Pasighat, Along, Walong, Zero and Tawang. The airfields and advanced landing grounds, depending on the location, will be used by different combat and logistics aircraft and helicopters. For example, while An-32 and C-130J aircraft can land at Pasighat, only the Dorniers can fly from the advanced landing ground at Along.

However, the toughest to be dealt with is the fact that the IAF faces numerous operational shortcomings. First and foremost is the combat strength. As we have seen, the IAF envisages having forty-two combat squadrons by 2027. These would be a mix of Su-30MKI, MiG-29, Mirage, Jaguar, Rafale, Light Combat Aircraft (LCA), one more combat aircraft sourced from a foreign manufacturer, and one or two squadrons of Fifth Generation Fighter Aircraft (FGFA). In 2016, the combat strength officially stood at thirty-four squadrons with uncertainty over when the LCA, a new combat aircraft and FGFA would arrive; the remaining fleet was ageing. Given the state of the combat fleet, there is no way that the IAF can fight a two-front war, let alone an air war with Pakistan.

The problem is compounded by low serviceability of the fighter fleet. Defence Minister Manohar Parrikar admitted in Parliament, 'During the period from January to December 2014, the average aircraft availability was about 55 per cent. Between 15 to 20 per cent of the aircraft fleet is grounded throughout the year due to shortage of spares.' In February 2015, there was a public row between the IAF and Russia's United Aircraft Corporation, the makers of frontline Su-30MKI aircraft, over perennial engine troubles. It was evident that the IAF had not given due importance to aircraft serviceability over its lifetime. On the one hand, the IAF has difficulty in maintaining its combat force levels; on the other hand, lifelong product support by manufacturers is not assured.

The answer lies in the IAF undertaking equipment rationalization by reviewing its operational doctrine based on thirty-two to thirty-four combat squadrons, and by striking a balance between manned aircraft, unmanned aircraft and surface-to-surface cruise missiles with precision attack capability. The cruise missile would not replace but supplement air power.

Another reason why the IAF should undertake equipment rationalization is that, unlike China, India does not have a robust indigenous aerospace industry. It is only a matter of time before China achieves a breakthrough with indigenous jet engines. Once that happens, India would find it impossible to maintain an unrealistic combat strength through imports to match China and Pakistan's combat strength.

The second issue concerns the doctrine. Instead of primacy of air power, the need in subcontinental wars is for greater interservice cooperation. This can only happen if the army and air force evolve a common operational doctrine to fight common rather than individual wars. To take the argument further, unless the two services involved in land war devise a common doctrine, have a good understanding of each other's core competencies at all staff and command levels, the idea of the chief of defence staff or permanent chairman of chiefs of staff committee doing joint operation planning is premature.

The third issue concerns the need for an excellent radar network for impregnable air defence. While the air force leadership has accorded importance to tangible assets, it has not kept pace with the infrastructure to support them. A few airborne warning and control systems and aerostat balloons are inadequate to meet the challenges on both fronts. Especially when Pakistan has a state-of-the-art ground-based air defence system on the border, and is developing airfields close to the Gwadar Port. Except for radar networks close to air bases, and designated vulnerable areas and vulnerable points, there are large voids in our air warning systems. For example, networking with civil radars in real time is not available. And the eastern front against China lacks radar cover or air defence network and integrated air defence cover between the army and the air force. Associated with this is the issue of ground-based air defence systems whose induction should be accelerated.

The next shortcoming is regarding electronic warfare, which China has elevated as the fourth dimension of warfare after land, air and sea. The Pakistan Air Force has a one to one ratio of electronic warfare pods for its fighters, something that the IAF lacks. Given the dense air defence environment at the border and tactical battle areas, the IAF needs electronic warfare pods for all fighters; unfortunately, foreign vendors are reluctant to sell these. The Pakistan Air Force also scores over the IAF in the ratio of pilots to fighters. The need is for more pilots than fighters to generate more sorties at the peak of war.

Another issue is the slow development of space-based assets in comparison with those available with China, and through it, with Pakistan. This is critical for timely and accurate round the clock intelligence, surveillance and reconnaissance.

For extended reach and capability, the IAF is acquiring network centricity so that it can use space-based assets along with a terrestrial backbone in real time. The IAF is interacting with the Integrated Defence Headquarters and Indian Space and Research Organisation on this. A clear distinction has been made between militarization and weaponization of space; the former relates to using space to enhance military capabilities, while the latter refers to using offensive capabilities such as anti-satellite capabilities demonstrated by China and the US. India's use of space will be for intelligence, surveillance and reconnaissance requirements. India has embarked upon a satellite-based navigation system project. Similarly, to ensure a high degree of communication security and connectivity, a satellite-based dedicated defence network has been planned for the armed forces. What is being attempted is the provision of 'informationalized' conditions backed by dedicated air and rotary wing assets similar but in much reduced quantity to those available to PLA forces.

Once the IAF acquires more airborne warning and control systems and with the expansion of the Air Force Net (AFNET), the stage will be set for ground networking (Integrated Air Command and Control System) and space networking (Operational Data Link). In conversations with senior air force officers, the authors were given to understand that progress was being made on this front through the introduction of airborne warning and control systems, unmanned aerial vehicles and high-altitude loitering munitions like the HAROP from Israel and other suppliers. The IAF is also acquiring additional air-to-air refuelling aircraft (eighteen aircraft are expected by 2020) and has bought strategic C-17 and operational lift capabilities with C-130J. Once all these capabilities are in place, the IAF will have the advantage of forward deployment of Su-30MKI and the ability to support operations in the Tibet Autonomous Region from bases as far as central India.

Yet another shortcoming usually overlooked is the security of air bases and vital installations. The terrorist attack on the Pathankot air base in Punjab in January 2016 should serve as a wake-up call. The need is for an outside security set-up with clearly delineated responsibility and accountability since the IAF does not have manpower for the task. Given the state of terrorism inside the country, high-profile and expensive air force and naval assets should be properly secured.

INDIAN NAVY

Like the other two services, the Indian Navy suffers from the malady of overstretched commitments (on naval diplomacy and constabulary roles) versus force level rationalization. The navy has justified the need for a balanced combat force to include submarines and aircraft carriers. However, it lacks an achievable military strategy.

According to the Indian Maritime Doctrine published in 2010, 'While China shares a long land frontier with India, in so far as our waters (Indian Ocean) are concerned her navy is an extra-regional one. A certain threshold of capability is therefore required, which will make the cost of intervention sufficiently high. Submarines are the most suited vehicles for such deterrence, largely because of their relative invulnerability to detection, particularly in tropical waters.'

The government had in 1999 cleared a thirty-year plan to build twenty-four conventional diesel submarines. Of these, six submarines each were to be procured under Project 75 and 75I, while the remaining twelve submarines were to be built by indigenous design with expertise obtained from building the initial twelve submarines. Now halfway through the plan period, in 2016, the first vessel of Project 75—INS *Kalvari* (built by the French DCNS company), undergoing sea trials—is expected to join the fleet by 2017; the others by 2022.

Within months of assuming office, the navy chief, Admiral Robin Dhowan, in April 2015, citing increased threat, sought to revise the thirty-year plan. According to him, 'We have proposed to the government that in lieu of the conventional submarines we would like to have more nuclear powered submarines (Ship Submersible Nuclear or SSNs).' Of the twelve indigenous submarines that are to be manufactured after Project 75 and Project 75I, the navy wants six of them to be SSNs. Their production needs to start now. The navy has leased the Russian SSN, renamed INS *Chakra* for ten years until 2022. It is expected to be replaced by another Russian SSN after 2022 and Russia is expected to support construction of India's six indigenous SSNs. Since SSNs can stay underwater for months (state-of-the-art SSNs can stay submerged all their operational life), they are ideal platforms for firing cruise missiles, intelligence gathering, and insertion and extrication of Special Forces. According to an admiral, 'Since the Chinese Navy and Pakistan Navy would have interoperability in the Indian Ocean soon, the Indian Navy would need to keep an eye on their activities from a greater distance. And hence the SSNs.'

As regards aircraft carriers, the Indian Navy, according to Admiral

Dhowan, 'is looking to have three sea-borne carriers in its fleet. The first indigenous carrier, INS *Vikrant*, will be inducted by 2018. All options are open for the second indigenous aircraft carrier. Nothing has been ruled out. It could be nuclear-powered or conventionally-powered.' These will be in addition to the recently acquired INS *Vikramaditya*.

Regarding the rationale of why the aircraft carriers are needed, according to the Indian Maritime Doctrine (2010), 'An enemy's littoral cannot be dominated unless his air and underwater forces are supressed. Strong air support is critical and navies with integral air capability, which only aircraft carriers can provide, are best positioned to deal with such a situation. Indeed, navies without such capabilities may never be able to achieve the kind of control that is required to achieve such domination. Once the domination is achieved a range of options become available. One can go for the hinterland, one can go for the coastal targets, one can impose a blockade, one can interdict his commerce, one can carry out amphibious operations—the possibilities are endless.'

Unfortunately for the Indian Navy, the possibilities for such combat operations no longer exist. Against the Pakistan Navy, the Indian Navy could perhaps have done aplenty. But with the Chinese Navy in the Indian Ocean with bases in Gwadar and bases/berthing and replenishment rights along numerous littoral nations, the Indian Navy needs to review its operational doctrine.

A good maritime strategy should have two major phases. The first is the establishment of sea control by ensuring one's own use of the sea (by aircraft carriers) and denying the enemy the use of the sea (by submarines). Appropriate naval strategies and naval tactics which take into account the adversary's strengths (in India's case maritime interoperability between the Chinese and Pakistani navies) determine the progress of struggle for control. After adequate control of the sea is established, the second phase, which involves projection of power both at sea and on land, is undertaken.

The question that the Indian Navy should ask is: considering the interoperability between the Chinese and Pakistani navies, will the Indian Navy have the capability and capacity to project sea power even in the Indian Ocean Region, never mind the Western Pacific? This question assumes importance since the Modi government has agreed to partner with the US Navy in the entire Asia-Pacific and Indian Ocean Region. In other words, there seems to be a mismatch between what India has agreed to do and what the Indian Navy can deliver.

The issue has been complicated with the acquisition of an indigenous nuclear-powered ballistic missile submarine (SSBN) by India. According to media reports, the INS *Arihant* with 6,000-ton displacement has an 83-megawatt nuclear reactor and can carry twelve K-15 (700-kilometre) ballistic missiles or four K-4 (3,000-kilometre) ballistic missiles. The complication stems from the fact that China has more potent SSBNs and could possibly share the technology with Pakistan.

To match India's sea-based deterrence, Pakistan is building the naval version of the Ra'ad cruise missile which it intends using with nuclear warheads on its (eight) submarines being acquired from China. According to an authoritative writer, 'Pakistan's Maritime Technology Organisation is nearing completion of the (Ra'ad) project, which, once tested or inaugurated, will be commissioned under the Naval Strategic Force Command, completing the third leg of the triad.' Since enough literature is available on China's formidable fleet of SSBNs, SSNs and conventional diesel submarines, some of which have made forays in the Indian Ocean, what exactly will India, with its limited ability to make nuclear reactors for big displacement submarines and equally abysmal capability to make weapons, do with INS *Arihant* series submarines?

Taking the fast changing regional combat environment into account, it becomes evident that navy chief Admiral Dhowan's call for six nuclear submarines and a possible nuclear-powered carrier is nothing more than a knee-jerk reaction. Since these assets are extremely expensive, India needs to review its strategic options in the Indian Ocean region before acquiring big-ticket items that fall short of political objectives (not given by the political leadership) and do not achieve desired combat aims.

CHAPTER 15

THE NUCLEAR OPTION

When India conducted its series of nuclear tests in May 1988, it said security concerns (with China in particular) were its reasons for doing so. Within days, Prime Minister Vajpayee announced (a) a voluntary moratorium on nuclear testing (b) a no-first-use (NFU) policy and (c) credible minimum deterrence (CMD). The draft nuclear doctrine issued on 17 August 1999 added the need for a triad—air, land and sea—of nuclear delivery vehicles. The final nuclear doctrine released on 3 January 2003 added 'massive retaliation (MR)' as another significant feature.

Eleven years later, the BJP election manifesto for the May 2014 General Elections, which brought Narendra Modi to power, mentioned the need to revisit the nuclear doctrine. Once in power, the Modi government backtracked, saying the doctrine needed no changes. It does.

To assess what changes would make India's nuclear deterrence credible and cost-effective it becomes imperative to assess the management of nuclear forces, its relationship with conventional capability and whether it contributes to overall military power.

India's Nuclear Command Authority (NCA) comprises a Political Council and an Executive Council. The Political Council, chaired by the prime minister, is the sole body to authorize use of nuclear weapons, comprising the Cabinet Committee on Security (CCS)—union ministers of defence, home, external affairs and finance—as members and the national security advisor as its member secretary. The Executive Council is chaired by the NSA; it provides inputs for decision-making to the Political Council and executes orders given by it.

The Executive Council has numerous members namely the chairman, Chiefs of Staff Committee (COSC); the commander-in-chief, Strategic Forces Command; scientists from the Department of Atomic Energy (DAE) and Defence Research and Development Organisation (DRDO), heads of intelligence agencies, secretaries of ministries headed by CCS members, and so on. In addition to providing inputs to the Political Council for nuclear use, the NSA does a host of things. He ensures availability of nuclear weapons, nuclear command and control structures, alternate chain of command, state of readiness, targeting strategy, update on delivery systems, operating procedures for various stages of alert and launch, and secure communications, to name a few. From time to time, the NSA updates the CCS on the above issues.

The above set-up suffers from a serious flaw—there is a total disconnect between the policymakers and executors. Since prime ministers have traditionally kept the atomic energy and space portfolios with them, the secretary of the Atomic Energy Commission had direct access to the prime minister. After the 1998 tests, like the NSA, the post of principal scientific advisor (PSA) was created to give the prime minister a combined view of the DAE and DRDO (responsible for nuclear cores and non-nuclear elements in a nuclear warhead). Dr A. P. J. Kalam was the first PSA.

With prime ministers having little inclination to understand warfare, the PSA and NSA decide nuclear capabilities and its international fallout. Select diplomats are roped in to buttress the decided capability with appropriate nuclear strategy. Given total opacity, where the scientists and defence forces operate in silos, large amounts are frittered away on technologies which are unnecessary and unattainable. In the absence of any audit, scientists continue to milk finances from dead projects by extolling the virtues of the spin-off technologies they generate. Moreover, the irrepressible urge to brag by scientists spurs the adversary to indulge in an arms race.

Sometime between 2008 and 2010, when the economy was galloping along, India's nuclear policy was altered surreptitiously, with dangerous implications, under Prime Minister Manmohan Singh. The threat from China as the original reason for nuclear tests was superseded. In a series of articles, Shyam Saran, the chairman of the National Security Advisory Board, placed India's nuclear weapons programme in a global context. India, he argued, needed a peaceful global environment shorn of all nuclear weapons for its economic rise and inclusive well-being. Thus, the 'minimum' of the credible minimum deterrence was pitted against the 'maximum' nuclear weapons capability nation, which is the US. While it would be preposterous to suggest that India needed deterrence against the US, the question that begged an answer was: why did Saran make India's 'minimum' open-ended, knowing well that it could lead to an unnecessary, wasteful, devastating and extremely expensive arms race? Are India's nuclear capabilities for deterrence (against China and Pakistan) or for prestige?

The Strategic Forces Command, on cue, sat down to work on future nuclear force levels based not upon the actual yields to weight ratios, which they do not know, but on nuclear theology extrapolated from reservoirs of western nuclear literature in the open domain. A new department under a three-star officer, called the Strategic Programme Staff, was created in 2010 to update nuclear doctrine, nuclear force levels, safety needs, and so on, for the 'minimal' placed in a global context by diplomats.

This was in addition to the Strategic Forces Command, which 'manages and administers the nuclear forces, and is responsible for conduct of retaliatory strikes. The command is tasked to carry out training and conduct test launches to guarantee operational preparedness.' The tests of delivery vehicles (ballistic missiles) are done from prepared DRDO sites under supervision of the scientists.

The nuclear execution chain of command runs from the national security advisor to the commander-in-chief, Strategic Forces Command, through the chairman, Chiefs of Staff Committee. India presently has two operational legs of the triad—aircraft and ballistic missiles. The aircraft being dual tasked (for conventional and nuclear roles) remain with the air force, while most ballistic missiles are with the Strategic Forces Command. At present, the Strategic Forces Command reportedly has three missile brigades; a mix of Prithvi, Agni-I and Agni-II missiles. The Agni-III missile brigade is becoming operational.

Being in the chain of command, the chairman, COSC, whatever his length in the office (sometimes just a few months), is required to liaise with services' headquarters to ensure availability of the delivery system, and to know the nuts and bolts of nuclear weapons. With few exceptions, most chairmen, COSC, continue focusing on their parent service rather than getting too involved in the nitty-gritty of nuclear matters. They will after all be remembered as the service chief rather than as chairman, COSC.

Nuclear warheads remain firmly in the custody of the Department of Atomic Energy and Defence Research and Development Organisation scientists. In a probable four-step cycle unique to India, scientists would mate nuclear cores with essential sensors and safety systems to make them into warheads; next, under the secure custody of scientists, the warheads would be moved to the actual firing site (by the air force) during a crisis or war situation. There, the scientists would mate the warhead with the ballistic missile or the aircraft. Once done, the nuke would be fired by the Strategic Forces Command. Why the defence forces cannot be trusted to carry out the first three steps is anyone's guess. The convoluted procedure puts a question mark over assurance and safety levels if not the accuracy of nuclear weapons.

There are essential steps to graduate from a nuclear test to a deliverable weapon where stakeholders should be in the loop. These include correct yield to weight ratio (for a specific target), reliability, fusing and arming, and safety features. About 4 per cent of a total of 1,050 nuclear tests done by the United States were to ensure complete safety.

Another area where scientists maintain total secrecy is secure communications and its redundancy, whether by satellite or fibre optics. Given India's no-first-use nuclear policy, this is a critical requirement. This means that having absorbed the enemy's nuclear strike where everything will be devastated, Indian nuclear stakeholders should be able to communicate amongst themselves to ensure a retaliatory nuclear strike. These communication channels should have redundancy implying duplications; if one fails, the other should work. Since the stakeholders, which include the military, would be involved in exercising the nuclear option, they should necessarily know about the communications.

As regards use, India's nuclear weapons are not meant for war-fighting. They are meant for deterrence and are strategic in nature. Thus, if an adversary fails to get deterred, India would still not use its nuclear weapons until the adversary uses them first—as per India's no-first-use policy. This means an adversary with formidable conventional war capability like China, or one with tested sub-conventional war capability (terrorism) like Pakistan, will not be deterred by India's nukes. India would need to confront such situations through either conventional capability providing deterrence or wait for the adversary to use nukes first which they might not do. Moreover, since India's nuclear forces are for strategic purposes only, the need for integration of conventional and nuclear plans is not believed to be necessary.

What if India's conventional forces were stronger than Pakistan's and manage to cross its nuclear redlines forcing it to use tactical nuclear weapons? Or, the PLA, unable to get a quick breakthrough against a strong and determined Indian Army holding a long front, uses tactical nuclear weapons in the Himalayas where collateral damage would be minimal? Both situations are unlikely but not inconceivable. To cater for such contingencies, India should integrate its conventional and nuclear forces into a single war plan. It should also have tactical nuclear weapons for deterrence. The low-yield tactical nuclear weapons could be held and operated like strategic nuclear weapons. This is important, as at present, India's nuclear weapons neither deter the two adversaries to start a conventional war nor to end it.

Now consider the key elements of India's nuclear doctrine: moratorium on testing, no first use, massive retaliation and triad. After five nuclear tests in May 1998, India declared that its weaponization was complete; it could make megaton thermonuclear weapons, low-yield (below 5 tons) nuclear weapons, and had enhanced its computer simulation capabilities substantially. It is known that India's 1974 nuclear test had a yield of 12 to 15 kilotons. To put it in perspective, the US has had a total of 1,050 tests, the USSR did 750 and China did 45 tests.

Immediately after the 1998 tests, Western as well as Indian nuclear scientists, led by P. K. Iyengar, former director, Atomic Energy Commission, cast grave doubts over India's claims which were brushed away. In August 2009, nuclear scientist K. Santhanam, who was intimately associated with the 1998 tests, announced that the thermonuclear test had failed. The government tried to defuse this bombshell by getting other scientists to assert that Santhanam's claim was not true. Indian nuclear experts argued that even if the megaton (1,000 kilotons) had not been successful, deuterium-tritium boosted fission weapons could generate yields of 200 to 500 kilotons, the standard nuclear yields used the world over. Whatever the truth, the incident cast doubts on Indian scientists' integrity.

This is worrisome since India has invested a huge amount of hope and finances in SSBNs and submarine-launched ballistic missiles. As we saw in the previous chapter, the first of the four planned SSBNs of the Advanced Technology Vessel programme which began amidst great secrecy in 1983, the 6,000-ton *Arihant* finally launched in July 2009, started sea trials in December 2014. Two nuclear-armed submarine-launched ballistic missiles, the single-stage 700-kilometre K-15 missile and the two-stage 3,000-kilometre K-4 missile, are reportedly to arm INS *Arihant* and its follow-on submarines.

From a purely scientific point of view, submarine-based missiles require careful miniaturization of weight without loss of yield and the ability to pack warheads with the same yield into smaller and smaller spaces. Weight-to-yield ratio is the main consideration for submarine-based missiles. It must be low weight so that the missile within the submarine can be carried without a problem and can launch the warhead to distances of upto 3,000 kilometres. Such nuclear missiles without validation by actual testing would not have the desired assurance levels even for the safety of the submarine crew. How can India, with scientists whose integrity has become questionable, and which has placed a voluntary moratorium on nuclear testing, be sure about the efficiency of its submarine-launched ballistic missiles without testing their warheads?

If India were to test, international opprobrium would dent its image, huge losses to its peaceful nuclear programme where India has signed nuclear energy agreements with eleven countries would follow, and the import of nuclear fuel for its separated civil nuclear reactors in the aftermath of the 2008 Indo-US civil nuclear deal would stop. Either way, India would lose.

Moreover, *Arihant* which reportedly joined service in August 2016 will be required to go on deterrent patrols with submarine-launched ballistic missiles on board. In a compartmentalized system where scientists do not share nuclear warheads details with defence services, how would this be possible? Will the DRDO scientists be on board INS *Arihant* during deterrent patrols? Or will these patrols be done without submarine-launched ballistic missiles on board? Both situations make no sense whatsoever.

Regarding no first use, experts believe that it should be revised to an ambiguity policy—that is, India should announce the withdrawal of its no-first-use policy and refuse to spell out the new one, like Pakistan, which has maintained a stony silence on the subject suggesting a nuclear first-use policy. Moreover, its acquisition of tactical nuclear weapons has made India's no-first-use commitment suicidal. Fortunately, the experts are wrong on both issues.

First and foremost, a nation's nuclear weapons declaratory and employment policies are not sacrosanct; a nation's leadership can change its intention on its nuclear-use policy anytime as long as the capability exists. A declaratory nuclear first or second use or ambiguity policy does not affect the conduct of war, which can be assessed by ground realities. If anything, a declared ambiguity policy which has first use inbuilt into it will raise international heat, spur an unnecessary arms race, and heighten suspicion amongst adversaries making nuclear confidence building measures more difficult.

What is important is the role assigned to nukes in war-fighting. For example, during the Cold War, the US-led NATO assessed that it could not match the Soviet-led Warsaw Pact's conventional weapons capability in the European war theatre. The answer was found in tactical nuclear weapons, which would halt the Soviet onslaught. Regarding the US continent, it was believed that the Soviets would attack it with their nuclear-tipped long-range ballistic missiles, hence the need for a ballistic missile defence, assured sea-based deterrence, and large numbers of ballistic missiles capable of striking the Soviet Union. The doctrine which purportedly prevented war between the big two was called Mutual Assured Destruction.

India's context is dissimilar. In Pakistan, where its army controls nukes, no serving officer has ever said that they would be used first in a war. If anything, during the 2001–02 Operation Parakram, Pakistan Army chief General Pervez Musharraf had consistently maintained that nukes would be weapons of last resort in war. He repeatedly spoke about 'restraint and responsibility' regarding nuclear weapons.

More to the point, the Pakistan military spends huge amounts on its conventional war-fighting capability to maintain an operational or theatre level parity with the Indian military with similar conventional war-fighting doctrines. What this means is that it is prepared to fight an all-out conventional war for seven to ten days before resorting to the nuclear option, if at all. In the clearest indication of its intent, in the absence of bilateral nuclear confidence building measures, the Pakistan Army has publicly spelt out its nuclear redlines, which should not be crossed by the Indian conventional war-fighting machine. These four thresholds laid out by retired Lieutenant General Khalid Kidwai, former head of Pakistan's Strategic Plans Division responsible for nuclear weapons, are:

- Space Threshold: India attacks Pakistan and conquers a large part of its territory;
- Military Threshold: India destroys a large part either of Pakistani land or air forces;
- Economic Threshold: India engages in economic strangling of Pakistan; and
- Domestic Threshold: India pushes Pakistan into political destabilization or creates a large-scale subversion in Pakistan.

The real reason why experts close to the government advocate a nuclear ambiguity policy is not difficult to find. Since India has elevated its thinking on 'minimum' to the global minimum, it desires to pursue the policy of ambiguity followed by four of the five nuclear weapon powers, namely, the US, Russia, the UK and France. China is the only nuclear power under the Non-Proliferation Treaty to have a declared no-first-use policy. Change of declaratory nuclear policy from no first use to ambiguity would allow Indian scientists to continue spending money on indigenous ballistic missile defence irrespective of results, and other offensive capabilities like MIRVs (Multiple Independently targetable Re-entry Vehicles) and MaRVs (Manoeuvrable Re-entry Vehicles).

A MIRV is a ballistic missile which has multiple small warheads packed in a single warhead capable of hitting different targets simultaneously. In military terms, MIRVs provide two advantages: they enhance first strike capability, and a single thermonuclear or boosted fission weapon is able to do greater damage. The MaRV on the other hand is a ballistic missile whose warhead is capable of shifting targets during flight by use of terminal active homing guidance.

The element of massive retaliation added in January 2003 pledges that India 'will respond with massive retaliation should deterrence fail', with the emphasis being on the word massive. This suggested that India will both have the capability to survive a nuclear first strike by Pakistan and China, and to retaliate menacingly, indicating a large inventory of possible high-yield warheads and a variety of delivery systems or vectors.

Neither adversary has been deterred by India's massive retaliation (MR) announcement. If anything, Pakistan has used India's declaration of MR along with its ballistic missile defence (BMD), its emerging sea-based deterrence, and the India-US civil nuclear deal as reasons to increase its fissile material stocks, procure more nuclear reactors from China, and enhance ballistic and cruise missiles. Clearly India's nuclear doctrine remains defanged and in urgent need of reassessment.

For use against Pakistan's elongated geography, where many of its high-profile strategic targets are close to the border, when its cities are congested with virtually non-existent civil defence, ill-equipped hospitals and other life-saving facilities, why does India need more than 20-kiloton yield nukes in limited (low double digits) quantities even with a declared no-first-use policy?

Let us review the triad thinking, which appears outdated. The use of aircraft, ballistic and cruise missiles, and submarine-based deterrence depends on India's indigenous technology-military-industrial base, and the ability of scientists to produce nuclear weapons with high yield to small weight ratios. The results thus far have not been promising. Interestingly, experts are lamenting the deficiency of long-range bombers with the capability to deliver cruise missile and nuclear capable stand-off air-to-surface missiles.

Making a virtue out of necessity, the air force vector should be removed from the triad and perhaps offered as a tempting nuclear confidence building measure to Pakistan. With two live borders, dwindling combat strength, and the need for long-range preponderant firepower against both adversaries in a conventional war, the Indian Air Force will find it virtually impossible to provide its assets for a nuclear mission. Moreover, a unilateral announcement of removing the IAF from the nuclear delivery role will help Pakistan not to misread its payload each time the IAF enters its airspace.

With conventional war at its peak, when the IAF's daily sorties will dip, can it afford to reserve nearly sixty combat aircraft for the nuclear mission? For example, two aircraft armed with nuclear weapons would require three to four electronic countermeasure escort aircraft, the same number of aircraft in an air defence role, and a few aircraft to engage the enemy's ground-based air defence systems, making a total of about fifteen to twenty aircraft for a single nuclear mission. With at least two to three decoy missions needed, the total number of aircraft which would get locked for the nuclear delivery role could be about sixty.

As far as sea-based deterrence is concerned, it is known that India is building three nuclear submarines (with 80-megawatt nuclear reactors, referred to as S2, S3 and S4 vessels. Considering that when the DRDO had started the secret advanced technology vessel programme, it had kept its sights low (on Pakistan), why not stop at S2 and S3 (which have reached advanced stages) and make bigger vessels with 180-megawatt nuclear reactors which would be credible against China? If India were to do it alone it could take up to a decade and might not be successful. Hence, outside handholding, perhaps from Russia, would be necessary.

Land-based ballistic and cruise missiles remain the best nuclear delivery vehicle for India. It is the same for Pakistan but for different reasons. The Pakistan Army chief, who derives his ultimate power from the custody of nuclear weapons, would ideally not like to share responsibility for nuclear weapons with the air force and navy.

BALLISTIC AND CRUISE MISSILES

India's Integrated Guided Missile Development Programme announced in 1984 had five missiles, two strategic and three non-strategic. The non-strategic systems were required to undergo user trials before acceptance and induction into service. The strategic systems, meant for nuclear weapons delivery, needed the Defence Research and Development Organisation's nod for operational acceptance; the services have little to do with them. The two strategic missiles were the battlefield support Prithvi ballistic missile and the long-range Agni, which since India was not a declared nuclear weapons state in 1984, was referred to as a technology demonstrator.

The three non-strategic missiles were two quick reaction surface-to-air missiles, the Akash and Trishul, and the anti-tank Nag missile. The defence services, not satisfied with them, had been reluctant to induct these missiles into service. The Trishul missile programme was finally closed in 2008, and the Nag is nowhere near completion. To respect indigenization, the Akash missile was finally accepted by the air force and army in 2013–14. Could the DRDO, which has not been able to meet the defence services' non-strategic missile needs, be trusted to have produced strategic missiles with good accuracy, assurance and reliability?

The Prithvi was first test-fired on 25 February 1988 when India was still a decade away from its nuclear tests. Within weeks, according to the DRDO chief, Dr Kalam, 'The army approached the cabinet committee for placing orders for Prithvi missile system'. In reality Prime Minister Rajiv Gandhi goaded the army to accept the project, after which staff requirements to check whether the missile met the operational needs of the army were firmed up. After India became a nuclear power, the other two services saw the prestige in having the Prithvi with its dual purpose warhead (conventional and nuclear) and asked for it.

It was decided to offer the Prithvi in three variants: 150-kilometre range with 1,000-kilogram payload for the army; 250-kilometre range with 500-kilogram payload for the air force; and the navy version called Dhanush to have a 350-kilometre range and lesser payload. There was a trade-off between weight and range, more weight to less range and vice versa. This indicated that the liquid propellant used in all Prithvi missiles had a restricted specific impulse which decides how far a payload would go.

In the 1980s, when the world had moved from liquid to solid propellants in ballistic missiles, the Prithvi series still used liquid propellant. The latter has a higher specific impulse than solid propellants but too many disadvantages. Liquid propellants are time-consuming and difficult to handle in field conditions, have restricted tactical movements because of the large logistics train required, and present a huge signature for enemy counter-bombardment. Since a single Prithvi missile battery needed as many as eight to ten logistics vehicles, they presented a huge target for enemy counter-fire. Other disadvantages are slow response time, poor accuracy (the missile does not have a seeker which homes in on the target for assured destruction), and importantly, its low terminal velocity, and hence inability to penetrate hardened fortifications. The reason for low terminal velocity, unlike the Chinese solid propellant M-11 missiles which were given to Pakistan and renamed Hatf-III, was that the body of the Prithvi does not separate from the warhead. Once the Strategic Forces Command was formed in 2003, Prithvi was withdrawn from the army and handed over as a strategic system to the tri-service command.

The Agni ballistic missile, first test-fired on 22 May 1998 days after the nuclear tests, has stabilized. All missiles of this series have solid propellant stages, carry a one-ton warhead, are road mobile, and use strap-down inertial navigation system (SDINS) for guidance. None have seekers for terminal guidance. Unlike the platform (gimballed) inertial navigation systems which are intricately designed and used in intercontinental ballistic missiles, the SDINSs use dry-tuned gyros strapped to the missile body. The SDINSs have good reliability up to a 5,000-kilometre range, are cheaper than platform inertial navigation systems, and are best employed against moving targets. Select countries, including China, have platform (gimballed) inertial navigation systems.

The 700-kilometre range single-stage Agni-1, and the 2,000-kilometre two-stage Agni-2 have been inducted into the Strategic Forces Command. Both missiles have a one-metre diameter. The two-stage Agni-3 with a two-metre diameter has a 3,500-kilometre range. Once Agni-3 enters service it will be part of missile brigades having a mix of both Agni-2 and Agni-3 missiles.

Two other missiles being test-fired are Agni-4 and Agni-5. The Agni-4 has a one-metre diameter, a two-stage rocket and can cover a distance of 4,000 kilometres. This is similar to Agni-2 in specifications except that it uses lighter composite material for rocket motors, and hence its payload travels a longer distance. Once Agni-4 enters service, the Agni-2 missile will be withdrawn.

The Agni-5, successfully test-fired for the third time in January 2015, has three stages (unlike previous missiles), a two-metre diameter and can reach 5,000 kilometres. The first stage uses a metallic rocket while the other two stages are with composite material. The problem of stage separation in ballistic missiles, where within a split second the stage two propellant should start burning before the stage one motor burns off and falls to the ground, is an intricate and delicate affair. The DRDO has overcome the difficulty of stage separation by use of a 'velocity trimming module' which helps the stage two propellant ignite before the stage one motor falls off. Once Agni-5 enters service, Agni-3 will be decommissioned. Eventually, there will be three Agni missiles—1, 4 and 5. While Agni-1's range can cover all of Pakistan, Agni-5 can reach Beijing.

The Agni-5's single warhead could have three multiple independently targetable re-entry vehicle (MIRV) warheads. Since the weight of a 20-kiloton warhead is about 400 kilograms (from open sources), three MIRVs would mean a total of 1.2 tons, a little more than the one-ton warhead carried by Agni-5. A 20-kiloton nuclear bomb would completely devastate an area of 5.5-kilometre radius, the spread of nuclear radiation would depend on winds prevalent at the time.

Enter the ambitious Agni-6. This, the DRDO announced in 2013, would carry a 3-kiloton payload (three times more than the present), have MIRVs and MaRVs, and reach ranges up to 8,000 kilometres. According to top DRDO sources in 2015, the design is ready and will be put up for government clearance and funding after Agni-5 joins the Strategic Forces Command. This will be a challenge on three counts. The DRDO does not have high specific impulse propellants, unless they are acquired from the space (ISRO) programme. ISRO uses large solid propellants in its polar space launch vehicle programme. Moreover, adding another stage with a velocity trimming module may not work. And more than anything else SDINS might not be accurate and reliable even with nuclear warheads at such long ranges. When there is no evidence to suggest that strategic nukes have a role in a border war with China, why does India need the Agni-6?

What India needs are cruise missiles. Pakistan's subsonic Babur cruise missile with turbofan technology is the gamechanger because India does not have a comparable weapons system. Test-fired for the first time in August 2005, Babur has been inducted into Pakistan's Army Strategic Force Command. Similarly, Pakistan tested its 350-kilometre range air-launched cruise missile Ra'ad in August 2007, which is now part of its Air Force Strategic Command.

Babur, with ranges between 500 to 2,000 kilometres, would be the platform of choice with both tactical nuclear weapons and conventional warheads, provided Pakistan has procured capability (which is likely) from China to make small compact warheads with high yield. Produced in large numbers (which appears to have been done), Babur is the answer to India's Cold Start Doctrine and would probably be used for non-contact war at the border with conventional warheads.

In an attempt to match Babur, the DRDO test-fired the subsonic, two-stage, 1,000-kilometre range Nirbhay cruise missile in 2013 and 2015; it failed both times. What was claimed to be an indigenous propulsion system was perhaps acquired from Russia. If senior DRDO scientists are to be believed, the DRDO chief V. K. Saraswat wanted a totally indigenous Nirbhay as the counter to Pakistan's Babur cruise missile.

Pakistan, in comparison, has a range of ballistic missiles with solid and liquid propellants, and cruise missiles. These include solid propellant Hatf-I, Hatf-II, Hatf-III (also called Ghaznavi), Hatf-IV and Hatf-V (also called Shaheen-1), and Hatf-VI (also called Shaheen-2) ballistic missiles. The liquid-propellant ballistic missiles are Ghauri, Ghauri II and III. Pakistan's

60-kilometre range Nasr or Hatf-IX battlefield ballistic missile successfully test-fired in April 2011 is believed to be capable of carrying a low-yield small nuclear warhead. Pakistan also has the 2,750-kilometre range Shaheen-3 ballistic missile, which can reach India's Andaman and Nicobar islands in the Indian Ocean. Rawalpindi's logic of procuring the Shaheen-3 missile is to be able to cover all areas where India could move its land-based second strike capability.

Pakistan has two cruise missiles: Babur surface to surface and Ra'ad air-launched missiles. It has also developed the 'Burraq Unmanned Aerial Vehicle', which, with Chinese help, could be armed like the US's Predator. Regarding sea-based deterrence, the capability 'would most likely be based on a naval version of the cruise missile. Pakistan's Maritime Technology Organisation is nearing completion [which, once tested,] will be commissioned under the Naval Strategic Force Command, completing the third leg of the triad.'

Given Pakistan's road map, the DRDO should focus on two major areas: building a turbofan propulsion system for long-range cruise missiles, and accuracy for ballistic missiles. India's supersonic cruise missile, BRAHMOS, is not the answer because, being a joint venture with Russia, Moscow will disallow its use with nuclear weapons. Moreover, the DRDO should develop better guidance systems for accuracy so that ballistic missiles can be used with conventional warheads. This is essential because the Chinese have converted their small- and medium-range ballistic missiles from nuclear to conventional roles; this is compatible with its stated conventional war-fighting doctrine that ballistic missiles will be used to supplement air force with tighter control. There is no question that Chinese guidance systems would have been given to Pakistan.

BALLISTIC MISSILE DEFENCE

An example of DRDO's technology overreach—India's indigenous ballistic missile defence—has national security implications. It does not contribute to military power, if anything, it jeopardizes it. Since, according to one DRDO source, more than ₹20,000 crore has been spent on the ballistic missile defence without much success, it would be interesting to trace its genesis.

The ballistic missile defence was not a consequence of debate between stakeholders as would happen elsewhere in the world. The nation and the defence forces were taken by surprise by the maiden flight-test of the indigenous anti-ballistic missile interceptor in the exo (outside) atmosphere (PAD project) at a 47-kilometre altitude on 27 November 2006. The dividing altitude between atmosphere and space is 40 kilometres, below which is atmosphere and beyond which is space. Even as the media went overboard in declaring that India had built a world-class ballistic missile defence, DRDO's Saraswat, announced that DRDO would conduct missile interception in the endo (inside) atmospheric zone (AAD project) followed by half a dozen tests over the next four years to validate the system as credible defence against incoming ballistic missiles.

Interceptions of hostile missiles are done in the exo and endo phases to ensure guaranteed success. The challenge of defeating a hostile missile armed with a nuke is that the interceptor should also have a nuclear warhead. It should be one's own nuclear bullet versus the enemy's nuclear bullet. Since interceptors, unlike ballistic missiles, have a much smaller diameter, it is uncertain if India has the capability to make small warheads of high yield for interceptors. In the event of interception with conventional warheads, a direct hit is a must for the kill. The DRDO has radio frequency seekers and claims to have imaging infrared seekers, yet none of the tests done have been direct hits.

Speaking with the authors, Saraswat declared that Phase I interceptors (PAD and AAD) to protect cities like Delhi and Mumbai from a hostile ballistic missile of 2,000-kilometre range would be deployed by 2013. He said, 'Our commitment is to complete the flight trials of Phase I interceptors (PAD and AAD) for the 2,000-kilometre range missile by 2011. By 2013, we will realize all other elements including radars required for strategic defence. In phase II, we plan to take on targets with ranges till 5,000 kilometres.'

The inspiration for the ballistic missile defence had come to the DRDO from two events at the turn of the century. On assuming office, US President George W. Bush announced his ballistic missile defence plans, with India becoming the first country, even before the US's close allies like Japan and South Korea, to endorse it wholeheartedly. To demonstrate Washington's pleasure with New Delhi's quick endorsement, US Deputy Secretary of State Richard Armitage travelled to New Delhi in April 2001 to explain the Bush initiative, a gesture that the US undertakes with a few valued countries to explain important decisions. The Bush ballistic missile defence, he said, was in two parts: national missile defence and theatre missile defence; and deeper nuclear cuts, even unilateral if Russia did not agree. With the proliferation of short- and medium-range ballistic missiles with China and Pakistan, the theatre missile defence caught New Delhi's interest. Moreover, it was argued that years of US pressure on India to slow its indigenous ballistic missile programme had taken their toll where it was felt that Pakistan had acquired a lead in ballistic missiles, clandestinely acquired from China and North Korea.

The answer for India lay in concentrating on the ballistic missile defence, where the US even offered its improved Patriot (PAC-3) system to New Delhi. While the PAC-3 is a state-of-the-art system, it had two drawbacks: it was too expensive for the number of vulnerable areas and vulnerable points to be guarded. Moreover, the system is endo-atmospheric, implying it can intercept a hostile missile within the atmosphere in the terminal phase, which would mean the debris would fall on our own territory.

Given the size of the subcontinent, what India needed was a large number of anti-ballistic missiles that could intercept both inside and outside the atmosphere. Ballistic missiles can be intercepted and shot down at three points in their flight: in the early boost phase, in mid-course when most of the missiles are outside the atmosphere, and in the terminal phase where they hit the target. The ideal point, and also the most difficult, is to kill the missile in the boost phase—this would require space-based sensors and directed-energy weapons such as jet-based lasers to destroy the missiles. The achievable objective for India was to attempt to kill the missile in exo- and endo-atmosphere during the mid-course and terminal phases. Just when the DRDO was mulling over how to do this, Israel sold two EL/M Green Pine ground-based phased-array L-band 600-kilometre long-range tracking radars to India in late 2001.

This was the beginning of the Indian ballistic missile defence which has four components: long-range, long-wavelength radar to spot the re-entry vehicle (which contains the warhead); short-range, short-wavelength radar that can determine the position of the attacking re-entry vehicle with precision and guides the interceptor missile towards it; many long-range (exo-atmospheric) and short-range (endo-atmospheric) interceptor missiles; and a launch control centre or the battle management and command, control, communication and intelligence centre.

The ballistic missile defence is conceived on two established principles. First, the trajectory of a re-entry vehicle after it is released by the missile is entirely predetermined; therefore, if one can observe an early portion of it, the rest of the trajectory can be calculated. And second, the exo- and endo-atmosphere have their unique characteristics. Unlike the atmosphere, in space, a bullet and a feather released at the same point with the same speed and in the same direction will continue to travel together indefinitely.

According to an analyst, 'A missile defence system is workable only in support of an offensive strike (by air or land firepower). The logic behind this is that one's counterforce strike would have knocked out most of enemy's missiles so the ballistic missile defence system will have to deal with only a few surviving ones. This is clearly not a scenario that applies to India... It is for this reason that, apart from the US (with its unlimited resources) and Israel (needing to defend only about 500 kilometres to protect three-quarters of its people), no other nuclear weapon state is pursuing a ballistic missile defence programme.'

On DRDO's ballistic missile defence, there is a need for technical re-evaluation on five major counts. One, hostile long-range ballistic missiles armed with nuclear warheads would be dangerous to intercept in endo-atmosphere as the debris from a successful engagement would fall on one's own soil. For successful interception in the exo-atmosphere, the need is for a high-energy propellant to reach higher altitudes. DRDO does not have high-energy propellants to intercept hostile missiles at altitudes of 100 kilometres and above. For years, unsuccessful efforts have been made to procure them from Russia and Israel.

Two, all interception tests done in exo- and endo-atmosphere are of Prithvi and boosted Prithvi missiles which have slow terminal velocity. Since Pakistani missiles such as Ghauri and Shaheen have faster speeds, the need for DRDO is to demonstrate successful interception of Agni series missiles, which are being avoided as it is likely that these experiments will fail.

Three, unlike ballistic missiles, interceptors need both strap-down inertial navigation systems for guidance and highly accurate seekers for terminal homing. The DRDO has radio frequency seekers and hopes to get better imaging infrared seekers. Both however, would be inadequate for an assured direct kill. According to DRDO sources, none of the interceptions done so far have been direct hits. Four, for quick acquisition of hostile long-range missiles for interception in the exo-atmosphere, space-based capabilities are needed, which India lacks. And India's capability to make small nuclear warheads with high yields for interceptors is highly suspect.

The ballistic missile defence system should have 100 per cent assurance as a single ballistic missile armed with a nuclear warhead slipping through its net would cause the desired devastation, especially in India's urban areas which have dense population and sparse assets to deal with the aftermath of nuclear fallout. The reality is that once re-entry vehicles leave the missiles that propel them to their trajectories, there is no ballistic missile defence system that can effectively prevent them from causing an enormous amount of destruction.

For these reasons, the US and Soviet Union signed the 1972 treaty banning further development and deployment of the anti-ballistic missile (ABM) or ballistic missile defence system. Moreover, it was concluded that the biggest flaw in the ABM system, that seeks to hit a missile with another missile, was that both travel at about the same speed. If the first ABM interceptor misses the hostile ballistic missile, there will be no time to try again. The answer found was in the use of directed-energy weapons, which derive their destructive power from electromagnetic energy that travels close to or at the speed of light. ABM systems create more problems than they resolve. The DRDO could argue that the present ABM building blocks are just technology demonstrators and the government would decide when to deploy the ABM system once it becomes productive. But until then, the ABM programme is a drain on resources.

Even this argument does not help. Considering that Pakistan has repeatedly said that India's budding ballistic missile defence system would lead to a ballistic missile race, it has a perfect case to enhance its inventory of ballistic missiles without bothering about pressure from the US. Pakistan will also legitimately seek, if it has not acquired it already from outside, the evasive re-entry vehicle technology. Considering that India and Pakistan do not have a ballistic missiles understanding, and are unlikely to have one given New Delhi's position that its arsenal is not Pakistan-centric, this should worry India. More so when Pakistan's ballistic missiles, firmly under the command and control of its army chief, are its principal nuclear vector. Not to be missed, Pakistan has already made the case for the Fissile Missile Control Treaty to not focus only on future fissile material but to also consider existing stocks.

Given the above scenario, it is not unrealistic to assume that India will be under outside pressure to both keep its ballistic missiles arsenal and fissile material stocks in check, while Pakistan would not be under any such stringent obligations. All this would happen because India is building its ballistic missile defence blocks and publicly gloating about it. Wouldn't it be better if the money, energy and capability are instead focused on speedy building up of necessary ballistic and cruise missiles, both land and sea-based?

CHAPTER 16

QUEST FOR TECHNOLOGY

Chief of Naval Staff Admiral D. K. Joshi's sudden resignation on 26 February 2014 taking moral responsibility for a spate of accidents involving submarines and surface ships was as much a surprise as was the government's acceptance of his resignation letter post-haste in less than forty-eight hours. Breaking his silence one year later he gave two reasons for his abrupt departure: moribund higher defence management where services had accountability without powers; and the media for sensationalizing mishaps since it had little understanding of military matters.

The admiral did not understand why the government had accepted his resignation so promptly. However, to outside observers, it was clear why this had happened. It was because he had exploded India's myth-making which held that the country had a muscular foreign policy. India's Look East policy enunciated in 1991, and carried forward by successive governments, was aimed at seeking closer economic, diplomatic and strategic ties with East Asian nations. There were two reasons for doing so. After the 1990 economic liberalization necessitated by circumstances it became necessary for India to seek closer trade and commerce ties with littoral Western Pacific nations. They in turn sought comfort in India's size, potential and purported naval power as a balance to China next door. Indian strategists sensed an opportunity in this symbiotic economic relationship. With China and Pakistan having stumped India's options in the Himalayas for strategic space, they argued that India's strategic space was along the Indian and Western Pacific oceans. This argument found favour with New Delhi as it was compatible with the US's reaching out to India since 1992 for increased naval cooperation.

The US in 1992 had its own dilemma. After the demise of the Soviet Union in 1991, the US, scouting around for a worthy foe, was confronted with the quandary described by George Bernard Shaw, 'There are two tragedies in life. One is to lose your heart's desire. The other is to gain it.'

Explaining it lucidly in his 1994 book, *Diplomacy*, Henry Kissinger writes, 'Used to the two-power world which existed during the Cold War, the US, at no time in its history had participated in a balance-of-power system.' The latter implies give and take cooperation, something that the US had little experience of. Caught in the emerging globalized world order where 'the US can neither withdraw from the world nor dominate it', it identified 'at least six major powers—the United States, Europe, China, Japan, Russia, and probably India'.

Since the balance of global economic power was fast shifting to the Asia-Pacific with the emergence of China, the US reasoned it had to be offset by its unrivalled military power in order to retain pre-eminence in the new world order. Given its geography, size and potential, India—jutting out into the Indian Ocean region through which the trade of East and Southeast Asian powers, namely, China, Japan, Vietnam, South Korea and ASEAN nations, as well as from Europe and the Middle East passed—was the right choice for partnership. With this in mind, Lieutenant General Claude M. Kicklighter, from the US Pacific Command, visited India in 1991 with an offer—known as the Kicklighter Proposal—for peaceful military cooperation across the three defence services.

Buoyed by the US's wooing, India, positioning itself as the major naval power in the Indian Ocean region, reached out to smaller littoral nations eastwards seeking security and military ties. This was confirmed by Shivshankar Menon, India's national security advisor from 2010–14. According to him, 'our strategy has shifted to the entire Asia-Pacific region as we are looking at the maritime strategy since 2004'. India's carefully built naval credibility across the oceans got a knock with Admiral Joshi indicating that the Indian Navy was not muscular enough. He had to go, and so he did without the government having to take the flak.

To lend credibility to its Look East policy (during ten years of the Manmohan Singh government from 2004–14), India projected itself as China's strategic rival in Asia where it announced there was enough space for both to grow. However, being equal to China meant playing down India's military weakness on the disputed land border. Since India's diplomats neither desired sharing the dais with military leaders nor understood military power, the appeasement policy towards China was the preferred option.

With the arrival of the Narendra Modi government in May 2014, India's Look East policy was rebranded as Act East, in sync with India's new emphasis on Modi's personal diplomacy. It was argued that Modi's personal connections with world leaders had raised India's stature. The

prime minister and the naval chief, Admiral Robin Dhowan (March 2014–
May 2016), who had replaced Admiral Joshi, showed admirable flair for
perception management by projecting India as a leading power. The Indian
Navy under Admiral Dhowan carried out astonishing naval diplomacy. Forty
naval frontline ships (comprising most of the seagoing vessels) were flying
the flag across Southeast and East Asia, the Middle East and Europe during
2015–16—something that a leading naval power would do.

According to the US Ambassador to India, Richard Verma, 'Indian
leaders have expressed a determination to leave behind the traditions of
non-alignment and strategic autonomy and, in the words of (Indian) Foreign
Secretary Jaishankar, to become a leading power.' India's Act East policy was
closely aligned with the US's rebalancing to Asia, and Japan's 'confluence of
the two seas—the Indian Ocean and Pacific Ocean'. During the January 2015
visit of then US President Barack Obama to India, the two sides signed the
'US-India Joint Strategic Vision for the Asia-Pacific and the Indian Ocean
Region', with the US unequivocally stating that 'the US-India strategic
partnership will be anchored in Asia'. Japanese Premier Shinzo Abe, during
his December 2015 India visit, wrote that 'Japan and India are natural
partners also in maritime security… As such, our countries share extensive
roles and responsibilities with regard to nurturing and enriching the Indian
Ocean and Pacific Ocean to become seas of the clearest transparency, and
keeping these seas open, free and safe.'

With China as the proverbial elephant in the room in the Western
Pacific and Indian Ocean, India's relations, especially with the US—the
leading naval power in the world—assumed criticality. What did India want
from the US and what would Washington get in return?

To answer this question, we need to step back to the 1980s when
India was perceived to be in the Soviet Union camp and the US was the
estranged superpower. Providing incremental correction to his mother's
foreign policy, Prime Minister Rajiv Gandhi decided to move beyond a
handshake with the US. High on his US agenda was the quest for high-
end technology to build indigenous defence production capabilities. Indian
policymakers, however, did not reckon that indigenous technology is germane
to becoming a geostrategic player.

Thus within a month of assuming office, Prime Minister Rajiv Gandhi
in December 1984 signed the memorandum of understanding on technology
with the US. This was hailed as a major policy shift where India, hitherto
completely under the Soviet Union's tutelage, had decided to warm up
to the United States. Under the memorandum, the two sides discussed

the US's concerns about diversion of its technologies to the Soviets and India's wish list from Washington. The US also proposed high-end technical cooperation for the manufacture of India's next-generation fighter aircraft, the Light Combat Aircraft, by offering the General Electric 404 engine as the power pack. However, when India sought the US's high-end Cray-XMP-24 supercomputer, which could ostensibly be used for the development of nukes and ballistic missiles as well as to aid agriculture, the US refused. Instead India was offered the much less powerful Cray-XMP-14 supercomputer. This was at a time when the US, having given F-16s to Pakistan, was considering providing them with the Boeing 707 advanced warning and control system supposedly to aid Mujahids combating the Red Army in Afghanistan.

The US's strategic objective in the bilateral relationship was clear: to wean India away from the Soviet camp. India, on the other hand, had two objectives. The stated objective was to get US high-end and dual-use technology; the unstated objective was to be identified as close to the US. Thirty-two years later, in 2016, India's objectives remained unchanged. The US's objectives, on the other hand, kept pace with geopolitics: from 1998 to 2008, it was non-proliferation. Since then, it has been twofold: defence trade and support for its security architecture in the Asia-Pacific and Indian Ocean region (against China). The ultimate proof of this would be joint patrols by the two countries, requiring commonality of equipment and sharing of operational communications, for common combat missions when required. In other words, without being a NATO member or a US ally, Indian and US militaries would have the ability to fight together.

Set as a benchmark, when Rajiv Gandhi became the first Indian prime minister in 1985 to address the US Congress, all Indian heads of governments have sought 'successful' rather than substantive US visits. This has helped the US extract concessions from India without much reciprocation.

For example, after the 1998 nuclear tests, Prime Minister Vajpayee wrote a confidential letter to US President Bill Clinton citing China as the reason for the tests. It was hoped that this would please the US—which was seeking close ties with Delhi—since it wanted India to balance the rising China. What better than a muscular India with nuclear weapons? What was forgotten was that the US as the leader of global non-proliferation would find India's tests unacceptable.

Once tempers cooled in Washington and sense prevailed that the nuclear genie could not be put back in the bottle, non-proliferation became the US's prime agenda for ties with India. This continued until the signing of the Indo–US nuclear deal on 10 October 2008.

The Clinton administration wanted India to sign the Comprehensive Nuclear Test Ban Treaty and define the concept of strategic (nuclear) restraint. The US interlocutor, Deputy Secretary of State Strobe Talbott told the authors, 'The essence of the concept of strategic restraint, which was not the phrase favoured by the Indian side (India preferred to call it defence posture), was essentially to take the slogan of the government of the time that is, minimum credible deterrence, and translate it into deployment and other practices that would be minimal as well as credible and would diminish the danger of an arms race in the region.'

With the Clinton administration ending its term in 2001, the incoming Bush administration picked up the threads from the unprecedented fourteen rounds of bilateral talks on how to manage India's nuclear arsenal held between Strobe Talbott and India's Jaswant Singh. To begin with, the US de-hyphenated its relations with India and Pakistan. De-hyphenating refers to a policy started by the US government under President Bush of dealing with India and Pakistan in different silos, without referring to their bilateral relations. It enabled the US to build closer military and strategic ties with India without factoring in the reaction from Pakistan, and to continue its own strategy in Afghanistan with the help of the Pakistan military without referring back to India. While this was hailed in India as its diplomatic victory, for the US, it was a necessary move. The US needed Pakistan to fight its war on terror, and India to limit its nuclear arsenal since it had a direct consequence on Pakistan's necessity for strategic parity with India. In return for its cooperation, the US dangled the offer of technology before India.

This was done in two steps. In November 2002, the two sides established the High Technology Cooperation Group—meant for commercial trade in high technology for civilian use. This was followed by the formulation of the Next Steps in Strategic Partnership (NSSP) on 13 January 2004 between Vajpayee and Bush.

The NSSP covered three strategic areas, namely, the civilian space programme, civilian nuclear activities and high technology trade as well as dialogue on missile defence. Trade in defence hardware was deliberately not included in the NSSP because it was felt that trade in weapons platforms should follow trade in technology. This was meant to ensure that enough strategic trust was built before India purchased war-fighting platforms which would need an uninterrupted supply of spares.

Speaking with the authors in June 2004, the US Undersecretary of

Commerce, Kenneth Juster, said, 'In some respects, the NSSP builds and expands upon the work being done in the High Technology Cooperation Group. The HTCG set up a framework for reviewing and analysing how technology commerce between the US and India could be expanded across a broad range of categories, including information technology, biotechnology, nanotechnology and defence technology.'

Thus the NSSP, a process touted as capable of fulfilling India's need of high technology and the US's need for the tightening of Indian laws for better export controls (a non-proliferation requirement) was meant to, in a subtle, progressive manner, help India and the US come geopolitically closer without ruffling China.

The slow movement of the NSSP did not diminish its importance. Given the distrust that existed on both sides, especially on the Indian side, the NSSP was possibly the best approach for the relationship to grow. This was confirmed by the then NSA, Brajesh Mishra, 'There were three phases in NSSP. In general terms there was a difference of opinion in what they (the US) were looking [for] and what we were looking [for]. At the end of NSSP, we were looking at lifting up of all restrictions on India's civilian nuclear and space programme. This is not what they had in mind. They were looking at end-use verification and fissile material. So when phase one was over, they said that a new phase has begun. What they meant (in that) is a promise to work with the Congress and their allies in Nuclear Suppliers Group.' This required that India place its nuclear reactors under the International Atomic Energy Agency's (IAEA) safeguard.

Given India's stated minimum credible deterrence, which Mishra said 'is a flexible concept', 'the NDA (Vajpayee) government had offered to put a few of our existing nuclear reactors under safeguards. The idea was that from the unsafeguarded reactors there would be enough fissile material for India's minimum credible programme. We have 14 reactors in operation and about nine under various stages of construction (this was in August 2005). I would have said that all future reactors either built by us or with others' cooperation will be put under safeguard. This way we would have had 10 to 11 unsafeguarded reactors. But this was not acceptable to the US.'

Just as the two sides started working on phase two of NSSP, the Vajpayee government was voted out of power. The Manmohan Singh government with J. N. Dixit as the national security advisor, taking ownership of the NSSP, initiated talks with the Bush administration on phase two of the NSSP in September 2004. However, given the US presidential elections, it was left to the second Bush administration to move the bilateral dialogue forward.

When the second Bush administration entered office, two major changes transformed the ongoing dialogue between India and the US: Condoleezza Rice, a Bush family friend, was elevated from the post of NSA to secretary of state, and on the sudden demise of Dixit, India got a new NSA, M. K. Narayanan, a former intelligence officer who was unaware of NSSP's technical nuances. It was in these circumstances that Rice, on her first overseas tour arrived in Delhi on 16 March 2005, and took the Indian dispensation by storm with her declaration that the US would help India become a major power.

There was excitement in Delhi and alarm in Islamabad and Beijing. While India had harboured ambitions of becoming a major power, it found it hard to believe that the foremost power of the time, while acknowledging India's potential, had promised to help it realize its dream. Pakistan was worried that by de-hyphenating it from India the US might lose strategic interest in it. China saw the partnership between India and the US as designed to contain Beijing.

After Rice's spectacular announcement in Delhi, the NSSP was ended abruptly and talks on the nuclear deal—Rice's brainchild—began. In her book, *No Higher Honor*, Rice writes, 'The key from our point of view was to get India within the IAEA… better to have India in the tent in some fashion, even if New Delhi could not formally sign the NPT… at least, new construction of (Indian) reactors would be under safeguard. India already had more than enough nuclear material for its military program. It needed help on the civilian side and we needed the strategic breakthrough with this emerging, democratic power.'

Rice's trick worked. The nuclear deal offered by her was too tempting for Prime Minister Manmohan Singh to let it go easily. While suggesting nothing more substantive than the NSSP, the nuclear deal by its over reach, all-inclusiveness, fast pace and pretence of equality between India and the US came across as an awesome proposition to the Indian side. According to the deal, India was to place certain numbers of its nuclear reactors under International Atomic Energy Agency safeguards. In return, the US promised to end India's nuclear apartheid by acknowledging it as a nuclear weapons power, agreed that India would have access to high and dual-use technologies, and offered to cooperate on civilian nuclear energy to meet India's growing energy demands.

It seemed that India would get the moon: it would become a nuclear weapons power (with freedom to maintain its credible minimum deterrence); be free to decide on more indigenous nuclear reactors for strategic purposes;

be part of the global restricted technology cartels, namely, the Nuclear Suppliers Group, Missile Technology Control Regime, Australia Group, and Wassenaar Arrangement (all led by the US but working by consensus); maintain strategic autonomy implying independent foreign policy; not be clubbed with Pakistan; be free to buy nuclear fuel (uranium), run the nuclear closed fuel cycle (including reprocessing and subsequently the indigenous three-stage Thorium cycle), and purchase state-of-the-art nuclear reactors and enrichment and reprocessing technologies for its energy needs. It appeared to be a win-win situation for India.

In reality, from the US perspective, the deal was about non-proliferation by coercing India to identify the maximum numbers of its reactors for civilian use, getting India to de facto sign the Comprehensive Nuclear Test Ban Treaty even when the US Senate had rejected it, getting India's foreign policy closely aligned with that of the US, doing commerce in civil nuclear reactors and defence (through a ten-year defence framework signed separately but highlighted in the 18 July 2005 framework agreement), and eventually having India as a junior strategic partner if not junior ally in the Asia-Pacific region.

What Mishra had foreseen seemed to have come true. Going public within days of the 18 July 2005 framework document (joint statement with the nuclear deal) being signed in Washington, Mishra said, 'My view is that if you offer to identify and separate the civilian and military nuclear facilities and programmes, it will have long-term national security impact.'

Having flown halfway across the globe, Prime Minister Manmohan Singh had a similar apprehension sitting in Washington's Willard Hotel a block away from the White House on the night of 17 July 2005, when he was to sign the framework document which was meant to transform the bilateral relationship the next day. He suddenly developed cold feet and, according to Rice, refused to meet her since he felt 'he cannot sell [the deal] in New Delhi'. The reason: the US had shifted the goalposts and wanted India to 'keep just two or three reactors outside safeguard', India's then National Security Advisor Narayanan disclosed on the tenth anniversary of the deal in July 2015.

Rice managed to coax the Indian prime minister to sign the 18 July 2005 framework agreement and the hard work for India, as the junior partner, began. While the excruciatingly long process with dramatic highs and lows—on account of the US's constant shifting of the goalposts and meeting its global non-proliferation obligations many of which were contrary to the nuclear deal promises—which concluded on 10 October 2008, with the signing of the Indo–US 123 agreement, have been documented, a few instances indicative of the US's seeming duplicity deserve highlighting.

Having signed the framework agreement, Manmohan Singh returned home to enormous scepticism. The Congress President Sonia Gandhi— the real power centre—and numerous Congress MPs were unsure about the deal. The Left parties—coalition partners of the government—were upset about closer ties with the US and wanted more transparency on the bilateral relationship. The opposition, led by the BJP, declared the framework document a sell-out to the US. And the diplomats and scientists were deeply divided on the strategic implications of the deal. In such a domestically charged atmosphere, US President Bush arrived on 2 March 2006 in Delhi to settle the deal's separation plan—which reactors would come under IAEA safeguards and which would not. This turned out to be an acrimonious bilateral exercise, especially because according to the framework document, India was to unilaterally take this decision.

When Manmohan Singh was informing the nation that with the separation plan, only 65 per cent of Indian reactors would be under safeguards, the US's main interlocutor, Nicholas Burns, told the media that 'in one generation 90 per cent of Indian reactors would be under safeguards'. Burns was clearly hinting that India's right to decide future indigenous reactors for strategic purposes as agreed to in the deal would be opposed by the US.

India was thus being subjected to restricted fissile material stocks even before the world had agreed to the terms of the Fissile Material Cut-off Treaty. Also, the India-specific Additional Protocol that India signed with the IAEA was extremely intrusive and could through technical means and unannounced sudden visits by the agency's inspectors monitor progress of the unsafeguarded reactors. The US relented on keeping India's research reactors out of safeguards because they have not yet harnessed the indigenous three-stage Thorium cycle (an example of technology overreach).

While Bush was pushing India's case for exemption from the global restrictive regimes and the US Congress, the US, under its global commitment, was also urging the Nuclear Suppliers Group (NSG)—the forty-eight-nation NSG was formed consequent to India's 1974 nuclear test—to review its export control rules to check proliferation.

What appeared to be duplicitous behaviour from the US perspective, was the right course to adopt. On the one hand, the US under its civil nuclear deal commitment made in the July 2005 framework agreement to India urged the US Congress, and the non-proliferation cartels, namely, the Nuclear Suppliers Group, Missile Technology Control Regime, Australia Group, and

Wassenaar Arrangement to allow a waiver to India to buy nuclear reactors (which can technically be used both for civilian and military purposes) despite India not having signed the Non-Proliferation Treaty (NPT). On the other hand, the US, as the leader of these cartels, asked them (especially the NSG which trades in nuclear reactors and its technologies) to tighten its trade rules against non-NPT nations (India bring the prime one).

A decade later, when the US's conduct would prove detrimental to India's interests, India's ire was, surprisingly, aimed at China. In July 2016, the Modi government—having undertaken intense global lobbying led by the prime minister himself—failed to make India an NSG member. This was because China and eight other smaller nations had argued that only those nations which had signed the NPT could be considered for NSG membership. A little known fact is that the smaller nations which had opposed India's entry into the NSG were also concerned about India's uncompleted nuclear separation plan (since India's military reactors are a spin-off of civilian reactors, separation of the two would be extremely difficult) which could result in undetected (by the IAEA, the nuclear watchdog) nuclear proliferation. While China certainly opposed India's NSG membership, the reality is that the tightened export control rules implemented at the US's behest would have disallowed NSG members' to trade with India in technologies needed to exploit the full nuclear fuel cycle even after India had acquired NSG membership.

To take the story further back, in July 2011, the NSG announced its new export norms: only those nations which had signed the NPT would be eligible for enrichment and reprocessing technologies. India was taken aback by this. While it would be allowed to trade for fuel with the NSG, it would be denied enrichment and reprocessing technologies because it had not signed the Non-Proliferation Treaty.

In simple terms, while India could buy nuclear fuel from the world, it could not use it fully as without reprocessing technologies it would be unable to use the nuclear waste for energy production. Especially since India has reprocessing capabilities although these are somewhat limited.

Regarding India's quest for membership of the Nuclear Suppliers Group—the club which works on a consensus principle—China had in July 2015 made it clear that signing of the NPT would be essential for new member states. What China had left unsaid was that India could become an NSG member only if it signed the NPT under United Nations article 1172 as a non-nuclear weapon state.

Even as the non-proliferation noose was being tightened on India (through the signing of the India-specific Additional Protocol with the International Atomic Energy Agency, shifting US goalposts by reinterpretation of the separation plan and new NSG export guidelines requiring signing of the NPT as a prerequisite), there was bilateral disagreement over how much India was obliged to align with the US's global strategic and security concerns.

India said that it would abide by the bilateral 123 Agreement that it had signed with the US on 10 October 2008, which did not mention India's obligation to abide by the US's strategic concerns worldwide. The US, on the other hand, was bound by its own domestic law, the Henry J. Hyde Act of 2006 (essential for the US administration to sign the 123 Agreement), which required India to respect the US's security agenda. This resulted in India's flip-flop Iran policy as Delhi was torn between its relationship with the US and the need for bilateral strategic ties with Tehran.

To add to this, two other contentious issues popped up: the US's disappointment over defence ties with India and India's 2010 Nuclear Liability Law. While the bilateral defence framework was signed in April 2005, three months before the July 2005 framework agreement, it got mentioned under the framework agreement. For this reason, the powerful US defence lobby, which had played a major role in the passage of the nuclear deal through the US Congress, expected, in a transactional fashion, to be rewarded. When neither of the two US fighter jets—the F-16 and Super Hornet—which had participated in the over US$ 40 billion Indian Air Force's Medium Multi-Role Combat Aircraft competition made it into the final round in 2012, numerous US Congressmen and leading analysts accused India of betrayal. A lot of pressure was put on New Delhi to consider another US platform—the F-35 aircraft—for the IAF.

Similarly the 2010 Indian Nuclear Liability Law was found unacceptable to the US which argued that in the event of an accident, the liability should be of the supplier rather than the operator. Thus, when Manmohan Singh's term in office ended in May 2014, few mentioned the nuclear deal as the outgoing government's achievement. Those who did obfuscated matters by arguing that the nuclear deal was a prime reason for overall improved ties between India and the US. The truth remained that both the strategic and commercial aspects of the nuclear deal had remained unfulfilled.

Nuclear commerce, which India had touted as the key reason for the deal, had not started. And India, despite having accepted non-proliferation measures, namely, signing the Additional Protocol with the International Atomic Energy Agency and undertaking the separation plan, had not operationalized the deal. The promised Nuclear Suppliers Group waiver fell short of expectations. While India could carry out nuclear fuel commerce, there remained uncertainty about India getting reprocessing and enrichment technologies to recycle spent fuel. Moreover, the high and dual-use technologies that were promised to India under the deal have not arrived.

The Modi government in May 2014 went along with the popular perception that the deal had transformed strategic relations between India and the US. Before Prime Minister Narendra Modi embarked on his US visit in September 2014, India, on 22 June 2014, ratified the Additional Protocol signed (on 15 March 2009) with the International Atomic Energy Agency, signalling its intention to bring the deal to a closure so that nuclear commerce with the US could commence. Between September 2014 and the visit of Obama as the chief guest on India's Republic Day in January 2015, 'experts, legal and nuclear, from both countries sat down and worked out an understanding (on India's Nuclear Liability Law)', as Richard Verma, the US ambassador to India, put it. It is another matter whether it would be acceptable to the business community in both countries.

Notwithstanding phrases like 'natural allies' used by Vajpayee for Indo-US ties, 'strategic partnership' cited by Manmohan Singh and the 'strategic plus partnership' by US Richard Verma in 2015, the spectre of mutual distrust has not gone away, especially as India did not get the US high and dual-use nuclear technologies that it had sought.

The next initiative to move the relationship forward was once again taken by the US. During the visit of US Defense Secretary Leon Panetta to India in June 2012, the US proposed the Defense Technology and Trade Initiative (DTTI), to be worked out between Panetta's deputy, Ashton Carter (defense secretary in 2015), and India's NSA, Shivshankar Menon.

Having secured its non-proliferation objectives, the US administration moved to mollify its exasperated defence industry which had helped push the nuclear deal through the US Congress. With the US entries to the big-ticket Medium Multi Role Combat Aircraft deal having been rejected, their grouse was that the Indian bureaucracy was too slow on outstanding defence deals. The first task of the DTTI was to secure fast closure of pending defence deals. This was not easy on two counts. One, Prime Minister Manmohan Singh was a political lightweight, while his defence minister, A. K. Antony, an indecisive leader more worried about his reputation than defence preparedness, was a political heavyweight. Given this, it was virtually impossible for the Prime Minister's Office to persuade the defence minister. The other reason was the Indian government's scepticism about dealing with the US especially since the nuclear deal had not enhanced strategic trust. In order to move the DTTI to the next level, the US had suggested that India sign four foundational agreements which the US routinely entered into with its allies. These are the General Security of Military Information Agreement, Logistics Support Agreement, Communication and Information Security Memorandum of Agreement (CISMOA), and Basic Exchange and Cooperation Agreement (BECA) for geospatial intelligence. With these agreements, the decks would be cleared for the two militaries to share classified communications with one another necessary for joint patrols.

While India signed the General Security of Military Information Agreement, it procrastinated on the others as they were perceived to be intrusive and detrimental to India's strategic autonomy. For example, the Logistics Support Agreement meant that two countries could avail of each other's military facilities like naval bases, fuel dumps, air force stations, and so on, for replenishment of their own equipment and forces in the region. Instead of carte blanche, India was willing to consider such US requests on a case-by-case basis. This was eventually agreed to by renaming the Logistics Support Agreement as the Logistics Exchange Memorandum of Agreement (LEMOA) which the Modi government signed in August 2016 to 'allow military logistics permission on a case-by-case basis to each other to facilitate joint exercises, humanitarian assistance and other relief operations'.

While basing rights or US warships anchored at Indian naval bases or US combat aircraft parked at India air force stations is not allowed under LEMOA, it is a definitive step towards interoperability necessary to conduct joint patrols at sea and joint air combat training. Once India signs the remaining two hold-out agreements (CISMOA and BECA), the two militaries (especially the navies and air forces) would be ready to commence training for common combat missions. After the LEMOA signing, defence minister Manohar Parrikar, when asked, had said that CISMOA and BECA signing by India would happen after a public debate.

What would be the purpose of joint patrols? This was spelt out by Prime Minister Modi while addressing the US Congress in June 2016. 'A strong India-US partnership can anchor peace, prosperity and stability from Asia to Africa and from Indian Ocean to the Pacific.'

Thus, depending upon the US President Donald Trump, and Modi securing a second term in office (in 2019), India could become the main security provider (with fulsome US political and military support) in the Indian Ocean region to uphold the existing security architecture. This would be at odds with China's ambitious Maritime Silk Road which follows the same path as the sea lanes of communications in the Indian Ocean region that India hopes to guard. In other words, there is the possibility of a direct clash between China's One Belt One Road project for global dominance and India's Act East and Think West policy.

India under Modi also committed to a political and military role in the Western Pacific (impinging on China's major concern in the South China Sea). This was evident from Modi's September 2016 visit to Vietnam when India granted US$ 500 million defence credit line and elevated the bilateral relationship to Comprehensive Strategic Partnership with emphasis on defence ties with Vietnam. Thus, Modi's India has challenged China in its own backyard.

Meanwhile, the US, after the signing of the LEMOA, conferred the title of major defence partner on India in June 2016. What it meant was that simultaneously with India signing the remaining foundation agreements and the two militaries moving towards interoperability through joint patrols, Washington would enhance the sharing of its technologies and defence sales to India to achieve commonality of equipment for interoperability. The US's 2016 offer of moving its F-16 aircraft production line to India was meant for this purpose.

Two other tasks of the DTTI were assistance in research and development (R&D) and co-production with India. On R&D, the US did make efforts under President Obama's 2010 export control reform initiative to revise its export list which was rigid in exports of technology. The problem came with the Indian Defence Research and Development Organisation (DRDO) which instead of assessing available US technologies was keen on the US's help to resolve its own technical problems which had prevented fructification of its military projects. While the US was involved with a few DRDO labs, nothing of significance happened.

On co-production, after years of proposals and counter-proposals, five projects were mutually agreed to and announced during Obama's January 2015 India visit. Two projects that caught the fancy of the services and the media related to jet engines technology and aircraft carrier development. While working groups were formed on the projects, it is anyone's guess how far they will go. There is an unbridgeable gap between the technology bases of the two countries. Then there are issues bothering the US government and US defence manufacturers. As Ashley Tellis puts it, 'Because the United States is a hegemonic power in the international system, all significant military technology transfers are conditioned fundamentally by an assessment of their impact on Washington's capacity to preserve its unique supremacy, their consequences for global or regional stability, and their benefits for strategic ties with the recipient'.

US defence manufacturers had other concerns. Since most US military technology is in the private sector, their proprietors were unlikely to part with it given India's cap of 49 per cent foreign direct investment in defence. Even when the Modi government raised the FDI cap to 100 per cent with strings attached, there were numerous hurdles (explained earlier in the book) along the way. These would not allow foreign manufacturers to make strategic decisions or protect their intellectual property rights. Unless India decides to completely revamp its defence policy to allow market forces freedom to operate, which is unlikely, India would at best be looking at foreign technology 'know-how' rather than 'know-why'. It becomes evident that in the defence ecosystem prevalent in India, the DTTI would not be able to achieve a major breakthrough in co-production.

The 'know-why' that the US might give India would not be high-end technology, and it would be linked to strategic trade-offs. No nation, least of all the US, which has a huge lead over the rest of the world in technology, will part with its high-end 'know-why' which is guarded as a state secret. Moreover, the procedure to even get the US's middle-level technology is not a one-stop shop; it is a constant tussle between the White House, the Pentagon, the commerce ministry and the US Congress to determine the transactional mathematics.

If this simple truth had struck India, it would not have given so much away for so little to the US. In the quest for US technology since 1985, which it got in driblets, it is debatable if India's 1998 nuclear tests were a strategic blunder. Because of the tests, the China-Pakistan clandestine nexus became overt; Pakistan acquired a lead over India in strategic weapons; the balance tilted in favour of Rawalpindi; and civil-military relations in Pakistan shifted decisively in favour of the Pakistan Army making it difficult for peace between India and Pakistan

India, in 2016, seemed agreeable to match its strategic objectives with those of the US in the Asia-Pacific and Indian Ocean region, something the Manmohan Singh dispensation had resisted. It is however debatable whether the Modi government, having expressed its willingness to sign the remaining US foundational agreements, and having Japan as a trilateral partner—US, India and Japan—through the Malabar series and strategic dialogue, will risk annoying China by having regular naval presence in the Western Pacific, especially in the South China Sea. Good strategy dictates that India should concentrate on peace and the rule of law in the

Indian Ocean region. Overreach to the contentious South China Sea is unnecessary, dangerous and counter-productive. China will hit back if its strategic objectives are harmed.

For technology, it is important for India to rebuild its traditional and time-tested relationship with Russia. Meeting with Viktor Komardin, deputy director general of Rosoboronexport, at the International Defence Maritime Show in St Petersburg in 2013 was a sobering experience. When the authors asked him why Russia gave 1970s' technology for India's submarine nuclear reactor (INS *Arihant*), his cryptic counter-question was, 'Do you have it?' Met with silence, which conveyed that India did not have the technology, he replied, 'In that case, it is state-of-the-art for you.'

This is par for the course. Instead of investing in know-why, the DRDO is constantly scouting around for quick fixes. In military circles it is common knowledge that Russian manufacturers have made tentative offers to share technology know-why with the DRDO. This has not come about because the DRDO has raised certain objections that have come in the way of deals being structured.

Thus, Indian-Russian military-technical cooperation, which is the backbone of the bilateral relationship is half served. Both sides are sufficiently hard-nosed at bargaining—Indians seek comparably good equipment and Russians demand competitive prices, among other things. Nevertheless, India's defence-related connection with Russia outweighs all the others. At least 70 per cent of cutting-edge equipment with all three Indian defence services is of Russian origin. More is in the pipeline, including fifth generation aircraft, major surface ships and tanks, indicating that India would remain dependent on Russian defence hardware for at least thirty to forty years. Defence ties will remain robust for four fundamental reasons: traditional comfort and trust, the possibility of getting restrictive technologies which the US and western countries will not part with, general compatibility with each other's world view, and Russia being a one-stop shop. Unlike the US, the Russian president's nod is sufficient to get things rolling.

The long-term optimism about the India-Russia relationship is underpinned by their mutual interest in Asia. When asked whether Russia sees itself more in Europe or Asia, the Russian Ambassador to India, V. I. Trubnikov, gave an interesting perspective in January 2006, 'Gone are the times when Russia, according to the great Russian poet Alexander Blok, "used to hold the shield between the two hostile races"—Europe and Asia. Now, Russia plays an absolutely different role of the link between the East and the West. This role is determined by Russia's multidirectional foreign policy with its European and Asian vectors complementing each other in order to reinforce the country's stand in the international arena.'

After the Yeltsin years, when Russia felt humiliated by the US's attitude, and with the arrival of Putin in 2000, Moscow saw itself as the champion of Asia. Consequently, it took two unusual steps. At Moscow's behest, the first trilateral meeting between the foreign ministers of Russia, India and China was held in Almaty in October 2004. Russia said this would help in the formation of real multipolarity in the world since the three nations' strategic interests, namely combating international terrorism, religious extremism and separatism, cooperation in economic development, joint exploration of energy resources, scientific, technical and cultural collaboration, were common. The natural convergence of the three nations would bring about the integration of resources and should not be viewed as a 'block' or 'axis'.

China, in 2005, had not adopted an aggressive foreign policy. While both China and Russia profess a strategic relationship, ten years later in 2016 it was of a different kind. Peeved with the US's perceived high-handedness, both are slowly inching towards building an alternative Asian security architecture; Moscow's partnership, however, is half-hearted as it does not relish the idea of China, with its deep pockets, being the big brother. Moreover, Russia is not happy with China building its military power with Russian know-why without either its consent or paying for it. The Chinese are past masters at reverse engineering equipment. They are known to have bought select Russian defence platforms, stripped them completely without permission, acquiring know-why which they have then used to make cheaper imitations for export. Russia does not have this fear from the DRDO scientists who are considered too disinterested to even attempt this.

While the US and Russia provide India with strategic advantages to conduct diplomacy with China, to derive fulsome gains India should know that diplomacy is only as good as its own two legs—economic and military power (including technology)—supporting it. Merely pretending to have military power will not enable India's desire to be a geostrategic player in the world.

CHAPTER 17

THE INDIGENOUS DEFENCE INDUSTRY

According to some analysts, in the next decade or so, China's defence exports may exceed Russia's because China will be in a position to offer a package deal to the buyer, given its economic strength and now the ambitious connectivity programme across land and sea. At least in four areas, China has been producing and exporting defence platforms and weapons to some Asian and African countries. These include fighter aircraft, submarines, tanks and missiles. In fact, the buzz is that the Chinese-built fifth generation fighter aircraft, J-31, may find export customers faster than Russia's PAK-FA, in which India is a supposed partner although the final agreement still hangs fire, primarily because the Russian fighter has already been doing test-flying for the last few years and the Indian partner Hindustan Aeronautics Ltd. (HAL) is yet to make any contribution. Given the enormous strides the Chinese defence industry has made in the past several decades, any idea that our indigenous defence industry can go some way towards catching up and thereby restore a bit of balance to the military–defence equation seems unrealistic.

India has not been able to produce something as basic as an acceptable rifle for its infantry soldiers or even a hand grenade, forget about high-technology guns, aircraft, submarines, etc. The supposed success of the Defence Research and Development Organisation (DRDO) in the area of ballistic missiles is notional, because the missiles have only been tested in a simulated environment and bank on imports for a number of crucial technologies. The Light Combat Aircraft, which has been in the making for nearly three decades, remains a work in progress. It is unlikely to be the mainstay of the Indian Air Force's combat fleet any time soon. Despite claims to the contrary by the Indian Navy, even it is heavily dependent on imports. The so-called indigenous content in the warships refers to the licensed production of foreign equipment in India. The story is more or less the same across technology domains with few variations.

Catching up with China is certainly not possible and not even desired. However, if India is able to produce mid-technology stuff, let's say, ammunition, without overwhelming dependence on foreign manufacturers then at least in the event of a clash (either with China or its proxy, Pakistan) it would not be required to run helter-skelter looking for war sustenance (as happened during the 1999 Kargil War). Complete dependence on imports, especially defence imports, impedes the growth of a nation.

Knowledgeable observers, and those of us who have focused on Indian military and defence matters know that the problem does not lie with the quality of India's scientists and engineers. The problem is the absence of sensible, pragmatic policymaking. Unfortunately, the Government of India is still in evolutionary mode. It is only tweaking the existing policy framework without disturbing the main structure and this is holding back progress.

The closing months of the United Progressive Alliance (UPA) government were rife with what was called policy paralysis in industry parlance. Despite several amendments and revisions, the defence procurement procedure (DPP) policy and the rules governing the flow of foreign direct investment (FDI) through which the government was trying to streamline purchase of equipment as well as kick-start the indigenous defence industry remained deeply flawed. Grappling with corruption charges and an economy that was threatening to go into reverse, the UPA government had hit the pause button; probably out of fear that anything it did was bound to create more problems; especially after AgustaWestland's VVIP helicopter programme started to unravel early in 2013 with allegations of kickbacks.

Given this, the global vendors of defence equipment, most of whom had set up shop in India during the glorious years between 2005–09, when the economy promised to breach the magical 10 per cent growth figure, had all gone into a wait and watch mode. Their Indian partners, consultants or agents told them that the situation would change dramatically with the arrival of the Narendra Modi government. There was much optimism in the last week of May 2014 as the new government took the oath of office. It seemed that the wait after all was worth every precious moment. When the prime minister asked Finance Minister Arun Jaitley to also take care of the defence portfolio, the industry read a positive message in that.

'It is no secret that Jaitley is the most influential minister in the Cabinet. By giving him charge of both the finance and defence ministries, the government is sending out a strong message that it is serious about building India's defence capabilities. Now the files will not gather dust shuttling from one ministry to another. Decision-making will be quicker and will have direct intervention of the prime minister,' a former military officer and a consultant with a US-based defence company had predicted then. The tussle between Defence Minister A. K. Antony and Commerce Minister Anand Sharma was probably at the back of his mind. In March 2013, Sharma had proposed raising the FDI in defence from 26 per cent to 74 per cent. In a letter to Prime Minister Manmohan Singh, he suggested that to allay fears of global companies overwhelming their Indian partners with the power of their shareholding, the secretary of defence production could be made a member of the Foreign Investment Promotion Board to oversee the FDI process. Nothing much came out of his proposal. In May 2013, he made a fresh proposal. Instead of 74 per cent, he now offered a modest 49 per cent to mollify the concerns of the Ministry of Defence, even though from an investors' point of view, there wasn't much difference between 26 or 49 per cent, because neither accorded them any influence on the joint holding. The defence ministry rejected even this proposal on the grounds of it being detrimental to indigenization. Clearly it was under pressure from both public and the private sector companies, who have also craved protection against global competition.

But with the coming of the Modi government, the overall feeling was that, given the national security challenges and the abject state of Indian military preparedness, the government's first priority would be to put the procurement process and the FDI issue in order. The optimists in the industry expected that by the time the government completed one hundred days, some announcements would be made.

Realizing that overhauling the DPP would require a lot of work and expertise, the government first tried to tweak the FDI limit. Within a month of taking charge, a Cabinet note was issued suggesting three tiers for FDI—49 per cent, 74 per cent and 100 per cent—depending upon the equipment and the quantum of technology transfer. Sure enough, alarm bells started ringing and articles started appearing in the media decrying the proposal. Despite that, in August 2014, the government raised the FDI limit to 49 per cent subject to certain conditions and safeguards. It also reiterated the previous government's claim that in certain areas, the government could consider 100 per cent FDI if it involved critical technologies.

Clearly this has not been enough. In March 2015, the government admitted in Parliament that since it raised the FDI figure, it had got proposals worth only US$ 15 million. Proposals do not imply that the FDI actually starts to flow in. In the decade from 2004 to 2015, the total FDI that the defence sector actually got was a measly US$ 5 million. The 100 per cent

FDI assertion was merely kite-flying as no project had ever been cleared under this. Moreover, the critical or state-of-the-art technologies that the government referred to, such as 'seeker' technology for ballistic missiles, is beyond the control of the industry. This can only be a government to government process.

Conscious of this reality, in June 2016, the government announced 100 per cent FDI without the clause of 'state-of-the-art' technologies and 'case to case clearance by the Cabinet Committee on Security'. According to the new announcement, the government would allow 100 per cent FDI in defence if 'modern technologies' or those not available in India are involved. Since this announcement, several analysts, apart from expressing hope that this will kick-start the government's ambitious 'Make in India' programme, have given a different interpretation to what this would mean for Indian defence manufacturing and modernization of the armed forces. While some decree the relaxation of 'state-of-the-art' to modern technology as a comedown, others claim that it is just semantics. Similarly, while some fear that this will harm the Indian private sector as foreign companies would no longer seek partnership with them, preferring to operate directly through their 100 per cent owned subsidiaries, others feel that since defence procurement procedure lays down the condition of Indian companies being the prime contractors, foreign original equipment manufacturers would have no choice but to seek partnership.

Clearly, there is no clarity about what the new FDI ruling will mean in practice. The only thing that seems plausible at the moment is that the government hopes that with this relaxation, more foreign companies will transfer their production facilities to India to take advantage of low costs of manufacturing, thereby creating more jobs in India. Helping India acquire technology is not central to the FDI relaxation.

What the Indian government does not seem to understand is that for the big manufacturers of the global defence industry to be interested in manufacturing in India, they need to be profitable. Let's take the French example and contrast it with India.

All leading French defence companies originally were government controlled as they needed both assured investment and sales, yet they were run by professionals and not bureaucrats. Over the years, the government gradually disinvested, bringing in greater private sector participation. However, even today, not all French defence companies are completely in the private sector; the French Ministry of Defence (MoD) still retains some control over them. Since the French MoD cannot buy everything produced by the French industry, manufacturers are allowed to export to stay profitable. But whether in the private or the public sector, the government has complete control over the technologies developed, because the government pays for their development. And only the government decides which of these technologies can be exported to which country. For example, the French shipbuilders DCNS make one type of submarines for export and another type (nuclear-powered) for the French Navy, which is non-exportable.

The French procurement model is also unique. The French government has a specialized procurement agency called Direction Générale de l'Armement (DGA). The DGA works closely with the military and industry. Based on the military's modernization vision, the DGA draws up the profile of the technology/platform the services would require in the coming years. This profile depends upon the vision of the military, the capabilities of French industry and the money that the government is willing to spend on that particular system. This is a three-way consultative process by the DGA involving the military, the MoD and the industry. Once the requirements are finalized, the DGA places the order with the selected manufacturing company and gives them a deadline. The DGA monitors the programme through its development, as based on that it seeks funds from the government. Once the system or the platform is developed, the DGA tests and certifies it, after which it is handed over to the military. In case certain technologies or systems that the military desires are not available or are not cost-effective within the French industry, the DGA either imports them or creates a joint venture with a foreign company, specific to that technology or system. Such is the DGA's reputation for professionalism that many French export customers buy equipment based solely on DGA certification.

Although India must evolve its own system, at the very least what should happen is that major public sector defence industries must be properly evaluated. Giant corporations need to be reconfigured so that they are better able to function and focus on core competencies.

The DRDO needs a major reorganization. Scientists and engineers cannot work in isolation. They have to be integrated. There is no point in evolving concepts and technologies which cannot be successfully produced.

Looked at from another angle, the problem that the Government of India has is that it has not been able to shed its historical baggage of distrusting the private sector and looking at the public sector undertakings (PSUs) as a means to keep control of key assets and revenues. The government funds the PSUs, who get licences from global vendors to assemble defence equipment in the country. The services buy the equipment (produced under licence) from the PSUs, often at rates higher than those supplied by the original equipment manufacturer, because of delays in delivery. The extra money that the PSUs make in the bargain is returned to the government as dividend. Since the services pay for the equipment from the defence budget allocated by the government, the annual dividend effectively discounts the equipment for the state and not the services. Clearly this well-oiled cycle will not work in the private sector.

Yet way back in 2001, the government realized that to develop indigenous defence capability, participation by the private sector was imperative. The public sector—comprising PSUs and ordnance factories—had not moved beyond assembling semi-knocked down or completely knocked down kits that were procured from foreign vendors. In fact, the state of the ordnance factories has been so pathetic that many operate below capacity and seldom keep their timelines. As a result of this, the defence forces are frequently compelled to procure their requirements from the open market. Even more tragic is the fact that sitting on prime land, throughout the country, ordnance factories manufacture items such as shoes, clothes, balaclavas and mosquito nets for soldiers, all of which can be bought in the markets at lower cost and of better quality and are often procured by the soldiers at their own expense or their units' expense. Both the comptroller auditor general (CAG) and Parliament's Standing Committee on Defence have frequently castigated ordnance factories and the PSUs for their failure to stick to timelines and minimum quality. Prime Minister Narendra Modi himself took the defence PSUs to task during the inauguration of Aero India 2015 in Bengaluru. He said in his address, 'In some areas we are still where we were thirty years ago. Our public sector units have not delivered as effectively as was expected of them. There is a need for greater accountability.'

The wake-up call for the government was the unexpected 1999 Kargil War. On discovery of the occupation, Defence Minister George Fernandes declared in June 1999 that the intruders would be thrown out within forty-eight hours. The government later discovered that it had spoken too soon. On 23 June 1999, as we know, in an interaction with the media, army chief General V. P. Malik said, 'We shall fight with whatever we have.' The government realized that the army was woefully short of something as basic as ammunition. Desperate Indian bureaucrats then flew from country to country (Israel to Russia) carrying foreign exchange in suitcases to buy off-the-shelf ammunition. The so-called Indian defence industry had failed the nation.

The government-appointed Kargil Review Committee faulted the

DRDO and the defence PSUs in its report (submitted in 2000) for the abject state of the defence forces. Finally, in May 2001, the government announced its intention to open the defence sector to private industry. To assuage the whimpering PSUs who felt threatened, the government announced two categories to re-emphasize their primacy as far as defence production went. The defence PSUs, depending upon their size and turnover, were accorded the titles of Navratna (nine jewels) and mini-Ratna. The status implied that in addition to relative autonomy these PSUs would also have complete government support; the government would not disinvest from them. Also, the Navratnas would be allowed to participate in global competitions, implying that they would be allowed to export to friendly countries—under government watch, of course.

As far as the private sector was concerned, the government announced that it would select some of the companies based upon their financial solvency and technological capability and give them the status of Raksha Udyog Ratna (defence industry jewel). The Raksha Udyog Ratnas would then be considered almost as good as PSUs insofar as delegation of defence contracts was concerned.

In 2003, the government released its defence procurement procedure policy, in which foreign equipment manufacturers were required to invest some percentage of the total value of the contract in the Indian defence industry as offsets. It was thought that this would give the needed thrust to the moribund defence industry. At least, that was the intent. Unfortunately, things did not work out quite like that. Under enormous pressure from the defence PSUs who had several fears, the government could never fulfil its Raksha Udyog Ratna promise. All the programmes in which the private sector was allowed to participate, such as the Future Infantry Combat Vehicle, Tactical Communication System or Battlefield Management System, never took off, despite several companies signing up partnership or joint venture agreements with foreign technology partners.

The government lost no opportunity to inform the world that it had deep pockets to modernize its armed forces. By early 2007, a figure of US$ 20 billion started being circulated in the media as money available to be spent on defence procurements over the next decade. The amount progressively increased each year. It became the habit of the defence minister to announce at defence trade shows that India was the biggest market for defence equipment and the world must come here.

The world did come, but the Indian defence industry remained where it was. Three primary reasons come to mind as to why the Indian defence industry remains mired in assembling and not manufacturing.

FLAWED MINDSET

Having internalized the notion of being a peace-loving nation, the government had traditional disdain towards building weapons. While peaceful scientific research and programmes like space exploration and research were acceptable, military modernization was not accorded similar primacy. From this basic abhorrence towards military power stemmed the lackadaisical attitude which resulted in India procuring a huge quantity of equipment from the USSR during the decades of Indo-Soviet friendship. The equipment came cheap with just a few conditions being imposed by the Soviets. None of these were seen as too onerous and over time Indian PSUs became used to assembling Soviet-made equipment. It was a comfortable, almost somnolent process with one government agency supplying another. When India finally woke up to the world of competitive buying in the 1990s after the implosion of the USSR, it was completely ill-prepared to deal with the reality that existed. The process worked something like this: military officers would look through international defence trade magazines and put to paper wish lists that would be sent to government departments. If it was affordable, the government went for outright purchase without giving a thought to technology transfer and its absorption in India.

FLAWED POLICY

In 1992, the government was compelled to come up with the defence procurement policy. Since there was no in-house expertise, either about defence technology or the procurement process, it was half-baked and borrowed heavily from whatever similar policies the bureaucrats could lay their hands on from across the world. It also suffered from the hangover of 'India being a peace-loving country', which would not profit from building weapons of destruction, at least not openly. In fact, there were agents galore, who not only greased the palms of government officials and politicians for the completion of a programme but also took a neat packet home. Publicly, these agents were reviled as arms dealers and treated as the scum of the earth. Privately, they played an important role in facilitating meetings between the industry and the government representative, because of complete opacity around defence procurement. These agents also helped the foreign vendors understand Indian regulations: how to stay within the rules and how to get around them.

Following the Kargil War, the defence procurement procedure was overhauled and the new version emerged in December 2002. A year later, the government discovered yet more lacunae and amendments were added in 2003, then again in 2005, 2006, 2008 and 2011. All these amendments only added to the bulkiness of the document, offered little clarity and left several loopholes for vested interests to thrive. Despite the inclusion of the 'integrity clause' for all deals worth ₹100 crore and more in 2006, practices of corruption continued to be reported. Interestingly, after all the amendments, in 2012 the finance ministry questioned the very method of calculating life cycle costs. One industry honcho, directly affected by this belated realization, told the authors in February 2013 during the Aero India defence show, 'This re-looking at the life cycle costs will affect the current programmes where technical/price negotiations are going on. Moreover, the finance ministry has also sent back a few proposals for future acquisitions to the Ministry of Defence asking it to review whether India can really afford such platforms.'

The 2013 amendment to the defence procurement procedure reinforced the government's desire for indigenization. It stated that the first option for purchase will be Buy (India) with Buy (Global) being the last choice. However, even this suffered from several flaws. For instance, transfer of technology was not part of the offsets, as is the practice in most developing countries. As a result, technology transfer was not included in the primary purchase contract. The reason for this is that because the government wants to maintain the façade of allowing the private sector an opportunity to participate in defence programmes, the original equipment manufacturer is allowed to choose any offset partner from the private sector. But it can only transfer the technology to a defence public sector undertaking. This attitude of protectionism towards defence PSUs has neither helped the public sector nor encouraged the private sector to invest in the defence business. After all, why would the offset partner (private sector) invest in creating a facility to absorb offsets in the form of small contracts for supply of low-technology stuff, if it is not getting any technology to develop its capability for designing and manufacturing complete equipment?

The other problem of the defence procurement policy was its rigidity. The original equipment manufacturers were not allowed to change their offset partners after the signing of the contract. Those who signed the contracts before the amendments of 2011, which opened the ambit of offsets to civil aviation and homeland security (after the government belatedly realized that there isn't much capacity in the defence sector to absorb technology), are governed by the previous defence procurement policies and are unable to fulfil their annual offset obligations. Yet they are not allowed to enlarge the ambit of their obligatory disbursal because the rules prevent them.

FLAWED INDUSTRIAL ATTITUDE

In May 2011, the authors visited the Pipavav Shipyard Ltd., whose introduction was always preceded by superlatives like the largest dry dock, the biggest Goliath cranes in the country, etc. Sprawled over 200 hectares with a sea front of nearly 720 metres, Pipavav Shipyard was the outcome of the grand vision, ambition and resources of its then owner. 'The focus of Pipavav was on creating general engineering skills and assets, which are germane to shipbuilding but not exclusive,' the company's chief operating officer, Debashis Bir, told the authors. 'The idea being that Pipavav Shipyard over time should become a national asset and not remain just a shipyard.'

But there was one very crucial link to greatness that the visionaries of Pipavav Shipyard Ltd. had overlooked: in-house design and research and development capabilities. Pipavav Shipyard had none. It did not even intend to invest in those. 'It is much cheaper to buy ship designs from professional design houses around the world,' explained Bir. Contrast this with the vision of the President and CEO, Saab Group, Hakan Buskhe, 'In 2010, when the global economy started to shrink and defence markets worldwide became stagnant, we increased our R&D budget from 18 per cent annually (of the turnover) to 28 per cent. In times like these, it is even more important to research and develop affordable and cost-effective technologies.'

In the last ten years, the authors have visited several defence facilities in Europe and the United States. We have met and interviewed presidents, chief executive officers and managing directors of several global companies. They take great pride in emphasizing the amount they reinvest in R&D every year, which varies from 10 to 15 per cent of the turnover. Companies like Airbus, MBDA, Boeing, DCNS, and so on, showcase future technologies that they are developing at international trade shows. The idea is to show potential customers what they are capable of delivering.

In India, the attitude towards research and development is just the opposite. It is viewed as avoidable and wasteful expenditure. The government itself allocates a mere 5 to 6 per cent of the Defence Research and Development Organisation budget for R&D. This is the reason India has never been able to manufacture and export any indigenously produced industrial goods. Outside defence too, all production essentially entails the assembly of good produced under licence. In the defence sector, R&D

is the job of the DRDO, which conducts research in fields as varied as missiles and ready-to-eat hydrogenized meals in its forty-eight laboratories across India. The developed technology, depending upon its criticality, is then shared with the industry (defence PSUs) for production.

In March 2015, Reliance Aerospace and Defence bought over Pipavav. Despite creating huge infrastructure, Pipavav eventually had to depend on government business to sustain itself. International orders did not come. But Pipavav is not alone. Most private sector companies are reluctant to invest in research and development. Like all businesses across the world, they are driven by the profit motive. But unlike all businesses across the world they want return on investment overnight. Hence, instead of creating new models, which entails the risk of failure, they prefer to buy mature technologies from abroad.

Unfortunately, defence technologies that are available on the market are not state of the art. No country has been able to buy them off the shelf. The exception was China, which cleverly did not buy the technologies, but the technologists, that is, the scientists. After the collapse of the Soviet Union, China employed out-of-work Russian scientists in large numbers and laid the foundation of its defence industry. Today, China builds its own fighter aircraft, ships, tanks and submarines, etc.

Clearly India needs similar hand-holding, because despite producing defence equipment under licence for decades, its public sector has still not imbibed the concepts clearly enough to successfully develop its own product. But the government's attitude of protectionism towards public sector undertakings and suspicion towards the private sector will not help in this process. It has to treat both as national assets.

In early 2015, the government appointed a committee led by former bureaucrat Dhirendra Singh to review defence procurement procedures and suggest reforms. The amount of time the committee took to submit its report led to speculation that the government wanted to drastically reform the procurement procedure and not merely tinker with the original framework. However, the defence procurement procedure 2016, which was announced by Defence Minister Parrikar at the inauguration of DefExpo 2016 in Goa, was as usual high on rhetoric and short on reforms; at best it could be seen as an amendment to the earlier version.

Amongst the drastic measures suggested by the committee, the government broadly accepted three, of which one—creation of strategic partners from among the private sector—has been withheld for further consultations with the stakeholders in both the public and the private sector. The two recommendations that form part of the report are raising the threshold for the application of the offsets clause from ₹300 crore to ₹2,000 crore. This means that the foreign original equipment manufacturers would be liable to disburse 30 per cent offsets if the value of the contract was ₹2,000 crore or more.

The second recommendation is the creation of yet another category of procurement: buy IDDM (Indian Designed, Developed and Manufactured). This will now be the most preferred category for procurement, instead of 'Buy Indian'. Buy IDDM must have at least 40 per cent indigenous content, or 60 per cent indigenous content if the product is not designed and developed in India.

The third recommendation that the government has accepted but yet not notified is the creation of strategic partnerships in the domain of aircraft; warships; armoured fighting vehicles; complex weapon systems that rely on guidance; C4ISTR (command, control, communication, computers, intelligence, surveillance, target acquisition and reconnaissance); and critical materials. The idea is that the government will identify certain private sector companies based on their turnover and technological base, and forge partnerships with them for one particular kind of platform or technology. For example, the government can identify a company like Reliance Aerospace and Defence for strategic partnership in the field of aircraft. This would mean that Reliance Aerospace and Defence would then be eligible to only bid for aircraft programmes, and junk its already-built facilities for warship building or helicopters. This is being resisted by everyone—the defence public sector undertakings, the large private conglomerates and the micro, small and medium enterprises. So the Ministry of Defence has gone back to the drawing board. However, by the end of 2016, speculation was rife that the government will soon announce its policy on strategic partners.

Today the most important issue for the government is to prioritize modernization of the armed forces rather than indigenization. Because our history shows that the two cannot go together. For the last decade, the government has been trying to do both, and has failed in both. The result is that the Indian military's conventional capabilities have been severely eroded. To make matters worse, the Indian defence industry is in a complete shambles. Its capacity to even maintain equipment is questionable. One of the reasons that defence partnerships with foreign original equipment manufacturers have not taken off is because once they realized what the Indian industry was capable of, they developed cold feet. Even for the most basic of technology transfers, they demanded more control over the business. The government's confidence in its own industry is so low that it urges foreign vendors to stand guarantee for platforms built in India under transfer of technology.

Under these circumstances and given the increasing threats to India's security (as well as credibility), the best way forward would be to delink war preparation from building indigenous capability. Let the government take stock of the most pressing military requirements on a fast-track basis through transparent competitive tendering. And, separately, let it engage with the industry within India and outside to generate ideas on the best way to revolutionize Indian defence manufacturing. Modi grandly announced that defence manufacturing lies at the heart of his 'Make in India' dream. To turn this dream into a reality, one needs to wake up and take stock of ground realities. In the globalized interdependent world, it only makes sense to buy defence equipment from the most affordable seller. And where technology is concerned, the DRDO should only focus on understanding and acquiring the most critical and cutting edge technologies. A combination of the two approaches is the best way forward to build this aspect of India's military power.

TIBET

CHAPTER 18

THE TIBETAN STRUGGLE

Losar, the Tibetan New Year, marks the onset of spring—the beginning of new life after the long, harsh winter. In McLeod Ganj near Dharamshala, which serves as one of the temporary homes for Tibetan exiles, including His Holiness the fourteenth Dalai Lama, Losar is a covenant of hope. Tibetans wrap white scarves on their doors and put out grains of rice at their doorsteps in an affirmation of life, even as multicoloured prayer flags are entrusted with entreaties to the gods in heaven.

Dressed in new clothes, Tibetans flock to the Dalai Lama's temple to hear his annual address to his people. Religion forms only a part of the Dalai Lama's annual preaching. Deeply religious Tibetans do not need a yearly renewal of faith. But they do need the rekindling of hope. And the Dalai Lama does not disappoint them. He tells the thousands yearning for the homeland who come to hear him every year, that 'until the last moment, anything is possible'. Perhaps he believes it himself. Perhaps he doesn't. He once remarked, 'What other option do we have?' But for Tibetans, this is enough to last another year. Their hope is sparked and their faith in their future is restored.

The Tibetans are a remarkably resilient people. Their trust in their leader, as well as their own destiny may have wavered from time to time, but just as Losar promises renewal of life, an address by the Dalai Lama reinforces the belief that theirs is a just struggle; and not in vain. Time is on their side.

'The Tibetan struggle has continued to exist through complex times and it will continue to do so even more strongly in the future,' the Tibetan Sikyong (head of the government-in-exile), Lobsang Sangay, said. He insists that the 'Tibetan spirit and unity will stand the test of time with democracy as one of its mechanism. And as in every struggle, optimism is a necessity and I believe Tibetans have never been more united than now.'

Overlooking the Kashag or Tibetan Parliament-in-exile, Sangay's office is perched on a low, steep hill between McLeod Ganj and Dharamshala. The panelled walls are adorned with portraits of the Dalai Lama and delicately painted tankhas. The bookshelves are lined with literature on Tibet and several small statues of the Buddha wrapped in orange scarves. There is a Tibetan flag behind him and one on his desk, as if making up for the lack of avenues where one can wave these.

There is nothing extraordinary about his office, except one tankha, in the middle of which is a scene depicting the Dalai Lama along with Sangay and some senior lamas from Tibet. The tankha came from Tibet. 'Isn't it extraordinary?' exclaimed Sangay. 'It is a crime in Tibet to possess a photograph of His Holiness. Yet somebody had the courage to paint this. They must have seen my photograph somewhere and made this tankha.' Courage was displayed not in the painting alone. It was also in smuggling the tankha out of Tibet, getting it through several known and unknown checkpoints all along the Tibet-Nepal Highway.

Resistance has many shades, courage being the boldest. The Tibetans lack neither hope nor courage. 'All resistance movements go through various stages from the time the conflict breaks out,' Sangay, a student of non-violent conflicts across the world, said. 'The first stage is to survive the conflict. Then one has to build resistance. The third stage is sustaining the movement.'

Sangay feels that the success of the Tibetan struggle can be gauged by the fact that they have reached the third stage without faltering and without loss of spirit. His optimism is echoed by several Tibetans, both government officials and ordinary citizens. A large part of this optimism stems from the example of the Indian freedom struggle. Most Tibetans use that to hold onto their faith—'Indians struggled without success for nearly two centuries, our struggle is merely fifty-eight years old', is the line frequently iterated by people in the streets and in the offices.

What adds to the Tibetan optimism is the Chinese inability to ignore it. Since the early 1990s, the State Council Information Office of the People's Republic of China (PRC) started issuing a white paper on the Tibetan issue. The most recent of these, the thirteenth white paper, was issued in May 2015. Titled 'Tibet's Path of Development is Driven by an Irresistible Historical Tide', the paper repeats the contents of the previous twelve papers. Running into more than thirty pages, the document chronicles Tibetan history as one of barbaric feudalism and abject poverty. Given this, the paper argues that the People's Army's peaceful liberation of Tibet was for the betterment of the Tibetans and to integrate them into the mainland.

It was the Dalai Lama who forced China into issuing the first white paper. In 1988, addressing the European Parliament in Strasbourg, the Dalai Lama enunciated the Tibetan demands for the first time in public, offering China what came to be known as the Strasbourg Proposal, whereby he gave up the earlier demand for complete independence for 'genuine' autonomy for Tibet under the Chinese constitution. Since then, this has been referred to as the Middle Path.

The Dalai Lama had taken his time to deliberate and evolve the concept of the Middle Path, having exhausted all other options. After his flight to India in 1959, the first priority of the exiled community was to hold itself together body and soul. Survival was of utmost importance. Moreover, for a semi-literate, impoverished and hapless community, there was no future road map then. The Tibetan fate was more in the hands of outside powers, especially the United States and, to a lesser extent, India, with Taiwan and the USSR also trying to pitch in with advice and offers of support. Over time the Tibetans realized that the support was not so much for them or the Dalai Lama but was intended to test the mettle and resolve of the newly formed People's Republic of China.

However, at that time, all foreign help was welcome. This was ironical. For centuries, Tibetan leaders had shunned outsiders, fearing that their influences would corrupt their society. This was a practice the Dalai Lama came to regret. In a conversation with author Pico Iyer, he said, 'Our worst mistake, our greatest mistake, was being isolated from the world.' This probably was the reason why the world has been ambivalent as far as Tibet's independent status vis-à-vis China is concerned.

Once the PLA started creeping up on Tibet, beginning in October 1950, the US reached out to the Tibetans in an effort to thwart the expansion of Communism. Through some American missionaries based in the Amdo region of Tibet, the American Committee for Free Asia (which later morphed into the Asia Foundation, a part of the newly created Central Investigation Agency), reached out to the Dalai Lama's older brother Norbu (Taktser Rinpoche), a monk who had to escape his monastery to save himself from the invading PLA troops. Norbu had settled in Kalimpong in the Indian state of West Bengal, where he met some Americans who invited him to settle down in the US.

With Norbu settled in the US, his interlocutors invited his younger brother, Gyalo Thondup (the only brother of the Dalai Lama who didn't become a monk) to study at Stanford University. While his visit to the US in October 1951 was facilitated by Chiang Kai-shek who had shifted to Taiwan after the revolution and was hopeful that the Tibetans would

help him overthrow the Communists, the Americans offered to pay for
Thondup's education. Thondup, who had been a student in the Chinese
capital of Nanjing for a few years before the revolution under the patronage
of Chiang, declined further education and returned to Tibet after spending
a few months travelling and living it up in the US. This was the time he
established several contacts in the US State Department, or rather, the
Americans established contact with him.

Thondup was an important, though gullible, member of the Dalai
Lama's government. Just as the senior lamas discovered the present Dalai
Lama, Tenzin Gyatso, as the latest reincarnation of Avalokiteshvara, the
Bodhisattva of Compassion, Thondup was chosen to be his main political
advisor when still a child. Hence, instead of being sent to the monastery
like all his other brothers, he was sent for secular education to China by
the then Tibetan regent as part of his grooming. According to the Tibetan
system, the country was administered by regents till the new Dalai Lama,
the spiritual leader of the Tibetan people, was old enough to take over as
the temporal head.

By early 1952, the situation in Tibet had started to deteriorate. The
Chinese controlled the countryside, the Dalai Lama was still underage
and the government functionaries were squabbling among themselves, with
each suspecting the other of being a Chinese spy. Threats to Thondup had
increased (as he was seen to be influencing his brother) both from the
Tibetan officials as well as the Chinese who wanted to make sure that he
was on their side. As a result, Thondup escaped to India via Tawang in
Arunachal Pradesh. Interestingly, the residents of Tawang (which was taken
over by the Indian government in February 1951 by chasing away the
Tibetan commissioner) thought that the brother of the Dalai Lama had
come to liberate them from Indian rule. 'I had to explain that I was running
away from the Chinese occupiers of Tibet and was in no position myself
to help free them from Indian rule,' he writes in his memoirs.

He settled in Darjeeling where mysterious American visitors started
to call upon him with veiled offers of help. Finally, the cards were put on
the table in 1954, when Thondup was convinced that the US was serious
about helping Tibet raise a resistance force and delivered the first group of
potential fighters for training to the CIA. His memoir, *The Noodle Maker
of Kalimpong*, has a fascinating account of how Pakistan helped the Tibetans
deliver the potential fighters to the US trainers. India, then, was nursing
its fledgling relationship with China.

While Thondup doesn't say whether the Dalai Lama was in the loop or not, it would be difficult to imagine that the Dalai Lama remained oblivious of this guerrilla force throughout its existence. From these original guerrillas emerged a dedicated band of the Dalai Lama's bodyguards, who helped escort him to India when he escaped in 1959. They kept the PLA troops at bay mostly by misleading them at certain places, but also by fighting in some areas.

Though the US kept up its support until the end of the 1960s, when it started making overtures towards China and pulled from supporting the Tibetans, the military assistance that it gave the resistance fighters was more notional than real. The training was inadequate and pertained essentially to spying on China, the equipment was mostly obsolete and there was never enough ammunition. According to Thondup, thousands of Tibetans died in 1954 because they were inadequately trained and armed.

However, as the US's interest started to wane, others stepped in. After the debacle of the 1962 war against China, India discovered the Tibetan guerrillas. In November 1962, the Government of India approved the raising of the Special Frontier Force (also referred to as Establishment 22) with some funding and weapons from the US, channelled through the CIA.

The objective was ambitious: to train all able-bodied Tibetan men in special operations so that they would be able to operate inside Tibet. With this in mind, till the 1980s, it was compulsory for all Tibetans to undergo six months training in the Special Frontier Force (SFF), beyond which the service was voluntary. Officered purely by the Indian Army and reporting to the cabinet secretary, the SFF was a secret force. 'Our mission was the liberation of Tibet,' said Samdup Gyaltsen, who was conscripted in 1977, but stayed on beyond the mandatory service period because he believed that he would one day march into Tibet.

Ironically, the only operation that the SFF carried out against China was planting some listening devices atop a mountain peak for intelligence gathering some time in 1965 and engaging the Chinese border forces in hit and run skirmishes on the Nepal-Tibet border in the area called Mustang. Gradually, the US lost interest in the SFF as its relations with China improved after Secretary of State Henry Kissinger's secret visit to China (facilitated by Pakistan) in 1971. India also lost both the nerve and direction as far as employing the SFF was concerned. It increasingly became just another regiment of the Indian Army, though remaining unaccounted for in the official record. Consequently, the only enemy it has seen action against has been Pakistan, starting with the 1971 war, in which it lost forty-six of its soldiers. Thereafter, it has operated alongside the Indian Army in Operation Bluestar, Operation Meghdoot (Siachen Glacier, 1984) and Operation Vijay (Kargil, 1999).

By 2009, the pretence of a secret force was dropped when the government approved pay and allowances, including pensions, for the Special Frontier Force at par with the rest of the Indian Army.

In 1967, Indian diplomat T. N. Kaul facilitated a meeting between Thondup and the Russians, who also offered to help train Tibetan fighters in Tashkent. Even though the meeting was proposed and organized by the former ambassador to Moscow, Thondup was wary of the offer, as disappointment with the Americans had started to set in. He consulted the founding chief of the recently raised Research and Analysis Wing, R. N. Kao, who told Thondup to steer clear of the Russians.

Given the apparently friendly overtures made by the Russians, Thondup urged them to support the Tibetans in the United Nations, where Russia had traditionally stood by China. The Russians resisted doing that and the communication petered out after a few years.

Interestingly, there was another Tibetan guerrilla force operating within Tibet. Raised by Phuntsok Wangyal Goranangpa in the 1940s, this force was aligned with the PLA and indulged in skirmishes against Chiang Kai-shek's Kuomintang government. Wangyal had established the Tibetan Communist Party in the hope that after the revolution, Communist China would help emancipate Tibetan society, get rid of feudalism, and yet let it remain an independent country. According to Thupten Samphel, director of the Tibet Policy Institute, Wangyal had apparently met Mao and had received such an assurance from him. His faith in the Chinese was belied soon after. In 1949, he was expelled by the Tibetan government once the PLA started moving on to the plateau. A man of extraordinary naiveté and courage, Wangyal devoted his life to the Communist Party of China even as he started criticizing the government for its aggression in Tibet. He was arrested in 1958 just before the invasion and remained in solitary confinement for nearly two decades.

It was this long history of fruitless violence, half-hearted support by the West, uncertainty about the Tibetan claim of independence and the growing influence of China that shaped the Dalai Lama's thinking on the possible future of Tibet and also about the place it should occupy in the mindscape of people worldwide. Conscious of the diminishing returns of violent resistance, the Dalai Lama gradually started to focus on a peaceful struggle to achieve the stated objectives of his people. When the US stopped military support to the Tibetan guerrillas, it also sought to close down their operations in the Mustang region of Nepal. When the guerrillas resisted, China got Nepal to arrest and torture them. Eventually in July 1974, the Dalai Lama had to personally request the guerrillas (through an audio recording) to lay down arms to avoid annihilation. This finally closed forever the option of the armed struggle against China.

Internationally, while Tibetan emissaries tried to make the case for Tibetan independence, they were conscious of the fact that historically their country's status vis-à-vis China had been a bit nebulous, at least in terms of a modern nation state. Tibet had been a loosely held country, which was frequently governed by China and even Mongolia whenever its rulers were weak. In an address to select Indian intelligentsia in June 2008, the last kalon tripa (senior-most minister reporting directly to the Dalai Lama), Samdhong Rinpoche, said that even the institution of the Dalai Lama as the temporal head of Tibet had come about because of the Mongol tribal leader Gushri Khan who invaded Tibet circa 1640 and handed it over to the fifth Dalai Lama in 1642 to govern. This established the Gaden Phodrang dynasty, vesting both the spiritual and temporal powers in the office of the Dalai Lama. The seat of the government was the Potala Palace. However, the influence of the palace did not reach the border areas of Tibet, which were vulnerable to encroachment, both physical and political, by China, especially in the east and the northeast.

According to Samphel, 'The Tibetan territories in the east and the northeast have often functioned as semi-autonomous areas. Depending upon who levied less tax, these provinces used to pay taxes to either the government in Lhasa or China.' These were the provinces of Amdo and Kham, which had ceased to be part of the Tibetan territory in the beginning of the twentieth century. However, insisted Samphel, 'Regardless of this, we see the whole of Tibet as one region, geographically, linguistically and religiously.'

Whenever there was a powerful Tibetan leader, his reign frequently extended to all of Mongolia and most of China. More than absolute sovereignty, what the Tibetan ruler or the Dalai Lama enjoyed throughout history in the areas removed from Lhasa was religious suzerainty. Even the rulers of Ladakh used to pay tributes to Lhasa instead of the government in Kashmir (or the British for that matter). Either way, for much of its history, a Chinese regent had been present in Lhasa, sometimes as a mere ambassador and sometimes wielding direct influence on the Tibetan government.

However, when the crisis broke out after the Chinese Revolution in 1949, and China sought the 'peaceful liberation of Tibet' (a euphemism for invasion), the British, who had three decades earlier hosted the tripartite agreement between British India, Tibet and China on the demarcation of the border between the three 'sovereign' countries at Simla in 1913–14, wrung their hands helplessly saying that they were not clear about the legal status of Tibet vis-à-vis China. Because of this, while the world sympathized with the justness of the Tibetan desire for independence, it just wasn't convinced about the historicity and legality of the issue.

Over time, there were occasionally some positive developments from the Tibetan point of view. As the relationship between the US and China grew warmer, the Tibetans benefitted to some extent. In late 1979, the Deng Xiaoping-led Chinese government got in touch with Thondup, who was then living in Hong Kong, and invited him to visit Beijing for a meeting with Deng. Thondup sought the Dalai Lama's clearance, which came immediately.

In his first meeting with Thondup, Deng came straight to the point. 'But for independence, everything is negotiable. Everything can be discussed,' he said. Having said his piece, Deng asked Thondup if he wanted to make any points. Most of the issues raised by Thondup pertained to the free movement of Tibetans in exile to the homeland and vice versa. In an unexpected display of open-heartedness, Deng agreed to everything raised by Thondup.

In 1979–81, many Tibetans in exile, including the Dalai Lama's family, were able to visit Tibet. While superficially it enhanced goodwill between the Tibetans and the Chinese, in reality it exacerbated the tension between the two. For the Chinese, it brought home the realization that twenty years of direct rule in Tibet had done little to wean the people away from the Dalai Lama. On the contrary, the yearning for the Dalai Lama peaked with the visits of his family members. Tibetans of all hues, even those who had never seen or met the Dalai Lama before, poured on to the streets for a glimpse of his family members, raised slogans against the Communist government and clamoured for the return of the Dalai Lama. At night, many slipped surreptitious notes to the visitors mentioning excesses by Beijing, despite the presence of Chinese escorts.

Meanwhile, the visiting Tibetans realized how much the Chinese had plundered and subverted Tibetan religious and cultural institutions. While several monasteries were completely destroyed, most were desecrated and robbed of their historical artefacts.

On both sides, the result was contrary to expectations. The visiting Tibetans were hurt and angry; the Chinese increasingly paranoid. The Chinese government had underestimated the Dalai Lama's and Buddhism's influence on ordinary Tibetans. With each visit to Tibet, Beijing became convinced that there was no way the Dalai Lama could be allowed to return to Tibet. He would simply be too strong a power centre.

As a result, while the fourth delegation of Tibetans was not allowed to visit Tibet in 1980, Thondup was invited for another meeting in 1981. He met the General Secretary of the Communist Party, Hu Yaobang, who handed over a written statement listing Chinese conditions for the betterment of relations. While the statement urged the Dalai Lama to observe the path of development that China had undertaken, it asked him not to raise the issue of Chinese repression in Tibet since 1959, and instead work for the unity of the country (China). It extended a warm invitation to the Dalai Lama, but made it clear that he would have to live in China, where he would be given a position appropriate to his status. 'It is necessary that he not live in Tibet or hold any position in Tibet,' the statement, preserved in the Kashag's office in Dharamshala, apparently said.

This brought the tenuous communication between the two sides to a standstill. While the Tibetans were distrustful of the Chinese, the PRC had started to grow weary of what it viewed as the growing stature of the Dalai Lama worldwide. Starting in 1967, he had started travelling outside India. One of his early destinations was Japan, where his eldest brother Taktser Rinpoche had established his own monastery and had settled down after having fallen out with the Americans. Though the Dalai Lama's earliest visits were purely spiritual in nature, where he gave sermons at monasteries or religious centres, gradually various heads of state started engaging with him. By the middle of the 1980s, he had traversed nearly the entire globe, meeting leaders in business, entertainment, civil society as well as politics.

In September 1987, he gave a talk at the US Congressional Human Rights Caucus, where he announced a five-point peace plan for Tibet. The plan called for the withdrawal of Chinese and Indian troops from the borders of Tibet so that it could once again become a peaceful buffer between the two nations. He also asked for a stop to the wholesale resettlement of the Han Chinese on the Tibetan plateau as it was creating a demographic imbalance. In addition to these, he urged respect for human rights and a nuclear weapons-free world. His final point was the beginning of serious negotiations between Tibet and China for the peaceful resolution of the Tibetan issue.

If this was not enough to raise China's hackles, the beginning of protests in Tibet (which the Chinese suspected were instigated by westerners travelling across Tibet as tourists) added to the Chinese paranoia. Beijing deployed additional troops to quell the disturbances on the plateau, which obviously meant further repression and even more protests. Meanwhile, the Dalai Lama had started to warm up to his theme of laying out his vision for the future of Tibet and its ties with China. Along with Michael van Walt van Praag, the lawyer-activist and intra-state conflict resolution scholar, the Dalai Lama drew up a vision statement for Tibet, which was delivered to a global audience through the European Parliament. The Dalai Lama proposed genuine autonomy within the Chinese constitution. However, there was a huge catch in this autonomy. 'The whole of Tibet known as Cholka-Sum (U-Tsang, Kham and Amdo) should become a self-governing democratic political entity,' he told the European Parliament. Hence, the Middle Path or the Strasbourg Proposal actually went well beyond the independence position in pure geographical terms. The Tibet that was governed or rather controlled by the regents in the Dalai Lama's name had been just a little more than a quarter of what he now claimed. Since 1912, independent Tibet had only been made up of the U-Tsang province and parts of Kham, which the Chinese had renamed the Tibet Autonomous Region (TAR) in 1965.

Once the PLA's annexation of the Tibetan plateau was complete (after the flight of the Dalai Lama in 1959), the Chinese government had restructured various provinces for security as well as taxation purposes. Most of Amdo, the current Dalai Lama's place of origin, has been incorporated into Qinghai; parts of southern Amdo and Kham are now in Sichuan and the Dechen area of Tibet is a part of Yunnan. So basically, what the Dalai Lama sought was a reorganization of Chinese provinces.

Justifying this reorganization, Tashi Phuntsok, secretary, Department of Information, Central Tibetan Administration (CTA), said, 'Since Tibet is a vast region, with very poor means of communications, retaining political control over all parts at all times was not possible. Yet at no point in history did these regions give up the Tibetan way of life or paying religious obeisance to the Dalai Lama.'

A historic Greater Tibet is not the only thing enunciated by the Middle Path. Much to China's horror, the Dalai Lama also laid claim to Tibet's natural resources, including minerals and water. 'The Government of Tibet would pass strict laws to protect wildlife and plantlife. The exploitation of natural resources would be carefully regulated,' the Dalai Lama said at Strasbourg. In the two domains that the Middle Path was willing to concede to China, external defence and foreign policy, the Dalai Lama added a rider, 'The Government of Tibet should, however, develop and maintain relations, through its own foreign affairs bureau, in the [fields] of commerce, education, culture, religion, tourism, science, sports and other non-political activities. Tibet should join international organizations concerned with such activities.'

So even though the Tibetans were at pains to explain that the Tibet autonomous government would function alongside the PRC, the Chinese rejected the Middle Path, calling it a veiled effort at splitting China. Their objection to the proposal stemmed from their belief that the Dalai Lama was seeking 'independence, semi-independence or independence in disguise'. On 21 September 1988, communicating through its embassy in Delhi, the Chinese government informed the Tibetan leadership that the Strasbourg Proposal could not be considered the basis for talks as it had not abandoned the concept of 'independence of Tibet'. Subsequently, the Chinese government set a precondition for talks: the Dalai Lama must accept and support the unity of the motherland.

This was the end of the talks. The Chinese government clamped down in Tibet, starting with the monasteries, as these were considered the hotbeds of dissent. This increased repression saw a series of violent protests in various parts of the Tibet Autonomous Region including Lhasa in 1987–89, prompting a vicious crackdown in which several monks were imprisoned or killed. Some simply disappeared. The brutal cycle of protest and repression spiralled out of Tibet and spilled onto the mainland, where students and young professionals rose up against the government demanding democratic rights. Incidentally, the clamour for democratic rights had started on the mainland almost a decade earlier, when human rights activists had started to call for democracy as the fifth modernization, alluding to Deng Xiaoping's four modernizations programme.

However, the situation got out of control in 1989. For a country like China, which since the time of Mao Zedong has internalized a persecution complex whereby the entire universe has consistently contrived against it, these series of events appeared to be some sort of a diabolical global conspiracy. Unable to either control the growing protest or hold talks with the protestors, Prime Minister Li Peng's government (with blessings from Deng Xiaoping), ordered the military to crush the protest. On 4 June 1989, tanks rolled down on Beijing's main square, Tiananmen. An untold number—the figure hovers between hundreds to thousands depending upon the narrative—of young people died. An equal number disappeared.

International opprobrium followed. Moreover, in recognition of the Dalai Lama's steadfast commitment to peace and perhaps to spite China, he was awarded the Nobel Peace Prize in December 1989. That proved to be the proverbial last straw that broke the camel's back. China imposed martial law in Tibet (as well as parts of the mainland) and closed it to the world, including foreign aid workers. As international sanctions and condemnation mounted, China was forced to issue a white paper on Tibet claiming that Tibet had always been a part of China and that vested interests in the West were stoking the so-called freedom movement. Since then, China has issued a white paper on Tibet once every two years; each paper has increasingly vilified the Dalai Lama.

By the time talks resumed in 2002, the world had changed; and China's position in that world had changed too. The four modernizations programme of Deng Xiaoping had borne fruit. TAR was transformed by the deliberate settlement of Han Chinese, massive infrastructural development and the overwhelming presence of the Chinese military. Secular education was made compulsory in Tibet and more Tibetans were encouraged, lured or simply coerced into not sending their children to the monasteries. Moreover, to let the world see what developments were taking place inside TAR and how the Tibetans were being assimilated into the mainstream, the Chinese government opened TAR to foreign tourists. Though tourism in the region had been sporadic earlier, the Chinese government now began to develop tourism as an industry.

On the mainland, a new assertive leadership had assumed office after the era of Deng Xiaoping. While it is quite possible that Deng was sincere in resolving the Tibetan issue with some amount of give and take when he initiated the dialogue with the Dalai Lama's representatives, his successors did not believe in serious engagement. When US President Bill Clinton urged his Chinese counterpart Jiang Zemin to start a dialogue with the Dalai Lama during his 1998 visit to Beijing, Zemin laid down two conditions for talks. One, the Dalai Lama must recognize that Tibet is an inalienable part of China; and two, Taiwan is a province of China.

China also gave up the pretence of reverence towards the Dalai Lama by publicly calling him names like 'splittist', a 'devil with horns', among others, to psychologically wound the Tibetans and to take away some of the international sheen that the Tibetan leadership had accrued before dialogue began in 2002.

With the outright rejection of the Strasbourg Proposal by the Chinese, there was no agenda on the table for discussion by the two sides. The reality that the Chinese were not serious about the talks that were held from time to time was not lost on the Tibetan leadership. According to a Tibetan official who attended one of the meetings with the Chinese and did not want to be identified, 'The talks were always held in China.

While we sent very senior officials representing the Dalai Lama, the Chinese government used to depute a few intelligence officers from the Central United Front Work Department. Sometimes, they also brought a Tibetan Chinese along for the talks. The idea was to impress upon us how advanced a country China had become. The actual talks formed a minuscule part of the visit because the greater part was spent showing the Tibetan delegation various developmental projects in different regions of China.' Interestingly, the Chinese government never allowed any Mandarin-speaking person to be included in the Tibetan delegation, even though they brought Tibetan-speaking Chinese with them.

Till 2007, the Tibetans held seven rounds of talks with the Chinese without an agenda. Finally, during the eighth round in October 2008, the Chinese—supremely confident after the successful completion of the Olympic Games in August 2008 (despite fears of disruption by Tibetan activists)—asked their interlocutors to submit their demands in writing. On 31 October 2008, the Tibetan government submitted a Memorandum on Genuine Autonomy for the Tibetan People. Even though the official document published by the Department of Information and International Relations claims that the memorandum is completely different from the Strasbourg Proposal, in essence the demands made in both documents were the same.

According to Samphel, 'The memorandum cited the Chinese constitution and the rights given to the minorities in the constitution under the national regional autonomy provisions to make our case for genuine autonomy. The Chinese constitution provides for this.' Among the main demands of the memorandum were the amalgamation of the three provinces of Amdo, Kham and U–Tsang as one unitary autonomous region to be governed by the government elected by the Tibetans. The Chinese government would have the right to formulate Tibet's defence and foreign policy in consultation with the Tibetan government, but all the other issues, like preservation of language, culture, religion, education, environment, utilization of natural resources, economic development and trade, public health, public security, regulation on population migration, and cultural, educational and religious exchanges with other countries would be the prerogative of the Tibetan government.

China rejected the memorandum on the same grounds that it had rejected the Strasbourg Proposal. 'The Chinese government said that we were again asking for freedom or semi-independence; that we were seeking Greater Tibet in the name of genuine autonomy,' said Samphel. Consequently, in the next round of talks, the Tibetan delegation offered notes to the memorandum explaining in desperate detail how it was not seeking to undermine the supremacy of the People's Republic of China.

Interestingly, through all these years of engaging with the Tibetan government in exile, China never made any counter-offer for resolution. It offered no sops to the Tibetans and no confidence building measures. As usually happens in negotiations, the Chinese government did not even adopt a step-by-step approach (which it has done in the case of border talks with India), addressing the doable issues first leaving the difficult ones for later. 'The Chinese government says that there is no Tibetan issue to be discussed,' said Samphel. 'The only issues that it is willing to talk about pertain to the status and the privileges of the Dalai Lama.'

Yet hope has refused to wilt. A day before the thirteenth white paper was issued in April 2015, the authors were chatting with Samphel at the Tibet Policy Institute in Dharamshala. According to him, 'Many Tibetans see hope in the new Chinese dispensation. Ever since he has assumed office, President Xi Jinping has not made any statement on Tibet. Perhaps he is still making up his mind. This is a positive sign. This shows that he is not carrying the baggage of his predecessors.' That Xi Jinping's mother and wife are sympathetic to Buddhism and have often engaged with lamas added to his optimism.

As it turned out, Samphel had spoken too soon. The thirteenth white paper concludes with Xi's statement in which he says, 'The central government has followed a clear and consistent policy towards the fourteenth Dalai Lama. Only when he makes a public statement acknowledging that Tibet has been an integral part of China since antiquity, and abandons his stance on independence and his attempts to divide China, can he improve his relationship with the central government in any real sense.'

Innumerable historical accounts would disprove China's assertion that Tibet has been an integral part of it since antiquity. The concept of the nation state is just a few centuries old. In ancient and even medieval times, borders were fluid and determined by the prevailing military power. The boundaries of countries continued to expand and shrink depending upon the influence and intent of the ruling class. For instance, the Indian border once included parts of Afghanistan but not the region south of the Deccan plateau. In another period it encompassed several parts of East Asia, including some portions of Indonesia, but not the western Indian states.

Ancient and medieval Tibetan and Chinese history was also determined by the logic of the sword. But history is susceptible to subversion by the powerful and hence China dismisses the Tibetan narrative as imaginary.

Yet some Chinese historians too dispute the government's version of history. In an article in the *China Review* magazine, Professor Ge Jianxiong, director of the Institute of Chinese Historical Geography and the Research Centre for Historical Geographic Studies at Fudan University in Shanghai, wrote in 2015 that during the Tang Dynasty (the largest dynasty during the seventh to tenth century), 'we cannot include the Qinghai-Tibetan Plateau, which was ruled by Tubo/Tufan… Tubo/Tufan was sovereignty independent of the Tang Dynasty. At least, it was not administered by the Tang Dynasty.'

According to Ge, 'It would be a defiance of history to claim that Tibet has always been a part of China since the Tang Dynasty; the fact that the Qinghai-Tibetan Plateau subsequently became a part of the Chinese dynasties does not substantiate such a claim.'

His article also questions the concept of Chinese nationhood as asserted by his government. He writes that in different periods throughout history, the Chinese nation, sometimes referred to the as 'Qing State', included all the territory that fell within the boundaries of the Qing empire; but during other periods, it referred to only '18 interior provinces', excluding Manchuria, Inner Mongolia, Tibet and Xinjiang.

In any case the struggle for self-determination is not led by historical traditions, but by the will of the people. And here the will of the people has remained steadfast; that is the reason why Tibet continues to be China's core concern, in its own words.

Ironically, despite hosting the largest Tibetan diaspora, including the government in exile, New Delhi's policy towards Tibet has been ambivalent. In the early years, it was partially guided by lofty humanitarian ideals and partially by a desire to spite China. However, after the 1962 war, India's view of the Tibetan refugees changed. As we have seen, the government came up with the idea of raising an all-Tibetan insurgency force, the Special Frontier Force (SFF), which could operate inside Tibet and instigate an uprising against the PLA. With this in mind, all arriving Tibetan refugees into India (until 2008, they used to number a couple of thousand) were enrolled into this secret force. For many years, Tibetan teenagers were picked up from villages spread across India for compulsory military service.

Yet, the Indian government could never muster enough courage to put into practice what it had conceived and the SFF was never deployed for the role for which it was created. Interestingly, in the early decades, some Indian intelligence officers used to goad Tibetan leaders to mount armed resistance against China even as the Government of India insisted that they indulge in no political activity from Indian soil. Driven by intelligence agencies, the thinking was that the refugees (and the Dalai Lama himself) were a 'Tibet card', which could be used against China at an opportune time. But the problem with policies driven by intelligence agencies is that they suffer from tunnel vision and rarely see the big picture. As a result, nothing came of this. Where the government's foreign policy initiatives on Tibet were concerned, no serviceable ideas have emerged yet. It is not that there haven't been attempts to back the Tibetan cause but these have been driven by various interest groups with their own agenda.

One of these groups has been the right-wing Hindu organization, the RSS. It has built relations with Tibetans for two reasons. One was to co-opt Buddhism (being a religion that sprouted in India) under the overarching umbrella of Hinduism. The other reason was the presence of Hindu pilgrimage sites like Mount Kailash and Mansarovar Lake in Tibet and Buddhist pilgrimage sites in India.

Tibetans have played along with these sentiments because it helps them delink themselves even further from China, historically, culturally and politically. Professor Samdhong Rinpoche said, 'I feel that India has more logic to claim Tibet as its territory than China, which has no logic at all. Our religion, language and culture are of Indian origin... So, if Indians claim Tibet as a part of this country, we will have a difficult time arguing otherwise.'

On Tibet's shared history with China, he said, 'We do not have any long history with China, whereas we do have a history with India. From China, the only thing that we have imbibed is our culinary system... everything else about the Tibetan culture is of Indian origin. In India, organisations like the RSS and Tibet Swaraj have always supported the cause of Tibetan independence.'

Given this, perhaps one of the things that India can do to help the Tibetan cause and acquire leverage against China is to build upon this religious-cultural legacy. Even supposedly godless China realized the importance of religion, when in 2011 it sanctioned US$ 3 billion for the renovation and development of Lumbini—the birthplace of the Buddha in Nepal—as an international pilgrim spot on the lines of Mecca in Saudi Arabia. After holding out for a year, asserting its sovereignty over Lumbini, the Nepalese government agreed to the Chinese proposal in 2012, causing much hand-wringing in India.

Successive Chinese governments have not only reviled Buddhism, but religion in general. Clearly they have not seen the light all of a sudden. Nor is the development of Lumbini a step towards forging better ties with Nepal, because for that China has already made adequate investments. The only reason China has 'discovered' the Buddha is to isolate the Tibetans and the Dalai Lama from the larger Buddhist community worldwide. Since the Dalai Lama escaped to India in 1959, he was allowed to visit and pray at Lumbini only once. That was in 1981.

China is obviously banking on the assumption that international sentiment towards Buddhism and the Tibetan issue is driven by the Dalai Lama's personality. Once he passes on, the Buddhist religious leadership will be up for grabs. Not only is religious tourism a very lucrative industry, it is a very powerful tool to politically and psychologically control the community.

Instead of protesting from the sidelines, India should step up and take on the 'leadership role on Buddhism', as Samphel puts it. While politics should not meddle in religious matters, given that the most sacred Buddhist sites like Bodh Gaya, Sarnath, Nalanda, Sravasthi are all located in India, there is merit in the argument that these should be developed as a proper pilgrimage circuit. Now that the Dalai Lama has given up his temporal role and is only a religious leader, he should be encouraged by the government to chalk out an annual pilgrimage programme for all Buddhists. Why can't the government facilitate an annual Buddhist festival on the lines of Durga Puja or Ganesh Mahotsav running into a few days at one of these places, say Bodh Gaya, with a prayer service by the Dalai Lama? Let Buddhists from all over the world attend this, and be allowed to visit revered monasteries like Tawang in Arunachal Pradesh and Rumtek in Sikkim as part of the pilgrimage.

Additionally, when the Government of India visualized reviving the Nalanda University, it should have done so in tandem with its Buddhist past. Instead of looking for international academics or politicians to head it, it should have chosen the tallest Buddhist leader—the Dalai Lama—as its chancellor. After all, it's only a ceremonial position. But it would have sent a message throughout Southeast Asia, where Buddhism is the dominant religion. Of course, this can be done even now.

There is a viewpoint amongst Indian intelligentsia that since India has a bona fide Buddhist legacy which predates Tibet, we need not give primacy to a Tibetan Buddhist leader. In isolation, perhaps this argument could have held ground. But when seen in the context of China and the way it is appropriating not just the religion but everything else associated with it, the Indian response must be pragmatic and far-sighted. The Dalai Lama is not a person, but an institution. The person may die, but the institution will live. How well it lives will depend on how well it is nurtured. This is an opportunity that India should not let slip.

CHAPTER 19

THE DALAI LAMA

Great leaders need great power and even greater public relations machinery to ensure long-term sustenance and relevance. In March 1959, when twenty-four-year-old Tenzin Gyatso fled to India from Tibet—in a boat, on horseback and by foot, covering the physical distance of roughly 240 kilometres—all he had was the faith of his people through the office he held and his own narrative of injustice and betrayal at the hands of the Chinese.

That he was the fourteenth reincarnation of the Dalai Lama was of little consequence to anyone except the Tibetans. A measure of how little the world understood or cared for the Tibetan form of Buddhism or the institution of the Dalai Lama can be gauged from the conversation Russian Premier (chairman of the council of ministers) Nikita Khrushchev had with the Chinese supreme leader, Chairman Mao Zedong, in 1959. After the Dalai Lama's flight to India, Khrushchev admonished Mao for not having killed the Tibetan leader before his escape. '[A]s to the escape of the Dalai Lama from Tibet, if we had been in your place, we would not have let him escape. It would be better if he was in a coffin. And now he is in India, and perhaps will go to the USA,' Khrushchev told Mao, during a visit to China. Russia, and to some extent China, believed at that point that it was possible to assassinate the Tibetan leader without much international opprobrium. At the time, perhaps they were right.

The Dalai Lama himself was not sure about his international stature. He wasn't even sure whether India would grant him and his escaping entourage asylum. He writes in his memoirs: 'We took the decision to send officials ahead of us to the border, with a message asking the Indian government for asylum. We did not want to cross the border before we had permission.' A few days later, when he embarked upon the rail journey from Tezpur, the last railhead those days in east India, to Mussoorie he was astounded to find hundreds of devotees seeking his blessings at different stations en route, in addition to the international press covering his travel. From the splendid isolation of Lhasa to being the centre of the 'story of the year' as his escape was being described in the foreign press, the Dalai Lama realized, perhaps for the first time, that at least some people (outside Tibet) were conscious of the importance of the institution he represented. Probably he also realized that a large part of this consciousness stemmed from curiosity about Communist China.

Sifting through a blizzard of conflicting advice from well-meaning supporters about handling the present and charting out a viable future course of action, the twenty-four-year-old had actually traversed the distance of a few decades in just a few days. As the spiritual and temporal head of his people, his word was law. He had to not only comfort his distraught people, who were arriving in India by the dozen every day, but he also had to ensure through his statements and actions that those who remained in Tibet were not made to suffer because of his escape and his actions in exile. At the same time, he understood that he had to position himself in such a way that the international interest in him and his beleaguered cause went beyond inquisitiveness or wariness about China. This was the hardest part. Most of the world didn't even know of Tibet or its geographical location. For explorers, Tibet was the enigmatic Shangri-La.

The miracle of the Dalai Lama lies not in the fact that he has outlived all his adversaries, from Mao to Deng, or outpaced his contemporary resistance fighters across the world. The miracle is in his building up of his cause as righteous and just (not merely dissident), and his own stature as a spiritual conscience-keeper of the world; even when realpolitik prevents world leaders from openly supporting the Dalai Lama's political cause, they still meet him and listen to him.

◆

However, when his exile began, the immediate priority for the Dalai Lama on reaching India was to broadcast the Tibetan narrative to as many people in the world as possible. Towards that end, the Dalai Lama issued a brief statement from Mussoorie in 1959 emphasizing the provocation and circumstances of his journey. Within two days, the Communist government in Beijing denounced the statement calling it crude and full of lies. It doubted the veracity of the statement, insisting instead that the Dalai Lama had been abducted by Tibetan rebels. The Chinese also castigated India, accusing it of being expansionist, following in the footsteps of the colonial power it had recently won independence from. Clearly the Chinese government was wounded and furious. It hadn't expected the Dalai Lama to successfully escape from Tibet or the Indian government to welcome him.

In 1956, before the Dalai Lama embarked upon a pilgrimage to India (on the invitation of the Mahabodhi Society of India to mark the 2,500th birth anniversary of Gautama Buddha), his interlocutors had requested the Government of India for political asylum, which was agreed in principle. When the Dalai Lama met Prime Minister Nehru during his visit, he repeated the request made earlier.

While Nehru weighed the request, Chinese Premier Zhou Enlai arrived in India. This was the era of Hindi-Chini bhai-bhai, with the Panchsheel Agreement between India and China having been signed two years earlier. In addition to the summit meeting with Prime Minister Nehru, Zhou also met the Dalai Lama. He impressed upon both, albeit separately, that it would be in the best interest of Tibet and its bilateral relationship with China if the Dalai Lama returned to Lhasa. Even though the Dalai Lama resisted Zhou's charm offensive, Nehru did not want to offend his guest, especially when in his mind a new era of India-China friendship was dawning, despite border issues. Moreover, the Bandung Conference of 1955, in which Nehru promoted the idea of the Non-Aligned Movement, and where he went out of his way to ensure that Zhou was not viewed with suspicion by participating African and Asian leaders, had created an image of Nehru as a righteous and a global leader. He couldn't let down that image by not believing Zhou's assurances. Hence, he politely refused to accept the request for asylum and persuaded the Dalai Lama to return.

Yet, contrary to what Nehru had expected, far from being grateful to him, both Mao and Zhou didn't think much of Nehru as a strategist or a strong leader. They viewed him as a person who was impractical and possibly even a little vain. Moreover, in the Chinese perception, India was not as great a country as was being projected by Nehru, having been colonized by several invaders and imperialists. Hence, they had little patience with India assuming the leadership of the newly independent Asian-African countries. That space was reserved for China. It was this perception that informed their view; they felt Nehru could be persuaded quite easily to defer to China's wishes.

Hence, when Nehru's government welcomed the escaping Dalai Lama in 1959 and gave him political asylum the Chinese were shocked. Let down by their assessment of Nehru, they called him duplicitous. But actually the budding friendship between the two countries was already on the rocks well before the Dalai Lama crossed over the Himalayan pass into Tawang. The continued Chinese incursions into Ladakh and maps depicting Indian territory as part of China, despite assurances given by Zhou to Nehru and the signing of the Panchsheel Agreement, had clouded Nehru's views on China. The Indian government was aware of Chinese excesses in Tibet, especially the mass killings of monks and civilians alike. The Chinese invasion of Tibet in 1950 had made news in India, with its sympathies clearly lying with the Buddhist people. Given all this, there was no way that the Indian government could have refused asylum to the Dalai Lama.

For the barely decade-old Communist regime, which was grappling with far too many issues, not least the hostility of most of the Western world, the Dalai Lama's escape was a huge blow. Just as the Dalai Lama was keen to reach out to the world with his story, the Chinese government was also trying to sell a narrative that would reinforce its claims on Tibet and its intentions about the future of Tibetan religious institutions.

Despite his inexperience in politics, the Dalai Lama was conscious of his stateless position vis-à-vis China, as well as the lack of clarity on Tibet's international status. As soon as he recovered from his arduous journey, he started consulting with legal experts on international law. Alongside, he established the government in exile, called the Central Tibetan Administration (CTA). This was the easy part, as he had come to India with his government, including the council of ministers. The difficult part was to construct a sensible, logical and righteous narrative that would get not just the sympathy but also the support of international institutions.

At the same time, the Dalai Lama had to be mindful of the sensitivities of India as the host country, especially as relations between India and China started to deteriorate rapidly. It is not difficult to imagine how insecure the exiled Tibetans would have been then; Indian hospitality could have run cold at any time.

This was one of the reasons the Dalai Lama was circumspect in his utterances on China: he didn't want his statements to further imperil the India-China relationship. He also did not want to close all doors to discussion with the supreme leaders of China, including Mao Zedong, whom he had met a number of times, both formally and informally during his stay in China in 1954–55. The Dalai Lama writes in his memoirs:

> Before I left China I was greatly impressed by Mao Tse-tung's outstanding personality. I met him many times on social occasions, apart from our private meetings... I was also convinced that he himself would never use force to convert Tibet into a Communist state.

Certainly, I was disillusioned afterwards by the policy of persecution which was adopted by the Chinese authorities in Tibet, but I still find it hard to believe that these oppressions had the approval and support of Mao Tse-tung.

Perhaps it was these meetings that the Dalai Lama refers to in his book that led even the Chinese to think, at least initially, that he wouldn't have thought of escaping of his own accord. When the Chinese military representatives first arrived in Lhasa in 1950, the Dalai Lama was a teenager, a mere fourteen years old. Clearly he was impressionable, vulnerable and given to taking the advice of his political office-bearers including the two prime ministers who were running the administration in his name. Four years later, when he went to China, he had already seen how the Chinese had systematically emasculated his government to the extent that he was forced to ask his prime ministers to resign on Chinese demand. His land was colonized and his people enslaved. He may have been drawing strength from his religious learning, but he was clearly vulnerable, impressionable and maybe afraid too.

Compared to the Dalai Lama, Mao was the fearsome ruler of his people. Even if he didn't strike terror in the hearts of the people, he did inspire awe. Given the difference in their age and power, it is not difficult to imagine how one-sided their meetings would have been. The Dalai Lama writes of their first meeting, 'I felt I was in a very difficult position. I was sure that unless I could maintain a friendly atmosphere, our country would suffer far more than it had already. So I told him that the people of Tibet had great hopes for their future under his leadership.'

The Chinese, particularly Mao, felt that they would be able to manipulate the Dalai Lama, and realize their intent of 'peaceful liberation of Tibet'. However, unfortunately for Mao, his foot soldiers in Tibet were both impatient and imprudent. Their arrogance and atrocities fuelled sporadic mini-rebellions in various parts of Tibet, which got the Chinese to inflict further hardships on the civilians. A cycle of revolt and repression commenced. Over the years, the mini-rebellions in various parts of Tibet converged in Lhasa leading to the Dalai Lama's flight in 1959.

He was no longer the naive, wide-eyed boy of eighteen who had met Mao; he was now the leader of his people, who had experienced at first hand Chinese double-speak and betrayal as well as witnessed the brutalization of fellow Tibetans.

In India after his escape, the Dalai Lama was more self-assured. Distance from China added to his courage and determination about taking on the

Chinese. It helped that for the first time he was able to consult dispassionate, secular, legal and political specialists who could give him opinions based on the documents—international treaties, agreements, land deeds, taxes, etc.—that the Tibetan government possessed to make its case of being an independent country. By the time he was ready to respond a few months later to China's assertions on Tibet and his abduction by the 'imperialists' he was better equipped.

He called a press conference where he asserted that he had left Tibet of his own accord because of the Chinese invasion and subsequent atrocities. He formally rejected the 17-Point Agreement which his government had signed under duress in 1951. His government also presented the Tibetan case for review to the International Commission of Jurists, which examined old treaties (which Tibet had entered into with other countries, including China, as a sovereign state) and statements made by Tibetans and the Chinese over the years. The International Commission of Jurists also interviewed refugees to get an understanding about living conditions in Tibet before and after the Chinese invasion.

In its report submitted in June 1959, the commission observed, 'From 1950 onwards as a result of Chinese aggression a practically independent country is being turned by force into a province of China and the struggle of the Tibetans has been to regain their independence... Even the terms of the 17-Point Agreement of 1951, guaranteeing broad autonomy to Tibet as mentioned above, have been consistently disregarded...'

Buoyed by the commission's report, the Dalai Lama decided to take his plea to the United Nations, despite India's advice to the contrary. He now had several advisors, both amongst Indians and westerners, who helped in making Tibet's case. Since both Tibet and China were not members of the UN (China's seat was represented by Chiang Kai-shek's Taiwan), the resolution was moved by Ireland and Malaya and was adopted in October 1959.

Though nothing much came out of it, just as the Indian government had advised the Dalai Lama, by now he was emerging as his own person—listening to everyone's opinion but relying on his instincts alone; a phenomenal leap of faith at age twenty-four. He recognized then that the only way he could reach out to the world was by establishing the justness of his cause, which was beyond compromise.

'We must never allow a belief to grow up abroad that Tibet will ever acquiesce in Chinese Communist domination. For I know it never will,' he wrote.

While he was reaching out to the world, his government was reaching out to the stream of Tibetan refugees pouring into India, following their leader's footsteps for a few years before China clamped down on the border. Through the Central Tibetan Administration, the Dalai Lama created an administrative infrastructure with ministers and secretaries responsible for various aspects of welfare, education and settlement of the refugee population. It was a select body of people directly answerable to the Dalai Lama.

Considering that the Dalai Lama's vision was global—to garner international support for his cause against China—it was important for him to travel. Unlike in the past, the Tibetan leader could no longer afford to be isolated from the world. He went outside India for the first time in 1967 and since then has never stopped travelling. He is probably one of the most widely travelled religious leaders in the world, visiting countries of all faiths and inclinations. His message to the world has consistently evolved and over time transcended his religion, focusing his fight on the injustice meted out to his people by the bigger and more powerful Chinese.

Quite early in his peripatetic career, the Dalai Lama realized that while the global political class was sympathetic to his narrative and was happy to meet him as a Buddhist leader, it was wary about supporting his cause against China. So he stopped seeking them out. Instead he shifted his attention to another constituency: Hollywood. Author Pico Iyer writes, 'In a curious way, therefore, without even necessarily intending to, the Tibetans had begun acting on the clairvoyant idea of Gore Vidal decades ago, that in a global world, the centre of power might be not just Washington but Hollywood. Having found that most politicians clamoured to see him but were reluctant, practically speaking, to do much to help him, the Dalai Lama had almost literally allowed his cause to be taken to the streets, permitting movie stars and rock musicians and artists to reach a greater global audience than any national politician could.'

This approach had another concomitant benefit. Aid flowed in. This paid salaries, strengthened the administration and also allowed it to undertake educational and developmental work for the refugees, thereby becoming one of the most 'serious' governments-in-exile, according to *The Economist*.

The Central Tibetan Administration continued with the administrative work of looking after the Tibetan diaspora under the close watch of the Dalai Lama till 2001, when the supreme leader embraced democracy and progressed from selection to election. The Tibetan diaspora was urged for the first time to vote for the people they wanted to see in the assembly as well as elect the kalon tripa, which, loosely translated, meant the minister-in-chief or the senior-most minister whom the other ministers would report to. The kalon tripa, in turn, was to continue to report to the Dalai Lama.

But such was the Tibetan people's absolute faith in the clergy that they could not look beyond a Rinpoche (a senior lama) as the political leader. The first elected kalon tripa, as we've seen, was Professor Samdhong Rinpoche, former vice chancellor of the Central Institute of Higher Tibetan Studies at Varanasi. Born in 1939, at the age of five he was recognized as the reincarnation of Samdhong Rinpoche.

Responding to Rinpoche's election, the Dalai Lama joked that he asked his people to choose their own political leader and they chose an old monk, instead of 'a young, energetic, educated and secular person'. Perhaps the people didn't have much to choose from, which is why the final authority rested with the Dalai Lama. He continued to be as much the face of the Tibetan struggle as the guiding light for the increasing tribe of restless people worldwide in need of spiritual succour and a cause to devote their energies to.

For much of his years in exile, the Dalai Lama's biggest challenge has been to create a corpus of well-educated (preferably Western-educated) professionals who would be taken seriously by the world when they spoke of Tibet. This was no easy task. Tibetan society traditionally was very primitive and the people who fled to India were not only impoverished but largely illiterate too. The literate and the learned ones were the lamas who only studied religious texts.

Indian Prime Minister Jawaharlal Nehru, who regarded the Dalai Lama as his friend, advised him to focus on the education of his people more than anything else. 'If the Tibetan people were educated, everything else will follow,' Thupten Samphel, a former member of the CTA and now director, Tibetan Policy Institute, recalled Nehru telling the Tibetan leader. The Dalai Lama heeded the advice, with support from India. Consecutive Indian governments supported the establishment and running of Tibetan schools and institutes of higher learning throughout the country.

The effort took time to bear fruit, but it did for sure. 'Today, amongst the Tibetans in exile, we have professionally qualified people from different streams,' Sikyong (leader of the CTA) Lobsang Sangay told the authors. 'From chartered accountants to lawyers, we don't have to look outside the community.'

For people like Sangay, the Tibetan struggle has many layers to it, with the right to return to a fully autonomous Tibet being just one part. Equally important is the overall upliftment of the Tibetan people, who despite fifty-six years of living in exile and hence no longer in the splendid isolation of the plateau, are still quite backward. For this reason, when Sangay took charge in 2011, skill development and dissemination was one of his primary objectives. This he tried to do through a four-pronged programme, at the heart of which is education. 'My vision is that in about a decade's time every member of the CTA should have a postgraduate degree from the best institutions of the world, right down to the junior-most person and not just the prime minister and the ministers,' said Sangay. In the last few years, the Tibetan administration has been focused on promoting higher and professional education.

The second prong of nurturing an intellectual corpus is the think tank, Tibetan Policy Institute, which was inaugurated by Sangay in February 2012. For far too long, the biggest spokespersons of the Tibetan issue, after the Dalai Lama, have been western celebrities, academicians and the voiceless self-immolating monks on the plateau. But with the Tibetan Policy Institute, the CTA wants to reclaim the narrative, through personal histories, research and information dissemination.

Amongst the objectives of the Tibetan Policy Institute is to create Tibetan-origin human resources on its history, religion, culture and present-day politics which could gradually help change the worldwide perspective on the Tibet-China issue. In popular perception, while the Tibetans have moral ascendancy because of their peaceful resistance and spiritual living, China has the economic clout to subvert that.

In the short term, the Tibetan Policy Institute is supposed to hold either one major conference on Tibet spread over a few days every year or a few day-long conferences. It also invites experts on the Tibet-China issue once a month to give a talk to CTA scholars and other members of the Tibetan diaspora, including non-governmental organizations. The institute is also supposed to make efforts to participate in international seminars or conferences on Tibet or China. However, the most important responsibility of the institute is to produce at least one authoritative paper on a subject that can impinge upon the Tibet-China issue.

Recently, the institute brought out a detailed dossier on the Chinese power structure starting with the president and down to the lowest party functionary in the government. The document lists their past and present positions with conjectures about possible future positions. This document has also been shared with the Government of India.

The third prong of developing educated and intellectually stimulating human resources is the Tibet Corps. 'With our emphasis on encouraging Tibetans to seek education abroad, there was a fear in the community that this youth would become self-centred and would forget about the Tibetan cause,' said the sikyong.

'Tibet Corps is a voluntary organization for Tibetans settled in around forty countries. The members of the corps return to Dharamshala once a year and work with the CTA; thereby they not only renew their connections but also bring global perspective, which will over time better equip the members of the CTA to address developing issues in our area of interest. The idea is, no matter how far he goes, a Tibetan must remain rooted to his land, culture, tradition and struggle,' he added.

The final prong is a replication of the concept of twin cities, albeit on a smaller scale. In the last few years the Tibetan administration has got sympathetic countries interested in adopting various Tibetan settlements across India and Nepal whereby small investments come in for welfare and infrastructural projects.

Isn't all this tantamount to making oneself comfortable in exile and putting the core issue of Tibet, whether complete independence or genuine autonomy, on the back-burner?

The sikyong does not agree. Having been a student of non-violent conflicts across the world, Sangay believes that the Tibetans have time on their side. According to him, conflict has various stages from the time its breaks out. The most important of these are surviving the conflict and sustaining the resistance movement.

'The early decades after His Holiness escaped from Tibet were spent merely in surviving the changed circumstances,' he said, referring to the survival not merely of human beings, but of religion, language, culture and cuisine. Through personal example, piety and development of Tibet-specific educational and cultural centres, the Dalai Lama and his CTA ensured that even as his exiled people learned the ways of the host country, they did not forget their own. To ascertain this fact one doesn't need empirical evidence. One only needs to eavesdrop on any two Tibetans talking to one another, whether in Delhi's Majnu ka Tila settlement of Tibetans or anywhere in Dharamshala. Even those born in exile as late as in the 1990s, use Tibetan as the first language.

As if giving voice to the Dalai Lama's and sikyong's thoughts, Samphel had earlier told the authors, 'The biggest indicator of the success of our movement is this. Despite being in exile and dispersed all over the world, we have retained our Tibetan-ness. If you see the odds, this is no mean achievement.'

Yet, despite all this, the future of the Tibetan struggle rests on the future of the Dalai Lama. For the Tibetans, life, religion and the Dalai Lama are intertwined in such a manner that no meaningful conversation about their future is possible without their spiritual leader playing a central role in it.

It is this that troubles the Chinese government. Despite running down the fourteenth Dalai Lama personally, it tries to uphold the institution, because it understands that to keep the Tibetans on its side in the long run, it will need the Dalai Lama on its side. Hence, the country which is ideologically opposed to religion took offence at the suggestion that the institution of the Dalai Lama may end with the death of the incumbent, as the Dalai Lama once mentioned. China has repeatedly said that only it has the right to identify and appoint the fifteenth Dalai Lama. It has rightly understood that no amount of oppression has been able to shake people's faith in the supreme leader. Not only have Tibetans rejected Chinese assertions, the fourteenth Dalai Lama has been extremely cautious and clever in speaking in multiple voices on this subject so as to retain the initiative vis-à-vis China. It is now near impossible for China to find favour for the fifteenth Dalai Lama of its choice. After all, it is not about a religious head, it is about the people's faith. And faith understands no strategy or logic.

In his address to the Tibetan people on 24 September 2011, the Dalai Lama spoke about his future. He said that he would decide at the age of ninety whether the institution should continue or not. Elsewhere he has said that perhaps there will be no Dalai Lama after him. In yet another conversation with a journalist he suggested that the next Dalai Lama could be a woman. He further added to the uncertainty by asserting that if the fourteenth Dalai Lama died leaving the task unfinished, then the next Dalai Lama would have to complete that task, which would be winning back the homeland for the Tibetan people. And because the homeland is under occupation at the moment, the fifteenth Dalai Lama would have to reincarnate in exile. He has also made it clear that if the Tibetan people desire, then he will reincarnate.

In the Tibetan belief, a high lama can reincarnate in three ways. One, he can be reborn after death; he is then recognized through a mystical process; two, he himself identifies his reincarnation while alive; and three, the Dalai Lama appoints his own successor (referred to as emanation) from among his disciples and personally grooms him to take over his responsibilities. Apparently, exceptional lamas have the capacity to be present in different bodies at the same time.

Given the way in which both the Chinese government and the Dalai Lama have been trying to outpace one another, the possibility of the latter selecting his own successor at the time of his choosing is high. By saying that it will depend upon the will of the people, the Dalai Lama has ensured that his choice will have the support of all Tibetans across the world; support that will be steered through the office of the sikyong and the CTA. By helping the office of the sikyong to grow outside his shadow, the Dalai Lama wants to make certain that after him the widespread Tibetan diaspora and the international community take the sikyong seriously, so that the unquestioning devotion that people have towards His Holiness is also extended to the political leadership of the community. Perhaps this is one of the reasons why the Dalai Lama is waiting before taking the final call on his reincarnation. He wants the office of the sikyong to attain a degree of authority and credibility worldwide, so that it is able to hold its own against China in the diplomatic arena.

In the last four years, Sangay has been travelling all over the world to establish his credentials, with many governments according him the status of a foreign minister. He has frequently been interviewed by the international media and has written articles in magazines like *Time* on the subject of the fifteenth Dalai Lama. In October 2015, he was accorded the presidential medal for 'leadership and forward thinking' by the Salisbury University of Maryland. Perhaps in his second term—he won the 2016 elections—his stature will grow enough to not only nurture the young reincarnation, but also to keep the Tibetans together under his leadership. It is not difficult to see why. Being the first Tibetan to get a doctorate from Harvard Law School on 'Democracy and History of the Tibetan Government in Exile from 1959–2004', and several post-doctoral diplomas on subjects as varied as environmental law and advanced study of non-violent conflict from institutions such as the Fletcher Summer Institute at Tufts University, Sangay probably has educational qualifications that are unmatched in the entire Tibetan diaspora.

His qualifications and years of employment in the US give him a clear edge as far as representing the Dalai Lama or the Tibetan cause is concerned. As usually happens, the Ivy League colleges of the US provide the student with not just education but an alumni network which seldom fails to deliver. The Dalai Lama has not been oblivious to this. He couldn't have found a better candidate to take on his temporal duties even as he continues to be the benign overseer. There is unity of purpose in this duality, a purpose both unambiguous and uncomplicated: to ensure that the Tibetan cause does not fall off the radar of the global community of sympathetic governments and well-meaning celebrities after the fourteenth Dalai Lama passes away.

Meanwhile the Dalai Lama has been strengthening the Tibetan administration to not only look after the day-to-day affairs of the diaspora but also to ensure that the flock stays together despite the multiplicity of voices that claim to speak for them. For instance, in spite of demanding 'Rangzen' or complete freedom, the Tibetan Youth Congress, which the Chinese white paper refers to as a terrorist organization, passed a resolution in 2013 promising that if the Tibetan issue is resolved, it will respect the majority decision, implying that it will forfeit claims of Rangzen in favour of the Middle Path.

In another show of foresight, all the departments of the CTA have been registered in India as independent societies. 'The reason for that is very obvious,' Sonam Dagpu, secretary, Department of International Relations, CTA, told the authors. 'For China, Tibet is the core issue. For India, border is the core issue. What if China tells India that it is willing to resolve the border issue if India orders closure of the CTA?' Dagpu said.

One of the Dalai Lama's recurring messages to his people is that 'anything is possible in the future', hence one must always be prepared. Clearly, he believes in following what he says. In this long-drawn battle of imaginary history and the will of the people, time, as the sikyong asserted, is on the side of the Tibetans. But in India's case, it cannot wait indefinitely to formulate a clear and effective strategy against China. As it is not beyond probability that the fifteenth Dalai Lama will incarnate on Indian soil, it is important for us to nurture the institution and figure out what place it will have in our future China strategy.

THE INSURGENCIES WITHIN

CHAPTER 20

THE INSURGENCIES WITHIN

In February 2014, the then union Minister of State for Home, R. P. N. Singh, in a written reply to the Rajya Sabha said, 'The CPI (Maoist) has developed close fraternal ties with Northeast insurgent groups like the Revolutionary People's Front and People's Liberation Army of Manipur. Both the outfits have agreed upon mutual cooperation in the areas of training, funding, supply of arms and ammunition.' He added, 'Upper Assam Leading Committee (UALC) of CPI (Maoist) is operating in Assam and Arunachal Pradesh…and [has] been engaged in recruitment and training of cadres for the outfit in Assam and these cadres have been utilised in extensive propaganda against mega dams in Assam.' His last words on the subject were, 'In this backdrop, the Assam-Arunachal Pradesh border has emerged as another theatre of Maoist activities. The outfit is also establishing separate channels in the Northeast, particularly in Nagaland for procurement of ammunition.'

Perhaps some of these channels have started to deliver. In early May 2016, the national media reported an unprecedented incident from the sensitive Tawang town of Arunachal Pradesh: two people, including a monk, were killed in police firing. The two were part of the 200-strong mob that had collected outside a police station to protest the arrest of their leader Lama Lobsang Gyatso the previous month. Gyatso is the general secretary of Save Mon Region Federation, an organization that has been protesting against building of dams in the region, a fear expressed two years earlier by the minister of state for home.

Earlier, in 2012, Home Secretary R. K. Singh admitted that the left-wing extremists or Maoists have presence and influence in fifteen states. After allying with movements in the Northeast, they are also trying to expand their operations into newer regions through the forests of Mysore in Karnataka onto Kerala. Despite this, Singh dismissed the Maoists as a ragtag bunch of criminals who are opposed to development. He said the Maoists are trying to exploit the regions where development is taking place. Given that almost all of India is pushing the envelope for rapid development, this is a bit ominous and more so in areas which are vulnerable to external exploitation.

Former army chief General Shankar Roychowdhury has said as much, 'Left-wing extremism offers the most attractive high-value, low-cost strategic option for external exploitation. Rest assured: Pakistan, Bangladesh, and perhaps even "Maobadi Nepal"—as proxy for the People's Republic of China—are eyeing it very closely indeed.'

In addition to the Indian heartland, Maoists have already established a base in the forested portions of the impoverished Wayanad region of Kerala. Admitting this, Kerala Home Minister Ramesh Chennithala said in a press conference in December 2014 that though the presence of CPI (Maoists) had been identified in some pockets in the Western Ghats region of the state, they were yet to influence the public, including tribesmen, in the area. But they were trying to influence the youth in cities. Interestingly, the people of Kerala have traditionally been opposed to big industrial projects which the locals feel threaten the environment or their natural habitat. The state has a history of violent protests against big and 'polluting' industry. So even if it is early days, the ground is ripe.

Chronicling the outreach mechanism of the Maoists since the late 1960s, author Sudeep Chakravarti refers to their earliest treatise called *Report from the Flaming Fields of Bihar by Communist Party of India (Marxist-Leninist)*, which was brought out in the 1980s. It laid down in minute detail the various fault lines in Bihar and its contiguous states where promising conditions for revolution existed. According to Chakravarti, the report was a handy manual for the next decade and more as the Maoists started penetrating the forests of central India. In 2004, CPI (M) released a document titled *Urban Perspective: Our Plan in Urban Areas*. Writes Chakravarti, 'It's a revealing, sometimes chilling, blueprint of thought and possible action that wove together networking with the disillusioned, dispossessed and plain angry in Indian cities—counting among them residents of slums, labourers, incensed students and intellectuals, even allies among so-called civil society groups.'

Kerala can be very lucrative for the Maoists. It has contiguous forests with Karnataka and Tamil Nadu. It has a coastline. And it has educated people temperamentally inclined towards Communist thinking. There are reports that Maoists are building up their base in Kerala by smuggling weapons through the remote fishing ports in neighbouring Tamil Nadu.

However, the most worrying development is the Maoist outreach in the northeastern states of Assam, Arunachal Pradesh, Manipur, Meghalaya and Nagaland, which gives the movement access not only to Myanmar, but China too. All these states, with the exception of Arunachal, have their own insurgencies, some as old as independent India. Almost all of them have been supported by China at various stages of their incubation. The earliest Chinese connection to India's Northeast was discovered in the 1960s, when Naga insurgents went into China's Yunnan province through Myanmar with an appeal for help. For several years, China's PLA trained the Naga rebels in guerrilla warfare, in addition to supplying them with arms. Once a secure connection was established, other insurgent groups from Assam and Manipur flocked to China.

In the early 1980s, following Indian objections, as well as the possibility of improving ties with India, China closed the Yunnan facilities, outsourcing the training to the Kachin Independence Army, an ethnic insurgent group based in north Myanmar. Even after the Kachin Independence Army stopped supporting the northeastern insurgent groups after an agreement with India, the Chinese continued the supply of arms through private players based in Yunnan.

The insurgents were a two-pronged weapon in the hands of China. They kept the Indian Army and its paramilitary forces bogged down in counter-insurgency operations spread across six states (Assam, Nagaland, Manipur, Meghalaya, Mizoram and Tripura), and they spied on India for China. Many of the insurgent groups believe that China will wage a debilitating border war against India which will give them the chance to break free of the union.

The Government of India has been struggling to contain if not completely finish off these insurgencies. Given that there are so many of them, most officials don't even remember who is fighting for what. This has also come in the way of pursuing peace, because the demands of one group conflict with another. For instance, the Greater Nagalim that the Nationalist Socialist Council of Nagaland (NSCN) has traditionally demanded includes parts of Assam, Arunachal Pradesh, Manipur and Myanmar in addition to the entire state of Nagaland. Conflicting demands apart, over a period of time, most of these groups have splintered into several factions, with one entering peace talks with the Government of India and the other continuing with violence.

For example, of the two organizations waging a war for Bodoland, the Bodoland Liberation Tigers Force entered into a peace agreement with the Government of Assam in February 2003, but the National Democratic Front of Bodoland continues its violent struggle. It has been held responsible for the worst ethnic violence in recent times in Assam, including the communal riot in August 2012 which left seventy-seven people dead. Nearly 400 villages were scorched and over 400,000 people were forced to shift into 270 relief camps, the biggest such displacement in independent India.

The trouble with the Northeast is that these multiple insurgencies have been allowed to go on for so long without a sincere effort to find a political solution to their demands that there is now even a vested interest against finding a solution by some government agencies and others. In a conversation with the authors, former Home Secretary G. K. Pillai alluded to this saying that resistance to resolution comes from the most unexpected quarters.

'The union government releases funds to the security forces battling insurgencies in the form of Security Related Expenditure to meet small/tactical requirements from time to time. In addition to this, funds are also given for tactical intelligence gathering. Both are unaccounted. Then, of course, there are opportunities for smuggling, if not directly then by turning a blind eye to the smugglers and extracting protection money,' he said. Even routine economic activities like trade, infrastructure building, supply of foodstuffs and other fast-moving consumer goods rake in a lot of unaccounted money.

Pillai narrated an interesting story about a road that never was in one of the northeastern states. When he was the home secretary, he received a file with a proposal for the construction of a 10-kilometre road which would provide connectivity to seven tribal villages. Convinced of the usefulness of the road, he recommended its construction. A few days later, one of his junior officers brought him another file, about five years old, in which a similar sanction had been given; the road had not only been completed but had been inaugurated by the oldest man, 'gaon burha', in that cluster of villages.

'I smelt a rat,' recounted Pillai. 'I asked one of my youngsters to visit the area to see the state of the road. There was no road. There was no sign of any road ever having been there. There are hundreds of roads, culverts, bus stops and water pipelines that have been built and inaugurated in these remote, conflict-ridden areas where hardly any government official ever goes. But only on paper.'

According to Pillai, the most important job in these areas is that of a government contractor. As the last recipient of developmental funds released by the central government, he has to ensure that the supply chain remains adequately greased and foolproof. It's a well-oiled conveyor belt which keeps all the stakeholders happy and gradually carries the contractor to the position of a minister in his state. 'If you trace the background of most politicians in the northeastern states, you will realize that they started off as government contractors,' laughed Pillai.

Hence it was with great optimism that the Government of India signed a reconciliation treaty with one faction of the Nationalist Socialist Council of Nagaland led by Isak Muivah (NSCN-IM) in August 2015, leading many to believe that this would eventually open the door to peace. However, as the NSCN-IM had been demanding Greater Nagalim until as recently as July 2015, it is difficult to see how this will play out in the days to come. If Greater Nagalim is part of the treaty, how will neighbouring states respond? And if it is not, then how will NSCN-IM sell the treaty to the Naga people?

The confusion is compounded by the other faction of the Nationalist Socialist Council of Nagaland, led by S. S. Khaplang (NSCN-K), who lives in Myanmar, ostensibly under the benign watch of the Myanmarese government who currently oppose any treaty with India. In February 2015, when Khaplang had fallen ill and needed to be evacuated to a hospital from his hideout in Tago on the Myanmar-China border, he was apparently taken in a government helicopter to Yangon, the capital of Myanmar. To be fair to the Myanmarese government, at that time the ceasefire agreement between the Government of India and NSCN-K (signed in 2001) was in force, so the Myanmarese had no reason not to extend such a courtesy to the dissident leader.

Interestingly, the dissident leader used this time to stitch up a broad alliance with the insurgent groups of Assam (United Liberation Front of Assam-Independent and National Democratic Front of Bodoland), Manipur (People's Liberation Army of Manipur, CorCom, United National Liberation Front, etc.) and West Bengal (Kamtapur Liberation Organisation) under the broad umbrella of the United National Liberation Front of Western South East Asia (UNLFWSEA). Following this the NSCN-K called off the ceasefire. According to analysts, NSCN-K has been encouraged to do this by the Myanmarese Army, which has also allowed them to set up training camps in forest areas close to the Indian border. Apparently, the Myanmarese Army is doing this with Chinese approval.

The end of the ceasefire in March 2015 was announced by two successive attacks on the Indian Army and the paramilitary forces in March and April in which eleven soldiers were killed. The biggest attack in recent times was mounted on 5 June 2015 in Chandel district of Manipur, about 80 kilometres from Imphal. The insurgents attacked an Indian Army convoy killing twenty soldiers. Though the Indian Army carried out an operation against the NSCN-K on the Nagaland-Manipur-Myanmar border subsequently and claimed that heavy casualties had been inflicted on the group, the primary perpetrators remained at large. In September 2015, the National Investigation Agency (NIA) announced cash rewards on Khaplang and his 'military commander' Niki Sumi. Finally, in November 2015, the NSCN-K was declared a terrorist organization under the Unlawful Activities (Prevention) Act.

Meanwhile the government has been trying to mainstream another insurgent group, the United Liberation Front of Assam (ULFA). The chairman, Arabinda Rajkhowa, has been pressing for peace with the Government of India, and his second-in-command Anup Chetia's return to India from Bangladesh gave a boost to the peaceniks. The euphoria however has been tempered by the formation of UNLFWSEA (an umbrella organization of major Northeastern insurgent groups) by NSCN-K's Khaplang, in which the rebel ULFA leader Paresh Barua is said to be the second-in-command after Khaplang. According to G. M. Srivastava, the former director general of police, Assam, 'Paresh Barua is now under total control of the Chinese agencies who will not let him come back to India so easily.'

In a telephone interview with Rajeev Bhattacharya, a freelance journalist and author who spent three months in Myanmar travelling across the insurgent camps for a book, Barua said, 'The United National Liberation Front of Western South East Asia will take the struggle to a higher level. There will be a constitution, a flag and campaigns on a global scale will be stepped up… There is realization that our movement has not been able to achieve much since Angami Phizo raised the banner of revolt. That is why all groups felt the urge to come together. We will strike wherever and whenever possible. We also hope to be able to form a government-in-exile by the end of this year.'

The speculation amongst some is that a government-in-exile, irrespective of its potency, is the handle China is developing to counter the Tibetan government-in-exile in India. Even if nothing much comes out of it, the UNLFWSEA will keep India's northeastern flanks not only vulnerable, it will stop India from redirecting resources, both man and material, to other theatres.

At the moment, barring Sikkim, all the northeastern states are either entirely under the Armed Forces (Special Powers) Act or partly, as in the case of Arunachal, Meghalaya and Mizoram. The central government has deployed 403 companies of paramilitary forces, including the COBRA commandos of the Central Reserve Police Force in the region. This amounts to roughly 60,000 central government troops deployed in this region in addition to the state police and the army. A total of 116 battalions of various paramilitaries are currently deployed to combat the Maoist insurgency. According to the Ministry of Home Affairs annual report for 2015–16, this number is likely to increase. The sheer amount of manpower deployed to stabilize internal security (excluding J&K) is a huge drain on national resources, apart from the sobering fact that such a large proportion of India's population remains disaffected and outside the national mainstream.

It was not without reason that, during his ten-year tenure, Prime Minister Manmohan Singh called left-wing extremists the biggest internal security threat the country faced on several occasions. His government also realized that, left to their own means, the states would not be able to handle it. Hence, an annual chief ministers' conference, with the union home minister was instituted in 2005. The government sanctioned rapid raisings of the Central Armed Police Forces (CAPF), to be inducted in the Maoist theatre to aid the state police. The government also approved of an Integrated Action Plan under which specific development activities are carried out. To ensure greater efficacy and non-partisanship, the Integrated Action Plan, with its focus on programmes like roads, drinking water facilities, schools and primary health centres, was put under the Planning Commission (now NITI Aayog) instead of the home affairs ministry.

To be fair to Prime Minister Manmohan Singh, he had reservations about the usefulness of the Integrated Action Plan. Registering his doubts, he said that the plan must be more focused to promote 'development and inclusiveness', and must ensure the utilization of funds in a target-oriented manner. He noted that in the past government efforts have not yielded the desired results and did not empower the people in the manner envisaged. However, in the absence of other ideas, the Integrated Action Plan was rolled out for the eighty-two worst-affected Maoist-affected districts (subsequently extended to eighty-eight), with an initial allocation of ₹6,090 crore in 2011. By 2013, less than two years after the plan was rolled out, the government announced, without any supporting evidence on the ground, that local support for the Maoists had declined in the areas in which the Integrated Action Plan has been most effective.

Ironically, soon after this, a government-commissioned committee to investigate the funding pattern and budget of the CPI (M) reported that the

Maoists generate at least ₹140 crore annually from extortion alone—from industrialists and government functionaries alike. Add to this the income from illegal mining and forest produce and their annual budget rakes in up to ₹1,500 crore. Not all of this goes into the purchase of weapons and paying of salaries. They also run parallel governments in certain districts; and by some estimates, despite the brutality of their jan adalats (people's courts), pretty efficient ones at that. So Prime Minister Manmohan Singh's misgivings were not unfounded after all.

In the last ten years, the government has tried to address the Maoist problem through the twin strategies of economics and policing. The idea has been to hit at the hard-core Maoist cadre wherever possible, while pushing through development projects to win over the local people. Yet if this strategy was working, some evidence would have shown on the ground. Given that the Maoists continue to expand their area of influence in India reaching out to new districts, shows that the two prongs of 'hard economics and hard policing' have not delivered.

The problem is not at the policymaking level alone. That is secondary. The problem is in the failure to recognize the issue for what it is. Through the 1990s, the Government of India's attitude towards the Maoists was inconsistent and fitful. It treated left-wing extremists as a law and order problem. Sometimes it buckled under the Maoists' pressure, fulfilling their extortionist demands, and at other times it allowed the police to carry out extrajudicial killings, sometimes through proxy armed groups. As a result of this approach, the Maoists became local heroes, turning the state and the police into public enemies. Over time, the Maoist movement, distinct from the insurgencies in the Northeast, went through an evolutionary process, responding to the changing geopolitical situation. In the early years, the October 1917 Russian Revolution was the inspiration. Communist parties worldwide took their cue from the Soviet Union; hence the names were drawn from Marx and Lenin. However, by the late 1960s, the Cultural Revolution of China caught the fancy of the ultra-radical leftists. A large number of Communist ideologues and leaders started to find merit in the action-oriented approach of Mao Zedong. Mao's famous phrase 'political power grows out of the barrel of a gun', became the guiding principle of those who sought to bring about a revolution; China was the ready reckoner. And gradually, Marxist-Leninist as the suffix of the Communist parties gave way to Maoist.

The first radical party, the Communist Party of India (Marxist-Leninist), formed in 1969, had sprouted several branches by the early 1970s. One such party called itself Dakshin Desh (southern land), in allusion to China being the uttar desh (northern land). In 1975, the party changed its name to Maoist Communist Centre of India, removing all ambiguity about its inspiration and to some extent its support. Kanu Sanyal, one of the earliest protagonists of the armed revolt, the famous Naxalbari movement of West Bengal (because of which Maoist extremists are also called Naxalites), had in his authorized biography lamented that while he received money and equipment from the Chinese government, he got little respect from them, because the Chinese thought Indians were an inferior race.

Even though the Indian Maoists have evolved in strategy and thinking since those early days, the Government of India continues to look at their movement from the old prism of a corridor linking India with Nepal. When the Communist Party of Nepal (Maoist) started the insurgency in their country (1996–2006), and the Indian Maoists had started entering Chhattisgarh in big numbers after being pushed out of Andhra, many Indian analysts floated the theory of a Red Corridor connecting the Deccan plateau of India with Nepal, weaving its way through the Dandakaranya forests, though why the Indian Maoists would want a physical land connection with the Nepalese Maoists was never fully understood nor explained. In those years, experts expended their intellectual resources on warnings of the Red Corridor and how it would be disastrous if it was to come true. The argument was that the Red Corridor would facilitate easy movement of men and material between the two countries. Eventually when the Red Corridor did not physically come about (the Nepalese Maoists succeeded in forming the government in Kathmandu in 2008), it was hailed as a measure of success. Reams were written on how Indian Maoists were losing their momentum.

However, the corridor concept did not go out of favour. In 2011, senior police officers, especially in Chhattisgarh, started talking about the Maoists' forays into the eastern parts of the country through West Bengal, instead of going up north towards Nepal. According to them, the direction of the Red Corridor had now shifted towards Myanmar. 'Because of our concerted efforts and pressure on them, they have been trying to build a parallel corridor now on the border of Chhattisgarh and Orissa. The idea is to move eastwards, into Myanmar,' Vishwa Ranjan, director general of police, Chhattisgarh, told the authors in 2011.

This theory presumes that Maoists are a cohesive group of people who move from place to place. It is true that the Maoists slipped into Chhattisgarh from Andhra Pradesh when the Greyhounds, an elite government force set up to combat the Maoists, went after them. But Chhattisgarh already had a substantive Maoist presence, complete with their administrative infrastructure and model villages well before the cadre from Andhra came in. Similarly, states like Orissa, Bihar, Jharkhand, West Bengal, Karnataka, Punjab, Uttar Pradesh, Kerala, etc. have their own local cadre, who respond to local issues. They may be one cohesive party, with central leadership, but the cadre is spread all over in pockets; hence they do not need to move from one place to another to spread the movement. Even in terms of arms and ammunition, the sources and routes are diverse.

The other folly that Indian experts commit is to measure the success or failure of the Maoists in India by the template of the old revolutionary literature. According to this, the Maoists are bound to follow a three-stage doctrine for total revolution, which is based on Mao Zedong's writings.

- First, organization, consolidation and preservation of base areas, usually in difficult and isolated terrain;
- Second, progressive expansion by terror and attacks on isolated enemy units to obtain arms, supplies and political support; and
- Third, progressive control of urban areas (through encirclement of small towns) and destruction of the enemy in battle.

Despite the vacuousness of these theories, most of which remain in the realm of theories (and are only periodically applicable), the Indian security establishment has been reluctant to let go of them, probably because they accord well with the government's position of futility of talks with the Maoists because they do not believe in parliamentary democracy. Common sense, however, dictates that in this age of the Internet, no insurgent or terrorist group needs a physical connection to organize sections of the populace or link up with other groups. More to the point, a corridor is just an amorphous concept, not an inviolable structure which the security forces cannot breach. Wouldn't it make more sense for the Maoists to create pockets of influence throughout India in places which they can dominate to put pressure on the state? In the last ten years, they have forced the government to hastily raise Central Armed Police Forces and deploy them in the districts where their diktat runs. Even the Indian Army and the air force have been providing training and logistics support to the Central Armed Police Forces in counter-Maoist operations. Isn't that itself a mini victory of sorts for the Maoist—that they have forced the Government of India to deploy even its military against them?

Since the assessment of the problem is faulty, the remedial measures are faulty too. Take economics, for instance. The government presumes that the people are backward and poor, which is why they veer towards the Maoists, because they offer a panacea which the government has failed to do in all these years. Hence if 'development', in the form of roads, schools, primary health centres, industry, etc. reaches them, they will move away from the Maoist influence. On paper, this is a reasonable approach. On the ground, the reality is somewhat more complex.

Development, like modernization, is an abstract concept. It is also subjective. One person's development could be another person's disaster. For some people, the ability to live life of their own choice is enough; all they ask for is to be left alone. From their perspective, they are not asking for much—just leave them to their forests or land. Recognizing this vast population which desired to be left untouched, the Fifth Schedule of the Indian Constitution specifies that the resources in the tribal areas belong to the tribal people. And to ensure that this is not violated, the Constitution gives special powers to the state governor to oversee this, irrespective of the state government. Hence, if at all these areas are to be developed, the process has to be bottom-up and not top-down.

For this reason, the only sensible way to ensure that the nation has access to these vast resources to fuel its overall economic growth without criminalizing the forest dwellers, the government must make them stakeholders in the growth. The first step would be to follow the provisions of the Scheduled Tribes and Other Traditional Forest Dwellers (Recognition of Forest Rights) Act of 2006, which returns the right of forest produce to the tribal, both in letter and spirit. This implies that the Government of India should direct state governments to stop all economic activities, like mining and culling of forests, in the tribal areas until the people themselves are shareholders. Just as a farmer has control of both his farm and its produce, let the tribal have control over his bit of land and its produce, so what if it's a forest. The government should enhance his skills to 'exploit' his produce more efficiently. However, they should let the tribal population decide for themselves at what pace they want to develop.

Offering compensation or alternative land means nothing. First of all, most poor and illiterate tribals do not understand hard currency; when it is given in huge amounts it is even more baffling to them. In most cases, the compensation is siphoned off by predators. And relocation is not only traumatic but also renders the people both unemployed and unemployable. How can a tribal used to picking forest produce shift to agricultural land and start growing potatoes or rice or vice versa? Very few relocated people have thrived; most have been reduced to farm labourers or urban labourers—both unacceptable conditions for people who take pride in their independence.

The second step would be to reach out to the tribals, the Dalits and the poor in Maoist-affected areas through the people they trust—not the politicians, not the bureaucrats and certainly not the uniformed class. Instead of ridiculing and vilifying social activists and volunteers, the government must co-opt them into helping with development. This is extremely important for the simple reason that the Maoists draw their support and sustenance from these people. These people are the centre of gravity of the so-called Maoist revolution.

This is not an impossible proposition. Not only the tribal, even the most fanatic Maoist ideologue remembers Dr Brahma Dev Sharma (who died in December 2015), an IAS officer. When he was the district collector of the undivided Bastar region of Madhya Pradesh in 1969–71, he won the trust of the locals through his sincerity and the effort he made to understand their concerns. When the state government tried to push for the expansion of Bailadila mines, the tribals urged him, even though he was no longer posted there, to stop it because it was affecting their habitat. He successfully argued their case with his own political and administrative masters. He realized early in his career that both the tribals and the Dalits were extremely vulnerable against the full might of the government, hence to ensure that they were not exploited or made use of, it was important that the government heed their concerns and allay their fears. When he was chairman, National Scheduled Caste & Scheduled Tribe Commission in 1986–91, he raised the issue of forest management, the rights of tribals over forest produce and payment of wages for forest produce, all of which subsequently led to the amended Right to Forest Act of 2006.

Unfortunately, people like Sharma are the exception. The majority of government representatives are guilty of greed, impatience, intolerance and short-sightedness. For them, the vulnerability of the people they are responsible for simply offers an opportunity to subjugate and exploit. Sharma himself was frequently vilified by the political class for his 'sympathy' for the tribal; he was even physically assaulted once by the right-wing student's organization, Akhil Bharatiya Vidyarthi Parishad. Official disdain created the vacuum into which the Maoists moved and became the voice of the downtrodden.

As far as hard policing is concerned, there is a need to replace the word 'hard' with sensible and sensitive policing. In a country like India, the armed Maoists cannot be a match for the might of officialdom. Their strength lies more in the realm of the mind. The government insists that people support them out of fear, but that is not entirely correct. No insurgency can survive and grow on the basis of fear alone. Several news reports have appeared from time to time, quoting government officials that the Maoists have been trying to 'mislead' the urban youth. Obviously this is not being done through the gun, but through ideological indoctrination. Even the Maoists understand that more than mindless, weapon-wielding foot soldiers, they need ideologically committed people to take the movement forward. This is the reason that, by and large, Maoists do not deliberately seek confrontation with the police. They retaliate when challenged. As long as they are not challenged, they prefer to operate below the radar screen.

Instead of helping the state, 'hard policing' actually helps the Maoists. Most police operations inadvertently leave behind some civilian casualties, which further fans public anger, propelling more people towards those who are ostensibly standing up for them against the government, represented by the police. If the police stop pushing inside the forest areas in an effort to breach the so-called Maoist bastion, the violence level will obviously come down. Then even if the government doesn't want to engage with the Maoist leadership directly, it can begin a civil conversation with the people.

For some reason the Government of India, irrespective of party persuasions, has been most reluctant to talk with the Maoists, even though it has engaged in conversation with all sorts of separatist groups. In 2010, Home Minister P. Chidambaram made a half-hearted attempt at talks. A social activist, Swami Agnivesh, was roped in to initiate talks with the Maoists. In a confidential letter sent to Swami Agnivesh, the government offered unconditional talks to the Maoists as well as a ceasefire for seventy-two hours as evidence of its intent. Based on the letter, Swami Agnivesh engaged with some people, including journalists and managed to make contact with the senior Maoist leader and spokesperson, Azad.

The first betrayal by the government came when Chidambaram revealed the process in a television interview. The second betrayal happened when Swami Agnivesh was to meet Azad for a preliminary talk in the Dandakaranya forest. Even as Swami Agnivesh was trailed by the Chhattisgarh police and heckled by the villagers (ostensibly at the police's instigation) when he was on his way, Azad, who was being accompanied by journalist Hem Chandra Pandey from a hideout in Andhra, was arrested by the Andhra police. Subsequently, both were killed by the police in what many, including Swami Agnivesh, claim was a fake encounter. That the government was never serious about any talks was clear when the twin deaths were shrugged off.

In April 2014, as the General Elections got under way, CPI(M) spokesperson Abhay offered conditional peace to the government. In a formal statement released to the press, he laid down five conditions. One, the government should recognize the Maoist movement as political; two, it should lift the ban on it and its frontal, mass organizations; three the 'killers' of Azad should be punished; four, the government should stop police action against the people in remote areas under partial control of the Maoists; and five, all veteran comrades in prisons should be released.

A day later, the union government asked the CPI (M) to withdraw the boycott call of the elections and shun violence. And the matter ended. Since the offer came from the Maoists, the government assumed that they were on the back foot and the government could dictate terms. The irony that was lost on the government was that the Maoists or any insurgent group will always be on the back foot, because they do not have the resources, both man and material, available to any government. Despite this, the people that they represent deserve peace and a life of dignity. Therefore, governments need greater resilience and magnanimity to effectively help them, something which successive Indian governments have failed to understand. The most unfortunate part of Indian government decision-making is that when it comes to dealing with our own unhappy people, the government goes by the advice of the police and the intelligence forces, instead of concerned citizens. It labels those who can bridge the gap as sympathizers and frequently harasses or vilifies them.

It is unlikely that Modi's government (or any that follow it) will depart from the policies followed so far. If at all, it is likely to push harder on tough police action because it has to show economic results to realize its electoral promise. The sign of the times to come can be gauged by the BJP election manifesto, where unlike the vacillations of the previous regimes, it did not hold back from qualifying the near civil war-like conditions in parts of central and southern India as 'Maoist insurgency'.

If this is also the government's position (not merely a party's manifesto), then it should signal not only a change in the nature of the problem but also in the government's response. Insurgency is an armed rebellion against the state. It presupposes the support of the people to the movement. With this clarity then, the Maoist insurgents are not a band of criminals terrorizing people for monetary gains. An insurgency should imply a direct intervention of the union government, but the manifesto makes it clear that the government will make its plans in consultation with the states. Hence, the drivers of the anti-Maoist operations will remain the states. How that will be different from the policies pursued by the earlier government remains to be seen. However, given that the states worst affected by Maoist violence are also the ones rich in partially tapped natural resources, the union government's focus is likely to keep the Maoist insurgents outside the area of economic activity, for instance, mining. After all, a country with a limited manufacturing and export base has to depend upon exploitation of natural resources to drive its economy.

Hence, one of the early pieces of legislation that the government undertook in March 2015 was amendment to the Right to Fair Compensation and Transparency in Land Acquisition, Rehabilitation and Resettlement Bill 2013. The amendment created five categories, namely, defence, rural infrastructure, affordable housing, industrial corridors and infrastructure projects in public-private partnership. These have been exempted from the land bill, which means that if the land needs to be acquired for the above categories, the government doesn't need to get the consent from 80 per cent of the affected population, as the original bill proposed. It does not require genius to see that the government has effectively defanged the earlier bill paving the way for indiscriminate land acquisition.

Considerable research has been done to establish how the discriminatory and high-handed laws of India, promulgated by the British, have contributed to the criminalizing of vast sections of the dispossessed Indian population, gradually nudging them towards left-wing extremism in various forms. Ideologies apart, the mass of the left-wing extremist movement comes from these dispossessed people.

While the erstwhile Forest Act robbed the forest dwellers of their right to forest produce thereby rendering them helpless in front of corrupt forest officials, the old land acquisition act which dates back to 1894, created a mass of displaced people, evicted from their places of habitat and employment without adequate compensation by a state in a hurry to grow.

With the limited success of 'hard economics' and 'hard policing', the government brought in a surrender policy a few years ago, which basically offers money to the Maoists to surrender. Talking to the authors, the Additional Director General Police, Chhattisgarh, R. K. Vij, said that the government has increased the surrender amount by nearly five times in the last few years. Though he does not make the connection, it does get established when he also mentions that the surrenders in Chhattisgarh have increased. He says that while in 2012 and 2013, about thirty to forty Maoists used to surrender every year, in 2014, over one hundred have surrendered.

'There are three reasons for this,'Vij said. 'One, the Maoist cadre are fed up with violence. They have realized that there is no ideology here, only a fugitive life. Two, in addition to an attractive surrender policy, the credibility of the state police has increased a lot. Those who have surrendered send out the message to others that the police do not harass the surrendered Maoists. This is encouraging others. And three, living in the forest takes a toll on their personal life. Everyone wants to lead a normal life.'

The idea behind urging the extremists to surrender is to rehabilitate them in society. But what if those who accept money for surrendering go underground after a while? 'While theoretically this is possible,' he said, 'it is not easy to do so. We give them the money only after their antecedents have been verified and they have been thoroughly interrogated. We also keep an eye on them.'

Seen from a distance, this seems to be the kind of strategy that the government has pursued in various insurgency-riddled areas: using brutal force and money. Probably that is the reason why the efficacy of this strategy is limited. The government frequently pats itself on the back claiming success against the Maoists, but actually there is no way of determining whether the insurgency is really gasping for breath.

Since 2005, when the first chief ministers' conclave was held to evolve a concerted strategy to take on the Maoist challenge, different state administrations including the police forces have repeatedly been insisting, as we have mentioned earlier, that the Maoists are on the back foot. Yet, despite being on the back foot for several years, their network continues to expand and enter new areas. Moreover, their collaboration with groups outside India also seems to be strengthening. In a written reply to Parliament on 15 July 2014, Kiren Rijiju, the minister of state for home affairs, said, 'CPI-M clandestinely getting foreign funds cannot be ruled out. Inputs also indicate that some senior cadres of the Communist Party of the Philippines imparted training to cadres of CPI-Maoists in 2005 and 2011.' It will not be inappropriate to quote a verse here by poet Kaifi Azmi:

> Ab gareebi jaane hi wali hai mulk se
> Yeh sunte umr ke sattar baras gaye
>
> (Poverty is about to be eliminated from the country
> Hearing this, seventy years of my life are gone)

If the end game is to finish the Maoist menace, what does 'finish' imply? Periodic leaks from the Ministry of Home Affairs seem to suggest that this entails, 'flushing them out of their hideouts'. What will happen after they are flushed out? What if thousands of hapless tribals are flushed out as well along with the Maoists? What will happen to them? What if they are not part of the dallam (armed militia), only members of the sanghams (people's militia)? Will they be collateral damage? More to the point, there is no one hideout. They are all over the country, in small pockets and big. The only way to defeat it is to challenge it ideologically. Instead of the Maoists representing the displaced, dispossessed people, why can't the government represent these people? Instead of being the predator, let it become the preserver of those resources which the tribals hold dear.

The situation today is more critical because the present government comes with the baggage of an ideology which is in violent opposition to everything that the Maoists represent, from people to thought. The fiercely independent, and to some extent, insular tribals have their own religious beliefs and customs. While most of them are animists, some believe in ancestral and nature worship. They don't follow any organized religion. While the missionaries started work among the northeastern tribes of India, which involved religious conversion as well, Hindu proselytizing organizations started the same with central Indian tribes. Humanitarian work aside, they also worked on 'bringing them back' into the Hindu fold on the assumption that all Indians were Hindus once.

Over time the work of purely socio-religious groups like the Ramakrishna Mission, etc. was supplemented by political-social organizations like the RSS. In 1952, it started an organization focused entirely on the tribal population called Vanavasi Kalyan Ashram, headquartered in Jashpur (now in Chhattisgarh). One of its founding missions was to counter the missionaries' appeal amongst the tribals and to inculcate in them a feeling of Hinduism and nationalism. Today in most parts of Chhattisgarh, the only educational system available to the backward and the tribal population is run through the RSS's Ekal Vidyalayas (single schools) and Vidya Bharatis (Indian education). This obviously is possible because of political patronage.

Talking to the authors in 2011, Sunil Kumar, editor and publisher of an evening newspaper called *Chhattisgarh*, said, 'Tribals, and other backward communities, do not consider themselves Hindus. They follow their distinctive sects like Satnami or Raedasi, which are monotheist in nature. However, RSS considers all of them to be Hindu. Apart from imparting its brand of education to the children, it is also gradually introducing religious rituals like jagrans and mass pujas (prayers) in the tribal areas which were unheard of till a decade ago. Several tribal communities resent this. The bigger cause of friction is the RSS's cultivation of non-tribal communities in the tribal belt. In the last few years, the government has encouraged junior government functionaries, like revenue or forest officers to settle down in the tribal areas after retirement by giving them cheap land. While on the one hand their status accords them privileges that the tribals don't get, on the other hand, these people comprise the support base for the BJP government in the state.'

While this may be clever politics, it doesn't help in strengthening India's core, which is its richest area in terms of natural resources. This is the area which will fuel future economic growth but not unless the people are on the side of the government. In the national interest, politics will have to be put on the back-burner. Because time is not on our side. In April 2015, after a series of attacks in Chhattisgarh in which seven security personnel were killed, Rijiju told television channels that the government would review its strategy against the Maoists.

No country can grow with a hollow middle. The Maoist insurgency, alone and in collaboration with other insurgent groups, is sapping India. Not only is it retarding the pace of development, it is also forcing the government to spend huge amounts of money on internal security. And most importantly, it is bringing the border into the heartland.

THE HIGH SEAS

CHAPTER 21

LANES OF INFLUENCE

India started its journey in 1947 with a world vision shaped by an assortment of dreams. In the early decades, it worked in spurts because of the overwhelming enthusiasm and passion of the people at the helm. But over the years that vision began to crumble. Foundational aspects of the Indian world view such as the Panchsheel Agreement and the Non-Aligned Movement, both of which were the result of moral idealism, but which did not take into account either the present facts or historical precedents, did not live up to their promise. The former ended in bloody war in the Himalayas and the latter became increasingly irrelevant.

After the reality check of the 1962 war, Prime Minister Nehru, the chief architect of the Non-Aligned Movement, sought support, including military support, from the US. However, with Pakistan firmly in the US camp, India gradually started veering towards the Soviet Union without entering into a military alliance. Ironically both history and mythology show that the strongest or the most bankable partnerships are the military ones, which test the sincerity of a relationship. Seeking a non-aligned foreign policy was and remains a laudable goal. Unfortunately, the most basic requirement for the success of such a policy is military power. If one doesn't have that, one needs to offset the weakness with a powerful partner; for a price of course. Prime Minister Indira Gandhi understood this. Hence, when she decided to wage war against Pakistan in 1971, she got the Soviet Union to look out for India.

Despite hard lessons, India's political class has continued to believe in grandiose dreams about the country's greatness and clout despite little evidence to back up these illusions. This national pastime afflicts the Indian military as well, which, like the political class, has delusions of grandeur and geostrategic importance. Its so-called perspective plans (which are supposed to lay out its vision for the next fifteen years) are mostly in the realms of fantasy. The officers who make these plans make assumptions about the world and their own capabilities that suit their plans and not as they exist or are likely to change; most of the time they underplay the opponent's capabilities, overplaying their own.

The fact that even today, Indian Army officers like to say that the 1962 war (with China) will not be repeated is evidence enough that their vision for the future is not firmly anchored in reality. In August 2010, the authors visited Tawang in Arunachal Pradesh, which was the site of the Indian collapse against the Chinese in 1962. All the officers that the authors met spoke of the previous war and were certain that all things being equal, the Indian soldier would give a bloody nose to his Chinese counterpart. Unfortunately, neither they, nor officers today, take into account that all things are not equal.

Of the other two services which are platform and technology-intensive, the Indian Air Force has more or less a considered position on its capability and reach. There was a flight of fancy in the middle years of the previous decade when the growing economy led to an increase in the defence budget and the IAF started talking in terms of strategic reach and out of area contingencies, but gradually it was tempered to a more realistic worldview. Since the end of the last decade, the IAF has become reasonably circumspect about what it can and cannot do. Senior IAF officers even admit the limited utility of advanced landing grounds, activated by the IAF in the forward areas facing China, many of which have become operational in the last ten years.

In sharp contrast, the navy has been charting a different course; partly of its own volition, and partly because some analysts, both domestic and international, have been pumping it up as a source of power projection. Former Foreign Secretary Shyam Saran encapsulated this wishful thinking in his talk at the Lowy Institute for International Policy, Sydney, Australia. He said, 'India has increased its presence in the South China Sea and the Western Pacific. This is likely to continue as India plans to devote a larger proportion of resources to its navy in the coming years. India sees its naval strength as compensating, to some extent, the sub-continental dilemma...' Shyam Saran is not the first one to expound upon this idea. In 2008, George Friedman, author and founder of the US-based private intelligence corporation Stratfor, wrote, 'Given the isolation of the subcontinent, any further Indian expansion is limited to the naval sphere. A robust navy also acts as a restraint upon any outside power that might attempt to penetrate the subcontinent from the sea. These imperatives shape the behaviour of every indigenous Indian government, regardless of its ideology or its politics.

They are the fundamental drivers that define India as a country, shaped by its unique geography. An Indian government that ignores these imperatives does so at the risk of being replaced by another entity—whether indigenous or foreign—that understands them better.'

In theory this is plausible and perhaps desirable too. The sea fosters global thinking and cooperation, which is why navies also act as a state's instrument for diplomacy and hence work closely with the external affairs ministry. Since navies mostly operate in international waters, their engagement with forces of other countries is deeper than that of the land-bound services. The air forces too, despite the range of their platforms, have to operate within the national airspace. Hence there is theoretical merit in the argument that with the boxing in of India's land borders (flanked on both sides by inimical Pakistan and less than friendly China), the only scope for expansion is in the seas. In this context Indian experts are also fond of quoting Chinese scholar Professor Lexiong Ni, who in an article on 'Sea Power and China's Development' in the *People's Liberation Daily* wrote, 'When a nation embarks upon a process of shifting from an "inward-leaning economy" to an "outward-leaning economy", the arena of national security concerns begins to move to the oceans. This is a phenomenon in history that occurs so frequently that it has almost become a rule rather than an exception.' For this reason, and given the length of its coastline (nearly half of its land borders), many experts have started calling India an island nation, especially as its economy overwhelmingly depends on the sea.

Trade and aspirations notwithstanding, exploitation of any medium depends on the ground realities of that country, its national policies and capabilities. This is where the conflict between vision and dream come about. The first part of Saran's statement is incorrect and reflective of the dreams that we tend to dream, based upon an imagined past. Forget the Western Pacific, the Indian Navy does not operate even in the South China Sea. A single naval vessel calling at a port once a year cannot be said to be 'operating'. As far as the Western Pacific is concerned, the Indian Navy has participated in three exercises of the Malabar series with the US off the coast of Japan, in which Japan was an invitee. The Malabar exercises, at the initiative of the US, were originally envisaged as Indian Ocean exercises.

The traditionally inward-looking Indian policymakers were invited to look outside India's Exclusive Economic Zone by the US military when it reached out to India in 1991. Though Prime Minister Rajiv Gandhi tried to break the ice during his 1985 visit to the US, President Ronald Reagan took a while to warm up to India. The baggage of history was still holding him back. As we have seen, in 1991, Claude M. Kicklighter, from the US Pacific Command, offered India the Kicklighter Proposal for peaceful military cooperation across services. The first visit led to several others and eventually executive steering groups were formed between the military services of the two nations to discuss greater cooperation. Even though Kicklighter was from the US Army and initially sought army to army exercises, it was the naval cooperation which was the first to get off the block with the exercise, named Malabar, that we have referred to, taking place in 1992. Having bracketed India in the US's Pacific Command area of responsibility (AOR), as opposed to Pakistan which the US clubbed with the Middle East and hence put in its Central Command's AOR, the US found it more useful to engage with the navy compared with the other two services. One of the reasons was that the US Pacific Command is overwhelmingly a naval command.

The next two exercises in the Malabar series followed in 1995 and 1996, including one between the Indian Navy's MARCOS (Marine Commandos) and US Navy SEALS (Sea, Air and Land Teams). The fledgling cooperation came to a halt in 1998 after India conducted the nuclear tests and the US led the world in imposing sanctions against India. However, the 11 September 2001 attacks in the US changed the discourse once again. The sanctions were lifted and military cooperation was restored. As the global war on terrorism progressed, the Indian Navy's offshore patrol vessels, INS *Sharda* and *Sukanya,* escorted high-value US Navy ships through the Straits of Malacca, from Singapore to the Andaman Sea in the Indian Ocean, thereby creating additional camaraderie between the two navies. Gradually other countries woke up to the idea of exercising with the Indian Navy and a series of bilateral exercises with Russia, France, the UK, Singapore, etc. commenced.

As the US became increasingly conscious of China's growing interest in its maritime capabilities—with the PLA Navy's ships calling at ports in countries in the US neighbourhood, such as Brazil and Peru—it sought to intensify the cooperation with the Indian Navy. For the first time, in 2007, the Malabar exercise was held not on India's western seaboard from where it draws its name, but in the east. The exercise itself was broken into two phases. The first part took place near Japan's Okinawa Island in April, with Japan participating as an invitee in the bilateral drill. For the second phase in September, the exercise moved to the Bay of Bengal, roughly 350 nautical miles southeast of the Andaman chain of islands, close to the Straits of Malacca. Here, the trio were joined by Australia and Singapore. A total of twenty-six ships participated in the month-long exercise, including Indian and American aircraft carriers, in addition to a number of fighter aircraft and helicopters. The Indian Air Force's Jaguars also participated in the exercise.

Expectedly, China saw this polygonal collaboration as 'ganging up' against it. It objected. To mollify China, Malabar 2008 stuck to the script—India and the US exercised in the Arabian Sea. This was also the year China started sending its ships to the Gulf of Aden on anti-piracy missions, all the way across the Indian Ocean. The following year, Japan once again participated in the Malabar exercise. But keeping in mind Chinese sensitivities, the exercise was held off the coast of Okinawa instead of the Indian Ocean. This set the pattern. Whenever Japan—which remained an invitee to the Malabar exercise instead of a formal partner—joined the exercise, it was held in the Western Pacific, off one of the Japanese islands. In the Indian Ocean, only the US exercised with India.

In 2015, during President Barack Obama's 26 January Republic Day visit, India and the US agreed to upgrade the level of the Malabar exercise. Clearly the US was keen that Japan should become a permanent member in the bilateral engagement. India, not wanting to needle China, was reluctant. However, things changed. The Modi government formally invited Japan to join the exercise as a partner and the first of the trilateral series took place in October 2015 in the Bay of Bengal. Apparently Prime Minister Modi's decision came after Chinese President Xi Jinping ignored his request for defining the Line of Actual Control. In any case, of all the exercises that the Indian military has been doing for the last decade and a half, the Malabar series of the Indian Navy is the one which has been thriving, and primarily because of the US's enthusiasm for it. Year on year, the US has been fielding its leading platforms during the exercise from aircraft carrier to submarines and Special Forces, thereby forcing the Indian Navy to shed its traditional cautiousness. Whether the US wants to prop up the Indian Navy as a counterbalance to the growing Chinese assertiveness is debatable, but what is clear is that the US desires greater interoperability, which it hopes will eventually lead to commonality of missions.

The second part of Saran's statement talks of the continental dilemma. That's putting it a bit too mildly. The so-called 'dilemma' is actually a threat posed by two inimical powers, which have nurtured an all-weather friendship aimed at keeping India vulnerable and boxed in. The Himalayan and the Karakoram ranges are not mere walls which prevent India's influence to extend up north, they are two prongs that are holding India's security and development by the neck. Hence, no matter how tempting the promise of the Indian Ocean may appear, the truth is the Indian Navy can go only as far as the chains around its neck allow.

In December 2012, during his annual press conference, the Chief of Naval Staff, Admiral D. K. Joshi, told the media in reference to the South China Sea, 'We are not direct claimants to the area. What concerns us is the issue of freedom of navigation in that area. This should not get affected. Not that we expect to be in those waters very frequently, but when the requirement is there for situations where the country's interests are involved, we will be required to go there. Now, for example, the Oil and Natural Gas Corporation Videsh is operating in that area; it is carrying out exploration work in three blocks in the region. If a need to secure those is felt, the navy will have to do that.'

This was the navy chief's way of assuring the nation that the navy is prepared to safeguard national economic interests across the seas, just as the army chiefs tell their countrymen every year in January that the army is prepared for any eventuality. Unfortunately, National Security Advisor Shivshankar Menon was visiting China at that time, touching base with the new Chinese pecking order. Indian newspapers carrying the chief of naval staff's statement that the Indian Navy would enter the South China Sea to protect Indian assets in the region was not the publicity he was looking for. Even before the Chinese could react, Menon clarified to his hosts that the navy chief was led into making such a statement by the media.

Thereafter, according to the rumour mills, the government reproached the navy chief. This was almost confirmed when former navy chief Admiral Sushil Kumar wrote an article in support of the chief, criticizing the government for its timidity. As a result, a year later, on the same occasion, at the same venue, Admiral Joshi dismissed the question on the South China Sea saying, 'We do not operate in the South China Sea on a regular basis. So the issue of airspace cover does not concern us.' This was in reference to the news (especially in the US media) that China was building up an Anti Access/Area Denial (A2/AD) capability to enforce navigational restrictions in the South China Sea. The American experts argued that China was resorting to a slew of measures, including both weapons and psychological warfare, to prevent others from freely flying or plying through the contentious areas. Additionally there has been periodic speculation that just as China enforced an air defence identification zone (ADIZ) in the East China Sea, it may do so in the South China Sea as well to increase its airspace.

In December 2014, Admiral Joshi's successor, Admiral Robin Dhowan,

brushed aside the question of China during his press conference by referring
to global commons. 'There is a thing called global commons; and the
Indian Ocean is part of that. China has been operating in the Indian
Ocean region since 2008, primarily in the anti-piracy role to ensure the
safety of its merchant vessels. We should not see more into this,' he told
the journalists, refusing to get into a discussion on the South China Sea.

Diffident power is the term often used for India. Strategy experts aside,
even senior naval officers are fond of using this term to suggest that India
punches below its weight. In an informal conversation with the authors, a
vice admiral said that while the world thinks highly of the Indian Navy and
its capabilities, the Indians doubt it. According to him, one of the measures
of how highly the world regards the Indian Navy is that everyone wants to
exercise with it, or at least engage with it in some manner. This is a self-
delusionary statement, not because the Indian Navy is not good enough,
but because the international praise comes with a purpose.

During the Indian Ocean tsunami of December 2004, where the Indian
and the US navies worked together closely in humanitarian assistance and
disaster relief operations, such was the bonhomie between the two that
Indian naval personnel, especially medical personnel, frequently operated
from the US ships. The US commander-in-chief of the Pacific Fleet during
the relief operations, Admiral Walter Doran, in many subsequent meetings
with the authors warmly recalled the efficiency with which the Indian and
the US naval personnel operated together. 'It was all so simple. I picked
up the phone and spoke with [Admiral] Arun [Prakash]. And he said "no
problem." That is how special the naval relationship is and this is how well
we work together,' he said about the relief operations in the Indonesian
archipelago, in which the Indian Navy operated closely with the US and
Japanese naval forces, without the UN flag.

However, Indian naval officers at that time bristled at such compliments,
which they considered condescending. From their perspective, the Indian
Navy had been carrying out extensive relief and rescue operations on its
own, both on mainland India and the Nicobar Islands, which were severely
affected by the tsunami, so they didn't need a certificate from anyone! The US
did not comprehend Indian sensitivities, and frequently resorted to praising
Indian military personnel across services, probably in an effort to get them
to open up a bit more. For example, in an air exercise called Cope-India
2004, the US Air Force's F-15C air superiority fighters competed against
the IAF's MiG-21, MiG-29, Su-30MKI and Mirage 2000 in simulated
beyond-visual-range combat and high-altitude combat missions. After the

exercise, the US observers praised the IAF pilots with some going to the extent of calling them better than the US pilots. Of course, the young IAF pilots were pleased. But the senior IAF brass resented this as a 'big brother' attitude which smacked of 'encouragement of the junior'. Some also felt that this was the US's way of familiarizing itself with the Russian equipment used by the Indian military.

The curiosity about the Russian equipment persists. At the Defence & Security Equipment International exhibition in London in September 2015, one of the highlights of the show from India's perspective was the presence (at static display) of the Indian Navy's frigate INS *Trikand*, the last ship of the second batch of the Talwar class built in Russia. INS *Trikand* was in the UK just before the show, participating in Indo-UK naval exercise Konkan in early September. After the exercise, the ship sailed down the Thames River to London and was anchored at the show for the entire week, during which it remained an object of great curiosity. Visitors from different militaries, the defence business and media flocked to the stealth guided missile frigate for conducted tours. While this added to the swagger of the Indian delegation—the Minister of State for Defence, Rao Inderjit Singh, hosted a reception on the ship for select guests—the interest in INS *Trikand* was accidentally put into perspective by a French defence company executive who had booked a slot to visit the ship. 'We don't have access to the Russian platforms. This is a good opportunity to see their capabilities,' said the Frenchman when asked why he was excited about visiting INS *Trikand*. He grinned sheepishly, 'We still have the Cold War mindset.'

This in no way suggests that all global engagements are superfluous. On the contrary, the Indian Navy needs to enhance and intensify its operational engagement, both with its sister services (Indian Army and the IAF) and other navies. Unfortunately, grandiose statements, an exaggerated sense of self and lack of imagination mar meaningful exercises.

In February 2008, the Indian Navy launched an ambitious multinational cooperative engagement forum called the Indian Ocean Naval Symposium (IONS), taking the plunge into the world of naval diplomacy, where so far it had only followed the Ministry of External Affairs' lead. Inspired by the US-led Western Pacific Naval Symposium, IONS aimed to give a common forum to Indian Ocean littoral countries, in which they could discuss shared concerns. The first session held in New Delhi was inaugurated by Prime Minister Manmohan Singh on 14 February. There was a full house at Vigyan Bhavan, the venue of the symposium, where he laid out his vision for the gathering. In his concluding remarks, Singh said, 'I also hope that the Symposium will harness the remarkable diversity among us and reinforce the commonalities that bind us. It should provide a platform for discussions on how we can further accelerate the pace at which we are engaging each other. We need greater connectivity among us, not just in trade and commerce but of ideas, people and cultures.'

Defence Minister A. K. Antony was a bit more forthcoming in his address. Blending optimism with caution, he told member countries, some of whom were also members of the Western Pacific Naval Symposium (WPNS), 'I would like to exhort all present and future members of the IONS initiative to resist the temptation of trying to provide a prescriptive set of answers to a prescribed set of problems or challenges. I would caution them against seeking to import extra-regional template... explore a variety of regionally-relevant and regionally-sensitive solutions to problems whose very definition is given form and shape—not by extra-regional players often pursuing agendas of their own—but by the regional players themselves, acting in close consultation with one another and cooperating freely for the common good of all.'

The Chief of Naval Staff, Admiral Sureesh Mehta, to whom the credit for conceptualizing IONS went, took care to point out that IONS was a non-competitive forum. 'NATO and the Warsaw Pact were competitive constructs that pitted combinations of nation-states against one another. The changed realities of our present time provide both strategic and intellectual space for other forms of collective groupings of states that are arrayed not against one another, but against security challenges and threats that are common to all,' he said in a conversation with the authors before IONS.

Hence, though the initiative came from India, it was not India-led. This was probably IONS's biggest undoing and stymied its development. It is leaderless, hence directionless. The IONS has brought together disparate Indian Ocean countries, from India, Australia and France to Timor Leste, Comoros and Iraq. Then there are countries like Pakistan, Myanmar and Saudi Arabia with greater interests outside the Indian Ocean framework than within. Even more importantly, there is a huge disparity in the economic and military strength of the member countries, with some not even holding navies—they only have coastguards. The result has been dissimilar priorities and availability of funds. Though the IONS's charter magnanimously suggests that stronger members help the weaker ones organize biennial meetings, the leaderless symposium is simply drifting on the high seas.

Admiral Mehta had envisioned that commonality of interests would propel IONS towards interoperability and maritime domain awareness, where each Indian Ocean nation is able to speak with others in the same language, where training and exercising together becomes routine. Clearly this was an ambitious goal, born of a dream which wasn't thought through. India held the membership for the first two years, after which the baton was passed on to the United Arab Emirates.

In January 2016, Indian Navy chief Admiral Dhowan attended the fifth edition of IONS in Bangladesh, which then took over the chair from Australia. The theme for that edition was 'Fostering Partnership in IOR: Charting Course for Maritime Cooperative Engagement' and India presented a paper on humanitarian assistance and disaster response. Even after almost a decade, the engagement has not gone beyond seminars and essay-writing exercises.

The future of IONS was written in its first edition itself. An initiative this ambitious, where all navy and coastguard chiefs of Indian Ocean littorals collected, along with several defence ministers, and which was inaugurated by the prime minister, was 'disowned' by India's own Ministry of External Affairs. The term naval diplomacy suggests the participation of both the military and the diplomats. But at the inauguration, the Indian Ministry of External Affairs sent no representation. Ironically, Prime Minister Manmohan Singh's written address, which was distributed to the media, started by greeting the ministers of defence and external affairs.

Once the baton passed on from India, the government, probably on the external affairs ministry's advice, lost all enthusiasm for the project initiated by its own navy. When the new chief of navy staff took over, there was no motivation to build on the dream of the predecessor, because no institutional building blocks were put in place. The navy got busy with coastal security and currying favour with the government of the day, while the diplomats started talking about the South China Sea and Western Pacific.

In contrast, the WPNS holds multinational exercises—mine counter-measure exercise, diving exercise, counter-piracy workshop, and so on. It also works collectively to formulate behaviour on the high seas. The most recent instance of that is the Code for Unplanned Encounters at Sea which had been under discussion amongst the members for at least a decade. When the issue was first brought up in the WPNS meeting in Kuala Lumpur in 2012, China was the only country to oppose it. Its objection was to the word 'code' which it considered as having legal implications. However, two years later at the next edition of the forum in the Chinese city of Qingdao, all members unanimously approved it. The Code for Unplanned Encounters at Sea is a voluntary agreement which puts in place a procedure by which ships and aircraft of different countries communicate if they encounter each other unexpectedly. Certain English words and colour-coded flares have been agreed upon to prevent such encounters from accidentally turning hostile.

At yet another function in May 2013, this time the foundation laying ceremony of the Indian National Defence University, Prime Minister Manmohan Singh said, 'Our defence cooperation has grown and today we have unprecedented access to high technology, capital and partnerships. We have also sought to assume our responsibility for stability in the Indian Ocean Region. We are well positioned, therefore, to become a net provider of security in our immediate region and beyond.'

Being a net security provider entails a minimum of three conditions. One, complete awareness, or what the navy calls maritime domain awareness, of both one's area of responsibility (AOR) and area of interest (AOI). The navy's AOR is the Indian Exclusive Economic Zone, including the island territories of Andaman-Nicobar and Lakshadweep, where ideally, nothing should move without the Indian Navy's knowledge; the AOI is the area where the navy would want to wield some amount of influence, if not control. Many years ago, the Indian Navy decided that the entire Indian Ocean region, from the Gulf of Aden at the tip of Somalia in the west to the Straits of Malacca (straddled by Malaysia and Indonesia) in the east and the eastern coastline of Australia in the southeast would be its area of interest. Of course, the navy participates in international maritime events, such as tall ships races, port-calling and bilateral/multinational exercises well beyond the Indian Ocean, but this is the region where it aspires to wield influence. According to the naval script, in addition to the naval intelligence, surveillance and reconnaissance platforms—surface, aerial and space-based—this influence or relationship with the Indian Ocean region littoral states helps keep it in the picture about various movements and happenings in this area.

Two, the navy must have the capability and reach to be able to answer any distress call from any IOR state in the shortest possible time. But more on that later.

Three, the IOR states should look upon India as the net security provider. Enabling this relationship is not in the navy's domain alone. The navy can at best be the executor of the national policy, but the building blocks have to be put in place through a political process, combining politics with economics, diplomacy, technology and military. As of now, China is already on its way to assuming that role in the IOR. Already Chinese flotillas comprising ships, and periodically, submarines, are all over the IOR ostensibly in an anti-piracy role. Besides, the entire IOR is dotted with naval ports being built with Chinese assistance from Myanmar in the east to Sri Lanka in the south and Tanzania in the west, among many others, with Gwadar in Pakistan being the flagship. Given the political situation in the Maldives, China may be able to persuade the island nation to allow it to establish a submarine building and berthing yard there. Moreover, once the road part of the Chinese One Belt One Road project gets under way, the Indian Ocean will become China's playground. Not only because of the presence of the Chinese vessels, but because all the Indian Ocean littoral states have been co-opted as beneficiaries of the China Dream.

As we have mentioned earlier, given the future role and scope of Gwadar Port, India's proposal to develop Chabahar port in Iran, a mere 92.98 nautical miles from Gwadar, now appears to be a wasteful venture. With the growing criticality of Pakistan for the future of Afghanistan, in which Iran has a substantial stake, Tehran is hardly likely to allow India to use its port for any activity other than trade. Strategically speaking, today Chabahar is a dead investment for India. India might as well use that money to develop Karwar naval base, south of Goa, which geographically has the potential of becoming one of India's largest ports.

Coming back to the capability aspect, the Indian Navy now visualizes a 200-ship force of surface and subsurface vessels. At the moment, the most generous estimate of the navy's seaworthy platforms is less than one hundred, though for the sake of number-crunching, the navy insists that it has about 135 ships of all shapes and sizes. In this, submarines and surface ships which should have been retired years ago are included. At the moment, forty-seven ships and submarines are under construction. In Indian shipyards, construction usually takes much longer than scheduled so it is safe to assume that the navy is unlikely to reach the figure of 198 ships anytime soon. Given the levels of obsolescence, each new induction will see some de-inductions, keeping the growth static.

But the problem is not of numbers alone. In the absence of indigenous technology, naval modernization is overwhelmingly dependent upon imports. In an interview in July 2014, Admiral Robin Dhowan explained the indigenization challenge, 'To fully understand the challenge of indigenization, we must break it down to three different segments. The first is the float segment, which basically involves the hull or the structure of the vessel. In this, we have 90 per cent indigenous content. The second is the move segment, which is about propulsion. In this we have achieved about 60 per cent indigenization. The third segment is fight, and this is where we need to focus on, because this deals with weapon systems and we only have about 30 per cent indigenous content here. This is the area where we really need to work hard because for the navy, platforms are meaningless without weapons.'

This, of course, is the palatable truth. The reality is somewhat more distressing. We tend to call anything which is physically made in India indigenous, irrespective of where the intellectual property rights lie. Hence, even platforms which are assembled in India from semi-knocked down kits supplied by the exporter are called indigenous. Or systems being produced in India under licence from foreign vendors are called Indian. Specific to the navy, it is true that Indian shipyards are now able to construct the hulls of the vessels. But they still do not have the expertise to design those hulls in detail. Hence, we seek consultancy from foreign vendors in that area. As far as propulsion is concerned, we do not make engines across the equipment domain, whether it is land, air or sea. All engines are imported. This reality means that we cannot claim 60 per cent indigenization based on assembly of systems and subsystems within the country. The same goes for weapons systems. It stands to reason that a country which has not been able to produce a basic 'acceptable' rifle for its soldiers can hardly produce more sophisticated naval weapons like missiles, torpedoes, naval guns, etc. Incidentally, many of them (unless direct imports) are made in India under licence from European and Israeli manufacturers. If the Indian companies had the capacity to absorb technology then based on their five-decade-long experience of license-production, they would have been able to produce an Indian weapon system by now. This has not happened as yet.

There is another factor that holds back the navy from realizing its potential. And that is the Government of India's lack of faith in the military. This is the reason that even hard-core military matters are dealt with by the bureaucrats, or diplomats, in the case of the navy.

In May 2016, the US held the first Maritime Security Dialogue with India. While the US side included Vice Admiral Aucoin, the commander, US Seventh Fleet, David Shear, the assistant secretary of defence for Asian and Pacific security affairs, and Manpreet Anand, deputy assistant secretary of state for South and Central Asian affairs, the Indian side comprised only bureaucrats from the ministries of external affairs and defence. Not a single naval officer was invited to discuss issues like Asia-Pacific maritime challenges, naval cooperation and multilateral engagement.

With this reality, the Indian Navy is not the force the world imagines it to be or the nation expects it to be. With the additional responsibility of coastal security, and the necessity of power projection every once in a while through overseas deployments and to satisfy the urges of the Indian diplomats, the navy is hard-pressed to train and prepare for its primary role, which is war-fighting or as the prime minister said 'net security provider'.

Perhaps, the Indian Ocean Naval Symposium was the result of this consciousness, where other Indian Ocean region countries were being co-opted as a mechanism of collective security. Even today, IONS probably is one of the better ideas to reinforce India's centrality to the Indian Ocean region. Instead of a hands-off approach, India should wholeheartedly embrace the symposium. It should create a financial corpus in partnership with the stronger members of the forum, like France, Australia, UAE, Saudi Arabia and Singapore so that more intense interactions and engagements can happen within the forum beyond seminars and debates. The multinational biennial Exercise Milan that India hosts off the Andaman archipelago for Indian Ocean region countries should be incorporated into IONS, rendering greater width and depth to it. Not only that, a half-baked project like Mausam should also come under the IONS umbrella.

Touted as Prime Minister Modi's riposte to China's Maritime Silk Road, Mausam envisions reviving ancient India's maritime links with the countries where traders went following the monsoon winds. In September 2014, Foreign Secretary Sujatha Singh confabulated with Culture Secretary Ravindra Singh to give shape to the idea. According to the Ministry of Culture website, 'Project "Mausam" is a ministry of culture project to be implemented by Indira Gandhi National Centre for the Arts (IGNCA), New Delhi as the nodal coordinating agency with support of Archaeological Survey of India and National Museum as associate bodies.' The website further states, 'Project "Mausam" aims to understand how the knowledge and manipulation of the monsoon winds has shaped interactions across the Indian Ocean and led to the spread of shared knowledge systems, traditions, technologies and ideas along maritime routes.'

To be of any consequence, Project Mausam will have to evolve beyond theory and understanding of history. And since it is premised on maritime trade routes, it would make more sense if it is spearheaded by the Indian Navy, which can be both a flagbearer for the nation's military might as well as a cultural ambassador. After all, the ancient mariners were not mere traders; they were ambassadors of Indian power, culture, religion and economy. That is how cross-pollination of culture, religion, language, cuisine, myths and customs happened all across the Indian Ocean region. If Mausam rises to its potential, perhaps in some areas it can coalesce with China's

Maritime Silk Road. Today, any project that promises cooperation instead of confrontation has greater chances of success.

This calls for vision, overriding turf wars between government departments and ministries. If India wants to retain its primacy in the Indian Ocean, it will have to call upon all the resources it can muster—military, economic and cultural. Half-baked schemes will yield only half-baked results.

CHAPTER 22

ADRIFT ON THE HIGH SEAS

The Indian Navy had its Kargil moment on 26 November 2008, when ten terrorists sailed into Mumbai from Karachi. The post-massacre deconstruction suggested that trained by Pakistan's ISI (and some elements of the Pakistan Navy), the LeT terrorists were escorted up to the high seas on a merchant vessel by their handlers. When they neared Indian territorial waters they waylaid an Indian fishing trawler, massacred the crew and sailed close to shore, where they abandoned the trawler and got into inflatable motorboats, which brought them ashore. All through this journey of roughly 590 nautical miles, they did not attract any suspicion, at least not seriously enough to merit action (notwithstanding the subsequent claims of the intelligence agencies). In a region rife with smuggling, nobody bothered about a suspicious vessel.

Coastal waters and Exclusive Economic Zone became household terms after the 26/11 attacks in the country, which has historically viewed only the land borders with suspicion. Even without the disputed northern borders on the east and the west, India had faced foreign invasions only through the land route, the formidable Himalayas notwithstanding. The sea has always been the benign medium which brought about trade and cultural confluence. On India's west coast, the sea brought prosperity, especially in states with natural harbours, such as Gujarat, Maharashtra, Karnataka and Kerala; in the east, the sea was the chosen medium for ancient Indian kings to reach out to lands as distant as Thailand, Malaysia, Indonesia and Vietnam, both militarily and culturally.

Such was the comfort associated with the sea that post-Independence, when India started to build its pillars of progress, it chose to do so as far away from the land borders as possible. The majority of national assets—public sector undertakings, research and development institutions, space and atomic energy agencies were all built south of the Vindhyas.

The insecurity associated with the land borders also ensured that the nation remained ambivalent towards the utility of naval power. This was ironic. The colonizers, from the Portuguese to the British, all arrived on our shores from across the seas. Perhaps because they came in the garb of trade and not as marauding hordes on horseback, their subsequent machinations did not malign the sea. Preoccupied with land, India focused only on its land forces; and rightly so. The nascent nation had to fight a war to protect its land within a year. Hence, the earlier vision for the air force also envisaged it to be primarily a weapon in the hands of the army, to be used in its support when requested by the army. The navy was on its own; both in its operations and aspirations to resurrect the grandeur of the erstwhile Royal Indian Navy. Great nations have great navies was the recurring suggestion.

'In my opinion, Jawaharlal Nehru's grand vision required that the Indian Navy become a true instrument of our nation's foreign policy and be capable of dominating the region. Perhaps, this was the basis of India's desire to develop a two-carrier navy by 1960 and a four-carrier one by 1968. It was so articulated in the initial plan papers prepared for government approval,' wrote Admiral S. M. Nanda, the man who also showed that the navy could actually participate in warfare.

But the vision that he laid out was unrealistic. Plying hand-me-downs from the retreating British empire, the Indian Navy's status in the national scheme of things was largely ornamental; something akin to a middle-class family acquiring a fancy gadget to be displayed on special occasions as a status symbol. Even today, India relies on second-hand aircraft carriers. The most recent induction, INS *Vikramaditya*, has been bought from Russia after its navy decommissioned it.

After the 1962 debacle, when the government took stock of Indian military preparedness, the services were asked to prepare lists of their requirements. The navy made a projection for 130 ships. 'But no one in the government at that time accepted that the navy had any significant role to play in the country's defence. The focus was in finding the means to counter major threats emanating from across the land borders.'

Sure enough the next challenge again manifested itself on land and ended up in the mountains, with the navy wondering what it could do beyond ordering its ships to be on full alert. Funnily enough, when the Modi government commemorated fifty years of the purported Indian victory over Pakistan in the 1965 war, the Indian Navy was hard-pressed to produce at least one press release stating that 'the Indian Navy remained vigilant to ensure the safety of Indian ports, guard the country's entire coast line and above all protect India's shipping from interference by the Pakistan Navy'.

A nation's history, especially that projected by government's PR flack, is often exaggerated. But there was one period when the Indian Navy's history was quite glorious. When India and Pakistan went to war again in 1971, Admiral Nanda, its chief, who was determined to push his service into the collective consciousness of the nation showed everyone just how potent an imaginative and audacious navy could be. Within days of the war commencing, the navy got its frigates to tow three missile boats at night close to the Karachi harbour. In the first attack, on the night of 4–5 December, the boats sank a Pakistan Navy destroyer, a minesweeper and a merchant ship resting in the harbour. The second attack was carried out in similar fashion on the night of December 8–9. The casualties this time were a Pakistan Navy oil tanker and a couple of merchant vessels. The attack also destroyed the oil tank farm in Karachi, resulting in a huge blaze that continued for a week.

In addition to this unprecedented attack, the Indian Navy played a deterrent and supportive role on the eastern seaboard as well, lending more than moral support to the Indian Army and the Air Force. Since then, 4 December became the navy's coming of age day, celebrated every year as Navy Day with consecutive events planned in various naval stations spread over a week throughout the country.

If 4/12 gave wings to the navy's aspirations of becoming a symbol of national power, shaping the maritime environment in its area of interest, 26/11 grounded it. The Mumbai mayhem was blamed squarely on the navy. After all, what good is the navy if it cannot stop terrorists from entering India using a boat? Isn't it the navy's job to protect the country from threats emanating from the sea? Once these questions were asked in the media and tacitly accepted by the government, primarily to divert attention from its own problems, there was no let-up of pressure on the navy. It did try to convey its position through the media, but the horror of Mumbai simply did not give it the space to argue why—if at all the navy must take responsibility for the failure—it was the last link in the chain of control that failed and not the first.

The Kargil conflict, barely a decade ago, had brought home the glaring gaps in intelligence gathering/sharing and border management, in addition to a whole gamut of issues pertaining to how the political class perceived military power. It forced the government to look at national security in a holistic way, perhaps for the first time, and led to the creation of various committees under the Group of Ministers focusing on issues like intelligence, border management, and so on. This exercise promised to deliver in two areas, border management and intelligence (with higher defence management remaining in cold storage), and it was these two that failed yet again. After the hard-won Kargil conflict, the government of the day realized that there was a serious lack of communication between all the multifarious intelligence agencies—turf war, lack of trust and sheer pettiness that the other should not get the credit—hence the government created a twenty-four-hour Multi Agency Centre within the Intelligence Bureau to work as a coordinator between all the intelligence agencies like the Research and Analysis Wing, military intelligence, state police, paramilitary forces, and so on. The idea was to create a seamless network of intelligence flow from the collector to the interpreter, analyser and the executor. But the Multi Agency Centre remained stillborn. The individual personalities, egos and absence of executive direction collectively buried what could have been the beginning of inter-agency cooperation.

Border management fared a little better, but was hampered by an overwhelmingly landlocked vision. So while the government enunciated and executed the policy of one border one force on the land, the coastal border remained less than effective, even though the Group of Ministers had proposed a coastal security scheme, it remained largely ignored. Despite the surprising breach of the Himalayan frontier, nobody in the government seriously thought that the sea would be no protection either. An ad hoc arrangement existed between the Indian Navy, Indian Coast Guard (ICG) and the underdeveloped entity called the coastal police to guard what was vaguely called the coastal border of India. Since the whole system was amorphous there was no accountability. And nobody knew where the buck stopped.

How loose the structures were and how petty institutional leadership was, became evident when the blame game started between various agencies after the 26/11 attack. Deliberate leaks were fed to the media by the intelligence agencies shoving the blame onto the Indian Navy, which in turn defended itself by rubbishing claims of timely intelligence by saying that they were not actionable. Meanwhile, the coastguard offered its stock of excuses for why it was not to blame. And nobody even bothered about the marine police because clearly nothing was expected of them. Since everyone was on their own in this, there was no fixing of responsibility. The navy's plaintive plea, 'Do you hold the army accountable when the terrorists come by road, like in the case of Indian Parliament?' found no takers, primarily because as a nation, Indians, led by the political class, have never had any real concept of maritime security.

This was ironical because the importance of the sea, both for trade (the sea being the biggest medium of transportation) and asserting national power was increasingly becoming more and more pronounced. In 1991, as the Cold War ended with the collapse of the USSR, the US started to reach out to the so-called other camp. As mentioned earlier, Kicklighter, from the US Pacific Command, visited India with an offer for peaceful military cooperation and by 1992, the Indian and the US navies had started exercising together. In just about a decade after that, the Indian Navy was exercising with a host of other navies.

Yet the government chose to conflate the coastline with the maritime border. Such is the preoccupation with land that the concept of a border ends where the land ends. The Ministry of Home Affairs, which lists the total length of India's borders in its annual report, only mentions the coastline (7,516.6 kilometres) and not the maritime border. Apparently no government has ever undertaken the exercise to measure India's maritime border, which lies 12 nautical miles further out from the coastline. But calculating the maritime border is not as simple as measuring the linear length along the coastline. The maritime border takes into account all the promontories along the coastline, drawing a line from one to another to create a baseline. A similar exercise would need to be carried out in the island territories. Instead of the coastline, the furthest landmass jutting into the sea would be taken as the baseline. From this baseline, 12 nautical miles into the sea would be India's territorial waters, which for all regulatory purposes would be considered a part of the landmass, as Indian law would apply in this region. Two hundred nautical miles beyond the territorial waters lie the country's Exclusive Economic Zone, beyond which are the high seas, which are treated as global or international commons, to be used by all for free transit.

Just as the army does not guard the land borders, which are the responsibility of the border guarding forces like the Border Security Force, Indo-Tibetan Border Police and Sashastra Seema Bal, the maritime borders, that is, the area between 12 to 200 nautical miles from the Indian coastline, were the responsibility of the Indian Coast Guard. The belt within 12 nautical miles was to be secured by the marine or coastal police of various states. The Indian Navy was meant to operate beyond the Exclusive Economic Zone.

However, as the ten Pakistan-trained terrorists held Mumbai to ransom for nearly three days, the shocked nation realized that Maharashtra's coastal police were next to useless, despite the supposed raisings a few years ago. A handful of coastal police stations were lying in disuse. Apparently the portly policemen assigned the coastal duties suffered from seasickness when asked to man the patrol boats! Over the next few months, more skeletons tumbled out. The coastal states of India had no concept of security. Most fishing trawlers and small boats were unregistered or were operating with expired licences. There were hundreds of unaccounted-for small, semi-developed ports, which over time had become hubs for smuggling and landing of contraband. Even more shockingly, the navy, the Indian Coast Guard and the various state governments had no formal mechanism of talking to one another. Everything had to be routed through New Delhi. In its report submitted to the US Senate committee, the Federal Bureau of Investigation noted that the Indian response to the Mumbai terror attack was hamstrung by lack of coordination between 'different levels of the government' and the local police's inadequate training and lack of 'powerful' weapons. 'Unified command system is of paramount importance if governments are to respond to terrorist attacks quickly and effectively.'

Even as the government ordered a holistic review of maritime security, with the suggestion of appointing a maritime security advisor being tossed around, the comatose Multi Agency Centre was revived. All intelligence agencies were asked to depute a representative to the centre. The union government also created the National Investigation Agency (NIA) specifically for terrorism-related incidents. Despite being the Central government's agency, states were asked to cooperate with the NIA whenever needed. The defence ministry drew lines of jurisdiction to fix responsibility for the future.

The navy was made the 'designated authority' responsible for complete maritime defence, with both coastal and offshore security under its control. The ICG was no longer to patrol the Exclusive Economic Zone. Instead it was told to focus on the territorial waters under the navy's supervision. 'Post 26/11, the Coast Guard has been given additional responsibility of coastal security in India's territorial waters, i.e., up to 12 nm from our coastline,' Director General, ICG, Vice Admiral Anil Chopra said in an interview. In addition to this, yet another effort was made to overhaul the moribund marine police, by bringing them closer to the shore. If at all they were to venture out to sea, they were to go only up to three to four nautical miles in a patrol craft, money for which was allocated and various state governments raced to procure them from India and abroad.

Making these announcements in February 2009, union Defence Minister A. K. Antony added, 'The navy will control all naval and coastguard joint operations. This will ensure that the assets are optimally deployed and there is synergy between the two organizations.' To facilitate this, a national command, control, communication and intelligence (NC3I) network was to be set up to ensure smooth coordination between the navy and the coastguard. Joint operation centres were to come up in Mumbai, Kochi, Visakhapatnam and Port Blair. The ICG was also allocated nine additional stations to be integrated with coastal police stations at Karwar, Ratnagiri, Vadinar, Gopalpur, Minicoy, Androth, Karaikal, Hut Bay and Nizampatnam. New posts of additional director general and three deputy director generals were sanctioned in addition to a 20 per cent increase in ships and 30 per cent increase for shore support. Basically, all services were brought closer home, thereby effectively clipping the Indian Navy's recently acquired wings.

If at all one needed evidence of a fearful nation, unsure of its own potential, this was it. Everyone, including the military, was asked to close in towards the coastline. How pervasive this hemmed-in mindset had become could be gauged by the statement of the Chief of Naval Staff, Admiral Robin Dhowan, during his annual press conference in December 2014. Calling coastal security 'work in progress', he said with a twinge of regret, 'After all, we cannot put a fence on the sea.' He then expounded on the initiatives that the navy had undertaken on its own to ensure better surveillance of the coastline. During the monsoon of 2014, the navy sent out its soldiers to map all coastal villages. 'My boys visited every village along the coast by whatever means possible, foot or a two-wheeler to reinforce an eyes and ears concept among the local population. We also want to win the trust of the locals so that they understand that we will not come in the way of their livelihood and that they can share any suspicious information with us without fear,' said the navy chief.

According to Admiral Dhowan, there are 250,000 registered fishing boats in India, and over a period of time biometric cards have been issued to these fishermen. 'We have also fitted transponders on boats of a certain size,' he said. In addition to these, the coastal surveillance network now has seventy-four automatic identification system receivers and an overlapping chain of forty-six coastal radars. All these, including the naval communication satellite Rukmini, now send their signals directly to the Information Management and Analysis Centre (IMAC) located in Gurgaon, which was inaugurated by Defence Minister Manohar Parrikar in November 2014. The information received at IMAC would give the navy a real-time picture of what moves where in the Indian territorial waters. In addition to fishing trawlers, the IMAC would also hopefully keep track of merchant vessels approaching

Indian shores. Gradually the network of radars would increase in density.

If the navy is doing this then what is the Indian Coast Guard—which has been given the direct responsibility for coastal security—doing? Shouldn't it be mapping the villages, building interdependent relationships with the border population? Brushing aside the ICG, Admiral Dhowan said, 'There are sixteen agencies, both state and Central, involved in coastal security.' While operationally the navy has the overall responsibility, at the command level a National Committee for Strengthening Maritime and Coastal Security has been instituted under the cabinet secretary which oversees the big picture.

Ideally the Indian Navy should manage the big picture with the Indian Coast Guard carrying out everyday operations. But the navy's fondness for coastal security has grown over time to such an extent that it is completely hands-on, leaving the ICG with a mere support role. In November 2015 the navy chief told select editors in an informal interaction inside his office in South Block, 'Coastal security is at an all-time high.'

But it wasn't always like this. Coastal security was a responsibility the navy accepted with a measure of reluctance and caution, conscious of the fact that this new responsibility came at a cost. And the cost would be paid by its primary and secondary roles: military preparedness for war and naval diplomacy. Its other two roles include constabulary and humanitarian assistance and disaster relief. Vice Admiral Sanjeev Bhasin, former flag officer commanding-in-chief, Western Naval Command (2009-11), based in Mumbai, said in an interview in August 2011, 'There was a bit of confusion about how to define the roles of the Indian Navy which was overall responsible for coastal defence and the ICG in its new avatar being responsible for coastal security. The understanding that I had was that the state police and the ICG would take on this job of normal patrolling for policing purposes to see there was no smuggling, landing of contraband and human trafficking along the coast. The Indian Navy would have no role in this.'

Things did not turn out the way the navy thought they should have. Just as the Government of India has little faith in the Central Reserve Police Force (despite calling it its lead counter-insurgency force while it continues to entrust counter-insurgency operations in J&K and the Northeast to the Indian Army), it has minimal confidence in the capabilities of the coastguard and none in the marine police. Since Pakistan's hand was spotted behind the 26/11 attacks, the government had to deploy its most potent force to prevent future Mumbai attacks. It never crossed the minds of the policymakers that just as there was no Kargil II, there may not be a Mumbai

II. Pakistan may think of another way of hurting India.

The initial government pronouncements were that the coast must be made impregnable even though senior naval officers argued that it was not possible. 'Coastal security is not like a polythene bag inside which you put India with all the bad people remaining outside,' a senior naval officer posted in Mumbai told the authors. According to him, surveillance and detection is a multi-asset, multilayered job. Only with a combination of shore-based, sea-borne, air-borne and space-based platforms and systems can one hope to get a comprehensive picture of what is happening or who is going where in the sea. But even when you get the complete picture, there is still no guarantee that your coastal borders will remain impregnable. 'After all, almost the entire land border of India has multilayered fencing with sensors. It is also vigorously patrolled. Yet there are frequent incidents of ingress (by terrorists, smugglers, illegal immigrants, and so on) throughout the length of the border fence, and not just in Kashmir,' he pointed out. 'How does that happen?'

The International Hydrographic Organization, which delimits the seas and ocean, puts the area of the Arabian Sea at roughly 38.6 lakh square kilometres. Since India considers the entire Arabian Sea as its area of interest, the job of patrolling (as well as sanitization) of this area is the responsibility of the Western Naval Command, which is the Indian Navy's largest command holding the maximum number of frontline warships and aircraft assets. A medium-sized ship's radar can detect an average-sized ship up to 20 nautical miles, which means an area of about 1,250 square nautical miles. A small ship's radar can detect other vessels up to a distance of 5 to 6 nautical miles. If the Indian Navy was to rely entirely on sea-based assets for surveillance, then it would need more than 900 ships to cover the entire Arabian Sea. Let alone the Western Naval Command, even the Indian Navy does not have such numbers and does not envisage having them. The most ambitious plan today talks of a 198-ship navy by the next decade, whereas at the moment, the navy has less than a hundred seaworthy ships of all sizes.

The story of the airborne platforms is only slightly better. Despite the concept of maritime domain awareness being in circulation for several years, the Indian Navy's air surveillance and reconnaissance capabilities are hugely inadequate, to put it politely. Though the induction of the long-range maritime reconnaissance aircraft P-8I has helped, they are not enough. Acquisitions for medium-range maritime reconnaissance aircraft and helicopters have been in the pipeline for a long time. The saga of shore-based coastal radars is even sorrier. They are neither enough nor very efficient. Most importantly, if the navy allocates its capital budget to build up its capabilities for coastal security, it will have that much less money for its conventional role. Realizing this, the navy deployed its existing conventional capabilities on the constabulary role, in an effort to ensure that the new acquisitions pertain to its primary role.

In an interview in July 2013, navy chief Admiral D. K. Joshi said, 'Not only our ships, but aircraft, unmanned aerial vehicles, etc. are stressed. What we need is efficient planning so that we retain the focus on our principal job.' Making a reference to the expansion and modernization of the Indian Coast Guard as well as the state marine police forces, he hoped that 'in the next few years, this will free the larger naval ships from the security role'.

Perhaps figures from the last few years were weighing on his mind. Since August 2010 all frontline warships of the Western Naval Command had been patrolling (in a constabulary role) for nearly 280 days in a year. In addition to needless wear and tear of expensive platforms, this additional responsibility was distracting the navy from one of its key operational objectives, which is to remain relevant to the land battle with Pakistan. Vice Admiral Bhasin feared as much and maintained that the navy needed to hand over the responsibility of coastal defence to the Indian Coast Guard at the earliest. 'The Indian Navy will be diluting its primary role of being a blue-water navy, if it continues to deploy its capital ships and aircraft on the policing role. This will be at the cost of exercising with friendly navies, and the need to refine its ability to network and concentrate on cooperative engagement capability. This will take a toll on expensive frontline warships which have limitations of engine hours, and if these are used at low speed they will have their own set of problems.'

The key to the navy's plan of gradually offloading the job of daily monitoring of the coastline to the ICG was the Coastal Security Bill, which the navy had prepared and submitted to the government by the end of 2013. The bill that was to delineate jurisdiction and fix responsibilities for all stakeholders to coastal security (Indian Navy, Indian Coast Guard, governments of the coastal states, ministries of shipping, environment, petroleum and natural gas, and the department of fisheries) was to be steered by the Ministry of Home Affairs as border security is its responsibility. Even seven years after the 26/11 attacks, the bill has not been tabled in Parliament.

For obvious reasons, the navy is keen to see that the bill is passed as an act. 'Who will do what, who is responsible for what and what are the powers that can be given to these agencies are all mentioned in the bill,'

Admiral Dhowan said in an interview in May 2015. More importantly the bill also gives punitive powers in small measures to the security/military forces for raiding or impounding suspect vessels at sea. The army in counter-insurgency ops operates under the Armed Forces (Special Powers) Act and can therefore carry out cordon and search operations or detain suspects or even kill in 'self-defence' without a legal consequence; the navy does not have this privilege. It can report suspicious movement but can only act when authorized through the proper channels (some of these even involve the Ministry of External Affairs), lest its suspicion turns out to be unfounded.

Even though the parliamentary committee on defence observed in 2015 that the Coastal Security Bill needs to be passed at the earliest, it is not a priority with the government. Since the navy is willing to flog its personnel and platforms on the job, why should the government trouble itself with policymaking? Moreover, from the government's perspective, the present arrangement is working successfully because no other Mumbai-like attack has taken place. Until a couple of years back the navy did appear worried about coastal security taking precedence over its primary role. However, with the government now identifying terrorism as one of the main military threats, it has given the navy a definitive reason to continue with the present arrangement. Like the army, it also offers an opportunity for public projection. The so-called silent service, which traditionally operated hundreds of miles off the coastline, is now the most visible service.

So in many ways, 26/11 has been the navy's Kargil moment. It has given a raison d'être to the service, which was always considered last after the Indian Army and the Air Force. So much so, there is speculation that in the coming decade, the navy's share of the defence budget would increase substantially at the cost of the other two services. Naval empire-building will commence because, as the chief himself has said, the sea is no longer benign. Just as on the land, there are non-state actors that the navy must factor in. In an ideal world, this wouldn't have been worrying. After all, if the army has perfected the job of the paramilitary, why should it matter if the navy is doing it too? The problem, however, is that the army is a personnel-intensive service, the navy is platform-intensive. If a ship worth ₹2,500 crore, that takes over five years to build, is deployed on a job that can be done by a smaller vessel less than half its cost then somebody needs to question the return on investment.

Even more worrisome is the growing maritime environment in India's neighbourhood, where China is no longer a mere visitor but a stakeholder too. Chinese-built submarines, including nuclear submarines, frequently operate here. Under the One Belt One Road programme, the ships from China or owing allegiance to China would be operating and anchoring all around India, from Pakistan's Gwadar to Sri Lanka's Hambantota to Bangladesh's Sonadia and Myanmar's Maday Island.

In a stroke of brilliance in Kargil in 1999, Pakistan trapped the Indian Army in internal security duties, thereby gradually whittling away its conventional edge. Handicapped by its lack of imagination, the army further hemmed itself in by building a fence all around itself. Nine years later, Pakistan struck again. The Mumbai attack helped the enemy in two ways. Not only did it cost us the lives of hundreds and damage worth crores, as well as a huge blow to our self-esteem and notions of defence preparedness, it succeeded in deflecting the Indian Navy from its real role, which is conventional war, and making it lament the impossibility of building a fence in the sea. What is most disturbing is the fact that a country that India expected would implode anytime has forced it to deploy the best of its resources to counter an 'invisible enemy'. What could be more emasculating than that?

THE WINNING STRATEGY

'India should grow from a balancing power into a global player,' Prime Minister Narendra Modi announced enthusiastically on the completion of one year in office in May 2015. The rather more circumspect foreign secretary, S. Jaishankar, wondered whether 'India should remain a balancing power or aspire to be a leading one?'

Both the prime minister and the country's top diplomat believed that given India's potential, size, geography and negotiating skills, the dividing line from one to the other could be crossed. A growing economy, and 'the confidence to speak with major powers—the US and China—as an equal', as the prime minister put it, were apparently all that India needed to influence events beyond its geographic borders.

Both these assumptions appear misplaced. As we have tried to show throughout the book, India lacks the military power required to compel or deter adversaries (Pakistan and China), and to exercise coercive diplomacy through an assertive foreign policy. To build military power, India requires military reforms. It also needs a plan which places an equal premium on a peaceful neighbourhood and partnership diplomacy (Act East, Think West policy) with major powers and friendly nations.

Such a plan, however, should first make India's home secure before it ventures out into the Indian and Asia-Pacific Oceans. The argument that India can balance China only by close ties with the US will no longer work. For instance, in 2005, when India signed the framework agreement with the US, China had agreed to 'political parameters and guiding principles' as the basis for a border resolution with India. In 2016, an assertive China which has locked horns with the US in South China Sea would do just the opposite. It might increase military pressure through Pakistan on the disputed borders where India would have to fend for itself.

For this reason, China and not the US should be the main focus of India's foreign policy. In short, here is what India must do to minimize the military threat from the Pakistan-China combine to become a leading power.

MILITARY REFORMS

Before enumerating the various steps that are needed to build military power, it is necessary to make two assertions, the reasons for which have been discussed at length. One, a possible war between India and Pakistan or India and China will be a conventional one. While the fact that all three possess nuclear weapons is a reality that needs to be factored into the overall military plan, there are military objectives that can be achieved that are short of a nuclear confrontation. And two, the idea of fighting a two-front war that the Indian military leadership talks about is, to say the least, suicidal. It will be well-nigh impossible to fight and defeat two nuclear-armed adversaries.

Military reforms must take into account an understanding of the adversaries, technology and nature of warfare. China is an unusual adversary which welcomes disequilibrium in the world and gives importance to deception in its foreign policy. In his book, *World Order*, Henry Kissinger writes, 'In July 1971—during my secret visit to Beijing—Zhou Enlai summed up Mao's conception of the world order by invoking the Chairman's claimed purview of Chinese emperors with a sardonic twist: "All under heaven is in chaos, the situation is excellent."' Given that Mao's portrait dominates Tiananmen Square in Beijing, the Chinese leadership endorses Mao's thinking wherein each cycle of less equilibrium and more disequilibrium brings a nation to a higher level of development.

So far as India is concerned, this should be taken to mean that China, which holds most of the cards on the disputed border, would neither settle the issue peacefully nor renege on its claims. China has no problems with a blow-hot-blow-cold relationship with India as long as its strategic objectives are met. The Pakistan Army, which controls Pakistan's India policy, remains fixated on the Kashmir resolution. Until this is settled, the possibility of war exists.

In a top-down approach, India's political leadership must first decide on the strategy to settle or make the Line of Actual Control with China and the Line of Control with Pakistan incident-free. Only this will ensure a peaceful neighbourhood for India. The foremost military reform, therefore, should be to make the defence minister, and not the defence secretary, responsible for India's defence. Once he assumes charge, joint-ness at the strategic level—which is a critical need—would become easy to accomplish. Bringing the defence services' chiefs constitutionally into the policymaking loop, reviewing the office of the National Security Advisor, and incremental steps to get the three services (army, air force, navy) to work together would follow.

There would be an added military gain: since political objectives and military aims to be achieved by military power would become clear, it would spur the defence services to review their force levels (or combat capabilities) holistically. The army could reduce its manpower, the air force could review its combat aircraft authorization, and the navy could review its roles and missions to balance its acquisitions.

Since military diplomacy is an essential feature of military power, the military leadership should become an integral part of diplomacy. Without clarity on operational matters (which diplomats do not have) it would not be possible to conduct meaningful military confidence building measures with our hostile neighbours, especially Pakistan. Because nuclear arms control and reduction must follow conventional arms control with Pakistan, it is vital that military leadership take the lead. Similarly, naval officers should lead naval diplomacy. With this in mind, the Indian Navy created the office of assistant chief of naval staff (foreign cooperation and intelligence) in 2005. With diplomats not willing to share space with the military, this did not go far.

India's nuclear policy needs to be reviewed, especially the delivery systems. Even when nuclear weapons are not meant for war, the need for tactical nuclear weapons with their command and control held firmly at the strategic level should be considered. Since both Pakistan and China have this capability, India too should have it. There is also the need to revisit the minimum nuclear deterrence concept, and the air component in the triad (involving air, land and underwater delivery systems). Given its paucity of combat aircraft, India would do well to review the triad. Until the underwater delivery component acquires the desired assurance level, the focus should be on ballistic and cruise missiles as nuclear delivery systems.

Regarding ballistic missiles, when India's security requirements are met with the 5,000-kilometre Agni-5, why does it need the longer range Agni-6? Since cruise missiles are a better delivery option than ballistic missiles, India should focus on them. Most of all, there is the need to technically review the indigenous ballistic missile defence program. Once India buys the Russian S-400 air defence missile system, the technically-reviewed indigenous ballistic missile defence system as well as other ground-based air defence equipment (the surface to air Akash missile) should become a part of it.

TECHNOLOGY ENHANCEMENT

India began its quest for high-end technology from the US in 1985. Three decades later, it has gained little and perhaps lost a lot. While the Next Steps in Strategic Partnership started in January 2004 between India and the US showed promise for India, its follow-on, the July 2005 India-US framework agreement, did not help India much. Focused on non-proliferation, the latter—between July 2005 and the signing of the October 2008 civil nuclear deal—helped the US's strategic goal of keeping India's nuclear arsenal in check. The promised high-end technology did not come to India because it is unlikely the US will share this know-why even with its closest allies. That said, the two nations have good possibilities of military cooperation for common strategic goals.

Russia could be a better bet for India to get technology for a number of reasons: it is a time-tested relationship that both sides are comfortable with, the Indian military has up to 70 per cent of Russian equipment with the possibility of acquiring even more sophisticated armaments and equipment in the future; Russia has helped India with its nuclear reactors; India is unlikely to steal Russian technology for reverse engineering without paying for it; and, unlike the US, the Russian president would be able to authorize the obtaining of sophisticated technology more easily than the US president even if the latter were inclined to part with it. Unfortunately, suspicion owing to geopolitical circumstances—Russia's growing military ties with Pakistan—has crept into the bilateral relationship. From Moscow's perspective, India's growing strategic and military ties with the US might compel it to reassess its traditional comfort quotient with Delhi. Russia worries about its military technologies leaking to the US.

DEFENCE INDUSTRY

The quest for technology will remain an exercise with modest returns unless the Government of India creates an ecosystem to absorb these. The first step in this direction would be to treat the defence industry—both public and private sector—as a national asset. The government needs to make long-term investments in them, encouraging research and development as well as exports, instead of expecting immediate returns. Most importantly, instead of indulging in technological overreach as the Defence Research and Development Organisation tends to do, the government must invest in technologies and systems that meet the operational requirements of the Indian armed forces.

Since this will take time, stock must be taken of the immediate requirements of the armed forces and steps should be taken to meet these either through direct imports or collaborative imports. No country can aspire to become a global or regional influencer without a sound defence-industrial base.

RESOLVE KASHMIR

What if the Kashmir issue is resolved? The enormous possibility of this 'what if' has been exercising many minds. And not just in the subcontinent. At an international seminar in New Delhi in October 2015, US analyst George Perkovich, the author of the award-winning book *India's Nuclear Bomb*, wrestled with this question. Will the Pakistan Army's outlook towards India change if this seeming impossibility is realized? he wondered. He answered the question himself, 'I do not think it would.'

It is quite likely that the Pakistan Army will continue to regard India as a threat, if not an existential threat. The baggage of history that it carries is too heavy to disappear with the disappearance of one issue. It is also likely that the Pakistan Army will continue to determine not only the country's India policy but foreign policy in general especially when it is gradually inching closer to realizing its strategic goals. As the nucleus of China's ambitious One Belt One Road plan, Pakistan today is in an enviable position. For far too long it has been striving to turn its geography into a strategic asset. Its long and sustained partnership with China, despite the opprobrium of being a lackey, will finally give it the stature it has feverishly craved.

Today, as it is seen as being integral to the future of Afghanistan (whatever shape it takes) Pakistan is critical to all countries which have or wish to have a stake in the landlocked but mineral-rich country, from the US to Russia, China, Iran and the Central Asian Republics. With its nuclear weapons (also a key instrument of its foreign policy), it is the pride of aspirational Middle Eastern Islamic countries. Pakistan has long coveted the leadership of the Islamic world. With China by its side (to whom it is opening the doors to the Gulf), it may well achieve this goal.

This rightly begs a question. What do we get out of resolving Kashmir if Pakistan will remain a thorn in India's side? Unfortunately, we no longer get to choose whether to resolve Kashmir or not. China and Pakistan's physical link-up in Gilgit-Baltistan has taken away that choice. Now that the CPEC has become operational with the first Chinese trade convoy arriving at Gwadar Port in November 2016, it's only a matter of time before the pressure, including military pressure, will build on Kashmir. This has been accentuated by Prime Minister Narendra Modi's Kashmir agenda disclosed in August 2016. Instead of bilateral talks on the entire undivided Jammu and Kashmir, India would only talk on terror emanating from Pakistan, and how to get Pakistan-occupied Kashmir and Gilgit-Baltistan back from Pakistan.

According to Government of India statistics, the level of militant violence until 2015 had consistently been reducing in Kashmir. Not only was there less violence in Kashmir, it had been directed largely towards the uniformed forces, the military, paramilitary and the state police.

However, only the naive will believe that Kashmir had less militant violence because the people of the state had found love for India. If Kashmir was relatively peaceful, it was because the violent phase of the insurgency had run its course. And Pakistan had been conscious of this fact since 9/11 when the war on terror changed international sentiment towards violent resistance movements. Since then, it has been trying to showcase Kashmiri insurgency as an indigenous movement with only moral and political links with Pakistan. The resurrection of the Hizbul Mujahideen in the last decade has been the result of that change.

Since 2008, when Pakistan discovered the potential of street protests, it has thrown its weight behind them. There are two ways in which these protests score over direct violence. One, they reflect large-scale public disaffection towards India. Sustained protests running into months get international coverage. Two, they put security forces on the back foot; there is still no incident-proof method of dealing with a mob running into the thousands armed only with stones. Inadvertently, a lot of people are gravely injured and a few die, further fuelling the rage which keeps the cycle of protests going.

It is these agitations which give Pakistan the moral high ground to counter India's protestations at its meddling in Kashmir. At the SAARC summit in Pakistan in August 2016, Pakistan's interior minister, Chaudhry Nisar Ali Khan, responded to India's home minister, Rajnath Singh's speech on terrorism by stressing that 'legitimate freedom struggles should not be suppressed in the name of the fight against terrorism'. He urged the world to differentiate between terrorism and freedom movements. According to Chaudhry Nisar, equating the movement for Kashmir's liberation with terrorism was being '[dishonest] with history'.

RECLAIM THE PEACE NARRATIVE
New geopolitical alliances propelled by economic interests are being forged in Asia. China is heralding this change which is being made possible by the

convergence of the interests of Russia, Pakistan, the Central Asian Republics and Iran, besides the Southeast Asian region. India and Pakistan are joining the Shanghai Cooperation Organization as members. India signed the memorandum on the commitments of applicant states in June 2016 and is likely to become a full-fledged member in about a year. Both Russia and China have made it clear that bilateral issues will either have to be resolved or kept out of the cooperative framework. If India is able to address its own bilateral issues in a win-win manner, it may be in a position to influence others on the emerging Asian chessboard.

Contrary to common wisdom, China wants permanent peace between India and Pakistan. Having used Pakistan against India over the decades, China today is way ahead of India in national power and international standing. It has managed to make an unassailable case—legally, militarily and psychologically—on the disputed border row with India. Peace between India and Pakistan would help China get both on board its One Belt One Road plan, further cementing its position as Asia's biggest power. With Kashmir settled, China may find a mechanism to address the concerns of the restive population of Xinjiang, which borders both Gilgit-Baltistan and Afghanistan. After all, China would want the One Belt to traverse the old Silk Route through the Wakhjir Pass into the Wakhan Corridor onwards to Afghanistan, Turkmenistan, Iran and beyond. China closed the pass, a shorter route to Iran via Afghanistan, two decades ago to prevent the Uyghurs of Xinjiang from having access to the Afghan Taliban. This route would also help China establish a closer land link with mineral-rich north Afghanistan.

Worried about terrorism in Afghanistan and its implications for Russia and the Central Asian Republics, Russia is seeking closer security ties with Pakistan. Both Russia and China believe that Pakistan, with its Islamic identity and close ties with the Middle East, would make an indispensable partner in standing up to US unilateralism in Asia. Once protracted issues like Kashmir are resolved, India would be viewed as a country capable of shedding its historical baggage. It will also help ease the instability on the Line of Actual Control with China. Perhaps India can then play the role of an honest peacemaker between the Tibetan government-in-exile in India and China. It can help open a sincere dialogue between the two sides, thereby assuming its role as a leading Asian country, with non-violence as the cornerstone of its foreign policy, and national (including military) power to steer the collective future of the region.

STABILIZE THE HEARTLAND

India is perhaps one of the few countries where a huge mass of population is removed from the national mainstream from north to northeast and central India. Of course, in terms of diversity, there is no country like India, but over the years this diversity has been edged out of the national mainstream. As a result, large chunks of the country are reeling under varying degrees of insurgent violence, many sustained by India's neighbours. Unless these conflicts, whether in central India or the Northeast, are resolved, India's global aspirations will remain only partially successful. After all, one cannot run far with a hole in the heart.

Unleashing the military and paramilitary on one's own people is not the answer, sincere and constructive dialogue is. The Government of India must open unconditional talks with everyone alienated from the national mainstream, irrespective of their professed public positions. Instead of testing them on the touchstone of nationalism, the government must accommodate their aspirations and concerns, most of which are simply the baggage of history. In this it should seek help from concerned members of civil society, co-opting them as foot soldiers to reach the disaffected masses.

Even the biggest of powers have not been able to withstand internal discord because they understand that the financial and military effort required to keep it in check debilitates the nation in the long term. If India is able to win over the tribal population of central India and the people from the northeastern states, it will be able to free up a substantive number of its soldiers from internal stability and counter-insurgency operations. Plus it can save money, which can then be utilized in social-development programmes. With improving relations in the neighbourhood, over time even China will have no reason to extend tacit support to Indian insurgent groups of the Northeast, who, squeezed of funds and weapons will be forced to join the constituency for peace.

Military power is indispensable for nation-building and projecting power. Without it India will remain high on rhetoric and low on substance: neither will it deter enemies nor will it command respect among friends. We owe it to our history and geography to become a geostrategic player.

ACKNOWLEDGEMENTS

This book flowed from numerous sources of inspiration. Our debt to each one of them is unmeasurable.

To China's strongman, Deng Xiaoping who established that a nation's foreign policy is as strong as its economic strength and military power. Today, the world listens to President Xi Jinping not because of his skill as an orator but because China's national power is extraordinarily potent.

To China's master strategist, Sun Tzu who said, 'the supreme art of war is to subdue the enemy without fighting.' China has used this strategy with great success. It has used its military power not for war but for successful military and diplomatic coercion. China's unchecked military intrusions and transgressions across the disputed border are examples of its military coercion. Xi's maiden visit to India in September 2014 when he was accompanied with PLA troops was diplomatic coercion.

To Jaswant Singh, a prominent figure in the Vajpayee government, for saying that India's foreign policy is chained by the Line of Control with Pakistan and the Line of Actual Control with China. This book has attempted to unchain India from these military lines which have strategic, political, military and economic implications.

To Prime Minister Manmohan Singh who understood that without peace with Pakistan, India's rise would remain uncertain. The Manmohan-Musharraf formula, which was supported by all stakeholders, has raised the bar for mutual peace; nothing less would ensure peace.

To FORCE newsmagazine that provided the reason for numerous visits over fifteen years to India's borders and turbulent heartland. Meeting with field commanders gave priceless inputs to the authors. These visits also gave us access to people outside the political mainstream, especially in Kashmir. Each of those insights has been useful. A special thank you is reserved for Professor Abdul Ghani Bhat for his time, perspective and ironies.

To FORCE subscribers, whose swelling numbers, encouraged us to believe in our opinions which did not always find favour with the establishment. We learnt that logically argued points find takers.

To the *FORCE* team for taking on added responsibilities while we were busy with the manuscript. Special thanks are due to James Rajan, our irreplaceable team member. *FORCE* could not have come this far without him.

To innumerable policy-makers, and military and paramilitary leaders (many of whom are friends), who for obvious reasons cannot be identified, but are deeply appreciated.

To David Davidar, our publisher, for accepting an unconventional and perhaps provocative manuscript. He proves that an exceptional writer makes for an equally exceptional publisher. To our editors, Pujitha Krishnan and Aienla Ozukum, for their support and patience.

◆

I (Pravin Sawhney) would like to thank my family for the support they have given me all these years; especially my son, Dhruv Sawhney, who gives me immense happiness with his liberal and progressive views.

I (Ghazala Wahab) would like to thank my father for instilling in me the importance of imagination right from my childhood; and my mother for ensuring that my imagination didn't fly too high above ground realities.

NOTES AND REFERENCES

PROLOGUE

ix 'Our [India's] conventional strength is far more than theirs [Pakistan's]': 'India warns Pakistan of "more pain" in border fighting', *Dawn*, 22 October 2014.

x 'It should also be noted at the outset that although all geostrategic players': Zbigniew Brzezinski, *The Grand Chessboard*, Basic Books, 1997, p. 41.

xvi I asked him about the popular Chinese game called wei qi: Henry Kissinger provides a keen insight into the two games: 'If chess is about the decisive battle, *wei qi* is about the protracted campaign. The chess player aims for total victory. The *wei qi* player seeks relative advantage… Chess teaches the Clausewitzian concepts of centre of gravity and the decisive point, the game usually beginning as a struggle for the centre of the board. *Wei qi* teaches the art of strategic encirclement. Where the skillful chess player aims to eliminate his opponent's pieces in a series of head-on clashes, a talented *wei qi* player moves into "empty" spaces on the board, gradually mitigating the strategic potential of his opponent's pieces. Chess produces single-mindedness; *wei qi* generates strategic flexibility', Henry Kissinger, *On China*, Penguin, 2011, p. 24.

Introduction: How We Got Here

2 Within days of the declaration of independence, the Muslims from Poonch: Unlike Kashmiris from the Valley, the Poonchis were not pastoral. Their primary economic activity was military service and Poonch was the British Indian Army's favourite recruiting ground. After Independence, while Kashmir's status remained undecided, Maharaja Hari Singh sent his troops to disarm them. This was resented by the people who were now unemployed and poor. Hence, when the tax was imposed, they revolted. A large number crossed the border into the then North-West Frontier Province and Punjab to buy arms. Comprehensive details of the rebellion are in Christopher Snedden, *Kashmir: The Unwritten History*, HarperCollins, 2013.

5 was informed in a telephone conversation by his colleague General Gracey: Major K. C. Praval, *Indian Army After Independence*, Lancer International, 1990.

6 Major O. S. Kalkat…accidentally chanced upon the plans: Ibid.

6 President (General) Ayub Khan, who took over power in October 1958: Ibid.

7 This was done by abolishing the designation of the commander-in-chief in 1955: Ibid.

11 'With the exception of the Hajipir offensive': Lt. Gen. Harbakhsh Singh, *War Despatches: Indo-Pak Conflict, 1965*, Lancer International, 1991, p. 193.

12 Yet another example of India's weak leadership: Operation Grand Slam was launched by President Ayub Khan against the towns of Chhamb and Akhnoor in India with the aim of capturing the bridge at Akhnoor. This would cut off India's vital communication links between Jammu and Kashmir. Details of the operation are in Praval, *Indian Army*, pp. 259-306.

14   **'The transformation of the ceasefire line into the line of control'**: P. N. Dhar, *Indira Gandhi, the 'Emergency', and Indian Democracy*, Oxford University Press, 2000, p. 192.

22   **He made it clear that the use of air power needed clearance from the government**: According to Air Chief Marshal A.Y.Tipnis who wrote an exclusive account of the air force operations, Safed Sagar, *FORCE*, October 2006.

23   **'I felt that the movement of additional units and sub-units at the brigade'**: V. P. Malik, *Kargil: From Surprise to Victory*, HarperCollins, 2006, p. 118.

23   **'Besides weapons and equipment, the ammunition reserves for many important weapons were low'**: Ibid., p. 288.

27   **Nearly three divisions (30,000 troops) were moved from the east against China**: The Indian Army has three strike corps, namely, 1, 2 and 21 against the Pakistan Army's two: 1 and 2.

28   **Given the official figures of 798 dead**: According to Colonel Anit Mukherjee, who participated in the operation and is now assistant professor, Nanyang Technological University, Singapore, the death toll was 2,165.

28   **'The very first few days of Operation Parakram exposed'**:   General V. K. Singh, *Courage and Conviction*, Aleph Book Company, 2013, p. 243.

28   **'Helplessly, the army kept sitting on the border'**: Ibid., p. 244.

28   **'If threat from coercive diplomacy is not credible'**: Joseph S. Nye Jr, *The Future of Power*, Public Affairs, 2011, p. 45.

CHAPTER 1: THE CHINESE THREAT

33   **'For bilateral relations with China'**: Doval speaking at the annual K. F. Rustamji Lecture in Delhi on 22 May 2015.

33   **Prime Minister Rajiv Gandhi's Cabinet during the 1986–87 Sumdorong Chu crisis**: The Indian Intelligence Bureau had an observation post at Sumdorong Chu in the Thagla Ridge area of eastern Arunachal Pradesh where the 1962 war had started. In June 1986, when Indian patrols left the post to collect their supplies, Chinese troops quickly occupied it. The Chinese refused to vacate the post and both sides hardened their positions and started a massive build-up of troops, which continued for a year. Just when war appeared imminent, China broke the stalemate and suggested talks to resolve the issue.

35   **Mao also got Soviet leader Nikita Khrushchev's nod**: Kissinger, *On China*.

36   **In a well-documented book, A. G. Noorani makes two pertinent points**: A. G. Noorani, *India-China Boundary Problem 1846-1947: History and Diplomacy*, Oxford University Press, 2011.

36   **'The treaty of 1842 between'**: Ibid. The letter was written on 22 March 1959.

36   **Another version argues that the Ladakh-Tibetan border**: According to P. Stopdan, diplomat and national security expert who hails from Ladakh, in an article in *The Pioneer*, 20 December 2013.

37   **'Nehru actually came out of the negotiating room'**: T. N. Kaul, *A Diplomat's Diary (1947-1999): The Tantalizing Triangle-China, India and USA*, Macmillan, 2000.

39   **Various generals approached the government for infrastructure building on the Chinese border:** 4 Corps is responsible for the NEFA region, now Arunachal Pradesh.

39   **'I must say that Prime Minister Gandhi had an excellent understanding of defence matters':** Interview with Gen. K. V. Krishna Rao in *FORCE*, December 2004.

40   **Tawang in Kameng district of Arunachal Pradesh must not fall again:** The sixth Dalai Lama was born at a place close to the Tawang monastery that is revered by Buddhists.

40   **'withdrew from the territories it occupied as a result of the 1962 operations':** Shyam Saran, '1962: The view from Beijing', *Business Standard*, 7 April 2014.

40   According to former Foreign Secretary Shyam: Shyam Saran, 'India-China border dispute—Coping with asymmetry', *Business Standard*, 13 April 2014.

42   **'in [his] fifty years' involvement in foreign affairs and diplomacy':** Natwar Singh, *My China Diary 1956–88*, Rupa Publications, 2009, p. 113.

42   **'If the choice is between believing what the Chinese say':** Ibid., p. 137.

42   **This included the 1987 Exercise Brasstacks:** When military commanders war game with or without troops, it is called an exercise. Operation, on the other hand, implies troops going to war. Exercise Brasstacks was a major Indian military exercise in the winter of 1986–87 conducted close to the Pakistan border, which the Pakistan Army interpreted as a launch pad for war. Both sides came close to war before matters were defused bilaterally. Following the Sumdorong Chu crisis in June 1986 when India and China dug in their heels and started military build-up, the Indian Army conducted a war game called Exercise Chequerboard to identify what capabilities would be needed to meet China's challenge. After the Indo-Sri Lanka Peace Accord of July 1987, India sent its military force to seek the surrender of the LTTE (Liberation Tigers of Tamil Eelam) from Jaffna. This was called Operation Pawan.

42   **'The fresh Chinese position was that since the largest dispute was in the Eastern sector':** Shyam Saran, 'India-China border dispute—Coping with asymmetry', *Business Standard*, 13 April 2014.

43   **Before the seventh round that took place in Beijing:** R. D. Pradhan, *Dragon's Shadow over Arunachal: A Challenge to India's Polity*, Rupa Publications, 2008, p. 139. In 1987, Pradhan was appointed the first governor of the new state of Arunachal Pradesh.

43   **'the Sumdorong Chu conflict showed the preparedness of the Indian Army':** Ram Madhav, *Uneasy Neighbours: India and China after 50 Years of the War*, Kaveri Books, 2014.

43   **The Chinese leadership was not impressed:** Natwar Singh, *My China Diary*, p. 115.

43   **The border issue was instead discussed between Prime Ministers Gandhi and Li Peng:** Ibid., p. 120.

46   **By early 2015, 'there were 12 areas of differences in LAC perception between the Indian and Chinese maps':** Shishir Gupta, 'India, China Set to Get Real on Border', *Hindustan Times*, 23 March 2015.

47   **The Chinese do not have this problem:** China created the Tibet Autonomous Region (TAR) by incorporating parts of western Kham and U-Tsang provinces

in 1965. The TAR is just a small part of Tibet, which comprises the provinces of Amdo (the fourteenth Dalai Lama belongs to Amdo), now part of Chinese Qinghai province; Kham, now part of Sichuan; and U-Tsang.

47   **India formally accepted the Tibet Autonomous Region:** The Tibetan population, led by the Dalai Lama, does not recognize the TAR. In deference to these sentiments, India also never referred to the Chinese formulation before Vajpayee. See Prabhu Chawla, 'Dancing with the Dragon,' *India Today*, 7 July 2013.

48   **Beijing, thus, hasn't given the formal recognition to Sikkim**: Sikkim, with about 200 km of border with Tibet, has the highest concentration of troops anywhere in the world. India's entire 33 Corps (about 40,000 troops) is responsible for the defence of Sikkim. North Sikkim is most vulnerable because of inadequate infrastructure. The other vulnerability is in the Chumbi Valley adjacent to the narrow Siliguri Corridor, India's only land lifeline to its northeastern states. China has built excellent road and rail connectivity deep inside the Chumbi Valley. It is also in talks with Bhutan to settle the disputed border with it and hopes to broaden the Chumbi Valley funnel to bring in more troops to heighten its offensive posture along Siliguri Corridor.

50   **At the time, China had responded with a studied and significant silence:** Noorani, *India-China Boundary Problem*, p. 222.

50   **If, instead, he was sent as a member of the delegation:** Pravin Sawhney, 'China has shrunk the border', *FORCE,* August 2012.

51   **As the PLA numbers starting increasing, army chief General V. K. Singh finally went public:** 'Chinese troops in POK: Gen.V. K. Singh', *Economic Times*, 6 October 2011.

51   **For this reason, President Xi, unlike his predecessors:** The Communist Party of China, at its plenum meeting in October 2016, named Xi Jinping 'core leader', putting him on par with strongmen Mao Zedong, Deng Xiaoping and Jiang Zemin..

51   **'China would try and do business with India':** Ashutosh Varshney, 'The Chinese would not make big concessions to win India's friendship', *Indian Express*, 27 September 2014.

52   **The army, out of domestic (media) pressure to do something:** Army chief General Bikram Singh told one of the authors that matters would have settled without kicking up any dust if the media had not got wind of the incident.

52   **Notwithstanding the ongoing crisis**: Hardeep S. Puri, 'Playing hardball with China', *Indian Express*, 18 May 2013.

52   **Without political direction, the general did nothing:** G. Balachandran, 'China's creeping cartographic aggression', *The Pioneer*, 13 December 2014.

53   **In reality this means that if a PLA patrol manages to find a gap:** Ajay Banerjee, 'Lining up to maintain peace along LAC', *The Tribune*, 21 December 2015. The Indian Army is projecting the BDCA as a positive move to maintain peace. The troops are told to 'take pictures and document' PLA troops who manage to intrude the LAC. These pictures are then used at local meetings to resolve issues locally.

53   **'accepted principle of mutual and equal security':** Pranab Dhal Samata, 'Border Pact with China does not tie India's hand', *Indian Express*, 24 October 2013.

54   **China has even expressed its displeasure at India's plan:** Vijaita Singh, 'India to build 1800-km highway along China border in Arunachal Pradesh,' *Indian Express*, 16 October 2014.

54   **Thus the new 'limit of patrol' has become the new LAC in Ladakh:** Shishir Gupta, 'PLA restricting Indian patrol areas', *Indian Express*, 3 September 2013.

54   **Meanwhile, to formalize its Depsang gains, the PLA issued new 'battle maps' to its troops:** Ananth Krishnan, 'China's PLA distributes new "battle maps" in border areas', *The Hindu*, 19 July 2014.

54   **General Xu Qiliang, vice chairman of the CMC:** Ananth Krishnan, 'China General Visited Disputed Region', *The Hindu*, 6 August 2014.

55   **Xi replied that 'both sides were fully capable of ensuring':** Shubhjit Roy, 'Determined to solve border question', *Indian Express*, 19 September 2014.

56   **'India will maintain [the] status quo at disputed pockets along the China border':** Vijaita Singh, 'Govt to maintain status quo along China border', *Indian Express*, 31 December 2014.

56   **In essence, 'the PLA had incrementally occupied near 640 sq km':** Ajai Shukla, 'NSAB chief denies reporting Chinese intrusions to PMO', *Business Standard*, 5 September 2013.

56   **India's Modi government quietly accepted the altered LAC:** Pravin Sawhney, 'China is winning without a fight', *The Pioneer*, 26 March 2015.

56   **'The present priority of both nations':** Sanjoy Narayan and Shishir Gupta, 'The Modi Interview', *Hindustan Times*, 9 April 2015.

57   **'Chinese negotiations use diplomacy':** Kissinger, *On China*.

57   **'A shadow of uncertainty always hangs over the sensitive border region':** Shishir Gupta, 'PM Modi's Message to Beijing', *Hindustan Times*, 18 May 2015.

57   **'If we find that clarification of the LAC is a building block':** 'China rejects India's proposal for LAC clarity', *The Pioneer*, 5 June 2015.

58   **'India-China border areas continue to remain peaceful':** Syed Akbaruddin, 'India-China border areas continue to remain peaceful: external affairs ministry spokesman', *Business Standard*, 28 April 2013.

58   **Today, China wants both Ladakh and Arunachal Pradesh:** In 2016, there are four mutually agreed flashpoints in Ladakh, namely Trig Heights, Demchok, Pangong Tso and Chushul; and three agreed flashpoints in Arunachal Pradesh, namely Bum La (Tawang), Fishtail area and Diphu. Moreover, in the comparatively calm Middle Sector where before 1998 China claimed only Barahoti, today it wants Lapthal, Sangcha, Palam Sumda and Kavriki in addition to Barahoti.

58   **According to Saran, 'One cannot see a solution that diverges significantly':** Shyam Saran, 'India-China border dispute—Coping with asymmetry', *Business Standard*, 13 April 2014.

59   **'China cannot lose one centimetre of the area it claims':** 'China Says "Cannot Lose One Centimetre" Of Disputed Area', NDTV, 15 July 2016.

CHAPTER 2: LINE OF CONSTRAINT

60   **Brigadier Ramesh Halgali, told the authors:** The authors were visiting the Uri brigade for a cover story on the Line of Control for *FORCE* magazine's inaugural issue ('Line of (No) Control', August 2003). In a short span of three days,

the *FORCE* team encountered enemy shelling thrice.

60   **Before the ceasefire and LC fence:** Pakistan President Pervez Musharraf announced the unilateral ceasefire on the LC on 24 November 2003. India accepted it on 26 November and the ceasefire came into force. The construction of the fence on the LC by the Indian Army started soon after that.

61   **In the aftermath of the ten-month-long Operation Parakram:** The authors visited both headquarters—Srinagar and Udhampur—in July 2003.

61   **'Our methods of interception have improved and we have started select fencing':** Pravin Sawhney and Ghazala Wahab, 'The Line of (no)Control', *FORCE*, September 2003.

62   **The 1999 Kargil conflict is the extreme example:** The then Pakistan foreign minister, Sartaj Aziz, justified the occupation of Indian territory close to the LC on the grounds that the LC was not delineated. The LC is marked on two sets of maps, each set consisting of twenty-seven map sheets formed into nineteen mosaics. Each individual mosaic of all four sets of maps was signed by the representatives of the chiefs of army staff of India and Pakistan, Lt. Gens. P. S. Bhagat and Abdul Hameed Khan. Sartaj Aziz's problem with the small maps used in 1972 for delineation was that they would make modern surveyors squirm. The line drawn on these maps could be off the mark by anything from 2 to 5 kilometres on a large modern map. Pakistan played up this technical shortcoming of the original map while making its claim. Had Pakistan not got carried away by its initial success and intruded as much as 15 kilometres inside Kargil (while India was oblivious), it could perhaps have justified its position that the LC was not clearly delineated.

64   **450 kilometres of the LC is mountainous with heights of up to 11,000 feet:** 10,000 feet and above is considered high altitude.

65   **Benazir Bhutto declared from Muzaffarabad in April 1990:** Muzaffarabad is the capital of what Pakistan calls Azad or independent Kashmir and India calls Pakistan-occupied Kashmir.

67   **General Joshi revived the idea of the Rashtriya (national) Rifles**: The Rashtriya Rifles was originally envisaged as comprising retired servicemen. At present, with a strength of over 80,000 troops, the Indian Army's Rashtriya Rifles is the largest counter-insurgency (CI) force in the world. There are a total of sixty-four RR battalions each with 1,147 troops comprising six rifle companies (unlike four in a standard infantry battalion). The infantry component in each RR battalion comprises 60 per cent troops in four rifle companies affiliated to various regiments of the infantry. Two rifle companies in each RR battalion are from other arms, chosen from the artillery, air defence corps, armour and engineers. The remaining comprises task-oriented troops from various services to provide logistics backup to an RR battalion. Since this force is engaged in counter-terrorism (CT) operations, it does not have heavy weapons like a regular infantry battalion and is without organic artillery. The tenure of troops, including officers, in an RR battalion is between two to three years. Two aspects of RR have transformed this force into what army chief in 2007, General J. J. Singh, called the 'Iron Fist'. One, the affiliated infantry regiments responsible for providing their assigned RR battalions ensure that the best men, equipment and weapon systems go to the RR battalions for CT operations. And, two, the modernization of the infantry battalions has benefitted the RR in terms of better firepower, communications and mobility.

While the command and control of Force Headquarters is the responsibility of 16 and 15 Corps Headquarters that have been designated as the operational level for CI operations, the administrative aspects of RR are looked after by the director general, RR, based in New Delhi.

73 **For these reasons, in 2011–12, 15 Corps did a successful pilot project of replacing the fence:** The authors visited 15 Corps in May 2011.

74 **'When Vij asked my opinion on the fence':** Pravin Sawhney and Ghazala Wahab, 'It's no Wall', *FORCE*, November 2005.

74 **'The army is not the only one to learn':** Ibid.

74 **people were full of praise for the Indian Army:** Pravin Sawhney and Ghazala Wahab, 'Lost to Nature', *FORCE*, November 2005.

76 **With a frontage of 243 kilometres, 25 Division extends from Surankot to Pir Panjal:** The authors visited the division in December 2013.

77 **'While CI ops require immediate and expeditious response':** 'How raw courage and grit triumphed', Lt. Gen. Mohinder Puri, *The Tribune*, 25 July 2014.

78 **'innovative troops deployment, efficient use of surveillance':** Pravin Sawhney, 'The Army is Not War Ready', *The Tribune*, 14 Feb 2016.

78 **'The new fence will be twice as effective as the existing one':** Rahul Singh, 'New "all-weather" fence to seal 100km of LoC in a year', *Hindustan Times*, 10 August 2015.

CHAPTER 3: NIGHTMARE ON THE LINE OF ACTUAL CONTROL

84 **17 Mountain Corps has two parts:** According to a general who was closely involved with the case for the raising of 17 Mountain Corps in conversation with one of the authors.

84 **The accretion forces totalling 30,000 troops:** One infantry brigade each in the Western and Middle sectors, one armoured brigade each in the Western and Eastern sectors, three artillery brigades with flexibility to shift between sectors and logistics units.

85 **According to Kiren Rijiju, the union minister of state for Home Affairs, there have been '1,612 transgressions':** Bharti Jain, 'No Chinese intrusion since 2010, only "transgressions": Govt', *Times of India*, 20 August 2014.

85 **'I do not think India has ever':** 'Three Turning Points,' *FORCE*, May 2008.

87 **'To make matters worse, our government is oblivious':** 'The Chinese are going to give us a major surprise', *FORCE*, May 2008.

87 **Fernandes conceded that 'politics and constraints as the defence minister':** George Fernandes, defence minister (1998-2004), in an interview to *FORCE* magazine, May 2008.

88 **'All reports in the Indian media on Chinese transgressions':** Pravin Sawhney, 'China has shrunk the Border', *FORCE*, August 2012.

90 **In January 2015, the union home minister announced an additional forty-nine battalions**: Before the announcement of ITBP new raisings, it had twenty battalions (eight each in the Western and Eastern sectors and four in the Middle sector) on the LAC.

91 **'The delay is on account of forest and wildlife clearances':** Lt. Gen. A. T. Parnaik, 'Challenges facing BRO', *FORCE*, May 2011.

91 **seventeen roads in 2016; nine roads in 2017:** Statement in Lok Sabha on 27

February 2015. Disclosing the shabby account on border road building by the Manmohan Singh government, Defence Minister Manohar Parrikar said that of the 3,000 kilometres of General Staff roads only 600 kilometres had been built in a ten-year period.

91   **'the director general of military operations was reportedly against building roads':** 'The Chinese threat in Kashmir', *The Pioneer*, 28 July 2016.

92   **There are hotlines and established procedures for formal flag meetings:** Border meeting points are at Spanggur Gap and Daulat Beg Oldi in Ladakh; Nathu La in Sikkim; and Bum La and Kibithu (Walong) in Arunachal Pradesh.

92   **'despite anxieties on frequent incursions across the disputed portions':** C. Raja Mohan, 'Chinese Takeaway: Border Paradox', *Indian Express*, 24 March 2015.

CHAPTER 4: COLD START TO A HOT WAR

95   **After the Pakistan Army-supported Lashkar terrorists:** Pravin Sawhney, 'Defence of India', *FORCE*, August 2010.

97   **'There is no Chinese threat in the near term':** Interaction with one of the authors in August 2010 at Air Headquarters, Delhi.

97   **'The military preparedness of any nation':** Interview with a senior officer at Eastern Air Command, October 2010, Shillong.

98   **it would be difficult for them to bring more than eighteen:** A senior army officer told one of the authors in an interaction in March 2011.

98   **Add to this the new raising of 17 Mountain Strike Corps:** '17 Corps Commenced Raising', Chief of Army Staff, Gen. Bikram Singh in an interview with Pravin Sawhney, *FORCE*, January 2014.

98   **The 17 Mountain Strike Corps will have two infantry divisions:** 17 Mountain Strike Corps will have two infantry divisions, three armoured and artillery brigades each, an engineer and aviation brigade each and logistics services. The total cost will be ₹92,000 crore (at 2013 prices) and added manpower will be 90,000 troops.

98   **The army also hopes to shift a few formations:** Army chief Gen. Bikram Singh in conversation with Pravin Sawhney in December 2013.

99   **the IAF has since 2008 built or activated:** In the Western Sector (Ladakh), three advanced landing grounds at altitudes of 13,000 to 16,000 feet have come up at Daulat Beg Oldi, Fukche and Nyoma. In the Eastern Sector there are six advanced landing grounds at Pasighat, Mechuka, Along, Vijaynagar and Ziro (just north of Itanagar, the capital of Arunachal Pradesh).

100   **Pakistan operates on interior lines and could mobilize its holding corps:** In warfare, interior lines imply that distances for movement, communication and supply within an area are shorter than the exterior lines. In the case of Pakistan, its geography and lack of depth ensures that it can move quickly to the war theatre.

106   **'conventional war plans would be independent of nuclear forces':** Feroz Hassan Khan, *Eating Grass: The Making of the Pakistani Bomb*, Stanford University Press, 2012.

112   **According to *FORCE* magazine, which did a comprehensive article after speaking with those who have knowledge of the matter:** Pravin Sawhney and Ghazala Wahab, 'Armed without Ammunition', *FORCE*, January 2013.

113   **War wastage reserves for most ammunition categories do not exist:** It is

mandatory for the army to have ammunition stocks (war wastage reserves) for forty days of intense war of the long shelf-life category, and twenty-one days intense fighting of short shelf-life category like anti-tank, rocket artillery and missiles. In addition, the army holds critical ammunition for two days of war as unit reserves, first and second line holdings.

CHAPTER 5: WAR IS NOT AN OPTION

114 **'As both sides have agreed to have peaceful borders, the [Indian] focus should not be on the border issue':** Pravin Sawhney, 'Seven Days in China', *FORCE*, August 2012.

114 **Instead, senior PLA officials took pains:** Pravin Sawhney was part of a group of visiting journalists attending a higher defence organization briefing.

115 **This PLA stance of non-contact war would also help in military coercion:** According to China's May 2015 military strategy, 'The revolution in military affairs (RMA) is proceeding to a new stage. Long-range, precise, smart, stealthy and unmanned weapons and equipment are becoming increasingly sophisticated. Outer space and cyberspace have achieved new commanding heights in strategic competition among all parties. The form of war is accelerating its evolution to informationization. The aforementioned revolutionary changes in military technologies and the form of war have not only had a significant impact on the international political and military landscapes, but also posed new and severe challenges to China's military security.'

115 **The other first was the decision to move beyond coastal defence to the open seas:** The PLA Navy will gradually shift its focus from 'offshore waters defence' to the combination of 'offshore waters defence' with 'open seas protection'.

115 **According to the May 2015 military strategy, 'China will optimise its nuclear force structure':** The full text of China's military strategy is here: http://www.chinadaily.com.cn/china/2015-05/26/content_20820628.htm.

122 **In India, there is no institutionalized system for the prime minister:** On assuming charge in May 2014, Prime Minister Narendra Modi sought an informal meeting with the three defence service chiefs once a month. Being informal, it is not a regular feature, and his meeting them individually indicates his desire to know each service's problems rather than to frame a defence policy.

123 **In 2013, China 'launched three small satellites into orbit as part of Beijing's covert anti-satellite warfare programme':** Pravin Sawhney, 'Voice of Reason', *FORCE*, March 2010. According to DRDO chief Dr V. K. Saraswat: '[D]emonstrating satellite interception is not something that is necessary to acquiring this capability. Satellite, as you know, has a predictable path, whether it is in the polar, low Earth or any other orbit. To check my interception capability, I can always simulate the satellite path electronically. I will generate an electronic scenario at the launch pad as if I am getting data from another satellite or ground-based radar and take that as the input for my mission-control centre. Then, I can launch an interceptor. Since the path is known, I will know if I have accurately hit the target or not. Unlike in ballistic missiles, where the path can be unpredictable, thanks to aerodynamic and other reasons. So technically, we have concluded that we do not need to check our building blocks to ascertain whether we have satellite interception capability.' When asked why the Chinese thought it necessary

to demonstrate anti-satellite capability, he replied, 'I do not know. Only they can answer this question.'

The answer probably lies in cold statistics. Satellites in Low Earth Orbit (LEO) are at heights of 300 kilometres above Earth—any lower and they will not be stable. The polar orbit is at a height of 843 kilometres. The demonstrated capability of DRDO's outside atmosphere interceptor is only 80 kilometres above Earth. Even if the DRDO were able to make an interceptor which could reach a height of 300 kilometres—satellites in LEO move at speeds of up to 28,000 kilometres per hour. Thus, to demonstrate assurance, there is a need to make a successful anti-satellite. India has enough commercial satellites in space. India has plans to launch dedicated military (navy, air force and then army) satellites for communications and targeting needs.

124 **No one will win the battle in the cyberspace:** Told to the author (Pravin Sawhney) during his August 2012 China visit.

124 **'If we could destroy the enemy's political, economic and military infrastructure':** Joel Brenner, *America the Vulnerable: Inside the New Threat Matrix of Digital Espionage, Crime, and Warfare*, Penguin, 2011, p. 118.

125 **The rail line from Lhasa has been extended to Shigatse:** Ananth Krishnan, 'Tibet rail extension to Nepal border', *The Hindu*, 7 March 2014.

125 **China also plans to construct rail lines:** Ananth Krishnan, 'Chinese Rail Lines up to India Border', *The Hindu*, 25 July 2014.

125 **'The Militia performs combat readiness':** Interaction at the Chinese Ministry of National Defence with the author in August 2012.

127 **What that means can be seen at Tawang:** The entire Tawang sector has been filled with tactically networked surveillance devices by the Chinese, which are monitored regularly. The Chinese Militia brigade (2 Border Guard Regiment) facing Tawang, is 40 kilometres in depth at Tsona Dzong. The regular forces, trained in mobile operations, are invisible. The road that leads to Tsona Dzong is a well-tarred gravel road, which allows better water drainage during monsoons. The tracks on the Indian side, if they exist at all, are pathetic. Tawang has over 200 posts. Many of them do not have tracks. Troops have to lug loads—walking from five hours to two days from the last track-head. A second road axis leading to Tawang (which is crucial for speedy troop build-up) was approved by the Vajpayee government in 2001. But work has not yet commenced. North Sikkim is another area of great sensitivity. Here also work on roads sanctioned in 2001 has not progressed.

128 **India deployed a few indigenous liquid-propellant:** According to senior defence sources.

128 **However, given the operational drawbacks of liquid propellants:** 'Prithvi to be replaced: DRDO chief, Avinash Chander', *LiveMint*, 30 June 2013. Avinash Chander's predecessor V. K. Saraswat had given the accuracy of Prithvi as 25 metres for 150 kilometres range ('Boosting the Arsenal', *India Today*, 29 February 1996). If Prithvi is indeed so accurate why has Avinash Chander given accuracy as a reason for replacing Prithvi with Prahaar, especially when liquid propellant gives better accuracy than solid propellant?

128 **Unlike Indian formations, the PLA forces are lightly armed for rapid deployments:** According to former DGMO Lieutenant General Vinod Bhatia, the PLA has the capability to store 4.1 lakh tons of war logistics in TAR. This is

enough to support fifty days of high-intensity war for thirty-four army divisions.

CHAPTER 6: CHINA'S GRAND STRATEGY

131 **Looking back, the year 2008 appeared to be the turning point:** Deng Xiaoping's twenty-four-character strategy translated into English from Mandarin would be: observe calmly; secure our position; cope with affairs calmly; hide our capabilities and bide our time; be good at maintaining a low profile; and never claim leadership.

134 **These included the Association of Southeast Asian Nations (ASEAN):** ASEAN comprises Indonesia, Malaysia, Singapore, Myanmar, Philippines, Vietnam, Laos, Thailand, Brunei and Cambodia.

134 **'may be remembered as the moment the US':** Myles Udland, 'Larry Summers has a major warning for the US economy, and everyone should be paying attention', *BusinessInsider*, 6 April 2015.

134 **In tune with Deng Xiaoping's twelve-character policy:** The twelve-character policy reads: 'Enemy troops are outside the wall. They are stronger than we are. We should be mainly on the defensive.'

135 **Undeterred, China continued with its assertiveness in the East China Sea over the Diaoyu Islands:** The Japanese call them Senkaku Islands.

135 **numerous prestigious US think tanks stuck to the US strategy being a 'pivot':** Pivot suggests military power. Rebalance on the other hand, suggests a combination of various elements including military, economic, culture and so on.

135 **'The purpose of rebalance was to reassure friends':** J. Stapleton Roy, former US ambassador to China, speaking at the 6th Xiangshan Forum in Beijing, 17 October 2015.

136 **However, the most important component is economic not military:** Admiral Harry Harris in conversation with the authors, 'Shifting Matters', *FORCE,* March 2015.

136 **China's narrative of why the SCS was important for it was explained by two senior officials:** Both spoke at the 6th Xiangshan Forum.

136 **'China is the largest stakeholder':** Major General Yao Yunzhu, 6th Xiangshan Forum.

140 **'Liu, a military hardliner at China's National Defence University, wrote in his 2010 book, *China Dream*':** The book, originally written in Mandarin, has been commented upon by Kissinger in *On China.*

142 **The Xiangshan dialogue Forum since 2006 by the PLA which in 2014 was upgraded to 1.5 track:** Track 1.5 accords it semi-official status. In addition to experts and scholars, serving government officials participate in it.

145 **According to a PLA document the shift was 'from quantity':** China's National Defence in 2010: Information Office of the State Council.

147 **a China-Pakistan economic corridor:** It will run from Kashgar in Xinjiang to Gwadar in Balochistan.

147 **He could finally realize the dream of his predecessor and military ruler:** Robert D. Kaplan, *Monsoon: The Indian Ocean and the Future of American Power,* Penguin, 2010, p. 69.

147 **China accepted Pakistan's offer and completed the first phase on the Gwadar Port:** A senior official in the Chinese Embassy in New Delhi told one of

the authors on 12 November 2015 that China's control over Gwadar management would be indefinite. He also hinted at the future militarization of the port with Pakistan's concurrence.

CHAPTER 7: THE CHOICES BEFORE INDIA

151   **'There is a direct interrelationship, a consequence':** Jaswant Singh, *India at Risk: Misconceptions and Misadventures of Security Policy*, Rupa Publications, 2013, p. 253.

153   'Thus far we have been a balancing power': Raj Chengappa, 'Call for achhe din was to get rid of the bad, we have achieved that', *The Tribune*, 30 May 2015.

153   **the 'personal chemistry [of the prime minister]':** 'All for cooperation with neighbours, firm if needed, says S. Jaishankar', *Indian Express*, 18 July 2015.

155   'Chinese strategists, realizing that a conventional confrontation': Joseph S. Nye Jr, *The Future of Power*, PublicAffairs, 2011.

158   **'In the short term, develop capability to thwart':** Lt. Gen. S. K. Gadeock, 'Geo-Politico Situation: Indian Armed Forces and Higher Defence Organisations—Transformation and Future Strategy', *Trishul*, 2014.

159   **Instead of doing that, the defence ministry decided to reform the ops:** Interaction with a recently retired chief of Integrated Defence Headquarters in September 2015.

160   **'Making strategy is by far the most difficult':** Colin S. Gray, *Explorations in Strategy*, Greenwood Publishing Group, 1996.

161   **'Our relations with Islamabad have their own agenda':** Interview with Russian Ambassador V. I. Trubnikov, January 2005.

162   **'Islamabad is a very important player in joint efforts':** Interview with Denis Alipov, Deputy Chief of Mission, Russian Embassy, New Delhi, October 2015.

162   **'to cooperate in counter-terrorism situation evaluation':** 'China mooted counter-terrorism takes shape', Inter-Services Press Release, 3 August 2016.

163   **'Our apparent tolerance towards these blatant terrorist attacks':** General Shankar Roychowdhury, *Officially at Peace*, Penguin Viking, 2002, p. 157.

165   **'China is the biggest trading country in the world':** Le Yucheng, 'Why India Must Track China's 13.5,' *Indian Express*, 6 November 2015.

166   **'It is my belief that the raison d'être':** Khurshid Mahmud Kasuri, *Neither a Hawk Nor a Dove*, Penguin Viking, 2015, p. 320.

168   **Reports indicate that Pakistan's Gwadar port will get linked through a railway line:** Saleem Shahid, 'Rail link planned between Gwadar and Iranian port', *Dawn*, 12 January 2016.

CHAPTER 8: POLITICAL GAMES AT WORK

173   **'Elections are not about the Kashmir issue':** Professor Abdul Ghani Bhat, interview with the authors, Srinagar, April 2014. The All Parties Hurriyat Conference (APHC) was created by Pakistan in March 1993 by bringing together over twenty-five smaller political parties that questioned Kashmir's accession to India and sought independence (Azadi). The formation of the group was announced by Abdul Ghani Lone in May 1993 in the US. Collectively referred to as separatists because of their demand for separation from the Union of India, several members of the Hurriyat Conference at the time of its amalgamation were

former mainstream politicians. APHC lent a semblance of a political struggle to the armed insurgency. In the early years, APHC had some traction with the militants, especially of the indigenous variety like Hizbul Mujahideen. But gradually as Pakistan started to side-line HM in favour of Pakistan-based organizations such as Lashkar-e-Taiba (LeT) and Jaish-e-Mohammad (JeM), the APHC lost its moderating effect on the Pakistani terrorists. In 2002, the APHC split into two groups. One was led by the conservative and hard-line leader of the Kashmir chapter of Jamaat-e-Islami, Syed Ali Shah Geelani. Called Hurriyat (G), it favours the merger of Kashmir with Pakistan. The other faction is led by a moderate cleric, Mirwaiz Umar Farooq, and is called Hurriyat (M). While this group favours independence from India, it has engaged in talks with the Government of India from time to time.

174 **'China is involved in mining of heavy metals':** Email interview with Senge Sering, 8 January, 2015.

174 **about 40 per cent of the inhabitants of Gilgit–Baltistan are Tibetan:** Ibid.

175 **While discounting China's claim to Kashmir, Mirwaiz Umar Farooq:** Interview with the authors, April 2014.

175 **Unlike most of his ilk in the Hurriyat Conference:** One of the provisions of Article 370, which covers states like Nagaland, Manipur, Mizoram and others, prohibits the Constitutional provision that allows citizens to buy, own or sell property anywhere in India. These special provisions also extend to the states of Andhra Pradesh, Maharashtra, Assam, Sikkim, etc. But none of them actually refer to anything pertaining to accession, not even in the case of Hyderabad. Only Article 370 says, 'the power of Parliament to make laws for the said State shall be limited to (i) those matters in the Union List and the Concurrent List which, in consultation with the Government of the State, are declared by the President to correspond to matters specified in the Instrument of Accession governing the accession of the State to the Dominion of India...' These special provisions were made in the case of J&K because the circumstances of it becoming part of India were special. It was not a merger as happened with other princely states. Moreover, over the years, various provisions of Article 370 were chipped away. What remains today is mere tokenism of a separate Constitution and a state flag. In reality, a chief minister of Uttar Pradesh or Tamil Nadu is more powerful than a chief minister of J&K, who cannot even appoint his own bureaucrats without consulting the central government.

175 **The overtures to Pakistan were followed by the first ever meeting:** 'India holds first talks with Kashmiri separatists', *The Guardian*, 22 January 2004.

175 **Meanwhile, the government in Kashmir had changed too:** Within a few months of winning the 1996 elections, the National Conference government, with Farooq Abdullah as chief minister, constituted a committee to draft an autonomy resolution, which was eventually passed by a voice vote by the state assembly in June 2000. The Government of India trashed it without discussion.

177 **'I did not even get an acknowledgement of receipt':** Pravin Sawhney and Ghazala Wahab, 'Summer 2011', *FORCE*, April 2011.

177 **The basis of the dialogue was Musharraf's publicly espoused:** The Manmohan Singh-Musharraf dialogue was based on the road map drawn up by the US-based think-tank, Kashmir Study Group (KSG). KSG was founded by Farooq

Kathwari, a Kashmiri businessman and chairman, president and chief executive officer of Ethan Allen Interiors Inc.

177	**Apparently, by early 2007, the two sides were very close:** Steve Coll, 'The Back Channel', *New Yorker*, 2 March 2009.

178	**The diplomats were also working on finalizing a visit by Manmohan Singh to Pakistan in late 2007:** Ibid.

178	**'we had reached an understanding in back channels':** Sachin Parashar, 'Manmohan Singh, Musharraf came close to striking Kashmir deal: WikiLeaks', *Times of India*, 3 September 2011.

178	**Satinder Lambah...made a reference to the process in a talk he delivered:** The talk was excerpted in *Outlook* magazine, May 2014.

178	**'What we were working on agreed there would be no reference to the United Nations':** Harinder Baweja, 'Almost had Kashmir deal with Pakistan: Ex-PM's envoy Lambah', *Hindustan Times*, 16 Oct 2015.

179	**'Who knows what sorting out Kashmir means':** Interview, Noida, September 2014.

179	**'As far as I understand, the Government of India':** Interview, Delhi, November 2014.

179	**Moreover, unlike Pakistan, where Musharraf sounded out:** Steve Coll, 'The Back Channel', *New Yorker*, 2 March 2009.

180	**Once this opportunity was lost, the situation in Kashmir started deteriorating again:** In early 2008, the state government signed an order transferring 100 acres of land to the Shri Amarnath Shrine Board. The initial murmurs of protest were about the environmental impact new constructions would have on the sensitive ecology of the Valley, but gradually as more facts tumbled out about the manner of transfer, conspiracy theories kicked in. Facing street protests in Kashmir and with the assembly elections due in October 2008, the state government withdrew the order. Now protests erupted in Jammu as well, with all political parties with a stake in the coming elections jumping into the fray. The situation turned ugly when a section of people in Jammu with support from the right-wing parties blockaded National Highway 1A for a few days. Details in Pravin Sawhney and Ghazala Wahab, 'Holding Peace to Ransom', *FORCE*, September 2008.
	On 30 April 2010, an Indian Army unit was found to have killed three youth in the Machil sector of north Kashmir in what proved to be an obvious case of fake encounters. In a subsequent protest against this fake killing, a student, Tufail Ahmed Mattoo, was accidentally killed by a tear gas shell. This started a cycle of protest and killing which continued unabated for nearly four months.

181	**the spirit of the Simla Agreement itself underlines the process of Kashmir resolution:** Sub-clause 4 (ii) of the Simla Agreement says: In Jammu and Kashmir, the line of control resulting from the ceasefire of 17 December 1971, shall be respected by both sides without prejudice to the recognized position of either side. Neither side shall seek to alter it unilaterally, irrespective of mutual differences and legal interpretations. Both sides further undertake to refrain from the threat or the use of force in violation of this line. See Dhar, *Indira Gandhi, the Emergency and Indian Democracy*.

181	**'opened a dialogue with Sheikh Abdullah':** Ibid., p. 195.

181 **The Indira Gandhi-Sheikh Abdullah Accord of 1974:** Nyla Ali Khan, *Islam, Women and Violence in Kashmir: Between India and Pakistan*, Northwestern University, 24 May 2011.

181 **Today, instead of building on the legacies of its predecessors:** In 1932, Maharaja Hari Singh, the ruler of the state of Jammu and Kashmir imposed a ban on the slaughter, sale and consumption of cows in deference to Hindu beliefs, despite the fact that the majority in the state did not believe that the cow was sacred. However, post-Independence, the implementation of the ban became lackadaisical, with successive state governments ignoring stray instances of cow slaughter in the state. Despite this, beef, even in the Muslim-dominated Valley, never became part of Kashmiri cuisine, which relies heavily on goat meat.

183 **'In the last twenty years, madrassas have mushroomed all over the state':** Pravin Sawhney and Ghazala Wahab, 'Closed Minds', *FORCE*, August 2015.

184 **the Hadith:** Compilations of habits, sayings and traditions of Prophet Mohammed, as remembered or understood by his successors.

186 **the Kashmiri Members of the Legislative Assembly (MLAs) went into hiding:** Hakeem Irfan Rashid, 'Jammu Kashmir separatists ask MLAs to abandon Mehbooba Mufti', *Economic Times*, 21 July 2016.

CHAPTER 9: THREAT TO LADAKH

191 **'while work on the 255 kilometres Darbuk-Shyok-DBO is progressing':** 'India ups military presence in Ladakh', *The Hindu*, 18 July 2016.

193 **believes that the situation is not so grim in north Ladakh:** Interaction with the former director general, Military Operations.

195 **In July 2016, according to media reports, Indian Army officers:** Dinakar Peri, 'Third regiment of T-72 tanks to be moved to Ladakh soon', *The Hindu*, 19 July 2016.

CHAPTER 10: AFSPA AND OTHER DISCONTENTS

198 **Halgali (along with the authors) was driving back to his headquarters:** 'Men with the Past', *FORCE*, May 2007. Ever since the state government instituted a surrender policy, whereby those surrendering with a weapon would get a fixed compensation and a chance of being employed either in the state police or a paramilitary force, many insurgents have been giving up their arms. During Maj. Gen. Halgali's tenure alone, 146 terrorists, owing allegiance to such outfits as Hizbul Mujahideen, Tehrik-e-Jihad, Hizb-e-Islami and Kashmir Revolutionary Force, had surrendered to the 19 Infantry Division. The ones who want to surrender send messages across to their families in Kashmir, who in turn inform the local army commander, and their crossing of the LC is facilitated. Sometimes, even Pakistan facilitates such crossing if the potential insurgent or terrorist is found unfit for operations.

199 **'to enable certain special powers to be conferred upon members of the armed forces':** Armed Forces (Jammu & Kashmir) Special Powers Act, 1990.

199 **he expedited the raising of Rashtriya Rifles:** These were not new raisings, only conversion of selected regular army units into RR units.

200 **'In view of peaceful elections, there is a case to be made for force':** Omar Abdullah in an interview to FORCE, January 2009.

200 **one of the members of the Justice Jeevan Reddy Committee:** In 2004, a Manipuri woman, Manorama Devi, was found dead after the Assam Rifles (a paramilitary force officered by the Indian Army) had picked her up for questioning. There was uproar in the state, with people alleging rape and extrajudicial killing. Such was the anger among the people that Manipuri women came out in the nude to protest, holding banners which read, 'Indian Army Rape Us'. Pushed into a corner, the Government of India appointed the Justice Jeevan Reddy Committee to study AFSPA. The committee was to explore either modifications in the Act or the possibility of its revocation. Headed by Justice Jeevan Reddy, the members of the committee included former jurist S. B. Nakade, former special secretary to the Ministry of Home Affairs, P. Shrivastav, former director general, Military Operations, Lt. Gen. V. R. Raghavan and activist-journalist Sanjoy Hazarika. The committee members travelled to several northeastern states, and spoke to a cross section of people before submitting their report to the government in 2005. The report recommended revocation of AFSPA from the Northeast. No action was taken on the report and its contents remained restricted, though some websites have uploaded the report.

200 **'Blaming the Act is wrong':** Ghazala Wahab, 'AFSPA is not perfect that it cannot be improved', *FORCE*, July 2010.

200 **Even as the debate on AFSPA raged:** Chief of Army Staff General V. K. Singh said, '…in J&K, the terrorist threat remains real and the terror infrastructure across the border remains active… Any dilution/withdrawal of AFSPA will lead to constraining our operations.' 'People want AFSPA withdrawal for political gains Army chief', *Times of India,* 26 June 2010.

200 **The three interlocutors appointed by the union:** Dilip Padgaonkar, Radha Kumar and M. M. Ansari.

201 **One of his slides read, 'While the State people were seeking bijli, sadak, paani':** Praveen Swami, 'Army raises "secession" spectre to counter plan to lift AFSPA', *The Hindu*, 11 November 2011.

201 **First it said that AFSPA could only be revoked if the state government**: Such is the shroud of misinformation around the legalities of AFSPA that when a National Conference MLA demanded that the Mufti Mohammed Sayeed government (formed in 2015 in an alliance with the BJP) withdraw the Disturbed Areas Act (the Act had lapsed in October 1998) the J&K Assembly said there was no question of lifting it. However, Sayeed clarified that Section 3 of AFSPA (J&K) enjoins upon the governor (upon the advice of the central government) to declare an area disturbed and enforce AFSPA. Given this technicality, the state chief minister actually has no power over AFSPA.

202 **When 'Kashmiri Pandits will feel confident enough to return…':** General N. C. Vij, 'Dilution is no Answer', *Indian Express,* 17 January 2014.

202 **'With very few terrorists left to eliminate, the path to conflict termination':** Lt. Gen. Syed Ata Hasnain, 'Rashtriya Rifles: The Fearless Force', *Defence and Security Alert*, January 2015.

204 **In 2015, the International People's Tribunal:** Jason Burke, 'Indian forces in Kashmir accused of human rights abuses cover-up', *The Guardian*, 12 September 2015.

204 **Another set of statistics comes:** Randeep Singh Nandal, 'State data refutes claim of 1 lakh killed in Kashmir', *Times of India*, 20 June 2011.

205 **In an interview in November 2011, M. M. Ansari:** 'A more civil way to peace', *Hindustan Times*, 6 November 2011.

205 **'We are not getting into infrastructure building anymore':** Pravin Sawhney and Ghazala Wahab, 'A Legacy of Good', *FORCE*, April 2014.

206 **Successive chiefs of army staff have voiced their concerns**: Both General V. K. Singh (*FORCE*, June 2010) and General Bikram Singh (*FORCE*, October 2012) have brought this up in their interactions with the media.

206 **'What was supposed to be a temporary arrangement has now become permanent':** Ghazala Wahab, 'AFSPA is not perfect that it cannot be improved', *FORCE*, July 2010.

CHAPTER 11: THE DEMOLITION OF THE BABRI MASJID AND ITS AFTERMATH

211 **Amongst the worst-affected places was Bombay, where over 900 people:** Ananya Sengupta, 'What about us, ask Bombay riot victims', *The Telegraph*, 30 July 2015.

212 **In a horrifying 1992 documentary,** *Ram Ke Naam*: *Ram Ke Naam* won the Filmfare Award for best documentary and the National Film Award for Best Investigative Film. The documentary is available here: https://www.youtube.com/watch?v=OO-VaJBHiik.

212 **In 1990, he set off on a journey through India, starting from Somnath**: Situated on the Saurashtra coast of Gujarat, Somnath temple is considered extremely sacred by Hindus for several reasons. The religious and mythological significance apart, the fact that the temple was plundered and destroyed several times, starting 725 CE by a number of Muslim rulers and invaders, including Mahmud of Ghazni in 1027, added to its significance as a symbol of Hindu resistance. The Portuguese also ransacked it in 1546.

213 **Moreover, as a subsequently released video shot by the state intelligence agencies showed:** Part of the speech is available on YouTube: https://www.youtube.com/watch?v=-EhMmJEwbTg.

213 **The M. S. Liberhan Commission, which was constituted by the union government:** The full text of the 'Report of the Liberhan Ayodhya Commission of Inquiry' is available in *The Hindu* archives: http://www.thehindu.com/multimedia/archive/00014/Full_text_of_Liberha_14061a.pdf.

214 **'After the demolition of the Babri Masjid':** SIMI (Students' Islamic Movement of India) was formed as a students' union in Aligarh in 1977. Over the years, the organization became increasingly radicalized and politicized, going beyond student activities. Accused of being involved in various acts of terrorism through the 1990s, usually in the wake of communal riots, the organization was banned in 2001. According to security agencies, after the ban, SIMI went underground and became even more vicious, gradually morphing into the Indian Mujahideen. See Ghazala Wahab, 'Jihad', *FORCE*, November 2003

215 **'If we look at triggers for radicalisation':** 'Islamic State May Join Hands with Lashkar for Attacks in India, says Army', NDTV, 19 November 2015.

216 **'There is no scope for Al-Qaeda and IS in Jammu and Kashmir':** Peerzada Ashiq, 'IS has no role in Kashmir: Lashkar', *The Hindu*, 22 November 2015.

216 **The annual candlelight vigil at the Attari-Wagah border:** Journalist and civil rights activist Kuldip Nayyar started the tradition of holding a candlelight vigil on

the Attari border since 1994 on Pakistan and India's Independence Days (14 and
15 August) in an effort to create a groundswell for peace on both sides. His efforts
remained unrequited until 2008, when, for the first time, a large number of people
joined him from across the border.

221   **'The two sides shall engage in bilateral consultations on security
       concepts':** Amit Baruah, 'The Bus to Pakistan', *Frontline*, 27 Feb–12 March 1999.

222   **Musharraf came to Agra for a summit meeting with Vajpayee in July
       2001:** A. G. Noorani, 'The Truth about Agra', *Frontline*, 16–29 July 2005.

223   **cricketing ties—were resumed in 2006:** They had been discontinued after the
       1999 Kargil War.

224   **At the UN General Assembly in September 2008, Zardari trashed the
       Pakistan Army's:** Pravin Sawhney and Ghazala Wahab 'Beyond the Peace
       Process', *FORCE,* November 2008.

225   **A month later the two sides agreed to ease the visa regime:** 'Pakistan and
       India agree on 8 visa categories', *News International*, 7 September 2012.

225   **Pakistan also converted the positive list of tradable goods:** 'India-Pakistan
       to establish reciprocal NDMA by Feb end', *The Hindu*, 18 January 2014.

226   **Yet the world has not given up hope**: Dalia Dassa Kaye, *Talking to the Enemy:
       Track II Diplomacy in Middle East and South Asia*, RAND's National Security
       Research Division, 2007.

226   **With the experience of the Cold War, the West felt:** Ibid.

CHAPTER 12: THE PAKISTAN ARMY

230   **After the Vajpayee government lost at the hustings, the Manmohan
       Singh-Musharraf duo:** Pervez Musharraf, *In the Line of Fire*, Simon and Schuster,
       2008.

230-231 **Providing details of the backchannel talks, Khurshid Kasuri,
       Musharraf's foreign minister:** Kasuri, *Neither a Hawk Nor a Dove.*

231   **'We realized fairly early that the peace process with India could not
       survive':** Ibid., p. 327.

232   **Finally, Indian diplomats detest the idea of sharing their exclusive space
       with military officers:** Khan, *Eating Grass*, p. 303.

233   **'That he (Holbrooke) got the Pakistan military to give its okay was a
       mighty achievement':** Vali Nasr, *The Dispensable Nation*, Doubleday, 2013, p. 47.

234   **'in quest for a negotiated settlement of the Kashmir':** Kasuri, *Neither a
       Hawk Nor a Dove*, p. 299.

235   **Meanwhile, the ice was once again broken at the Paris climate change
       meet in December 2015:** The Composite Dialogue was the result of a series
       of talks between the two foreign secretaries between March 1997 and September
       1998. An agreement on the new format was formally announced in New York in
       September 1998. It was decided that the Composite Dialogue would comprise
       eight subjects, each being given equal importance to move the bilateral relations
       forward for building trust and confidence. The new format was a significant
       departure from the earlier format under which the foreign secretaries conducted
       talks without any fixed agenda. Under the Composite Dialogue, two subjects,
       peace and security including CBMs and Jammu & Kashmir, were to be discussed
       by the foreign secretaries. The Siachen issue was to be discussed by defence

secretaries; Tulbul navigation project by the secretaries of water and power; Sir Creek by the additional secretaries of defence; terrorism and drug trafficking by home/interior secretaries; economic and commercial cooperation by commerce secretaries; and promotion of friendly exchanges by culture secretaries in various fields. Interestingly, Musharraf, during his tenure when backchannel diplomacy was moving apace and showing promise, had called CBMs under the Composite Dialogue as 'mere irritants'. The underlying sense was they could be skipped when talking with the Pakistan Army which desired Kashmir resolution.

236 **'The session with Advani was unnerving'**: Strobe Talbott, *Engaging India*, Penguin Viking, 2004, p. 101.

238 **Far from talk of nuclear war**: 'Ex-President discusses nuclear program, politics', Foreign Broadcast Information Service, 26 July 1993; and 'Gen. Beg claims country conducted cold nuclear test', FBIS, 3 August 1993.

238 **'1990 was one instance when Pakistan's nuclear capability'**: 'Securing nuclear peace', *International News*, 5 October 1999.

238 **He suggested that the three rounds of the India-Pakistan conflict**: General K. Sundarji, 'Is Pakistan's nuclear deterrence losing credibility,' *Indian Express*, 15 September 1994.

239 **Prime Minister Benazir Bhutto offered a zero-missile status**: That both sides will not use ballistic missiles against one another.

240 **This was not difficult, as Pakistani nuclear interlocutors were well versed**: In his book, *Eating Grass: The Making of the Pakistani Bomb*, Brig. Feroz Hassan Khan writes that Gen. Beg had initiated a programme to send military officers to Western civil universities for advanced degrees. By the early 1990s, several military officers had postgraduate degrees from top Western universities in nuclear operational and technical fields.

240 **It consisted of 'three interlocking elements'**: Khan, *Eating Grass.*

241 **'The Indian delegation had no military officer at the meeting'**: Ibid.

242 **The contours of a regional regime that includes reciprocal restraints on nuclear**: Gen. Jehangir Karamat, 'The Burden of Power', *FORCE*, October 2003.

CHAPTER 13: A NEW DECISION-MAKING STRUCTURE

247 **'Politicians enjoy power without any responsibility'**: He was quoted by Admiral Arun Prakash while delivering the third K. Subrahmanyam Memorial Lecture in Delhi. The lecture can be found here: http://www.globalindiafoundation.org/Admiral%20Arun%20Prakash%20Speech[1].pdf.

249 **'During these meetings of about thirty minutes duration'**: V. P. Malik, *India's Military Conflicts and Diplomacy*, HarperCollins, 2013, p. 264.

251 **'the NSA's beat, with foreign affairs, defence and nuclear strategy was allotted'**: Sanjaya Baru, *The Accidental Prime Minister*, Penguin, 2014, p. 43.

251 **When asked for advice following Dixit's sudden death**: Ibid.

256 **The CISC prepares the nuclear targets list which is updated annually**: Interaction with a recently retired CISC who did not want to be named.

257 **Headed by two-star rank officers, the Defence Space Agency interacts**: According to defence sources, both the National Technology Research Organisation and the Defence Cyber Agency have offensive capabilities.

257 **Against this backdrop, the Naresh Chandra task force**: Malik, *India's Military*

Conflicts and Diplomacy.

258   **One, as another department of the defence ministry, the IDH would no longer:** 'Today the three services speak in one voice': Chief of Integrated Staff to Chairman (CISC) Lt. Gen. Pankaj Joshi, *FORCE* September 2003.

258   **Working with the commander-in-chief, Strategic Forces Command, the PCCOSC and the services chiefs:** The nuclear weapons targeting list indicates which enemy targets are to be hit by nuclear weapons if the option is to be exercised. This is updated periodically depending on the prevailing threat assessment.

CHAPTER 14: THE INDIAN ARMED FORCES

264   **The long list of tasks that the Indian Army has taken upon itself:** Four battalions of the army will work under the ministry of water resources, river development and Ganga rejuvenation. 'Army Called In', *Times of India*, 4 January 2015.

265   **'The strength of the standing army is around 1.23 million':** Manu Pubby and Deepshikha Hooda, 'Private sector has a strong role to play in modernisation efforts in defence sector: General Dalbir Singh', *Economic Times*, 21 January 2016.

265   **'Worried about shortage of finances':** 'Army corps would be pruned', *Hindustan Times*, 16 April 2015.

266   **'a target was kept of nine years':** 'Raising of Mountain strike corps on track', *The Tribune*, 15 January 2016.

266   **Except for Ladakh where China says it does not have a border with India:** According to a director general of military operations.

266-267   **The Chinese proposal of June 2015 for a 'code of conduct':** Atul Aneja, 'Beijing for code of conduct', *The Hindu*, 5 June 2015.

267   **According to the National Security Advisor, Ajit Doval:** Doval spoke about defensive-offence against Pakistan and said Pakistan would lose Balochistan if there was another Mumbai attack. The video can be found here https://www.youtube.com/watch?v=N7ESR5RU3X4.

268   **Yes, according to army chief General Bikram Singh:** Interview, army chief's office, South Block, New Delhi, January 2013.

272   **'During the period from January to December 2014':** 'Government admits only 55 per cent fighter fleet operational', *Economic Times*, 16 December 2015.

273   **A few airborne warning and control systems and aerostat balloons are inadequate:** The IAF has sought twelve airborne warning and control systems by 2022.

275   **'We have proposed to the government that in lieu of the conventional submarines':** Ajay Banerjee, 'Navy's Wish List: 6 nuke subs, N-powered carrier', *The Tribune*, 7 May 2015.

276   **It could be nuclear-powered or conventionally-powered:** Ibid.

277   **'Pakistan's Maritime Technology Organisation is nearing completion':** Khan, *Eating Grass*, p. 396.

CHAPTER 15: THE NUCLEAR OPTION

280   **'manages and administers the nuclear forces':** Lt. Gen. B. S. Nagal (former commander-in-chief, Strategic Forces Command), 'Perception and Reality',

FORCE, October 2014.

287 **'The army approached the cabinet committee'**: A. P. J. Abdul Kalam, *Wings of Fire: An Autobiography*, Universities Press, 1999, p. 155.

288 **Unlike the platform (gimballed) inertial navigation systems:** A missile can be brought to bear accurately on the target by two means: inertial navigation system (INS) and terminal homing (done by various kinds of seekers) which direct the missile when close to the target. The INS system comprises three accelerometers (one each to measure the missile during flight in all three dimensions—roll, pitch and yaw) to ensure corrections are provided to the missile to keep it moving steadily towards the target. These accelerometers could either be suspended in a liquid-filled container (called a gyroscope or gyro) as a separate unit close to the moving missile where they rotate freely, or they could be housed in dry gyros which are strapped on the body of the missile itself. The latter, called strap-down inertial navigation system, is cheaper and easier to acquire but less accurate.

289 **Pakistan, in comparison, has a range of ballistic missiles:** More details are available in the chapter Pakistan's Missile Quest in Khan, *Eating Grass*.

290 **'would most likely be based on a naval version':** Khan, *Eating Grass*, p. 396.

290 **The nation and the defence forces were taken by surprise:** PAD and AAD were arbitrary acronyms given by the DRDO. According to the media, PAD stands for Prithvi Air Defence and AAD stands for Akash Air Defence, but top DRDO scientists confirmed to one of the authors that this is not so. Since the missiles are at a project stage, the acronyms have been used for identification purposes only.

291 **'Our commitment is to complete the flight trials of Phase I interceptors':** Interview with Dr V. K. Saraswat, *FORCE*, March 2010.

293 **'It is for this reason that':** Verghese Koithara, *Managing India's Nuclear Forces*, Routledge, 2012, p. 224.

CHAPTER 16: QUEST FOR TECHNOLOGY

295 **'There are two tragedies in life':** George Bernard Shaw, *Man and Superman*, 1905.

297 **'Japan and India are natural partners':** Shinzo Abe, 'India, Japan are natural partners: this relationship has the greatest potential in the world, I will turn it into reality', *Times of India*, 11 December 2015.

299 **'the essence of the concept of strategic restraint':** 'Unequal Music', *FORCE*, October 2004.

300 **'In some respects, the NSSP builds and expands upon the work':** 'US Believes India Can Play a Role in Increasing Stability in Asia': US Under Secretary of Commerce, Kenneth Juster in an interview with Pravin Sawhney, *FORCE*, July 2004.

300 **'There were three phases in NSSP':** *FORCE*, August 2005.

300 **the NDA (Vajpayee) government had offered:** Ibid.

301 **'The key from our point of view':** Condoleezza Rice, *No Higher Honor*, Simon & Schuster, 2011, p. 440.

308 **'Because the United States is a hegemonic power in the international system'**: Ashley Tellis, 'Beyond Buyer-Seller', *FORCE*, August 2015.

309 **It is however debatable whether the Modi government:** The first trilateral meeting between the foreign ministers of India, the US and Japan elevated from bureaucratic level was held in New York in September 2015.

310-311 This role is determined by Russia's multidirectional foreign policy: 'India Must Enjoy All The Rights Of Permanent Membership, Including The Veto Power': Russian ambassador to India, Vyacheslav I. Trubnikov, in an interview to *FORCE* magazine, January 2005.

CHAPTER 17: THE INDIGENOUS DEFENCE INDUSTRY

312 China will be in a position to offer a package deal to the buyer: Robert Farley, *Russia vs China: The Race to Dominate the Defense Market*, nationalinterest.org, July 2015.

312 In fact, the buzz is that the Chinese-built fifth generation fighter aircraft, J-31: Ibid.

312 (HAL) is yet to make any contribution: Despite the joint venture inter-governmental agreement on the Fifth Generation Fighter Aircraft (the Russians call it PAK-FA), the Russians have only been interested in a financial contribution from India. They have not allowed HAL to participate in the design and development stage nor let the Indian fighter pilots fly the version being made for the Russian Air Force. The Russians repeatedly assure India that once the fighter is operational they will let HAL suggest or carry out India-specific modifications to the fighters made for India. The story of the so-called successful joint venture, the BRAHMOS cruise missile, is somewhat similar. While India has inducted the missile into its army and navy (the air force version is under way), the Russian military has not inducted the missile in its military. They have their own cruise missiles for their armed forces.

312 and bank on imports for a number of crucial technologies: Essentially from Russia, which is also the biggest arms supplier to China. In fact, Russia's biggest dilemma is violation of its intellectual property rights by China, which reverse engineers Russian equipment to make their own, which it then supplies to other countries.

315 'Make in India' programme: Prime Minister Narendra Modi coined this slogan soon after assuming office to lay focus on indigenization. Subsequently, while inaugurating the Aero India 2015 exhibition in Bengaluru, he told the audience that defence production lay at the heart of his 'Make in India' programme.

317 In fact, the state of the ordnance factories has been so pathetic that many operate below capacity: 'CAG Slams OFB for Slippages in Providing Equipment to Armed Forces', *Times of India*, 13 December 2013.

317 Even more tragic is the fact that sitting on prime land, throughout the country: There are a total of forty-one factories and six headquarters spread across the country.

317 'We shall fight with whatever we have': Pravin Sawhney and Ghazala Wahab, 'Silence of the Guns', *FORCE*, June 2012.
In 2006, Gen. V. P. Malik wrote in his book, *Kargil: From Surprise to Victory*, 'When the Kargil war began, it was not the vintage but the deficiencies of weapons, equipment, ammunition and spares that worried us more. Even infantry weapons such as medium machine-guns, rocket launchers and mortars, apart from signal equipment, bulletproof jackets and snow clothing for high-altitude warfare, were in short supply. Besides weapons and equipment, the ammunition reserves for many

important weapons were low.'

318   **Under enormous pressure from the defence PSUs who had several fears:** The defence PSUs have traditionally run like extensions of government departments and not as an industry. They have strong unions and permanency of jobs, which do not depend on performance. All this has led to inefficiency, which will become glaringly obvious if they are pitted against the private sector.

318   **defence trade shows:** Organized by the Ministry of Defence, the shows take place every alternate year—DefExpo in even years and Aero India in odd years.

319   **In 1992, the government was compelled to come up:** Maj. Gen. Mrinal Suman (retd), 'Acquisition Syndrome', *FORCE*, March 2012.

321   **'The idea being that Pipavav Shipyard over time should become a national asset':** 'Eyes on the Future', *FORCE*, June 2011.

321   **Contrast this with the vision of the President and CEO, Saab Group:** Saab is a Swedish aerospace and defence company with interests in India. The Indian Army has been using Saab's Carl Gustav anti-tank recoilless rifle for decades.

322   **Clearly India needs similar hand-holding:** Bharat Dynamics Ltd has been license-producing MBDA's anti-tank missile, Milan, for the last forty years but has not yet been able to produce a new anti-tank missile of its own.

CHAPTER 18: THE TIBETAN STRUGGLE

331   **'1971 war, in which it lost forty-six of its soldiers':** According to the reports of the SFF, interview, McLeod Ganj, 14 April 2015.

327   **'What other option do we have?':** Pico Iyer, *The Open Road: The Global Journey of the Fourteenth Dalai Lama*, Penguin Viking, 2008, p. 228.

329   **Norbu had settled in Kalimpong in the Indian state of West Bengal:** Gyalo Thondup and Anne F. Thurston, *The Noodle Maker of Kalimpong: The Untold Story of My Struggle for Tibet*, PublicAffairs, 2015.

330   **This was the time he established several contacts in the US State Department:** Ibid.

330   **'I had to explain that I was running away from the Chinese occupiers of Tibet':** Ibid.

331   **After the debacle of the 1962 war against China:** Samdup Gyaltsen, vice chairman, ex-servicemen Welfare Association, Special Frontier Force, in an interview with the authors. Gyaltsen retired from the SFF in 2009.

331   **'Our mission was liberation of Tibet':** Ibid.

332   **The Russians resisted doing that and the communication petered out after a few years:** Thondup and Thurston, *The Noodle Maker of Kalimpong*.

332   **Wangyal had established the Tibetan Communist Party in the hope:** Melvyn C. Goldstein, Dawei Sherap and William R. Siebenschuh, *A Tibetan Revolutionary: The Political Life and Times of Bapa Phuntso Wangye*, University of California Press, 2004.

334   **'But for independence, everything is negotiable. Everything can be discussed':** Thondup and Thurston, *The Noodle Maker of Kalimpong*, p. 258.

334   **Deng agreed to everything raised by Thondup:** Ibid.

335   **'It is necessary that he not live in Tibet or hold any position in Tibet':** Tsering Shakya, *Dragon in the Land of Snows*, Penguin, 2000, pp. 384–385.

338   **One, the Dalai Lama must recognize that Tibet is an inalienable part of**

China: Thondup and Thurston, *The Noodle Maker of Kalimpong.*

338   **China also gave up the pretence of reverence towards the Dalai Lama by publicly calling him names like 'splittist':** 'Sikyong Lobsang Sangay', 'Tibetan Leader: Chinese Government Can't Choose Next Dalai Lama, *Time*, 30 March 2015.

CHAPTER 19: THE DALAI LAMA

344   **In March 1959, when twenty-four-year-old Tenzin Gyatso fled to India from Tibet:** The Dalai Lama, *My Land and My People: Memoirs of His Holiness*, Srishti Publishers and Distributors, 1997.

344   **'As to the escape of the Dalai Lama from Tibet, if we had been in your place':** Kissinger, *On China,* p. 171.

345   **The Chinese also castigated India:** The Dalai Lama, *My Land and My People.*

345   **When the Dalai Lama met Prime Minister Nehru during his visit:** Thondup and Thurston, *The Noodle Maker of Kalimpong.*

346   **it would be in the best interest of Tibet and its bilateral relationship with China:** Ibid.

347   **Before I left China I was greatly impressed by Mao Tse-tung's:** The Dalai Lama, *My Land and My People.*

348   **'I felt I was in a very difficult position':** Ibid., p. 115.

349   **'We must never allow a belief to grow up':** Ibid., p. 231.

CHAPTER 20: THE INSURGENCIES WITHIN

359   **In February 2014, the then Union Minister of State for Home:** 'Assam-Arunachal border a new theatre of Maoists: Govt', http://arunachalpradesh.nic.in/csp_ap_portal/pdf/Documents/assam-arunachal-border-maoists.pdf.

360   **'Left-wing extremism offers the most attractive':** 'China-Naxalite linkages: Gauging its dimensions', Vivekananda International Foundation, 25 March 2011.

360   **But they were trying to influence the youth in cities: South Asia Terrorism Portal, 'Kerala Time Line 2014',** http://www.satp.org/satporgtp/countries/india/maoist/timelines/2014/kerala.htm.

360   **Chronicling the outreach mechanism of the Maoists since the late 1960s:** Sudeep Chakravarti, *Clear. Hold. Build: Hard Lessons of Business and Human Rights in India*, HarperCollins, 2014.

360   **'It's a revealing, sometimes chilling, blueprint of thought':** Sudeep Chakravarti, 'The curious case of Maoists in Kerala', *LiveMint*, 28 November 2014.

360   **And it has educated people temperamentally:** 'Naxal Movement in Kerala is a Matter of Concern', oneindia.com, 10 December 2014.

361   **Even after the Kachin Independence Army stopped:** Bertil Lintner, *Great Game East: India, China and the Struggle for Asia's Most Volatile Frontier*, HarperCollins, 2012.

361   **They kept the Indian Army and its paramilitary forces bogged down:** Arunachal Pradesh has been a later addition to the list, while Tripura has been peaceful now, primarily because of the sagacious political leadership of Chief Minister Manik Sarkar.

361   **The Government of India has been struggling to contain if not completely finish off these insurgencies:** Of the sixty-five recognized terror

organizations in India, fifty-seven are from the Northeast, out of which thirty-four are from Manipur alone. Under the Unlawful Activities (Prevention) Act of 1967, thirty-eight terror organizations are banned by the Union home ministry. Ten are from the Northeast.

363 **Interestingly, the dissident leader used this time to stitch up a broad alliance:** CorCom is a Manipur-based umbrella of six outfits that includes the Kangleipak Communist Party (KCP), Kanglei Yawol Kanna Lup (KYKL) and People's Revolutionary Party of Kangleipak (PREPAK).

364 **The euphoria however has been tempered by the formation of UNLFWSEA:** '9 NE militant groups form joint front', *NorthEast Today* (http:// thenortheasttoday.com/9-ne-militant-groups-form-joint-front/).

364 **travelling across the insurgent camps for a book:** Rajeev Bhattacharya, *Rendezvous with Rebels: Journey to Meet India's Most Wanted Men*, HarperCollins, 2014

364 **since Angami Phizo raised the banner of revolt:** Angami Phizo was the first Naga leader to seek secession from India. He also tried to mobilize various northeastern tribes such as Garo, Khasi, Lushai, Mikir, Abor, Mishmi and Meitei across states to seek independence from India. He died in exile in London in 1990, where he had been living since 1960.

364 **'The United National Liberation Front of Western South East Asia will take the struggle to a higher level':** Rajeev Bhattacharya interviews Paresh Barua, 'A Govt in Exile by Year End', *Outlook*, 22 June 2015.

364 **At the moment, barring Sikkim, all the northeastern states:** Annual Report 2014–2015, Ministry of Home Affairs.

364 **UNLFWSEA (an umbrella organization of major Northeastern insurgent groups):** UNLFWSEA was formed in the spring of 2015 by Paresh Barua's faction of ULFA, NDFB, Kamatapur Liberation Organisation (KLO) of Bengal and the Khaplang faction of the NSCN-K in Myanmar. Gradually, other insurgents groups of the Northeast extended support to UNLFWSEA. See http://www.idsa. in/system/files/jds/jds_9_4_2015_UNLFWSEA.pdf.

365 **The Central government has deployed 403 companies:** The Central Reserve Police Force (the largest Central Armed Police Force in India), which has been declared the lead agency for counter-Maoist operations, now has over 229 battalions, at least half of which have been raised hastily without commensurate training facilities. Several battalions have been inducted in the theatre after only basic training in their group centres instead of the training academies, since all of them have been overbooked. No surprise then that the CRPF continues to suffer maximum casualties in the Maoist theatre.

366 **Mao's famous phrase 'political power grows out of the barrel of a gun':** The statement comes from Mao Zedong's speech at the conclusion of the 6th Plenary Session of the Communist Party in November 1938. He said, '[E]very Communist must grasp the truth, "political power grows out of the barrel of a gun." Our principle is that the Party commands the gun, and the gun must never be allowed to command the Party. Yet, having guns, we can create Party organisations... We can also create cadres, create schools, create culture, create mass movements. Everything in Yenan has been created by having guns. All things grow out of the barrel of a gun. According to the Marxist theory of the state, the army is

the chief component of state power. Whoever wants to seize and retain state power must have a strong army. Some people ridicule us as advocates of the "omnipotence of war". Yes, we are advocates of the omnipotence of revolutionary war; that is good, not bad, it is Marxist'. (*Selected Works of Mao Tse-tung*, Vol. II, Marxist Internet Archive).

CHAPTER 21: LANES OF INFLUENCE

379 **Hence, when she decided to wage war against Pakistan in 1971:** The Indo-Soviet Treaty of Peace, Friendship and Cooperation was signed on 9 August 1971. Amongst its various provisions was one 'to support the just aspirations of the peoples in their struggle against colonialism and racial domination'. This covered the war to help the Bangla people realize their 'just aspirations'.

380 **George Friedman, author and founder of the US-based private intelligence**: Among his famous books are *America's Secret War*, *The Intelligence Edge*, *The Coming War With Japan* and *The Future of War*.

381 **An Indian government that ignores these imperatives:** 'The Geopolitics of India: A Shifting, Self-Contained World,' George Friedman, 16 December 2008 (https://wikileaks.org/gifiles/attach/57/57115_THE_GEOPOLITICS_OF_INDIA.pdf).

382 **As the global war on terrorism progressed:** The US campaign, mainly in Afghanistan, against Al-Qaeda after the 9/11 attacks, though subsequently the attack on Iraq to depose Saddam Hussein was also brought under the umbrella of the global war on terror.

383 **A total of twenty-six ships participated in the month-long exercise:** The US's nuclear-powered aircraft carrier USS *Nimitz* participated in the Bay of Bengal phase along with the nuclear-powered submarine USS *Chicago*.

383 **upgrade the level of the Malabar exercise:** See https://www.whitehouse.gov/the-press-office/2015/01/25/us-india-joint-statement-shared-effort-progress-all

383 **The American experts argued that China was resorting to a slew of measures:** Deng Cheng, 'The U. S. needs an integrated approach to counter China's anti-access/area denial strategy', www.heritage.org, 9 July 2014.

384 **the army is prepared for any eventuality:** Making this assertion year after year has become a sort of tradition now, which even the army probably does not take seriously. For example, in January 2012, Chief of Army Staff General V. K. Singh assured the nation that the army was prepared for the entire spectrum of war. Two months later he wrote a letter to Prime Minister Manmohan Singh pointing out how the army was 'devoid of critical ammunition' in addition to having an obsolete air defence system, basic infantry weaponry, etc. According to the letter, the army was ill-prepared even for a war with Pakistan. The following year, his successor, General Bikram Singh once again told the media, 'Indian Army is prepared for war on the strength of the steel armour of its men.' *FORCE*, February 2013.

384 **Additionally there has been periodic speculation that just as China enforced:** 'China Should Not Declare New South China Sea ADIZ: Top Chinese Expert', *The Diplomat*, July 2015.

385 **'It was all so simple. I picked up the phone and spoke with [Admiral] Arun [Prakash]':** Admiral Arun Prakash, Indian chief of naval staff at that time. 'That is how special the naval relationship is and this is how well we work together': The Government of India allows the Indian military to operate outside India only under the UN flag in UN-mandated peacekeeping missions. India does not participate in any out of area operations in a coalition with another country. The international cooperation is limited to exercises alone.

386 **Inspired by the US-led Western Pacific Naval Symposium:** WPNS started in 1988. It has twenty members including the US, China, Australia, Russia and Singapore, among others. India has frequently been invited as an observer and has participated in WPNS exercises. In 2014, China hosted the symposium and even invited Pakistan as an observer along with India.

386 **IONS aimed to give a common forum to Indian Ocean littoral countries:** IONS has thirty-five members who have been divided according to their geographical location. The South Asian Littoral comprises Bangladesh, India, Maldives, Pakistan, Seychelles and Sri Lanka. The West Asian Littorals include Bahrain, Iran, Iraq, Kuwait, Oman, Qatar, Saudi Arabia, UAE and Yemen. The East African Littorals have Comoros, Djibouti, Egypt, Eritrea, France, Kenya, Madagascar, Mauritius, Mozambique, Somalia, South Africa, Sudan and Tanzania. The Southeast Asian and Australian Littorals include Australia, Indonesia, Malaysia, Myanmar, Singapore, Thailand and Timor Leste. China and Japan have observer status.

387 **'NATO and the Warsaw Pact were competitive':** Ghazala Wahab, 'Taking the Lead: Naval who's who from the IOR attend the IONS inauguration', *FORCE*, March 2008.

388 **However, two years later at the next edition of the forum in the Chinese city of Qingdao:** 'Small but positive signs at Western Pacific Naval Symposium', *The Diplomat*, 24 April 2014.

389 **We are well positioned, therefore, to become a net provider of security in our immediate region and beyond:** 'India well positioned to become a net provider of security: Manmohan Singh', *The Hindu*, 24 May 2013.

389 **According to the naval script, in addition to the naval intelligence:** Intelligence, surveillance and reconnaissance can be done through surface ships, aircraft/helicopters as well as satellites.

390 **At the moment, the most generous estimate of the navy's seaworthy platforms:** In response to a question by one of the authors whether the navy has at least one hundred seagoing ships, a recently retired vice admiral said, 'Yes, there should be about one hundred ships.'

390 **At the moment, forty-seven ships and submarines are under construction:** Figure given by Chief of Navy Staff Admiral Robin Dhowan during his Navy Week media interaction.

392 **The multinational biennial Exercise Milan that India hosts:** At the last edition of Milan in February 2014, sixteen countries participated. These were Australia, Bangladesh, Cambodia, Indonesia, Kenya, Malaysia, Maldives, Mauritius, Myanmar, New Zealand, the Philippines, Seychelles, Singapore, Sri Lanka, Tanzania and Thailand (in addition to India).

392 **In September 2014, Foreign Secretary Sujatha Singh:** Sachin Parashar, 'Narendra Modi's "Mausam" manoeuvre to check China's maritime might', *Times of India*, 16 September 2014.

CHAPTER 22: ADRIFT ON THE HIGH SEAS

394   **south of the Vindhyas:** The Vindhyas, which run west to east, south of Madhya Pradesh, are considered the traditional boundary between north and south India. Historically, they used to be considered the border of most north Indian empires.

395   **'In my opinion, Jawaharlal Nehru's grand vision required that the Indian Navy':** Admiral S. M. Nanda, *The Man Who Bombed Karachi: A Memoir*, HarperCollins, 2004, p. 114.

395   **'The focus was in finding the means to counter major threats':** Ibid., p. 120.

396   **Within days of the war commencing:** Missile boats are small warships fitted with anti-ship missiles. They are similar in concept to the torpedo boats of World War II. Because of their size they have little endurance and range, therefore they need to be close to the target for a successful attack. Their size also works to their advantage as they have insignificant radar signature. At least in 1971, operating in the night, they were undetectable by the Pakistan military.

396   **The attack also destroyed the oil tank farm in Karachi:** The event won Admiral Nanda the sobriquet of the man who bombed Karachi, which eventually became the title of his memoirs, where he recounts the attack in detail.

396   **Once these questions were asked in the media and tacitly accepted by the government:** While the attack definitively ended the Composite Dialogue process with Pakistan, the government's dilemma was to figure out an adequate response to Pakistan's perfidy. Should it announce mobilization of the military as the NDA government had done after the Parliament attack in 2001? Should it carry out precision air strikes against Pakistan? Should it suspend all diplomatic ties with it? Even today the Government of India has not been able to figure out a way in which it can deter Pakistan.

397   **So while the government enunciated and executed the policy:** The Group of Ministers-proposed coastal security scheme was approved by the Cabinet Committee on Security in 2005 and was to be implemented over the next five years. Under the scheme, the union government was to provide assistance to nine coastal states and four Union Territories for setting up of 73 coastal police stations, 97 check posts, 58 outposts and 30 barracks. These were to be equipped with 204 boats, 153 jeeps and 312 motorcycles. The manpower was to be provided by the states and UTs. The scheme was allocated one-time funding of Rs 400 crore and Rs 151 crore for recurring expenditure on incidentals and training of marine police personnel. But as 26/11 showed, implementation was largely on paper.

398   **The maritime border takes into account all the promontories:**   A promontory is a foreland, headland or rocky cliff jutting into the sea. In the case of India, it would imply the jagged coastline especially in the region of Gujarat, Tamil Nadu and West Bengal.

398   **This was ironical because the importance of the sea:** 90 per cent of India's trade by volume and 70 per cent by value is seaborne, thereby contributing nearly 42 per cent to the national GDP.

398   **The Ministry of Home Affairs, which lists the total length of India's borders:** Ministry of Home Affairs' Annual Report 2014–2015 (http://mha.nic. in/sites/upload_files/mha/files/AR(E)1415.pdf).

399   **In its report submitted to the US Senate committee, the Federal Bureau**

of Investigation: The US carried out its own investigations because several US citizens were killed in the attacks. Also, the person accused of co-plotting and carrying out the reconnaissance for the attack, David Coleman Headley, is a US citizen.

400 **To facilitate this, a national command, control, communication and intelligence (NC3I):** NC3I was finally operationalized in November 2014 by the setting up of the Information Management and Analysis Centre in Gurgaon.

400 **Joint operation centres were to come up in Mumbai, Kochi, Visakhapatnam and Port Blair:** The Navy established Joint Operation Centres (JOCs) to coordinate security/patrolling operations between the Navy, ICG, state police, customs and port authorities, etc. by the middle of 2009. But setting up of JOCs did not automatically lead to cooperation between these agencies. Even as the navy was at pains to explain that the JOCs were coordination and not command centres, the inherent mistrust and turf-protection mentality stymied them. In the absence of this jointness, hotlines were established between these agencies as an interim solution, though some existed between the navy and the ICG even before the November 26 attacks. Gradually, the JOCs started to function by 2011, which basically implied that the state police, customs and port authorities started sending their officials to these centres.

401 **'India has increased its presence in the South China Sea':** The talk was excerpted in *The Tribune*, 23 November 2015

401 **And the cost would be paid by its primary and secondary roles:** Naval diplomacy includes port-calling, naval exercises with friendly navies, participation in international maritime events like fleet reviews, joint patrolling, etc.

401 **Its other two roles include constabulary:** This involves both coastal security and anti-piracy operations.

402 **Despite the concept of maritime domain awareness:** The term was first mentioned to the authors by the navy's Eastern Naval Commander, Vice Admiral Sureesh Mehta, in February 2006 in Vishakapatnam. Vice Admiral Mehta's concept of maritime domain awareness involved interacting closely with littoral and neighbouring countries, to build bridges with them, 'so that in times of need they will be with us'. For him, MDA had to be driven by human interface and not mere technology. Vice Admiral Mehta subsequently became the Chief of Naval Staff.

403 **'The Indian Navy will be diluting its primary role of being** a blue-water navy': 'It Was Very Clear in the Government Order That the Responsibility and Accountability for Coastal Defence was of the Indian Navy': Vice Admiral Sanjeev Bhasin, FOC-in-C, Western Naval Command (30 April 2009-30 April 2011) in an interview to FORCE, September 2011.
A blue-water navy refers to the capability of operating across the deep waters of open oceans, well away from the country of origin, like the US Navy.

404 **'Who will do what, who is responsible':** Kalyan Ray, 'Coastal Security Bill Caught Red', *Deccan Herald*, 25 May 2015.

404 **However, with the government now identifying terrorism as one of the main military threats:** 'The threats may be known, but the enemy may be invisible,' Prime Minister Modi told the armed forces in October 2014 (http://www.narendramodi.in/pms-address-at-the-combined-commanders-conference-6766).

404   **the navy's share of the defence budget would increase:** In the Confederation of Indian Industry's assessment, the navy's share of the annual defence budget would be 40 per cent of capital allocation. *FORCE*, December 2015.

404   **the sea is no longer benign:** Admiral Dhowan at the annual press conference, Kota House, New Delhi, December 2014.

404   **If a ship worth ₹2,500 crore:** Cost of the indigenous frigate INS *Satpura*, built by Mazagon Dock Shipbuilders Limited, which was commissioned into the navy in August 2011.

INDEX